Encyclopedia of Social Work

19th
Edition

1997 Supplement

Encyclopedia of Social Work

19th
Edition

1997 Supplement

Encyclopedia Update Committee
Richard L. Edwards, *Editor-in-Chief*

Ira C. Colby   Ruth G. McRoy
Alejandro Garcia   Lynn Videka-Sherman

NASW PRESS

National Association of Social Workers
Washington, DC

Josephine A. V. Allen, PhD, ACSW, *President*
Josephine Nieves, MSW, PhD, *Executive Director*

Encyclopedia of Social Work, 19th Edition, 1997 Supplement

Executive Editor	Nancy A. Winchester
Director of Member Services and Publications	Jane Browning
Project Manager	Patricia D. Wolf
Assistant Project Manager	Melissa D. Conroy

NASW Press Staff Editors
Christina A. Davis
Sarah Lowman   Marcia Roman

NASW Press Editorial Secretary
Heather Peters

Editorial Assistants
Cynthia Hargett   Meredith Welty

Copy Editors
Kendall W. Sterling
Patricia Borthwick   Donna Verdier

Proofreaders
Louise Goines
Donna Verdier
Annette Hansen   Elizabeth Reynolds
Joanne Lockard   Ronald W. Wolf

The Encyclopedia Update Committee expresses its gratitude to Linda Beebe, former NASW associate executive director for communications and director of the NASW Press, for her major contribution to the development of the 1997 Supplement to the Encyclopedia of Social Work, 19th Edition.

ISSN: 0071-0237

First printing September 1997

Second printing January 1998

Printed in the United States of America

Encyclopedia Update Committee

Contents

Preface and Acknowledgments   ix
How to Use the Encyclopedia   xi
Introduction *by Paula Allen-Meares*   xv

Biographies   361

Appendixes

Index   409

Preface and Acknowledgments

This update of the 19th edition of the *Encyclopedia of Social Work* has been made possible by advances in technology. Because the 19th Edition was produced both in print and CD-ROM formats (as *The Social Work Reference Library*), it has been possible to revise many of the entries in that edition in the CD-ROM format, as well as to add new entries. The new entries are included not only on the CD-ROM but in this print *Supplement* to the 19th Edition. The 2nd edition of the *Social Work Almanac* also has been updated on the CD-ROM and is fully linked to both the updated *Encyclopedia* and *The Social Work Dictionary*, 3rd Edition.

The 19th edition of the *Encyclopedia* was released in March 1995, not long after the mid-term elections of 1994, in which Republican majorities were elected in both the U.S. Senate and House of Representatives. The Republicans campaigned vigorously on their "Contract with America" and, once in office, began attempting to implement many of its provisions. At that point, the chances that President Clinton would be re-elected in 1996 looked slim. However, he rebounded and was indeed re-elected. Before the election, he signed legislation related to welfare reform, which promised to bring about a number of significant changes in the way public welfare is administered in the United States. The legislation gave further impetus to what many have called the "devolution revolution" (that is, the shifting of responsibilities from the federal to the state and local levels). Additionally, since the 19th Edition was published, there have been a number of other changes that affect social policy and the profession of social work.

A great deal of effort has gone into producing these updates and new entries. I have been fortunate to work with an extremely dedicated group of colleagues who composed the Update Committee. These include the following social work educators: Ira Colby, from the University of Central Florida; Alejandro Garcia, from Syracuse University; Ruth McRoy, from the University of Texas at Austin; and Lynn Videka-Sherman, from the University at Albany, State University of New York. The committee reviewed every entry in the 19th Edition to determine which should be updated and solicited input from a variety of sources, including various NASW committees, to determine where gaps existed that might be filled by commissioning new entries. Update Committee members then identified potential authors for the new entries and worked with them through the process of producing their manuscripts. The dedication and effort of my committee colleagues made this update possible. I also want to commend the authors of entries included in the 19th Edition who produced updates, as well as those authors who wrote new entries. Their cooperation in meeting tight timelines was critical.

No publication effort of this magnitude can succeed without excellent staff support. We were fortunate to be able to work with a cadre of individuals who were extremely competent and dedicated. Linda Beebe, former director of the NASW Press and executive editor of the 19th Edition, provided staff leadership throughout the development of the 19th Edition and for most of the work on this update. She was very ably assisted by Nancy Winchester, publications manager and executive editor for this update, who assumed overall responsibility for NASW publications when Linda left NASW in winter 1997. These two individuals are really exceptionally well-qualified professionals and, on behalf of the entire committee, I would like to express our appreciation for their support, their good humor, and their dedication to this project. We also thank Sarah Lowman, who was formerly editorial secretary and is now a staff editor at the NASW Press, for her efforts. In addition, we would like to acknowledge Patricia D. Wolf, Melissa D. Conroy, and the staff of Wolf Publications for ably handling the editorial production and project management activities.

We hope that those who use the CD-ROM version of *The Social Work Reference Library* find that the new DynaText search engine makes it even more user friendly than the previous version. We further hope that those who read the new entries, either in the CD-ROM or print version, will find that they address a range of issues of great import to our profession and that they provide useful information. Our goal was to provide a useful tool for social work practitioners, educators, researchers, managers, and students. This update represents our best effort toward that end.

Richard L. Edwards, PhD, ACSW, *Editor-in-Chief*
Dean and Professor
School of Social Work
University of North Carolina at Chapel Hill

July 1997

How to Use the Encyclopedia

For the 19th edition of the *Encyclopedia of Social Work,* the editorial board attempted to collect the most current scholarly analyses of practice and research. Reflecting the breadth of the diverse social work profession, the three-volume set, published in March 1995, contains 290 entries, representing the work of nearly 350 authors. The 1997 print *Supplement* to the *Encyclopedia* adds 30 brand new entries. It also includes the same search tools for readers featured in the 19th Edition.

CONTENT

The editorial board sought to make the 19th Edition the most comprehensive reference in social welfare. Numerous areas of interest are covered in much greater depth than in previous editions. Among the topics with greatly enhanced content are

- Corrections and Justice
- Cultural Competence
- Direct Practice
- HIV/AIDS
- International Social Work
- Management
- Racial and Ethnic Groups
- Research
- Sexual Orientation.

For the 1997 *Supplement*, the Encyclopedia Update Committee commissioned 30 new entries to address emerging topics and to reflect changes in the profession and in society. New entries expand coverage of such areas as

- Adoption
- Aging
- Children
- Community
- Domestic Violence
- Electronic Technologies
- Ethics
- Health Care
- Managed Care
- Management
- Mental Illness
- Spirituality.

The *Supplement* also includes 15 new biographies and the 1996 *NASW Code of Ethics.*

ORGANIZATION OF THE PRINT VERSION

The print version of the 19th Edition, which consists of 290 entries and 142 biographies, is published in three volumes:

Volume 1: A–E
Volume 2: F–O
Volume 3: P–Y and biographies

Each volume contains a full table of contents and an index to make it easier for readers to locate entries. The *Supplement* contains many of the same search features as the 19th Edition.

Entries have been placed in alphabetic order, word by word; colons within a title precipitate a secondary sort. The following example illustrates the pattern:

Asian Americans Overview
Asian Americans: Chinese
Asian Americans: Japanese
Asian Americans: Southeast Asians
Asian Indians

SEARCH TOOLS

Readers may open a volume and turn to the appropriate place in the alphabet to find the information they seek. We have also incorporated several tools to help you find a specific topic or a set of related topics.

Detailed Table of Contents

At the beginning of each volume, there is a complete table of contents for the full *Encyclopedia.* Entry titles, stated as simply and descriptively as possible, are listed in alphabetic order, and the names of authors and the opening page number are given.

Subject Cross-References

Although we have attempted to place entries where readers might be most likely to look, many terms might be used interchangeably. Therefore, numerous subject cross-references have been inserted in the 19th Edition and the *Supplement* to help readers find entries quickly. Some examples:

Native Americans
See American Indians

Refugees
   See Displaced People

Comprehensive Index

The highly detailed, easy-to-follow index is your best source for people, organizations, federal legislation, and places. Browsing through the index will lead you to a wide range of key topics. The index also includes cross-references (such as OAA. *See* Old Age Assistance—Title I) and "see also" references (such as Prisons. *See also* Community-Based Corrections; Family-Based Corrections).

Reader's Guides

Reader's Guides will help you locate entries on related topics. In the 19th Edition, Reader's Guides are interspersed with entries in alphabetic order. The *Supplement* lists all of the Reader's Guides in appendix 2 at the back of the book. Titles of new entries (those included in the *Supplement*) appear in boldface. These guides list the pertinent entries related to the subject. For example:

READER'S GUIDE

HIV/AIDS

The following entries contain information on this general topic:

HIV/AIDS Overview
HIV/AIDS: Direct Practice
HIV/AIDS: Men
HIV/AIDS: Pediatric
HIV/AIDS: Women

We have attempted to provide as many ways to find a subject as possible. For example, you will find entries related to people of color in several Reader's Guides:

   Cultural Competence
   National Origin Groups
   People of Color
   Racial and Ethnic Groups
   Special Populations

A full listing of Reader's Guides appears on page xxii in the 19th Edition and immediately following this section.

For Further Information

Another way to find related entries is to review the additional entry titles listed at the end of each entry. For example, the "Aging: Alzheimer's Disease and Other Disabilities" entry includes the following:

For further information see

Adult Day Services; Adult Protective Services; Aging Overview; Aging: Direct Practice; Aging: Public Policy Issues and Trends; **Aging: Racial and Ethnic Groups;** Aging: Services; Aging: Social Work Practice; Bereavement and Loss; Brief Therapies; **Christian Social Work;** Clinical Social Work; Direct Practice Overview; Families Overview; Group Practice Overview; Human Development; Interviewing; **Jewish Communal Services; Managed Care: Implications for Social Work Practice;** Mental Health Overview; Natural Helping Networks; Public Social Services; Self-Help Groups; **Serious Mental Illness: A Biopsychosocial Perspective;** Social Work Practice: Theoretical Base.

Entries in the new *Supplement* contain cross-references to other new entries as well as to entries in the 19th Edition. Titles of entries contained in the *Supplement* are boldface.

Key Words

Authors have supplied up to five key words or key word phrases that most succinctly describe the content of the entry. You may use these to search for other entries in the index.

Authors

Authors are listed with the title of the entry in the table of contents, and there is a byline immediately following the entry title in the text. At the end of each entry, you will find the author's position and address as they were at the time the *Encyclopedia* or *Supplement* was published.

Bibliographic Information

Because of the number of entries and the extensive reference and reading lists for them, the 19th Edition provides perhaps the most comprehensive bibliographic database extant in social work. The reference style is the author–date citation style used in all NASW Press publications. References are listed immediately following each entry.

   Most entries also include a "Further Reading" list. The materials in these listings, although not specifically mentioned in the text of the entry, provide additional helpful information on the topic.

BIOGRAPHIES

The 19th Edition, like previous editions, includes biographical information on people who had a major impact on the profession during their lives. The biography section for the 19th Edition immediately follows the "Youth Services" entry in Volume 3 and includes 142 biographies. The *Supplement* carries an additional 15 biographies. These individuals, all of whom are deceased, are recognized for their significant contributions.

Not all of the people whose biographies appear are social workers, but the work they did during their lives influenced social work significantly or made a major difference in the delivery of social services. The editorial board was particularly concerned about adding people from many racial and ethnic groups.

STATISTICS

Previous editions of the *Encyclopedia* included a specific section devoted to statistics, generally within the body of the *Encyclopedia.* Concerned that a statistics section would not serve readers well for the life of an edition, the editorial board of the 18th Edition commis-

sioned a separate volume of statistical tables, charts, and graphs.

In 1992 the NASW Press released the *Social Work Almanac,* by Leon Ginsberg, which is a full book of data related to social services. Rather than duplicate this effort, the editorial board of the 19th Edition requested that Ginsberg update the volume; the 2nd Edition of the *Social Work Almanac* was published simultaneously with the 19th Edition in 1995. It has now been revised and is included on *The Social Work Reference Library, 1997 Update,* on CD-ROM.

CONCLUSION

The *Encyclopedia of Social Work* was three years in development, and the *Supplement* nearly two. Many people—the editorial board, the update committee, a total of nearly 400 authors, and staff—have collaborated to create an up-to-date reference work that presents the richness, the vitality, and the depth of social work knowledge. We hope that it will be useful to scholars, practitioners, and students as they continue to expand the knowledge base of the profession.

Listing of Reader's Guides

(For full Reader's Guides, see appendix 2.)

Adolescents
Adults
African Americans
Aging
AIDS/HIV
Asian Americans
Assessment
Budgeting
Child Abuse
Children and Youths
Clinical Social Work
Community
Computer Use
Courts and Corrections
Crisis Intervention
Cultural Competence
Death and Dying
Direct Practice
Disabilities
Education
Employment
Ethics
Families

Feminist Practice
Fields of Practice
Finances
Foster Care
Fundraising
Gay Men
Gerontology
Group Work
Health
Hispanics/Latinos
History
HIV/AIDS
Homelessness
Homosexuality
Immigrants
Income Security
Information Systems
International Issues
Justice
Legal Issues
Legal Regulation
Legislation
Lesbians

Management
Medical Care
Men
Mental Health
National Origin Groups
Needs Assessment
Parenting
People of Color
Planning
Poverty
Professional Associations
Public Assistance
Public Policy
Public Social Services
Racial and Ethnic Groups
Regulation of Social Work
Religion and Spirituality

Research
Residential Care
Sexual Abuse
Sexuality
Social Services Delivery
Social Supports
Social Work Education
Social Work Profession
Special Populations
Staff Development
Substance Abuse
Third-Party Payments
Treatment Approaches
Vendorship
Violence
Welfare
Women

Introduction

Paula Allen-Meares

The NASW Press published the 19th edition of the *Encyclopedia of Social Work* in March 1995 in both print and CD-ROM formats. Advances in technology have made it possible for NASW to update the CD-ROM about every two years to accompany the print supplement of new entries. Shortly after the 19th Edition appeared, NASW President Jay Cayner appointed the Encyclopedia Update Committee. The committee met several times in 1996 to discuss which of the 290 entries in the 19th Edition would be updated and on what topics new entries would be commissioned. Their work resulted in a revised CD-ROM that includes 65 updated entries, 30 new entries, 15 new biographies, the *NASW Code of Ethics* and the *NASW Bylaws* as approved by the 1996 Delegate Assembly, a revised *Social Work Almanac,* 2nd Edition, and the 1995 *Social Work Dictionary,* 3rd Edition. The print supplement includes the 30 new entries and the 15 biographies, as well as the *Code of Ethics.*

Updating the 19th edition of the *Encyclopedia of Social Work* has been an enormous task. At moments it seemed nearly as difficult as producing an entirely new edition. Issuing periodic updates is critically important, however, because many practitioners and educators rely on the information in the *Encyclopedia.* This edition is 19th in a series of premier reference works for the profession that began in 1929 when the Russell Sage Foundation published the first *Social Work Year Book.* Ten editions of the year book were published by Russell Sage, first at two-year and later at three-year intervals, between 1929 and 1949. The American Association of Social Workers (AASW) published the 11th and 12th editions in 1951 and 1954, respectively. In 1955 AASW merged with six other organizations to form the National Association of Social Workers, which continued to publish the year book until 1960, when a special committee was appointed to re-evaluate the nature and use of the publication. In 1965 the first edition to be titled the *Encyclopedia of Social Work* was published; subsequent editions appeared in 1971, 1977, and 1987, along with occasional supplements. The 19th Edition was the first to include three volumes and the first to be published in CD-ROM format.

Throughout its history, the *Encyclopedia* retained its prominence and served as a resource to practitioners, those in academia, and many other groups and individuals needing information about the social work profession. The 19th Edition has ably upheld this tradition of excellence: Among other honors it was named one of the outstanding reference books of 1995 by *Choice,* the journal of college and research librarians, and it received a silver medal for excellence in print from Washington Edpress, a major professional publishing organization in Washington, DC. One of the strengths of the *Encyclopedia* has always been its breadth: It provides a wonderful historical account of many key areas and is written by a diverse group of practitioners and academics. For this update to the 19th Edition, the specially appointed Update Committee strove to maintain the quality of the original publication and the 19th Edition and at the same time to include new material to keep abreast of changes in the profession and society at large.

Issuing an update to the 19th Edition affords an excellent opportunity to take stock of the profession and to carefully examine recent changes and their implications. Analyzing the way social work is practiced today reveals a continuing commitment to the ideals of the profession even as cultural norms are shifting. The social work profession is undergoing rapid change, particularly as the network of federal and state social services is transformed in the wake of welfare reform. We cannot yet anticipate all the effects of welfare reform, but to assist social workers and other professionals in learning to navigate their new environment, the Update Committee included the latest research and information in the relevant entries.

Changes in the 1997 Update

Welfare reform is not the only change social work professionals are facing. This update attempts to address a wide variety of emerging trends and new emphases by including new entries and revising old ones. It features 65 revised entries, some with only slight changes and some with extensive alterations. It includes the latest information on medical advances, social services programs, local and national laws and regulations, theoretical perspectives, and research results. It also includes 30 new entries and 15 new biographies. The new information spans the breadth of social work practice and research, touching on the most important and timely issues confronting the profession—both in newly emergent areas and in long-established ones. Following are some of the areas that have seen the most far-reaching changes since the publication of the 19th Edition just over two years ago.

International Social Work

Social work professionals have been increasingly concerned with international issues, partly as a result of escalating globalization. Since World War II, the United States has increasingly renounced its former isolationism as it recognizes the interdependency among nations. As Franklin Roosevelt said, "We have learned that we cannot live alone, at peace; that our own well-being is dependent on the well-being of other nations, far away. . . .We have learned to be citizens of the world, members of the human community." During the past several years, there have been significant advances in global trade and economy, including the passage of the North American Free Trade Agreement and the implementation of the European Union. New technology has similarly brought people together across nations; today we can e-mail a colleague across the globe as easily as across the hall. These developments have heightened researchers' interest in international issues; similarly, recent events have required some practitioners to develop new skills and knowledge in response to shifting responsibilities. Accordingly, the updated *Encyclopedia* offers new entries titled "Adoption: International" and "World Social Situation." The fall of communism in Eastern Europe in the 1990s increased public awareness of the differences—and in some cases the similarities—among government systems and their social services networks. For example, the plight of Romania's orphaned and abandoned children received much attention in the mainstream press and spurred social work researchers to conduct cross-national studies. At the same time, some practitioners found themselves needing specialized knowledge to help their

clients involved in various ways with international adoption. The knowledge gained through this recent research is not limited to practitioners working with international issues; whatever our field of practice or area of interest, cross-national comparisons give us greater insight into the strengths and weaknesses of our own systems and habits.

Demographics

The continuing "graying" of the American population prompted the Update Committee to commission entries titled "Aging: Alzheimer's Disease and Other Disabilities" and "Aging: Racial and Ethnic Groups." Recent research has developed our understanding of the particular issues affecting elderly people and of the importance of devising strategies for dealing with aging clients that address their long-term medical, mental heath, and family needs. As life expectancies have expanded, older people are finding themselves more in need of health and social services and, at the same time, less likely to have a family member close by to provide care and to coordinate services. In addition, because the fiscal future of the social security system remains precarious, elderly people and those approaching retirement are facing economic uncertainty on a scale not seen in the United States since the passage of the Social Security Act in 1935. These changing demographics are creating an additional demand for social workers and—combined with the growth in managed care—are redefining practice with elderly people.

Managed Care

Health care in the United States is undergoing a revolution as managed care increasingly becomes the norm. In response, this update includes four new entries: "Managed Care: Implications for Social Work Practice," "Managed Care: A Review of Recent Research," "Health Care Practice Overview," and "Health Care: Policy Development." Social workers are finding that clients with mental and physical health issues are receiving care in an entirely new environment. The committee has tried to include both the positive and the negative aspects that researchers and practitioners see in the move to managed care. The new emphasis on the bottom line has led some to believe that economic status is increasingly dictating the quality of health care a patient receives. However, managed care's emphasis on team approaches enables the breadth of client/ patient difficulties to be addressed as social workers and health care providers share information and work together. As social workers increasingly practice in teams with other professionals, new challenges must be met, and the literature has reflected the need to find new solutions. Research is sorely needed to study the current systems; we still need to understand better the role of the managed care environment in social work and the implications it holds for education preparation.

Religion and Spirituality

Recent social work literature shows an expanded interest in issues of spirituality and religion, and accordingly this update includes new entries titled "Christian Social Work," "Jewish Communal Services," and "Spirituality." Researchers have found many fruitful areas of inquiry concerning individuals and cultures with a strong religious base, and practitioners are responding positively to the new knowledge and suggested approaches researchers are disseminating. The emphasis on spirituality seems to result not so much from an increase in religious practices and beliefs as from a heightened awareness on the part of social work professionals that our practice needs to be as sensitive to religious issues as to gender, socioeconomic, and ethnic ones. The recent emphasis on spirituality is a new development in our tradition of addressing the needs of the total person, rather than merely treating the symptoms of individual problems.

Electronic Resources and the Internet

Perhaps the biggest change in the two years since the 19th Edition was published has been the phenomenal growth of the Internet and the emergence of the World Wide Web as an amazingly powerful information resource and research tool. This update includes entries titled "Social Work Education: Electronic Technologies" and "The Internet," although continued rapid growth in electronic technology and resources will no doubt produce yet more changes. The Internet is still young, and we have only begun to discover the informational, educational, and research opportunities it offers. Two years ago, many of us had only the most rudimentary acquaintance with the World Wide Web, but today we use it daily for the easy access it provides to a range of information. The Internet is more than the conglomeration of information that is the World Wide Web. Currently, many universities are developing distance learning techniques and programs in which the Internet is used to link physically distant students and teachers. In addition, researchers are exploring the capabilities of the Internet to connect groups of people into electronic communities with their own distinct culture and norms. The Internet will thus become an even more powerful means of connection and communication in the future, one that will present new challenges and opportunities for social work research and practice.

Conclusion

The NASW Press looks forward to producing future revisions of the 19th edition of the *Encyclopedia of Social Work*. Rapid advances in technology have made more frequent updates in electronic formats possible, and future revisions will no doubt be available online.

The 19th Edition and the 1997 revised CD-ROM and print supplement offer a contemporary, forward-looking reference tool serving social workers in every environment. It is the Update Committee's pleasure to present this 1997 update to you and its wish that it will prove useful in navigating the rapidly changing landscape of our profession.

Paula Allen-Meares, PhD, LCSW, is chair, NASW Communications Committee, and dean and professor, School of Social Work, University of Michigan, 1065 Frieze Building, Ann Arbor, MI 48109.

A

Adoption: International
Victor Groza

International adoptions have increased since World War II. This entry reviews practice and research literature on international adoption, offers a typology for classifying children adopted internationally, and reviews the services and issues encountered in international adoption, from preparing families for adoption through post-legalization issues. Results from a study of Romanian children adopted into the United States are used to elucidate the discussion.

Adoption has been a family structure since recorded history, and international adoptions have increased since the end of World War II. Initially most children adopted internationally became available for adoption as a result of being abandoned or orphaned in times of war. After World War II children were abandoned or orphaned more often as a result of poverty and overpopulation rather than war (Ngabonziza, 1988; Resnick, 1984). Beginning in 1955, as the number of European children available for adoption began to decrease, children were adopted from less-developed countries (Resnick, 1984). International adoption represents approximately 10 percent of all adoptions in the United States (Barth, 1995). According to estimates provided by Adoptive Families of America and based on the number of visas issued, more than 7,000 children are adopted internationally each year.

Before 1990, most international adoptees came from Asia or South America, with Korea and Colombia having the most children placed for adoption. Beginning in 1990, the fall of communism throughout the Soviet Union and Eastern and Central Europe added new children to those adopted internationally; there was a steady decrease in the number of children adopted from Asia and an increase in adoptions from Europe. European adoptions, particularly in 1990 and 1991, were predominantly from Romania. By 1992, however, the number of Romanian adoptions ranked second

to the number of children adopted from the republics of the former Soviet Union. In 1995, there was an increase in children arriving from Asia; most of these children were predominantly from China as a result of increased flexibility in adoption regulations in that country. Thus, since the 1950s, different countries have been sources for international adoption. Although the histories and cultures of these countries differ, there are many similarities in their child welfare systems.

Child welfare systems in most developing or war-torn countries are predominantly institutional or group care–based systems, unlike the that in the United States, which is predominantly a foster family–based system. Thus, the overwhelming majority of children adopted internationally have spent time in institutional settings. Many of these children are placed in institutions at infancy or shortly thereafter. To have an accurate understanding of international adoption, practitioners must also have an understanding of the risk inherent to children who are institutionalized early in their lives.

The negative effects of early institutionalization have been known since the beginning of the 20th century. Early institutionalization interrupts the parent–child bonding cycle, which can result in attachment difficulties and can slow the child's emotional, social, and physical development (Bowlby, 1951; Dennis, 1973; Freud & Burlingham, 1944; Goldfarb, 1943a, 1943b, 1944, 1955; Kaler & Freeman, 1994; Provence & Lipton, 1962; Spitz, 1945; Tizard & Hodges, 1977; Tizard & Joseph, 1970; Tizard & Rees, 1974, 1975). It also increases the likelihood that the child will have psychiatric impairments as an adult (Frank, Klass, Earls, & Eisenberg, 1996).

The author would like to thank Daniela Ileana for her assistance in preparing this manuscript and Thais Tepper from the Parent Network for the Post-Institutionalized Child, who commented on an earlier version of this manuscript.

Early deprivation tends to affect the child's ability to make smooth transitions from one developmental stage to another. The unique risks to children raised in congregate care are outlined in Table 1. Concerns about the effects of early deprivation have received renewed attention recently as a result of the influx of international adoptees from former communist countries, particularly given the poor conditions of many institutions caring for orphaned or abandoned children.

This entry outlines issues related to the international adoption of children placed from institutional settings. It includes information for practitioners to assist families in preparing for international adoptions, as well as information on services families who have adopted internationally may need.

THE CHILD ADOPTED INTERNATIONALLY

As stated previously, the vast majority of children adopted internationally have spent

---

TABLE 1
Risks to Children from Early Institutionalization

Health risks
  Increased risk for TB and hepatitis
  Below-normal weight and height
  Increased risk for opportunistic infection
  Feeding difficulties at placement

Developmental risks
  Delay in fine and gross motor skills
  Delay in social skills
  Delay in language skills
  Learning problems

Personality risks
  Passive or apathetic
  Defiant or aggressive
  Depression
  Personality disorders
  Hyperactivity
  Immaturity
  Hoarding food or objects

Attachment risks
  Overfriendliness to strangers
  Indiscriminate with strangers
  Poor relationship boundaries
  Lack of trust
  Unwillingness or inability to be comforted
    when upset
  Avoidance of close, intimate relations
  Clinginess and anxiety
  Oversensitivity to touch
  Fearfulness

---

time living in group or institutional settings. Based on my research and experience in international adoption, I propose the following classification for the types of children adopted from institutions. The first group of children is the "resilient rascals." These children, regardless of their circumstances, seem to survive relatively well. Some come from horrific conditions but, for the most part, fare well in orphanages. Some were favored children and received a great deal of attention. Others who did not receive the needed attention from adults turned to their peers. Resilient rascals usually adjust well in family settings. About one-fifth of internationally adopted children fall into this category.

The second group of children, the "wounded wonders," demonstrate significant effects from institutionalization. However, families often report, with awe and astonishment, the changes that occur (for example, rapid weight and height gains) after these children enter their adoptive homes. This group of children represents the majority of children from institutions. Initially they can be a real challenge—with marked difficulties in development and problems with other life transitions—but over time these children seem to respond favorably to the home environment. For the most part the wounded wonders fare adequately in their families and make tremendous gains in their health and development. About 60 percent of children fall into this category.

The third group of children is the "challenged children." These children are severely affected by their institutionalization. Many have special needs, and although they show improvement, the effects of institutionalization continue to have considerable impact on their lives and the lives of family members. It is interesting that the same circumstances can result in different outcomes for children—that is, children who experience the same conditions can have markedly different outcomes. Outcomes are influenced, in part, by prenatal care, prenatal exposure to toxic substances, heredity, and temperament. Not surprisingly, parents have the most difficulty with this group of children. They are also a challenge to school systems and require special services. Many families are not adequately prepared to parent these types of children, who offer unique challenges; some interventions work for short durations, and then families have to try new interventions. There is still much to be learned about these children and what happens to the families who adopt them over the course of their lives together. The families who unknowingly adopt these children remain at risk for disruption, dissolution, and other negative adoption outcomes. About one-fifth of children fall into this category.

Although institutionalization poses risks to children, results from adoption studies (Harvey, 1983; Kim, Hong, & Kim, 1979; Rathbun, DiVirgilio, & Waldfogel, 1958; Rathbun, McLaughlan, Bennett, & Garland, 1965), a review of adoption studies (Tizard, 1991), and recent reports about children from Romania (Groze & Ileana, 1996; Groze & Schmidt, 1995) are generally quite positive. For example, Rathbun et al. (1965), in a study of 38 children adopted internationally, suggested that only 20 percent of the children had severe adjustment difficulties. Five years later, of the 33 children participating in the second part of the study, fewer than 10 percent (n = 2) needed professional assistance. Twenty-five percent of the children continued to have some adjustment problems, but the majority (more than 65 percent) experienced positive outcomes. Kim et al. (1979), in a follow-up of 21 Korean children adopted by 15 white couples living in New York, found only one child with severe psychiatric problems; other areas of growth and development showed no remarkable differences, and although the authors were not explicit in their comments, these adoptions seemed to be progressing quite well. Harvey (1983), in his follow-up of 102 Vietnamese children adopted into 93 Australian families, reported that more than 94 percent of adoptions were successful. Initially most parents reported that their children had adjustment problems, but at the time of the study, the vast majority of parents were very positive about their children's development and behavior. Groze and Ileana (1996), in a follow-up study of 475 children from Romania adopted by 399 American families, found that most families reported that behavior difficulties or health problems were not apparent and were as described by the agency or individual involved in the adoption process. Children with preadoptive histories of institutionalization are more likely to suffer from delays in development and have more handicaps or difficulties. They also are more likely to be below normal weight and height at placement. However, in general, the outcomes reported in this study

were very hopeful. Overall, parent–child relationships were positive, most children had made up delays in development, the majority did not have behavior difficulties, and about 91 percent of respondents rated their adoptions as having a positive effect on their families.

However, there is at least one study that raises concerns about outcomes for international adoptees. Verhulst, Althaus, and Bieman (1990) compared parent perceptions of behavior and emotional problems of 2,148 international adoptees ages 10 to 15 with parent perceptions for a same-age sample of 933 nonadopted children from the general population. Data were gathered through surveys (for international adoptees) and home interviews (for adoptees from the general population); the Child Behavior Checklist was used to assess behavior and emotional problems (Achenbach, 1991; Achenbach & Edelbrock, 1983). The adopted group obtained significantly higher total scores in problem areas than the nonadopted group. However, only 16 percent of the children ages 10 and 11 and 23 percent of the children ages 12 to 15 had scores that would place them in the clinical range (that is, scores similar to those of children receiving mental health services). Although these percentages were greater than those for the nonadopted general population sample, it is important to note that the vast majority of international adoptees did not show behavior problems. In addition, the adopted children showed some strengths: They were scored as more skillful in sports and nonsports activities and were more active in organizations than the general population sample.

Thus, in the extant studies of international adoption, there is much reason for cautious optimism. However, social workers also must be knowledgeable about issues faced both by families considering international adoption and by families who have adopted internationally.

The sections that follow highlight issues related to international adoption. To illustrate specific points, data collected by Groze and Ileana (1996) in their sample of 399 American families who adopted 475 children from Romania are reported. This is the largest data set collected to date on children recently adopted from Eastern Europe. Although the information is based on the experiences of families who adopted children from Romania, the similarities between institutional and societal structures for children adopted from other countries suggest the usefulness of these data in understanding issues for many international adoptees. The estimated percentages are based on the quantitative and qualitative data reported by families. Details of the sample and other adoption outcomes are available elsewhere and are not presented here (Groze & Ileana, 1996; Groze & Schmidt, 1995).

PREPARING FAMILIES WHO ARE CONSIDERING INTERNATIONAL ADOPTION

Adoption preparation is an important part of the adoption process. There are long-term benefits to preparing families for adoption, whereas lack of preparation has serious negative effects. Adoption home studies are part of the preparation process. The primary purpose is to screen adoptive families to protect children from harmful situations. These studies also help families clarify their intentions and flexibility regarding the characteristics of the child or children they desire to adopt (Barth, 1995). In addition, structured and educational adoption preparation and training—resources provided by agencies and social workers—can assist families in being successful. Families need training about the process of adoption, issues that are unique to life as an adoptive family, and characteristics that may place them at risk for adoption problems, as well as characteristics that may strengthen their lives as adoptive families. Some families, given accurate information about adoption issues and the adoption process, will decide against pursuing adoption when they recognize that they may not be successful or that there is an incongruity between their expectations and the realities of adoption. Others may need assistance in making the decision whether to pursue adoption. Still other families are able to make the changes necessary to be successful adopters. Katz (1986) highlighted the benefits of preparation and training, particularly when the preparation focuses on characteristics that families can be taught to maximize their success in adoption. These characteristics include the ability to (1) deal with strong, negative emotions; (2) delay gratification of parental needs, including the desire for reciprocity from the child; (3) rejoice in small achievements; (4) be flexible, patient, and humorous; and (5) know their limits so they can do what is necessary to take care of themselves. It is also helpful for families to have a strong support system (see Groze, 1996; Katz, 1986; Rosenthal & Groze, 1992).

There are many prepackaged curricula for adoptive families. Local departments of human services often have preparation activities and educational–training programs that are beneficial for potential adoptive families. At a minimum, parents should either receive training or, in the event the agency facilitating the adoption does not provide training, attend seminars or read books in the following areas:

- details on the legal and social process of adoption in both the United States and abroad
- issues of abandonment, separation, grief, loss, and mourning for adoptees that are evident throughout the life cycle
- issues of separation, grief, loss, and mourning for infertile couples that are evident throughout the life cycle
- the adoptive family's life cycle and unique issues in family formation
- individual and family identity development in adoption
- unique issues of attachment in adoption
- outcomes and risks in international adoptions.

Adoption preparation helps families understand the unique issues in forming families or adding to families through adoption. A successful adoption depends less on the child and more on parental and family characteristics that allow the child to be incorporated into the family without an intolerable level of family distress or chronic crises. The lack of preparation cannot be easily compensated for later (Aldridge & Cautley, 1975), and adequate preparation reduces the risk of negative adoption outcomes (Barth, 1988; Barth & Berry, 1988). Social workers can play active roles in helping families successfully prepare for adoption. The list above serves as a guide for the type of content that should be included in preparing families, as well as the areas of knowledge that are important for social workers to master if they practice in this arena.

As part of the preparation, it is the family's responsibility to develop a cultural plan that will help their child build an identity as a cultural and ethnic person. As part of this plan, it might be helpful for the adoptive family to prepare a family life book, similar to a child's life book, that would include information about the child as a cultural person. (A life book is a scrapbook that contains photos, mementos, drawings, and stories that form the child's life experiences and is used to help the child connect and integrate the past and the present.) The family life book is developed by the family before adoptive placement and includes all the information leading up to the adoptive placement. Although typically the book includes pictures and stories, it could also have a section on the cultural history and identity of the biological family. Also, as part of the family life book, a plan should be developed to keep the child connected to his or her culture, history, and traditions. Such a plan might include celebrating certain dates that are important in the child's country of origin, preparing foods native to that country, and ensuring access to culturally significant music and books. The exact content and plan are less important than having the family think about these issues and how they can integrate this part of the child's life into their lives as an adoptive family.

In addition to these preparation activities, social workers can help families understand the financial and medical issues in international adoption.

Finances

Social workers, as part of adoption preparation, must assist families in understanding the financial issues in international adoption. About one-third of families who adopted children from Romania commented about unanticipated costs in the adoption process before placement; 16 percent indicated they needed adoption subsidies after placement, and 13 percent indicated they needed additional financial support (Groze & Schmidt, 1995).

Social workers should explore the following financial issues with families as they make their decisions to adopt. Adoptive families should

- make sure they understand the fees they are being charged and how the fees were determined
- know that they have the right to question any item or charge incurred
- determine whether they are responsible for traveling costs and arrangements in a host country, and whether they might be required to pay any additional fees once they leave the United States
- assess whether their adoption agency will pay for needed services after the child is placed in their home and the adoption is legalized

- discern what expenses they will be responsible for if they are not approved to adopt children or if information included in a home study disqualifies them from adopting in their country of choice
- negotiate what expenses they will be responsible for in the event they change their minds about adopting or change their minds about a child chosen for them if they do not believe an appropriate match has been made.

To assist families who want to adopt, flexible and creative opportunities can be developed to provide funding for agency costs in adoption; these might include low-cost loans, unsecured loans, and grants. In some instances airlines have donated tickets—or greatly reduced ticket prices—to modest-income adoptive parents who need to travel to the country in which they are adopting to finalize the adoption. International hotel chains may offer discounts for adoptive parents when they travel internationally on behalf of their children. Social workers may be able to play both advocacy and brokering roles as they assist families with the financial component of international adoption. On an individual-case basis, some families have already taken advantage of these kinds of opportunities.

In addition, social workers need to advocate for regulation of adoption expenses for several reasons. First, compromises are made in agency decision making and in the quality of services given to parents before and after adoption—including the information given to prospective adoptive families—when children become a commodity in a market economy and families are seen as consumers. These compromises occur in several ways. There is a conflict of interest when professionals in "sending countries" are paid only when placements are finalized. In such cases either the information about the child is not gathered properly, or information about health, development, and living conditions are purposely ignored to facilitate a placement. Once the agency receives funds from the adoptive family, the adoption is usually approved, even if there are reservations about the appropriateness of the family. If the family is unwilling to participate in preparation activities, the agency may not force the issue because it must compete for its market share of adoptive families. If the family believes that preparation activities are an additional hassle to the adoption process, they may choose an agency that does not require participation in such activities. Thus, when adoption as a practice becomes a business enterprise, it often loses focus and integrity.

Second, there is wide variation in the costs of international adoptions for different agencies or individuals in the same country. A 1994 survey of agencies providing international adoption from Romania revealed that costs ranged from $8,000 to $20,000 (Groze, 1995). Although the exact reason for this discrepancy is not known, its existence should be of concern. The amount of money is related both to the philosophy of the agency or individual facilitating the adoption and the amount of money paid by the family for the adoption. The more desperate the family (which often means the adopter is a single individual or an older couple, or there has been a long waiting period), the higher the costs. In addition, the profitability of international adoptions has allowed unscrupulous individuals and agencies to prey on naive or unsuspecting potential adoptive parents. For example, some families have paid fees and acquired children through medical visas. The stipulation for this type of arrangement is that once a child's medical needs are met, he or she is to be returned to the country of origin. Some families have been traumatized because they did not understand the agreement and, having spent a great deal of money for the placement and medical care of their child, thought they had a legal and clear adoption. In other instances families continue to pay fees to agencies or individuals who have no legal authority to conduct international adoptions to keep their cases "pending." The evidence suggests that federal oversight into costs and regulation of fees for international adoptions is warranted.

Third, when families pay fees for adoptions, then the emphasis becomes finding "a child for a family" (parent-centered focus) and not "a family for a child" (child-centered focus). Contemporary adoption practice has moved to a child-centered model because it is in the best interest of the child. However, the fee-for-service arrangement undermines this philosophy and often results in compromised adoption practices.

Children and families will benefit from regulation of the costs associated with adoption. Regulation of adoption financing remains an advocacy issue for social workers.

Medical Care

Medical information received about children from developing countries is often inaccurate. Information indicating that the child is healthy should be viewed with as much concern as information that the child has a medical problem or handicapping condition. The training of professionals in modern child development assessment and diagnosis is woefully lacking or substandard in many parts of the world. Medical testing information, although better in U.S. embassies, is still problematic.

As much information as possible should be obtained from the country of origin before placement. However, families should get a complete medical assessment by qualified U.S. medical personnel once the child is placed in the United States. One of the sites for medical assessment of international adoptees is the International Adoption Clinic at the University of Minnesota Hospital and Clinic in St. Paul–Minneapolis, Minnesota. (For more information about the International Adoption Health Center, contact Dr. Dana Johnson, International Adoption Clinic, University of Minnesota Hospital and Clinic, Minneapolis, MN 55455 [1-800-688-5252].) Accurate and comprehensive information at the time of placement can be used to plan medical follow-ups in the future. At the very least it gives parents peace of mind about the health of their children.

In addition, families may encounter problems with their health insurance. Although some insurance companies easily add children to insurance policies once they are adopted, others do not cover adopted children without a waiting period of six months to two years. Some insurance carriers will not pay for medical testing for some diseases, such as hepatitis B. Some refuse to pay any costs toward immunizing the family if an adopted child has a medical problem such as hepatitis or tuberculosis. Families are well advised to gain a thorough understanding of their health insurance coverage and to be certain they have written documentation of coverage for any medical problems and for health care of their adoptive child.

As part of preparing families for adoption, social workers can assist families in understanding the medical issues they may face and serve as brokers in helping families obtain access to the medical services they need for diagnosis and intervention.

ISSUES FOR PARENTS WHO ADOPT CHILDREN INTERNATIONALLY

This section discusses issues for parents who have adopted internationally. The primary focus is on post-institutionalized children, because the vast majority of international adoptees have been institutionalized. It is important to note that although some institutionalized children have complex difficulties, the effects of institutionalization are influenced by multiple factors, such as the child's age at placement, prenatal care, quality of institutional care, and heredity. The following section highlights issues in caring for post-institutionalized children and makes recommendations for interventions.

As a general rule, parents should obtain as much complete and accurate information as possible to make informed decisions and pursue early intervention programs. Early intervention may not help a child with severe problems become normal, but there is ample evidence to support the many positive effects of early intervention. Early intervention can (1) support the family, (2) provide the appropriate environment for the child's level of functioning, (3) prevent the worsening of any difficulties, and (4) enhance the child's ability to develop to the fullest extent of her or his potential (Kenny & Culbertson, 1993).

Day-to-Day with the Adopted Child

Many international adoptees come from institutional settings where their needs were not consistently met. Also, these institutions have too many children, too few caregivers, and lack individual programming or attention to meet the children's needs. It is important for children to know that they can trust their caregivers to respond to their needs on demand. International adoptees, especially those who come from institutions, should have full-time caregivers and should not be placed in group situations immediately after placement. If they are immediately placed in group settings, such as day care, they may not learn to trust the adults in their lives to meet their needs. Although a full-time caregiver may be an additional burden for many families who have two adults working outside the home, it may be in the best interest of the child to be consistently cared for by specific attachment and family figures as he or she adjusts to a family setting initially after placement.

Adoptive parents need to provide structure, consistency, nurturance, and love. Most institutionalized children respond favorably to this type of environment. Any interruption or inconsistency in day-to-day routines may be stressful to the parents and disruptive to the child. Parents need to take breaks in their daily parenting tasks to function optimally. In a subsequent analysis of the data collected by Groze and Ileana (1996), about 6 percent of adoptive families used respite care, but almost 10 percent believed that respite care would have been helpful to their families. Thus, almost one-fifth of families could have benefited from this type of support.

Parents also need to recognize what they can and cannot change. Children are born with certain characteristics—namely, physical genetic makeup, intellectual capacity, and temperamental makeup. Thus, parents (both biological and adoptive) are limited in their ability to change their child's basic personality traits. Parents do, however, exert major influences on the way children express themselves. Parents need to begin the process of understanding their child and the influence they have on that child. For some parents this means asking themselves what they expect from their children. When children do not meet parents' expectations, the parents have several choices. First, they can reject the child. Second, they can attempt to make the child fit their expectations, which can be frustrating for both the parent and the child and can put the adoptive placement at risk. Third, the parents can accept the fact that the child will not meet their expectations and can change the expectations to match what the child can accomplish. This is a very difficult process, but successful adoptive families are able to modify their expectations to meet the capabilities of their children (Groze, 1996).

The addition of a new child to any family is a stressful event. Family members need support and guidance as they integrate a new child into the family system. Whether this integration is a stressful event or a crisis will depend on the combination of resources and stressors in the adoptive family system. Stress occurs in all families, but crisis occurs when existing resources are not sufficient to meet current demands. Crisis is characterized by family disorganization or disruptiveness when old patterns and capabilities are no longer adequate and change is necessary (Patterson,

1988). All families use their capabilities (resources and coping behaviors) to meet the demands (stressors and strains) of maintaining family balance. When stress occurs, the family musters the resources to deal with it. In a sense, it balances the stressor with a resource. Crisis occurs when there are too many stressors and not enough resources, or when there is a buildup of stressors such that the family cannot accommodate quickly enough to garner its resources. So both the lack of resources and an overload of stressors can place a family in crisis. Social workers can play significant roles in helping families manage the stress of day-to-day life with their adopted children and in identifying or developing resources for the adoptive family. Concrete resources, depending on the needs of the child, are identified below.

Self-Stimulating Behaviors

Self-stimulating behaviors, such as rocking, slapping, pinching, or banging the head, are a great concern for parents and practitioners. Most parents report a decrease in self-stimulating behaviors over time (see Marcovitch, Cesaroni, Roberts, & Swanson, 1995). Sweeney and Bascom (1995) reported that rocking and other self-stimulating behaviors decreased after involvement in developmental intervention programs. However, rocking became evident again when children were bored; other behaviors, such as face guarding or wrist slapping, became evident when children were exposed to new situations or stress. Parents should be aware that boredom, stress, or change may result in a reappearance of self-stimulating behaviors.

In addition to involvement with developmental intervention programs, parents may need to use behavior modification techniques. Some behaviors, when ignored, will disappear over time. However, for persistent behaviors, families are encouraged to have assessments conducted with specialists who work with children with developmental disabilities. Most county departments of mental retardation and developmental disabilities can refer these families to competent professionals. In some cases these families may want to explore the use of medication prescribed by pediatricians who have knowledge about the effects of deprivation on children. Because many families may not have access to pediatricians with this expertise, they may want to consult with programs such as the International Adoption Health Center in Minneapolis–St. Paul, Minnesota. Parents may also want to contact the Head Start Program or Early Childhood Intervention Program in their area. Many of those programs can be reached by contacting the local department of human services or the health department.

Attachment Difficulties or Disorders

An attachment difficulty or an attachment disorder is not a diagnosis; these usually fall under childhood diagnoses such as anxiety or separation disorders. The closest diagnosis to attachment difficulties is found in DSM-IV and is referred to as "reactive attachment disorder of infancy or early childhood." Attachment disorders are hard to identify in infants and toddlers, although recent research (Zeanah, Mammen, & Lieberman, 1993) and popular books (Magid & McKelvey, 1987) have made professionals and the public more aware of attachment issues. Because of the lack of set definitions and accurate diagnoses, some current treatment programs for children with attachment disorders are questionable in terms of their validity and utility. Some therapies, such as rage induction and holding techniques, are highly experimental and unusual. One holding technique involves holding children against their will until they are in a rage and then comforting them as a vehicle for promoting attachment. The belief is that the most opportune time for building a connection or attachment is after the child experiences stress and starts to relax. The relaxation process makes the child vulnerable to building an emotional connection to the parent, especially if the parent provides comfort and consolation as part of the relaxation process. These techniques are clinically rather than empirically based—that is, in carefully constructed research studies, the more intrusive techniques have not been shown to be effective, because little research has been conducted (Groze, 1992; Groze & Rosenthal, 1993). Parents should avoid rage induction therapies and use their own judgment in working with therapists who use holding techniques.

There are several ways to strengthen the bond between the child with an attachment difficulty and the adoptive parents. One way, mentioned earlier, is to educate the child about his or her history by developing a life book, or a scrapbook of mementos, drawings, pictures, and other memories from the child's life experiences (Aust, 1981; Wheeler, 1978). The life book helps the child understand his or her history and integrate and connect the past with the present. It gives the child and family a sense of history from which they can continue to build their relationship and life together. Families should be encouraged to get as much information as possible, including photos of their child's orphanage and caregivers in the orphanage, once their child has been selected. Also, with the wide accessibility of videotaping, many families can obtain videos of their children and should be encouraged to get as much visual information as possible.

Another way to help adopted children who have attachment difficulties is through behavioral approaches. Parents should model how to express feelings and use positive physical contact. Modeling expressed feelings is essential to facilitating attachment between child and parent (Groze & Rosenthal, 1993). One intervention to help parents in this process is the Steps Toward Effective Enjoyable Parenting (STEEP) program. STEEP is a comprehensive and intensive intervention program whose goal is to develop good-quality relationships between parent and child (Erickson, Korfmacher, & Egeland, 1993). The program focuses on modifying parents' inner working model of relationships developed during their own childhoods. It is designed to help parents examine their own developmental history and how it has affected their parenting skills and aims at empowering the adult to become a better parent.

A third approach to building attachment is "theraplay." *Theraplay* is an intensive, structured, short-term approach designed to enhance attachment as well as build self-esteem, trust, and mutual engagement between parent and child. The ultimate purpose is to create effective connections. The technique is a combination of structured activities for both play and therapeutic interventions (see Jennberg, 1979, 1993; Morin, 1993; Rubin & Tregay, 1989).

In addition to the type of intervention provided, parents and professionals must be very careful about the labels used to describe children. Labels such as "unattached" automatically put parents on the defensive, thinking that there is something wrong with their children. Parents and professionals would better serve children by describing them as having an attachment problem or difficulty.

There remains a serious gap in the area of attachment disorders and treatment that suggests a need for more research. Much of the knowledge about how to effectively intervene with children who have attachment difficulties is anecdotal and unscientific, which means families may struggle with these children without having access to valid treatment resources.

In addition, the following points are important for parents to know if they are to gain an understanding of how to intervene with adoptive children who display attachment difficulties:

- Behaviors that are not reinforced lose their effectiveness over time, and behaviors that are praised and reinforced are repeated.
- As children experience positive caregiving consistently over time, they change their behaviors and their cognitive models of caregivers and themselves, and attachment difficulties become less pronounced.
- The parent–child relationship is the best mechanism for promoting change in attachment; parents can use their relationships with their children to help them restructure their representation of school, others, themselves, and their relationship to others.
- Attachment patterns change over time as a result of the maturation process; parents can help their child examine and understand his or her past, giving the child a vision for the future, and can use appropriate and positive physical contact.
- Parents need to model and express feelings; modeling and expressing feelings are essential components to facilitating attachment between parent and child.
- Parents need to look for opportunities to promote attachment, such as when their child expresses anxiety or fear, or when he or she is ill or fatigued.
- Parents may need to learn how to change their expectations of their child and of their relationship with their child.

In the Groze and Ileana study (1996), fewer than 10 percent of the parents who adopted Romanian children indicated that their child had attachment problems, although anecdotal comments suggested that up to 20 percent may have had attachment difficulties. This is consistent with impressions formulated from previous researchers (Tizard & Rees, 1974,

1975). For children with severe attachment problems, parents should seek qualified professionals who have training and expertise in working with attachment difficulties. Word-of mouth recommendations from other adoptive parents are frequently the best reference for various resources. In addition, support groups composed of parents who have adopted children with attachment difficulties may be a major resource for families (Groze, 1996; Proctor, Groze, & Rosenthal, 1996). These groups often provide emotional and concrete support that helps families manage the stress of caring for special needs children. In Groze and Schmidt's (1995) study of Romanian adoptees, about one-fourth of the families who adopted Romanian children were involved in parent support groups, and another 17 percent reported that they would like to be involved in support groups.

Language Impairments

Locke (1994) described two early phases of language development that occur during the first year of life. The first phase is vocal learning, during which the child becomes oriented toward voices and faces. The second phase begins when the child develops word patterns and phrases. The lack of adequate verbal stimulation, which often occurs in institutions, may affect a child's ability to acquire language dexterity. As a result, the child is destined to be a late talker and to experience difficulty in developing expressive language, nonverbal skills, and the use of symbols. The child also may experience difficulty with receptive and expressive language skills. In the Groze and Schmidt study (1995), almost one-fourth of the families who adopted Romanian children reported obtaining speech therapy services after placement.

Wilson (1993) identified the symptoms of developmental language disorders that are evident in children who have spent formative months or years in institutions. She described a number of manifestations that are apparent in some post-institutionalized children. She also described receptive disorders as an inability or a limited ability to comprehend vocal language. Expressive disorders are characterized as an inability to express thoughts in vocal language or a limited ability to use gestures or to sign for communication purposes. Clark (1996) offered a list of language development intervention resources,

most of which focus on the family. Although the subject of Clark's writing is children exposed prenatally to alcohol and other drugs, many of the resources she highlighted are appropriate for children with preadoptive histories of institutionalization. In particular, families should have their children evaluated by speech therapists and should work with these therapists to develop language intervention programs.

Auditory Processing Problems

Related to problems with language development are problems with listening and with processing and integrating information, which are underlying sources of many learning, language, and relationship problems. Children with auditory processing problems may appear to lack interest or curiosity; be aggressive or angry; or demonstrate problematic peer relations, such as playing only by themselves, playing with younger children, or being trouble-makers or scapegoats in their peer groups. Children with auditory processing problems often have speech and language difficulties as well as general learning problems (Duchan & Katz, 1983; Lubert, 1981). Without professional assistance for at least a multifaceted assessment, parents may not understand the nature of their child's problems or the appropriate intervention strategy. There are many intervention programs and strategies for helping children who have auditory processing problems (Butler, 1983; Hoffman, 1983; Lasky & Cox, 1983). Families should contact local or regional speech and hearing centers or programs for information, assessment, and recommendations. Only a small percentage of parents (fewer than 5 percent) identified auditory processing problems in their adopted children from Romania (Groze & Ileana, 1996). Language difficulties are easier to identify, but if a child has a language difficulty, he or she may also be at risk for auditory processing problems.

Educational Difficulties

Language impairments and auditory processing problems often result in educational difficulties. Verhulst and colleagues (1990) commented on the high proportion (13 percent) of international adoptees in special education programs. About one-third of the families adopting Romanian children were involved in educational testing, assessment, or planning for their children (Groze & Schmidt,

1995). It is important for families to know that federal laws require local school districts to provide educational, developmental, and related services to children who have, or who are at risk of having, handicapping conditions (Kenny & Culbertson, 1993). Educational institutions play major roles in screening children for difficulties. Services include remedial education as well as early intervention. Families may experience reluctance or refusal on the part of local school authorities to meet the needs of their children, but by federal law they are mandated to meet these children's needs, regardless of how the needs developed.

Some adopted children have difficulties with hyperactivity (Rosenthal & Groze, 1992), and parents' reports suggest that internationally adopted children are vulnerable to attention deficit difficulties, hyperactivity, or both. These children present unique challenges in the classroom as well as in their homes. Parents need to learn negotiating skills to deal with the educational maze, as well as advocacy skills to get educational needs met for their children. Social workers can play educational and advocacy roles in assisting parents to get the educational needs of their children met within their communities.

Mental Health and Psychiatric Difficulties

Emotional and behavioral problems can lead to more serious mental health difficulties. Comprehensive, multidisciplinary assessment and treatment by trained and qualified child mental health specialists often are essential for intervention in mental health concerns. About one-fifth of Romanian adoptees and their families receive outpatient psychiatric services (Groze & Schmidt, 1995). Some international adoptees are particularly vulnerable to posttraumatic stress disorder (PTSD) as a result of their preadoptive histories. Several families who had adopted Romanian children suggested that their children had symptoms of PTSD (Groze & Schmidt, 1995).

Although a rarity, some children have or may be vulnerable to more serious psychiatric difficulties. Previous research has suggested that some of these children are at risk for serious mental health problems (Frank et al., 1996). Fortunately, however, a relatively small percentage of them evidence significant mental health difficulties (Verhulst et al., 1990). As with other concerns, social workers may play a brokering role to help families locate services,

or they may actually deliver mental health services to this population of children.

Other Behavior and Developmental Concerns

Parents may have other behavior and developmental concerns that are not reviewed here. For example, Federici (1995) cautioned that some children may be misdiagnosed with psychiatric or behavior difficulties when they really have neuropsychological deficits. Children have such deficits as a result of prenatal exposure to risk factors such as poor nutrition and environmental neglect. These risks also occur postnatally and are often found in institutions. Federici suggested that these risk factors may alter neuronal (nerve) development, brain chemistry, and molecular genetic functions. Although these claims cause many parents alarm, Federici acknowledged that there is no test to confirm or negate these declarations; they are largely based on theory, without confirmation from scientific studies. Nevertheless, Federici's suppositions are based on sound related research and theory suggesting that the part of the brain that affects personality development, emotional responsiveness, and control over emotions such as anger, love, affection, and rage could be seriously and negatively affected in post-institutionalized children. He recommended, in addition to a comprehensive neuropsychological evaluation, that parents work with professionals to develop multiple intervention strategies.

Sometimes the best interventions for children are not formal services but activities that stimulate their growth and development. In addition to the recommendations above, imaginative play training (which comprises exercises and games to encourage and endorse imaginative play) has been reported to help children. This technique is similar to play therapy and has been demonstrated to help children improve their creativity (Dansky, 1980; Udwin, 1983), improve language and verbal skills (Freyberg, 1973; Lovinger, 1974; Udwin, 1983), increase group problem solving, interaction, and critical thinking skills (Freyberg, 1973; Rosen, 1974; Udwin, 1983), and decrease aggression and hyperactivity (Freyberg, 1973; Udwin, 1983).

It is important for families to recognize that international adoption poses some risk with children who come from institutions. Although most institutionalized children recover from the trauma, others continue to have special needs. Parents must be prepared and flexible if they plan to be successful as adoptive families.

SUMMARY

There are many issues that must be sorted through by all adoptive parents. In addition, there are many special or unique issues that must be addressed by parents who are considering international adoption. Social workers employed in the area of international adoptions must effectively prepare families for adoption, including assisting those who adopt transculturally to be sensitive to issues of culture and ethnicity. They also may have to assist families with financial and medical issues. It is important that social workers be knowledgeable about policies and procedures in sending countries, as well as the legal and financial issues families may face domestically. In addition, social workers must be aware of service resources for families who adopt, in the event that these families need preventive, diagnostic, or remedial assistance.

Fortunately, many adoptive families have not needed professional services after adoptive placement. However, most families who adopt internationally need to work with social workers who will listen to them, accept the choices they make, and empower them to take charge of the services and interventions available to them and their children. Although many complicated issues exist, there are also many rewards for working in international adoption. Social work has and will continue to play a major role.

In addition, as the 21st century approaches, the Hague Conference on Private International Law may have a profound effect on international adoption (American Society of International Law, 1993). This conference offers a process for standardizing international adoption practices by establishing guidelines for cooperation between countries for the purpose of exchanging information on process and law. The conference also attempts to minimize child trafficking by setting minimal standards for accreditation, adoption processes, and reporting of noncompliance. In addition, the convention puts intercountry adoption ahead of intracountry foster care or institutionalization as the best option for children.

There are still many issues to be settled regarding implementation of the Hague Conference recommendations. Although there are many problems, the conference represents one of the first universal attempts to regulate international adoptions. The impact of this treaty and how it is codified in policy in various countries will be a major area of activity as international adoption moves into the 21st century. For a listing of those countries that have signed the Hague Convention, please go to the following web site: http://www.gov.state.md.us/sos/admin/html/certif.html.

REFERENCES

Achenbach, T. (1991). *Manual for the child behavior checklist/4–18 and 1991 profile.* Burlington: University of Vermont, Department of Psychiatry.

Achenbach, T., & Edelbrock, C. (1983). *Manual for the child behavior checklist.* Burlington: University of Vermont, Department of Psychiatry.

Aldridge, M., & Cautley, P. (1975). The importance of worker availability in the functioning of new foster homes. *Child Welfare, 54*(6), 444–453.

American Society of International Law. (1993). Hague Conference on Private International Law: Final act of the 17th session, including the Convention on Protection of Children and Co-operation in Respect to Intercountry Adoption, May 29, 1993. *International Legal Materials, 32,* 1134–1146.

Aust, P. H. (1981). Using the life story book in treatment of children in placement. *Child Welfare, 60,* 535–560.

Barth, R. (1988, winter). Disruption in older child adoptions. *Public Welfare,* pp. 323–329.

Barth, R. (1995). Adoption. In R. L. Edwards (Ed.-in-Chief), *Encyclopedia of social work* (19th ed., Vol. 1, pp. 48–60). Washington, DC: NASW Press.

Barth, R. P., & Berry, M. (1988). *Adoption and disruption: Rates, risks, and response.* New York: Aldine de Gruyter.

Bowlby, J. (1951). *Maternal care and mental health* (World Health Organization Monograph No. 2). Geneva: World Health Organization.

Butler, K. G. (1983). Language processing: Selective attention and mnemonic strategies. In E. Z. Lasky & J. Katz (Eds.), *Central auditory processing disorders* (pp. 297–318). Baltimore: University Park Press.

Clark, J. C. (1996). Language development in children prenatally drug exposed: Considerations for assessment and intervention. *Source, 6*(1), 12–14.

Dansky, J. L. (1980). Cognitive consequences of sociodramatic play and exploration training for economically disadvantaged preschoolers. *Journal of Child Psychology and Psychiatry, 21,* 47–48.

Dennis, W. (1973). *Children of the creche.* New York: Appleton-Century-Crofts.

Duchan, J. F., & Katz, J. (1983). Language and auditory processing: Top down plus bottom up. In E. Z. Lasky & J. Katz (Eds.), *Central auditory processing disorders* (pp. 31–45). Baltimore: University Park Press.

Erickson, M. F., Korfmacher, J., & Egeland, B. R. (1993). Attachments past and present: Implications for therapeutic intervention with mother–infant dyads. *Annual Progress in Child Psychiatry and Child Development, 4*(4), 459–476.

Federici, R. S. (1995). Commentary on neuropsychological evaluation of post-institutionalized children. *Post, 3/4,* 2–3.

Frank, D. A., Klass, P. E., Earls, F., & Eisenberg, L. (1996). Infants and young children in orphanages: One view from pediatrics and child psychiatry. *Pediatrics, 47,* 569–578.

Freud, A., & Burlingham, D. T. (1944). *Infants without families.* New York: International University Press.

Freyberg, J. T. (1973). Increasing the imaginative play of urban disadvantaged kindergarten children through systematic training. In J. L. Singer (Ed.), *The child's world of make-believe.* New York: Academic Press.

Goldfarb, W. (1943a). Effects of early institutional care on adolescent personality. *Journal of Experimental Education, 12,* 106–129.

Goldfarb, W. (1943b). Infant rearing and problem behavior. *American Journal of Orthopsychiatry, 15,* 249–265.

Goldfarb, W. (1944). Effects of early institutional care on adolescent personality: Rorschach data. *American Journal of Orthopsychiatry, 14,* 441–447.

Goldfarb, W. (1955). Emotional and intellectual consequences of psychologic deprivation in infancy: A re-evaluation. In P. Hoch & J. Zubin (Eds.), *Psychopathology of childhood* (pp. 105–119). New York: Grune & Stratton.

Groze, V. (1992). Adoption, attachment and self-concept. *Child and Adolescent Social Work Journal, 9,* 169–191.

Groze, V. (1995, April 28–29). *Post adoption family issues.* Keynote address presented at the Annual Conference of the American Academy of Adoption Attorneys, Atlanta.

Groze, V. (1996). *Successful adoptive families: A longitudinal study of special needs adoption.* New York: Praeger.

Groze, V., & Ileana, D. (1996). A follow-up study of adopted children from Romania. *Child and Adolescent Social Work Journal, 13,* 541–565.

Groze, V., & Rosenthal, J. (1993). Attachment theory and the adoption of children with special needs. *Social Work Research & Abstracts, 29*(2), 5–13.

Groze, V., & Schmidt, D. (1995, August 3–6). *Adopted children from Romania: Myth and reality.* Paper presented at the 21st Annual North American Council on Adoptable Children Conference, Norfolk, VA.

Harvey, I. J. (1983). Adoption of Vietnamese children: An Australian study. *Australian Journal of Social Issues, 18,* 55–69.

Hoffman, M. (1983). Psychological interventions for the child with central auditory processing disorder. In E. Z. Lasky & J. Katz (Eds.), *Central auditory processing disorders* (pp. 319–330). Baltimore: University Park Press.

Jennberg, A. M. (1979). *Theraplay: A new treatment program using structured play for problem children and their families.* San Francisco: Jossey-Bass.

Jennberg, A. M. (1993). Attachment formation. In C. E. Schaefer (Ed.), *The therapeutic powers of play* (pp. 241–265). New York: Jason Aronson.

Kaler, S. R., & Freeman, B. J. (1994). An analysis of environmental deprivation: Cognitive and social development in Romanian orphans. *Journal of Child Psychology and Psychiatry and Allied Disciplines, 35,* 769–781.

Katz, L. (1986). Parental stress and factors for success in older-child adoption. *Child Welfare, 65,* 569–578.

Kenny, T. J., & Culbertson, J. L. (1993). Developmental screening for preschoolers. In J. L. Culberston & D. J. Willis (Eds.), *Testing young children: A reference guide for developmental, psychoeducational, and psychosocial assessments* (pp. 73–100). Austin, TX: Pro-Ed.

Kim, S. P., Hong, S., & Kim, B. S. (1979). Adoption of Korean children by New York area couples: A preliminary study. *Child Welfare, 57,* 419–427.

Lasky, E. Z., & Cox, L. C. (1983). Auditory processing and language interaction: Evaluation and intervention strategies. In E. Z. Lasky & J. Katz (Eds.), *Central auditory processing disorders* (pp. 243–268). Baltimore: University Park Press.

Locke, J. (1994). The gradual emergence of developmental language disorders. *Journal of Speech and Hearing Research, 37,* 608–616.

Lovinger, S. (1974). Sociodramatic play and language development in preschool disadvantaged children. *Psychology in Schools, 11,* 313–320.

Lubert, N. (1981). Auditory perceptual impairments in children with specific language disorders: A review of literature. *Journal of Speech and Hearing Disorders, 46,* 3–9.

Magid, K., & McKelvey, C. A. (1987). *High risk: Children without a conscience.* New York: Bantam Books.

Marcovitch, S., Cesaroni, L., Roberts, W., & Swanson, C. (1995). Romanian adoption: Parents' dreams, nightmares, and realities. *Child Welfare, 74,* 991–1017.

Morin, V. (1993). *Messy activities and more.* Chicago: Chicago Review Press.

Ngabonziza, D. (1988). Inter-country adoption: In whose best interest? *Adoption & Fostering, 12*(1), 35–40.

Patterson, J. M. (1988). Families experiencing stress. *Family Systems Medicine, 6,* 202–237.

Proctor, C., Groze, V., & Rosenthal, J. A. (1996). *Social support and adoptive families of children with special needs.* Unpublished manuscript, Mandel School of Applied Social Sciences, Case Western Reserve University, Cleveland, OH.

Provence, S. A., & Lipton, R. C. (1962). *Infants in institutions.* New York: International Universities Press.

Rathbun, C., DiVirgilio, L., & Waldfogel, S. (1958). The restitutive process in children following radical separation from family and culture. *American Journal of Orthopsychiatry, 27,* 408–415.

Rathbun, C., McLaughlan, H., Bennett, O., & Garland, J. A. (1965). Later adjustment of children following radical separation from family and culture. *American Journal of Orthopsychiatry, 35,* 604–609.

Resnick, R. P. (1984). In P. Bean (Ed.), *Essays in social policy, law and sociology* (pp. 273–287). London: Tavistock.

Rosen, C. E. (1974). The effects of sociodramatic play on problem-solving behavior among culturally disadvantaged preschool children. *Child Development, 45,* 920–927.

Rosenthal, J., & Groze, V. (1992). *Special needs adoption: A study of intact families.* New York: Praeger.

Rubin, P., & Tregay, J. (1989). *Play with them: Theraplay groups in the classroom.* Springfield, IL: Charles C Thomas.

Spitz, R. A. (1945). Hospitalism: An inquiry into the genesis of psychiatric conditions in early childhood. *Psychoanalytic Study of the Child, 1,* 53–74.

Sweeney, J. K., & Bascom, B. B. (1995). Motor development and self-stimulatory movement in institutionalized Romanian children. *Pediatric Physical Therapy, 7,* 124–132.

Tizard, B. (1991). Intercountry adoption: A review of the evidence. *Journal of Child Psychology and Psychiatry, 32,* 743–756.

Tizard, B., & Hodges, J. (1977). The effect of early institutional rearing on the development of eight-year-old children. *Journal of Child Psychology and Psychiatry, 19,* 99–118.

Tizard, B., & Joseph, A. (1970). Cognitive development of young children in residential care: The study of children aged 24 months. *Journal of Child Psychology and Psychiatry, 11,* 177–186.

Tizard, B., & Rees, J. (1974). A comparison of the effects of adoption, restoration to the natural mother, and continued institutionalization on the cognitive development of four-year-old children. *Child Development, 45,* 92–99.

Tizard, B., & Rees, J. (1975). The effect of early institutional rearing on the behaviour problems and affectional relationships of four-year-old children. *Journal of Child Psychology and Psychiatry, 75,* 61–73

Udwin, O. (1983). Imaginative play training as an intervention method with institutionalized preschool children. *British Journal of Educational Psychology, 53,* 32–39.

Verhulst, F. C., Althaus, M., & Bieman, H. J. M. V. (1990). Problem behavior in international adoptees: I. An epidemiological study. *Journal of the American Academy of Child and Adolescent Psychiatry, 29,* 94–111.

Wheeler, C. (1978). Where am I going? Making a life story book. *Child Welfare, 60,* 535–560.

Wilson, B. C. (1993). Assessment of young children with communication disorders. In J. L. Culbertson & D. J. Willis (Eds.), *Testing young children: A reference guide for developmental, psychoeducational, and psychosocial assessments* (pp. 192–236). Austin, TX: Pro-Ed.

Zeanah, C. H., Mammen, K. O., & Lieberman, A. F. (1993). Disorders of attachment. In C. H. Zeanah (Ed.), *Handbook of infant mental health* (pp. 332–349). New York: Guilford Press.

Victor Groza, PhD (formerly Groze), is associate professor, Mandel School of Applied Social Sciences, Case Western Reserve University, 10900 Euclid Avenue, Cleveland, OH 44106-7164.

For further information see

Adoption; Child Care Services; Child Foster Care; Child Welfare Overview; Children: Mental Health; Children's Rights; Families Overview; International and Comparative Social Welfare; International Social Welfare: Organizations and Activities; **Oppression;** Organizations: Context for Social Services Delivery; **World Social Situation.**

Key Words	
child welfare	postadoption services
international adoption	Romania
orphanages	

Aging: Alzheimer's Disease and Other Disabilities

Sheldon S. Tobin

Alzheimer's disease, the most common form of dementing illness, is a progressive, irreversible neurological disorder of unknown etiology. As the average life span has increased, so too has the prevalence of this dreaded disease. Concurrently, incapacities in activities of daily living (ADL) from other causes have apparently decreased. Moreover, if cardiovascular diseases and cancer were cured, people would live close to 115 years or so—their genetic endowment—but with unavoidable musculoskeletal degeneration, loss of neurons, and a greater possibility of Alzheimer's disease. Although Alzheimer's disease can be definitively diagnosed only at autopsy, a provisional diagnosis can be made by a history that reveals an insidious course of memory loss, confusion, and personality changes. Social workers, therefore, have an important role in history taking and in referring assumed victims and their families for medical workups to rule out physical causes for symptoms, being mindful that anxiety, relocation, and depression must also be ruled out. If Alzheimer's disease is the provisional diagnosis, victims and their families can be assisted initially and helped in their caregiving throughout the lengthy progression of the disease. Workers can help make the meanings of seemingly irrational behaviors understandable and can teach management techniques useful to family and nonfamily caregivers.

Alzheimer's disease has become a major cause of disability among the elderly. The incidence of clinical dementia increases exponentially with age; an acceptable estimate is that one of three persons 90 years of age and older will be its victim (Katzman, 1987; Katzman & Kawas, 1994). A higher estimate of prevalence—48 percent of those 85 years of age and over—was obtained in the much-quoted community study in East Boston, Massachusetts (Evans et al., 1989). This appears, however, to be an overestimate, because mildly to moderately cognitively impaired persons were included (Weiner, 1991). Whatever the true prevalence, there is no doubt that the percentage and number of persons afflicted with Alzheimer's disease are increasing as people are living longer.

While Alzheimer's disease has increased, there has been an apparent decrease in disability from other diseases, particularly cardiovascular disease (Manton, Corder, & Stallard, 1993; Manton, Stallard, & Corder, 1995). However, a decrease in the percentage of elderly persons with other disabilities, as assessed by incapacity to carry out ADL, must not obfuscate the fact that the number of persons with chronic disabilities is increasing because more people are living to older ages.

Alzheimer's disease as a cause for incapacity to carry out ADL is decidedly different from causes such as stroke and heart disease, because Alzheimer's disease is a mental disease without accompanying physiological deficits until very late stages. In contrast to Alzheimer's disease, cardiovascular disease and cancer, in common with respiratory impairments, fractures, and other diseases, necessitate medical intervention in their acute phases and usually continual treatment thereafter. Patients in the acute phases of these diseases are usually treated in hospitals, with medical social workers now largely practicing geriatric social work.

LIVING LONG WITH IMPAIRMENTS

Although the average life span in the United States is increasing, the longevity of human beings is not increasing, but instead is fixed at approximately 115 years (Hayflick, 1994). The ability to live this long (especially in contrast to higher-order apes, which do not live beyond the menopause) is assumed to be a by-product or counterpart of human evolution that ensures survival through years of nurturing offspring until their maturity. As human beings have evolved from lower mammalian forms, there has been an increasing redundancy in biological systems, as well as an increase in the ability of the central nervous system to maintain integration of these systems (Hayflick, 1994). For example, in mammals the ratio of brain weight is associated with longevity; this ratio is greatest for humans (Sacher, 1977). This integrative capacity and redundancy also facilitate transcendence of physical pathology, maintaining ADL, and living well beyond the child-rearing years. The average life span in 1990 at birth was 78.6 years for women and 71.8 years for men; at age 65 it was 83.8 for women and 80.2 for men (U.S. Bureau of the Census, 1990). Although women apparently have a genetic advantage, both men and women can expect to live many years after age 65 before they begin to experience the incapacities of advanced age. Using ADL incapacity as a gauge, advanced or extreme old age is now considered to be 85, with slightly less than one half (45.4 percent) of adults of age 85 and older needing assistance with ADL (U.S. Bureau of the Census, 1990).

Inevitable Normative Deterioration
Therefore, although more than half of individuals age 85 and older do not need assistance with ADL, people experience musculoskeletal deterioration and loss of neurons well before age 65. These most obvious underlying age-associated changes in organs and tissues are manifested in the inelasticity of smooth muscle tissue and a decrease in bone density. These decrements can be remediated, however, by prostheses, including eyeglasses and hearing aids; by exercise; and by hormonal replacement therapies that enhance bone density for most menopausal women. Age-associated chronic impairments thus are not cured but are partially corrected with intervention.

Loss of neurons has two major effects: a decrease in reaction time and a decay in immediate memory. A decrease in reaction time per se may have minimal negative effects, but, when combined with vision impairment, may make driving quite hazardous. An inability to drive can be quite devastating to elderly individuals. Although visual impairments can sometimes be corrected, there is no correction for slowed reaction time.

With age there is an increasing inability to recall familiar names and places. Although this change is bothersome, most elderly people adapt to it. Unfortunately, however, with the attention now given to Alzheimer's disease, many older people interpret forgetfulness as the beginning of this dreaded disorder. Augmenting this interpretation are problems in registering information because of sensory losses or anxiety. To be specific, memory necessitates registration, retention, and recall of information. If there is no registration, nothing becomes stored to be recalled; for example, a physician's or nurse's instructions may not be recalled because the words did not register. In turn, social workers sometimes label the inability of an older person to respond adequately to a query as denial, when in fact the initial information never registered because of anxiety interacting with sensory deficits.

Cardiovascular Disease and Stroke
If the two leading causes of death in old age were cured, the average life span from birth would increase by an estimated 17 years, and life span from age 65, by 15.2 years (Hayflick, 1994). Most deaths, other than those from Alzheimer's disease, would occur from "natural causes," a kind of general exhaustion of human vitality. Until cures are discovered, however, cardiovascular disease and cancer will continue to take a toll on capacity to carry out ADL. This toll is exacted not only on people with these diseases but also on family caregivers. Spouse and parent caring has now become normative (Brody, 1985) and especially burdensome because hospitalized patients are discharged home "quicker and sicker." Caregiving burden can be reduced by services that include support groups (Toseland, Smith, & McCallion, 1995) during the lengthy period of home care before caregivers become exhausted and seek institutional care. It is very common for families to suffer in silence without benefit of any ameliorating service. Nearly three times as many older people whose deteriorated status approximates that of nursing home residents are being cared for at home rather than in a nursing home (14.2 percent versus 5 percent, respectively) (Weissert, 1985).

Idiosyncratic Causes of Disability
Idiosyncratic causes of disability can be divided into adverse lifestyle causes and genetic deficits. Adverse lifestyle causes encompass early developmental deficiencies, noxious environments, and problematic behaviors that result in health problems. Growing up in poverty causes problems from birth that affect morbidity and mortality later in life. Environmental pollution also makes inroads on morbidity and mortality, but noxious environments must be broadly defined when considering the health problems of elderly people. The death of a spouse can cause a mourning process that, when combined with a

weakened biological substratum, can lead to death. Similarly, relocating to a nursing home can have lethal consequences (Lieberman & Tobin, 1983; Tobin & Lieberman, 1976). Lack of a sense of control over one's life when living in a nursing home can also hasten death (Rodin & Langer, 1977). Personal behaviors—for example, inadequate coping with stress, smoking, and Type A behavior—can lead to premature illness and then to death.

Genetic deficits refer to inherited organ weaknesses that lead to illness and death. It is a rare person who has not inherited a weakness in one or more organs. Thus, even if cardiovascular diseases and cancer were cured, inherited organ weaknesses alone would cause morbidity and mortality.

ALZHEIMER'S DISEASE

The unknown etiology of Alzheimer's disease necessitates making a provisional diagnosis by ruling out other possible causes for senile dementia. "Senile," of course, refers to onset late in life and "dementia," to regression from previously sound mental functioning. Originally Alzheimer's disease was a diagnosis reserved for presenile, hereditary dementia. Alois Alzheimer, a German neurologist, identified the disease in 1907 when he reported the perplexing case of a 51-year-old woman whose intellectual functioning progressively deteriorated. When death occurred four years later, she was bedridden and incontinent. An autopsy of her brain revealed "tangles" and "yellow plaques," features that have persisted as neuropathologic indicators of the disease that bears Alzheimer's name. For this reason, until the 1970s heredi-tary, presenile dementia was known as Alzheimer's disease, whereas late-life dementia was referred to as senile dementia, chronic brain syndrome, or organic brain syndrome.

As senile dementia became more preva-lent, scientists began focusing attention on the disease, and neuroanatomists and pathologists discovered that the microscopic changes found at postmortem examination were the same in senile dementia as in Alzheimer's (presenile) dementia. Although the post mortem pathological changes in the brain were the same, there was an initial resistance to grouping them together, because it was unusual to have a family history of the disease in senile dementias of unknown etiology. Senile dementia became rather common in the 1960s and 1970s as people lived longer; most experts

attributed the cause of the disease to deterio-rative brain changes associated with aging, a normative degenerative process associated with long life. However, when Congress was debating establishing the National Institute on Aging (NIA) as a new research institute of the National Institutes of Health (NIH), less money would be allocated to the NIA if senile demen-tia was considered a normal process. Robert Butler, the first director of the NIA, argued convincingly that senile dementia was a disease and not a normal process, thus warranting the targeting of funds and research efforts toward finding a cure for the disease. The disease thereafter was named senile dementia of the Alzheimer's type (SDAT), but even though there have been vigorous re-search efforts to determine its cause, to date the etiology of SDAT remains elusive.

A consequence of grouping early- and late-life dementias under the rubric of Alzheimer's disease, however, is that relatives of late-life victims of senile dementia fear the disease is familial. The situation can be confusing, because some families manifest hereditary dementia in the older years. Yet clinical wisdom has it that one identical twin may become a victim of SDAT, but not the other, which suggests a nonfamilial etiology. Still, as with some other ailments, a genetic predisposi-tion may be necessary for Alzheimer's disease to be manifested in later life. Although genetic markers will provide a better understanding of familial etiology, there is a negative aspect of this discovery. Any person who belongs to a family with a history of dementia must decide whether to have the test that can determine whether he or she is carrying the gene for this dreaded disease.

DIAGNOSIS

Alzheimer's disease is an insidious disease that progresses slowly and inexorably from islets of confusion to total confusion within a period of time that can range from a few years to more than a decade. Dementia, in its essential meaning of deterioration from former cognitive functioning, entails the diminishing of such intellectual abilities as short-term memory, judgment, and language, without a loss of consciousness. Personality changes can be expected. A well-groomed person may develop a disheveled appearance; an outgoing indi-vidual may become withdrawn and silent. However, because Alzheimer's disease is insidious, the sine qua non of diagnosis is the slow progression of confusion. In normative aging, losses in short-term memory cause modest forgetfulness but do not expand to disorientation in familiar settings or to erratic judgment. A history of undiminished intellectual functioning can quickly rule out Alzheimer's disease. Similarly, if confusion is acute, its suddenness rules out Alzheimer's disease.

Psychological Causes for Dementia

Psychological causes for confusional states include anxiety, depression, and effects from relocation (Tobin, 1991). An elderly patient examined in the physician's office to confirm a presumptive diagnosis of Alzheimer's disease often becomes beset with anxiety and cannot correctly answer the doctor's queries on orientation to time and place. A hospital patient may become depressed about the possibility that a medical condition could necessitate transferring to a nursing home rather than returning home. An elderly person relocated to a nursing home may become confused in a foreign environment, displaying a "first-month syndrome" characterized by disorientation, anxiety, depression, and sometimes psychosis.

Anxiety at any age can fractionate behavior. Students know only too well how anxiety can affect their performance on tests. A little anxiety in a very old person who has the modest impairments in short-term memory associated with aging (for example, being unable to recall in the morning where their eyeglasses were placed the night before) can quickly decompensate into massive confusion when experiencing anxiety.

Depression causes a pseudo, or false, dementia. A depressed person who is apathetic may have the capacity to be oriented to time, place, and person, but may be too withdrawn to respond to queries about his or her orientation. It is essential, however, not to overlook depression in the presence of dementia. As noted by G. Cohen (1988), cognitive dysfunction is "all the greater when depression accompanies the disorder" (p. 97).

Relocation is disorienting, regardless of age. Young, healthy Peace Corps volunteers experience culture shock, becoming disoriented in a foreign culture where they cannot communicate with those around them and sometimes suffering acute psychotic breakdowns. Relocation effects are evident not only when someone enters a hospital or nursing home but also when people, regardless of age, change their community residences (Lieberman & Tobin, 1983; Tobin & Lieberman, 1976).

Noncurable Medical Conditions

Slowly developing confusional states can be caused by medical conditions that may not be curable—specifically, tumors or cerebral ministrokes. Arteriosclerosis does not cause dementia but is associated with ministrokes, which may account for as much as one-third of senile dementias with unknown etiologies. More than two-thirds of nursing home residents, whose average age is approximately 85, have senile dementia (Strahan & Burns, 1991), and in possibly one-third of these residents, senile dementia is caused by ministrokes. Cerebrovascular accidents (strokes), which are more damaging than a series of ministrokes, can be diagnosed from both their suddenness and their accompanying impairments, such as slurred speech and motor dysfunction. Ministrokes and SDAT, however, cannot be differentiated because their course is the same, and therefore a differential diagnosis can be made only by autopsy.

Overdiagnosis

The eagerness to diagnose Alzheimer's disease, which results from the best of intentions, can cause a provisional diagnosis to be communicated to patients and families, with devastating consequences. There are many treatable medical conditions that can cause slowly developing intellectual dysfunction, including malnutrition; drug intoxication from a single drug or from the interaction of medications, as often occurs in the polypharmacy of older people; thyroid imbalance; vitamin B_{12} deficiency; fecal impaction; or a mild heart attack. If such a condition is correctly diagnosed and treated, the confusion will be ameliorated.

Assessing Confusion

Confusion per se is assessed for orientation to time, place, and person by a mental status examination that requires patients to state the day, month, and year; the place where they are; and who they are. Patients who are very anxious, especially if they fear a diagnosis of Alzheimer's disease and are in a foreign setting such as a physician's office, may respond incorrectly to queries regarding time and place. Disorientation to person occurs late in the disease. To rule out anxiety, some neurologists ask the patient for a valued personal possession, such as a wallet or house keys, before beginning the examination. If answers to queries as to time and place are incorrect but the patient asks the neurologist to return the wallet or house keys on leaving the office, then a diagnosis of a pathological process is not made. However, if the valued personal possession is not requested by the patient and Alzheimer's disease is suspected, then examination for treatable medical conditions should follow.

The Social Worker's Role in Diagnosis

Social workers must take a careful history to determine whether the dementia has occurred slowly and insidiously rather than suddenly. A second task is to stabilize the person to rule out anxiety and depression as causes and to determine whether relocation is a cause for symptoms. Next, referral to a physician, preferably a geriatrician, is essential to rule out obvious causes for an insidious process, such as a nutritional deficiency, overmedication, and drug interaction.

INITIAL ASSISTANCE TO VICTIMS AND FAMILIES

When a presumptive diagnosis of Alzheimer's disease has been made, victims must be helped to maintain as much autonomy as possible. Bumagin and Hirn (1990) believed the elderly person assumed to have Alzheimer's disease should be included in the evaluation process and, if amenable, involved in arranging the evaluation appointment with the physician. Later, clients' autonomy can be enhanced by, for example, making living wills and assigning durable powers of attorney (Brechling & Schneider, 1993).

Concurrently, the family must be apprised of the diagnosis without overwhelming them. Professionals must allow time for questions and clarifications, and families should be told that current deficits may persist for an indefinite period without worsening, as the course of the disease is slow and variable. At this point the focus must be on "management, the need for caregiving or other auxiliary services, and the maintenance of physical and mental health" (Bumagin & Hirn, 1990, p. 184). Ways that family members can be helpful in providing a secure, stable environment must be discussed in detail. Also, it is best to encourage families to join the Alzheimer's Association so that caregiver loneliness is diminished, families can share ways of caring, and families can be empowered through advocacy as their family member experiences further deterioration.

CARING FOR PEOPLE WITH ALZHEIMER'S DISEASE

As Alzheimer's disease is diagnosed and then progresses, the nature of caring changes. When the disease is initially diagnosed and the person with Alzheimer's disease becomes aware of its insidious de-selfing process, assurance must be communicated that care will be given. Reactions of victims and family members, of course, will vary. Those with the disease who are more intellectually oriented appear to respond more adversely. One who has not been particularly interested in intellectual pursuits may not be as devastated by the diagnosis as someone who derives stimulation from his or her intellect. Deriving gratification, as well as identity, from simpler pleasures seems to facilitate adaptation when care is provided by spouses and other family members, who relate to victims of the disease in essentially the same ways they have always related to them. The goal in doing so is to prevent any excess disability in clients with dementia (Gwyther, 1990).

The struggle to retain the self among those with Alzheimer's disease has been observed not only by family members but also by practitioners. D. Cohen and Eisdorfer (1986) titled their book on family caring for Alzheimer's disease patients *The Loss of Self*. They begin their book with quotes from the diary of James Thomas. "Help me to be strong and free until my self no longer exists" and "Most people expect to die some day, but who ever expected to lose their self first?" The dissolution of the self is catastrophic for the person who is aware of the dissolution in him- or herself. Apparently, a similar process occurs in the early stage of schizophrenia, when the victim of this disease becomes aware that inner mental processes are becoming destructured. Indeed, the early paranoid ideation in schizophrenia may be a way of coping with this awareness, in the same way that similar ideation may be a way of coping with the early awareness of Alzheimer's disease.

Walter Lyons (1982), a caseworker and administrator in the Bay Crest Home for the Aged in Toronto, reported on his frustrating experiences caring for his wife, who was afflicted with Alzheimer's disease. Because of his background, he understood not only some of the principles in providing care but also his wife's internal feelings. He wrote the following as if these words were hers: "You only know me from the outside, through my 'abnormal behavior.' Will you see me inside, struggling to maintain my assaulted personhood? Will you mistake my struggle to retain some dignity, some feeling of self, for organic disease rather than its consequences?" (p. 3).

Most essential to Lyons's care for his wife was providing assistance to her in being the same person she had always been. However, not all family caregivers are as aware as Lyons that seemingly bizarre and aimless activities may have purposeful meanings and may not be aimless. Snyder, Rupprecht, Pyrek, Brekhus, and Noss (1978), for example, identified three motives for the common and annoying behavior of wandering: (1) release of tension by using a lifelong pattern of coping with stress by taking a brisk walk or a long stroll, (2) searching for security ("Where is my mother?"), and (3) carrying out a work role. People who wander may be going to their jobs, to the grocery store, or to the kitchen.

Families can be assisted to help individuals with Alzheimer's disease retain a sense of self. Just as Lyons learned that his wife was struggling to be herself, family members must learn that bizarre behaviors often have meanings related to the striving for preservation of self. Once this principle is understood by family members, it becomes increasingly possible for them to understand the continuity between current bizarre behaviors and past normal behaviors. As bizarre behaviors become intelligible, they can be tolerated or even encouraged to the extent that the aberrant behaviors help the patient to be her- or himself. Feil (1992) based her validation approach on this perspective. In my own experience (Tobin, 1991), a woman who constantly touched the breasts of another resident in Drexel Home for the Aged was a survivor of a concentration camp. She and her husband were always touching each other, as if physical distance were tantamount to destruction. This fearful woman was terrified of people, especially men, and once she was in a delusional, psychotic state, her best solution for retaining psychological intactness and avoiding further dissolution was to touch women in intimate places.

When seeking to understand the meanings of behaviors, caregivers must penetrate and look beyond exaggerated and inappropriate expressions of emotions, a lack of personal hygiene, and unintelligible communication (Shomaker, 1987). Because unintelligible communication often masks residual cognitive abilities that make it possible to understand simple conversations, tactless discussions of childlike behaviors in front of patients with Alzheimer's disease cause them to become enraged. Caregivers are disturbed not only by childlike behaviors but also by changes in personality and bizarre behaviors. The man who has always been fastidious in his appearance may scatter all his clothes on the floor while searching for a favorite tie. When a woman talks to her long-dead mother as if she were alive and in the room, it is certainly abnormal, but she is also seeking security and expressing her lifelong identity.

The woman or man may not be completely the "same person," but she or he is still a person, and in many ways is the same person. The extent to which the patient with Alzheimer's disease feels like the same person he or she has always been—no matter how bizarre his or her behavior—must be accepted as that individual's reality. The distortions that are so very painful to family members as they watch a loved one lose contact with reality may indeed serve the patient's purpose of retaining a sense of self while providing assurance as the disease follows in its inexorable course.

An example of an inappropriate response to a family member who was a victim of Alzheimer's disease occurred when a husband tied his wife to a chair while he cooked the meals. To the home care worker involved and the husband, restraints made sense, because his wife had previously not allowed him to prepare food in her kitchen. When she refused to talk to him after he began to restrain her, the husband and home care worker became alarmed because the relationship between the husband and wife immediately deteriorated. The husband did not object to adopting the role and responsibilities of "housewife," but he did object to his wife's incessant interference. He tied her down only after he had frequently and painstakingly explained why she should not interfere. She would "shadow" him by standing at his elbow whenever he was in the kitchen, and her interference turned the kitchen into a complete mess. Now he felt that she was being unduly angry at him for taking a necessary step. I suggested to the worker that the husband allow his wife to have the use of the kitchen, use a space for meal preparation that she did not ordinarily use, and call me if he believed that the restraints were still needed. The worker did not call back, hopefully because the wife was not tied down and, although the kitchen was messier, was again talking to her husband, and life was calmer.

Inability to Differentiate Thoughts and Actions

Too often, overwhelmed spouses and children of family members with Alzheimer's disease interpret behaviors as motivated by vindictiveness, as illustrated in the previous case. At other times, behavior is interpreted as lying, or the purposeful telling of untruths. The bewilderment produced by strange behaviors during caregiving can indeed lead to a perception that the care receiver is doing spiteful things, which unfortunately can be a projection of one's own frustrations and angry feelings. When a daughter asks her confused mother, who has disheveled hair, to comb her hair and her mother answers that she just did, the mother is not "lying." Instead, it is her inability to differentiate between thoughts and actions that causes her to say this. Her transient thought of hair combing becomes the belief that she did so. Zarit, Orr, and Zarit (1985) provided many other examples of misinterpretation of the effects of memory loss. For example, repetitive questions may be misconstrued as a wish to be annoying or to attract attention, and thus the reaction becomes, "He should control himself." This behavior more likely reflects an inability to remember asking the question or the loss of skills needed to gain attention in appropriate ways. As another example, a family may say that their mother is denying her memory loss, when in fact she cannot remember. Too often explanations that seem plausible to families are not at all accurate. More than anything else, acceptance is beneficial to, and has a calming effect on, both the patient and the family.

When Memories Fade

The loss of resemblance of self is accelerated when long-term memory begins to fade, when memories of the past become dim and are difficult to recapture. One of my students who was working in a medical day care program took daily walks with an elderly gentleman who lucidly discussed this terrible problem. The student reported that the man said that he and his wife had been comforting each other with their past. However, now that he was losing his past, he would no longer be able to share their history.

Family Intervention

Whereas previously it was thought that families become increasingly unable to withstand the mental deterioration, Zarit et al. (1985) reported that family caregivers experience less burden over time, even though the physical burden may be appreciably greater, as described by Mace and Rabins (1981) in their book, *The 36-Hour Day*. This seemingly counterintuitive finding apparently demonstrates that the most trying times are (1) when the victim and the family first become aware of the disease and (2) in the subsequent phase, when the de-selfing process causes a marked deterioration from the premorbid state. The shift that later occurs from a moderate or extreme nonresemblance of self to a total nonresemblance is easier to accept, probably because family members have already begun to successfully mourn the loss of identity of the person.

Still, living with and caring for a family member with Alzheimer's disease has a profound effect on mental health. Schulz, O'Brien, Bookwala, and Fleissner (1995) reviewed the 40 studies since 1989 of the effects on people caring for demented family members. Virtually all studies reported elevated levels of depression, and many reported heightened physical morbidity. The extent of psychological morbidity among family caregivers was associated with increased problem behaviors of care receivers with Alzheimer's disease, less income, poorer self-ratings of health, more perceived stress, and less life satisfaction. Physical morbidity was associated with problem behaviors and cognitive impairment and with caregiver depression, anxiety, and perceived lack of social supports. Although there are measurable effects on health, most effects are primarily psychological.

Meaningful variations by cultural backgrounds, however, were not found by Schulz et al. (1995) in their review of studies. For example, Mintzer and Macera (1992) found some greater depression in an African American than in a white caregiving sample, whereas Hinrichsen and Ramirez (1992) found their samples in a larger study to be similar in their adaptation to dementia responsibilities. African American caregivers, however, reported less burden, less desire to institutionalize their relatives, and more unmet service needs. In the third of the 40 studies that included culture as a variable, Mintzer et al.

(1992) reported no differences between Cuban American and white caregivers. Yet of the six studies investigating socioeconomic status as a correlate of morbidity, five revealed that low income was associated with greater psychiatric morbidity. Given the greater percentage of people of color in lower socioeconomic strata, it could be expected that psychiatric morbidity would be greater among people of color than among white caregivers.

Race was also found not to determine the structure of informal care in the large 1989 National Long-Term Care Survey (Burton et al., 1995). Size of caregiving networks and unpaid networks did not differ by race. However, widowhood, which was appreciably higher for African Americans in this national survey, was associated with more caregivers who were non-immediate family members and also non-kin.

When there are family caregivers, the nature of the consanguinal relationship and gender influence the psychological state of caregivers (Horowitz, 1985). Female caregivers, (for example, wives, daughters, and daughters-in-law) tend to be more depressed than male caregivers (for example, husbands and sons). Males cope better by focusing on instrumental assistance, whereas females cope more poorly because of their greater emotional concerns. Caregivers in general, however, are concerned about losing control, because they perceive the situation as worsening, have conflicts with in-home service providers, and experience problems with how to relate to other family members. Spouses, for example, are often ambivalent about asking children for assistance, and daughters are especially concerned about taking time away from husbands who may be contemplating retirement or may have retired. These daughters, as well as daughters-in-law, are caught in the middle between elderly parents and husbands. Note that for past generations, "caught in the middle" referred to being caught between responsibilities to infirm parents and dependent children. Now, however, with parent-caring likely to begin when parents are in their 80s and caregiving children in their late 50s and 60s, grandchildren are invariably well beyond the dependency years.

Although differences produced by consanguinal relationship to the care receiver apply to family members with or without Alzheimer's disease, problem behaviors as a source of stress are unique to caregiving for an Alzheimer's disease victim. Interventions to help caregivers cope better with those problem behaviors have had some limited success (Schulz et al., 1995). Although short-term group interventions, whether led by peers or professionals, have helped caregivers cope better (Toseland, Rossiter, & Labrecque, 1989), interventions focused specifically on lifting depression among caregivers have not been very successful.

Mittelman and colleagues have reported, however, that a comprehensive support program delayed institutionalization (Mittelman et al., 1993) and also reduced depression (Mittelman et al., 1995) among spouses caring for a wife or husband with Alzheimer's disease. In this support program, caregiving spouses in a treatment group not only participated in an Alzheimer's disease caregiver support group, in which they were taught how to reduce stress and manage care to reduce the frequency and intensity of troublesome behaviors, but also received individual and family counseling and were provided with informal consultation when requested by the caregiver or other family members. Conflicts with family members were apparently sufficiently resolved to increase satisfaction and thereby enhance the perception of family cohesion without increasing interaction with or assistance from significant others.

Research has suggested additional approaches to families. Because there is a relationship between health status of caregivers and institutionalization (Lieberman & Kramer, 1991), then enhancing the physical health of caregivers, for example, should reduce institutionalization of dementia victims. Monahan and Hooker (1995) found that a perception of less social support and higher levels of neuroticism were associated with poorer health of caregivers. Providing social supports and counseling family caregivers, as well as helping family members understand the unavoidable strain in the marital relationship (Sherman, Ward, & LaGory, 1988), are all ways in which social workers can ameliorate distress among family caregivers. Use of respite and adult day services can also reduce burden (Rathbone-McCuan, 1990).

The 1993 study by Mittelman et al. also revealed that after placement of a family member in a nursing home, care burden and depression may continue among spouses and other relatives who previously provided care at home because of (1) feelings of guilt related to abandoning the family member, (2) the time required to travel and visit their relative, and (3) concerns that adequate care and supervision are not being provided in the facilities. Monahan (1995), who developed support groups and workshops to alleviate burden levels after nursing home placement, reported that support group attendance was significantly associated with lower burden levels.

Management Techniques

People with Alzheimer's disease who are cared for at home or in long-term-care settings can be assisted in many concrete ways. Mace and Rabins (1981) provided many recommendations, derived from the experience of family caregivers, for simplifying daily routines. Examples include laying clothes out in the order they will be put on; guiding by touch rather than calling out instructions; using pictures when the ability to comprehend the written word has been lost; and, above all, maintaining calmness. Burnside (1981), a nurse with years of experience in nursing homes, in synthesizing techniques for managing patients with cognitive impairments, divided these techniques into three categories: (1) techniques for the helper, (2) techniques for memory development, and (3) techniques for manipulation of the environment. Her bedside-helper techniques included reinforcing reality, using touch, supporting denial if it is therapeutic, and helping clients to express feelings. Reducing duress is particularly important. Situations that provoke agitation, including most new situations, must be recognized. Obviously, when the victim of the disease cannot communicate the source of the agitation, disorganized and aberrant behavior is likely to escalate. Education in communication is very helpful, because it enables family members and nursing home staff to become more comfortable and more competent and feel more efficacious in working with individuals with dementia. Our observations at Drexel Home have shown that it is possible to enhance staff's functioning and feelings, but only with support and reassurance of the more professional staff. The more output expected from staff, the more "nourishment," or input, staff must be provided.

With regard to retention of memory, Burnside (1981) has provided a list of ideas that are appropriate for any setting. She suggested providing sufficient cues to aid memory and orientation (for example, props to indicate change of seasons), consistent cues that encourage recognition instead of recall, and multiple cues; avoiding pressure to perform; being sure to communicate what is expected to be remembered; and being sure that familiar objects that reaffirm the continuity of the sense of self are on display. Bourgeois (1991, 1994) increased beneficial family-patient interaction by use of personal memory albums, which consist of particularly meaningful photographs that are carried around by Alzheimer's victims. Woods and Ashley (1995) suggested the use of memory audiotapes. In turn, Pietrukowicz and Johnson (1991) showed that life history boards placed outside the rooms of nursing home residents enhanced resident-staff interaction.

Most environmental manipulations are rather obvious, such as using night lights and bright colors. In nursing homes it is sensible to color-code doors, keep the same staff working with individuals, provide a safe and nonthreatening environment that is not too boring but also not overstimulating, provide clocks and calendars, and make special efforts to provide a milieu that reduces "sundowner's syndrome." When family and other familiar people are present to affirm the persistence of the self and use several kinds of management techniques, there may be a maximization of residual cognitive capacities that at times can be startling (Edelson & Lyons, 1985).

The End Stage

The final stage of the disease is marked by a shrunken brain and the loss of vital functions. The victim, at this point in a vegetative state, may remain fixed in a fetal position, incontinent of urine and feces. If, as is common, a respiratory infection develops, little will usually be done to maintain life (a form of passive euthanasia). By this time in the progression of the disease, family members have usually mourned the loss of their loved one and should have been helped to accept this inevitable outcome. It is not uncommon for family members as well as nonfamily caretakers to say that death at this time is a blessing.

REFERENCES

Bourgeois, M. S. (1991). Communication treatment for adults with dementia. *Journal of Speech and Hearing, 34,* 831–844.

Bourgeois, M. S. (1994). Teaching caregivers to use memory aids with patients with dementia. *Seminars in Speech and Language, 15,* 291–305.

Brechling, B. G., & Schneider, C. A. (1993). Preserving autonomy in early stage dementia. *Journal of Gerontological Social Work, 20,* 17–33.

Brody, E. M. (1985). Parent care as a normative stress. *Gerontologist, 25,* 19–29.

Bumagin, V. E., & Hirn, K. F. (1990). *Helping the aging family: A guide for professionals.* Glenview, IL: Scott, Foresman.

Burnside, I. M. (1981). *Nursing and the aged.* New York: McGraw-Hill.

Burton, L., Kasper, J., Shore, A., Cagney, K., LaVeist, T., Cubbin, C., & German, P. (1995). The structure of informal care: Are there differences by race? *Gerontologist, 35,* 744–752.

Cohen, D., & Eisdorfer, C. (1986). *The loss of self.* New York: W. W. Norton.

Cohen, G. (1988). One psychiatrist's view. In L. F. Jarvik & C. H. Winograd (Eds.), *Treatment for the Alzheimer patient: The long haul* (pp. 96–104). New York: Springer.

Edelson, J. S., & Lyons, W. (1985). *Institutional care of the mentally impaired elderly.* New York: Van Nostrand Reinhold.

Evans, D. A., Funkenstein, H. H., Albert, M. S., Scherr, P. A., Cook, N. R., Chown, M. J., Hebert, L. E., Hennekens, C. M., & Taylor, J. O. (1989). Prevalence of Alzheimer's disease in a community population of older persons: Higher than previously reported. *Journal of the American Medical Association, 262,* 2551–2556.

Feil, N. (1992). *V/F validation: The Feil method.* Cleveland: Edward Feil Productions.

Gwyther, L. P. (1990). Clinicians and family: A partnership for support. In N. L. Mace (Ed.), *Dementia care: Patient, family and community* (pp. 193–230). Baltimore: Johns Hopkins University Press.

Hayflick, L. (1994). *How and why we age.* New York: Random House.

Hinrichsen, G. A., & Ramirez, M. (1992). Black and white dementia caregivers: A comparison of their adaptation, adjustment and service utilization. *Gerontologist, 32,* 375–381.

Horowitz, A. (1985). Family caregiving to the frail elderly. *Annual Review of Gerontology/Geriatrics, 5,* 194–246.

Katzman, R. (1987). Alzheimer's disease: Advances and opportunities. *Journal of the American Geriatrics Society, 35,* 69–73.

Katzman, R., & Kawas, C. (1994). The epidemiology of dementia and Alzheimer's disease. In R. Katzman, R. D. Terry, & K. L. Bick (Eds.), *Alzheimer's disease* (pp. 105–122). New York: Raven Press.

Lieberman, M. A., & Kramer, J. H. (1991). Factors affecting decisions to institutionalize demented elderly. *Gerontologist, 31,* 37–374.

Lieberman, M. A., & Tobin, S. S. (1983). *The experience of old age.* New York: Basic Books.

Lyons, W. (1982). Coping with cognitive impairment: Some family dynamics and helping roles. *Journal of Gerontological Social Work, 4,* 3–21.

Mace, N. L., & Rabins, P. V. (1981). *The 36-hour day: A family guide to caring for persons with Alzheimer's disease, related dementing illnesses, and memory loss in later life.* Baltimore: Johns Hopkins University Press.

Manton, K. G., Corder, L. S., & Stallard, E. (1993). Estimates of change in chronic disability rates and institutional incidence and prevalence rates in the U.S. elderly population from the 1983, 1984, and 1989 National Long-Term Care Survey. *Journal of Gerontology: Social Sciences, 48,* S153–S166.

Manton, K. G., Stallard, E., & Corder, L. (1995). Changes in morbidity and chronic disability in the U.S. elderly population: Evidence from the 1982, 1984 and 1989 National Long-Term Care Surveys. *Journal of Gerontology: Social Sciences, 50B,* S194–S204.

Mintzer, J. E., & Macera, C. A. (1992). Prevalence of depressive symptoms among white and African-American caregivers of demented patients. *American Journal of Psychiatry, 149,* 575–576.

Mintzer, J. E., Rubert, M. P., Lowenstein, D., Gomez, E., Millor, A., Quinteros, R., Flores, C., Miller, M., Rainerman, A., & Eisdorfer, C. (1992). Daughters caregiving for Hispanic and non-Hispanic Alzheimer's patients: Does ethnicity make a difference? *Community Mental Health Journal, 28,* 293–303.

Mittelman, M. S., Ferris, S. H., Shulman, J., Steinberg, G., Ambinder, A., Mackell, J. A., & Cohen, J. (1995). A comprehensive support program: Effect on depression in spouse-caregivers of AD patients. *Gerontologist, 35,* 792–802.

Mittelman, M. S., Ferris, S. H., Steinberg, G., Shulman, E., Mackell, J. A., Ambinder, A., & Cohen, J. (1993). An intervention that delays institutionalization of Alzheimer's disease patients: Treatment of spouse caregivers. *Gerontologist, 33,* 730–740.

Monahan, D. J. (1995). Informal caregivers of institutionalized demented residents: Predictors of burden. *Journal of Gerontological Social Work, 23,* 652–681.

Monahan, D. J., & Hooker, K. (1995). Health of spouse caregivers of dementia patients: The role of personality and social support. *Social Work, 40,* 305–314.

Pietrukowicz, M. A., & Johnson, M. M. S. (1991). Using life histories to individualize nursing staff attitudes towards residents. *Gerontologist, 31,* 102–106.

Rathbone-McCuan, E. (1990). Respite and adult day services. In A. Monk (Ed.), *Handbook of gerontological services* (2nd ed.). New York: Columbia University Press.

Rodin, J., & Langer, E. (1977). Long-term effects of a control-relevant intervention with institutionalized aged. *Journal of Personality and Social Psychology, 35,* 897–902.

Sacher, G. A. (1977). Life table modification and life prolongation. In C. E. Finch & L. Hayflick (Eds.), *Handbook of the biology of aging.* New York: Van Nostrand Reinhold.

Schulz, R., O'Brien, A. T., Bookwala, J., & Fleissner, K. (1995). Psychiatric and physical morbidity effects of dementia caregiving: Prevalence, correlates and causes. *Gerontologist, 35,* 771–791.

Sherman, S. R., Ward, R. A., & LaGory, M. (1988). Women as caregivers to the elderly: Instrumental and expressive support. *Social Work, 33,* 164–167.

Shomaker, R. (1987). Problematic behavior and the Alzheimer patient: Retrospection as a method of understanding and counseling. *Gerontologist, 27,* 370–375.

Snyder, L. H., Rupprecht, P., Pyrek, J., Brekhus, S., & Noss, T. (1978). Wandering. *Gerontologist, 18,* 372–380.

Strahan, G., & Burns, B. (1991). Mental illness in nursing homes: United States, 1985. In *Vital and health statistics* (No. 13). Hyattsville, MD: National Center for Health Statistics.

Tobin, S. S. (1991). *Personhood in advanced old age: Implications for practice.* New York: Springer.

Tobin, S. S., & Lieberman, N. A. (1976). *Last home for the aged.* San Francisco: Jossey-Bass.

Toseland, R. W., Rossiter, C. M., & Labrecque, M. (1989). The effectiveness of peer-led and professionally-led groups to support family caregivers. *Gerontologist, 29,* 465–471.

Toseland, R. W., Smith, G. C., & McCallion, P. (1995). Supporting families in elder care. In G. C. Smith, S. S. Tobin, E. A. Robertson-Tchabo, & P. Powers (Eds.), *Strengthening aging families: Diversity in practice and policy* (pp. 3–24). Thousand Oaks, CA: Sage Publications.

U.S. Bureau of the Census. (1990). *The need for personal assistance with everyday activities: Recipients and caregivers.* Washington, DC: U.S. Government Printing Office.

Weiner, M. F. (1991). Introduction. In M. F. Weiner (Ed.), *The dementias: Diagnosis and management* (pp. xvii–xx). Washington, DC: American Psychiatric Press.

Weissert, W. C. (1985). Estimating the long-term care population: Prevalence rates and selected characteristics. *Health Care Financing Review, 6,* 83–91.

Woods, P., & Ashley, J. (1995). Simulated presence therapy: Using selected memories to manage problem behaviors in Alzheimer's disease patients. *Geriatric Nursing, 16,* 9–14.

Zarit, S. H., Orr, W. K., & Zarit, J. M. (1985). *The hidden victims of Alzheimer's disease.* New York: New York University Press.

Further Reading

Aronson, M. K. (Ed.). (1994). *Reshaping dementia care: Practice and policy in long-term care.* Thousand Oaks, CA: Sage Publications.

Gruetzner, H. (1988). *Alzheimer's: A caregivers guide and sourcebook.* New York: John Wiley & Sons.

Light, E., Niederhe, G., & Lebowitz, B. D. (1994). *Stress effects on family caregivers of Alzheimer's patients.* New York: Springer.

Silverstone, B., & Burack-Weiss, A. (1983). *Social work practice with frail elderly and their families: The auxiliary function model.* Springfield, IL: Charles C Thomas.

Smith, G. C., Tobin, S. S., Robertson-Tchabo, E. A., & Powers, P. (Eds.). (1995). *Strengthening aging families: Diversity in practice and policy.* Thousand Oaks, CA: Sage Publications.

Weiner, M. F. (Ed.). (1991). *The dementias: Diagnosis and management.* Washington, DC: American Psychiatric Press.

Sheldon S. Tobin, PhD, is professor, School of Social Welfare, University at Albany, State University of New York, 135 Western Avenue, Albany, NY 12222.

For further information see

Adult Day Services; Adult Protective Services; Aging Overview; Aging: Direct Practice; Aging: Public Policy Issues and Trends; **Aging: Racial and Ethnic Groups;** Aging: Services; Aging: Social Work Practice; Bereavement and Loss; Brief Therapies; **Christian Social Work;** Clinical Social Work; Direct Practice Overview; Families Overview; Group Practice Overview; Human Development; Interviewing; **Jewish Communal Services; Managed Care: Implications for Social Work Practice;** Mental Health Overview; Natural Helping Networks; Public Social Services; Self-Help Groups; **Serious Mental Illness: A Biopsychosocial Perspective;** Social Work Practice: Theoretical Base.

Key Words	
Alzheimer's disease	disabilities
caregiving	morbidity
cognition	

Aging: Racial and Ethnic Groups

Marta Sotomayor

Elderly people of color continue to encounter many more hardships than the elderly population in general. Their socioeconomic status is disquieting, and substantial numbers experience substandard living conditions. These conditions affect their physical health, mental well-being, and ability to function to their fullest capability and undermine the overall quality of their lives (Crystal & Shea, 1990). Their socioeconomic status and demographic characteristics are distinctly different from those of the general population, whether living in rural or in urban areas. Elderly people of color have lower incomes and less education and are more likely to live in poverty or near poverty, more likely to live in substandard housing, and more likely to be disabled than elders in the general population. They are at increased risk because of dietary patterns, poor health care, and decreased access to care, factors that also affect health care utilization. Gender-specific differences and increasing numbers of the old-old with a number of chronic health conditions also differentiate this group from other elderly populations in the United States (Kitagawa & Hauser, 1973).

The doubling and even tripling in the numbers of elders of color is a significant part of the demographic transformations taking place in the United States. These changes, coupled with changes in the economic, political, and social arenas, will continue into the next century and will significantly affect the quality of life of everyone in the United States and of elderly people of color specifically.

Diversity among Diversity

Overall, the elderly population is a diverse group defying generalizations and simple characterizations. Elders of color differ not only from the white elderly population but also from elders in other ethnic and racial groups and even among themselves. Elders of color differ in many ways, including race, ethnicity, country of origin, educational level, language, religious orientation, and date and reason for migration. Greater diversity exists among Latinos and Asian Pacific Island groups and, to a considerable degree, among Native Americans. Latino elders include people who identify with or whose country of origin is Mexico, Central or South America, and the Caribbean. Native Americans include American Indians and Native Alaskans (Eskimos/Aleuts). Asians and Pacific Islanders include people who identify with or whose country of origin is located in southeast Asia, China, the western Pacific (excluding Australia and New Zealand), Japan, Korea, and all other countries of the Pacific Rim. During the latter half of the 20th century, immigrants from the Caribbean and Africa and Latinos of African descent have added to the numbers and diversity of African Americans (Reid, 1986).

Immigration

"Latino" is an umbrella term for people who identify with the language and certain cultural components that characterize Spanish-speaking countries in the Americas, including the Caribbean. Americans of Mexican descent have been in the southwestern United States since the 16th century, but substantial immigration waves in the early part of the century and in the 1990s and high birth rates have increased their numbers considerably. Currently they constitute the largest sector among Latinos in this country. It is estimated that approximately 60 percent of Latinos in the United States are of Mexican descent, and although the group is relatively young, the age group that is growing fastest is the group 65 years old and older. Puerto Ricans constitute the second largest Latino group and often prefer to, and do, return to the island on retirement. Substantial numbers of Cuban Americans came to the United States as political refugees in the 1960s. Many of them were middle aged on arrival and are now 65 years or older. Central Americans—particularly from El Salvador, Nicaragua, and Guatemala—are relatively recent immigrants, having arrived in the 1980s and 1990s after fleeing their countries' bitter and protracted civil wars. The numbers of immigrants from other Central and South American countries are not as large, and these immigrants have significantly different life experiences and styles related to racial or ethnic identification and different reasons for migration.

There is great diversity among Asian and Pacific Islander elders as well. The 1990 censuses tabulated data on 24 ethnic populations within the Asian and Pacific Islander group. Asians of Chinese, Filipino, and Japanese origin each represent about one-fourth of elderly Asian people in this country; many immigrated early in the century or are the children of such immigrants. The proportion of immigrants admitted to the United States from other Asian countries increased considerably beginning in the mid-1960s. Most Vietnamese and Cambodians came to this country as political refugees after immigration quotas were lifted in 1965. Although those entering the United States between 1961 and 1970 composed only 1 percent of the total Asian immigrant population, approximately 15 percent of Asian immigrants between 1981 and 1987 were from Vietnam (U.S. Bureau of the Census, 1990a).

Since the early 19th century, immigrants from the Caribbean have added to the numbers of African Americans who are descendants of slaves who were transported from Africa and the Caribbean from the 17th to 19th centuries. International migration from the Caribbean and Africa assumed importance once again during the latter half of the 20th century. Two million, or three-fourths, of all legal immigrants to the United States from this region were admitted between 1971 and 1990 (U.S. Immigration and Naturalization Service, 1991). After 1965, the number of immigrants from Sub-Saharan African countries, such as Nigeria, increased sixfold (Ewbank, 1987). By the 1990 census, foreign-born people accounted for approximately 5 percent of African Americans nationwide. This percentage is projected to increase to 10 percent by the year 2010 (Reid, 1986).

SIZE OF THE OLDER POPULATION

In 1900, there were only 3 million older adults in the United States, and they made up one in 25 Americans. Their numbers have doubled since 1950 and are expected to rise by 28 million, or 39 percent of the projected growth by 2025, and to almost double again to 65.6 million by 2030. One-fifth or more of the population of 27 states will be elderly. Although demographic projections indicate that in the next century the majority of elderly people will be white, there will be virtually no increase in the number of these elders from 2030 to 2050. The young-old (ages 65 to 74) will continue to make up the majority of older Americans until about 2030. Those age 75 and older will account for more than half of all

elders after 2030. The number of those age 85 and older more than tripled between 1980 and 1995; this group is expected to become the fastest growing age group in the United States (Tauber & Smith, 1988; U.S. Bureau of the Census, 1993a, 1996).

THE GROWING SIZE OF POPULATION OF ELDERLY PEOPLE OF COLOR

According to the U.S. Bureau of the Census (1996), elderly people of color 65 years and over are currently the fastest growing segment of the older population; this population will continue to grow dramatically until 2050. By the year 2000, the 65 and older nonwhite population will increase by 34 percent. By 2025, 15 percent of the elderly population will be nonwhite, and this percentage will increase to approximately 21 percent by 2050. Overall the percentage of nonwhite elders is expected to nearly double by 2050. During the same period, the white elderly population will increase by 9.6 percent.

The African American elderly population will grow at a faster rate than the white elderly population into the 21st century. Although the African American population as a whole increased by only 11 percent in 1990, the number of those 65 years and older increased by 18 percent. In the same year there were more than 2.6 million elderly African Americans, or 8 percent of the total elderly population. The number of African American seniors is projected to grow by 10.6 percent by the year 2000, by 84.3 percent by the year 2020, and by 234 percent by the year 2050.

The proportion of elders among the Native American population increased by 35 percent between 1980 and 1990. In 1980, there were approximately 80,000 Native Americans 65 and older, or approximately 5 percent of the total Native American population, less than 1 percent of the total elderly population of color. About 6 percent of the Native American population were over 65 in 1990, of whom about 37 percent were 75 and over. Between 1970 and 1980, the older Native American population grew at nearly twice the rate of the populations of elderly whites or African Americans. The number of Native American elders has grown by nearly 7.6 percent per year since 1960 and will grow almost 5 percent annually by 2020; it will remain at 2 percent of total elderly people of color until the year 2050. Although the numbers of African American and

Native American seniors will grow at a slower pace, the most remarkable increase in this age group is projected for Latinos and Asians and Pacific Islanders. In 1990, the white population was a slow-growing, fast-aging population whose growth was largely fueled by immigration of young people and their growing families. Although Asian and Pacific Islander elders made up 2 percent of older Americans in 1995, their numbers more than doubled between 1980 and 1990. Taking into consideration variations within this population group, the proportion of those 65 years and over is expected to grow to 7 percent in 2050. A decrease in population size as a whole and a decrease in the number of seniors are expected among Japanese Americans owing to low birth rates and low immigration rates. However, Filipinos, Koreans, Vietnamese, and other groups that have high immigration and high birth rates are expected to increase in numbers and age by the 21st century. Smaller percentages of Asians and Pacific Islanders were 65 to 84 years old or 85 years and older.

The Latino and Asian population together will increase by 44 million and constitute 24 percent of the total population in 2025, up from 14 percent in 1996. The numbers of Latinos will grow faster than the rest of the population, and they will become the largest minority group in the United States, accounting for one-fourth of the nation's total growth by the year 2010 and for 61 percent of the population growth by 2025. By the middle of the 21st century, 22.7 percent of the total U.S. population will be Latino, and one in six will be age 65 and older. This age group grew from approximately 4 percent in 1980 to 6 percent in 1990 and is expected to double to 13 percent by 2030. The 1.2 million Latinos (about 6 percent) who are now 65 years of age or over are expected to increase to 2.5 million by 2010, to nearly 5.6 million by 2030, and to 7.9 million by 2050. Higher birth rates contribute significantly to population increase, but growth for Asians, Pacific Islanders, and Latinos is primarily the result of high immigration rates. More than half of the 40,000 persons age 65 and older who were granted permanent residency in 1993 were born in Asia or the Pacific region. Although approximately 23 percent of legal immigrants age 65 or older admitted in 1993 were refugees, most older immigrants came to join family members already in the United States. There are no official government data

regarding the number of Central American elders, particularly from San Salvador, Guatemala, and Nicaragua, who came to America to escape the civil wars and to join their families. The National Hispanic Council of Aging (1995) estimated that at least 15 percent of such families brought their middle-aged or elderly parents and grandparents with them.

In 1990, 10 percent of foreign-born people age 65 and older were recent immigrants (that is, they arrived during the 1980s). Those who arrived prior to 1950 were younger and were able to participate in the labor force. Those who migrate after retirement age have fewer economic assets to sustain themselves in their old age and depend on family and government programs. More than one-fourth of the elderly immigrants who entered the United States since 1980 received financial assistance in 1989 compared with about 7 percent of the total U.S. elderly population (Fix & Passel, 1994). The numbers of the very old have increased considerably since 1990 among all groups of color. Whereas fewer than one in 10 elders of color currently are very old, this proportion will increase to one in five by 2050. The number of African Americans 85 years and older increased from 67,000 in 1960 to 251,000 in 1990 and is expected to grow to one-half million by 2010 and to 1.8 million by 2050. The numbers of oldest-old Latinos (85 years and older) nearly doubled between 1980 and 1990, increasing from 49,000 to 95,000, with a dramatic increase projected to occur between 2020 and 2050.

MALE-TO-FEMALE RATIO
The ratio of males to females among elders of color varies considerably between age groups. In younger age cohorts, there are generally fewer men relative to women in each ethnic or racial group compared with white older people in the same age groups. In the older age cohorts, the ratio of males to females is consistently greater for each racial or ethnic group and decreases for the white population, in which elderly women outnumber men by three to two. In 1990, the sex ratio among elders 65 to 74 years old was 71 among African Americans, 100 among Puerto Ricans and Mexican Americans, 91 among other Latinos, 95 among Asian Pacific Americans, and 81 among non-Latino whites. Although the relative deficit of males in the African American population is most striking among young

adults and middle-aged people, it is also evident in older age groups. For example, 62 percent of elderly African Americans are women. The differences in male deficit among African Americans reflect the combined effects of undercounting African American males (particularly young inner-city males) during the census and of excessive premature mortality from injuries and chronic diseases (U.S. Department of Health and Human Services [DHHS], 1994). For Latino and Asian Pacific elders, the sex ratio variation occurs because of both the gender imbalance in early migration streams and the variation in female survival rates (Treas, 1995). In 1990, the sex ratio imbalance among Native American elders was not very different from that among white elders. Approximately 56.6 percent of the Native American population age 60 and over was female, compared with 58.1 percent of the white elderly The sex ratio, however, differs substantially between urban and rural Native American seniors. Females make up 59 percent of the urban elderly but only 53 percent of the rural elderly Native American population.

LIVING ARRANGEMENTS

There are striking differences by race and ethnicity in the living arrangements of older people. Elders of color are more likely than white elders to live with relatives other than a spouse. The majority of American Indians and Alaska Natives do not live on reservations. Approximately 22 percent live on 314 reservations and historic trust lands, and another 15 percent live in tribal or Indian village statistical areas. Multigenerational households are quite common, although more must be learned about the precise family structures of these households (U.S. Bureau of the Census, 1990b, 1993c). In 1990, 65.7 percent of male American Indian elders were married and remained so until advanced old age, whereas 61.8 percent of female elders did not. When gender and age are considered together, female American Indian elders are far more likely to live alone than males. Only 9 percent of female elders still have a spouse after age 85 living with them; thus they are at higher risk of social isolation and economic hardship, with related health consequences, as they age. African American elders are more likely to live alone than elders of other racial or ethnic groups. In 1990, only 39 percent of African Americans were living with a spouse compared with 56 percent of whites. In 1990,

one-third of African American women age 85 and older had no living children (Himes, 1992). African Americans and Latinos who left home in their youth for better job opportunities often retire to the state of their birth where they have kin (Longino & Smith, 1991).

LIFE EXPECTANCY

Life expectancy, the most comprehensive indicator of patterns of health, disease, living standards, and societal development, has improved for all groups since 1900. Overall, in 1995 it matched the record high of 75.8 years attained in 1992 and was slightly higher than the 1994 estimate of 75.6 years. Women generally live longer than men and have made greater gains in life expectancy during the 20th century. Although the sex differential was dramatically higher in 1993 than it was at the beginning of the century, the gender gap in life expectancy—6.8 years in 1993—has narrowed by a full year since 1979. However, gender and racial and ethnic disparities are clear. For example, the survival rate for women of color (78 percent) surpasses that for white men (75 percent), making gender a more important factor than race.

Since the 1970s, the average life expectancy for African Americans has remained six to eight years lower than that for whites. In 1995, life expectancy for African American men rose to 65.4 years and that for African American women rose to 74 years, but it remained unchanged for white women (79.6 years). In 1993, African American men age 65 could expect to live another 13.4 years, compared with 15.4 years for white men of the same age. Sixty-five-year-old African American and white women had an estimated 17.0 and 19.0 remaining years of life, respectively, in the same year (National Center for Health Statistics [NCHS], 1995). Age-adjusted death rates are much higher among African Americans than among whites because of two factors: infant mortality, which is double the rate for whites, and a greater likelihood of dying from certain preventable causes of death, such as homicides and accidents.

Life expectancy at birth increased by more than 20 years for American Indians, from 51 to 71.5 years, between 1940 and 1989. In comparison, life expectancy at birth for the white population increased by only 11 years during the same period. By 1980, life expectancy at birth for American Indian females had increased by 23 years (to 75.1 years), whereas American Indian male life expectancy had increased by approximately 16 years (to 67.1 years). The remarkable improvement in life expectancy at birth for American Indians is largely attributable to the efforts to eliminate infectious disease and to meet the acute care needs of this population of seniors (Indian Health Service, 1990).

During 1979 through 1981, the overall life expectancy at birth for all Asian and Pacific Islander groups in the United States was 81.9 years. In California, Japanese Americans and Chinese Americans combined were expected at birth to live eight years longer than were whites (82.5 years versus 74.9 years, respectively) (Gardner, 1994). Among Asians and Pacific islanders in Hawaii, the estimated life expectancy at birth in 1980 was 80.2 years for people classified as Chinese, 79.7 years for Japanese, 78.8 years for Philipinos, and 74 years for Hawaiians or part-Hawaiian individuals. Data collected from Asians and Pacific Islanders residing in the United States indicate that life expectancy for Chinese, Japanese, and Filipinos is higher than that for whites. Data closely reflecting the full diversity among all Asian and Pacific Islander ethnic groups, including Asian Indians, Pakistanis, Vietnamese, and other Southeast Asians, may substantially alter these life expectancy estimates. Although these data must be interpreted cautiously because of small samples, they do give an indication of life expectancy differentials (U.S. DHHS, 1994).

Currently, national estimates of life expectancy are not available for all Latino subgroups. There are some data for those groups that have been in this country longer than others. For Puerto Rican men, life expectancy at birth decreased from 71.1 years in 1987 to 69.6 years in 1991; for women, life expectancy at birth dropped from an estimated 79.4 years in 1987 to 78.5 years in 1991. For Latinos residing in Texas (mostly Mexican Americans), life expectancy at birth was similar to that for whites and higher than that for African Americans. For Mexican American men born in 1992, life expectancy is 74.0 years; for Mexican American women, 79.2 years (NCHS, 1990). If national life expectancy estimates for Latinos are similar to life expectancy estimates for Latinos in Texas, the number of Latinos who are more than 65 years old will continue to grow.

POVERTY

In recent years the percentage of all older people who are below the poverty level has diminished. The median income of older people in 1995 was up slightly from the previous year for men ($16,484) and less so for women ($9,355). In 1995, some 3.7 million elders were below the poverty level, and another 2.3 million were classified as near poor. Social security was the most-cited source of income for older couples and individuals (42 percent).

However, for elders of color the poverty rate or near-poverty rate over the life course remains disproportionately high. Although data show a wide range of socioeconomic indicators across and within the ethnic subgroups, those groups who have been in the United States for a longer time have the highest economic indicators. In 1990, 10.7 percent of white people of all ages were below the poverty level compared with 32 percent of African Americans. Poverty rates are highest among African American elders. In 1992, 62.3 percent of African Americans 65 years of age and older (88.9 percent of women and 76.9 percent of men) were poor, marginally poor, or economically vulnerable. Poverty rates increase for women 65 years and over, of whom more than 46.4 percent are in or near poverty compared with 15.7 percent of white women. Poverty rates are even more dramatic for African American elders living alone or with nonrelatives.

There is great socioeconomic diversity across and within the different Latino subgroups. Years of formal education, income, and home ownership are highest for Cuban Americans in general. Cuban refugees who came to this country at midlife or older and are now 65 and over have limited financial resources because of limited experience in the labor force in this country, which leads to small social security benefits or pensions. The percentage of Latino elders with incomes below the poverty level was 22.5 percent, or twice that of elderly whites; older Latinos' poverty level is also lower than that of whites at 22.7 percent (Administration on Aging, 1996). Dominicans and Puerto Ricans have the highest poverty rates. The median income of Latino men 65 years of age and over is only 62 percent that of white men of the same age. Latino elders, primarily Mexican American and Puerto Rican, depend mostly on small social security benefits supplemented by Supplemental Security Income (SSI) (Cuban American National Council, 1996). A study by the Urban Institute (Burt, 1993) pointed out that being Latino and elderly is a precursor to suffering food deprivation (hunger).

The percentage of Asian and Pacific Islander elderly people living below the poverty level (13 percent) is slightly higher than that for the white elderly population, but there are significant variations among subgroups. Per capita income for Japanese, Asian Indians, and Chinese Americans is higher than the national per capita income yet well below the national level for Vietnamese, Laotians, Cambodians, and Hmong (U.S. Bureau of the Census, 1993b). Per capita income for all of the Pacific Islander groups falls below the national per capita income, possibly reflecting the larger average family size compared with the general U.S. population. Because such large numbers of Asian and Pacific Islanders 65 and older are foreign born, they are far less likely than whites to receive social security benefits.

The economic well-being of American Indian elders is far worse than that of any other elderly population of color. Overall, 20 percent of Native Americans live below poverty levels, but 24 percent of those residing in nonmetropolitan areas live below this level. In 1994, 28.5 percent of all American Indians age 60 and older lived in poverty, but this percentage increased to 63 percent for those residing in rural areas. Approximately 9 percent of all impoverished American Indian families were headed by a householder age 65 years or older. The high poverty rates for American Indian elders are largely the result of low educational attainment and limited economic opportunities over the life course. Between one-third and one-half live in houses that lack complete plumbing facilities and have no mode of transportation and no telephone. Most American Indians rely on social security, SSI, and other public assistance programs.

The official poverty level is a poor predictor of hunger. Hunger is certainly highest among people who are officially classified as poor, but it does not drop off substantially until incomes rise to at least 150 percent of the poverty level. Only 12.9 percent of all seniors are officially poor, but another 14.7 percent have incomes between 100 and 150 percent of the poverty level. More than twice as many seniors face a serious risk of hunger than if only those

officially classified as poor are considered. Many elders of color whose income is above this artificial cutoff face difficult choices every day about how to ensure that they will have enough food to eat. The gap between the rich and the poor, together with the upward trend in poverty rates, will be widened by recently approved national welfare and immigration reform policies that exclude elderly immigrants from basic entitlement programs.

Although there are some variations (Cuban, Japanese, and Chinese elders have an education level comparable to that of white elders), the majority of elders from the four racial and ethnic groups discussed here have limited formal education. Low levels of educational attainment are often associated with low incomes and labor participation rates, concentration in low-paid employment, limited pension coverage, and class differences. Age, added to a limited knowledge of English and limited work-related marketable skills, diminishes opportunities in the labor force, often resulting in exclusion from employment. Higher rates of lifelong unemployment or underemployment reduce the potential for accumulation of retirement income. Although there is a distressingly high level of nonparticipation in social security and SSI by elderly people of color, their greater reliance on such income sources predicts higher levels of poverty and hunger and, consequently, poor health.

Low educational attainment is an important underlying cause of poverty. The lower the education level, the poorer a household is and the higher its risk for poor nutrition or hunger and poor health. More education, not having to pay for housing, and living with a spouse are all associated with having a higher income and therefore with lower levels of poverty, better health, more years of self-sufficiency, and independent living.

HEALTH

Differences in levels of educational attainment, perhaps more than any other sociodemographic characteristic, influence income, lifestyle, health care needs, and health care received. Class, together with race and ethnicity, creates an almost insurmountable barrier for elders of color in accessing health care. Acute and chronic stress and work-related hazards, as well as a sense of self-efficacy and control, social relations, and support are factors that have additive and cumulative effects on health and physical functioning in the life course (House, Kessler, Herzog et al., 1990).

The types of health conditions older people experience vary by economic status, gender, race, and ethnicity. For example, older people with higher incomes report their health as being much better than do older people with less income. Older men are more likely than older women to experience acute illnesses that are life threatening, whereas older women tend to experience more chronic illnesses that cause functional limitations. Also, poor people are at a disadvantage regarding many psychosocial and environmental risk factors associated with the etiology and course of disease and functional limitations.

Although there is a dearth of health and vital statistics data that take into account race and ethnicity, the information that is available points out that elders of color are disproportionately affected by a wide range of chronic illnesses and injuries that are more often than not preventable (Jackson, 1991; Jackson & Perry, 1989, 1991). There are similar and different health conditions among the various groups of elders of color that affect their daily lives, compromising their ability to live independently and productively. For example, African Americans, Native Americans, and Latino elders have rates of diabetes that are four to five times that of older white Americans. Because of the prevalence of obesity and hypertension among these three groups, their risk of stroke and cardiac disease is increased, with one-third of all deaths attributable to cardiovascular diseases. At the same time, up to age 65 American Indians have higher mortality rates than the general population; after age 65, they have lower age-specific mortality rates than the general U.S. population (U.S. DHHS, 1994). Cancer affects all groups of elders of color, both men and women. More African Americans and Latino elders report their health as fair or poor and rate it poorer compared with white elderly individuals (Markides, Coreil, & Rogers, 1989). Asian American elders report lower rates of activity limitations and better health status than the general population (Yu, Liu, & Kyrzeja, 1985). However, one-fourth of Native American elders report limitations in mobility or the ability to care for themselves (AoA, 1996). The proportion of older people with functional limitations is slightly higher among African Americans

than among whites or Latinos, with 26.3 percent of African American elders reporting at least some functional impairment compared with 19 percent of white and 25 percent of Latino elderly (Leon & Lair, 1990). The incidence of disability is much higher still for migrant and seasonal workers, most of whom are Mexican Americans and Filipinos. Elderly people of color in general have a higher rate of noncompliance than their white counterparts when it comes to taking their medication, exercising, or modifying their diets. This higher rate of noncompliance translates into an increased number of acute episodes resulting in longer hospital stays (Hernandez, 1996).

With advancing age, debilitating chronic conditions, many of which interact with one another, are likely to increase. Lack of affordable health insurance, the high cost of health care, large bureaucratic and impersonal health care systems, lack of transportation to reach available services, and a dearth of bilingual and bicultural personnel to reach those with limited English language skills are formidable barriers to access to health care services.

The implementation of Medicare was necessary to provide access to care for elderly people. However, the differential patterns in the use of many specific services according to race and income indicate that the provision of health insurance alone is not sufficient to promote effective patterns of use by all beneficiaries (Gornick et al., 1996). There are wide disparities between white elders and elders of color in the use of many Medicare services. Disparities are illustrated by utilization patterns of several types of services by low-income beneficiaries: They have fewer visits to physicians for ambulatory care, fewer mammograms, and fewer immunizations against influenza, but they are hospitalized more often and have higher mortality rates, suggesting that these beneficiaries may be receiving less primary and preventive care than either white or more affluent beneficiaries. In 1967, the first full year of Medicare, the hospital discharge rate was 29 percent lower among beneficiaries of color, most of whom were African American, than among white beneficiaries; by 1987, the rate among African Americans was 4 percent higher than among white elders (U.S. DHHS, 1987). Studies of the use of services in the first two decades of the Medicare program showed that racial disparities were disappearing with regard to overall measures, such as rates of visits to physicians and hospital discharges (Navarro, 1990). More recent analysis, however, shows wide racial disparities in the use of many medical and surgical services (Gornick et al., 1996).

The increased size and numbers of old-old elders of color present many potential problems, the most obvious being the increased need for long-term care. Individuals whose functional capacities are chronically impaired require services on a sustained basis to maintain maximal levels of psychological, physical, and social well-being (Kane & Kane, 1987). Generally, older people who live alone—particularly women, people of color, and those 85 or older—have lower incomes than couples. Thus, they are more vulnerable and more likely to have chronic health conditions that threaten their independence. Caregiving services that take into consideration the unique characteristics of the various elders of color will need to expand as the number of older people of color in need of long-term care services increases. As is the case with most elders, the family remains the main mechanism of social support for elders of color. Most elders of color have close family ties and place a strong value on caring for elderly family members but lack the economic resources or access to community services to support their caregiving functions. Although social support and support exchanges vary in significant ways by racial and ethnic group, little is known abut how caregiving patterns are affected by the various stresses imposed on families of color.

FINDING SOLUTIONS

The main political and social challenge in the coming decade is accepting a multiracial and multigenerational society. Diversity, cultural pluralism, and aging of the population are forces that will affect the future of the United States as growing numbers of ethnic and racial populations become the majority in various regions of the country (Torres-Gil, 1992). To be effective in diagnosing illness and creating wellness programs, providers must acknowledge that these diverse groups of clients use different paradigms in interpreting illness, health, long-term care, and quality of life. Lack of culturally competent providers may lead to misdiagnosis, delayed healing, and distrust, affecting the overall patient-health care giver relationship.

Older people represent only one end of the human life span and are clearly affected by the life situations of people younger than 65. Socioeconomic conditions that promote poverty, hunger, poor health—all issues facing elderly people of color—must be considered within an intergenerational context. The effects of limited educational opportunities, economic inequalities, discrimination in entering the labor force, poor health, and barriers to access to health care are cumulative over the life span, and thus interventions to deal with these complex forces must begin early in life. These problems affect not only elders' well-being, but also that of their children and grandchildren.

Program planning and development must consider the uniqueness of the various racial and ethnic groups, as well as their strengths. For example, with the exception of Cuban Americans, who cannot travel to Cuba, there are several significant characteristics about Latino elders that influence their worldview. Proximity to their country of origin and families on both sides of the border who encourage frequent travel back and forth result in a culture of migration that often strengthens transnational families. Frequent visits to their homeland and the strong influence of Spanish-language radio, television, and the written word reinforce language and culture on an ongoing basis, allowing preservation of language and culture. Family migration has been a significant characteristic of recent migrant waves from Latin America, specifically from Central America, swelling the numbers of middle-age and elderly family members and allowing continuation of functions and roles, particularly as they pertain to grandparenting and child-rearing practices. The indigenous and African American influences of immigrants, particularly those from Mexico, Central America, Peru, and the Caribbean, add important dimensions with the potential to develop bridges of understanding among the different racial and ethnic groups in this country.

American Indians and Alaska Natives, to varying degrees, incorporate traditional folk medicine into healing practices amid current medical approaches. Some folk medicine practices continue to be used on reservations by medicine men and other healers using dozens of native plants that have been officially recognized by the U.S. Pharmacopeial Convention (1994). Acknowledgment of the wisdom that comes with experience and age promotes respect for elderly family members and meaningful roles that, in turn, nurture an ongoing sense of well-being and belonging.

A variety of religions, such as Buddhism, Hinduism, Islam, Catholicism, and other Christian religious traditions, are practiced by Asians and Pacific Islanders. These traditional philosophies may well serve as a reference from which Asian and Pacific Islander immigrant families build their understanding and practice of health in their new country. For example, holistic health and traditional medicine emphasize elements of prevention, such as a balance for good health, the importance of good diet and healthy behaviors, and the use of herbs and acupuncture. There is a great need to recognize the heterogeneity of the African American population, to identify and build on the many coping skills that have allowed them to survive to old age in the most hostile environment. The role of the church and the family in caring for older members must also be recognized and used to reach younger generations. Their strong sense of justice and equity has provided leadership in movements of liberation. Younger generations have much to learn from these values as they forge a better future for themselves and their children.

Policy

Budgetary constraints raise serious concerns about the country's capacity to address policies and programs associated with the aging of the population in general, and of elders of color specifically. Federal policymakers concentrated on programs for poor people to an unprecedented degree in the 104th Congress, which affected virtually all categories of poor people and elders in particular (Center on Budget and Policy Priorities, 1996). In the past most national organizations in the aging network have had to address the competing agendas of their constituencies. In the face of diminishing resources, competition will increase and mechanisms for the voices of elders of color will need to be strengthened. The Black Caucus and Center on Aging; the National Asian Pacific Center on Aging; the National Indian Council on Aging; and two Latino organizations—the National Hispanic Council on Aging and Asociacion Pro Personas Mayores—have articulated the needs of the various elders of color. Advocacy has been carried out in the form of policy analysis and monitoring, collection and interpretation of data, develop-

ment of educational materials, institution and capacity building, leadership development, and increasing the level of awareness of decision makers and the aging network in general. These national organizations are the recog nized voice for elders of color, presenting their needs and advocating for solutions in a variety of public forums and a variety of forms. For example, these national organizations played important leadership roles when changes were proposed to social security and SSI, Medicaid and Medicare, welfare, and immigration reform law that threatened the livelihood of many elders of color.

References

Administration on Aging. (1996). *AoA Update, 1*(5).

Burt, R. M. (1993). *Hunger among the elderly: Local and national comparisons*. Washington, DC: The Urban Institute.

Center on Budget and Policy Priorities. (1996). *Older Americans Report, 20,* 412.

Cuban American National Council. (1996). *The Council Letter, 11*(2).

Crystal, S., & Shea, D. (1990). Cumulative advantage, cumulative disadvantage, and inequality among elderly people. *Gerontologist, 30,* 437–443.

Ewbank, D. C. (1987). History of black mortality and health before 1940. *Milbank Quarterly, 65*(Suppl. 1), 100–128.

Fix, M., & Passel, J. S. (1994). *Immigration and immigrants: Setting the record straight* (p. 63). Washington, DC: Urban Institute.

Gardner, R. W. (1994). Mortality. In N. Zane, D. Takeuchi, & K. Young (Eds). *Confronting critical health issures of Asian and Pacific Islander Americans*. Thousand Oaks, CA: Sage Publications.

Gornick, M. E, Eggers, P. W., Reilly, T. W., Mentnech, R. M., Fitterman, L. K., Kuchen, L. E., & Vladeck, B. C. (1996). Effects of race and income on mortality and use of services among Medicare beneficiaries. *The New England Journal of Medicine, 335,* 791–816.

Hernandez, G. G. (1996). Managed care: A cultural perspective. *Minority Faces, 2*(1).

Himes, C. L. (1992). Future caregivers: Projected family structures of older people. *Journal of Gerontology, 47*(1), S23.

House, J. S., Kessler, R. C., Herzog, R. A., et al. (1990). Age, socioeconomic status, and health. *Milbank Quarterly/Health and Society, 168,* 383–411.

Jackson, J. S. (1988). *The black American elderly: Research on physical and psychosocial health*. New York: Springer.

Jackson, J. J., & Perry, C. (1989). Physical health conditions of middle-aged and aged blacks. In K. S. Markides (Ed.), *Aging and health: Perspectives on gender, race, ethnicity, and class* (pp. 111–176). London: Sage Publications.

Kane, R., & Kane, R. L. (1987). *Long-term care: Principles, programs and policies*. New York: Springer.

Kitagawa, E. M., & Hauser, P. M. (1973). *Differential mortality in the United States: A study in socioeconomic epidemiology*. Cambridge, MA: Harvard University Press.

Leon, J., & Lair, T. (1990). *Functional status of the non institutional elderly: Estimates of ADL and IADL difficulties* (Publication No. PHS 90-3462). Washington, DC: U.S. Government Printing Office.

Longino, C. F., & Smith, K. J. (1991). Black retirement migration in the United States. *Journal of Gerontology, 46,* S125–S132.

National Center for Health Statistics. (1990). Life tables. In *Vital statistics of the United States 1988* (Vol. 2, pp. 183–204). Hyattsville, MD: Author.

National Center for Health Statistics. (1995). *Births and deaths for 1995* (DHHS Publication No. PHS 91-1232). Hyattsville, MD: Author.

National Hispanic Council on Aging. (1995). Washington, DC: Author.

National Indian Council on Aging. (1981). *American Indian elderly: A national profile*. Albuquerque, NM: Author.

Navarro, V. (1990). Race or class versus race and class: Mortality differentials in the United States. *Lancet, 336,* 1238–1240.

Reid, J. (1986). Immigration and the future U.S. black population. *Population Today, 14*(2), 6–8.

Tauber, C., & Smith, D. (1988). *Minority elderly: An overview of demographic characteristics and 1990 census plans*. Paper presented to the National Council on Aging symposium, Washington, DC.

Torres-Gil, F. (1992). *The new aging: Politics and change in America*. Westport, CT: Auburn House.

Treas, J. (1995). Older Americans in the 1990s and beyond. *Population Bulletin, 50*(2).

U.S. Bureau of the Census. (1989). Projections of the population of states, by age, sex, and race: 1988 to 2080. In *Current population reports* (Series P25, No. 1018). Washington, DC: U.S. Government Printing Office.

U.S. Bureau of the Census. (1990a). United States population estimates, by age, sex, race, and Hispanic origin: 1980–1988. In *Current population reports* (Series P25, No. 1045). Washington, DC: U.S. Government Printing Office.

U.S. Bureau of the Census. (1990b). *Statistical abstract of the United States: 1990* (110th Ed., No. 7). Washington, DC: U.S. Government Printing Office.

U.S. Bureau of the Census. (1993a). Population projections of the United States, by age, sex, race, and Hispanic origin: 1993 to 2050. In *Current population reports* (Series P25, No. 1104, Table 2). Washington, DC: U.S. Government Printing Office.

U.S. Bureau of the Census. (1993b). *We, the American Asians*. Washington, DC: U.S. Government Printing Office.

U.S. Bureau of the Census. (1993c). *We, the first Americans*. Washington, DC: U.S. Government Printing Office.

U.S. Bureau of the Census. (1996). *Census brief.* (CENBR/96-1). December 1996. Washington, DC: U.S. Department of Commerce.

U.S. Department of Health, Education, and Welfare, Social Security Administration, Office of Research and Statistics. (1987). Short-stay hospital utilization. In *Medicare: Health insurance for the aged* (Section 4.1). Washington, DC: U.S. Government Printing Office.

U.S. Department of Health and Human Services. (1994). *Chronic disease in minority populations*. Atlanta: Centers for Disease Control and Prevention.

U.S. Immigration and Naturalization Service. (1991). *Statistical yearbook of the Immigration and Naturalization Service, 1990*. Washington, DC: U.S. Government Printing Office.

U.S. Pharmacopeial Convention. (1994). *The national formulary* (23rd rev.). Rockville, MD: Author.

Yu, E. S., Liu, H., & Kyrzeja, W. T. (1985). Physical and mental health status indicators for Asian-American communities. In *DHHS: Black and minority health: Cross-cutting issues in minority health*. Washington, DC: U.S. Department of Health and Human Services.

FURTHER READING

Kunitz, S. J. (1983*). Disease change and the role of medicine: The Navajo experience.* Berkeley: University of California Press.

Kunitz, S. J., & Levy, J. E. (1989). Aging and health among Navajo Indians. In K. S. Markides (Ed.), *Aging and health; Perspectives on gender, race, ethnicity and class* (pp. 211–254). London: Sage Publications.

Markides, K. S., Coreil, J., & Rogers, L. P. (1989). Aging and health among southwestern Hispanics. In K. S. Markides (Ed.), *Aging and health: Perspectives on gender, race, ethnicity, and class* (pp. 177–210). London: Sage Publications.

Marta Sotomayor, PhD, is president and chief executive officer, National Hispanic Council on Aging, 2713 Ontario Road, NW, Washington, DC 20009.

For further information see
Aging Overview; Aging: Direct Practice; Aging: Public Policy Issues and Trends; Aging: Social Work Practice; Deinstitutionalization; Ethnic-Sensitive Practice; Income Security Overview; Long-Term Care; Managed Care Overview; Mental Health Overview; **Oppression;** Poverty; Social Security.

Key Words	
aging	health care
demographics	race
ethnicity	

Alzheimer's Disease

See **Aging: Alzheimer's Disease and Other Disabilities**

B

Baccalaureate Social Workers

Lorrie Greenhouse Gardella

Baccalaureate social work is generalist social work at the basic level of professional practice (National Association of Social Workers [NASW], 1981). Known informally as BSWs, baccalaureate social workers in the United States hold a baccalaureate degree (which may be designated as BA, bachelor of arts; BS, bachelor of science; or BSW, bachelor of social work) with a major in social work from a program accredited by the Council on Social Work Education. Baccalaureate social work practice is currently licensed in 33 states. With more than 400 accredited programs, baccalaureate social work education provides a critical entry point to the profession for students of color, students with low incomes, returning adult students, and students in rural areas. Empirical research on practice reveals the contributions of baccalaureate social workers to the profession. In comparison with master's degree social workers, BSWs tend to practice in distinct employment settings and professional roles.

This entry traces the history of baccalaureate social work in the United States, including the development of baccalaureate social work education, and profiles baccalaureate social work practice. Job analyses comparing BSW and master's-level social work (MSW) practice reveal the distinct contributions of baccalaureate social work to the profession. Baccalaureate social workers are twice as likely as MSWs to practice in the public sector. As a result, social work's support for baccalaureate education has waxed and waned with its commitment to public social services (Hoffman & Kolevzon, 1992; Teare, Sheafor, & Shank, 1995). The profession has alternately excluded and included baccalaureate social work through policies of its national educational and practice associations (Leighninger, 1987; Sheafor & Shank, 1986).

HISTORY OF BACCALAUREATE SOCIAL WORK

The history of baccalaureate social work reflects competing visions of the profession (Leighninger, 1987). Early social work leaders favored a private model of professionalism in which social workers, like doctors or lawyers, would practice in private agencies for the benefit of their clients. Other leaders in social work, including baccalaureate educators, sought a public model of professionalism, with social workers practicing in public social services agencies for the common good (Morales & Sheafor, 1995).

During the first quarter of this century, the Association of Training Schools for Professional Social Workers and its successor, the American Association of Schools of Social Work (AASSW), encouraged the shift from agency-based training to university- or college-based professional education. Most university or college courses in social work were offered through undergraduate departments of sociology (Sheafor & Shank, 1986). Influenced by Abraham Flexner, a medical educator, the social work educational associations sought increasingly selective educational standards for the profession. Graduate educators such as Edith Abbott and Sophonisba Breckinridge "were insulted when their programs were compared to those in nursing or public school teaching" (Leighninger, 1987, p. 127). They believed that social work would gain the professional status of medicine or law only when professional preparation for social work was limited to graduate education (Stuart, Leighninger, & Donahoe, 1993).

By 1932 AASSW required member schools to provide at least one year of graduate social work education. By 1939 only schools with a two-year graduate program were eligible for membership. The national social work practice association, the American Association of Social Workers (AASW), followed suit. In 1933 membership in the practice association was limited to graduates of schools approved by AASSW (Sheafor & Shank, 1986; Stuart et al.,

1993). In the face of the Great Depression, baccalaureate social work educators believed this emphasis on professional status was misplaced. Social work was failing to meet the tremendous social services needs emerging in the 1930s. Limited by size, located primarily in major urban areas, and focused on casework, graduate social work programs could not respond to the rapid expansion of public social services. By 1942 graduate social work enrollments were 4,000 to 5,000 students per year, in contrast to the 40,000 to 50,000 positions in state social services (Leighninger, 1987).

Land-grant universities, state colleges, and some private colleges offered baccalaureate social work education. These institutions supported a public model of professionalism for social work. W. B. Bizzell, president of the University of Oklahoma and of the National Association of State Universities, argued that if "social workers in the public welfare services are paid with public funds, so universities with state support should be allowed to train them for these positions" (Leighninger, 1987, p. 131).

Supported by their institutions, baccalaureate educators established an alternative social work educational association, the National Association of Schools of Social Administration (NASSA). State welfare departments and the national accrediting committee of state and land-grant colleges and universities supported NASSA, which by 1943 "was recognized as the official accrediting body for undergraduate social work programs" (Stuart et al., 1993, p. 3). In response to the formation of NASSA, the graduate education establishment began to accommodate undergraduate educators. AASSW offered a consulting service to assist colleges and universities in developing "preprofessional" social work programs. AASSW also opened membership to state universities with a one-year master's degree program in social work. Through this strategy "the larger and more established graduate association" tried to regain control of social work education (Stuart et al., 1993, p. 3).

Federal social welfare officials encouraged the two educational associations to work together, and AASSW and NASSA jointly commissioned a comprehensive study of social work education. Ernest Hollis of the U.S. Office of Education and Alice Taylor, a prominent practitioner and educator, completed the study in 1951. The Hollis–Taylor report brought together elements of the private and public professional models for social work. In keeping with the private professional model, the report recommended graduate-level professional education based on a mandatory preprofessional preparation at the baccalaureate level. In keeping with the public professional model, Hollis and Taylor advised graduate educators to place less emphasis on casework and give greater attention to "generic" social work education. In this way professional education would prepare social workers not only for practice in private agencies but also for practice in public health and social services (Leighninger, 1987).

Although graduate educators rejected the suggestion of mandatory baccalaureate preparation in social work, the Hollis–Taylor report forecast the direction of social work education in the years to come. Baccalaureate and master's-level education each would provide a common educational base (the "professional foundation") for social work practice.

The Hollis–Taylor report also supported a merger of the two educational associations into a single organization to represent the entire profession, and, in 1952, AASSW and NASSA merged into CSWE. In the new organization, undergraduate programs and their commitment to public social welfare "took a back seat to graduate interests" (Leighninger, 1987, p. 143). Social work practice organizations also came together to form a single professional association, NASW, in 1955. NASW required graduation from a CSWE-accredited school of social work as the basic membership criterion.

Consistent with the private model of professionalism, NASW assumed a limited political role in the 1950s. Although they avoided partisan politics, social workers provided consultation and expertise to government. Some writers in the field questioned the profession's emphasis on selective educational standards, its focus on casework practice in private agencies, and its retreat from political activism (Morales & Sheafor, 1995). In the 1960s, however, social work rediscovered its commitment to social change. The civil rights movement renewed social workers' interest in social policy. A 1966 editorial in *Social Work* noted that "the dazzle that once hovered over casework—especially psychiatric social work—now lights up social policy" (Morales & Sheafor, 1995, p. 72).

Federal social welfare services expanded once again under the Great Society programs of the Johnson administration. Projecting thousands of new social welfare jobs, the Department of Health, Education and Welfare (HEW) recommended federal support for professional baccalaureate social work education. In 1967 Congress appropriated $5 million to social work education to be divided equally between undergraduate and graduate programs, under Section 707, Title VII of the Social Security Act. Social workers within the federal government interpreted Section 707 to promote and strengthen baccalaureate programs in historically black colleges and universities and to provide training opportunities for American Indian and Latino students (Stuart et al., 1993).

By the late 1960s baccalaureate degrees in social work were recognized by state civil service boards. Undergraduate social work enrollments expanded from 12,500 in 1967 to 19,000 in 1970 (Stuart et al., 1993). A comprehensive study of baccalaureate social work, commissioned by the U.S. Veterans Administration, documented the competence of baccalaureate social workers for professional practice in a variety of settings (Sheafor & Shank, 1986).

In the face of workforce needs, federal support for baccalaureate social work education, and the growth of baccalaureate social work programs, NASW members voted in 1969 to recognize baccalaureate social work as the first level of professional practice. Effective in 1970, NASW opened membership to graduates of baccalaureate social work programs that had been approved by CSWE (Sheafor & Shank, 1986; Stuart et al., 1993). CSWE, meanwhile, instituted an approval system for professional baccalaureate social work education. In 1974, when CSWE implemented baccalaureate accreditation standards, 135 baccalaureate social work programs received accreditation (Morales & Sheafor, 1995).

Despite formal recognition by NASW and CSWE, baccalaureate social work was not fully integrated into the national practice and educational associations. In the early 1970s baccalaureate social workers had no representation on the NASW Board of Directors and sparse representation on committees. High fees for NASW membership presented a barrier to many baccalaureate social workers, who earned significantly lower salaries than their MSW colleagues. Some social workers with master's degrees did not accept the BSW

as a professional credential, and there was particular resistance from clinical social workers (Leighninger, 1987). A perceived chilly reception for baccalaureate social workers in many state chapters further discouraged their participation (Sheafor & Shank, 1986).

In CSWE some graduate educators did not accept the BSW as a meaningful professional credential. Baccalaureate educators had 10 seats on the CSWE governing board, compared with graduate educators' 20, and they were a distinct minority on commissions and policy-making groups (Stuart et al., 1993).

In response, undergraduate educators organized on behalf of baccalaureate social work. The Southern Association of Baccalaureate Social Workers identified the need to strengthen the voice of undergraduate educators in NASW and CSWE and to advocate for continued federal support for baccalaureate social work education. Following the lead of the Southern Association, baccalaureate program directors developed goals for a new national organization. Unlike the founders of NASSA, the 1940s-era undergraduate organization, they would support and work within established professional structures. In 1975, at the CSWE annual meeting, baccalaureate educators founded the Association of Baccalaureate Social Work Program Directors (BPD) (Stuart et al., 1993).

In addition to advocating for baccalaureate social work education and practice, BPD provided formal professional development opportunities to baccalaureate program directors and informal opportunities for networking and consultation (Stuart et al., 1993). As the organization developed, BPD became a general resource for baccalaureate educators, with faculty as well as program directors participating in the annual conference, the publications program, and other services. In 1995, with the inauguration of the *Journal of Baccalaureate Social Work*, BPD reached beyond education to practice. Baccalaureate practice had been nearly invisible in social work's professional literature. The new journal had the mission of "nurturing scholarship, contributing to the social work knowledge base, advocating for professional [baccalaureate] practice, and developing leadership within the baccalaureate community" (Mission Statement, 1996, p. 6).

BACCALAUREATE SOCIAL WORK EDUCATION

In the 1970s, when the BSW was first accepted as a professional degree, researchers began to develop a competency-based generalist curriculum for professional baccalaureate social work. Leaders in baccalaureate curricular research were active participants in CSWE and BPD (personal communication with M. Charles, Dean, School of Social Work, Southern University at New Orleans, March 8, 1997). Their proposals reached BSW programs nationally through CSWE approval or accreditation processes and through BPD's professional development services.

With HEW funding the Southern Regional Education Board (SREB) engaged in a curricular project (McPheeters & Ryan, 1971) that considered the roles of baccalaureate social workers from the perspective of clients, including individuals, groups, and communities. This study developed the concept of generalist practice. The Veterans Administration sponsored a comprehensive study (Barker & Briggs, 1968) of baccalaureate social work, conducted at Syracuse University, in which researchers identified specific tasks performed in baccalaureate practice. Educators at the University of Montana developed a competency-based examination (Arkava & Brennen, 1976) for baccalaureate social workers, and the West Virginia Curriculum Project (Baer &

Federico, 1978), funded by HEW and staffed by Betty Baer and Ron Federico, identified 10 competencies for baccalaureate social work practice and associated curricular content (Baer & Federico, 1978, Sheafor & Shank, 1986; Stuart et al., 1993).

These studies informed baccalaureate social work education, which "prepares students for generalist social work practice with systems of all sizes" (CSWE, 1994a, Curriculum Policy Statement [CPS] B6.9). As in the West Virginia Curriculum project, baccalaureate educators designed competency-based programs, with educational competencies or outcomes providing a basis for program evaluation. The current CSWE Curriculum Policy Statement (1994a) specifies a minimum of 12 educational outcomes for baccalaureate social work education, as shown in Figure 1.

Today baccalaureate and master's-level social work programs share a common educational base, known as the "professional foundation." The professional foundation includes knowledge, values, and skills related to social work values and ethics, diversity, social and economic justice, populations-at-risk, human behavior in the social environment, social welfare policy and services, social work practice, research, and field practicum (CSWE, 1994a, CPS B6.1). The baccalaureate field practicum includes a minimum of 400

FIGURE 1

Curriculum Policy Statement B5.7

Graduates of a baccalaureate social work program will be able to:

1. Apply critical thinking skills within the context of professional social work practice.
2. Practice within the values and ethics of the social work profession and with an understanding of and respect for the positive value of diversity.
3. Demonstrate the professional use of self.
4. Understand the forms and mechanisms of oppression and discrimination and the strategies of change that advance social and economic justice.
5. Understand the history of the social work profession and its current structures and issues.
6. Apply the knowledge and skills of generalist social work to practice with systems of all sizes.
7. Apply knowledge of bio-psycho-social variables that affect individual development and behavior, and use theoretical frameworks to understand the interactions among individuals and between individuals and social systems (i.e., families, groups, organizations, and communities).
8. Analyze the impact of social policies on client systems, workers, and agencies.
9. Evaluate research studies and apply findings to practice, and, under supervision, to evaluate their own practice interventions and those of other relevant systems.
10. Use communication skills differentially with a variety of client populations, colleagues, and members of the community.
11. Use supervision appropriate to generalist practice.
12. Function within the structure of organizations and service delivery systems, and under supervision, seek necessary organizational change.

SOURCE: Council on Social Work Education. (1994a). Curriculum policy statement for baccalaureate degree programs in social work education. In *Handbook of accreditation standards and procedures* (p. 99). Alexandria, VA: Author.

hours of professionally supervised social work practice (CPS B6.14).

Baccalaureate education integrates professional education with a liberal arts perspective, which promotes "an understanding of one's cultural heritage in the context of other cultures; the methods and limitations of various systems of inquiry; and the knowledge, attitudes, ways of thinking, and means of communication that are characteristic of a broadly educated person" (CSWE, 1994a, CPS B5.9). The liberal arts perspective is "prerequisite to the master's professional program in social work" (CSWE, 1994b, CPS M5.9).

The Curriculum Policy Statement (CSWE, 1994a, CPS B5.2) begins to distinguish between baccalaureate and master's-degree social work education, but the continuum from one educational level to the next is not clearly defined. Although they share a professional foundation and a liberal arts perspective, baccalaureate and master's-degree education "differ from each other in . . . depth, breadth, and specificity." Baccalaureate education prepares students for generalist social work practice, whereas master's-degree education prepares students for "advanced social work practice in an area of concentration."

In considering curricular content, social work educators have difficulty in making these distinctions between BSW and MSW education. Some master's degree programs offer "advanced generalist" concentrations (Gibbs, Locke, & Lohmann, 1990; Schatz, Jenkins, & Sheafor, 1990). How should the generalist and advanced generalist curricula differ? Some undergraduate educators and social services agencies call for areas of concentration, such as child welfare, in baccalaureate social work programs (Alperin, 1996; Baer & McLean, 1996). How should the generalist curriculum accommodate specialized knowledge, such as intensive study for child welfare practice? Where is the boundary between basic and advanced specialized knowledge?

This educational continuum raises structural as well as curricular issues. According to the Curriculum Policy Statement (CSWE, 1994a, CPS M5.8), baccalaureate social workers who enter master's degree programs "should not repeat professional foundation content . . . that has been mastered in the BSW program." Master's degree programs may avoid redundancy through advanced placement of qualified BSW graduates. Although most accredited MSW programs have policies and procedures for advanced standing, "these vary tremendously across programs" (Aguilar, Brown, Cowan, & Cingolani, 1997, p. 59).

To resolve issues in the educational continuum, social work needs to assess education and to research practice at every educational level. Unfortunately, the profession has not yet made a sustained commitment to educational assessment or to practice research. In the area of educational assessment, a BPD-sponsored project provides undergraduate programs with standardized instruments to measure educational outcomes as assessed by students, alumni, and their employers. A national database allows programs to compare their findings with those of other social work programs (Rogers, 1996). In contrast to baccalaureate educational assessment, master's degree programs, with their various concentrations and curricular designs, "lack standardized or national norms to compare MSW alumni responses from various schools" (Hull, Mather, Christopherson, & Young, 1994, p. 395).

In the area of practice research, national empirical studies of social work practice, including the NASW-sponsored job analysis (Teare et al., 1995) and the BPD-sponsored outcome study project (Rogers, Smith, Hull, & Ray, 1995) identify patterns in demographics, employment settings, and fields of practice. These studies, which were conducted independently, are based on data collected from 1989 to 1990. More recent general information is provided by a job analysis conducted from 1995 to 1996 by the American Association of State Social Work Boards (AASSWB, 1996). A 1996 NASW-sponsored job analysis updates information on MSW practice but not BSW practice.

The profession lacks information critical to improving social work education across the continuum because of inconsistent research on educational assessment, particularly at the MSW level and inconsistent research on practice, particularly at the BSW level. Nonetheless, the available research shows that baccalaureate educators have realized the goals of a public model of professionalism: providing access to the profession for underrepresented groups and preparing social workers for professional practice in the public social services.

BACCALAUREATE SOCIAL WORK PRACTICE

Baccalaureate social work education has provided a "critical entry point" to the profession for students from ethnic minorities, students with low incomes, returning adult students, and students in rural areas (Berger, 1992; Lennon, 1995; Morales & Sheafor, 1995). An estimated 10,500 degrees in baccalaureate social work were awarded in 1995 by 387 accredited programs and 38 programs in candidacy status (Lennon, 1995). Baccalaureate social work practice was licensed in 33 states in 1997.

Trends in baccalaureate social work education suggest that the BSW workforce is becoming more diverse, with increasing proportions of men and people from ethnic minorities entering the field (Lennon, 1995; Teare et al., 1995). The NASW study data found that, in 1990, nearly 90 percent of baccalaureate social workers were women, compared with 86 percent of BSW graduates in 1995. Only 13 percent of BSWs were members of ethnic minorities in 1990, compared with 24 percent of BSW graduates in 1995.

Other demographic patterns from the NASW study, which are shown in Table 1, appear to be holding true. Baccalaureate social workers range in age from young to older adulthood, with an average age in the mid-30s, and African Americans represent the largest ethnic minority group. The greatest numbers of baccalaureate social workers are concentrated in the Northeast and the northcentral states, yet most BSWs practice in small communities with populations of less than 44,000 (AASSWB, 1996; Rogers et al., 1995; Teare et al., 1995).

Research shows that the majority of baccalaureate social work graduates succeeds in finding social work jobs, with more than 80 percent of BSW graduates entering professional social work practice. Most baccalaureate social workers are employed in public and not-for-profit agencies and provide direct services to individuals and families in such fields as health care, gerontology, mental health, and child welfare. Their clients are culturally and ethnically diverse, ranging from infancy to old age (AASSWB, 1996; Rogers et al., 1995; Teare et al., 1995). BSW employment settings and fields of practice are shown in Table 2.

Although baccalaureate social workers find themselves well prepared for their responsibilities in practice, most BSWs intend to continue their social work education. More

TABLE 1
Personal Characteristics of Baccalaureate Practitioners (N = 1,449)

Characteristic	Percentage[a]	Years
Location		
Northeast	29.2	
Northcentral	38.8	
South	21.2	
West	10.4	
Ethnicity		
Asian/Pacific Islander	0.6	
African American	7.3	
Chicano/Mexican American	1.2	
Puerto Rican	0.5	
Other Hispanic	0.5	
White	87.4	
Gender		
Male	8.9	
Female	90.8	
Mean Age		33.4
Mean Yrs. in Present Position		3.2
Mean Yrs. in Social Work		5.3

[a]Percentages may not total 100 because of missing values on some variables.
SOURCE: Reprinted with permission from Teare, R. J., Sheafor, B.W., & Shank, B.W. (1995). Baccalaureate-level workers: Who they are and what they do. In *Practice-sensitive social work education: An empirical analysis of social work practice and practitioners* (p. 34). Alexandria, VA: Council on Social Work Education. Copyright 1995 by the Council on Social Work Education, Inc.

than 30 percent go on to earn the MSW, with an additional 38.5 percent planning to do so (Hoffman & Kolevzon, 1992; Rogers et al., 1995; Teare et al., 1995). As summarized by Teare and Sheafor (1991, p. 7), "It is clear that the BSW is an entry point to the profession. It is equally clear that those who stay in social work do not see the BSW as a terminal degree."

Researchers comparing BSW and MSW practice agree that baccalaureate social workers and social workers with master's degrees are employed in different settings or professional roles (AASSWB, 1996; Rogers et al., 1995; Teare et al., 1995). Baccalaureate social workers tend to practice in public social services agencies, community agencies, nursing homes, and group homes, and most work in small cities and towns. Master's-level social workers tend to practice in hospitals, mental health clinics, private practice, and schools, and most MSWs work in major metropolitan areas. In the field of health care, baccalaureate social workers practice primarily in nursing homes, hospices, or residential settings, whereas MSWs practice primarily in hospitals. As shown in Table 3, baccalaureate

TABLE 2
Employment Characteristics of Baccalaureate Practitioners (N = 1,449)

Characteristic	Percentage[a]
Primary Job Function	
Direct service	80.9
Supervision	6.6
Management/admin.	8.2
Other	3.5
Size of Practice Community	
Fewer than 10,000	16.7
10,001–40,000	27.2
40,001–100,000	.25.3
100,001–500,000	19.1
More than 500,000	11.7
Perceived Autonomy	
Almost complete	19.7
Considerable	42.4
Moderate	26.1
Little	9.1
Almost none	2.7
Practice Setting	
Social service agency	46.4
Hospital	13.7
Nursing home/hospice	11.5
Outpatient facility	8.7
Group home/residential care	6.3
Psychiatric institution	4.4
Courts/criminal justice	2.8
Elementary/secondary school	2.1
Non–social services agencies	1.2
Private Practice	0.9
Other	1.7
Primary Practice Area	
Children and youth	18.8
Services to the aged	16.5
Family services	13.7
Medical and health care	12.8
Mental health	9.9
Dev. disabilities/mental retardation	9.6
Alcohol and substance abuse	3.2
Public assistance/public welfare	3.1
Corrections/criminal justice	2.7
School social work	1.4
Other	8.3

[a]Percentages may not total 100 because of missing values on some variables.
Source: Reprinted with permission from Teare, R. J., Sheafor, B.W., & Shank, B.W. (1995). Baccalaureate-level workers: Who they are and what they do. In *Practice-sensitive social work education: An empirical analysis of social work practice and practitioners* (p. 35). Alexandria, VA: Council on Social Work Education. Copyright 1995 Council on Social Work Education, Inc.

TABLE 3
Distribution of BSWs and MSWs by Employment Setting

Employment Setting	Percent BSWs	Percent MSWs
Social service agency	46.4	26.7
Hospital	13.7	21.4
Nursing home/hospice	11.5	1.0
Outpatient clinic	8.7	19.4
Group home/residential care	6.3	1.6
Psychiatric institution	4.4	3.7
Court/criminal justice	2.8	1.4
Elementary/secondary school	2.1	7.2
Private practice	0.9	7.9
College or university	0.6	4.8

Source: Reprinted with permission from Teare, R. J., & Sheafor, B. W. (1995). *Practice-sensitive social work education: An empirical analysis of social work practice and practitioners* (p. 100). Alexandria, VA: Council on Social Work Education. Copyright 1995 Council on Social Work Education, Inc.

TABLE 4
Distribution of BSWs and MSWs by Primary Practice Area

Primary Practice Area	Percent BSWs	Percent MSWs
Children and youth	18.8	13.1
Services to the aged	16.5	3.7
Family services	13.7	13.7
Medical and health care	12.8	13.5
Mental health	9.9	28.3
Dev. disabilities/mental retardation	9.6	3.6
Alcohol and substance abuse	3.2	2.2
Public assistance/public welfare	3.1	1.5
Corrections/criminal justice	2.7	1.3
School social work	1.4	6.3
Education	0.6	3.4
Community organization	0.5	1.5

Source: Reprinted with permission from Teare, R. J., & Sheafor, B. W. (1995). *Practice-sensitive social work education: An empirical analysis of social work practice and practitioners* (p. 101). Alexandria, VA: Council on Social Work Education. Copyright 1995 Council on Social Work Education, Inc.

social workers are nearly twice as likely as MSWs to practice in public social services.

As shown in Table 4, baccalaureate social workers are more likely than master's-level social workers to identify primary practice areas in gerontology, developmental disabilities, public welfare, or criminal justice. MSWs are more likely to identify primary practice areas in mental health, school social work, and education.

When they are employed in similar practice settings, such as family services or health care, BSWs and MSWs have different responsibilities. Baccalaureate social workers are more likely to provide direct services, and master's-level social workers are more likely to provide indirect services, such as administration and supervision. In direct service positions, BSWs and MSWs assume different practice roles

(Rogers et al., 1995; Teare et al., 1995). For example, both baccalaureate and master's-level social workers engage in direct practice in the field of family and children's services. The baccalaureate social workers tend to focus on tangible services, such as those related to health, disabilities, financial assistance, and housing. The social workers with master's degrees tend to focus on clinical issues, such as those related to anxiety, depression, interpersonal relations, and family functioning. BSWs engage in case management activities, connecting people with services, whereas MSWs use "formal therapeutic models and techniques in individual, family, and group treatment" (Rogers et al., 1995; Teare et al., 1995, p. 108).

Similarly, in hospital settings, BSWs are more likely than MSWs to engage in activities such as protective services, case management and referral, dispute resolution, and provision of tangible services. Social workers with master's degrees are more likely to engage in formal treatment activities and, even when primarily in direct practice positions, to have supervisory responsibilities (Rogers et al., 1995; Teare et al., 1995).

Most BSWs and MSWs engage in professional development activities, such as participating in conferences, workshops, and continuing education programs. However, social workers with master's degrees are twice as likely as baccalaureate social workers to join NASW (Rogers et al., 1995).

Research on practice challenges three widespread assumptions about baccalaureate social workers. First, it is clear that baccalaureate social workers do not compete with master's-level social workers for the same professional positions (AASSWB, 1996; Rogers et al., 1995; Teare et al., 1995). As Teare and Sheafor (1995, p. 101) stated, baccalaureate social workers "have carved out a distinct niche in the human services."

Second, the NASW job analysis (Teare et al., 1995) revealed that baccalaureate social workers have considerable autonomy in their practice, including discretion as to choice of method or intervention strategy, prioritization of tasks, and determination of performance standards. With 62 percent reporting considerable to almost complete job autonomy and an additional 26 percent reporting moderate autonomy, baccalaureate social workers have more autonomy in practice than suggested by NASW's classification system.

Finally, a comparison of the data gathered from 1989 to 1990 (Rogers et al., 1995; Teare et al., 1995) with the more recent AASSWB (1996) data suggests that baccalaureate social workers may be assuming increasing responsibilities for indirect practice. In the NASW job analysis (Teare et al., 1995), 80.9 percent of baccalaureate social workers were employed as direct service providers. In the AASSWB job analysis, the proportion of direct service providers fell to 67.7 percent. Although further data are needed, researchers have hypothesized that baccalaureate social workers may supervise paraprofessionals, lay staff, and volunteers in such settings as nursing homes, where few MSWs are available. Rogers and his colleagues (1995) suggested that social workers with master's degrees are moving into managed care settings, where they provide direct clinical services. Baccalaureate social workers, meanwhile, are assuming indirect practice roles in environments outside managed care.

As indicated by the data on direct and indirect practice, changing contexts for master's-level social work affect baccalaureate social work and vice versa. Without information on one level of practice, researchers face difficulty in interpreting information about the other. In a time of fundamental economic and political change, the profession must be studied as a whole.

A commitment to educational assessment and practice research at the baccalaureate, master's, and doctoral levels would help social work identify its strengths and agree upon its goals. As health services are delivered through managed care and as social welfare programs devolve, privatize, or disappear, the distinctions between public and private models of professionalism no longer apply. Social work needs a new model of professionalism, an inclusive model in which "previously unheard voices . . . join in professional conversations about what is good, effective social work education and practice" (Schriver, 1995, p. 10). Baccalaureate social workers have much to contribute to these conversations: a vision of social work that combines high educational standards with commitment to practice for the common good.

REFERENCES

Aguilar, G. D., Brown, K., Cowan, A., & Cingolani, J. (1997). Advanced standing revisited: A national survey. *Journal of Social Work Education, 33,* 59–75.

Alperin, D. E. (1996). Graduate and undergraduate field placements in child welfare: Is there a difference? *Journal of Baccalaureate Social Work, 2*(1), 109–124.

American Association of State Social Work Boards. (1996). *Social work job analysis in support of the American Association of State Social Work Boards Examination Program: Final report.* Culpeper, VA: Author.

Arkava, M. L., & Brennen, E. C. (Eds.). (1976). *Competency-based education for social work: Evaluation and curriculum issues.* New York: Council on Social Work Education.

Baer, B. L., & Federico, R. (1978). *Educating the baccalaureate social worker.* Cambridge, MA: Ballinger.

Baer, B. L., & McLean, A. (1996). *Report on the interdisciplinary child welfare training project.* Green Bay, WI: University of Wisconsin Social Work Program.

Barker, R. L., & Briggs, T. L. (1968). *Differential use of social work manpower: An analysis and demonstration study.* New York: National Association of Social Workers.

Berger, R. (1992). Student retention: A critical phase in the academic careers of minority baccalaureate social workers. *Journal of Social Work Education, 28,* 85–97.

Council on Social Work Education. (1994a). Curriculum policy statement for baccalaureate degree programs in social work education. In *Handbook of accreditation standards and procedures* (pp. 96–104). Alexandria, VA: Author.

Council on Social Work Education. (1994b). Curriculum policy statement for master's degree programs in social work education. In *Handbook of accreditation standards and procedures* (pp. 134–144). Alexandria, VA: Author.

Gibbs, P., Locke, B. L., & Lohmann, R. (1990). A paradigm for the generalist-advanced generalist curriculum. *Journal of Social Work Education, 26,* 232–244.

Hoffman, K. S., & Kolevzon, M. (1992). Should we support the continuum in social work education? *Journal of Social Work Education, 28,* 6–17.

Hull, G., Mather, J., Christopherson, P., & Young, C. (1994). Quality assurance in social work education: A comparison of outcome assessments across the continuum. *Journal of Social Work Education, 30,* 388–397.

Hull, G. H., Ray, J., Rogers, J., & Smith, M. (1991). BPD outcome study: Report of phase I. In B. W. Shank (Ed.), *BPD forum* (pp. 54–63). St. Paul, MN: Association of Baccalaureate Social Work Program Directors and University of St. Thomas.

Leighninger, L. (1987). *Social work: Search for identity.* Westport, CT: Greenwood Press.

Lennon, T. (1995). *Statistics on social work education in the United States: 1995.* Alexandria, VA: Council on Social Work Education.

McPheeters, H. L., & Ryan, R. M. (1971). *A core of competence for baccalaureate social welfare.* Atlanta: Southern Regional Education Board.

Mission Statement. (1996). *Journal of Baccalaureate Social Work, 2*(1), 6.

Morales, A. T., & Sheafor, B. W. (1995). *Social work: a profession of many faces* (7th ed.). Needham Heights, MA: Allyn & Bacon.

National Association of Social Workers. (1981). *NASW standards for the classification of social work practice.* Washington, DC: Author.

Rogers, J. (1996, November). The BPD outcomes group. *BPD Update,* 12.

Rogers, J., Smith, M. L., Hull, G. H., & Ray, J. (1995). How do BSWs and MSWs differ? *Journal of Baccalaureate Social Work, 1*(1), 97–110.

Schatz, M. S., Jenkins, L. E., & Sheafor, B. W. (1990). Milford redefined: A model of generalist and advanced generalist social work. *Journal of Social Work Education, 26,* 217–231.

Schriver, J. M. (1995). As we begin: Collaboration, listening and diverse research methods. *Journal of Baccalaureate Social Work, 1*(1), 9–13.

Sheafor, B. W., & Shank, B. W., 1986. *Undergraduate social work education: Survivor in a changing profession.* Austin, TX: University of Texas at Austin School of Social Work.

Stuart, P. H., Leighninger, L., & Donahoe, J. N. (1993). *Reviewing our past: A history of the Association of Baccalaureate Social Work Program Directors.* Eau Claire, WI: Association of Baccalaureate Social Work Program Directors.

Teare, R. J., & Sheafor, B. W. (1991). Separating reality from fantasy: A depiction of BSW practice. In B. W. Shank (Ed.), *BSW education for practice: Reality and fantasy* (pp. 1–18). St. Paul, MN: Association of Baccalaureate Social Work Program Directors and University of St. Thomas.

Teare, R. J., & Sheafor, B. W. (1995). *Practice-sensitive social work education: An empirical analysis of social work practice and practitioners.* Alexandria, VA: Council on Social Work Education.

Teare, R. J., Sheafor, B. W., & Shank, B. W. (1995). Baccalaureate-level workers: Who they are and what they do. In *Practice-sensitive social work education: An empirical analysis of social work practice and practitioners* (pp. 33–57). Alexandria, VA: Council on Social Work Education.

FURTHER READING

Bisno, H. (1956). How social will social work be? *Social Work, 1,* 12–18.

Bisno, H. (1958). *The place of the undergraduate curriculum in social work education.* New York. Council on Social Work Education.

Bracy, W., & Cunningham, M. (1995). Factors contributing to the retention of minority students: Implications for incorporating diversity. *Journal of Baccalaureate Social Work, 1*(1), 85–96.

Carillo, D., & Thyer, B. (1994). Advanced standing and two-year program MSW students: An empirical investigation of foundation interviewing skills. *Journal of Social Work Education, 30,* 377–387.

Dhooper, S. S., Royse, D. D., & Wolfe, L. C. (1990). Does social work education make a difference? *Social Work, 35,* 57–61.

Flexner, A. (1915/1961). Is social work a profession? In R. E. Pumphrey & M. W. Pumphrey (Eds.), *The heritage of American social work* (pp. 301–307). New York: Columbia University Press.

Gross, G. (1992). A defining moment: The social work continuum revisited. *Journal of Social Work Education, 28,* 110–118.

Gibbs, P. (1995). Accreditation of BSW programs. *Journal of Social Work Education, 31,* 4–16.

Hollis, E. V., & Taylor, A. L. (1951). *Social work education in the United States.* New York: Columbia University Press.

Knight, C. (1993). A comparison of advanced standing and regular master's students' performance in the second-year field practicum: Field instructors' assessments. *Journal of Social Work Education, 29,* 309–317.

Lowe, G. R. (1985). The graduate only debate in social work education, 1931–1959, and its consequences for the profession. *Journal of Social Work Education, 21,* 52–62.

Macy, H. J., Sommer, V. L., Flax, N., & Swaine, R. L. (1995). *Directing the baccalaureate social work program: An ecological perspective.* Jefferson City, MO: Association of Baccalaureate Social Work Program Directors.

Schindler, R.. & Brawley, E. A. (1993). Community college programs for the human services: A continuing challenge for social work education and practice. *Journal of Social Work Education, 29,* 253–262.

Westphal, C. A. (1996). Right to resources or competency in the age of privatization. *Journal of Baccalaureate Social Work, 2*(1), 125–132.

For further information see

Direct Practice Overview; Generalist and Advanced Generalist Practice; Licensing, Regulation, and Certification; National Association of Social Workers; Social Work Education Overview; Social Work Practice: Theoretical Base; Social Work Profession Overview.

Lorrie Greenhouse Gardella, JD, ACSW, is associate professor and chair, Department of Social Work, Saint Joseph College, 1678 Asylum Avenue, West Hartford, CT 06117-2700.

Key Words	
baccalaureate social work	generalist
	professional
educational continuum	foundation

Behavioral Theory

Eileen Gambrill

Behavioral theories are described with an emphasis on social learning theory and radical behaviorism. Common features include an interest in pursuing a science of behavior and an emphasis on the reciprocal interaction between environments and organisms. Distinguishing features of different kinds of behaviorism are also described, including assumptions about the role of thoughts, degree of attention given to classical conditioning, and preferred methodologies. Common misunderstandings about radical behaviorism are described. Evolutionary influences are highlighted, including variability of behavior as a key building block.

In behavioral theory, actions, thoughts, and feelings are considered to be largely a function of our learning history. (The term "behavioral" is also used to describe rational emotive theory, cognitive-behavioral theory, and certain decision theories.) Behavioral theory has been used to achieve a wide range of outcomes of interest to social workers and their clients at many different levels, including individuals, families, groups, organizations, and communities (see, for example, Fawcett, Seekins, Whang, Muiu, & Suarez de Balcazar, 1984; Fawcett et al., 1994; Giles, 1993; Seekins & Fawcett, 1987; Thomas & Ager, 1993). It is assumed that evolutionary as well as current environments influence what we do, think, and feel. Biochemical and genetic influences are assumed to play a role; however, their interaction with learning variables is emphasized. All behavior is considered to be influenced by the interaction between the kinds of learning experiences we have and our genetic endowment. In addition, there are unique "biological boundaries" on learning in different species and unique physiological influences on individuals (Domjan, 1983). There is an emphasis on the role of learning in developing and maintaining behavior and a rejection of special causative factors related to "problematic" behavior (that is, a "disease model" of mental illness). All behavior is considered to be influenced by the same principles of behavior. Varied social and genetic histories result in a wide range of behavior. Behavior that may seem bizarre typically serves adaptive functions; however, only when contingencies of reinforcement are clarified may these functions become apparent (see, for example, Carr et al., 1994; Goldiamond, 1984; Layng & Andronis, 1984). Behavior always "makes sense" in this manner.

Behavioral principles describe relationships that have been found between behavior and environmental events. "Respondent behaviors" include those that involve the autonomic nervous system, such as heart rate and blood pressure, whereas "operants" (behavior that "operates" on or affects the environment) involve the skeletal muscles. The term "operant" refers to a class of behaviors, all of which have the same effect on the environment. The concept of the operant highlights both the fact that different forms of behavior can have the same function and the futility of punishing only one behavior in an operant. In the past a wide separation was made between operant and respondent behavior in terms of their controlling variables. Respondent behavior was thought to be influenced mainly by what happened before the behavior and operant behavior by what happened after the behavior. We now know that the separation between these two types of

reactions, in terms of whether they can be influenced by their consequences, has been exaggerated. Recent discussions of Pavlovian (respondent) conditioning have emphasized the overlap between cognitive and conditioning principles. The associations formed are influenced by the "net" of associations related to a particular stimulus, including inhibitory as well as excitatory associations (Rescorla, 1988).

TERMS AND PRINCIPLES OF BEHAVIORAL THEORY

Key principles and procedures of behavioral theory include reinforcement, punishment, establishing operations, extinction, differential reinforcement, shaping, conditioned reinforcement, and discrimination training (see, for example, Malott, Whaley, & Malott, 1993; Michaels, 1993). "Contingencies" refer to relationships between behavior and the events that follow behavior (consequences) and precede it (antecedents). Contingencies of reinforcement (for example, positive and negative reinforcement, punishment, and extinction) are defined not only by a certain procedure but also by the effect they have on behavior. Some contingencies, such as punishment and response cost, decrease behavior, whereas others, such as positive reinforcement and negative reinforcement, increase its probability on future occasions. Nonreward (extinction) creates emotional effects similar to those of punishment. Gray (1987) viewed these as so similar that he defines anxiety in terms of both frustration (nonreward) and punishment. Both increase arousal and attention and behavioral inhibition.

The "schedule of reinforcement" refers to the particular pattern that describes the relationship between a behavior and its consequences. Different schedules produce different patterns of behavior. What constitutes reinforcement or punishment varies depending on an individual's learning history and biological characteristics, as well as the particular setting, including competing contingencies. Because of different learning histories, current situations, and biological characteristics, an event that functions as a reinforcer for one person may not do so for another; each person has a unique reinforcer profile (that is, the list of events that function as reinforcers). Thus, reinforcers are known not by their physical characteristics but by their functional effects. Antecedent events acquire influence over behavior through their association with reinforcement or its absence.

Different response systems may or may not be related, depending on the unique learning history of each person. Response systems include overt behavior (for example, avoidance of crowds and verbal reports of anxiety), cognitions (thoughts about crowds), and physiological reactions (increased heart rate). Anxiety is viewed as a conditioned response acquired through unique learning histories. Changes in anxiety reactions are made by arranging new conditioning experiences (Barlow, 1988; Levis, 1990b). Wolpe (1958, 1995) emphasized reciprocal inhibition as the basis for changes in anxiety.

Motivational variables are related to the different reinforcing effectiveness of environmental events. Motivation can be viewed as a relationship between a set of operations (for example, deprivation of a reinforcer such as social approval) and the effects of these operations on behavior (that is, increased persistence in overcoming obstructions and increased resistance to extinction) (Millenson & Leslie, 1979). Establishing operations (for example, deprivation of water) influence motivational conditions (that is, the conditions of the body or the environment) that in turn influence motivational level (sensitivity to reinforcement). Matching theory is concerned with choice behavior and has a number of implications for understanding and altering behavior (McDowell, 1988).

Verbal behavior also has an influence over our actions because of its association on past occasions with certain consequences. It may have all the functions other kinds of behavior may have (for example, it may cue overt behavior, elicit emotional reactions, and function as a reinforcer). Our feelings and behavior are affected by what we say to ourselves (Bandura, 1986). Instructional control (by either others or ourselves) is created through individual learning histories. Lately a great deal of attention has been devoted to language, including rule-governed behavior in which behavior is influenced by descriptions of contingencies (for example, in a book or lecture) and equivalence relations (see, for example, Hayes, 1989; Hayes, Hayes, Sato, & Ono, 1994; Sidman, 1994). Rule-based learning differs from contingency-shaped behavior involving direct experience (Skinner, 1969). Rule-governed behavior is more vari-

able. Rules are often incomplete (that is, the required behaviors, the consequence, or related antecedents may not be described). They may not reflect real-life contingencies and so may result in punishing consequences (Poppen, 1989).

Behavioral theories differ in what causes they focus on, the closeness of the tie between theory and its testing, and the methodologies preferred (intensive study of individuals or the study of group differences). They also differ in the extent to which they focus on the influence of respondent or operant conditioning, in the breadth of environmental factors considered, and in whether an initiating causal status is attributed to thoughts. Although some scholars argue that integration of diverse behavioral perspectives is possible, others argue that it is not, because of different assumptions about the causes of behavior. Behaviorism and cognitivism have different goals. "The object of behaviorism is to establish the relation between behavior and the context of its occurrence. The object of cognitivism is to establish the design of the internal machinery through whose functioning organisms are capable of behaving in context" (Schnaitter, 1987, p. 1).

RADICAL BEHAVIORISM
There are different kinds of behaviorism, and these are often confused. Radical behaviorism is the philosophy related to applied behavior analysis, as well as a theoretical account of behavior (see, for example, Catania & Harnad, 1988; Skinner, 1969, 1971, 1974). It "is the attempt to account for behavior solely in terms of natural contingencies—either contingencies of survival, contingencies of reinforcement, or contingencies of social evolution" (Day, 1983, p. 101). Applied behavior analysis involves the application of findings from the experimental analysis of behavior to concerns of social importance (Baer, Wolf, & Risley, 1968, 1987). Although terms such as "ecobehavioral" (Lutzker & Campbell, 1994) and "contextualism" (Hayes, Hayes, Reese, & Sarbin, 1993; Morris, 1988) may be more "user-friendly" in relation to communicating with the public, they are misleading if meant to connote that radical behaviorism and applied behavior analysis do not involve a contextual approach (see, for example, Kunkel, 1970; Skinner, 1953).

It is assumed that most behaviors are selected by their consequences (that is, learned through interaction with the environment). Behavior is considered to be "the joint product of (i) the contingencies of survival responsible for the natural selection of the species and (ii) the contingencies of reinforcement responsible for the repertoires acquired by its members, including (iii) the special contingencies maintained by an evolved social environment" (Skinner, 1981, p. 502). Pursuit of a "science of behavior" is a basic goal. It is not claimed that a radical behavioral perspective is the only scientific psychology, but it is contended that a scientific approach is more likely than other approaches to yield knowledge about behavior and how it can be altered.

It is not assumed, however, that contingencies *cause* any behavior. To assign causal power to contingencies is what is meant by radical environmentalism. Radical behaviorism does not advocate this. Behavior is not endlessly malleable. Research in the experimental analysis of behavior shows that contingencies of reinforcement influence behavior, which is not to say that they are the only influence on behavior or to imply that all behavior is learned. Genetic and biological factors also influence behavior.

Differences in cultural norms and values reflect different reinforcement histories. Culture is viewed "as the contingencies of social reinforcement maintained by a group" (Skinner, 1987, p. 74). "It is the effect on the group, not the reinforcing consequences for individual members, that is responsible for the evolution of culture" (p. 54) (see also Glenn, 1991). Cultural practices affect our behavior, and we in turn affect cultural practices. A cultural practice may survive or disappear, depending on its consequences. Different cultures create different learning histories as a result of different social reinforcement patterns. Events have different meanings (that is, influences on thoughts, feelings, and behavior) for different people because of unique histories in particular groups. Contingencies at one level (for example, individual, family, group, community) influence those at other levels. Because natural contingencies related to behavior of interest (for example, wearing seat belts) are often remote, aversive, or inconsequential, we often must arrange contingencies at different system levels to support valued behaviors (Malott, 1994). We can examine problem-related contingencies at different levels (individual, family, group, organization, legislation, policy), including their interrelationships (see also Biglan, 1995; Kunkel, 1970; Mattaini, 1991). This analysis can help us understand who benefits and who loses from a certain policy or program.

Racial behaviorism is perhaps more misunderstood and misrepresented, and it attracts more objections, than any other perspective in psychology (see, for example, Catania, 1991; Todd, 1992). One objection is that it ignores the meaning of events. In fact, attention is devoted to discovering the unique individual meanings of events (their functions) through a detailed exploration of the relationships between behavior and related cues and consequences (see, for example, Carr et al., 1994; Goldiamond, 1984; Mattaini & Thyer, 1996). Radical behaviorism does not embrace associationism, operationism, positivism, or environmental determinism (Day, 1980). According to Skinner (1974), "It does not deny the possibility of self-observation or self-knowledge or its possible usefulness, but it questions the nature of what is felt or observed and hence known" (p. 16). Skinner's radical behaviorism explicitly rejected the methodological behaviorist's form of operationism and instead embraced a nonmediational, environmentally based account focused on the direct relationship between environmental events and behavior. "[Radical behaviorism] does not insist upon truth by agreement and can therefore consider events taking place in the private world within the skin. It does not call these events unobservable and it does not dismiss them as subjective" (Skinner, 1974, p. 16).

Methodological behaviorism also viewed publicly observable behavior as the only appropriate data of psychology, but this data was to be used to infer inner processes and underlying structures that were given special explanatory status. Although S-R (stimulus-response) links were considered to be important, these links had to be mediated by processes within the organism to account for variability in behavior. . . . Skinner explicitly included private events in his behavioristic account; however, private events were distinguished by their inaccessibility to an observer or interpreter of behavior, not by any special causal role (e.g., Skinner, 1984). (Lonigan, 1990, p. 1180; see also Day, 1983; Zuriff, 1985)

A radical behavioral perspective differs from Watsonian associationism. It is historic, (that is, historical influences are given a major role), selective, and consequential (Skinner, 1981). "Watsonian behaviorism insisted that the only acceptable area of inquiry in psychology was the study of behavior (as in the publicly observable responses of an organism). In this version of behaviorism, thoughts, feelings, and other internal states either did not exist or were considered epiphenomenal" (Lonigan, 1990, p. 1180). Watsonian associationism is explicitly rejected in a radical behavioral approach (Schnaitter, 1984).

In radical behaviorism, not only are private events such as thoughts and feelings not dismissed, but they are considered to lie in the behavioral domain. They are viewed as behaviors that themselves require an explanation (traced to their environmental, evolutionary, or physiological origins) (see Hayes & Brownstein, 1987, for further discussion). The difference between private and public behaviors is in their observability. Thoughts and feelings are assumed to have the same functions as public stimuli and responses. They can serve as eliciting events for emotional reactions, as discriminative stimuli for operant behavior, or as responses in their own right. The advantage of viewing thoughts and feelings as behaviors is that they cannot as readily be inaccurately presumed to be the initiating causes of behavior, thereby obscuring environmental causes. They themselves are behaviors in need of explanation. "The objection to [focusing on] the inner workings of the mind is not that they are not open to inspection but that they have stood in the way of the inspection of more important things [contingencies of reinforcement that would offer a much more effective analysis]" (Skinner, 1974, p. 165).

In a radical behavioral perspective, the causes of behavior are sought in the relationships between behavior and environmental changes, not in the feelings and thoughts that are considered to be collateral effects or by-products of these contingencies. "Whatever the ultimate consequences, the origination of behavior is still to be sought in natural selection, operant conditioning, and the evolution of cultural practices" (Skinner, 1984). "Troublesome behavior is due to troublesome contingencies of reinforcement, not to troublesome feelings or states of mind, and to correct the trouble we should correct the contingencies"

(Skinner, 1988, p. 172). Thus, private events can be called causes, but they are not initiating causes. Expectations and feelings are viewed as "surrogates" of histories of reinforcement. Those things that are introspectively observed are viewed as collateral products of genetic and environmental histories. Private events such as thoughts and feelings are believed to operate as elements in chains that begin with observable environmental events and end with observable responses. Both thoughts and feelings may play a mediating role in chains of behavior. Baer (1982) offered the example of using an algorithm for determining the square root of a real number. Once we memorize the algorithm, we can apply it to relevant problems. The algorithm mediates correct answers. (Here, the word "mediate" implies an intermediate relation.) So one could say (given that this algorithm is essential to solving square root problems) that this response (the algorithm) is causal to solving square root problems. Feelings are considered to be collateral effects or by-products of reinforcement contingencies (relationships between behavior and the environment) (Skinner, 1971)—that is, instead of a feeling causing a certain behavior, the feeling itself is considered to be a product of what we have experienced. For example, punishment for a behavior generates certain feelings. We may feel guilt, shame, or anger. "We do not cry *because* we are sad or feel sad *because* we cry, we cry *and* feel sad because something has happened" (Skinner, 1988, p. 172).

Behavior analysis involves the systematic investigation of variables that influence behavior. There is a focus on the relationship between behavior and the current antecedent and consequent environmental events that influence behavior. Attention is directed toward the change of "deviant" environments. Behavior—what people do—and the translation of problems into behaviors that if changed would resolve them is the central subject matter. "Analytic" requires "a believable demonstration of the events that can be responsible for the occurrence or nonoccurrence of that behavior" (Baer et al., 1968, p. 94). One of the hallmarks of applied behavior analysis is the translation of personal and social problems "into observable behaviors that, if changed, would constitute a solution to the problems" (Baer, 1982, p. 281).

The aim is to translate problems "into a set of behaviors which, once changed, satisfies the complaint" (p. 287). The challenge is "(1) to restate the complained of problem in behavioral terms; (2) to change the behaviors indicated by that restatement; and then, (3) to see whether changing them has decreased the complaining response" (p. 284). The analysis of behavior has been achieved when it can be influenced in predicted ways. This description illustrates the close tie between theory and testing in this approach to understanding behavior. Social validity (that is, acceptability of procedures, goals, and outcomes to clients and others affected) is a key concern (Schwartz & Baer, 1991).

SOCIAL LEARNING THEORY

Social learning theory (SLT) provides "an integrating framework for a broad swath of empirical data" (Rosenthal, 1982, p. 340; see, for example, Bandura, 1986). As in radical behaviorism, a reciprocal interaction is assumed between people and their environments (that is, people both influence and are influenced by their environment). Both applied behavior analysis and cognitive-behavioral approaches emphasize evaluation of results, relying on observable outcomes. Thoughts are given a causal initiating and explanatory role in social learning theory, in contrast to radical behaviorism, in which private events such as thoughts and feelings are viewed as covert behaviors that may be part of chains of behavior but do not have a causal initiating role. This key role is also emphasized in definitions of cognitive-behavioral therapy: "Specifically, cognitive-behavioral therapy is defined as those sets of therapeutic procedures that (1) embody theoretical conceptualizations of change that place primary importance on cognitive process, and that (2) procedurally target at least some therapeutic maneuvers specially at altering aspects of cognition" (Ingram & Scott, 1990, p. 55). It is assumed that thoughts and feelings influence behavior as eliciting, discriminative, and reinforcing events in both perspectives. They may function as eliciting events for emotional reactions, as discriminative cues for operant behaviors, as responses in their own right, and as negative or positive consequences.

Within SLT, thoughts are assumed to play an important role in the complex processes that affect attention. It is assumed that we present an important part of our environment through our expectations, goals, and standards (Bandura, 1986). Cognition is assumed to play a role in verbal and classical conditioning, social influence, incentive effects, and self-referent mediation. Thus, SLT includes appeals to cognitive explanations, in contrast to applied behavior analysis and behavioral approaches, which appeal to changes in conditioning as explanatory (Wolpe, 1990). Many procedures developed early in the history of the use of behavioral methods, such as systematic desensitization, depend heavily on changing unobservable events such as thoughts and images. However, conceptually, the explanatory focus is on conditioning and changes in conditioning (Wolpe, 1958, 1989). In SLT thoughts are considered to play a critical role in the degree to which different kinds of interventions are effective in altering "self-efficacy," which in turn is assumed to influence behavior (Bandura, 1986). "Performance efficacy" refers to expectations that a behavior can be carried out; "outcome efficacy" refers to expectations that the behavior will be effective if it is carried out. It is assumed that the extent to which different kinds of interventions alter self-efficacy determines their effectiveness. Observational learning—the acquisition of new behavior via an observer's exposure to modeled behavior—is given a key role in SLT. Bandura (1986) argued that cognitive mediation is required for delayed performance of observed behavior. Radical behaviorists do not think that recourse to symbolic causes is required to account for the experimental data in this area (see, for example, Deguchi, 1984). Instead of attributing similar behaviors on the part of many people in a situation to "imitation effects," it is suggested that all individuals involved may have experienced similar contingencies in that situation (whether this be leaving a church, entering a restaurant, sitting in a movie, or starting a conversation at a party).

The work of Gerald Patterson and his colleagues with antisocial children and their families illustrates the close connection among theory, measurement, and intervention in developmental social learning perspectives. This work suggests a developmental sequence in which children and parents actively participate in creating their family environments (Biglan, Lewin, & Hops, 1990; Patterson & Forgatch, 1990; Patterson, Reid, & Dishion, 1992). Inconsistent, harsh, and ineffective parenting practices result in increasingly deviant child behavior and association with other deviant peers (Dishion, Patterson, & Griesler, 1994). "The coercion process begins with something that is intrinsically normal, a rather high level of child noncompliance and continued employment of aversive behaviors that are maintained because they work (escape conditioning). The parents fail both to teach the prosocial behaviors that would replace the coercive ones and to use effective discipline strategies for the deviant behaviors that do occur. The process moves out of control when the frequencies of these coercive behaviors reach very high levels" (Chamberlain & Patterson, 1995, p. 213). Family members in turn are influenced by their environment, including the quality of social contacts of mothers outside of the home (Wahler, 1980). Discovering the contingencies related to behaviors of interest may require a fine-grained analysis. "Child behavior is functional (affects others) at the micro-social level [the child's unique environment] and theory building [guesses about what may be maintaining problem-related behaviors] at a minimum, needs to focus on understanding processes that are actually formative to the [unique] response styles children display in various settings" (Dishion, Patterson, & Kavanagh, 1992).

Radical behaviorists argue that cognitive-behavioral methods can be conceptualized within the framework of applied behavior analysis—that is, without reliance on unobservable events such as thoughts (Deguchi, 1984; Ledwidge, 1978). They contend that cognitive-behavioral methods involve the rearrangement of environmental cues and consequences and that it is these changes, rather than the alteration of cognitive events, that are responsible for change. Wolpe (1995) argued that cognitivists overlook the reciprocally inhibiting effects of positive helper-client relationships in accounting for decreases in anxiety reactions. Applied behavior analysts argue that key explanatory concepts in SLT, such as self-efficacy, are not explanatory, do not account for research data, and are superfluous constructs (Biglan, 1987; Lee, 1989). They argue that judgments of self-efficacy are covert behaviors that themselves require an explanation. Efficacy expectations are viewed as the product of environmental contingencies. Behaviorists note that environmental contingencies associated with feelings, expectations, moods, or "states of mind" often remain

unknown in cognitive accounts of behavior. They suggest that to understand thoughts and feelings, we have to explore past and present environmental histories. Skinner (1969) suggested that expectancy "is a gratuitous and dangerous assumption if nothing more than a history of reinforcement has been observed" (p. 147). To enhance efficacy in a given situation, positive contingencies allowing successful experiences should be arranged. The key question from a scientific perspective is whether assumptions are testable. If, for example, it is assumed that behavior can be changed via verbal instructions, then this can be tested with an appropriate research design focusing on changes in behavior.

NEOBEHAVIORISM AND PARADIGMATIC BEHAVIORISM

The term "neobehaviorism" is used by some investigators who focus on the treatment of stress and anxiety disorders. For example, Levis (1990a) used this term to refer to the accumulation of evidence about behavior and how it can be altered. There is an emphasis on respondent conditioning (rearrangement of antecedents) when compared with applied behavior analysis, in which operant conditioning and its effects are emphasized (Eysenck, 1982; Wolpe, 1993). It is argued that cognitive approaches disregard accumulated findings in psychology, appealing instead to ill-defined entities. As with other kinds of behaviorism, there is an interest in discovering the lawful processes involved in developing, maintaining, and altering behavior. Some writers (for example, Eysenck, 1982) emphasize the role of genetic factors in influencing personality characteristics, such as introversion and extroversion (in relation to understanding the ease of conditioning).

Paradigmatic behaviorism (PB) attempts to unify psychology, including all current theories of learning and conditioning (Staats, 1990). Vicarious learning processes are of particular interest, emphasizing how language is learned and how it functions in providing the basis for additional learning. The basic behavioral repertoire is central to PB's theory of personality (Staats & Staats, 1968). These include sensory-motor, language-cognition, and emotional-motivational. Staats's interest is in creating a "bridging theory framework under which to provide new directions in the fields of personality measurement and behavioral assessment" (1990, p. 49). He viewed SLT as falling somewhere between operant behaviorism and PB. Staats viewed learning as basic to personality and personality as basic to abnormal behavior and argued that "PB constitutes a comprehensive united theory as well as a philosophy-methodology for constructing such theories" (p. 52). Critics of PB argue that proponents overlook the attention given to symbolic events in behavioral therapy and related theory (Wolpe, 1993), misrepresent radical behaviorism, and attempt to integrate incompatible approaches (for example, psychiatric classification and behavioral assessment) (see Staats, 1993).

EVOLUTIONARY INFLUENCES

Behavioral theory emphasizes our history both as individuals and as a species. Both histories influence what environments we create and their risks and opportunities. Anatomical, physiological, and psychological characteristics related to our evolutionary history influence biological selection (some living beings are more likely to survive), behavioral selection (we act on the environment and are affected by the consequences), environmental selection (through our behaviors we create our own unique environments), and cultural selection (patterns of behavior in a network of individuals). Lewontin (1994) contended that based on what little we know about genes, organisms, and environments, a more accurate metaphor than adaptation is that of construction. "If we want to understand evolution, we must understand it as construction because the actual situation is that . . . there are powerful causal pathways that go from organism to what we call 'environment'" (p. 36). "What is the 'environment' to one differs dramatically from what it is for others. There is an external world but there is no single environment out there" (p. 38). "The evolution of organisms is a co-evolution of organisms and environment. Just as there is no change in the world that does not change organisms, so there is no change in organisms that does not change the world" (p. 44). Variability of behavior is a key building block of evolutionary theory. We evolve in certain ways depending on our experiences. In this sense, we are "embodied theories" about what works and has worked in the past (what has solved problems we confront) (Munz, 1985). Variations followed by positive consequences or the removal of

negative consequences are likely to recur. Those that are followed by the removal of positive consequences or the presentation of negative ones are less likely to recur. There is a complex interaction among biological, behavioral, and cultural selection. Behavior changes over time for an individual, family, and culture in accord with changes in contingencies.

An evolutionary perspective adds a historical dimension to understanding aggression and caregiving in society, as well as what Gilbert (1989) referred to as "defeat states" such as depression and the experiences that may be responsible (see also Gilbert, 1993; Trower, Gilbert, & Sherling, 1990). Defeat states are assumed to be involved in depression, whereas submissive behavior is assumed to reflect anxiety (Gilbert, 1992). Threats to survival and ecological imbalances are just as important now as they were millions of years ago, and phylogenetic carryovers influence our behavior, especially our emotions in certain situations (for example, when we are threatened). An evolutionary view highlights the communication and survival functions of emotions. For example, emotions mobilize us to deal quickly with environmental threats (for example, from predators). Gilbert (1989) suggested that social defense systems evolved to facilitate interaction within species (for example, to regulate control over territory and allow breeding) and to protect against predators (for example, parents act to reduce physical dangers to their offspring). Contingencies critical to our survival in early times may now hamper rather than help us. For instance, we seem to have difficulty decreasing our use of punishment, with all the negative consequences of relying on coercion (Sidman, 1989). Threats occur both from outside organized groups (for example, predators, strangers) and within them (from dominant individuals). "The defense system is essentially concerned with the avoidance of all forms of threat, injury and attack. It is a self-protective system with attentional, evaluative, affective and behavioral components designed to protect the animal" (Gilbert, 1989, pp. 42-43). The nonsocial defense system evolved to defend against predators. This includes "(1) hypersensitivity to sensory data; (2) rapid increases in arousal—startle, alertness; and (3) rapid, non-predictable discharges of arousal and movement, as in rapid flight, zigzagging, freezing, bouncing, automatic aggression, and catelepsy" (p. 43). Once initiated, it tends to be controlled internally. Ohman (1993) wrote: "Responses of fear and anxiety originate in an alarm system shaped by evolution to protect creatures from impending danger. This system is biased to discover threat, and it results in a sympathetically dominated response as a support of potential flight or fight. This response system can be triggered from three different levels of information processing, the first two of which are inaccessible to intro-spection" (p. 529). MacLean (1993) noted that the two older formations of our brain "lack the capacity for verbal communication with the parts of the human brain accounting for speech" (p. 67) (see also Berkowitz, 1994). This has important implications for the potential of higher-level cognitive influences on our emotions. There also are social and nonsocial safety systems. Cooperative behavior can be viewed as evolutionary adaptation designed to permit caregiving to infants who cannot defend themselves. Defense and safety systems interact. For example, anxiety may result because of an increase in fear or a loss of safety.

An evolutionary perspective gives us a view of human nature that builds on cross-cultural work. It can help us answer the question, "What is human nature?" An appre-ciation of the evolutionary roots of human behavior allows us to realistically view the potential for change. For example, the evolu-tionary functions of status hierarchies (rank-ing) suggest how difficult it will be to alter the reinforcing value of status and dominance (Gilbert, 1989).

CONCLUSION

Behavioral theory emphasizes the role of learning. It "is largely about the interactive control of behavior by environment and control of environment by behavior" (Baer, 1996, p. 83). It has provided guidelines for achieving a wide range of valued outcomes within a scientific approach to knowledge in which claims are critically tested.

REFERENCES

Baer, D. M. (1982). Applied behavior analysis. In G. T. Wilson & C. M. Franks (Eds.), *Contemporary behavior therapy: Conceptual and empirical foundations* (pp. 277–309). New York: Guilford Press.

Baer, D. M. (1996). On the invulnerability of behavior-analytic theory to biological research. *Behavior Analyst, 19*, 83–84.

Baer, D. M., Wolf, M. M., & Risley, T. R. (1968). Some current dimensions of applied behavior analysis. *Journal of Applied Behavior Analysis, 1*, 91–97.

Baer, D. M., Wolf, M. M., & Risley, J. R. (1987). Some still current dimensions of applied behavior analysis. *Journal of Applied Behavior Analysis, 20*, 313–327.

Bandura, A. (1977). *Social learning theory.* Englewood Cliffs, NJ: Prentice Hall.

Bandura, A. (1986). *Social foundations of thought and action.* Englewood Cliffs, NJ: Prentice Hall.

Barlow, D. H. (1988). *Anxiety and its disorders: The nature and treatment of anxiety and panic.* New York: Guilford Press.

Berkowitz, L. (1994). Is something missing? Some observations prompted by the cognitive-neoassociationist view of anger and emotional aggression. In L. R. Huesmann (Ed.), *Aggressive behavior: Current perspectives* (pp. 35–57). New York: Plenum Press.

Biglan, A. (1987). A behavior-analytic critique of Bandura's self-efficacy theory. *Behavior Analyst, 10*, 1–15.

Biglan, A. (1995). *Changing cultural practices: A contextualist framework for intervention research.* Reno, NV: Context Press.

Biglan, A., Lewin, L., & Hops, H. (1990). A contextual approach to the problem of aversize practices in families. In G. R. Patterson (Ed.), *Depression and aggression in family interaction* (pp. 103–129). Hillsdale, NJ: Lawrence Erlbaum.

Carr, E. G., Levin, L., McConnachie, G., Carlson, J. I., Kemp, D. C., & Smith, C. E. (1994). *Communication-based intervention for problem behavior: A user's guide for producing positive change.* Baltimore: Paul H. Brookes.

Catania, A. C. (1991). The gift of culture and elo-quence: An open letter to Michael J. Mahoney in reply to his article "Scientific psychology and radical behaviorism." *Behavior Analyst, 14*, 61–72.

Catania, A. C., & Harnad, S. (Eds.). (1988). *The selection of behavior: The operant behaviorism of B. F. Skinner: Comments and consequences.* New York: Cambridge University Press.

Chamberlain, P., & Patterson, G. R. (1995). Discipline and child compliance in parenting. In M. H. Bornstein (Ed.), *Handbook of parenting: Applied and practical parenting* (Vol. 4, pp. 205–225). Hillsdale, NJ: Lawrence Erlbaum.

Day, W. (1983). On the difference between radical and methodological behaviorism. *Behaviorism, 11*, 89–102.

Day, W. F. (1980). The historical antecedents of contemporary behaviorism. In R. W. Rieber & K. Salzinger (Eds.), *Psychology: Theoretical-historical perspectives* (pp. 203–262). New York: Academic Press.

Deguchi, H. (1984). Observational learning from a radical-behaviorist viewpoint. *Behavior Analyst, 7,* 83–95.

Dishion, T. J., patterson, G. R., & Griesler, P. C. (1994). Peer adaptations in the development of antisocial behavior: A confluence model. In L. R. Huesmann (Ed.), *Aggressive behavior: Current perspectives* (pp. 61–95). New York: Plenum Press.

Dishion, T. J., Patterson, G. R., & Kavanagh, K. A. (1992). An experimental test of the coercion model: Linking theory, measurement, and intervention. In J. McCord & R. E. Tremblay (Eds.), Preventing antisocial behavior: *Interventions from birth through adolescence* (pp. 253–282). New York: Guilford Press.

Domjan, M. (1983). Biological constraints on instrumental and classical conditioning: Implications for general process theory. In G. H. Bower (Ed.), *The psychology of learning and motivation* (pp. 215–277). New York: Academic Press.

Eysenck, H. J. (1982). Neobehavioristic (S-R) theory. In G. T. Wilson & C. M. Franks (Eds.), *Contemporary behavior theory: Conceptual and empirical foundations* (pp. 205–276). New York: Guilford Press.

Fawcett, S. B., Seekins, T., Whang, P. L., Muiu, C., & Suarez de Balcazar, Y. (1984). Creating and using social technologies for community empowerment. In J. Rappaport, C. Swift, & R. Hess (Eds.), *Studies in empowerment: Steps toward understanding and action* (pp. 145–171). New York: Haworth Press.

Fawcett, S. B., White, G. W., Balcazar, F. E., Suarez de Balcazar, Y., Mathews, R. M., Paine-Andrews, A., Seekins, T., & Smith, J. (1994). A contextual-behavioral model of empowerment: Case studies involving people with physical disabilities. *American Journal of Community Psychology, 22,* 471–496.

Gilbert, P. (1989). *Human nature and suffering.* New York: Guilford Press.

Gilbert, P. (1992). *Depression: The evolution of powerlessness.* New York: Guilford Press.

Gilbert, P. (1993). Defense and safety: Their function in social behavior and psychopathology. *British Journal of Clinical Psychology, 32,* 131–153.

Giles, T. R. (1993). *Handbook of effective psychotherapy.* New York: Plenum Press.

Glenn, S. S. (1991). Contingencies and metacontingencies: Relations among behavioral, cultural, and biological evolution. In P. A. Lamal (Ed.), *Behavioral analysis of societies and cultural practices* (pp. 39–73). New York: Hemisphere Press.

Goldiamond, I. (1984). Training parent trainers and ethicists in nonlinear analysis of behavior. In R. F. Dangel & R. A. Polster (Eds.), *Parent training: Foundations of research and practice* (pp. 504–546). New York: Guilford Press.

Gray, J. A. (1987). *The psychology of fear and stress* (2nd ed.). Cambridge, England: Cambridge University Press.

Hayes, S. C. (Ed.). (1989). *Rule-governed behavior: Cognition, contingencies, and instructional control.* New York: Plenum Press.

Hayes, S. C., & Brownstein, A. J. (1987). Mentalism, private events, and scientific explanation: A defense of B. F. Skinner's view. In S. Modgil & C. Modgil (Eds.), *B. F. Skinner: Consensus and controversies* (pp. 207–218). New York: Falmer Press.

Hayes, S. C., Hayes, L. J., Reese, H. W., & Sarbin, T. R. (Eds.). (1993). *Varieties of scientific contextualism.* Reno, NV: Context Press.

Hayes, S. C., Hayes, L. J., Sato, M., & Ono, K. (Eds.). (1994). *Behavior analysis of language and cognition.* Reno, NV: Context Press.

Ingram, R. E., & Scott, W. D. (1990). Cognitive behavior therapy. In A. S. Bellack, M. Hersen, & A. E. Kazdin (Eds.), *International handbook of behavior modification and behavior therapy* (2nd ed., pp. 53–65). New York: Plenum Press.

Kunkel, J. (1970). *Society and economic growth: A behavioral perspective of social change.* New York: Oxford University Press.

Layng, T.V.J., & Andronis, P. T. (1984). Toward a functional analysis of delusional speech and hallucinatory behavior. *Behavior Analyst, 7,* 139–156.

Ledwidge, B. (1978). Cognition-behavior modification: A step in the wrong direction? *Psychological Bulletin, 85,* 353–375.

Lee, C. (1989). Theoretical weaknesses lead to practical problems: The example of self-efficacy theory. *Journal of Behavior Therapy and Experimental Psychiatry, 20,* 115–123.

Levis, D. J. (1990a, November 4). *Behaviorism and cognitivism in behavior therapy.* Paper presented at the 24th Annual Convention of the Association for Advancement of Behavior Therapy, San Francisco.

Levis, D. J. (1990b). The experimental and theoretical foundations of behavior modification. In A. S. Bellack, M. Hersen, & A. E. Kazdin (Eds.), *International handbook of behavior modification and therapy* (2nd ed., pp. 27–52). New York: Plenum Press.

Lewontin, R. C. (1994). *Inside and outside: Gene, environment, and organism.* Worcester, MA: Clark University Press.

Lonigan, C. J. (1990). Which behaviorism? A reply to Mahoney. *American Psychologist, 45,* 1179–1181.

Lutzker, J. R., & Campbell, R. V. (1994). *Ecobehavioral family interventions in developmental disabilities.* Pacific Grove, CA: Brooks/Cole.

MacLean, P. D. (1993). Cerebral evolution of emotion. In M. Lewis & J. M. Haviland (Eds.), *Handbook of emotions* (pp. 6–83). New York: Guilford Press.

Malott, R. W. (1994). *Rule-governed behavior, self-management, and performance management.* Kalamazoo, MI: Western Michigan University Department of Psychology.

Malott, R. W., Whaley, D. L., & Malott, M. E. (1993). *Elementary principles of behavior* (2nd ed.). Englewood Cliffs, NJ: Prentice Hall.

Mattaini, M. A. (1991). Choosing weapons for the war on "crack": An operant analysis. *Research on Social Work Practice, 1,* 188–213.

Mattaini, M. A., & Thyer, B. A. (1996). *Finding solutions to social problems: Behavioral strategies for change.* Washington, DC: American Psychological Association.

McDowell, J. J. (1988). Matching theory in natural human environments. *Behavior Analyst, 11,* 95–109.

Michaels, J. L. (1993). *Concepts and principles of behavior analysis.* Kalamazoo, MI: Society for Advancement of Behavior Analysis.

Millenson, J. R., & Leslie, J. L. (1979). *Principles of behavioral analysis* (2nd ed.). New York: Macmillan.

Morris, E. K. (1988). Contextualism: The world view of behavior analysis. *Journal of Experimental Child Psychology, 46,* 289–323.

Munz, P. C. (1985). *Our knowledge of the growth of knowledge: Popper or Wittgenstein.* London: Routledge & Kegan Paul.

Ohman, A. (1993). Fear and anxiety as emotional phenomena: Clinical phenomenology, evolutionary perspectives, and information-processing mechanisms. In M. Lewis & J. M. Haviland (Eds.), *Handbook of emotions* (pp. 511–534). New York: Guilford Press.

Patterson, G., Reid, J., & Dishion, T. (1992). *A social interactional approach. Volume 4: Antisocial boys.* Eugene, OR: Castalia.

Patterson, G. R., & Forgatch, M. S. (1990). Initiation and maintenance of process disrupting single-mother families. In G. R. Patterson (Ed.), *Depression and aggression in family interaction* (pp. 209–245). Hillsdale, NJ: Lawrence Erlbaum.

Poppen, R. L. (1989). Some clinical implications of rule-governed behavior. In S. C. Hayes (Ed.), *Rule governed behavior: Cognition, contingencies and instructional control* (pp. 325–357). New York: Plenum Press.

Rescorla, R. A. (1988). Pavlovian conditioning: It's not what you think it is. *American Psychologist, 43,* 151–160.

Rosenthal, T. L. (1982). Social learning theory. In G. T. Wilson & C. M. Franks (Eds.), *Contemporary behavior therapy: Conceptual and empirical foundations* (pp. 339–363). New York: Guilford Press.

Schnaitter, R. (1984). Behavior as a function of inner states and outer circumstances. In T. Thompson & M. D. Zeilor (Eds.), *Analysis and integration of behavioral units.* Hillsdale, NJ: Lawrence Erlbaum.

Schnaitter, R. (1987). Behaviorism is not cognitive and cognitivism is not behavioral. *Behaviorism, 15,* 1–11.

Schwartz, I. S., & Baer, D. M. (1991). Social validity assessment: Is current practice state of the art? *Journal of Applied Behavior Analysis, 24,* 189–204.

Seekins, T., & Fawcett, S. B. (1987). Effects of a poverty-client's agenda on resource allocations by community decision makers. *American Journal of Community Psychology, 15,* 305–320.

Sidman, M. (1989). *Coercion and its fallout.* Boston: Authors Cooperative.

Sidman, M. (1994). *Equivalence relations and behavior: A research story.* Boston: Authors Cooperative.

Skinner, B. F. (1953). *Science and human behavior.* New York: Macmillan.

Skinner, B. F. (1969). *Contingencies of reinforcement.* New York: Appleton-Century-Crofts.

Skinner, B. F. (1971). *Beyond freedom and dignity.* New York: Alfred A. Knopf.

Skinner, B. F. (1974). *About behaviorism.* New York: Alfred A. Knopf.

Skinner, B. F. (1981). Selection by consequences. *Science, 213,* 501–504.

Skinner, B. F. (1984). The operational analysis of psychological terms. *Behavioral and Brain Sciences, 7,* 547–581.

Skinner, B. F. (1987). *On further reflection.* Englewood Cliffs, NJ: Prentice Hall.

Skinner, B. F. (1988). The operant side of behavior therapy. *Journal of Behavior Therapy and Experimental Psychiatry, 19,* 171–179.

Staats, A. W. (1990). Paradigmatic behavior therapy: A unified framework for theory, research, and practice. In G. H. Eifert & I. M. Evans (Eds.), *Unifying behavior therapy: Contributions of paradigmatic behaviorism* (pp. 14–54). New York: Springer.

Staats, A. W. (1993). Personality theory, abnormal psychology, and psychological measurement: A psychological behaviorism. *Behavior Modification, 17,* 8–42.

Staats, A. W., & Staats, C. K. (1968). *Complex human behavior: A systematic extension of learning principles.* New York: Holt, Rinehart & Winston.

Thomas, E. J., & Ager, R. D. (1993). Unilateral family therapy with spouses of uncooperative alcohol abusers. In T. O'Farrell (Ed.), *Treating alcohol problems: Marital and family interventions.* New York: Guilford Press.

Todd, J. T. (1992). Case histories in the great power of steady misrepresentation. *American Psychologist, 47,* 1441–1453.

Trower, P., Gilbert, P., & Sherling, G. (1990). Social anxiety, evolution, and self-presentation. In H. Leitenberg (Ed.), *Handbook of social and evaluation anxiety* (pp. 11–45). New York: Plenum Press.

Wahler, R. G. (1980). The insular mother: Her problems in parent-child treatment. *Journal of Applied Behavior Analysis, 13,* 207–219.

Wolpe, J. (1958). *Psychotherapy by reciprocal inhibition.* Stanford, CA: Stanford University Press.

Wolpe, J. (1989). The derailment of behavior therapy: A tale of conceptual misdirection. *Journal of Behavior Therapy and Experimental Psychiatry, 20,* 3–15.

Wolpe, J. (1990). *The practice of behavior therapy.* Elmsford, NY: Pergamon Press.

Wolpe, J. (1993). Commentary: The cognitivist oversell and comments on symposium contributions. *Journal of Behavior Therapy and Experimental Psychiatry, 24,* 141–147.

Wolpe, J. (1995). Reciprocal inhibition: Major agent of behavior change. In W. O'Donohue & L. Krasner (Eds.), *Theories of behavior therapy: Exploring behavior change* (pp. 23–58). Washington, DC: American Psychological Association.

Zuriff, G. E. (1985). *Behaviorism: A conceptual reconstruction.* New York: Columbia University Press.

Eileen Gambrill, PhD, is professor of social welfare, School of Social Welfare, University of California at Berkeley, 120 Haviland Hall, Berkeley, CA 94720.

For further information see

Assessment; Brief Therapies; Clinical Social Work; Cognition and Social Cognitive Theory; Cognitive Treatment; Direct Practice Overview; Ecological Perspective; Families: Direct Practice; Family Therapy; Genetics; Goal Setting and Intervention Planning; Group Practice; Human Development; Person-in-Environment; Psychosocial Approach; Single-System Design; Social Development; Social Skills Training; Social Work Practice: Theoretical Base.

Key Words

applied behavior analysis	radical behaviorism
behavior theory	social learning theory

C

Chaos Theory and Complexity Theory

Keith Warren
Cynthia Franklin
Calvin Streeter

During the past 30 years, chaos theory and complexity theory have grown out of a variety of fields, including physics, biology, and social science, in which researchers grapple with the often-paradoxical nature of complex, nonlinear systems as those systems change through time (Gleick, 1987; Waldrop, 1992). Chaos theory addresses feedback systems that show complicated and unpredictable behavior despite their underlying simplicity (Briggs & Peat, 1989; Gleick, 1987; Peak & Frame, 1994). Complexity theory seeks an understanding of the ways in which large, complex systems emerge from local interactions as well as the ways in which they change over time (Bak, 1996; Holland, 1995; Kauffman, 1995; Resnick, 1994). These theories offer a lens through which to examine human social systems ranging from families (Ward, 1995) to bureaucracies (Wheatley, 1996) and even entire societies and international systems (Richards, 1996; Saperstein, 1996). Social work, with its traditional broad focus on multiple systemic levels, stands to learn much from these disciplines.

The purpose of this article is to explain the theoretical foundations of chaos theory and complexity theory and relate them to contemporary social work practice and research. The presentation is conceptual rather than mathematical, first emphasizing the central ideas of chaos theory and complexity theory and then moving on to their implications for social work.

Numerous introductory books on chaos theory exist. For those with a modest background in calculus, either of two books by Devaney (1989, 1992) is an excellent introduction to the mathematics involved. Kaplan and Glass (1995) also provide an excellent introduction, with an emphasis on biological applications. The mathematics is actually more advanced than in the two Devaney texts, but the discussion is easier to follow. The same can be said for Cambel (1993). Peak and Frame (1994) provide a thorough introduction without using mathematics more complicated than high school algebra. Edward Lorenz (1993), one of the pioneers of chaos theory, has provided a delightful and almost wholly nonmathematical introduction. Kellert (1993) also introduces chaos theory in a nonmathematical manner that still manages to catch many of the technical nuances in addition to discussing its implications for the future of science.

THEORETICAL FOUNDATIONS

Dynamics
Chaos theory and complexity theory are *dynamical* theories, which means that they study the way in which systems change over time. Social workers also study the ways in which human systems such as groups or families change over time. Chaos theory and complexity theory offer a variety of new and intriguing models of systemic change.

Deterministic Chaos
Just what is the "chaos" that chaos theory addresses? It is technically known as *deterministic chaos*. The name comes from the fact that some completely deterministic systems can produce thoroughly unpredictable behavior. The easiest of these systems for most people to imagine is an old-fashioned taffy machine, with two arms that first stretch the taffy into a long, thin rope and then fold it back together again (Stewart [1989] had a similar discussion of a candy cane machine.) Imagine that two raisins start out side by side in the taffy (perhaps they fell in from the oatmeal cookie machine). The stretching of the taffy will pull the raisins far apart, and the folding will bring them close again but not quite to the exact position at which they started. The motion of the raisins is

bounded, because they cannot escape the sticky taffy, and the motion shows an irregular oscillation (Brown, 1995). The stretch-and-fold motion of the taffy moves the raisins back and forth, but they never follow exactly the same path twice. The system is also nonlinear. Any mathematical equation that sought to describe the motion of the raisins would have to include terms that described the curving, stretch-and-fold motion of the taffy.

The area in which the raisins move is known as a *strange attractor*. An attractor is exactly what the name implies—it attracts the moving system over time. For instance, a pendulum will eventually come to rest pointing straight down. This position is the attractor for the pendulum. What is "strange" about strange attractors is the irregular movement inside the bounded region. The raisins will be somewhere in there, but it is not clear where. Moreover, if the raisins had started a tenth of an inch farther apart, the stretching motion of the taffy machine will pull that initial tenth of an inch into two or three inches, which will be folded into one or two inches, which may soon be pulled into several feet. This means that you cannot tell where the raisins will be in the future, even if you know where they are today, because the stretching and folding motion exaggerates tiny initial differences to enormous size. This is known as *sensitive dependence on initial conditions* or, more poetically, the *butterfly effect*. The latter name has arisen because, when applied to weather patterns, sensitive dependence on initial conditions implies that the flapping of a butterfly's wings in the Amazon jungle can affect the path of a tornado in Texas (Lorenz, 1993; Stewart, 1989). Sensitive dependence on initial conditions implies that a tiny cause can have an enormous effect, assuming a system is chaotic.

Readers can reproduce the taffy and raisins example with two marbles stuck in some Silly Putty. The taffy model is not a metaphor for deterministic chaos; such real-world stretching and folding processes really are chaotic. The mathematics behind them is known as the "baker's map" (Ott, 1993). Those who would like to experiment with chaotic systems in more depth will find the article by Kiel and Elliott (1996) on exploring nonlinear dynamics with a spreadsheet to be a good place to start. (The authors thank Eric Weeks [Center for Nonlinear Dynamics, The University of Texas at Austin, personal communication, January 29, 1997] for

drawing their attention to the centrality of stretching and folding.)

Thus, deterministic chaos is an irregular oscillation that occurs in a bounded system. This oscillation is inherently unpredictable because of sensitive dependence on initial conditions. Why should this be expected in human systems? Notice that the stretch and pull of the taffy machine constitutes a simple feedback system. Any feedback system might show sensitive dependence on initial conditions, as initially small differences grow with each trip through the loop. In fact, it seems likely that deterministic chaos is ubiquitous in feedback systems (Briggs & Peat, 1989; Mees, 1986), and human systems include numerous feedback loops. One can easily think of examples in which deterministic chaos might arise in human systems. Consider a couple who have just had an argument. Each would like to apologize, but each wants the other to apologize first. Each is committed to the relationship, and so neither simply leaves. Instead they become stuck in an oscillating pattern, as each approaches the other, attempts to draw out an apology, and is rebuffed. In fact, numerous interpersonal problems might be chaotic in nature, because each person is forced to adjust to the other in a continuous, chaotic dance. The preconditions for deterministic chaos, a bounded system with tight feedback loops, are common in human systems.

However, deterministic chaos is not necessarily a bad thing. Unpredictability gives life much of its spice, and nonlinearity in general implies the possibility of rapid change (Holland, 1995). The attempt to understand the place of nonlinearity and deterministic chaos in a wide variety of physical, biological, and human systems is one of the roots of a rapidly expanding field called *complexity theory* (Lewin, 1992; Nicolis & Prigogine, 1989; Waldrop, 1992).

Complexity Theory

Complexity theory bears some resemblance to the systems theories with which social workers are already familiar, particularly the general system theory of Ludwig von Bertalanffy (1968). However, whereas systems theorists tend to emphasize the ways in which developed systems maintain themselves, complexity theorists focus on the ways in which systems arise and change (Bak, 1996; Holland, 1995; Kauffman, 1993, 1995). Nobel Prize–winning physicist Philip Anderson (1996) has pointed out that complexity is an inherently holistic approach. Science has traditionally proceeded through a process of reductionism, seeking to explain macroscopic phenomena by microscopic laws, but complexity theory focuses on *emergent* qualities. These are qualities of one systemic level that cannot be explained solely by the laws that pertain to the level below it. Anderson uses the laws of computation as an example. These laws do not vary depending on the physical mechanism doing the computing, and therefore they cannot be explained by the laws of physics that pertain to transistors, vacuum tubes, and so on.

In the view of complexity theorists, systems self-organize from a myriad of local interactions (Resnick, 1994). Stuart Kauffman (1995), a pioneer in complexity theory, has developed a simple computer model that addresses the problem of how local interactions can give rise to a global system. This model consists of "threads" and "buttons," and interested readers can easily replicate it with real threads and buttons. The idea is to randomly scatter a group of buttons and then connect them randomly with threads. The word "random" is key here— no planning is allowed. Kauffman found that, even under random conditions, at about the time that the number of threads passes half the number of buttons, a steep rise in the interconnectedness of all of the buttons occurs. This is a nonlinear change that happens quite rapidly. Soon, most of the buttons are connected in one large network. Kauffman called this "order for free," and added, however, that in living systems the order is not for free but must be paid for by the expenditure of energy. This last point is reminiscent of the work of Nobel Prize–winning chemist Ilya Prigogine in nonequilibrium systems. Prigogine argues that many systems, including biological and human social systems, are able to move against the second law of thermodynamics, which states that order will decline in a closed system such as the universe, and entropy will increase, by importing energy from the environment, using that energy to build up order, and then exporting the entropy that results from using the energy back into the environment. Such systems are able to operate far from thermodynamic equilibrium and exhibit nonlinear behavior (Nicolis & Prigogine, 1989; Prigogine & Stengers, 1984).

How are complex systems able to adapt quickly to change and still maintain coherence?

Kauffman and his colleague Christopher Langton have argued that such systems operate at the "edge of chaos" and they combine the potential for rapid change that is typical of chaotic systems with the greater stability of ordered systems (Kauffman, 1993, 1995). The physicist Per Bak (1996) has suggested that systems could evolve to such a state through local interactions. Bak's original model of a system was a pile of sand, built up one grain at a time. As more and more grains are added, the slope of the sand pile will grow steeper and steeper. Eventually, avalanches begin. The actual size of any given avalanche depends on the slope of the sand pile and the nature of the local interconnections between the grains of sand. If the slope is steep and the interconnections many, a large avalanche will result. A shallow slope with few interconnections will cause a small avalanche. Bak and other researchers (Bretz, Cunningham, Kurczynski, & Nori, 1992; Frette et al., 1995) have found that sand piles and other piles of granular objects such as rice tend to organize to the point where avalanches are characterized by a *power law*. This means that small avalanches are common and large avalanches are rare. This is similar to the edge of chaos idea: Small amounts of disorder happen frequently, with occasional large, truly chaotic, disorderly interludes. It is easy to see how this might work. A large avalanche will rearrange the entire structure of the sand pile, breaking the network of connections between the grains, and each small avalanche will allow the grains to form new subnetworks, which will eventually link into a network that covers the entire pile and is ripe for another large avalanche. This is a nonlinear phenomenon. The same falling grain of sand might set off a small avalanche, a large avalanche, or no avalanche, depending on the interconnectedness of the entire pile. Similar models have been applied in an attempt to understand economic fluctuations. Again, such behavior requires a network of local and nonlinear interactions (Scheinkman & Woodford, 1994).

Such edge of chaos behavior is strikingly similar to that observed by family therapists. Olson (1986, 1989), in his circumplex model, sees the healthiest families as dwelling in the center of a curve of flexibility. Families falling to the extremes on this curvilinear model, showing too little or too much change, are not as adaptive as families in the middle. Olson thinks of family cohesion in the same way: Families are less adaptive when they are either too close or too distant. They function best and can face the demands of development when they have close-knit organization and boundaries—but not too close. The perspective of self-organized criticality adds a dynamic element to this situation and implies that family connections will tighten or loosen repeatedly as family members adapt to each other.

APPLICATIONS TO SOCIAL WORK PRACTICE AND UNDERSTANDING

Both chaos and complexity theorists have stated that their findings might be applicable across a variety of systems (Cambel, 1993; Holland, 1995; Kauffman, 1995). This is a reasonable claim from both a theoretical and an empirical point of view. Theoretically, what determines a chaotic or complex system is not the nature of the subsystems but the connections between them. Any system that has interconnections that allow for nonlinear behavior has the potential to demonstrate chaotic or complex behavior. Empirically, evidence of deterministic chaos has been found in electroencephalograms (Freeman, 1991), monetary aggregates (Chen, 1988), stock markets (Chen, 1996), and political systems (McBurnett, 1996) as well as in a great variety of physical and biological systems. Power laws, which have been taken as evidence of evolution to the edge of chaos, are ubiquitous in both human and natural systems (Bak, 1996; Mandelbrot, 1983).

Any such broadly applicable theory would be of interest to social workers who work with and in a wide range of human social systems. Advocates of the use of systemic and ecosystemic models in social work practice have long argued that the breadth of such models encourages social workers in a broad practice focus (Germain, 1991; Martin & O'Connor, 1989). However, will chaos theory and complexity theory add something that the systems theoretical frameworks with which social workers are familiar do not?

The ideas associated with nonlinear dynamics seem likely to alter the underlying metaphors of social work practitioners. The nonlinear view of systems as evolving in sudden and often unexpected ways is in striking contrast to the emphasis on equilibrium to be found in many earlier systemic theories (Harvey & Reed, 1994). Although

recent social work systems theorists have struggled to overcome this limitation by adapting from the work of Bertalanffy (Martin & O'Conner, 1989) or by inserting concepts such as self-direction into their overall ecological and systemic framework (Germain, 1991), a nonlinear framework implies that complex systems must by nature be unpredictable because of sensitivity to initial conditions—social workers should expect the unexpected. In fact, this view of systems as continuously and unpredictably changing in both large and small ways is itself an apt description of human social systems as many of us experience them and may account for much of the recent social science interest in nonlinear dynamics. In an inherently nonlinear, unpredictable world, it might make sense to consciously train social workers to think creatively and flexibly, perhaps using the techniques pioneered by Edward DeBono (1973).

Deterministic chaos may play a central role in systemic change. Recent research (Ott, Grebogi, & Yorke, 1990; Ott & Spano, 1995) in nonlinear dynamics has focused on the "control of chaos." This is possible because numerous unstable orbits exist within any attractor. It is therefore possible, at least within laboratory conditions, to stabilize the entire system around one orbit with a small nudge. Systems that are not chaotic are not sensitive to stimuli of this magnitude because they lack the extreme sensitivity to initial conditions that characterize chaotic systems. It would appear that a system in a state of deterministic chaos has the potential to change in a multiplicity of different ways with relatively little effort. It has been argued that such flexibility is necessary to higher life forms (Ott et al., 1990; Ott & Spano, 1995).

This is a particularly intriguing idea for social workers because it has long been observed that times of change often appear chaotic and disorderly, whether on the level of the individual (Golan, 1986), the group (Mackenzie, 1994; Toseland & Rivas, 1984), or even the entire society (Harvey & Reed, 1994). Such disorder can be quite frightening, but if such times of change do in fact show deterministic chaos, social workers and their clients will know that they include an enormous number of possible paths to a more ordered state. Some cognitive constructivist therapists already view crises in this way. As discussed by Franklin (1995), "the disorganizing influence of distressing emotions is believed to represent a normal stage in reconstructing oneself to meet the demands of one's own development and social environment. In systemic terms, this process is referred to as 'self organizing and autopoietic development'" (p. 400).

Social workers might also develop systematic methods of nudging systems that are in a crisis toward a more ordered state. Sensitive dependence on initial conditions—the butterfly effect—implies that slight interventions will often be sufficient to do this (Ott & Spano, 1995). When a system is in a chaotic state, smaller interventions are likely to be better interventions. There are intriguing parallels in the social work literature. Crisis workers have long noted that small interventions with clients in crisis can have a disproportionate effect (Golan, 1986). This makes little sense within traditional, linear models—a serious crisis should require a powerful intervention if the effect is directly proportional to the cause—but such clients might well be exhibiting sensitive dependence on initial conditions. Similar dynamics could—and do—work in large-scale social systems. The actions of a single individual can alter a system in unexpected ways. Rosa Parks began the Montgomery bus boycott by refusing to give up her seat to a white person. Henry David Thoreau spent one night in jail to protest the policies of the U.S. government; the essay he wrote about that experience, "Civil Disobedience," came to influence generations of social change advocates.

Policymakers could, in theory, use the inherent nonlinearity of complex systems to make small changes that would have large effects. Complexity theorist John Holland (1995) referred to the points when small interventions are likely to be most effective as *lever points*, and argued that the inherently nonlinear nature of complex systems must mean they are common, even when the system is not in a state of true deterministic chaos. The organizational theorist Peter Senge (1990) has made a similar argument about lever points in corporations. Of course, the difficulty is in finding the lever points. Policymakers in at least one field, criminology, seem to have succeeded in finding some of them. Criminologists have recently begun to adapt nonlinear models from epidemiology. Within these models, the spread of crime is seen literally as an epidemic. A distinguishing characteristic of epidemics is that the models that describe

them are nonlinear. These models include *tipping points*, similar to Holland's lever points; if the new infection rate falls below the tipping point, the epidemic will go into a steady decline and soon disappear. Reductions in the new infection rate that still leave it above the tipping point will not lead to such a self-sustaining decline. Similar principles have been applied to the reduction of crime in New York City. When the New York City Transit Authority wanted to crack down on crime in the subway system in the late 1980s and early 1990s, it began by removing graffiti from all the cars and punishing turnstile jumpers, under the assumption that such trivial acts were tipping points that invited further disorder and more serious crimes. The strategy worked: Felonies in the subway system have decreased by more than 50 percent during the 1990s (Gladwell, 1996).

Complexity theory makes at least two other important contributions to social work. The first is the idea that systems self-organize from local interactions. Again, there are parallels in the existing social work and social science literature. Group workers and group therapists have long known that groups can be counted on to organize themselves (Schwartz & Zalba, 1972; Yalom, 1985). Group work has always been distinguished by an emphasis on a democratic style of leadership (Lewin, 1951; Schwartz & Zalba, 1972). Self-organization makes such a leadership style both possible and necessary. Schwartz and Zalba noted that it is possible because groups will organize and regulate themselves. Lewin noted that it is necessary because an attempt to control a group through authoritarian means will result in anger among group members, which damages the network of relationships that allows the system to organize itself. The need for local interactions implies that social workers who want to foster a self-organized system might begin by encouraging numerous one-to-one relationships. The work of Kauffman (1995) indicates that the one-to-one relationships will soon coalesce into a larger group system.

The phrase "foster a self-organized system" is used deliberately. As Margaret Wheatley (1996) pointed out, people have come, during the last few centuries, to view the world as a machine, and our organizations as if they were machines as well. From this point of view, one builds a system or an organization. Complexity theory, on the other hand, would say that the fundamental goal is to take advantage of the tendency toward order that is innate in any group. Wheatley argued that the primary issue any organization needs to address is that of its own purpose and intent: Once these are clear, the system will tend to self-organize.

Complexity theory's second contribution is the idea of systems evolving to a critical state on the edge of chaos, a state that is identifiable by a power distribution of crises (Bak, 1996). This implies that occasional crises are an unavoidable aspect of the functioning of any system and may be an indication of systemic health (Bak, 1996). (Continual, debilitating crises are, of course, a different matter.) It also gives theoretical backing to the point some systems theorists in and out of social work have made that healthy systems are in flux rather than equilibrium (Bertalanffy, 1968; Martin & O'Connor, 1989).

Both chaos theory and complexity theory emphasize the importance of context and timing in determining the success or failure of social work interventions, because within these frameworks virtually any difference might turn out to be critical. Parallels with contemporary social work literature are apparent. Coulton (1996a) had begun to examine the social properties of neighborhoods, seeking information about the availability of services, social interactions with neighbors, fear of violence, and willingness to intervene with children, among numerous other variables, in an attempt to link such variables to risk of maltreatment of children.

A complexity theorist would add, however, that it is just as important to understand the development and growth of neighborhoods and other social systems. The idea that a system cannot be understood apart from its history, that its history constrains the options available to the system for growth and change, and that small differences can lead to radically different histories, is known as *path dependence* (Arthur, 1990; Cowan & Gunby, 1996). A classic example is the rivalry between the Beta and VHS videocassette recorder formats in the early 1980s. They began as equals, and the Beta format may actually have been of slightly superior technical quality. At some point, however, probably through a random fluctuation, VHS sold a few more units. Once this had happened, video stores began to rent and sell more VHS tapes. It then became advantageous to own a VHS recorder because of the greater

selection of tapes. The initial small advantage of VHS over the Beta format became locked in and soon became overwhelming (Arthur, 1990; Waldrop, 1992). Such path dependence and eventual lock-in can be imagined to be capable of damaging or even destroying any system— for example, a social service organization. Many organizations are heavily dependent on a core of experienced social service staff members. If several of those members were to leave at once, the cost in years of social work experience might be far greater than the cost in actual work hours lost. The loss of several experienced staff members could easily initiate a decline in organizational performance, which could become locked in as the organization began to get a bad reputation among local professionals. This scenario unfortunately seems likely to become more common as the American work force becomes more mobile. Lest this seem too pessimistic, however, it should be pointed out that path dependence could also work in the other direction: A talented social worker could arrive at the agency, begin to attract skilled coworkers because of his or her own reputation, and set in motion a cycle of increasing excellence.

Previous systems models have often been criticized as being inherently conservative. This criticism was particularly telling when leveled against the functionalist systems model of Parsons (1949) (Bailey, 1994; Harvey & Reed, 1994). The reasoning in this case was that, because a functionalist model seeks to define a set of functions that are necessary for the survival of the system, the model could not account for change. Any function that disappeared would need to be immediately replaced by an identical function. Because complexity theory is not a functionalist model, and because it is fundamentally concerned with processes of systemic change, it appears to avoid this trap.

Chaos theory and complexity theory show that the timing of an intervention is often as important as, if not more important than, the content of the intervention. They also show that an intervention can be too powerful as well as too weak; that self-organizing systems require democratic leadership; that change can develop in a rapid, nonlinear fashion from small interventions; and that surprises are an inescapable part of any complex system. Complexity theorists have also argued that the theories actually offer more than this collection of observations—they offer the possibility of a science of human systemic development and change (Bak, 1996; Holland, 1995; Kauffman, 1995). Such a science would be of immense value to social workers, other helping professionals, and their clients, but will it ever live up to its promise? To begin to answer this question, the implications of chaos and complexity for social work research must be examined.

IMPLICATIONS FOR SOCIAL WORK RESEARCH

The developing sciences of chaos and complexity carry implications for social work research as it is practiced today and for its future directions. Social science research has traditionally drawn on linear cause–effect models. Chaos theory and complexity theory say, in effect, that such models can never capture the true richness and unpredictability of human change (Thelen & Smith, 1994). Although an experiment may show that a group of subjects suffered from a greater level of anxiety on average before an intervention than six months after that intervention, it cannot show the paths that each individual subject took during those six months. If the paths were nonlinear, perhaps slow at first and then picking up speed, or showing both increases and decreases in anxiety on the way to an eventual decrease, then the experimental design may give the deceptive impression of an orderly process that never really existed. The sensitive dependence on initial conditions that chaotic systems demonstrate also implies that one of the traditional goals of science, prediction, is simply unattainable, at least in the long term. Even the slightest measurement error will eventually render predictions useless (Kellert, 1993).

The goal of empirical research in chaos theory and complexity theory is to illuminate the nonlinear processes that standard linear models are likely to miss. This requires data in the form of a long time series of hundreds or thousands of points (Cambel, 1993). It also requires the researcher to examine one case at a time, because combining a number of cases and then averaging their changes will, in effect, average out the evidence of nonlinearity in the data (personal communication with P. Chen, research scientist, Ilya Prigogine Center for Studies in Statistical Thermodynamics and Complex Systems, University of Texas at Austin, May 2, 1995; personal communication

with L. Reichl, professor and faculty member, Ilya Prigogine Center for Studies in Statistical Thermodynamics and Complex Systems, University of Texas at Austin, May 2, 1995). This superficially resembles the single-subject design strategy that has been popular in social work during the past decade, but there is a critical difference. In a single-subject design based on linear research models, the researcher records client behaviors over a baseline period, then introduces an intervention and looks for a change in the behaviors during a follow-up period (Rubin & Babbie, 1997). In a nonlinear single-subject or single-system design, a researcher would examine the entire time series for evidence of nonlinear activity.

The techniques for doing this are fundamentally holistic. They involve testing for the presence of specific characteristics that are typical of underlying nonlinear activity, such as the presence of a strange attractor or sensitive dependence on initial conditions (Abarbanel, 1996; Kaplan & Glass, 1995). As Kaplan and Glass have noted, such tests will not allow for an analysis to show exactly where the nonlinearity comes from. Stephen Kellert (1993) has suggested that the attempt of chaos theorists to comprehend the overall dynamics of systems by the examination of such mathematical patterns as strange attractors represents a fundamentally new kind of scientific understanding. Traditional scientific understanding seeks causal laws; the chaos theorist seeks an underlying order expressed in models that may have little to say about cause and effect. Although this may be less than the ideal for a reduction-minded researcher, the presence of nonlinearity carries its own implications as to the predictability of systems and their capacity to change.

In the densely interconnected world that chaos theory and complexity theory reveal, reductionist methodology shows itself to be limited and at times deceptive. Reductionism by nature ignores the connections that make complex systems complex (Bertalanffy, 1968) and has almost invariably ignored the historical development of systems (Chen, 1993). When reductionist cause–effect models are applied to single-subject time series, the results are frequently unclear (Rubin & Knox, 1996). This is not to say that social scientists should always avoid reductionist research methodologies. Like any other research strategy, reductionism is more useful in some situations, and with some kinds of data, than in others.

It has been argued that chaos theory and complexity theory imply an interdisciplinary research agenda (Anderson, 1996; Waldrop, 1992). To the extent that these theories have in fact described interactions that occur in a variety of systems, this argument is clearly correct. For social scientists, these theories probably imply a multimethodological approach as well, if only because of the difficulties involved in the research (personal communication with P. Chen, research scientist, Ilya Prigogine Center for Studies in Statistical Thermodynamics and Complex Systems, University of Texas at Austin, May 2, 1995; Gregerson & Sailer, 1993). These difficulties are likely to be formidable. The length of a time series that is necessary to demonstrate the presence of deterministic chaos is considerable—on the order of hundreds of points or more. It is also clear that social science data are far more noisy than data from the physical sciences. Distinguishing chaos from noise is a significant methodological challenge (Holton & May, 1993). Given such requirements, a two-pronged research strategy involving both quantitative and qualitative methods might be useful in the exploration of deterministic chaos. In such a strategy, quantitative methods would be used when time-series data of sufficient quality were available. Researchers would also try to use qualitative methods as part of these studies in an attempt to develop a set of qualitative markers that would indicate the likely presence of deterministic chaos. They could then begin to pursue a wider variety of studies by use of qualitative methods. Calls for such studies of complex systems that combine qualitative and quantitative methods and emphasize processes of change are beginning to appear in the social work literature (Coulton, 1996b).

REFERENCES

Abarbanel, H.D.I. (1996). *Analysis of observed chaotic data.* New York: Springer-Verlag.

Anderson, P. (1996). Physics: The opening to complexity. *Proceedings of the National Academy of Sciences, 92,* 6653–6654.

Arthur, B. W. (1990). Positive feedbacks in the economy. *Scientific American, 263,* 92–99.

Bailey, K. D. (1994). Talcott Parsons, social entropy theory, and living systems theory. *Behavioral Science, 39,* 25–45.

Bak, P. (1996). *How nature works: The science of self-organized criticality.* New York: Springer-Verlag.

Bertalanffy, L. von. (1968). *General system theory: Foundations, development, applications.* New York: George Braziller.

Bretz, M., Cunningham, J. B., Kurczynski, P. L., & Nori, F. (1992). Imaging of avalanches in granular material. *Physical Review Letters, 69*(16), 2431–2434.

Briggs, J., & Peat, F. D. (1989). *Turbulent mirror: An illustrated guide to chaos theory and the science of wholeness.* New York: Harper & Row.

Brown, C. (1995). *Chaos and catastrophe theories.* Thousand Oaks, CA: Sage Publications.

Cambel, A. (1993). *Applied chaos theory: A paradigm for complexity.* San Diego: Academic Press.

Chen, P. (1988). Empirical and theoretical evidence of economic chaos. *System Dynamics Review: The Journal of the System Dynamics Society, 4,* 1–2, 81–108.

Chen, P. (1993). China's challenge to economic orthodoxy: Asian reform as an evolutionary, self-organizing process. *China Economic Review, 4*(2), 137–142.

Chen, P. (1996). A random walk or color-chaos on the stock market? Time-frequency analysis of S&P indexes. *Studies in Nonlinear Dynamics & Econometrics, 1*(2), 87–103.

Coulton, C. (1996a). Measuring neighborhood context for young children in an urban area. *American Journal of Community Psychology, 24*(1), 5–32.

Coulton, C. (1996b). Poverty, work and community: A research agenda for an era of diminishing federal responsibility. *Social Work, 41,* 509–519.

Cowan, R., & Gunby, P. (1996). Sprayed to death: Path dependence, lock-in and pest control strategies. *Economic Journal, 106,* 521–543.

DeBono, E. (1973). *Lateral thinking: Creativity step by step.* New York: Harper & Row.

Devaney, R. L. (1989). *An introduction to chaotic dynamical systems.* Menlo Park, CA: Benjamin/Cummings.

Devaney, R. L. (1992). *A first course in chaotic dynamical systems: Theory and experiment.* New York: Addison-Wesley.

Franklin, C. (1995). Expanding the vision of social constructionist debates: Creating relevance for practitioners. *Families in Society, 76*(7), 395–407.

Freeman, W. J. (1991). The physiology of perception. *Scientific American, 264*(2), 78–85.

Frette, V., Christensen, K., Malthe-Sorensen, A., Feder, J., Jossang, T., & Meakin, P. (1995). Avalanche dynamics in a pile of rice. *Nature, 379*(1), 49–52.

Germain, C. (1991). *Human behavior in the social environment: An ecological view*. New York: Columbia University Press.

Gladwell, M. (1996). The tipping point. *New Yorker, 72*(14), 32–40.

Gleick, J. (1987). *Chaos, the making of a new science*. London: Heinemann.

Golan, N. (1986). Crisis theory. In F. J. Turner (Ed.), *Social work treatment: Interlocking theoretical approaches*. New York: Free Press.

Gregerson, H., & Sailer, L. (1993). Chaos theory and its implications for social science research. *Human Relations, 46,* 777–802.

Harvey, D. L., & Reed, M. H. (1994). The evolution of dissipative social systems. *Journal of Social and Evolutionary Systems, 17,* 371–411.

Holton, D., & May, R. M. (1993). Distinguishing chaos from noise. In T. Mullin (Ed.), *The nature of chaos*. Oxford, England: Clarendon Press.

Holland, J. H. (1995). *Hidden order: How adaptation builds complexity*. Reading, MA: Addison-Wesley.

Kaplan, D., & Glass, L. (1995). *Understanding nonlinear dynamics*. New York: Springer-Verlag.

Kauffman, S. A. (1993). *The origins of order: Self-organization and selection in evolution*. New York: Oxford University Press.

Kauffman, S. A. (1995). *At home in the universe: The search for the laws of self-organization and complexity*. New York: Oxford University Press.

Kellert, S. H. (1993). *In the wake of chaos: Unpredictable order in dynamical systems*. Chicago: University of Chicago Press.

Kiel, L. D., & Elliott, E. (1996). Exploring nonlinear dynamics with a spreadsheet: A graphical view of chaos for beginners. In L. D. Kiel & E. Elliott (Eds.), *Chaos theory in the social sciences: Foundations and applications*. Ann Arbor: University of Michigan Press.

Lewin, K. (1951). *Field theory in social science*. New York: Harper & Row.

Lewin, R. (1992). *Complexity: Life at the edge of chaos*. New York: Collier Books.

Lorenz, E. (1993). *The essence of chaos*. Seattle, WA: University of Washington Press.

Mackenzie, K. R. (1994). Group development. In A. Fuhriman & G. M. Burlingame (Eds.), *Handbook of group psychotherapy: An empirical and clinical synthesis*. New York: John Wiley & Sons.

Mandelbrot, B. (1983). *The fractal geometry of nature*. New York: W. H. Freeman.

Martin, P. Y., & O'Conner, G. G. (1989). *The social environment: Open systems applications*. New York: Longman.

McBurnett, M. (1996). Complexity in the evolution of public opinion. In L. D. Kiel & E. Elliott (Eds.),

Chaos theory in the social sciences: Foundations and applications. Ann Arbor: University of Michigan Press.

Mees, A. (1986). Chaos in feedback systems. In A. V. Holden (Ed.), *Chaos*. Princeton, NJ: Princeton University Press.

Nicolis, G., & Prigogine, I. (1989). *Exploring Complexity: An introduction*. New York: W. H. Freeman.

Olson, D. H. (1986). Circumplex Model VII: Validation studies and FACES III. *Family Process, 24,* 203–207.

Olson, D. H. (1989). Circumplex Model of Family Systems VIII: Family assessment and intervention. In D. H. Olson, C. S. Russell, & D. H. Sprenkle (Eds.), *Circumplex model: Systemic assessment and treatment of families*. New York: Haworth Press.

Ott, E. (1993). *Chaos in dynamical systems*. New York: Cambridge University Press.

Ott, E., Grebogi, C., & Yorke, J. A. (1990). Controlling chaos. *Physical Review Letters, 64*(11), 1196–1199.

Ott, E., & Spano, M. (1995). Controlling chaos. *Physics Today, 48*(5), 34–40.

Parsons, T. (1949). The structure of social action. In P. Hamilton (Ed.), *Readings from Talcott Parsons*. London: Tavistock Publications.

Peak, D., & Frame, M. (1994). *Chaos under control: The art and science of complexity*. New York: W. H. Freeman.

Prigogine, I., & Stengers, I. (1984). *Order out of chaos: Man's new dialogue with nature*. New York: Bantam Books.

Resnick, M. (1994). *Turtles, termites, and traffic jams: Explorations in massively parallel micro worlds*. Cambridge, MA: MIT Press.

Richards, D. (1996). From individuals to groups: The aggregation of votes and chaotic dynamics. In L. D. Kiel & E. Elliott (Eds.), *Chaos theory in the social sciences: Foundations and applications*. Ann Arbor: University of Michigan Press.

Rubin, A., & Babbie, E. (1997). *Research methods for social work*. Pacific Grove, CA: Brooks/Cole Publishing.

Rubin, A., & Knox, K. S. (1996). Data analysis problems in single-case evaluation: Issues for research on social work practice. *Research on Social Work Practice, 6*(1), 40–65.

Saperstein, A. M. (1996). The prediction of unpredictability: Applications of the new paradigm of chaos in dynamical systems to the old problem of the stability of a system of hostile nations. In L. D. Kiel & E. Elliott (Eds.), *Chaos theory in the social sciences: Foundations and applications*. Ann Arbor: University of Michigan Press.

Scheinkman, J. A., & Woodford, M. (1994). Self-organized criticality and economic fluctuations. *American Journal of Economics, 84*(2), 417–421.

Schwartz, W., & Zalba, S. R. (1972). *The practice of group work*. New York: Columbia University Press.

Senge, P. M. (1990). *The fifth discipline: The art and practice of the learning organization*. New York: Doubleday.

Stewart, I. (1989). *Does God play dice?* Cambridge, England: Blackwell.

Thelen, E., & Smith, L. (1994). *A dynamic systems approach to the development of cognition and action*. Cambridge, MA: MIT Press.

Toseland, R. W., & Rivas, R. F. (1984). *An introduction to group work practice*. New York: Macmillan.

Waldrop, M. M. (1992). *Complexity: The emerging science at the edge of chaos*. New York: Simon & Schuster.

Ward, M. (1995). Butterflies and bifurcations: Can chaos theory contribute to our understanding of family systems? *Journal of Marriage and the Family, 57*, 629–638.

Wheatley, M. J. (1996). Breathing life into organizations: A new world view based on chaos and complexity. *Public Management, 78*(9), 10–14.

Yalom, I. (1985). *The theory and practice of group psychotherapy* (3rd ed.). New York: Basic Books.

Keith Warren, MSSW, is graduate research assistant, Center for Social Work Research, **Cynthia Franklin, PhD,** is associate professor, School of Social Work, and **Calvin Streeter, PhD,** is associate professor, School of Social Work, University of Texas at Austin, 1925 San Jacinto Blvd., Austin, TX 78712.

For further information see

Assessment; Citizen Participation; Cognition and Social Cognitive Theory; Community Oganization; Ecological Perspective; Epistemology; Experimental and Quasi-Experimental Design; Gestalt; Group Practice Overview; Intervention Research; Meta-Analysis; Person-in-Environment; Psychometrics; Recording; Research Overview; Single-System Design; Social Development.

Key Words

chaos	deterministic chaos
complex systems	nonlinear dynamics
complexity theory	systems theory

Christian Social Work
Mary P. Van Hook

Christian social work is guided by the goals of restoring justice to the community; enabling people to participate in the community; and responding to the needs of suffering, vulnerable people. It is characterized by Biblical teachings that transcend methods and settings. Important beliefs include the identity of people as children of God who are thus deserving of worth and dignity. Charity and social justice approaches are both important responses. Social worker-client relationships are based on a sense of grace. Indeed, social work had its original impetus in the Christian traditions of charity and social justice but subsequently entered a period of secularization. This entry analyzes the history and current state of Christian social work in Protestant and Roman Catholic traditions. Professional organizations and journals support Christian social work, and religious issues can be important to include when assessing client systems. Complex legal issues influence government and sectarian agency relationships.

Christian social work is distinguished by a basic worldview and set of beliefs about the nature of human beings, the world at large, and the purpose of social work. These beliefs represent the core of Christian social work, which transcends a variety of methods, target populations, settings, and theoretical orientations. In practice, Christian social work ranges from social advocacy to individual and family treatment, from child welfare administration to outreach services to the homeless, and from international development to case management. Although some social work organizations have a specifically Christian identity, the practice of Christian social work as defined in this entry is not limited to these organizations. This entry examines the major set of beliefs that characterize Christian social work, its historical origins and current organizational structures, and some implications for practice and current controversies. The related topics of church social work and spirituality have been discussed in length by Garland (1995) and by Canda elsewhere in this supplement.

BELIEF SYSTEM

Christian social work is set within the beliefs of the Christian faith. Although theological doctrines vary widely among specific Christian groups, certain core beliefs traditionally provide the foundation for Christian social work across the Roman Catholic, Eastern Orthodox, and the many Protestant denominations. These beliefs center around the nature of human beings, the world at large, and God. The beliefs about human beings provide a distinctive foundation for many of the basic values of social work.

Human beings are viewed as "children of God" and as created in the image of God (Keith-Lucas, 1985; Loewenberg, 1988; Niebuhr, 1932). This view has several important implications in terms of both rights and responsibilities of human beings. First, it gives human beings great worth and dignity, with accompanying rights in the area of basic material and social well-being (Mott, 1996). Within Christian social work this belief—rather than a humanistic or enlightenment foundation—provides the basis for the inherent worth of human beings that is an integral part of the basic social work value system. The second implication is the interrelatedness of all human beings as members of a single "family" that transcends racial and cultural boundaries (Keith-Lucas, 1985; Niebuhr, 1932). People are created to be part of a social community, and as a result, they have an inherent obligation to promote the welfare of others ("love one another"). Loving God is demonstrated through loving our neighbors (Catholic Charities USA, 1992; Niebuhr, 1932). This in turn has implications—namely, the concept of mutual individual responsibility and of a just society that protects and provides opportunity to all members (Catholic Charities USA, 1992; Mott, 1996).

These beliefs about the nature of human beings encourage Christian social workers to view themselves as fellow children of God along with their clients and to recognize a calling of responsibility for others who are fellow members of the family of God. These statements reflect ideals and goals about how people should relate to others. Christian social workers recognize that bitter battles have been fought among Christians and by Christians against members of other groups in the name of God.

A belief that people are created in the image of God and have dignity and worth also means that people have the capacity and right to make choices. The Bible describes human beings as created with a free will to make important decisions and contains stories of the choices people have made, the consequences of those choices, and God's response. In terms of social work practice, this means that Christian social workers should favor methods that enhance a person's right to choose (Keith-Lucas, 1985). This belief thus underlies the social work value of self-determination.

Human beings are "of infinite worth, irrespective of their behavior" (Keith-Lucas, 1985, p. 13). The worth of human beings is not predicated on a belief that people always act in good and positive ways (Loewenberg, 1988). Instead, the Christian view of human beings includes the concept of sin and a falling away from the image of God, as manifested in harmful actions and intentions toward others. Despite this, God acted in love through Jesus to bring a gratuitous gift of restorative grace to human beings. Christian social workers are aware of the unity between them and the people they serve as fellow recipients of grace. Recognition of sin can also be a moment of hope in which growth is possible (Catholic Charities USA, 1992; Keith-Lucas, 1985, 1992; Loewenberg, 1988; Mott, 1996; Niebuhr, 1932).

Christian social work views the world at large as part of God's creation. The "world is charged with the grandeur of God" (Catholic Charities USA, 1992, p. 27). In this context, human beings have important responsibilities as stewards and caretakers of the world.

Christian social work views God as taking an ongoing active and caring role in the world. God grants human beings the responsibility for carrying out God's purposes of healing in the world (Keith-Lucas, 1985). Love of God is expressed concretely in the form of love of others (Catholic Charities USA, 1992; M. Joseph, 1982).

FOUNDATION OF CHRISTIAN SOCIAL WORK

The Bible

The Bible, the basic religious document of Christianity, is replete with statements and stories describing how people should relate to each other. Because God has created human beings and continues to care about their well-being, oppressive or kind acts are not only done to fellow human beings but also to God

("He who oppresses a poor man insults His Maker" [Prov. 14:31 NIV]. "Whatever you did for one of the least of these brothers of mine, you did for me" [Matthew 25:40 NIV]. "Whatever you did not do for the least of these, you did not do for me" [Matthew 25:45 NIV].).

The injunctions in the Bible provide the basis for two approaches reflecting important strands within social work: charity and social justice. Charity consists of making helpful responses to specific crises without attempting to change the basic social structure of the local or global community. Social justice seeks to correct the social structures that create and perpetuate suffering and oppression.

Biblically, charity is supported by injunctions to protect two groups at great risk in a patriarchal society: fatherless children and widows. People are required to care not only for their own kinship or other community group but also for those who are aliens in the community (Deut. 10:18-19). Jesus told the story of the Good Samaritan, in which a "neighbor" is defined both as a person in need and as a person who responds to those needs (Luke 10:25-37).

However, the Bible makes it clear that God also requires a concern for just social structures. Under the principle of Jubilee, every seven years land reverts to the original owner, and slaves are to be given their freedom. Although implementation of these arrangements was probably limited, the prophets of the Old Testament repeatedly called for social justice. For the prophets, knowing God and doing justice—including evidencing concern for the poor and oppressed—were synonymous. Poor people have rights. God's justice required just treatment, not only for group members but also for aliens. Leaders, the community as a whole, and individuals were called to establish justice (Catholic Charities USA, 1992; Jer. 22:13-16; Keith-Lucas, 1996; Mason, 1996; Mott, 1996; Paget-Wilkes, 1981; Sider, 1982; Van Hook, 1996). Justice as intended by God is a restoration to the community. Individuals are to be empowered to be strong enough to participate in the community. Believers are enjoined to address any barriers to this participation (Mott, 1996).

Purpose of Christian Social Work

Biblical mandates and teachings about the relationships between God and human beings and among human beings set the direction for Christian social work. It is guided by the goals of restoring a just community, enabling people to participate in this community, and responding to the needs of suffering and vulnerable people. As a result, Christian social work encompasses social policy; advocacy; community practice; prevention; administration; and remedial efforts with individuals, families, and groups. The activities of specific Christian social workers can emphasize different aspects to accomplish these goals.

HISTORICAL BACKGROUND

Christian social work has its historical origins in the early Christian and medieval churches, the monastic movement, the Protestant Reformation, and early relief and missionary efforts. Charity was the dominant theme of these efforts (De Santa Ana, 1980; Niebuhr, 1932). The early Christian church, a marginalized and often persecuted group, stressed the principle of mutual obligation among members, as well as the general principle of charity (Conrad, 1980; Sider, 1982). With the blending of religious and civic life during the Middle Ages, the church was the primary institution charged with the welfare of the poor but received legal support for this role from civil authorities. The monastic movement served as a refuge and source of aid for those in need.

The church's capacity to care for the poor had declined substantially by the time of the Protestant Reformation (Hall, 1979). Under the leadership of Martin Luther and John Calvin, however, the Protestant Reformation brought an impetus for a greater responsibility on the part of the state to care for the poor, with accompanying religious support for the established civil authorities (Hall, 1979; Loewenberg, 1988; Mott, 1996; Niebuhr, 1932).

Christian missionaries frequently combined preaching with health measures, education programs, and efforts designed to reduce poverty and improve the general well-being of people. The goals of these activities were typically to further the missionary work itself rather than to address social issues. The Salvation Army, however, has long been noted for its combination of missionary and social services efforts.

African American churches traditionally have taken a leadership role within their communities and instituted a variety of social services programs. These churches helped provide the impetus and support for a major social justice struggle, the civil rights movement. Many African American churches currently have important social programs with both advocacy and service components as inherent aspects of their ministry.

Despite Biblical mandates to support a social justice agenda, the church and Christian community have frequently supported and legitimized a status quo that created and perpetuated inequalities (Bieler, 1980; Niebuhr, 1932; White, 1980). As Christians encountered the problems of the urban poor in the 1880s, some leaders "accepted poverty as a result of divine ordination and viewed the poor as existing in their condition because of sin or sloth" (White, 1980, p. 51). Although charity for worthy individuals was encouraged, public relief was viewed as contrary to the economic system and degrading to the poor themselves (White, 1980). The principle of "subsidiarity" in the Roman Catholic tradition, in which help begins at the personal level and moves up through the levels of society and government to meet social responsibilities, has supported broader community intervention (Tropman, 1986).

Several more recent movements within Protestant and Roman Catholic circles have promoted social justice concerns. In terms of Protestant churches, the Social Gospel movement, born in the United States after the Civil War, sought to apply the teachings of Christ to social institutions as well as to individuals. The movement was the product of an increased understanding of the nature of poverty along with the personal experiences of several pastors with the reality of the urban poor. These pastors returned to the Old Testament prophets and their message to the poor. Viewing the corporate nature of the Kingdom of God, they stressed the "Fatherhood of God and the brotherhood of man" and a view of people as brothers and sisters rather than economic commodities (White, 1980, p. 55). Christian leaders in this movement joined forces to work toward social action rather than just providing social services (White, 1980). Currently, the National Council of Churches, an affiliation of mainline Protestant groups, speaks out on social justice issues such as poverty and hunger. Major Protestant denominations have programs that address social justice issues domestically and abroad. Evangelical Christian groups have traditionally been hesitant to affirm social justice strategies because such efforts tended to be identified with the "social gospel," which they viewed as not adequately concerned about individual salvation. Recently the stark inequities present in Third World nations have forced some evangelical church leaders to consider the need for social justice strategies. Several meetings involving evangelical leaders and statements resulting from those meetings (For example, Consultation on the Theology of Development, 1980; Consultation on the Church in Response to Human Needs, 1983) have supported a social justice approach (Sider, 1982).

The Roman Catholic Church seeks to address social justice issues through many avenues. The U.S. Catholic bishops have asserted that basic human rights must also include a person's economic life—for instance, productive employment, just wages, and adequate income (Branner, 1980). Every four years the U.S. Bishops Conference states its position on human justice issues and produces a statement of political responsibilities. The U.S. Catholic Conference provides the U.S. Bishops Conference with information needed for policy development and collaborates with state and local dioceses by informing them about current church stands and the theological and social needs basis for these stands to mobilize individuals to influence social policy. The Bishops Conference also presents testimony to legislative committees on issues such as economic justice, minimum wage, and family health care legislation. Conference-level directors and officers at the state level also address state and local issues. The Campaign for Human Development raises about $10 million annually to support community organization to create structural change (Nancy Wisdow, U.S. Catholic Conference, personal communication, September 23, 1996). Catholic Charities, the largest nonprofit organization in the country, engages in extensive social action efforts and provides extensive direct services; for example, 11.1 million persons received emergency and other social services in 1994 (Catholic Charities USA, 1995). It also has a mandate to convene people of good will to share this joint vision by promoting compassion and responsible action at the local level (Catholic Charities USA, 1992; Ryle, 1992). Liberation theology, born within the Latin American Roman Catholic Church, has stressed the need to redress social inequality, emphasizing God's identification with the poor and the communal nature of the journey of faith (Gutierrez, 1984). It has influenced the contemporary direction of U.S. Catholic thinking about response to social concerns (Ryle, 1992).

MODERN CHRISTIAN SOCIAL WORK

History

In response to the social stresses and changes that accompanied the Industrial Revolution, expanding immigration, and increased urbanization during the 20th century, many voluntary benevolent groups were established to respond to problems of poverty, health, and child welfare. Church groups (often with a specific ethnic membership) typically would identify a need within their community and respond with a particular program designed primarily to serve the group's own members (Gallagher, 1965; Hugen, 1994). These programs formed the basis for the multitude of sectarian social services organizations in the United States. Although these agencies met important needs within the community, the process of their development resulted in important gaps and overlapping of services. In an effort to close these gaps and coordinate services, many nonsectarian organizations (for example, the Charity Organization Society) grew out of these sectarian agencies (Hugen, 1994). The growing array of Roman Catholic social services organized at the diocesan level has been coordinated at the national level by the National Conference of Catholic Charities (Gallagher, 1965).

Given the financial burden imposed by these growing services, church leaders supported the development of nonsectarian organizations. Because Protestants had the "security of being the majority group in many communities—culturally, financially, and religiously—many Protestant church group leaders were not concerned about letting the support and administration of these societies become community-wide" (Hugen, 1994, p. 87). Thus, Protestant groups continued their efforts through agencies that were conducted under secular auspices. For many individuals who initiated nonsectarian social work programs— for example, Robert Hartley, founder of the Association for Improving the Conditions of the Poor in 1843; Jane Addams, founder of Hull House; and Charles Loring Brace, founder of the Children's Aid Society—Christianity

represented one of the motivating factors for founding such organizations (Abbott, 1963; Costin, 1983; Garland, 1995; Hugen, 1994). Social work thus represented a natural joining of Christian concern and social change efforts without a specific demarcation of Christian and secular social work. As a result, the value base of social work has important religious roots (Constable, 1983; Siporin, 1986).

Despite these early links between social work and Christianity, several factors, identified by Hugen (1994), contributed to the secularization of social work. As social welfare efforts became more community based, a growing division occurred between community welfare concerns and the orientation to Christian charity in terms of control of the purpose and activities of these organizations. The large-scale involvement of the federal government in social welfare efforts furthered this process. In addition, the increased professionalism of social work, with its reliance on science, also hastened the trend toward secularization. Motive (viewed by Mary Richmond as furnished by the church [Gordon, 1965]) and method (based on science) were compartmentalized. Gordon (1965) distinguished between the role of social worker as scientific practitioner and that of social worker as social norms enforcer, with a preference for the neutral scientific practitioner.

However, social work as a vocation or calling as well as a profession continued to remain important for many who viewed themselves as Christian social workers (Keith-Lucas, 1985). The growing emphasis on ethnicity and spirituality (see Canda, "Spirituality," in this supplement) has renewed interest in issues pertaining to religion and social work. Studies of African American, Hispanic, Irish, and Italian groups, for example (McGolderick, Pearce, & Giordana, 1982), pointed out the need to understand the religious beliefs and practices of group members. Other studies have indicated how religious beliefs and organizations can influence the coping efforts of individuals and families generally and especially during times of crisis (Austin & Lennings, 1993; Carlson & Cervera, 1991; Dwyer, Clarke, & Miller, 1990; Hathaway & Pargament, 1991; M. A. Joseph, 1988; Koenig, George, & Siegler, 1988; Loewenberg, 1988; Mailick, Holden, & Walther, 1994).

With greater emphasis within all theoretical models on the need to understand the paradigms and beliefs that shape the life experiences of both social workers and their clients and the recognition that religion can be a crucial element in how people construct their life experiences and the world around them, there has been an increased awareness of the value of including religion when assessing individuals and families (DiBlasio, 1988; Loewenberg, 1988; Lovinger, 1996; Simpson & Ramberg, 1992). Religious beliefs of counselors can also influence how client problems are interpreted and which intervention strategies are viewed as appropriate (Canda, 1988). This greater interest in religion is reflected in articles regarding whether religion should be included as part of the curriculum in schools of social work to help social workers become more knowledgeable about religion, along with suggestions as to how this might be done (Canda, 1989; Netting, Thibault, & Ellor, 1990; Sheridan, Wilmer, & Atcheson, 1994).

Organizational Support for Christian Social Work

Christian social workers have developed professional forums to provide support and advance knowledge in critical areas. Several professional journals are currently devoted to religious and spiritual issues in social work. *Social Work and Christianity: An International Journal* (formerly *Paraclete*) has been published by the North American Association of Christians in Social Work since 1974. *Social Thought,* formerly edited by the National Conference of Catholic Charities and the National Catholic School of Social Services of Catholic University of America, is currently published by Haworth Press as *Social Thought: Journal of Religion in the Social Sciences.*

Christian social workers have also developed professional organizations. The Evangelical Social Work Conference was established in 1950. The name of the organization was changed in 1957 to the National Association of Christian Social Workers and then, six months later, to the National Association of Christians in Social Work as a result of the ongoing dialogue regarding whether "Christian" social work is different from other forms except in its purposes and philosophical underpinnings. The organization was again renamed as the North American Association of Christians in Social Work to acknowledge its active Canadian chapter. It publishes a journal (*Social Work and Christianity: An International Journal,* mentioned

above) and a newsletter (*Catalyst*) and holds professional conferences. The history of the organization reflects some of the struggles and controversies within Christian social work generally—for example, how inclusive or exclusive should Christian social work be, what is the mission of Christian social work, what distinguishes Christian social work, how should one seek to integrate religion and social work, and where does Christian social work stand on public matters (North American Association of Christians in Social Work, 1994).

Social work degree programs, both bachelor of social work and master's of social work programs, have been established at many Roman Catholic and Protestant colleges. However, the extent to which these programs (1) integrate a specifically Christian approach to social work into the typical social work curriculum and (2) work collaboratively with the church community varies widely.

RELIGIOUS ISSUES AND CURRENT SOCIAL WORK PRACTICE

Merely stating that religion (whether it be Christian, Jewish, Hindu, Islam, or other types) should be included in the process of assessing individuals and families does not provide an answer regarding how one should address religious issues in social work counseling or community practice. Astute clinical skills and knowledge of religious beliefs and practices are required, for example, to identify when religious beliefs and practices represent pathological defensives, coping strategies, or manifestations of group membership (Loewenberg, 1988). It is essential to place religion within a broader psychosocial perspective to examine ways in which it serves functional or dysfunctional purposes in the lives of clients (M. V. Joseph, 1987; Loewenberg, 1988; Lovinger, 1996; York, 1987, 1989). Experienced Christian social workers recognize that simplistic religious responses by counselors or others are not helpful and instead can create further burdens for individuals. Thus, Christian social workers must recognize not only the importance but also the complexity of religious issues in any counseling endeavor. In addition to their own efforts toward incorporating religious issues into the counseling process with individuals and families, social workers can work as partners with pastoral counselors, as well as others in the clergy, who have special training in this area (Nakhaima & Dicks, 1995). Including religion in community practice also involves an understanding of the views of church groups toward issues facing the community, as well as such groups' traditions of leadership, organizational structure, and integration with the community at large.

Social work organizations with an explicitly Christian identity sometimes have the challenge of interpreting to the church and the community at large the nature of their purpose. Some community members erroneously assume that these organizations exist to proselytize or to have people adopt a specific Christian code of behavior, or that their staff draw primarily on religious injunctions and practices when working with people.

Religious social work programs generally face new challenges in the contemporary context, in which social work programs are increasingly working under contractual arrangements, with specific criteria for staff and the nature of services. These criteria are particularly present in government contracts. Lutheran Social Services, Catholic Charities USA, the Salvation Army, and other sectarian organizations increasingly are seeking government funds to carry out their social ministry, and these funds come with requirements regarding staffing and programs that go beyond professional standards. Government funds are important for the operation of sectarian agencies (Netting, 1982), with government funding accounting for about half of sectarian agency funding in 1982 (Smith & Lipsky, 1993). Although the government is currently reducing support for social services generally, sectarian organizations such as Catholic Charities USA have become increasingly dependent on funding from government sources. In 1994, Catholic Charities received 62 percent of its income from such sources (Catholic Charities USA, 1995). All agencies, including sectarian ones such as the National Conference of Catholic Charities and the Lutheran Social Service System, that are accredited through the Council on Accreditation of Services for Families and Children must not only document accountability in terms of services provided (Catholic Charities USA, 1992) but also present a statement of affirmative action and hire staff without discrimination, including discrimination on the basis of religion (Loewenberg, 1988), something that obviously is very difficult for sectarian organizations to do.

Everson v. Board of Education (1947) established that no government aid may be given in support of religion, whether a religious group or religion generally, thus creating a wall of separation between church and state (Monsma, 1996). At the same time, a distinction was created between the sacred and secular parts of an organization. Public funds could thus flow to the secular, but not to the sacred, part of an organization. This required proof that an organization and its services were not pervasively religious. Furthermore, the question was raised as to how religious a nonprofit organization could be without being considered pervasively sectarian, with public funds inevitably aiding religion. Sectarian social services agencies have been allowed greater latitude than sectarian educational programs in implementing policies relating to separation of sectarian and secular activities.

These standards of separation can have an important impact on agency decisions in the critical area of hiring. Agencies vary widely in terms of how extensively staff must share the religious perspective of the organization. In *Dodge v. Salvation Army* (1989), a federal district court stated that a publicly funded domestic violence shelter run by the Salvation Army in Mississippi could not fire a domestic abuse counselor, who was a follower of Wicca, on the basis of her religious beliefs; the Salvation Army settled the case out of court instead of appealing to a higher court (Monsma, 1996). However, many organizations appear able to receive large amounts of public funds and still maintain much of their religious autonomy. In *Bowen v. Kendrick* (1988), the Supreme Court further defined the criteria by which social services agencies could obtain government funds. It stated that the government may provide funds to social services agencies with religious ties as long as those agencies are not pervasively sectarian. In practice this means that organizations must make decisions regarding what arrangements and policies will allow them to receive government funding to help them carry out their charitable mission and yet retain the autonomy they need to preserve their religious character. Implementation of these legal decisions can also vary widely depending on the region and the individuals involved. Some have argued that although their motivations to care for the poor are religious, the acts themselves are secular. Others believe that making such a distinction violates their religious identity, because they regard life as an integrated whole (Stronks, 1996).

Although Christian social work is not limited to practice within sectarian agencies, there is evidence that agencies with a religious focus can be especially helpful to some individuals who, because of their culture or religion, are particularly responsive to such an approach. Hispanic drug users, for example, responded especially well to a program incorporating their religious beliefs (Desmond & Maddux, 1984). Belief in a higher power has long been an essential part of the Alcoholics Anonymous movement. People may also feel more comfortable with social workers who they anticipate will understand and respect their view of the world.

CURRENT CONTROVERSIES

Although Christian social workers can agree on certain general positions, their practice in specific situations can vary depending on individual theoretical orientations. Although Christian social workers endorse grace as an essential aspect of life, they vary in their emphasis on the role of sin in the lives of human beings (Loewenberg, 1988). In addition, important differences remain with regard to key issues. These include the legitimacy of abortion (Loewenberg, 1988) and the view of homosexuality as a valid alternative life style (Sherwood, 1993). These differences become especially apparent as social work practice moves beyond direct practice with clients to the realm of policy.

CONCLUSION

Christian social work grew out of a long tradition within both the Christian faith and the origins of social work. It is based on a belief system in which human beings are seen as created in the image of God and on a theology of grace that extends to all people. As defined in this entry, Christian social work is not limited to practice within sectarian social work programs. Social workers who share this Christian vision of social work are employed by both secular and sectarian agencies in virtually all forms of social work practice, encompassing micro-level and macro-level roles, and with a variety of client groups. Christian social work agencies can play an important role for people who are seeking services that specifically address their religious beliefs. Sectarian

agencies face challenges in retaining their unique identity because of greater dependence on government funding and recent legal decisions. Central to all forms of Christian social work are the goals of relief of suffering, empowerment of people to reach their potential as image bearers of God, and restoration of justice.

REFERENCES

Abbott, E. (1963). *Some American pioneers in social welfare.* New York: Russell & Russell.

Austin, D., & Lennings, C. (1993). Grief and religious belief: Does belief moderate depression? *Death Studies, 17,* 487–496.

Bieler, A. (1980). Gradual awareness of social, economic problems (1750–1900). In J. de Santa Ana (Ed.), *Separation without hope? Essays on the relation between the church and the poor during the Industrial revolution and the western colonial expansion.* (pp. 3–29). Maryknoll, NY: Orbis Books.

Bowen v. Kendrick, 487 U.S. 589 (1988).

Branner, G. (1980). Economic justice. *Social Thought, 6*(1), 3–16.

Canda, E. (1988). Spirituality, religious diversity, and social work practice. *Social Casework, 69,* 238–247.

Canda, E. (1989). Religious content in social work education: A comparative approach. *Journal of Social Work Education, 25*(1), 36–45.

Carlson, B., & Cervera, D. (1991). Incarceration, coping, and support. *Social Work, 36,* 279–285.

Catholic Charities USA. (1992). *Cadre Study: Toward a renewed Catholic Charities movement.* Alexandria, VA: Author.

Catholic Charities USA. (1995). *Annual report: The servant leader proclaiming charity and justice.* Alexandria, VA: Author.

Conrad, A. P. (1980). Social ministry in the early church: An integral component of the Christian community. *Social Thought, 6*(2), 41–52.

Constable, P. (1983). Values, religion, and social work practice. *Social Thought, 9*(4), 29–34.

Costin, L. (1983). *Two sisters for justice.* Urbana: University of Illinois Press.

de Santa Ana, J. (Ed.). (1980). *Separation without hope? Essays on the relation between the church and the poor during the Industrial revolution and the western colonial expansion..* Maryknoll, NY: Orbis Books.

Desmond, D., & Maddux, J. (1984). Religious programs and careers of chronic heroin users. *American Journal of Drug Abuse, 8*(11), 7–83.

DiBlasio, F. (198). Integrative strategies of family therapy with evangelical Christians. *Journal of Psychology and Theology, 16,* 127–134.

Dwyer, J., Clarke, L., & Miller, M. (1990). The effect of religious concentration and affiliation on county cancer mortality rates. *Journal of Health and Social Behavior, 31,* 185–202.

Everson v. Board of Education, 330 U.S. 1 (1947).

Gallagher, R. (1965). Catholic social services. In H. Lurie (Ed.), *Encyclopedia of social work* (15th ed., pp. 130–137). New York: National Association of Social Workers.

Garland, D. (1995). Church social work. In R. L. Edwards (Ed.-in-Chief), *Encyclopedia of social work* (19th ed., Vol. 1, pp. 475–483). Washington, DC: NASW Press.

Gordon, W. (1965). Knowledge and value: Their distinction and relationship in clarifying social work practice. *Social Work, 10,* 32–39.

Gutierrez, G. (1984). *We drink from our own wells.* Maryknoll, NY: Orbis Books.

Hall, S. (1979). The common chest concept: Luther's contribution to the 16th century poor relief reform. *Social Thought, 5*(1), 43–54.

Hathaway, W., & Pargament, K. (1991). The religious dimension of coping: Implications for prevention and promotion. *Prevention in Human Services, 9*(2), 65–92.

Hugen, B. (1994). The secularization of social work. *Social Work and Christianity, 21*(2), 83–102.

Joseph, M. (1982). The developmental process of parish social ministries: A decade of experience. *Social Thought, 8*(2), 22–36.

Joseph, M. A. (1988). Religion and social work practice. *Social Casework, 70,* 443–452.

Joseph, M. V. (1987). The religious and spiritual aspects of clinical practice: A neglected dimension of social work. *Social Thought, 13*(1), 12–23.

Keith-Lucas, A. (1985). *So you want to be a social worker: A primer for the Christian student.* St. Davids, PA: North American Association of Christians in Social Work.

Keith-Lucas, A. (1992). Biblical insights into the helping process. *Social Work and Christianity, 19*(1), 6–14.

Keith-Lucas, A. (1996). A Christian response to welfare reform. *Social Work and Christianity, 23*(1), 66–74.

Koenig, H., George, L., & Siegler, I. (1988). The use of religion and other emotion regulation coping strategies among older adults. *Gerontologist, 28,* 303–310.

Loewenberg, F. (1988). *Religion and social work practice in contemporary American society.* New York: Columbia University Press.

Lovinger, R. (1996) Considering the religious dimension in assessment and treatment. In E. Shafranske (Ed.), *Religion and clinical practice of psychology* (pp. 327–364). Washington, DC: American Psychological Association.

Mailick, M., Holden, G., & Walther, V. (1994). Coping with childhood asthma: A caretaker view. *Health & Social Work, 19,* 103–111.

Mason, J. (1996). Biblical teaching and the objectives of welfare policy in the United States. In S. Carlson-Theis & J. Skillen (Eds.), *Welfare in America: Christian perspectives on a policy in crisis* (pp. 145–185). Grand Rapids, MI: Wm. B. Eerdmans.

McGolderick, M., Pearce, J., & Giordana, J. (1982). *Ethnicity and family therapy.* New York: Guilford Press.

Monsma, S. (1996). Overcoming poverty: The role of the religiously based nonprofit organizations. In S. Carlson-Theis & J. Skillen (Eds.), *Welfare in America: Christian perspectives on a policy in crisis* (pp. 426–453). Grand Rapids, MI: Wm. B. Eerdmans.

Mott, S. (1996). Foundations of the welfare responsibility of government. In S. Carlson-Theis & J. Skillen (Eds.), *Welfare in America: Christian perspectives on a policy in crisis* (pp. 189–208). Grand Rapids, MI: Wm. B. Eerdmans.

Nakhaima, J. M., & Dicks, B. H. (1995). Social work practice with religious families. *Families in Society, 76,* 360–368.

Netting, F. (1982). Secular religious funding of church-related agencies. *Social Service Review, 56,* 586–604.

Netting, F. E., Thibault, J. M., & Ellor, J. W. (1990). Integrating content on organized religion into macropractice. *Journal of Social Work Education, 26,* 15–24.

Niebuhr, R. (1932). *The contribution of religion to social work.* New York: Columbia University Press.

North American Association of Christians in Social Work. (1994). *Integrating faith and practice: A history of the North American Association of Christians in Social Work, 1950-1993.* St. Davids, PA: Author.

Paget-Wilkes, M. (1981). *Poverty, revolution, and the church.* Exeter, England: Paternoster Press.

Ryle, E. (1992). The Cadre Study: Twenty years later. In Catholic Charities USA, *Cadre Study: Toward a renewed Catholic Charities movement* (pp. 4–16). Alexandria, VA: Catholic Charities USA.

Sheridan, M. J., Wilmer, C. M., & Atcheson, L. (1994). Inclusion of religion and spirituality in the social work curriculum: A study of faculty views. *Journal of Social Work Education, 30,* 363–376.

Sherwood, D. (1993). Context for dealing with the issue of homosexuality: Love, justice, freedom, diversity. *Social Work and Christianity, 20*(2), 88–95.

Sider, R. (1982). *Evangelicals and development: Toward a theology of change.* Philadelphia: Westminster Press.

Simpson, W., & Ramberg, J. (1992). The influence of religion on sexuality: Implications for sex therapy. *Bulletin of the Menninger Clinic, 56,* 511–523.

Siporin, M. (1986). Contributions of religious values to social work and the law. *Social Thought, 12*(4), 35–50.

Smith S., & Lipsky, M. (1993). *Nonprofits for hire: The welfare state in the age of contracting.* Cambridge, MA: Harvard University Press.

Stronks, J. (1996). Social services agencies and religious freedom: Regulation, funding, and the first amendment. In S. Carlson-Theis & J. Skillen (Eds.), *Welfare reform: Christian perspectives on a policy in crisis* (pp. 480–503). Grand Rapids, MI: Wm. B. Eerdmans.

Tropman, J. E. (1986). The "Catholic ethic" vs. the "Protestant ethic": Catholic social service and the welfare state. *Social Thought, 12*(1), 13–22.

Van Hook, M. P. (1996). Rural poverty: Christian charity and social justice responses. In S. Carlson-Theis & J. Skillen (Eds.), *Welfare reform: Christian perspectives on a policy in crisis* (pp. 348–368). Grand Rapids, MI: Wm. B. Eerdmans.

White, R. (1980). Social reform and the social gospel in America. In J. de Santa Ana (Ed.), *Separation without hope? Essays on the relation between the church and the poor during the Industrial revolution and the western colonial expansion.* (pp. 50–59). Maryknoll, NY: Orbis Books.

York, G. (1987). Religious-based denial in the neonatal intensive treatment unit: Implications for social work. *Social Work in Health Care, 12*(4), 31–45.

York, G. (1989). Strategies for managing the religiously based denial of rural clients. *Human Services in the Rural Environment, 13*(2), 16–22.

Mary P. Van Hook, PhD, ACSW, is associate professor, School of Social Work, University of Central Florida, Orlando, FL 32816-3358.

For further information see
Advocacy; Church Social Work; Citizen Participation; Community Building; Community Organization; Ecological Perspective; Families Overview; **Jewish Communal Services;** Mutual Aid Societies; Natural Helping Networks; Organizations: Context for Social Services Delivery; Sectarian Agencies; Self-Help Groups; Settlements and Neighborhood Centers; Social Welfare History; Social Work Practice: History and Evolution; **Spirituality.**

Key Words

Christian social work	religion
church	spirituality

Code of Ethics
See **Ethical Standards in Social Work: The *NASW Code of Ethics***

Community Building
Arthur J. Naparstek
Dennis Dooley

Certainly the idea of community-based interventions is not new to social work or to work in low-income neighborhoods. Community development has old roots in 19th century utopian and communitarian thought and in the later initiatives of 20th century black leaders and community activists. Comprehensive community strategies were also part of the settlement house movement of the late 19th century and more recently re-emerged in the War on Poverty programs of the 1960s and the community development work done since the mid-1970s (Connell, Kubisch, Schon, & Weiss, 1995).

For social work practice, community has been central for more than 100 years. Spergel (1972), Rubin and Rubin (1992), and Garvin and Cox (1995) each identified major periods in the development of community organization practice. Each author provided a broad overview of the social, political, and cultural forces that have defined the various periods or eras of community organization practice.

Events since the mid-1970s have stimulated the development of new approaches to community intervention. First, major community improvement experiments managed by the federal government (for example, model cities and the Community Action Program) were phased out in the 1970s. Second, in the 1980s, President Reagan put the nation on a fundamentally different course, reducing the federal role in eight areas: income security, health, social services, transportation, housing and community development, employment, training and economic development, and education (Palmer & Sawhill, 1982).

As a result, changes in three broad thematic areas emerged: (1) the shifting of responsibility from state to local governments, (2) a greater reliance on the private sector and the mechanisms of the market, and (3) a narrower targeting of benefits to individuals (Palmer & Sawhill, 1982).

A third change factor that influenced community building came from a ground-breaking 1987 research study in which Wilson documented the internal dynamics of several poor Chicago neighborhoods, suggesting that persistent poverty—the kind of poverty that endures over many years and, with increasing frequency, is passed from one generation to another—is concentrated in geographic areas. He found this kind of poverty in neighborhoods marked by a deteriorated social infrastructure, with fraying or absent networks of churches, schools, banks, businesses, neighborhood centers, and families. The connection between dedicated social support systems and persistent poverty was established; conversely, Wilson also demonstrated the correlation between a strong community and the ability of its residents to get out of poverty (Wilson, 1991).

In response to these three factors, human services agencies and foundations began to seek new ways of thinking about and responding to poverty. During the 1980s, the Ford, Annie E. Casey, and Rockefeller Foundations initiated major community-building programs, often in partnership with community foundations and state and county human services agencies. Kingsley (1996) stated,

Although there are no precise measures, there are indications that community-based action is accelerating in the 1990s. There is also evidence that the approaches of practitioners who come out of very different backgrounds are beginning to converge. CDCs [community development corporations] are now reaching out and working with residents to address a broad range of social issues beyond housing. Community organizers who once focused only on "fighting city hall" are now also working on constructive self-help projects and partnering with outside agencies. Neighborhood leaders are now working together with Police Departments on community policing programs and partnering with city agencies in social service delivery. National foundations are sponsoring *comprehensive community initiatives* in neighborhoods of several cities that attempt to bring together the many strands of the new approach. Local foundations (e.g., in Cleveland and Boston) have sponsored the development of citywide strategies based on the community-building approach and a number of city governments are adapting their own programs to work with community associations as partners. (p. 5)

Today's changing policy environment is causing community organizers and developers to seek new ways to use the largely untapped resource of the low-income community itself: the self-help energy of residents. Organizers and developers are helping residents work on combating crime and drug activity, improving their children's school performance, providing child care, creating small service businesses, learning trade through apprenticeship programs, and linking people to jobs. Moreover, they are coming to appreciate that directing efforts toward strengthening the community itself can build a supportive social environment that creates a more fertile ground for the struggle for independence of individuals.

The dynamic of community building tends to operate spontaneously in neighborhoods marked by a strong social infrastructure (that is, an extensive grassroots network of churches, schools, banks, businesses, and neighborhood centers) that nourishes and supports the life of the community. The purpose of community-building activities as described in this article is to develop and strengthen the basic dynamic of community functioning in neighborhoods where it is not operating well.

Beneath the obvious problems of even the most distressed low-income urban neighborhood lies a great reservoir of human energy and aspiration. However, many residents in these neighborhoods are paralyzed, trapped in poverty—in part because the intangible catalysts found in a community's social life, institutions, and relationships have become weakened.

THE APPROACH: HOW DOES COMMUNITY BUILDING WORK?

Community building is an organized effort to make older and lower-income neighborhoods self-sustaining parts of a productive economy. It builds on traditional social work and community-based intervention strategies by enabling neighborhoods to acquire, develop, and use human, economic, and institutional resources for the benefit of their residents.

It establishes a process that promotes people working together for a common purpose in groups and organizations. The process builds trust and sociability by strengthening family structure and connecting residents to structures such as churches, clubs, unions, community organizations, and other networks of civic engagement (Cleveland Foundation Commission on Poverty, 1992).

Unlike most approaches, community building is not about simply giving money or services to poor people. Its aim is developmental rather than transactional, community-oriented rather than focused on individuals; that is, unlike traditional supportive approaches, it is not centered on transmitting a specific service or "package" of services to an individual in need, performing a transaction that can be clearly defined and completed. Instead, community building is a process. Its goals are the building of the independence of individuals and increasing the healthy functioning of a community. These goals are seen as reciprocal, each strengthening the other (Naparstek, Dooley, & Smith, 1997).

In the past strategies to improve conditions in poor neighborhoods have tended to be categorical in nature. Traditional human services programs—sometimes called *people-based strategies*—offer a defined service or package of services to individuals. *Place-based* community development, in contrast, focuses on physical development, such as housing or commercial structures (Sviridoff, 1994). Community building is both people and place based. It tries to join perspectives from the top down and from the bottom up. In effect, it brings all sides together.

Walsh (1996) noted that community building is complicated in theory and practice. She stated,

> It analyzes urban poverty not simply as a lack of jobs or income, but as a web of interwoven problems—poor schooling, bad health, family troubles, racism, crime and unemployment—that can lock families out of opportunity permanently. Thus, one watch word of the field is "comprehensiveness": to reduce urban

poverty, community builders believe, initiatives must untangle the knot of troubles that trap the urban poor today. Some projects—known as "comprehensive community initiatives"—tackle all those issues themselves in a given neighborhood; others may address a single issue, like infant mortality, comprehensively dealing with the employment, education, health and parenting issues that lead to high infant death rates in poor neighborhoods. Most initiatives fall somewhere in between. Community building is more a framework for analysis and problem solving than a blueprint for urban action. (p. vi)

The question of definition is complex, yet it is clear that a consensus is emerging as to the application of a community-building approach. The consensus relates to a set of community-building principles that, when woven together, set community building apart from other neighborhood-based programs of the past.

Community-building principles are becoming evident in citywide improvement planning in cities throughout the country and are also guiding major public policy initiatives in housing and community development. The principles result from the work of the Cleveland Commission on Poverty (sponsored by the Cleveland and Rockefeller Foundations). The commission report recommended reorienting the city's entire strategy for inner city revitalization around the community-building approach, and it became the basis for the city's successful application for funding under the Empowerment Zone program that is currently in implementation.

The four general principles that have emerged were first put forth by Naparstek, who served as director and principal author of the 1992 *Cleveland Community-Building Initiative: The Report and Recommendations of the Cleveland Foundation Commission on Poverty* (Cleveland Foundation Commission on Poverty, 1992). It is these four principles, taken together, that make this approach distinctive and maximize its chances for success.

COMMUNITY-BUILDING PRINCIPLES

Principle I: Community Building Is Comprehensive and Integrative

Poverty-related problems are interlocking and overlapping, yet previous attempts to combat poverty have ignored this fact, instead isolating specific problems such as housing or job training. Research shows, for example, that there is a relationship among the proliferation of female-headed households, the persistence of poverty over two or more generations, the concentration of poor households in the inner city, and quality-of-life issues such as health and poor outcomes for school-age children. If one is to deal with the issue of female-headed households, unemployment—particularly male unemployment—must be addressed, because the shortage of "marriageable" males in the inner city is directly related to the shortage of employed males. If existing transportation systems are not getting inner-city residents to available jobs, or if the available jobs require a different level of skills from that available in the community, efforts aimed merely at employment are of little use. Similarly, it does little good to offer a young inner-city mother a job if she lacks proper day care for her children or adequate health coverage, or is struggling with other problems in her family that continually deplete her energy and discourage her (Coulton, 1990).

Unfortunately, the social services system as it is currently set up tends to isolate and address various needs as though they were unrelated. Areas of need such as housing or jobs are typically addressed, for example, as if they had nothing to do with health or education.

Housing projects become prisons for the poor and the elderly when issues of crime, security, or city services are not also dealt with. However, the entire system of human services is set up in such a way as to separate all such issues—for example, children's needs from the needs of their parents, health care from job training, and food stamps from completing an education. Each system has evolved its own separate bureaucracy and set of rules and regulations. When systems do not acknowledge these linkages and fail to act with the bigger picture in mind, failure is inevitable.

A community-building approach to alleviating poverty acknowledges the interconnectedness of problems confronting families and recommends a course of action in which solutions are tied together.

Principle II: Community Building Takes Advantage of the New Forms of Collaboration and Partnerships

Because government roles are changing, new ways of proceeding through collaborative decision making are being developed. The movement toward devolution of program authority from the federal to the local level (state and county) through block grants puts substantial pressure on local health, education, and social services agencies to meet local needs. Through devolution of authority to lower levels of government, the federalism of the 1990s is intended to stimulate innovations in service delivery, streamline bureaucracy, and reduce dependency. The key to making this devolution process work, advocates of the community-building approach believe, is the movement away from the categorical approach and toward comprehensive block grants.

In effect, devolution is both a "top-down" and a "bottom-up" process. Experience has shown that either an exclusively top-down or an exclusively bottom-up approach to alleviating poverty is inadequate. An exclusively top-down strategy lacks significant contributions from practitioners, stakeholders, and the intended beneficiaries. On the other hand, approaches that are solely bottom-up, though often effective for building support for single issues, are less likely to produce the comprehensive policy changes that are needed to address more complex realities. Decision-making efforts that concentrate on achieving full consensus are frequently characterized by "least-common-denominator" thinking. In an attempt to reach consensus, these efforts often fail to raise the level of discussion.

Successful strategies borrow effective aspects of each approach by combining leadership and potential for large-scale impact with the impending nature of community-driven initiatives. This new form of collaboration has to be a strategy that strengthens the traditional sources of support in communities— families, churches, social clubs, and other voluntary associations.

In many poor communities informal support and networks that help people are not as effective as they could be. An organization needs to be designed that will (1) support collaboration and build relationships among different organizations; (2) serve as a resource for new ideas and approaches; and (3) provide assistance to build the capacity of local groups to address the community's needs and, most significantly, to link the neighborhood to the larger metropolitan economy. As community-building strategies support residents in many informal, decentralized ways, business and labor force development strategies must be used that are intended to make the neighborhood a source of employees, a place to locate or start a business, or a place to invest money.

Principle III: Community Building Targets Neighborhoods to Enhance Resident Participation

When specific neighborhoods are targeted for intervention, residents become more involved in shaping strategies. The temptation is often to attack the problem of poverty by instituting citywide or metropolitan programs, but we now know that such "macro" approaches are doomed. It is at the neighborhood level that people feel the consequences of policy and planning decisions. Residents have knowledge about their neighborhood, and this knowledge is an essential ingredient to a responsive planning effort. Residents' values, their insights, and their needs as they perceive them must be incorporated into any process for it to be meaningful.

A small-scale focus also minimizes the possibilities of unintended consequences of the sort that can result from defining a program for broad application in a wide variety of circumstances.

Community building involves many intangible forces, such as informal networks of support and leadership, that are critical to any long-term effort. Such relationships must be nurtured and encouraged as part of the process. Any effort directed at changing systems and social structures must focus on a distinct geographic area whose residents are linked by, and who identify with, a cluster of local institutions such as schools, churches, or community centers.

Principle IV: Community Building Builds on Neighborhood Assets

Past efforts have failed to link services and development initiatives to the asset base of a community. Human services practitioners have traditionally taken a deficit- or need-based approach to those being served, focusing on what is lacking. Kretzmann and McKnight (1993) offered a different strategy for empowering low-income communities, starting with the idea that poor neighborhoods also have assets. They likened it to viewing the glass as half full instead of half empty. Mental health, human services, and community and economic development initiatives based on the strengths, resources, and diversities existing in

local communities, they argued, are far more likely to succeed.

Indeed, currently there is empirical evidence that supports the efficacy of community-based networks. Putnam's (1993) comparative study of communities in northern and southern Italy has revealed that networks of civic engagement, such as guilds, religious fraternities, cooperatives, mutual aid societies, and neighborhood associations, are preconditions for economic development.

Two kinds of existing community associations are suited to the job of building a neighborhood's assets and capacities. One is the multi-issue community organization built along coalition lines. Community organizers understand the importance of associational life to the well-being of neighborhoods. Another is the community development corporation (CDC). The CDC's distinguishing characteristics are the comprehensive nature of its purpose and its flexibility. Many CDCs work with a range of neighborhood-based assets in the form of small business, commercial ventures, finance, and housing, often relying on a social planning approach.

When various social work approaches to community interventions are guided by community-building principles, a new approach to practice emerges. For example, Rothman's (1995) three modes of intervention—locality development, social planning and policy, and social action—when taken together or through various configurations, offer the social work field a conceptual framework for a community-building discipline. The broad approaches and set of practice variables Rothman put forth for each mode of intervention offer a range of interrelated possibilities for designing community-building intervention strategies (Rothman, 1995).

The concept of empowerment is integral to community building. Rothman (1995) pointed out that each intervention approach (locality development, social planning, and social action) values empowerment but uses it in a different and sometimes contradictory fashion. For example, for locality development, empowerment signifies the gaining of community competence—that is, the skills to make decisions that people can agree on and enact together. Social planning empowerment is associated with information. In a planning context, empowerment occurs when residents are asked to inform planners about their needs and preferences so that these can be incorporated into a design. Within a social action framework, empowerment means acquiring objective, material power that leads to residents becoming equal partners in decision-making bodies such as agency boards.

Regardless of which mode of intervention is used, the process calls for designing specific mechanisms that allow neighborhood residents to hold the larger systems that ought to be serving them more accountable. At the same time, community-building professionals can assist residents in the shaping of their indigent community's future economic development, along with the development of its human and material resources.

In other words a community-building approach to alleviating poverty helps create a context in which neighborhood residents can rebuild or strengthen the kind of community-based institutions, organizations, and networks that would allow them to escape poverty. It is in the neighborhoods where people live, among familiar faces and relatively accessible institutions, that people most easily can become involved and stand the best chance of regaining some measure of control over their own destinies.

SUPPORTING THE KEY FUNCTIONS OF A HEALTHY COMMUNITY

Proponents of new community-building polices argue that the mistakes made by previous attempts to combat poverty have been in isolating specific needs or problems, such as housing or job training, for intensive intervention. A community-building approach looks at the whole picture, acknowledges the interconnectedness of issues confronting poor families, and recommends a course of action in which solutions are tied together in a neighborhood and in a way in which they reinforce one another. Such an approach calls for specific mechanisms to be used that will give neighborhood residents more control over their lives and the ability to hold accountable the large systems that ought to be serving them. At the same time the community-building process supports the attempts of residents of poor neighborhoods to become active players in the shaping of their community's future competitiveness in such areas as economic development and in all issues confronting family and children.

In January 1990 the Cleveland Foundation's Commission on Poverty was convened in response to growing concerns about the steadily deteriorating conditions in Cleveland's inner-city neighborhoods. Persistent poverty in neighborhoods around the city had reached alarming proportions and threatened to engulf three-fourths of the city by the year 2000.

The commission's proposal for combating poverty through community building is organized in five program frameworks that roughly correspond to the five functions of a healthy community: investment, family development, education, health, and human resource development. Each program area suggests appropriate goals for a neighborhood, evaluates existing assets, and identifies critical components needed to realize the plan as well as a series of practical steps leading to the realization of the neighborhood's goals. The human resource strategy will be discussed in the context of building the capacity of social work education to support community-building initiatives.

FIVE PROGRAM FRAMEWORKS FOR COMMUNITY BUILDING

The fields of activity summarized here* are not ranked in order of importance. The functions they represent are present in all healthy communities. Indeed, activity must take place simultaneously in all of them.

Investment

Investment includes not only jobs but also housing and commercial revitalization—all the things that constitute a community's economic base. The goals that are encouraged or developed, therefore, are (1) establishing healthy residential market forces, (2) establishing communities as competitive locations, (3) reconnecting the resident labor force to the mainstream job market, and (4) fostering the capacity of individual entrepreneurs and organizations to carry out community renewal. Programs leading toward these goals are being carried out by the Enterprise Foundation of Columbia, Maryland, the Local Initiative Support Corporation of New York City, and the Shore Bank Corporation of Chicago.

Each of these goals, pursued strategically, reinforces the others, eventually creating the critical mass of activity necessary to change community market perceptions, both internal and external, which in turn will generate additional investment and reduce the need for subsidy. Special emphasis is placed on minority business development and minority ownership at the neighborhood level through initiatives linked comprehensively to education, training, and the creation of family support services such as health care or day care. A neighborhood asset that often serves as a key building block is the CDC. By using a social planning strategy, the CDC can organize and build partnerships with agencies representing family services, health care, and education (Rothman, 1995).

Family Development

Family development is key to building the community. When the community's support falls short or disappears, the family has trouble fulfilling its basic functions. In recent years this fundamental truth has become clearer than ever. The community and the family are inextricably intertwined: what hurts one hurts the other; what strengthens one strengthens the other. When the family fails to function as it should, the community suffers.

Community building can support families by working to (1) enhance critical family and parenting skills, (2) keep families intact through crisis, (3) build economic opportunities for families, (4) strengthen family-to-family connections, and (5) increase the commitment of families to the community. Programs working toward these goals are being carried out by the Annie E. Casey Foundation's New Future Program, the Child Welfare Reform Initiative, and the Family to Family Cities Program.

Assets that are needed to achieve these family development goals might include centralized facilities that house support network services and provide a communal place for family-oriented programs and activities; a library; child care facilities (comprising infant, toddler, and after-school care for older children); educational facilities; financial services; safe houses and emergency shelters for women and children who are homeless or victims of abuse; and communal associations such as churches, block clubs, parent groups, and play groups that support family activities. An existing neighborhood center or settlement house is an ideal place around which to develop a system of family-centered activities. Key to implementation is the family center.

A community board of parents, residents, service professionals, educators, and business people is set up to guide the design and ongoing development of this family center, offering a constellation of activities for families. Families are not categorized by specific problems but are seen in holistic ways, thus setting the stage for comprehensive approaches.

A support network of resources to help families remain intact and learn parenting skills might include family life, counseling, child development screening, temporary child care, mentoring, and family recreational or social activities. Meanwhile, outreach and home visit services are provided by residents trained to contact isolated families, identify family needs, initiate family center participation, and facilitate access to services in and outside the center.

Achieving the goal of enhancing child development and parenting skills requires the establishment of early childhood education programs in the community, if they do not already exist, along with flexible child care drop-in services convenient to parents who choose to avail themselves of educational and employment services.

The family center can be built around a child care drop-in center developed specifically with early childhood activities in mind. Here parents can interact with their children, with other parents, and with trained staff in a nonthreatening, hospitable environment. Center staff help parents learn how to support their children's healthy development by showing them, for example, how best to advocate for their children in school and how best to work with the school in planning their children's education.

Education

Education focuses on (1) encouraging and enabling high academic performance among elementary school children; (2) providing education readiness for preschool children; and (3) expanding educational opportunities for adults, both for them to grow in their understanding of their children's development and for them to acquire the training necessary to get and hold jobs. Programs leading to these goals are being carried out by the Beacon School program in New York City and selected charter schools throughout the United States.

To achieve the first of these goals, a community focuses its energies on elementary education, with a view to building traditions of excellence from the early years. Ways are also found to provide family and community supports that will enable children to benefit from effective elementary education.

A community embarking on such a highly collaborative undertaking should be able to identify in its midst a number of indispensable assets that can be built on to provide a comprehensive approach. Such assets include families involved in their children's education, both at home and in the classroom; residents and business and professional people willing to use their skills and resources to support activities; educators ready to commit time and effort both in and outside the classroom; and a facility of sufficient capacity to support planned uses without overcrowding.

The community also needs access to two critical resources: (1) innovative models for urban education, development of school staff, and parent involvement and (2) key assets whose control lies outside the community, such as libraries, institutions of higher learning, cultural organizations, facilitators, and technical consultants.

A community advisory group composed of parents, residents, leaders, business people, educators, and service professionals is formed to guide school curriculum and program design as well as community participation. Programming that results must be flexible enough to accommodate the educational initiatives and priorities adopted by the advisory group and the community. The school building should be seen as a community resource for pursuing those priorities and initiatives.

To achieve the second goal—providing educational readiness for preschool children—the community first identifies a core group of families in its midst who are committed to developing their children's capabilities from birth; professionals in early childhood development and family outreach services who can help families help their children; as well as facilities and other personnel (existing or potential) that can provide early childhood development supports. The community then sets about building informal networks of residents with knowledge, skills, and time to invest in young children.

As in meeting the first goal, the same or a different advisory group guides the design of integrated services for preschool children. These services might include such things as pre- and postnatal health care; the identification and treatment of illness, environmental contaminants, or handicapping conditions that, if undetected and untreated, could reduce a child's ability to benefit from effective education; and parent support such as family literacy and parenting programs.

Early childhood facilities and programs (both day care and preschool) that maximize parent access and participation are set up, along with a family support system, to involve and track families from the prenatal stage onward, troubleshoot family problems, and identify needs for intervention and opportunities for improving services. Opportunities must be created for parents to grow in their understanding of child development and share these skills with other parents in the community.

Health

Health affects many areas of an individual's, and a family's, life. Minorities, despite recent advances in medical science and health care, continue to experience illness and death at disproportionately higher rates than the rest of the population.

Community-building activities are focused, therefore, on three program goals:

1. increasing, both in quantity and quality, community and primary health care services available to the residents of the community, with emphasis on the prevention and treatment of those conditions that afflict inner-city and poor people of color at disproportionate rates
2. implementing effective services aimed at treatment and control of existing health conditions that are accessible to community residents
3. devising programs to alleviate and reduce disability resulting from disease and poor health conditions and to restore effective functioning by making existing rehabilitation services more accessible.

Programs working toward these goals can be found in the Metro Hospital Health Program in Cleveland, Ohio.

In addressing the first goal, major emphasis should be put on preventing and treating heart disease and stroke, cancer, diabetes, substance abuse, infant mortality, and both unintentional and intentional injuries, with specific goals and priorities established by the residents of the neighborhood. In addition to a system of trained outreach workers, other entities that constitute community assets in achieving the first goal are families, schools, centers, churches—even gangs willing to identify and encourage individuals to participate in violence reduction and programs teaching alternative means of conflict resolution—as well as courts and police willing to refer individuals to and cooperate and participate in such programs.

With regard to the second goal, such an undertaking usually begins by identifying the epidemiology of treatable diseases in the community and then determining the residents' understanding of the impact and pathophysiology of these diseases, including their relationship to sociocultural practices such as smoking, eating habits, and methods of dealing with psychological stress. A community health advisory board or subcommittee of a neighborhood council, at least 40 percent of whose members are local residents (with providers and others constituting the remainder), then sets the community's own priorities for the implementation of secondary prevention services.

Finally, with regard to the third goal, many such programs are currently provided by medical centers and outpatient clinics, public and private agencies, and self-help groups. Neighborhood residents who have already been through such programs are recruited along with others and trained as outreach referral and "health aides." A network of rehabilitation service providers is simultaneously established that consists of professionals and agencies willing to accept referrals of individuals of all ages for assessment and remedial and rehabilitation services. Eligible people are sent to the state office of vocational rehabilitation.

Providing community-based tertiary care requires the availability of, or arrangement for, outreach services from a neighborhood service center and special transportation services to specialized rehabilitation centers and sheltered workshops. A network of neighborhood-based self-help organizations can provide some services directly to people recovering from illness and their families.

Human Resource Development

Human resource development is the most important ingredient in the recipe for community building. The key to alleviating poverty is the people whose job it is to make change happen. It is people who drive the process, and people who must provide the skills, knowledge, or facilitation necessary to achieve progress.

For that reason, a plan for identifying, developing, and training those individuals for community building is an essential part of the approach. One component of the plan is to link community building to social work education in the form of a new speciality that requires competency in the processes of place-based, people-based strategies. Familiarity with community theory, community organization, and competency in the process of physical and economic development combined with core knowledge of social work values and commitment to grassroots participation is needed.

Community building requires that different roles be played by those engaged in services that have traditionally supported inner-city communities. Building on the principles of community building and using Rothman's (1995) intervention strategies, new approaches to work in the community must be developed in the following areas: investment in housing, jobs and economic development, health, education, human services, and family development.

Community building is best done by a professional who has competence in relating macrolevel relationships to microlevel practice. Rothman (1995) noted that in this pattern, macro-oriented community intervention, with its emphasis on structural change, prevention, and social reform, is matched with micro-oriented intervention (that is, casework, counseling, case management, clinical treatment), with an emphasis on personal renewal. Thus, a social worker practicing community building needs to be a versatile professional who can relate to various generic practice approaches (Rothman, 1995).

In 1991, a faculty committee at the University of Pittsburgh School of Social Work proposed a framework for a new specialty within the Master of Social Work major in community organization skills. The faculty committee proposed that the social worker have competence in both the processes of grassroots decision making and the valued skills of human services, economic development, and housing. The technical skills required include those related to (1) organizing the construction of affordable housing, (2) starting and expanding small businesses, (3) linking unemployed persons to training and jobs, and (4) planning and promoting private and public projects that help achieve social equity through redistribution of resources.

The challenge for the field is to develop a curriculum in support of community building that is interdisciplinary and part of a continuum of educational opportunities from high school to college (Associate of Arts programs in human services, Bachelor of Social Work programs, and Master of Social Work programs). Work in this area is being carried out at the Mandel School of Applied Social Sciences, Center for Community Development at Case Western Reserve University, Cleveland, Ohio. A Kellogg Foundation grant is supporting the effort.

Any program that is developed should be comprehensive in design, providing opportunities for education and training of community leaders. The program should be guided by the following four goals:

1. Educational programs should be developed to educate students in a perspective that begins with assets, values, and self-reliance and respects the wholeness and complexity of families and communities.
2. The number of minority professionals active in, and available to, community-building institutions should be increased.
3. Opportunities should be taken to build the capacity of neighborhood leaders to bring about community building through the empowerment of people.
4. A large number of staff workers in community organizations and specialized agencies should be recruited and trained in the principles and techniques of community building to help implement these new programs for these workers, who would be given the option of obtaining a degree or credentials in social work or human services at the associate, bachelor's, or master's degree level.

The key to the viability of a human resource strategy is establishing a partnership between schools of social work and the community to collaborate on achieving the four goals. For example, to achieve several of these goals, a community must be able to identify and build on a number of assets. These include high schools and nearby institutions of higher education that are interested in training workers in this perspective; agencies and professionals living or working in the community who are willing to create opportunities for community members to join them in the decision-making process and the workplace; educators able to share their knowledge and experience concerning such things as building from strength, empowerment, and holistic approaches to building neighborhoods; and, last but not least, locations convenient to the three groups just mentioned where training can occur.

Other institutions of higher learning that offer certificate programs or degrees in related fields (health, recreation, public administration, law), as well as periodic workshops on issues of special interest, would also be helpful, as would high schools offering a concentration in community building, a Young Leaders program, or a program of community service in which students can participate.

Similarly, a community's ability to address the second goal requires that there be minority members of the community, especially community-based organization leaders, interested in being trained for leadership positions and in training others in various capacities; training locations convenient to these groups; and agencies and institutions in both the public and private sectors willing to provide minority opportunities.

Talent could also be recruited from historically black colleges and universities for positions in this initiative, with similar assets being identified in the case of each of the respective goals outlined. An example includes a neighborhood-level leadership development program and collaboration workshops for all professionals involved, focusing on the key concepts of and the skills needed for community building.

A FRAMEWORK FOR THE IMPLEMENTATION OF A COMMUNITY-BUILDING APPROACH: VILLAGE-BASED DEVELOPMENT

As noted, the research findings of Wilson (1991), Putnam (1993), and Naparstek, Biegel, and Spiro (1982) compellingly establish the connections between poverty and weakened community support networks—beginning with the family. A community-building approach seeks to combat poverty through strengthening community at the neighborhood level.

Community-based activities of a positive nature must be identified; supported; fostered, where necessary; and, perhaps most important, linked together so that they reinforce one another and build the capacity of residents to manage their own lives.

In most low-income inner-city communities, the obstacles to progress are formidable. Jobs are scarce. Many city neighborhoods lack an adequate economic base with which to generate jobs or further development. The housing stock is deteriorating. Crime abounds, inhibiting normal commerce and new investment and offering self-destructive alternatives to disillusioned youth. Positive role models tend to move away. Schools are failing as the gateway to a better life. Furthermore, the current system of meeting human needs is having the unintended effects of fostering dependency and fragmenting family life instead of making it stronger.

The community-building approach, in brief, is a plan for organizing residents to overcome obstacles and meet challenges. It begins with a process, not a prescription, because it is important to discover what will work in a particular neighborhood and how real solutions can most effectively be crafted and put into place. The process, in other words, is as important as the product; for constructive measures to be meaningful, the parties involved must take ownership of them—indeed, they must have a hand in determining the shape they take.

Different neighborhoods have different needs and meet those needs in different ways. Therefore, a strategy for a neighborhood composed of seniors will be different from a strategy for neighborhoods of young families. However, the keys to each community-building strategy are the four guiding principles. The strategies for implementation must be (1) both comprehensive and integrated; (2) actively involve residents; (3) develop new forms of partnerships and collaboration; and (4) begin by focusing on assets, not deficits.

The principles suggest that implementation of the program areas be targeted to specific geographic areas in a city. The Cleveland Foundation Commission on Poverty report (1992) recommended that these targeted areas be defined as *villages*. The report stated that

the urban village has been chosen as the ideal unit for testing such community-building approaches. This microcosm of urban society, with its web of interdependent relationships and readily accessible institutions, offers both

the opportunities and to a large extent the means of building community. It is at the village level that individuals and families function most comfortably and knowledgeably and, therefore, have the best chance of regaining control over their lives. (p. 6)

It was the strong concurrence of the commission that villages must be geographically and socially defined with the participation of those individuals and institutions who are stakeholders in the area; that assets, both in and out of the village, must be identified that will support the development of initiatives in the fields of investment, education, family development, health, and human resources; and that a significant part of a village's overall strategy should be concerned with assisting its residents to gain access to assets located in the village. (It is currently accepted by many urban scholars that the ability to find and hold jobs is tied to neighborhood job networks and the support, both moral and practical, of neighborhood institutions. Creating linkages between these networks and assets therefore should be central to a village's strategy to combat poverty.)

It was further agreed that each village chosen for participation ought to have an existing indigenous institution of some stature—for example, a hospital, a major community development corporation, a well-regarded neighborhood center, a church, or an appropriate school—and the village should be situated in sufficient proximity to a major institution or commercial development that can provide access to jobs and economic development.

In large part the definition of the village will be based on the perceptions of the residents. The commission recognized that within each of these villages, there are distinct community identities and differing neighbor-to-neighbor expectations that have a profound influence on community building. For this reason, it is crucial that the residents be invited and encouraged to identify with the village's program.

Two interrelated challenges confront a community-building implementation plan. First, the relationships between the residents of a community are not always geographic in nature but frequently develop through institutions such as churches and voluntary associations or an individual's or family's social networks. Thus, a goal must be to identify an effective way to mesh a strategy of geographic targeting with one that works with, and strengthens, informal human support networks that are independent of place. These networks can also be used by residents to reach the goals in each of the program fields. Second, there is a need to coordinate the program framework so as to avoid fragmentation and establish linkages between program areas. To this end, village councils need to be organized. The councils should be made up of residents and other village stakeholders and should take a leadership role in defining the specifics of the intervention to be undertaken; fostering collaborative action; and implementing strategies in the areas of investment, education, family development, and human resource development. The councils should bring these diverse entities together around an agreed-on set of goals for the village and link them as a group to external institutions and other entities outside the village.

Conclusion

Since the 1930s, programs have looked at poverty and need as if they were a seamless problem, unrelated to other forces and amenable to monolithic solutions "parachuted in" from somewhere above. More recently, however, communities around the nation are turning away from piecemeal efforts and beginning instead to act in a concerted fashion to create the context and the mechanisms through which residents of persistently poor neighborhoods can regain some control over their lives. In cities throughout the country, local networks have created new organizations that are bottom-up development efforts. Thus, a new form of empowerment based on old social work values is emerging.

The stresses on our social system have forced communities to draw on hidden resources to create new modes of problem solving and new ways of distributing power. These new social forms of partnerships and networking are arising within the organizing shell of community building. Social work values are consistent with this new form of practice.

References

Cleveland Foundation Commission on Poverty. (1992). *The Cleveland community-building initiative: The report and recommendations of the Cleveland foundation commission on poverty.* Cleveland: Case Western Reserve University.

Connell, J., Kubisch, A., Schon, L., & Weiss, C. (1995). *New approaches to evaluating community initiative: Concepts, methods and contexts.* Washington, DC: Aspen Institute.

Coulton, C. (1990). *Neighborhood profiles: A profile of social and economic conditions in the city of Cleveland.* Cleveland: Case Western Reserve University, Mandel School of Applied Social Sciences, Center for Urban Poverty and Social Change.

Garvin, C., & Cox, F. (1995). A history of community organizing since the Civil War with special reference to oppressed communities. In J. R. Rothman, J. Erlich, & J. Tropman (Eds.), *Strategies of community intervention.* Itasca, IL: F. E. Peacock.

Kingsley, G. T. (1996). *Community building: Coming of age.* Draft paper prepared for the Development Training Institute/Urban Institute. Washington, DC: Urban Institute.

Kretzmann, J., & McKnight, J. (1993). *Building communities from the inside out: A path toward finding and mobilizing a community's assets.* Evanston, IL: Northwestern University Center for Urban Affairs and Policy Research.

Naparstek, A., Biegel, D., & Spiro, H. (1982). *Neighborhood networks for human mental health care.* New York: Plenum Press.

Naparstek, A., Dooley, D., & Smith, R. (1997). *Community building in public housing: Ties that bind people and their communities.* Washington, DC: U.S. Department of Housing and Urban Development.

Palmer, J., & Sawhill, J. (1982). Perspectives on the Reagan experiment. In J. Palmer & J. Sawhill (Eds.), *The Reagan experiment* (p. 5). Washington, DC: Urban Institute.

Putnam, R. (1993). *Making democracy work: Civic traditions in modern Italy.* Princeton, NJ: Princeton University Press.

Rothman, J. (1995). Approaches to community interventions. In J. R. Rothman, J. Erlich, & J. Tropman (Eds.), *Strategies of community intervention.* Itasca, IL: F. E. Peacock.

Rubin, H., & Rubin, I. (1992). *Community organization and development.* New York: Macmillan.

Spergel, J. (1972). *Community organization: Studies in constraint.* Beverly Hills, CA: Sage Publications.

Sviridoff, M. (1994). The seeds of urban revival. *The Public Interest, 114,* 82–103.

Walsh, J. (1996). *Stories of renewal: Community building and the future of urban America.* New York: Rockefeller Foundation.

Wilson, W. J. (1991). Public policy research and the truly disadvantaged. In C. Jencks & P. Peterson (Eds.), *The urban underclass* (pp. 460–482). Washington, DC: Brookings Institution.

Arthur J. Naparstek, PhD, is Grace Longwell Coyle Professor of Social Work, Mandel School of Applied Social Sciences, Case Western Reserve University, 10900 Euclid Avenue, Cleveland, OH 44106-7164. **Dennis Dooley, MA,** is consultant, Cleveland, OH.

For further information see
Advocacy; **Chaos Theory and Complexity Theory; Christian Social Work;** Citizen Participation; Civil Rights; Community; Community Development; Community Needs Assessment; Community Organization; Community Practice Models; Ethics and Values; Fundraising and Philanthropy; Human Rights; Interdisciplinary and Interorganizational Collaboration; **Jewish Communal Services;** Management Overview; Mass Media; Mutual Aid Societies; Natural Helping Networks; **Oppression;** Peace and Social Justice; Poverty; Rural Social Work Overview; Settlements and Neighborhood Centers; Social Planning; Social Welfare; Social Workers in Politics; Unions; Volunteer Management.

Key Words	
community building	community
community	organizing
development	village development

Complexity Theory

See **Chaos Theory and Complexity Theory**

Confidentiality

See Legal Issues: Confidentiality and Privilege; **Legal Issues: Recent Developments in Confidentiality and Privilege**

Cost Measurement

See **Management: Cost Measurement**

D

Divorce
Ellen B. Bogolub

The divorce rate in the United States rose rapidly in the 1960s and 1970s and stabilized at a high level during the 1980s and 1990s (Greenstein, 1995; Simons & Associates, 1996). Approximately one in every two marriages currently ends in divorce (Johnson & Wahl, 1995), with a slightly higher rate for second marriages (Ganong & Coleman, 1994).

Although divorce settlements among the rich garner much public attention, most divorces occur among ordinary people. Specifically, divorce correlates with low income (Ganong & Coleman, 1994; Guttmann, 1993) and low educational level (Guttmann, 1993). It also correlates with a couple's young age at marriage (Guttmann, 1993; Kitson, 1992). Although most divorces take place during young adulthood (Bee, 1994), marital rupture has been on the rise among midlife and older couples since the mid-1980s (National Center for Health Statistics, 1992).

Divorce is far more common among African Americans than among whites (Lawson & Thompson, 1995, 1996), occurring in two out of three African American couples (Staples, 1985). Among Hispanic Americans, the divorce rate is similar to that of non-Hispanic whites (Longres, 1995), but the divorce rate for Puerto Ricans is much higher than that for other Hispanic subgroups (Chillman, 1993). Asian Americans are at very low risk for marital disruption (Chiriboga, Catron, & Associates, 1991; Yu, 1993), and little is known about divorce among other ethnic groups (Chiriboga et al., 1991). Overall, when working with divorcing and divorced families, social workers encounter couples who are usually young, although the number of middle-aged or older couples is increasing; limited in their employment options and earnings; and ethnically diverse.

REASONS FOR DIVORCE
Most divorces are initiated by women (Mitchell-Flynn & Hutchinson, 1993), and the main reason for the high divorce rate is generally thought to be women's labor force participation (Cherlin, 1992; Guttmann, 1993; Johnson & Wahl, 1995). Paid employment lessens women's economic dependence on men and increases their ability to reject objectionable marital situations ranging from lack of affection to physical abuse. Marriages beset by a lack of communication are often rejected after a husband dismisses his wife's views on a life that violates her values or is unappealing; when the wife becomes exasperated and wishes to file for divorce, employment can enable her to proceed.

Female employment may also encourage male divorce initiation; with the decline in full-time homemaking among women, motivation for men to stay married for payment in kind for earning a living has waned (Bogolub, 1995). In addition, men who do not have an exclusive "breadwinning" responsibility for their children may have fewer qualms about leaving them than did their counterparts in a more traditional era (Furstenberg, 1988).

Feminism, which promotes the value and social acceptability of women regardless of marital status, is an influence on some divorcing women. However, other divorcing women— for example, Hispanic Americans and Asian Americans reared traditionally—may believe in traditional gender roles and remain uninfluenced by feminist views (Del Carmen & Virgo, 1993; Yu, 1993).

The high divorce rate among African Americans can be attributed to several factors. First, African American husbands may experience difficulty fulfilling breadwinning responsibilities because of employment discrimination (Franklin, 1992) or changes in the economy that limit black male labor force participation (Lawson & Thompson, 1995); financial strain can lead to marital tension. Second, the high female-to-male ratio among African Americans (Bulcroft & Bulcroft, 1993; Lawson & Thompson, 1995) may lead African American men to consider dissolution as a response to marital problems (Taylor, Chatters, Tucker, & Lewis, 1990). Third, the widespread economic independence of African American women and the tradition of supportive extended family may combine to deplete marriage of some of its importance as a basis for family life among African Americans (Bulcroft & Bulcroft, 1993; Cherlin, 1992).

ADULTS AND OFFSPRING AFTER DIVORCE: AN OVERVIEW

The vast majority of divorces involve offspring (Arendell, 1995), but a minority occur in brief, child-free marriages that end before age 30 (Schupack, 1994). Such dissolutions may constitute a time-limited trauma for both men and women (Schupack, 1994), but the ongoing responsibilities and ties that characterize divorced parents are absent.

In offspring-involved divorce, depending on the length of the marriage, children, adolescents, or young adults may be affected. A small proportion of divorced couples with children opt for joint residential custody (Maccoby & Mnookin, 1992), and the small proportion of divorced fathers with sole custody is increasing (Eggebeen, Snyder, & Manning, 1996). Nonetheless, more than 85 percent of children whose parents are divorced are currently in the custody of their mothers (Arendell, 1995).

Economic Issues

Mother-custody families. When compared with the predivorce intact family, the postdivorce mother-custody family almost always experiences a long-term decrease in standard of living. Although the well-known 73 percent decrease Weitzman (1985) reported has been revised to 27 percent by Peterson (Peterson, 1996; Weitzman, 1996), both Weitzman and Peterson, as well as others, agree that the income decrease in mother-custody homes is major (Arendell, 1995; Kitson, 1992; Maccoby & Mnookin, 1992; Peterson, 1996; Weitzman, 1996).

Income decline may occur because a mother, now on her own, works in a low-paying, sex-segregated field. It may also occur because of the gender-wage gap: When women work in fields that are not sex segregated, they receive less pay than men doing the same work (Kissman & Allen, 1993). In addition, women

are less likely than men to have uninterrupted work histories. Finally, child support from a noncustodial father, which may or may not be available (Meyer & Bartfield, 1996; Meyer, Bartfield, Garfinkel, & Brown, 1996), does not fully compensate for the paternal salary provided before divorce.

Two-thirds of women remarry within three to five years after divorce (Cherlin, 1992). Most experience some improvement in their financial situation but without duplication of the predivorce standard of living (Morgan, 1991). Because the remarriage rate is dropping (Ganong & Coleman, 1994) and the average remarriage lasts only five years (Bray & Berger, 1993), the financial bonus of remarriage is less and less likely, and usually temporary. In addition, compared with white women, African American women are less likely to remarry (Del Carmen & Virgo, 1993), in part because of the high female-to-male ratio among African Americans (Bulcroft & Bulcroft, 1993; Lawson & Thompson, 1995). Hispanic women are also less likely than white women to remarry (Del Carmen & Virgo, 1993), in part because of Roman Catholic views about divorce. Overall, it is incorrect to assume that remarriage will eventually solve a custodial mother's financial problems, although it does help somewhat (Morgan, 1991).

Father-custody families and joint custody families. Divorce-generated financial problems in father-custody families and joint residential custody families are fewer, as the parents involved tend to have relatively high incomes (Eggebeen et al., 1996; Maccoby & Mnookin, 1992). In addition, in these family types, the father's financial commitment is not limited by the amount of a child support award. Still, economic constraints arise, largely because in both cases mothers' and fathers' incomes must sustain two postdivorce households.

Psychosocial Issues

Because divorce entails massive changes, both ex-husbands and ex-wives are at risk for anxiety, depression, loneliness, and anger during the two to three years following the divorce (Bogolub, 1995). For those who initiate marital rupture as well as those who assent to it, divorce-generated losses (for example, of shared life, income, and social status) may create a sense of bereavement (Butler, Mellon, Stroh, & Stern, 1995; Guttmann, 1993; Kitson, 1992). However, by three to $3^{1}/_{2}$ years after the separation, most adults are coping well with their responsibilities and feeling much better emotionally than when they were recently separated (Kitson, 1992; Maccoby & Mnookin, 1992). And, some adults—particularly those who initiate divorce—experience feelings of independence, mastery, and relief as soon as marital rupture occurs. A minority of adults, mostly women, remain depressed after divorce (Kitson, 1992).

Parallel to adults, daughters and sons are likely to exhibit temporary upset and behavioral deterioration after divorce (Curtner-Smith, 1995; Furstenberg & Cherlin, 1991). It is interesting to note that such responses occur among African American offspring as well as among other offspring; neither the frequency of divorce in the African American community nor the relative ease African American mothers demonstrate in assuming postdivorce responsibilities (Bussell, 1995; Kitson, 1992) appears to decrease the impact of divorce on African American youths. Like other youths, they demonstrate a wide range of cognitive and emotional responses to parental marital rupture (Bussell, 1995).

As custodial parents regain the parenting skills that are temporarily diminished by divorce, most offspring resume normal development (Curtner-Smith, 1995; Furstenberg & Cherlin, 1991). Resumption of normal development is also affected by temperament (that is, level of innate vulnerability to external events) (Bee, 1994). Compared with daughters and sons with sensitive temperaments, those with resilient temperaments often take less time to accept marital rupture and return to their prior functioning level. Sibling support, when present, can also facilitate this process (Bogolub, 1995).

Although children who experience parental divorce are at some risk for low educational attainment, early childbearing, limited labor force participation (McLanahan & Sandefur, 1994), and divorce (Kitson, 1992), most children who experience parental divorce do not experience these outcomes. Rather, most are reared to competent adulthood by custodial mothers, regardless of whether the noncustodial father remains in contact (Furstenberg & Cherlin, 1991; McLanahan & Sandefur, 1994).

Mother-Custody Families

A mother-custody family has distinct divorce-generated experiences, both in its transactions with the environment and in its family relationships.

Transactions with the Environment

Household moves. Because of decreased income, a divorcing woman and her children typically face a household move, sometimes to a substandard or dangerous neighborhood. Schools may be inferior to those the children previously attended, and postdivorce families are more likely to be crime victims than predivorce families (McLanahan & Sandefur, 1994). If the woman is not employed when she exits the marriage, the first move may be to a shelter for the homeless rather than to a house or an apartment. If the woman is fleeing domestic violence, the first move may be to a shelter for battered women. Perhaps because of the many economic and social transitions marital rupture entails, divorced women tend to move more than their married counterparts (McLanahan & Sandefur, 1994).

Relative to white women, African American and Hispanic women are more likely to double up with extended family when divorce occurs (Walsh, 1991). Such a move generally results in lowered housing costs and assistance with child rearing, although intergenerational conflict may arise (Boyd-Franklin, 1989; Timberlake & Chipungu, 1992).

Increasing income. Once housed, a woman must often upgrade her income situation by beginning or resuming employment, increasing her work hours, or seeking advancement. If this is not possible, either because of labor market constraints or emotional stress, she may seek public assistance. Employed, younger divorced mothers almost always experience responsibility overload and time poverty as they juggle employment and child rearing, even when the extended family assists. If they are on their own and dependent on day care, the burden is even greater.

Older divorced mothers with adolescent and young adult children generally do not face the physical drain that younger mothers do. However, as they enter or re-enter the labor force, these women may face age discrimination or difficulty in obtaining up-to-date skills for a changed job market. In addition, middle- and upper-middle-class divorced women who were raised in a prefeminist era may resent having to earn a living (Wallerstein, 1986).

Among both younger and older mothers, African American women, because of a cultural emphasis on women's employment (Fine,

McKenry, & Chung, 1992), may be particularly well prepared for economic survival after divorce. In contrast, Hispanic women, depending on the degree of traditional emphasis in their upbringing, may be more oriented to homemaking than to economic self-sufficiency (Longres, 1995); traditionally reared Hispanic women may experience conflict as they begin job searches.

Obtaining legal assistance. A divorcing woman with children needs to obtain the services of a private attorney, legal services attorney, or divorce mediator to arrange a legal agreement with her ex-husband regarding custody, visitation, and child support. Agreement about custody and visitation matters, even if a father lacks interest in his children; divorce terms can serve as "insurance" against any unpredictable future behavior. A child support award is increasingly important, because the federal and state laws that establish award amounts and collection procedures are increasingly strict (Meyer & Bartfield, 1996; Meyer et al., 1996). Although women on public assistance should apply for awards, they may be discouraged to learn that local governments keep most, but not all, of any child support collected (Eckholm, 1992).

Less often, women should pursue alimony awards and property division agreements. Alimony is received by only 10 percent to 20 percent of divorced women (Fine & Fine, 1994). Generally, they are middle-aged and originally of relatively high income status (Weitzman, 1988). The current trend toward short-term or "rehabilitative" alimony (Fine & Fine, 1994) is based on the erroneous assumption that middle-aged women, with training, can earn income commensurate with that of their ex-husbands (Weitzman, 1988). Still, women receiving alimony awards do gain a temporary financial boost.

Most divorcing couples have little property to divide (Seltzer & Garfinkel, 1990). However, when property is an issue, custodial mothers need to be concerned about obtaining a distribution that takes into account the large size of the mother-custody household relative to the size of the father's household.

Family Relationships

Custodial mothers and their offspring. The many life changes in the two- to three-year transition after divorce diminish the security, stability, and routine that all children need

(Curtner-Smith, 1995). Children and adolescents may react strongly, often expressing in behavior rather than words emotions such as anxiety or anger about financial deprivation. Although young adult offspring were initially presumed to be relatively unaffected by marital disruption (Cooney & Kurz, 1996), research indicates they may experience emotions such as depression (Cooney & Kurz, 1996) or guilt that parents postponed ending an unhappy marriage because of them (Cain, 1989).

During this period of increased offspring need, many custodial mothers have difficulty parenting optimally (Cherlin, 1992; Guttmann, 1993). Preoccupied and overwhelmed, they may minimize or ignore offspring responses to divorce (Kitson, 1992; Walsh, 1991). Custodial mothers may also be unable to provide appropriate affection, role models, or discipline.

To compensate, children, adolescents, and young adults sometimes rely on other sources for attention. These include siblings, grandparents and other extended family members, and teachers. African American youths are likely to find supportive adults through churches (Boyd-Franklin, 1989; Ho, 1992), whereas Hispanic youths may develop connections with *compadrazgo,* or nonblood kin, created during life-cycle events such as baptism (Chillman, 1993).

A minority of custodial mothers have continued difficulty parenting after the divorce transition, but most gradually resume competent maternal functioning (Cherlin, 1992; Walsh, 1991)—that is, they are less self-absorbed and demonstrate adequate zest, affection, consistency, and ability to discipline.

As mother-custody homes stabilize, particular patterns are likely to arise. For example, relative to their counterparts in two-parent families, custodial mothers are more likely to delegate responsibility (Del Carmen & Virgo, 1993). Children may perform household chores, and adolescents and young adults may contribute money in addition to household chores; young adults may provide emotional support to the mother as well (Cooney, Hutchinson, & Leather, 1995). Although excessive demands on offspring may impede normal development (Kissman & Allen, 1993), a degree of extra responsibility may in fact heighten offspring competence (Del Carmen & Virgo, 1993). With some exceptions, over the long run the custodial mother generally learns to respond constructively to the needs generated in this distinct family form.

Noncustodial fathers and their offspring.
Daughters and sons experience a major loss when their fathers move out. If the relationship with the father was warm and loving, the loss is particularly painful. Even if the relationship was distant or troubled, the change is still unsettling. However, exceptions occur in cases of paternal brutality, when a father's departure may evoke relief.

A minority of fathers, most often those of relatively high socioeconomic status, maintain regular financial support (Meyer & Bartfield, 1996) and visitation (Stephens, 1996) after a divorce. Such fathers are generally able to put aside interparental conflict (Arendell, 1995), which can be a major obstacle to father–offspring contact. Involved, supportive noncustodial fathers are just as important in their children's lives as residential fathers (Munsch, Woodward, & Darling, 1995).

However, historically, most noncustodial fathers have rapidly faded to postdivorce noninvolvement with regard to both financial support (Arendell, 1995) and visitation (Arendell, 1995; King, 1994). Child support is typically received in full by only half of mothers who obtain child support awards, whereas one-fourth receive part and one-fourth receive nothing (Arendell, 1995; Meyer & Bartfield, 1996).

Changes in federal law may improve noncustodial fathers' compliance rates. Beginning in 1994, child support was routinely withheld from the paychecks of these fathers (Meyer et al., 1996); under the previous system, delinquency was necessary for withholding (Meyer & Bartfield, 1996; Meyer et al., 1996). Currently, enforcement of routine withholding varies widely according to locale (Meyer et al., 1996). Although national data are not yet available (Meyer et al., 1996), more circumscribed data indicate that enforcement, when it does occur, increases noncustodial fathers' compliance (Meyer et al., 1996).

It remains to be seen whether increased compliance owing to routine withholding will stimulate increased noncustodial father visitation; in the past, child support payment and visitation have correlated (Stephens, 1996). Over time, visitation rates have been low (King, 1994; Stephens, 1996). For example, most recently, Stephens (1996) found that among

children of divorced parents, 47 percent see their fathers several times a year or less, whereas only 27 percent see their fathers once a week or more. However, these findings do not take into account any impact that routine withholding may have on visitation.

With regard to payment and visitation, it is important to avoid stereotyping noncustodial fathers as uncaring. Even though only a minority maintain high-quality relationships with their children (Munsch et al., 1995), there are many reasons underlying seemingly "deadbeat" behavior. For example, fathers may withdraw to distance themselves from the pain of loss of day-to-day contact with their children (Kruk, 1994) or because they underestimate their own importance (Del Carmen & Virgo, 1993).

FATHER-CUSTODY FAMILIES

Although fathers are more likely to obtain custody now than in the past (Eggebeen et al., 1996), custodial fathers remain a minority among divorced parents. Custodial fathers tend to be white, well educated, and employed and belong to the middle- and upper-income brackets (Eggebeen et al., 1996; Guttmann, 1993).

For several reasons, most custodial fathers adapt well to parenting (Guttmann, 1993). They generally have actively sought custody (Fox & Kelly, 1995; Kissman & Allen, 1993) and are motivated to succeed. They generally do not have serious financial problems, so they can often afford concrete support for child rearing, such as household help. Furthermore, they frequently are able to obtain emotional support for child rearing from others (Guttmann, 1993). Finally, compared with custodial mothers, they are more likely to have older children in their care (Depner, 1993; Fox & Kelly, 1995). When custodial fathers do have difficulty raising their children, the source is likely to be a lack of norms for parental role performance (Germain, 1991) or a gender-based difficulty in deep interpersonal engagement with offspring (Downey, 1994).

Contrary to popular thinking, noncustodial mothers are as a rule neither unfit nor self-centered (Depner, 1993). Often, they are simply the less affluent spouse (West & Kissman, 1991). Compared with their male counterparts, noncustodial mothers are less likely to be under child support orders (Depner, 1993). Also, even though custodial fathers usually prefer to minimize contact with noncustodial mothers (Maccoby, Depner, & Mnookin, 1990), these women tend to assume an active postdivorce role with offspring, seeing them more frequently than do noncustodial fathers (Depner, 1993).

JOINT-CUSTODY FAMILIES

Like paternal custody, joint custody is a less common custody form (Maccoby & Mnookin, 1992). In both joint legal custody and joint physical custody, parents share legal rights and responsibilities. When joint legal custody children reside with their mother, custody in practice is not very different from sole maternal custody, except that fathers are more likely than other nonresidential fathers to pay child support and visit (Arditti, 1992). In joint physical custody, which is far less common (Arditti, 1992), children divide time between the residences of both parents. Joint physical custody is rare, because it requires relatively high income and the ability to sustain two domiciles of adequate size.

Compared to their sole-custody counterparts, joint physical custody parents experience less stress (Maccoby & Mnookin, 1992). They may experience some of the problems affecting sole-custody mothers (for example, time poverty, loneliness) or sole-custody fathers (for example, lack of norms), but the stress is less intense because of the recurring respites. Interestingly, however, joint custody parents experience only slightly less discord than other divorced parents (Maccoby et al., 1990). This may be because joint custody, as part of a divorce settlement, is not always desired by both parties (Maccoby & Mnookin, 1992). Although the purpose of joint physical custody is to enrich children's lives, interparental conflict can greatly interfere with its achievement (Arditti, 1992; Arendell, 1995; Maccoby & Mnookin, 1992).

SOCIAL WORK WITH DIVORCING AND DIVORCED FAMILIES

Direct Practice

Social workers encounter divorcing and divorced populations in numerous fields of practice, including family service, mental health, child welfare, occupational social work, and school social work. Attention to the divorced as a group with distinct economic and psychosocial features reflects social work's recognition of family diversity (Proctor, Davis, & Vosler, 1995). Assessment of the divorced is routinely family centered (Proctor et al., 1995), and intervention is geared to helping both adults and offspring.

Direct practice during the divorce process. Because of the many environmental challenges that arise during divorce (for example, obtaining legal assistance, applying for public assistance, job hunting, and moving a household), social workers often help divorcing adults delineate tasks and obtain resources (Haffey & Cohen, 1992; Strand, 1995). When clients do not speak English (sometimes because they have recently emigrated), social workers may advocate for them by telephone or in person. When traditional gender roles (for example, among Hispanic or Asian women) inhibit female clients' proactive behavior, social workers help clients consider the conflict and resolve it for themselves.

Although problem solving is emphasized, a focus on mourning of divorce-generated losses is sometimes a necessary preliminary or accompaniment to a challenge to clients to move ahead. The multiple demands of day-to-day life may mask loss issues among those with young children; consequently, loss issues may be more vivid among those with older children or no children. Whether bereavement issues are buried or readily accessible, many divorcing adults need professional assistance as they express, control, and ultimately let go of divorce-generated pain.

Direct practice with custodial parents and their offspring. When addressing family issues, the social worker communicates the view that the divorced family is not a deficient or substandard family (Kissman & Allen, 1993; Strand, 1995). In part, this occurs through recognition of client strengths (Proctor et al., 1995). For example, even though employed custodial mothers of young children sometimes need help with circumscribed issues, their sheer physical stamina, as well as their coping and organizational abilities, usually warrant the greatest respect.

Because of the fatigue and loneliness of solo parenting, a common dilemma for custodial parents is learning to establish consistent discipline. This dilemma is less likely among African American families, where cultural mandates of strict discipline (Hines, Preto, McGoldrick, Almeida, & Weltman, 1992; Ho, 1992) and extended family input (Ho, 1992) may buffer the disorganizing impact of marital rupture. Other common themes in practice with divorced families include appropriate demands on children, adolescents, and young adults; appropriate response to offspring reactions to the divorce; maintaining contact with children's and adolescents' schools within the constraints of a time-poor life; and pleasurable activities mothers and offspring can carry out together.

Individual sessions for custodial parents can promote ventilation about stress and strengthened parental behavior. Family sessions can facilitate feedback from offspring to parents and resolve extended family conflicts. For example, such conflicts may arise when employed African American grandmothers are strained by providing assistance to grandchildren (Timberlake & Chipungu, 1992) or when traditional Catholic Hispanic grandparents question maternal employment, or divorce itself. Cognitively based skills, such as psychoeducation, are particularly relevant to custodial fathers, who may be somewhat uncomfortable with emotions (Bogolub, 1995). A focus on the regular separation from sons and daughters is important for parents with joint residential custody.

Direct practice with noncustodial parents.

Generally, social workers should reach out to noncustodial parents (overwhelmingly fathers), even when they do not pay support or visit. The purpose is to heighten their involvement with offspring. Because a seemingly uncaring father is likely to expect the social worker to chastise him, the social worker should begin by respectfully acknowledging the father's diminished postdivorce status. This issue is particularly salient for Hispanic men, who generally assume an authoritative or *macho* role in their families of procreation (Del Carmen & Virgo, 1993). Then the focus should move to a heightened awareness of postdivorce paternal importance and more consistent contact with sons and daughters. When raising the issue of nonpayment, social workers should balance attention to any difficulties in budgeting or paying with an emphasis on responsibility.

However, social workers should not reach out to all noninvolved, noncustodial fathers (Curtner-Smith, 1995). For example, children, as well as their mothers, are better off without men with a history of violence or sexual abuse.

Direct practice with former spouses as a dyad.

In situations of parallel parenting, where there is little or no contact between former spouses (Furstenberg & Cherlin, 1991; Maccoby & Mnookin, 1992), social workers focus on increased child-centered parental contact. The purpose is to promote complete knowledge of offspring functioning for both parents and a postdivorce environment that is relatively free of contradictions for daughters and sons.

In situations of high interparental conflict, social workers aim to diminish or encapsulate such conflict, which is a major source of offspring difficulty after divorce (Curtner-Smith, 1995; Maccoby & Mnookin, 1992). Insofar as possible, former spouses learn to separate adult and parental roles and develop a business-like, cooperative relationship (Butler et al., 1995; Curtner-Smith, 1995; Maccoby & Mnookin, 1992). When working with former spouses, social workers must take into account that remarriage, particularly paternal remarriage, decreases the possibilities for co-parental cooperation (Christensen & Rettig, 1995).

Groups.

Groups for divorcing and divorced adults address a wide range of topics, including vocational development, postdivorce socializing, and parenting (Bogolub, 1995). Beyond their overt content, groups normalize the life situation of the divorced and thus raise self-esteem (Strand, 1995). The mutual support among group members is particularly important for middle-aged and older women; if such women came of age before the birth of feminism, they may be galvanized by younger women's ideas about independent living. Group support is also particularly helpful for isolated people, such as recently emigrated Hispanic women with no extended family nearby (Chillman, 1993).

Groups for young adults and adolescents typically focus on the impact of parental divorce on age-specific identity struggles (Bogolub, 1995). School-based groups for children of divorced parents typically focus on self-esteem, coping strategies, and related matters (Farmer & Galaris, 1993; Frieman, Garon, & Mandell, 1994). When social workers work with parents as well as students, the effectiveness of school-based groups is increased (Skitka & Frazier, 1995).

Family Life Education

Because participation does not require extensive personal disclosure and is sometimes mandated (Frieman et al., 1994), family life education (FLE) reaches divorcing and divorced parents who might not otherwise seek professional help. Typically, divorce-related FLE addresses topics such as child rearing and relationships with former spouses (Frieman et al., 1994). It is especially relevant for noncustodial fathers, who in general need help in understanding their impact on offspring (Arendell, 1995; Simons & Associates, 1996), and for parents of color, who tend to underuse family services (Proctor et al., 1995). For example, FLE leaders who present programs in nontraditional locations (for example, African American churches) and choose culturally relevant topics (for example, grandparents as resources for children) create rapport with participants of color; then, when indicated, leaders can sometimes refer for ongoing services individuals and families who might otherwise perceive such services as foreign and unhelpful.

DIVORCE: IMPLICATIONS FOR SOCIAL POLICY AND LEGAL REFORM

If a social policy helps families, it is likely to help financially stressed divorced families even more. Initiatives widely recognized as desirable include an increase in the minimum wage (Arendell, 1995); increased numbers of flex-time jobs (McLanahan & Sandefur, 1994; Simons & Associates, 1996); expansion of the earned income tax credit program (McLanahan & Sandefur, 1994; Simons & Associates, 1996); increased availability of affordable, high-quality day care (McLanahan & Sandefur, 1994; Simons & Associates, 1996); and an assured child support benefit (Arendell, 1995; Garfinkel, 1992). Garfinkel (1992) is the leading proponent of such a benefit, which would guarantee custodial parents the support they are owed, even if nonresidential parents have not paid. Also recognized as important are elimination of court-ordered joint physical custody when it is not desired by both parents (Arendell, 1995) and reversal of the current bias against lesbians in custody decisions (Duran-Aydintug & Causey, 1996).

SUMMARY AND CONCLUSION

Divorce is common and is likely to remain so. To assist divorcing and divorced adults and their offspring, social workers in agency practice address psychosocial issues, such as mourning and parenting, and environmental issues, such as household moves and employment shifts. Whether working with individuals, families, or groups, social workers routinely rely on knowledge of client ethnicity, gender, age, and income level to guide intervention with those whose lives have been affected by marital rupture. Furthermore, social workers should keep informed of needed divorce-relevant policy and legal initiatives and work to implement them.

To become increasingly effective, social workers need to draw on current research findings, which can suggest ways to develop and refine practice with the divorced population. For example, the findings of Lawson and Thompson (1995), who interviewed divorced African American men, suggest that services for these men can be improved by teaching postdivorce counseling skills to men traditionally viewed as helpers in the African American community, such as clergy. Likewise, the findings of Arbuthnot, Poole, and Gordon (1996), who mailed FLE booklets on coping with children's divorce-related problems to parents filing for divorce, suggest that the number of divorced parents helped by FLE can be increased by such mailings. Overall, by remaining open to the implications of research, social workers assisting those affected by marital dissolution can create diverse new practices to supplement extant ones.

REFERENCES

Arbuthnot, J., Poole, C. J., & Gordon, D. A. (1996). Use of educational materials to modify stressful behaviors in post-divorce parenting. *Journal of Divorce and Remarriage, 25,* 117–137.

Arditti, J. A. (1992). Differences between fathers with joint custody and noncustodial fathers. *American Journal of Orthopsychiatry, 62,* 186–195.

Arendell, T. (1995). *Fathers and divorce.* Newbury Park, CA: Sage Publications.

Bee, H. (1994). *Lifespan development.* New York: Harper Collins.

Bogolub, E. B. (1995). *Helping families through divorce.* New York: Springer.

Boyd-Franklin, N. (1989). *Black families in therapy: A multi-systems approach.* New York: Guilford Press.

Bray, J. H., & Berger, S. H. (1993). Nonresidential parent–child relationship following divorce and remarriage: A longitudinal perspective. In C. E. Depner & J. H. Bray (Eds.), *Nonresidential parenting* (pp. 156–181). Newbury Park, CA: Sage Publications.

Bulcroft, R. A., & Bulcroft, K. A. (1993). Race differences in attitudinal and motivational factors in the decision to marry. *Journal of Marriage and the Family, 55,* 338–355.

Bussell, D. A. (1995). A pilot study of African American children's cognitive and emotional reactions to parental separation. *Journal of Divorce and Remarriage, 24,* 1–22.

Butler, B. O., Mellon, M. W., Stroh, S. E., & Stern, H. P. (1995). A therapeutic model to enhance children's adjustment to divorce: A case example. *Journal of Divorce and Remarriage, 22,* 77–90.

Cain, B. S. (1989). Parental divorce during the college years. *Psychiatry, 52,* 135–146.

Cherlin, A. (1992). *Marriage, divorce, remarriage.* Cambridge, MA: Harvard University Press.

Chillman, C. S. (1993). Hispanic families in the United States: Research perspectives. In H. P. McAdoo (Ed.), *Family ethnicity: Strength in diversity* (pp. 141–163). Newbury Park, CA: Sage Publications.

Chiriboga, D. A., Catron, L. S., & Associates. (1991). *Divorce: Crisis, challenge, or relief.* New York: New York University Press.

Christensen, D. H., & Rettig, K. D. (1995). The relationship of remarriage to post-divorce co-parenting. *Journal of Divorce and Remarriage, 24,* 73–88.

Cooney, T. M., Hutchinson, M. K., & Leather, D. M. (1995). Surviving the breakup? Predictors of parent-adult child relations after parental divorce. *Family Relations, 44,* 153–161.

Cooney, T. M., & Kurz, J. (1996). Mental health outcomes following recent parental divorce. *Journal of Family Issues, 17,* 495–513.

Curtner-Smith, M. E. (1995). Assessing children's visitation needs with divorced noncustodial fathers. *Families in Society, 76,* 341–348.

Del Carmen, R., & Virgo, G. N. (1993). Marital disruption and nonresidential parenting: A multicultural perspective. In C. E. Depner & J. H. Bray (Eds.), *Nonresidential parenting* (pp. 13–36). Newbury Park, CA: Sage Publications.

Depner, C. E. (1993). Parental role reversal: Mothers as nonresidential parents. In C. E. Depner & J. H. Bray (Eds.), *Nonresidential parenting* (pp. 37–57). Newbury Park, CA: Sage Publications.

Downey, D. B. (1994). The school performance of children from single-mother and single-father families: Economic or interpersonal deprivation? *Journal of Family Issues, 15,* 129–147.

Duran-Aydintug, C., & Causey, K. A. (1996). Child custody determination: Implications for lesbian mothers. *Journal of Divorce and Remarriage, 25,* 55–72.

Eckholm, E. (1992, July 20). Fathers find that child support means owing more than money. *New York Times,* pp. A1, A13.

Eggebeen, D. J., Snyder, A. R., & Manning, W. D. (1996). Children in single-father families in demographic perspective. *Journal of Family Issues, 17,* 441–465.

Farmer, S., & Galaris, D. (1993). Support groups for children of divorce. *American Journal of Family Therapy, 21,* 40–50.

Fine, M. A., & Fine, D. R. (1994). An examination and evaluation of recent changes in divorce laws in five Western countries: The critical role of values. *Journal of Marriage and the Family, 56,* 249–264.

Fine, M. A., McKenry, P. C., & Chung, H. (1992). Post-divorce adjustment of black and white single parents. *Journal of Divorce and Remarriage, 17,* 121–134.

Fox, G. L., & Kelly, R. F. (1995). Determinants of child custody: Arrangements at divorce. *Journal of Marriage and the Family, 57,* 693–708.

Franklin, A. J. (1992). Therapy with African American men. *Families in Society, 73,* 350–355.

Frieman, B. B., Garon, R., & Mandell, B. (1994). Parenting seminars for divorcing parents. *Social Work, 39,* 607–610.

Furstenberg, F. F. (1988). Good dads–bad dads: Two faces of fatherhood. In A. J. Cherlin (Ed.), *The changing American family and public policy* (pp. 193–218). Washington, DC: Urban Institute.

Furstenberg, F., & Cherlin, A. (1991). *Divided families: What happens to children when parents part.* Cambridge, MA: Harvard University Press.

Ganong, L. H., & Coleman, M. (1994). *Remarried family relationships.* Newbury Park, CA: Sage Publications.

Garfinkel, I. (1992). *Assuring child support: An extension of social security.* New York: Russell Sage Foundation.

Germain, C. B. (1991). *Human behavior in the social environment.* New York: Columbia University Press.

Greenstein, T. N. (1995). Gender ideology, marital disruption, and employment of married women. *Journal of Marriage and the Family, 57,* 31–42.

Guttmann, J. (1993). *Divorce in psychosocial perspective: Theory and research.* Hillsdale, NJ: Lawrence Erlbaum.

Haffey, M., & Cohen, P. M. (1992). Treatment issues for divorcing women. *Families in Society, 73,* 142–148.

Hines, P. M., Preto, N. G., McGoldrick, M., Almeida, R., & Weltman, S. (1992). Intergenerational issues across cultures. *Families in Society, 73,* 323–338.

Ho, M. K. (1992). *Minority children and adolescents in therapy.* Newbury Park, CA: Sage Publications.

Johnson, G. B., & Wahl, M. (1995). Families: Demographic shifts. In R. L. Edwards (Ed.-in-Chief), *Encyclopedia of social work* (19th ed., Vol. 2, pp. 936–941). Washington, DC: NASW Press.

King, V. (1994). Non-resident father involvement and child well-being: Can dads make a difference? *Journal of Family Issues, 15,* 78–96.

Kissman, K., & Allen, J. (1993). *Single-parent families.* Newbury Park, CA: Sage Publications.

Kitson, G. C. (1992). *Portrait of divorce.* New York: Guilford Press.

Kruk, E. (1994). The disengaged noncustodial father: Implications for social work practice with the divorced family. *Social Work, 39,* 15–25.

Lawson, E. J., & Thompson, A. (1995). Black men make sense of marital distress and divorce: An exploratory study. *Family Relations, 44,* 211–218.

Lawson, E. J., & Thompson, A. (1996). Black men's perceptions of divorce-related stressors and strategies for coping with divorce. *Journal of Family Issues, 17,* 249–273.

Longres, J. (1995). Hispanics: Overview. In R. L. Edwards (Ed.-in-Chief), *Encyclopedia of social work* (19th ed., Vol. 2, pp. 1214–1222). Washington, DC: NASW Press.

Maccoby, E. E., Depner, C. E., & Mnookin, R. H. (1990). Coparenting in the second year after divorce. *Journal of Marriage and the Family, 52,* 141–155.

Maccoby, E. E., & Mnookin, R. H. (1992). *Dividing the child: Social and legal dilemmas of custody.* Cambridge, MA: Harvard University Press.

McLanahan, S., & Sandefur, G. (1994). *Growing up with a single parent.* Cambridge, MA: Harvard University Press.

Meyer, D. R., & Bartfield, J. (1996). Compliance with child support orders in divorce cases. *Journal of Marriage and the Family, 58,* 201–212.

Meyer, D. R., Bartfield, J., Garfinkel, I., & Brown, P. (1996). Child support reform: Lessons from Wisconsin. *Family Relations, 45,* 11–18.

Mitchell-Flynn, C., & Hutchinson, R. L. (1993). A longitudinal study of the problems and concerns of urban divorced men. *Journal of Divorce and Remarriage, 20,* 161–182.

Morgan, L. A. (1991). *After marriage ends: Economic consequences for midlife women.* Newbury Park, CA: Sage Publications.

Munsch, J., Woodward, J., & Darling, N. (1995). Children's perceptions of their relationships with coresiding and non-coresiding fathers. *Journal of Divorce and Remarriage, 23,* 39–54.

National Center for Health Statistics. (1992). Annual summary of births, marriages, divorces, and deaths: United States, 1991. *In Monthly vital statistics report (40).* Washington, DC: U.S. Public Health Service.

Peterson, R. R. (1996). A re-evaluation of the economic consequences of divorce. *American Sociological Review, 61,* 528–536.

Proctor, E. K., Davis, L. E., & Vosler, N. (1995). Families: Direct practice. In R. L. Edwards (Ed.-in-Chief), *Encyclopedia of social work* (19th ed., Vol. 2, pp. 941–950). Washington, DC: NASW Press.

Schupack, D. (1994, July 7). "Starter" marriages: So early, so brief. *New York Times,* pp. C1, C6.

Seltzer, J. A., & Garfinkel, I. (1990). Inequality in divorce settlements: An investigation of property settlements and child support awards. *Social Science Research, 19,* 82–111.

Simons, R. L., & Associates. (1996). *Understanding differences between divorced and intact families.* Newbury Park, CA: Sage Publications.

Skitka, L. J., & Frazier, M. (1995). Ameliorating the effects of parental divorce: Do small group interventions work? *Journal of Divorce and Remarriage, 24,* 159–179.

Staples, R. (1985). *Black masculinity: The black male's role in American society.* San Francisco: Black Scholar Press.

Stephens, L. S. (1996). Will Johnny see daddy this week? *Journal of Family Issues, 17,* 466–494.

Strand, V. (1995). Single parents. In R. L. Edwards (Ed.-in-Chief), *Encyclopedia of social work* (19th ed., Vol. 3, pp. 2157–2164). Washington, DC: NASW Press.

Taylor, R. J., Chatters, L. M., Tucker, M. B., & Lewis, E. (1990). Developments in research on black families: A decade review. *Journal of Marriage and the Family, 52,* 993–1014.

Timberlake, E. M., & Chipungu, S. S. (1992). Grandmotherhood: Contemporary meaning among African-American middle-class grandmothers. *Social Work, 37,* 216–222.

Wallerstein, J. (1986). Women after divorce: Preliminary report from a ten-year follow-up. *American Journal of Orthopsychiatry, 56,* 65–77.

Walsh, F. (1991). Promoting healthy functioning in divorced and remarried families. In A. S. Gurman & D. P. Kniskern (Eds.), *Handbook of family therapy* (Vol. 2, pp. 525–545). New York: Brunner/Mazel.

Weitzman, L. (1988). Women and children last: The social and economic consequences of divorce law reforms. In S. M. Dornbusch & M. H. Strober (Eds.), *Feminism, children, and the new families* (pp. 212–248). New York: Guilford Press.

Weitzman, L. J. (1985). *The divorce revolution.* New York: Free Press.

Weitzman, L. J. (1996). The economic consequences of divorce are still unequal: Comment on Peterson. *American Sociological Review, 61,* 537–538.

West, B., & Kissman, K. (1991). Mothers without custody: Treatment issues. In C. A. Everett (Ed.), *The consequences of divorce* (pp. 229–38). New York: Haworth Press.

Yu, M. (1993). Divorce and culturally different older women: Issues of strategies and interventions. *Journal of Divorce and Remarriage, 21,* 41–54.

FURTHER READING

Marshall, R. (1991). *The state of families* (Vol. 3). Milwaukee: Family Service America.

Ellen B. Bogolub, PhD, is assistant professor, School of Social Work, Adelphi University, Garden City, NY 11530.

For further information see

Brief Therapies; Clinical Social Work; Conflict Resolution; Domestic Violence; **Domestic Violence: Gay Men and Lesbians;** Ethnic-Sensitive Practice; Families Overview; Family Life Education; Family Planning; Gay Men Overview; Goal Setting and Intervention Planning; Human Sexuality; Intervention Research; Interviewing; Lesbians Overview; Marriage/Partners; Men Overview; Person-in-Environment; Sexual Distress; Women Overview.

Key Words

custody	family
divorce	

Domestic Violence: Gay Men and Lesbians
Bonnie E. Carlson
Katherine Maciol

Recognition of domestic violence in the intimate relationships of gay men and lesbians is a recent phenomenon. Physical, sexual, and emotional abuse do occur in same-sex relationships, probably with similar frequency and severity as abuse in heterosexual relationships, although more research is needed to establish the extent of such abuse. Domestic violence in gay and lesbian partnerships shares other similarities with abuse in heterosexual relationships, including similar contributing factors (for example, exposure to abuse during childhood), dynamics (for example, power and control issues), and consequences for victims and perpetrators (for example, shame, guilt, and self-blame among victims and disavowal of responsibility among perpetrators). However, some unique factors also affect how abuse is experienced in gay and lesbian relationships, including homophobia, heterosexism, and discrimination; difficulty acknowledging being a victim or perpetrator because of gender-role stereotypes; frequent alienation from potentially supportive families of origin; and limited availability of services for victims or perpetrators. Special issues for gay men, lesbians, and gay men and lesbians of color are discussed in this entry, along with implications for intervention with victims and batterers.

INTRODUCTION

Until fairly recently, violence in gay and lesbian relationships had been a hidden problem. However, since the mid-1980s, recognition of this form of domestic abuse has been growing. Violence and abuse in lesbian relationships was first publicly acknowledged at the 1983 meeting of the National Coalition Against Domestic Violence by the Lesbian Task Force (Leeder, 1988). Recognition of violence and

abuse in gay male relationships occurred somewhat later, perhaps because substantial energy was devoted to the human immunodeficiency virus (HIV) issue by the gay community during the 1980s, when lesbian battering was uncovered (Elliott, 1996). Initially, the gay and lesbian communities were reluctant to recognize existence of same-sex violence and abuse, particularly its frequency and severity, and responded to reports of such abuse with denial and minimization (Byrne, 1996; Island & Letellier, 1991; Merrill, 1996). Elliot (1996) noted, "The myth that lesbian relationships are more peaceful and egalitarian than heterosexual unions has been shattered by the reality of lesbian battering. Even the presumption that gay males, who are believed to be more enlightened and sensitive than their heterosexual counterparts . . . has been exposed as fantasy by evidence of same-sex violence" (p. 1).

Part of the reason that same-sex couple abuse has been overlooked is that the domestic violence movement, which had focused almost exclusively on the abuse of heterosexual women, has used a feminist, sociopolitical analysis of the problem, framing domestic abuse largely in terms of gender (Letellier, 1994). Heterosexual domestic violence has been said to occur as a result of the sexism and patriarchy that are deeply rooted in our culture. In this widely accepted explanation, victims are assumed to be female and perpetrators to be male, making partner abuse within same-sex relationships appear to be an exception to the rule (Merrill, 1996). Hamberger (1996) has observed that although "gender issues are important in heterosexual intimate violence, they may be less relevant, or take a substantially different form, in homosexual relationships" (p. 84). The fact that women, who are assumed to be nonviolent, would intentionally abuse other women, and that men, who are assumed to be strong and independent, could be victimized by intimate male partners, has called for a different level of analysis and explanation for intimate partner abuse (Hammond, 1989; Letellier, 1994). As a result, the current literature on violence in gay and lesbian relationships has focused on power and control, rather than gender, as the central dynamic.

DEFINITIONS AND EXTENT OF THE PROBLEM

A variety of terms and definitions has been used for abuse occurring in same-sex relationships. It is variously described as domestic violence, abuse, or battering, and it carries no universally agreed-on definition. One of the first definitions of *lesbian battering* was offered by Hart (1986) and has been widely used by others: "A pattern of violent [or] coercive behavior whereby a lesbian seeks to control the thoughts, beliefs, or conduct of her intimate partner or to punish the intimate for resisting the perpetrator's control" (p. 173).

Island and Letellier (1991) have defined gay *male domestic violence* as "any unwanted physical force, psychological abuse, or material or property destruction inflicted by one man on another" (p. 20). Their definition of physical abuse includes sexual violence.

Some writers use the terms violence, abuse, and battering interchangeably, whereas others differentiate among them. For example, Hammond (1989) defined *abuse* as "any behavior intended to cause harm or damage to the victim, or behavior that systematically disregards the basic human needs of the victim," whereas battering was "a *pattern* of physical abuse or intimidation in which the batterer uses the actuality or threat of physical force or violence to exert control over the victim" (p. 90, italics added).

Regardless of the definition preferred, there is broad agreement that same-sex abuse can take many forms, including physical violence such as shoving, punching, or beating up; emotional or psychological abuse (for example, threats, ridicule, or damage to possessions); and sexual abuse, such as nonconsensual sex or rape. An alternative typology differentiates among *situational physical abuse,* which occurs only once or twice in response to a situational crisis; *chronic physical abuse,* a recurrent, escalating pattern of destructive abuse that occurs among couples who generally live together and that can lead to injury and police intervention; and *emotional abuse* consisting of insults, threats of violence, harassment, and other types of psychological abuse (Leeder, 1988). In addition, a unique form of psychological abuse for gay men and lesbians is *outing*—that is, disclosing or threatening to disclose one's sexual identity to others (Elliot, 1996).

Research on the extent of lesbian or gay male violence and abuse is quite limited. There have been more studies on the incidence and prevalence of lesbian battering than on gay male abuse, as can be seen in the list of references at the end of this entry. However, confidence in the validity of findings in such studies is limited by the use of nonrandom convenience samples, often small in size and biased in favor of white, middle-class respondents. Lack of consensus on an operational definition of violence or abuse also has contributed to widely varying estimates of the extent and seriousness of the problem. Depending on the sample and on how abuse is defined, lesbian violence or physical abuse has been said to occur in one-third to two-thirds of past or current relationships; the incidence increases if psychological or sexual abuse are included in the definition (Lie & Gentlewarrier, 1991; Lockhart, White, Causby, & Isaac, 1994; Renzetti, 1992; Schilit, Lie, Bush, Montagne, & Reyes, 1991).

Elliot (1996) cited an unpublished survey of 1,000 gay men in Minnesota in which 17 percent had experienced physical violence at the hands of their partner. Island and Letellier (1991) speculated that half a million gay men may be battered yearly. This number is based on an estimated 9.5 million adult gay men, of whom 64 percent (6 million) are thought to be in couple relationships, and a 10.9 percent rate of abuse, which is derived from the violence rate for heterosexual men. One survey of gay men and lesbians in therapy found that 80 percent of the men and 94 percent of the women admitted to abusing their partners, although the type of abuse was not specified and may have included psychological abuse (Farley, 1996). Several authors have speculated that the prevalence of same-sex domestic violence is probably at least as high as that of abuse in heterosexual couples (Elliot, 1996; Island & Letellier, 1991; Renzetti, 1989). Emotional and psychological abuse are thought to be more common in same-sex couples than physical violence (Farley, 1996; Lockhart et al., 1994; Renzetti, 1992).

When abuse occurs in same-sex relationships, it is often not a one-time occurrence and may escalate to serious, injurious, and even life-threatening acts of violence. For example, in Lockhart et al.'s (1994) study of 284 predominantly white, professional lesbians, 11 percent reported at least one act of severe violence, such as being punched, kicked, or beaten up. In addition, as with abuse in heterosexual relationships, once violence has occurred, it can create sufficient fear that its mere threat can be effective in imposing power and control over the terrified victim (Hammond, 1989).

COMMONALITIES OF VIOLENCE IN HETEROSEXUAL COUPLES AND SAME-SEX COUPLES

Abuse in gay and lesbian partnerships has much in common with abuse as it occurs in heterosexual couples. Although much remains to be learned about same-sex couple abuse in terms of incidence, frequency, and severity, the frequency with which such abuse occurs, its seriousness, and the forms it takes appear to be quite similar to violence and abuse as they are manifested in heterosexual couples (Elliot, 1996; Hammond, 1989; Island & Letellier, 1991). There is also considerable commonality in the contributing factors and dynamics that surround physical and emotional abuse. For example, exposure to sexual, physical, or emotional abuse or neglect during childhood may be a risk factor for being an abuser or victim (Island & Letellier, 1991; Lockhart et al., 1994; Schilit et al., 1991). Often conflict about financial concerns, either partner's job, housekeeping issues, relatives, and jealousy over one or both partner's involvement with other people precede abuse (Leeder, 1988; Lockhart et al., 1994).

Other dynamics also may be operating. For example, substance use or abuse may be involved, and once violence has occurred more than once, it may recur in a cyclical fashion (Island & Letellier, 1991; Leeder, 1988; Lockhart et al., 1994). Tension may build over time, culminating in a violent incident and followed by a "honeymoon" period, which often involves sexual activity that comes to serve as a powerful reinforcer for making up (Walker, 1984). Power and control issues are likely to play a role as well, operating similarly to the way in which they play out in heterosexual relationships in some respects and differently in others.

Gender often has been viewed as the basis for power inequities in heterosexual relationships, with men seen as more powerful than women, not only physically but also on the basis of social status indicators such as education, income, or employment status. However, the basis for interpersonal power is much broader than gender. If its role in relation to violence in interpersonal relationships is to be understood, power must be viewed multidimensionally. Power can be viewed as physical (for example, size and strength), social (for example, connectedness to other people), vocational (for example, education, employment status, income), or psychological (for example, self-worth). Apart from gender, two partners in a couple may be similar or different along any of the power dimensions described above. Thus, many factors other than gender can form the basis for power inequities, including education, verbal skills, interpersonal skills, physical attractiveness, and age (Renzetti, 1989). In addition, factors that contribute to interpersonal power can shift over time, so that the partner who was more powerful at one point in time may hold less power at another (Elliot, 1996). Thus, differences in power as well as differences in the need or desire to be in control in a relationship can lead to violence and abuse, irrespective of the couple's sexual orientation. The literature on gay males suggests that the abusive partner tends to be more powerful, although not necessarily physically stronger, and to use violence to maintain control (Island & Letellier, 1991). However, one study of abuse in lesbian couples suggested a more complex power dynamic in which the aggressor has greater power in terms of more influence over decision making or more resources compared with the victim, but is also more dependent on the victim and thus perceives herself as having less power (Renzetti, 1988). Lockhart et al.'s (1994) research also supports the idea that a lesbian may resort to abuse if she feels too dependent on her partner. In this view, abuse is seen as a mechanism for equalizing power rather than asserting it (Renzetti, 1993).

There are also many similarities in the consequences of abuse between heterosexual and gay and lesbian couples. Physical injury is one obvious consequence. Hammond (1989) and Morrow and Hawxhurst (1989) noted that the belief that women are not capable of physical harm to another person detracts from recognition that lesbians can use the full "range of violence" on one another, including homicide. Emotional reactions such as fear, stigma, shame, guilt, and a sense of responsibility for the abuse on the part of the victim are reported by gay male and lesbian as well as heterosexual female victims (Island & Letellier, 1991; Renzetti, 1989). Often the abuse is a secret that the victim works very hard to maintain. Lesbian victims as well as gay male victims often have difficulty establishing their legitimacy or worthiness as "true victims," because they are members of devalued social groups (Renzetti, 1992). Often this feeling leads to difficulty in accessing assistance to end the abuse.

Another similarity between victims of abuse in same-sex relationships and those in heterosexual relationships is the reluctance to end the battering relationship and the reasons for remaining in the relationship: love for the abuser, feeling responsible for the abuse, belief that the abuser will change, learned helplessness, fear of retaliation by the abuser, and difficulty accessing help from others or having nowhere else to go (Elliot, 1996; Island & Letellier, 1991; Renzetti, 1992). Yet another similarity is that, like male heterosexual batterers, gay and lesbian abusers typically fail to take responsibility for their abusive behavior or to seek help voluntarily (Island & Letellier, 1991).

FACTORS UNIQUE TO VIOLENCE AND ABUSE IN SAME-SEX RELATIONSHIPS

There are also factors that may play a unique role in gay and lesbian couple violence. The most obvious factor is that both partners are of the same gender, so that "the opportunity to abuse can go both ways with lesbians and gay men" (Elliot, 1996, p. 4). Perhaps it is this potential that has given rise to the widespread "myth of mutual battering" (Renzetti, 1992)—the idea that virtually all abuse in same-sex relationships is reciprocated—as discussed later in this summary.

The prevalence of homophobia and heterosexism are also unique factors that affect abuse as it occurs in same-sex couples (Byrne, 1996; Hammond, 1989; Island & Letellier, 1991; Leeder, 1988). Elliot (1996) noted that "sexism creates the opportunity for heterosexual men to abuse their partners, and homophobia, a tool of sexism, creates the opportunity for gays and lesbians to abuse their partners" (p. 3). Merrill (1996), too, observed that environments characterized by prejudice or discrimination, such as homophobia, racism, and heterosexism, increase the opportunities for abuse, perhaps in part because prejudice and discrimination can increase the stress and isolation in a relationship. External homophobia and heterosexism also can fuel internalized homophobia, which consists of conscious or unconscious "feelings of self-hate and fear" about one's homosexuality that can affect self-concept and self-esteem (Byrne, 1996).

The literature on battering in gay and lesbian relationships has indicated a greater reluctance on the part of gay men and lesbians to acknowledge violence, abuse, or battering because of the myth that domestic violence happens only in heterosexual relationships (Island & Letellier, 1991; Leeder, 1988; Renzetti, 1988). Thus, in lesbian relationships it is difficult to identify a batterer because both partners are female, and in gay relationships it is hard to find a victim because both partners are male. This difficulty is experienced by the partners themselves as well as by others—friends, family members, formal help providers—who also may have trouble labeling the behavior they see as domestic violence, abuse, or battering (Renzetti, 1988). This difficulty is especially problematic when the perpetrator and victim share the same social network, which is often the case with lesbians (Hammond, 1989; Morrow & Hawxhurst, 1989).

Another factor unique to same-sex couple violence is that gay men and lesbians are often alienated from their families of origin, who may not be aware of their sexual orientation or, if they know about it, disapprove of it. This lack of connectedness and validation means that emotional and instrumental support from extended family, which is often extremely helpful for heterosexual battered women trying to leave abusive relationships (Davis & Srinivasan, 1995), is not forthcoming. In addition, it means that the lesbian or gay couple relationship assumes an even greater importance than a similar relationship might for heterosexual couples, taking on an "'us against the world' quality" (Island & Letellier, 1991, p. 23).

A final factor that is unique to same-sex couple violence, as mentioned previously, is the fear that disclosing or confronting the abuse in any way may lead to the revelation of the victim's sexual orientation (Elliot, 1996; Island & Letellier, 1991). Disclosing a partner's sexual orientation, or threatening to do so, which Morrow and Hawxhurst (1989) called "homophobic control," may be used as a control tactic by the abusive partner who fears embarrassment or stigma if the victim shares that abuse is occurring or wants to end the relationship. The disclosure also may occur in the context of seeking help from friends, family, or professional providers (for example, police, counselors, or shelters), at which time it may be necessary to "come out" to explain the abuse.

SPECIAL ISSUES FOR GAY MEN

Gay men who are abused by their intimate partners also have special concerns. Letellier (1994) observed that battered gay and bisexual men have more difficulty seeing themselves as victims than do battered women because our culture's view of victimization is incompatible with masculinity. Gay men have been said to be confused about masculinity and typically lack role models for healthy male-male relationships (Island & Letellier, 1991). As a result, they may not see themselves as victims of abuse, particularly emotional abuse, especially if they have not been physically injured. In turn, not labeling themselves as victims makes it more likely that an abusive relationship will continue and they will not seek help (Letellier, 1994). Some gay men may see intermittent violence as normal among men, an expression of masculinity or just a matter of "boys being boys." They may assume that a fight in which both partners are males is a fair fight between equals. Others may assume violence is an aspect of acceptable sadomasochistic sexual behavior (Island & Letellier, 1991). In addition, internalized homophobia has been fanned by the acquired immune deficiency syndrome (AIDS) crisis. Some gay or bisexual men may feel that violence or abuse is a punishment for being gay, the price they must pay for having a relationship with another man (Letellier, 1994).

Finally, mutual combat or reciprocal battering is often assumed when there is abuse, especially because both parties are male, or if both partners are about the same size. If women, either lesbian or heterosexual, use violence toward intimate partners, it seems reasonable to expect that male partners would be at least as likely to reciprocate, either in self-defense or retaliation, if their partners initiated violence. Moreover, if the victimized partner resorts to violence himself, it is even more difficult for him to perceive that he is a victim (Letellier, 1994).

SPECIAL ISSUES FOR LESBIANS

Because both partners are women, lesbian relationships are frequently idealized as being more cooperative, noncompetitive, and egalitarian than intimate relationships between men. Many within the lesbian community believe that acknowledging the existence of partner abuse may reinforce homophobia and threaten this image (Morrow & Hawxhurst, 1989). Victim and abuser often have the same friends, who may have conflicting loyalties and may find it difficult to recognize the existence of battering within the relationship as readily as they would in a heterosexual relationship in which the man was the batterer. Mainstream services are premised on the assumption of a male perpetrator, with the abuse resulting from gender-related factors. When the misperception that women are not capable of harming or inflicting serious injury on others is applied to lesbian relationships, "a profound misunderstanding and minimization of the impact of the battering and other abuse occurs" (Hammond, 1989, p. 91).

Three types of conflicts in lesbian relationships can contribute to partner abuse, "dependency versus autonomy, jealousy, and the balance of power between partners" (Renzetti, 1992, p. 29). Lesbians have been described as having higher levels of attachment and commitment to their partners than occurs in gay male relationships. The intensity that is characteristic of lesbian relationships can be problematic when one partner is overly dependent on the other and loses her sense of individuality and separateness, a phenomenon described as "merger" or "fusion" (Renzetti, 1992). This attachment is heightened by the lack of outside support and societal validation for the relationship. The overdependence of one partner may conflict with the other partner's need for independence, leading to abuse.

COUPLE VIOLENCE IN GAY MEN AND LESBIANS OF COLOR

Domestic violence in the relationships of lesbians and gay men of color presents special issues. Most information available on violence and abuse in gay and lesbian relationships is written "by and of white lesbians" (Kanuha, 1990). Because they are female, nonwhite, and homosexual, battered lesbians of color are faced with three forms of oppression and discrimination. Despite the development of lesbian culture, Kanuha (1990) pointed out the substantial effects of racism, from which lesbian communities are not exempt. In their struggle against racism, lesbians of color are connected to their ethnic communities in a special way. As Kanuha (1990) has noted, "due to racism and the concomitant need for people of color to bond together against it, however, lesbians of color are inextricably bound to their racial-ethnic communities and therefore to men of color" (p. 172). This association can be perceived as a threat to white lesbians.

Many battered lesbians of color may be socially isolated, having little contact with other lesbians and trusting only their partners, whom they also fear. Racism can intensify this isolation and be used as a warning by the

batterer to discourage the victim from seeking help. The batterer may also threaten to "out" the victim by disclosing her homosexuality to the community, which may have serious consequences resulting from the "widespread existence of negative and hostile attitudes toward homosexuals within communities of color" (Waldron, 1996, p. 45). As a result of this isolation and fear, the victim may attempt to protect her partner by not seeking help to end the domestic violence.

Within communities of color, because of the combined effects of sexism and racism, feminists and lesbians are perceived to be a "white phenomenon" (Kanuha, 1990). Another dimension is that a gay or lesbian person may be perceived as a threat to the potential reproduction of the ethnic group, contributing to perceptions of genocide within communities of color. In describing lesbians of color, Kanuha (1990) concluded that "the fear of increased homophobic retaliation towards the entire lesbian and gay community will surely be intensified by lesbians of color coming out about their abusive relationships" (p. 177).

IMPLICATIONS FOR INTERVENTION

Because of the relatively recent recognition of domestic violence as a problem within the gay and lesbian communities, research and literature on interventions with gay and lesbian clients are limited. No well-articulated treatment models have been developed, and none of the discussions about intervention issues are grounded in a particular theoretical approach. To date, no research evaluating clinical interventions with abused lesbians or gay men has been published.

Service Delivery Issues

There is a strong consensus on two issues: (1) gay and lesbian victims confront special service barriers and (2) helping professionals and agencies need information and training to address homophobia and avoid precluding same-sex couples from using necessary services. As Lie and Gentlewarrier (1991) have noted, "Service providers need to examine their existing service protocol for heterosexist language which presumes that the perpetrator is male and/or that the survivor is in a heterosexual relationship" (p. 56). Agencies must provide staff with appropriate training regarding issues specific to the gay and lesbian community and encourage staff to become aware of their feelings regarding homosexuality and the possibility of homophobia. Because seeking help from a mental health professional requires disclosing one's status as gay or lesbian, special attention must be given to issues of confidentiality. To effectively enhance the well-being of victims, service providers must understand what the risk of coming out means to a client and approach the issues of domestic violence and sexual orientation with sensitivity (Hammond, 1989). Hammond also pointed out that "lesbian identified therapists, as a rule, are not more highly trained in the intricacies of domestic violence" (p. 99) and may make mistakes similar to those of other therapists who provide services to lesbian victims of battering. This is assumed to be true for gay-identified therapists as well.

Research indicates that many lesbian victims of domestic violence seek help from counselors, second only to friends as the most frequent source of assistance (Renzetti, 1989). Because violence in gay male relationships has only recently been acknowledged, little is known about the extent to which abused gay men seek mental health assistance, and few mental health professionals specialize in this area (Island & Letellier, 1991).

Although there is a general lack of domestic violence services for gay and lesbian victims, gay men are especially disadvantaged. There are no shelters for gay men, and only about six agencies nationally specialize in services for gay male victims and perpetrators, despite the estimated 500,000 gay men who are battered (Island & Letellier, 1991). This lack of services can be attributed primarily to denial of the problem in the gay male community and the fact that most domestic violence services are targeted at female victims. An integrated approach to interventions with gay and lesbian victims and batterers has been recommended. Such an approach would include creating safe homes and shelters, educating members of the gay community and others about same-sex couple violence, using lesbian- and gay-sensitive staff and advocates in hospital emergency departments and the criminal justice system, and ensuring quality treatment programs (Hamberger, 1996).

Treatment of Victims
Research on gay and lesbian domestic violence indicates that victims are more likely to reach out for services and psychotherapy than the

battering partner (Margolies & Leeder, 1995). Renzetti (1993) recommended using Walker's (1979) suggestions regarding counseling battered heterosexual women in crisis situations for clinical work with lesbian victims. Renzetti (1992) further pointed out that when "a third party from whom help is sought excuses the battering, implies that the victim contributed to or precipitated the abuse in some way, or denies that the battering even occurred, a victim, who already has had her self-esteem diminished by the battering itself, is likely to experience increased self-blame and isolation" (p. 89).

Mental health professionals who behave in this manner fail to hold the batterer accountable. Service providers should encourage victims to tell their stories, and they should understand the importance of believing what clients tell them. Belief is especially important, because the fear of not being believed can be a barrier to seeking help. This belief is essential for work with gay men, who have difficulty perceiving themselves as victims, even in the face of serious violence by their partners (Letellier, 1995). It is important to be nonjudgmental. Linking the word "battered" with lesbian or gay assists in labeling the experience and helps to penetrate denial.

Hammond (1989) offered several recommendations to counselors who work with lesbian clients. She stressed the importance of asking all clients at intake about both physical and emotional abuse, including a thorough assessment of severity. It may be helpful to understand the client's personal history and background and how it may "collude" with battering. Because the victim's safety is of primary importance, when abuse is uncovered, it is important to assist with the development of protection plans that help clients tune into cues that violence or abuse may be forthcoming. At the assessment stage it is also appropriate to differentiate between violence that is initiated by the client and that used in self-defense (Hammond, 1989; Renzetti, 1993).

Individual treatment for the victim should focus on defining self-esteem issues; recognizing and constructively expressing emotions such as anger, guilt, and self-blame; and addressing the victim's desire to stay in the relationship and tolerate violent or abusive behavior (Leeder, 1988; Renzetti, 1993). It is important to be supportive while emphasizing that the victim is not at fault (Hammond, 1989).

In addition, the worker can assist clients to become assertive and use community supports (Leeder, 1988).

Island and Letellier (1991) offered two chapters on how to end and stay out of a violent gay male relationship, at the same time acknowledging the difficulty of leaving an abusive relationship. They began by noting the importance of admitting the abuse and sharing it with trusted others. Also important is finding a safe place and developing a plan for leaving, including having a separate bank account. They suggested using a "lay helper" to develop a plan, advising that discretion be used when choosing that special friend. It may be helpful to call a domestic violence program, a gay-lesbian hotline, or an antiviolence program, if there is one, and to seek a restraining order. To stay out of the relationship, it is important that survivors find support from friends or professional helpers to combat feelings of loneliness, guilt, fear, or self-doubt that may undermine the decision to end the relationship.

Treatment of Batterers

There is limited research examining the personality characteristics of lesbian and gay batterers or effective models of treatment. Margolies and Leeder (1995) observed that although the lesbian batterers they treated were a diverse group, all had witnessed or experienced abuse as children. They exhibited low self-esteem despite appearing charming, even charismatic. These abusers in treatment perceived their abusive behavior to be ego-dystonic and demonstrated empathy with their victims and shame because of their abusive behavior, which they said occurred in "an altered state of consciousness" (p. 143).

Island and Letellier (1991) portrayed gay batterers as men confused about masculinity who lack healthy role models for intimate relationships in a context in which being gay is perceived as unmasculine. Such men may resolve this confusion by equating masculinity with violence and aggression. Abuse is seen as a psychological disorder that results from cultural socialization and dysfunctional experiences in the family of origin. The "personality profile" of the gay batterer is one of low self-esteem, insecurity, depression, inappropriate expectations of self and partner, jealousy, excessive emotional dependency on the partner, and unwillingness to acknowledge abusive behavior (Island & Letellier, 1991).

Treatment for gay and lesbian batterers can include individual, group, or couples therapy, with all models stressing the importance of a comprehensive clinical assessment of the batterer at the outset of treatment. Minimally, this assessment should include attention to history of violence and abuse committed as an adult, abuse witnessed or directly experienced in the family of origin, the meaning and function of the violence, conflict and roles in the relationship, and sexual identity and orientation issues that can provide insight into the extent of internalized homophobia (Byrne, 1996; Hamberger, 1996).

In discussing individual treatment of the lesbian batterer, Leeder (1988) noted that the batterer should be seen as the primary focus for change and that such a viewpoint is important to developing a therapeutic alliance based on trust. Other treatment goals include helping the clients to recognize and manage anger and improve their ability to communicate their own needs and emotions. In discussing intervention with gay batterers, Byrne (1996) suggested that treatment begin with a written contract signed by the client to refrain from perpetrating emotional, psychological, or physical violence or abuse within the current or any subsequent relationships. The overall goal of treatment with gay batterers is to "create, nurture, and strengthen the individual's capacity to maintain intimate relationships which are free of violence and abusive behavior" (p. 111). Other treatment goals can include heightened self-esteem; increased awareness of triggers for violence; and appropriate expression of feelings, especially anger. An individualized safety plan should be developed to which the abused partner should also provide input. It is important that the worker communicate empathy and optimism that the abusive client can change and learn to become violence and abuse free (Byrne, 1996).

Group treatment is most often suggested in combination with individual treatment, although it is not as strongly recommended as the preferred modality for gay batterers as it is for heterosexual batterers (Byrne, 1996). According to Margolies and Leeder (1995), groups provide for peer support, shatter the secrecy of domestic violence, and serve "as an alternative to the norms of a violent lesbian subculture" (p. 149). Core issues identified in group treatment focused on anger management, negotiation, and the effective resolution of conflict. Finding a sufficient number of gay or lesbian batterers willing to participate in a group may be a problem in smaller communities.

Margolies and Leeder's (1995) community model was developed based on the premise that batterers are reluctant to enter treatment on their own. Their approach consists of three stages: (1) therapy with the couple together, (2) individual psychotherapy with the victim and perpetrator separately, and (3) conjoint work with the couple. Family members and friends also may be included. Therapy with the couple together, especially at the outset of treatment, is a controversial issue among those who write about same-sex domestic violence and is seen as contraindicated by most.

There are many cautions against couples counseling in the literature on the treatment of battering in gay and lesbian relationships (Morrow & Hawxhurst, 1989; Renzetti, 1993). Many therapists who use couples counseling, both heterosexual and lesbian, attempt to preserve the relationship, failing to address the violence issue directly and thereby missing the seriousness of the situation. "Couple counseling is usually unsuccessful because it overlooks the power differences between the partners, in particular the psychological and physical intimidation of the victim by the abusive partner" (Renzetti, 1993, p. 189). In support of Margolies and Leeder's approach, Istar (1996) observed that "while the safety of the battered partner is always of primary importance, in order to accurately diagnose the nature of power and control dynamics within the relationship, it may be necessary to work with both partners initially in an assessment process" (p. 104). As a final stage of treatment, precluding individual therapy, Margolies and Leeder suggested couples counseling to enhance communication and teach the batterer to compromise and understand the victim's perspective while implementing time-out to deal with anger and finding new ways of interacting.

With regard to gay men and lesbians of color, there is a need for mental health professionals who are culturally competent to have domestic violence training, as well as a need for research on gay men of color. To be more responsive to the violence-related needs of gay men and lesbians of color, Mendez (1996) and Waldron (1996) advocated the use of more creative outreach strategies. Advertis-

ing in publications read by people of color, regardless of sexual orientation; connecting with leaders in communities of color; and obtaining support from organizations used by people of color are suggested ways of reaching out to abused gay men and lesbians within their larger ethnic communities. In hiring direct services staff, Mendez (1996) suggested obtaining a staff that represents the population one is serving, although being a lesbian or gay man and a person of color is not necessary as long as the staff member is cognizant of racism, homophobia, and sexism (Kanuha, 1990). Service providers must be sensitive to long-standing tense relationships between the police and communities of color, as well as the prevalence of homophobia. As in all domestic violence situations, systems advocacy is important.

CONCLUSIONS AND RECOMMENDATIONS

Violence and abuse in lesbian and gay couple relationships has just recently been acknowledged. It shares many commonalities with domestic violence in heterosexual couple relationships. For example, it appears to occur with similar frequency and severity, has similar contributing factors and dynamics, and has similar consequences for its victims. However, there are also some features that are unique to abuse in same-sex relationships. These include the homophobia and discrimination suffered by gay men and lesbians, which create barriers to acknowledging the abuse and seeking and receiving help, and alienation from families of origin, which often provide assistance to heterosexual victims seeking to escape abuse. Because of gender-based stereotypes about who becomes a batterer and who becomes a victim, it is often difficult for people to perceive gay men as victims and lesbians as abusers. The reluctance to see same-sex couples as legitimate family units also may interfere with recognition of domestic violence among lesbians and gay men. Lesbians and gay men of color face particular problems in addressing issues of abuse, including conflicting loyalties to their ethnic communities and to the gay and lesbian communities.

As recognition of this problem has grown, so has the demand for services. Services are in short supply, especially for gay men, and must be expanded. Social workers also need to better educate professionals about this problem and encourage heterosexual treatment providers to carefully examine their beliefs and feelings about same-sex couples and possible homophobia. Gay and lesbian practitioners, too, may need to examine their preconceptions about the nature of same-sex relationships and acknowledge the existence of abuse in such relationships. Because the treatment literature is extremely limited, practitioners may be advised to consult the larger bodies of literature on intervention with heterosexual batterers and victims, much of which may be appropriate for use with gay men and lesbians, although modifications may be necessary.

More and better quality research is needed on virtually every aspect of abuse in same-sex relationships. Research is needed on the nature and extent of abuse, as well as the causes and consequences of violence and abuse in lesbian and especially gay couple relationships. This research should ideally be based on more representative samples that reflect the social class and ethnic diversity within the gay and lesbian communities, and abused lesbians and gay men should be compared with matched, nonabused counterparts. Abuse must be more carefully defined, and emotional, physical, and sexual abuse must be differentiated in terms of their antecedents and consequences. Equally important is research on intervention that investigates a variety of clinical approaches in terms of their effectiveness with gay men and lesbians. Couples-based approaches should be examined critically to determine their safety as well as efficacy and compared with clinical approaches that focus on work with individuals and groups.

Little has been written about the social policy implications of violence and abuse in gay and lesbian relationships. A more concerted effort must be made to disseminate information about such abuse among those who might be in a position to assist an abused gay man or lesbian, such as social workers and other mental health practitioners, police officers, and health care providers. More and better research is essential for this goal to be accomplished effectively. However, information about abuse in and of itself is not sufficient because of the pervasiveness of homophobia and widespread myths about homosexuality, which should be addressed systematically in the curricula of schools of social work and other mental health care training programs. Social agencies should also be encouraged to

critically examine the language used in service protocols and written materials, adopting more inclusive language where appropriate. Additional resources must be allocated to support the development of a range of services for both victims and perpetrators of same-sex violence and abuse, at least some of which should be made available to community-based programs for gay men and lesbians. Safe home and shelter services are especially needed for gay men, who do not have access to battered women's shelters, but may also be needed for lesbians, who may not be accommodated comfortably in shelters for heterosexual women. Finally, coordination with the battered women's movement and with programs for heterosexual batterers has been recommended, as well as continued lobbying for legislative changes to extend to gay men and lesbians the same protections afforded to heterosexuals with respect to intimate violence (Hamberger, 1996).

REFERENCES

Byrne, D. (1996). Clinical models for the treatment of gay male perpetrators of domestic violence. *Journal of Gay & Lesbian Social Services, 4,* 107–116.

Davis, L. V., & Srinivasan, M. (1995). Listening to the voices of battered women: What helps them escape from violence. *Affilia, 10,* 49–69.

Elliott, P. (1996). Shattering illusions: Same-sex domestic violence. *Journal of Gay & Lesbian Social Services, 4,* 1–8.

Farley, N. (1996). A survey of factors contributing to gay and lesbian domestic violence. *Journal of Gay & Lesbian Social Services, 4,* 35–42.

Hamberger, L. K. (1996). Intervention in gay male intimate violence requires coordinated efforts on multiple levels. *Journal of Gay & Lesbian Social Services, 4,* 83–91.

Hammond, N. (1989). Lesbian victims of relationship violence. *Women & Therapy, 8,* 89–105.

Hart, B. (1986). Lesbian battering: An examination. In K. Lobel (Ed.), *Naming the violence: Speaking out about lesbian battering.* Seattle: Seal Press.

Island, D., & Letellier, P. (1991). *Men who beat the men who love them: Battered gay men and domestic violence.* New York: Haworth Press.

Istar, A. (1996). Couple assessment—Identifying and intervening in domestic violence in lesbian relationships. *Journal of Gay & Lesbian Social Services, 4,* 93–106.

Kanuha, V. (1990). Compounding the triple jeopardy: Battering in lesbian of color relationships. *Women & Therapy, 9,* 169–184.

Leeder, R. (1988). Enmeshed in pain: Counseling the lesbian battering couple. *Women & Therapy, 7,* 81–99.

Letellier, P. (1994). Gay and bisexual domestic violence victimization: Challenges to feminist theory and responses to violence. *Violence and Victims, 9,* 95–106.

Lie, G. Y., & Gentlewarrier, S. (1991). Intimate violence in lesbian relationships: Discussion of survey findings and practice implications. *Journal of Social Service Research, 15,* 41–59.

Lockhart, L. L., White, B. W., Causby, V., & Isaac, A. (1994). Letting out the secret: Violence in lesbian relationships. *Journal of Interpersonal Violence, 9,* 469–492.

Margolies, L., & Leeder, E. (1995) Violence at the door: Treatment of lesbian batterers. *Violence Against Women, 1,* 139–157.

Mendez, J. M. (1996). Serving gays and lesbians of color who are survivors of domestic violence. *Journal of Gay & Lesbian Social Services, 4,* 53–60.

Merrill, G. S. (1996). Ruling the exceptions: Same-sex battering and domestic violence theory. *Journal of Gay & Lesbian Social Services, 4,* 9–22

Morrow, S. L., & Hawxhurst, D. M. (1989). Lesbian partner abuse: Implications for therapists. *Journal of Counseling and Development, 68,* 58–62.

Renzetti, C. M. (1988). Violence in lesbian relationships: A preliminary analysis of causal factors. *Journal of Interpersonal Violence, 3,* 38–399.

Renzetti, C. M. (1989). Building a second closet: Third party responses to victims of lesbian partner abuse. *Family Relations, 38,* 157–165.

Renzetti, C. M. (1992). *Violent betrayal: Partner abuse in lesbian relationships.* Newbury Park, CA: Sage Publications.

Renzetti, C. M. (1993). Violence in lesbian relationships. In M. Hansen & M. Harway (Eds.), *Battering and family therapy* (pp. 188–199). Newbury Park, CA: Sage Publications.

Schilit, R., Lie, G. Y., Bush, J., Montagne, M., & Reyes, L. (1991). Intergenerational transmission of violence in lesbian relationships. *Affilia, 6,* 72–87.

Waldron, C. M. (1996). Lesbians of color and the domestic violence movement. *Journal of Gay & Lesbian Social Services, 4,* 43–52.

Walker, L. E. (1979). *The battered woman.* New York: Harper & Row.

Walker, L. E. (1984). *The battered woman syndrome.* New York: Springer.

FURTHER READING

Edleson, J. L., & Tolman, R. M. (1992). *Intervention for men who batter: An ecological approach.* Newbury Park, CA: Sage Publications.

Elliott, P. (1990). *Confronting lesbian battering.* St. Paul: Minnesota Coalition for Battered Women.

Guth, J., & Elliott, P. (1990). *Confronting homophobia.* St. Paul: Minnesota Coalition for Battered Women.

Renzetti, C. M., & Miley, C. H. (1996). *Violence in gay and lesbian domestic partnerships.* Binghamton, NY: Haworth Press.

Roberts, A. R. (1996). *Helping battered women: New perspectives and remedies.* New York: Oxford University Press.

Bonnie E. Carlson, PhD, CSW, is associate professor, School of Social Welfare, University at Albany, State University of New York, 135 Western Avenue, Albany, NY 12222. **Katherine Maciol, CSW,** is clinical supervisor, Unified Services, Rensselaer County Department of Mental Health, Troy, NY 12180.

For further information see

Alcohol Abuse; Conflict Resolution; **Divorce;** Domestic Violence: Legal Issues; Drug Abuse; Gay Men Overview; Homicide; Lesbians Overview; Marriage/Partners; Men Overview; Sexual Assault; Substance Abuse: Direct Practice; Victim Services and Victim/Witness Assistance Programs; Violence Overview; Women Overview.

Key Words

abuse	homosexuality
domestic violence	lesbians
gay men	

E

Electronic Technologies
See **The Internet: Accessing the World of Information; Social Work Education: Electronic Technologies**

Ethical Standards in Social Work: The *NASW Code of Ethics*
Frederic G. Reamer

One of the hallmarks of a profession is its willingness to establish ethical standards to guide practitioner's conduct (Greenwood, 1957; Hall, 1968; Lindeman, 1947). Ethical standards are created to address ethical issues in practice and to provide guidelines for determining what is ethically acceptable and unacceptable behavior.

Professions typically publicize their ethical standards in the form of codes of ethics (Bayles, 1986; Kultgen, 1982). According to Jamal and Bowie (1995), codes of ethics are designed to address three major issues. First, codes address "problems of moral hazard" (pp. 703–704), or instances when a profession's self-interest may conflict with the public's interest (for example, whether accountants should be obligated to disclose confidential information concerning serious financial crimes that their clients have committed, or whether dentists should be permitted to refuse to treat people who have an infectious disease, such as the acquired immune deficiency syndrome [AIDS]). Second, codes address issues of "professional courtesy"—that is, rules that govern how professionals should behave to enhance and maintain a profession's integrity (for example, whether lawyers should be permitted to advertise and solicit clients, or whether psychiatrists should be permitted to engage in sexual relationships with former patients). Finally, codes address issues that concern professionals' duty to serve the public interest (for example, the extent of physicians', nurses', or social workers' obligation to assist when faced with a public emergency).

Like other professions such as medicine, nursing, law, psychology, journalism, and engineering, social work has developed a comprehensive set of ethical standards. These standards have evolved over time, reflecting significant changes in the broader culture and in social work's mission, methods, and priorities. They address a wide range of issues, including,

for example, social workers' handling of confidential information, sexual contact between social workers and their clients, conflicts of interest, supervision, education and training, and social and political action.

Ethical standards in social work appear in various forms. The *NASW Code of Ethics* (NASW, 1996) is the most visible compilation of the profession's ethical standards. Ethical standards can also be found in codes of ethics developed by other social work organizations (for example, the National Association of Black Social Workers [NABSW] and the National Federation of Societies for Clinical Social Work [NFSCSW]), regulations governing state licensing boards, and codes of conduct promulgated by social services agencies. In addition, social work's literature contains many discussions of ethical norms in the profession (Loewenberg & Dolgoff, 1992; Reamer, 1990, 1994, 1995; Rhodes, 1986).

THE PROFESSION'S EARLY YEARS
During the earliest years of social work's history, few formal ethical standards existed. The earliest known attempt to formulate a code was an experimental draft code of ethics printed in the 1920s and attributed to Mary Richmond (Pumphrey, 1959). Although several other social work organizations formulated draft codes during the profession's early years (for example, the American Association for Organizing Family Social Work and several chapters of the American Association of Social Workers), it was not until 1947 that the latter group, the largest organization of social

113

workers of that era, adopted a formal code (Johnson, 1955). In 1960 NASW adopted its first code of ethics, five years after the association was formed. Over time, the *NASW Code of Ethics* has been recognized as the most visible and influential code in social work.

In 1960 the *NASW Code of Ethics* consisted of 14 proclamations concerning, for example, every social worker's duty to give precedence to professional responsibility over personal interests; to respect the privacy of clients; to give appropriate professional service in public emergencies; and to contribute knowledge, skills, and support to human welfare programs. First-person statements (that is, "I give precedence to my professional responsibility over my personal interests" and "I respect the privacy of the people I serve" [p. 1]) were preceded by a preamble that set forth social workers' responsibility to uphold humanitarian ideals, maintain and improve social work service, and develop the philosophy and skills of the profession. In 1967 a 15th principle pledging nondiscrimination was added to the proclamations.

Soon after the adoption of the code, however, NASW members began to express concern about its level of abstraction, its scope and usefulness for resolving ethical conflicts, and its provisions for handling ethics complaints about practitioners and agencies (McCann & Cutler, 1979). In 1977 NASW established a task force to revise the code and enhance its relevance to practice; the result was a new code adopted by NASW in 1979.

The 1979 code included six sections of brief, unannotated principles with a preamble setting forth the code's general purpose and stating that the code's principles provided standards for the enforcement of ethical practices among social workers. The code included major sections concerning social workers' general conduct and comportment and ethical responsibilities to clients, colleagues, employers, employing organizations, the social work profession, and society. The code's principles were both prescriptive ("The social worker should act to prevent the unauthorized and unqualified practice of social work" [principle V.M.3]) and proscriptive ("The social worker should not exploit relationships with clients for personal advantage" [principle II.F.2]). Several of the code's principles were concrete and specific ("The social worker should under no circumstances engage in sexual activities with clients" and "The

social worker should respect confidences shared by colleagues in the course of their professional relationships and transactions" [principle III.J.2]), whereas others were more abstract, asserting ethical ideals ("The social worker should promote the general welfare of society" [principle VI.P] and "The social worker should uphold and advance the values, ethics, knowledge, and mission of the profession" [principle V.M]).

The 1979 code was revised twice (NASW, 1990, 1993), eventually including 70 principles. In 1990 several principles related to solicitation of clients and fee splitting were modified following an inquiry into NASW policies by the U.S. Federal Trade Commission (FTC), begun in 1986, concerning possible restraint of trade. As a result of the inquiry, principles in the code were revised to remove prohibitions concerning solicitation of clients from colleagues or one's agency and to modify wording related to accepting compensation for making a referral. NASW also entered into a consent agreement with the FTC concerning issues raised by the inquiry.

In 1993 the NASW Delegate Assembly voted to further amend the code of ethics to include five new principles, three related to the problem of social worker impairment and two related to the problem of dual or multiple relationships. The first three principles addressed instances when social workers' own problems and impairment interfere with their professional functioning, and the latter two addressed the need to avoid social, business, and other nonprofessional relationships with clients because of the possibility of conflicts of interest (NASW, 1993).

The 1993 Delegate Assembly also passed a resolution to establish a task force to draft an entirely new code of ethics for submission to the 1996 Delegate Assembly. The task force was established in an effort to develop a new code of ethics that would be far more comprehensive in scope and relevant to contemporary practice. Since the adoption of the 1979 code, social workers had developed a keener grasp of a wide range of ethical issues facing practitioners, many of which were not addressed in the NASW code. The broader field of applied and professional ethics, which had begun in the early 1970s, had matured considerably, resulting in the identification and greater understanding of novel ethical issues not cited in the 1979 code. Especially during the 1980s and early 1990s, scholarly analyses of ethical issues in the professions generally, and social work in particular, burgeoned. This occurred for a variety of reasons, including the emergence of complicated ethical issues in health care (for example, public debate about the ethics of allocating scarce vital organs, genetic engineering, abortion, and euthanasia); sustained debate about ethical issues identified in the 1960s concerning patients' rights, welfare rights, prisoners' rights, and civil rights; increased litigation alleging ethical misconduct by professionals; and widespread publicity about professionals' ethical misconduct (for example, physicians and nurses who use illegal drugs, clergy who are sexually involved with minors, police officers who accept bribes, and social workers who submit fraudulent Medicaid claims). (For additional discussion of ethical issues in social work, see the entry "Ethics and Values" elsewhere in this encyclopedia.)

A by-product of this trend was that social workers as a group began paying much more attention to ethical issues in the profession. For example, presentations on social work ethics at professional conferences, sponsored by NASW, the Council on Social Work Education (CSWE), and other social work organizations, increased significantly. In addition, the CSWE (1992) strengthened the language in its *Curriculum Policy Statement* requiring instruction on ethical issues and ethical decision-making in undergraduate and graduate social work education programs.

THE CURRENT *NASW CODE OF ETHICS*

The Code of Ethics Revision Committee was appointed in 1994 and spent two years drafting a new code. The committee, which was chaired by this author and included a professional ethicist and social workers from a variety of practice and educational settings, carried out its work in three phases. The committee first reviewed literature on social work ethics and on applied and professional ethics generally to identify key concepts and issues that might be addressed in the new code. The committee also reviewed the 1979 code to identify content that should be retained or deleted and areas where content might be added. The committee then discussed possible ways of organizing the new code to enhance its relevance and use in practice.

During the second phase, which overlapped with phase one activities, the committee issued formal invitations to all NASW members and to members of various social work organizations (for example, the NABSW, the CSWE, the American Association of State Social Work Boards, and the NFSCSW) to suggest issues that might be addressed in the new code. The committee then reviewed its list of relevant content areas drawn from the literature and from public comment and developed a number of rough drafts, the final of which was shared with a small group of ethics experts in social work and other professions for their comments.

In the third phase, the committee made a number of revisions based on the feedback it received from the experts who reviewed the document, published a copy of the draft code in the January 1996 issue of the *NASW News,* and invited NASW members to submit comments to be considered by the committee as it prepared the final draft for submission to the 1996 NASW Delegate Assembly. In addition, during this last phase members of the committee met with each of the NASW Delegate Assembly regional coalitions to discuss the code's development and receive delegates' comments and feedback. The code was then presented to and ratified by the Delegate Assembly in August 1996 and implemented in January 1997.

The code, which contains the most comprehensive statement of ethical standards in social work, includes four major sections. (The complete text of the 1996 code is presented in this 1997 supplement.) The first section, "Preamble," summarizes social work's mission and core values. This is the first time in NASW's history that its code of ethics has contained a formally sanctioned mission statement and an explicit summary of the profession's core values. The mission statement emphasizes social work's historic and enduring commitment to enhancing human well-being and helping meet the basic needs of all people, with particular attention to the needs and empowerment of people who are vulnerable, oppressed, and living in poverty. The mission statement clearly reflects social work's unique concern about vulnerable populations and the profession's simultaneous focus on individual well-being and the environmental forces that create, contribute to, and address problems in living. The preamble also highlights social workers' determination to promote social justice and social change with and on behalf of clients.

The preamble also identifies six core values on which social work's mission is based: service, social justice, dignity and worth of the person, importance of human relationships, integrity, and competence. The Code of Ethics Revision Committee settled on these core values after engaging in a systematic review of literature on the subject.

The second section, "Purpose of the NASW Code of Ethics," provides an overview of the code's main functions and a brief guide for dealing with ethical issues or dilemmas in social work practice. This section alerts social workers to the code's various purposes:

- to set forth broad ethical principles that reflect the profession's core values and establish ethical standards to guide social work practice
- to help social workers identify relevant considerations when professional obligations, conflicts, or ethical uncertainties arise
- to socialize practitioners new to the field to social work's mission, values, and ethical standards
- to provide ethical standards to which the general public can hold the social work profession accountable
- to articulate standards that the profession itself (and other bodies that choose to adopt the code, such as licensing and regulatory boards, professional liability insurance providers, courts of law, agency boards of directors, and government agencies) can use to assess whether social workers have engaged in unethical conduct.

This section's brief guide for dealing with ethical issues highlights various resources social workers should consider when faced with difficult ethical decisions. Such resources include ethical theory and decision making, social work practice theory and research, laws, regulations, agency policies, and other relevant codes of ethics. Social workers are encouraged to obtain ethics consultation when appropriate, perhaps from an agency-based or social work organization's ethics committee, regulatory bodies (for example, a state licensing board), knowledgeable colleagues, supervisors, or legal counsel.

One of the key features of this section of the code is its explicit acknowledgment that instances sometimes arise in social work in which the code's values, principles, and

standards conflict. The code does not provide a formula for resolving such conflicts and "does not specify which values, principles, and standards are most important and ought to outweigh others in instances when they conflict" (NASW, 1996, p. 3). The codes states that "reasonable differences of opinion can and do exist among social workers with respect to the ways in which values, ethical principles, and ethical standards should be rank ordered when they conflict. Ethical decision making in a given situation must apply the informed judgment of the individual social worker and should also consider how the issues would be judged in a peer review process where the ethical standards of the profession would be applied. . . . Social workers' decisions and actions should be consistent with the spirit as well as the letter of this code" (NASW, 1996, p. 3).

The code's third section, "Ethical Principles," presents six broad ethical principles that inform social work practice, one for each of the six core values cited in the preamble. The principles are presented at a fairly high level of abstraction to provide a conceptual base for the profession's ethical standards. The code also includes a brief annotation for each of the principles. For example, the ethical principle associated with the value "importance of human relationships" states that "social workers recognize the central importance of human relationships" (p. 6). The annotation states that "social workers understand that relationships between and among people are an important vehicle for change. Social workers engage people as partners in the helping process. Social workers seek to strengthen relationships among people in a purposeful effort to promote, restore, maintain, and enhance the well-being of individuals, families, social groups, organizations, and communities" (p. 6).

The code's final section, "Ethical Standards," includes 155 specific ethical standards to guide social workers' conduct and provide a basis for adjudication of ethics complaints filed against NASW members. The standards fall into six categories concerning social workers' ethical responsibilities to clients, to colleagues, in practice settings, as professionals, to the profession, and to society at large. The introduction to this section of the code states explicitly that some of the standards are enforceable guidelines for professional conduct and some are standards to which social workers should aspire. Furthermore, the code states, "the extent to which each standard is enforceable is a matter of professional judgment to be exercised by those responsible for reviewing alleged violations of ethical standards" (p. 7).

In general, the code's standards concern three kinds of issues (Reamer, 1994). The first includes what can be described as "mistakes" social workers might make that have ethical implications. Examples include leaving confidential information displayed on one's desk in such a way that it can be read by unauthorized persons or forgetting to include important details in a client's informed consent document. The second category includes issues associated with difficult ethical decisions—for example, whether to disclose confidential information to protect a third party from harm or whether to continue providing services to an indigent client whose insurance coverage has been exhausted. The final category includes issues pertaining to social worker misconduct, such as exploitation of clients, boundary violations, or fraudulent billing for services rendered.

Ethical Responsibilities to Clients
The first section of the code's ethical standards is the most detailed. It addresses a wide range of issues involved in the delivery of services to individuals, families, couples, and small groups of clients. In particular, this section focuses on social workers' commitment to clients, clients' right to self-determination, informed consent, professional competence, cultural competence and social diversity, conflicts of interest, privacy and confidentiality, client access to records, sexual relationships and physical contact with clients, sexual harassment, the use of derogatory language, payment for services, clients who lack decision-making capacity, interruption of services, and termination of services.

Unlike the 1960 and 1979 codes, the 1996 *NASW Code of Ethics* acknowledges that although social workers' primary responsibility is to clients, instances can arise when "social workers' responsibility to the larger society or specific legal obligations may on limited occasions supersede the loyalty owed to clients" (standard 1.01, p. 7). Examples include when a social worker is required by law to report that a client has abused a child or has threatened to harm self or others. In a similar vein, the code also acknowledges that clients' right to self-determination, which social workers ordinarily respect, may be limited when clients' actions or potential actions pose a serious, foreseeable, and imminent risk to themselves or others.

Standards on informed consent were added to the 1996 code specifying the elements that should be included when social workers obtain consent from clients or potential clients for the delivery of services; the use of electronic media, such as computers, telephone, radio, and television, to provide services; audio- or videotaping of clients; third-party observation of clients who are receiving services; and release of information. These include the use of clear and understandable language to explain the purpose of services to be provided, risks related to the services, relevant costs, reasonable alternatives, clients' right to refuse or withdraw consent, and the time frame covered by the consent. Social workers are also instructed to inform clients of any limits to services because of the requirements of a third-party payer, such as an insurance or managed care company. This is a critically important provision in light of the growing influence of third-party payers in recent years.

A new section in the current code pertains to the subject of cultural competence and social diversity. In recent years social workers have enhanced their understanding of the relevance of cultural and social diversity in their work with clients. Cultural and ethnic norms, for example, may shape clients' understanding of issues in their lives and affect their response to available social services. Consequently, the code requires that social workers take reasonable steps to understand and be sensitive to clients' cultures and social diversity with respect to race, ethnicity, national origin, color, sex, sexual orientation, age, marital status, political belief, religion, and mental or physical disability.

The code's standards concerning conflicts of interest alert social workers to their obligation to avoid circumstances that might interfere with the exercise of professional discretion and impartial judgment. This includes avoiding any dual or multiple relationships with clients or former clients in which there is a risk of exploitation or potential harm to the client. Social workers are also urged to take special precautions when they provide services to two or more persons who have a relationship with each other. Social workers who anticipate having to perform in potentially conflicting roles are advised to clarify their obligations with the parties involved and take appropriate action to minimize any conflict of interest (for example, when a social worker is asked to testify in a child custody dispute or divorce proceedings involving clients).

The 1996 code substantially expanded the profession's standard on privacy and confidentiality. Noteworthy are details concerning social workers' obligation to disclose confidential information to protect third parties from serious harm; confidentiality guidelines when working with families, couples, or groups; disclosure of confidential information to third-party payers; discussion of confidential information in public and semipublic areas, such as hallways, waiting rooms, elevators, and restaurants; disclosure of confidential information during legal proceedings; protection of the confidentiality of clients' written and electronic records and of information transmitted to other parties through the use of such devices as computers, electronic mail, facsimile machines, and telephones; the use of case material in teaching or training; and protection of the confidentiality of deceased clients. Social workers are advised to discuss confidentiality policies and guidelines as soon as possible in the social worker–client relationship and as needed throughout the course of the relationship.

The 1996 code also added considerable detail on social workers' sexual relationships with clients. In addition to prohibiting sexual relationships with current clients, which was addressed in the 1979 code, the current code also generally prohibits sexual activities or sexual contact with former clients. This is a particularly important development, considering intense concern among social workers about practitioners' possible exploitation of former clients. The code also prohibits sexual activities or sexual contact with clients' relatives or other individuals with whom clients maintain a close, personal relationship whenever there is a risk of exploitation or potential harm to the client. Furthermore, social workers are advised not to provide clinical services to individuals with whom they have had a previous sexual relationship because of the likelihood that such a relationship would make it difficult for the social

worker and client to maintain appropriate professional boundaries.

In addition to its greatly expanded detail on sexual relationships, the *NASW Code of Ethics* also comments on other physical contact between social workers and clients. The code acknowledges the possibility for appropriate physical contact (for example, holding a distraught child who has been removed from his or her home because of parental neglect or holding the hand of a nursing home resident whose spouse has died) but cautions social workers not to engage in physical contact with clients, such as cradling or caressing, when there is a possibility that psychological harm to the client could result. Social workers are also admonished not to sexually harass clients.

The 1996 code added a specific provision concerning the use of bartering—that is, accepting goods or services from clients as payment for professional service. The code stops short of banning bartering outright, recognizing that in some communities bartering is a widely accepted form of payment. However, the code advises social workers to avoid bartering because of the potential for conflicts of interest, exploitation, and inappropriate boundaries in social workers' relationships with clients. For example, if a client "pays" a social worker for counseling by performing some service—such as painting the social worker's house or repairing the social worker's car—and the service is somehow unsatisfactory, attempts to resolve the problem could interfere with the therapeutic relationship and seriously undermine the social worker's effective delivery of counseling services.

In addition to advising social workers to terminate with clients properly when services are no longer required or no longer serve the clients' needs or interests, the code permits social workers in fee-for-service settings to terminate services to clients who are not paying an overdue balance. However, services may be terminated in these circumstances only when the financial arrangements have been made clear to the client, the client does not pose an imminent danger to self or others, and the clinical and other consequences of the client's nonpayment have been discussed with the client.

The code advises social workers who are leaving an employment setting to inform clients of all available options for the continuation of services and their benefits and risks. This is an important standard, because it permits a social worker to discuss the advantages and disadvantages associated with a client's decision to continue receiving services from the social worker in her or his new setting, obtain services from another practitioner in the setting the social worker is leaving, or seek services from another practitioner or agency. In addition, the code prohibits social workers from terminating services to pursue a social, financial, or sexual relationship with a client.

Ethical Responsibilities to Colleagues

This section of the code addresses issues concerning social workers' relationships with professional colleagues. These include respect for colleagues; proper treatment of confidential information shared by colleagues; interdisciplinary collaboration and disputes among colleagues; consultation with colleagues; referral for services; sexual relationships with and sexual harassment of colleagues; and dealings with impaired, incompetent, and unethical colleagues.

The code encourages social workers who are members of an interdisciplinary team, such as in a health care or school setting, to draw explicitly on the perspectives, values, and experiences of the social work profession. If disagreements among team members cannot be resolved, social workers are advised to pursue other avenues to address their concerns (for example, approaching an agency's administrators or board of directors). Social workers are also advised not to exploit disputes between a colleague and an employer to advance their own interests, or to exploit clients in a dispute with a colleague.

The 1996 code includes a number of new standards concerning consultation and referral for services. Social workers are obligated to seek colleagues' advice and counsel whenever such consultation is in clients' best interest, disclosing the least amount of information necessary to achieve the purposes of the consultation. Social workers are also expected to keep informed of colleagues' areas of expertise and competence. In addition, social workers are expected to refer clients to other professionals when a colleague's specialized knowledge or expertise is needed to serve clients fully or when social workers believe they are not being effective or making reasonable progress with clients.

This section of the code also addresses dual and multiple relationships, specifically with respect to prohibiting sexual activities or contact between social work supervisors or educators and supervisees, students, trainees, or other colleagues over whom supervisors or educators exercise professional authority. In addition, the code prohibits sexual harassment of supervisees, students, trainees, or colleagues.

The 1996 code strengthens ethical standards pertaining to impaired, incompetent, and unethical colleagues. Social workers who have direct knowledge of a social work colleague's impairment (which may be caused by personal problems, psychosocial distress, substance abuse, or mental health difficulties, and which interferes with practice effectiveness), incompetence, or unethical conduct are required to consult with that colleague when feasible; assist the colleague in taking remedial action; and if these measures do not address the problem satisfactorily, take action through appropriate channels established by employers, agencies, NASW, licensing and regulatory bodies, and other professional organizations. Social workers are also expected to defend and assist colleagues who are unjustly charged with unethical conduct.

Ethical Responsibilities in Practice Settings

This section of the code addresses ethical issues that arise in social services agencies, human services organizations, private practice, and social work education programs. Standards pertain to social work supervision, consultation, education, or training; performance evaluation; client records; billing for services; client transfer; agency administration; continuing education and staff development; commitments to employers; and labor–management disputes.

One major theme in this section is that social workers who provide supervision, consultation, education, or training should do so only within their areas of knowledge and competence. Also, social workers who provide these services are to avoid engaging in any dual or multiple relationships when there is a risk of exploitation or potential harm. Another standard requires that social workers who function as educators or field instructors for students should take reasonable steps to ensure that clients are routinely informed when services are being provided by students.

Several standards pertain to client records. These require that records include sufficient, accurate, and timely documentation to facilitate the delivery of services and ensure continuity of services provided to clients in the future. Documentation in records should protect clients' privacy to the greatest extent possible and appropriate, including only that information that is directly relevant to the delivery of services. In addition, the code requires social workers to store records properly to ensure reasonable future access; records should be maintained for the number of years required by state statutes or relevant contracts.

Social workers who bill for services are obligated to establish and maintain practices that accurately reflect the nature and extent of services provided. Thus, social workers must not falsify billing records or submit fraudulent invoices.

Social workers are urged to be particularly careful when an individual who is receiving services from another agency or colleague contacts a social worker for services. Social workers should carefully consider the client's needs before agreeing to provide services. To minimize possible confusion and conflict, the code states that social workers should discuss with potential clients the nature of their current relationship with other service providers and the implications, including possible benefits or risks, of entering into a relationship with a new service provider. If a new client has been served by another agency or colleague, social workers should discuss with the client whether consultation with the previous service provider is in the client's best interest.

The 1996 code greatly expands coverage of ethical standards related to agency administration. The code obligates social work administrators to advocate within and outside their agencies for adequate resources to meet clients' needs and provide appropriate staff supervision; also, they must promote resource allocation procedures that are open and fair. In addition, administrators must take reasonable steps to ensure that the working environment for which they are responsible is consistent with and encourages compliance with the *NASW Code of Ethics*. They must also take reasonable steps to provide or arrange for continuing education and staff development for all staff for whom they are responsible.

The code also includes a number of ethical standards for social work employees. Although social work employees are generally expected to adhere to commitment made to their employers and employing organization, they should not allow an employing organization's policies, procedures, regulations, or administrative orders to interfere with their ethical practice of social work. Thus, social workers are obligated to take reasonable steps to ensure that their employing organizations' practices are consistent with the *NASW Code of Ethics*. Also, social workers should accept employment or arrange student field placements only in organizations in which fair personnel practices are exercised. Social workers should conserve agency funds where appropriate and must never misappropriate funds or use them for unintended purposes.

A novel feature of the code is its acknowledgment of ethical issues social workers sometimes face as a result of labor–management disputes. Although the code does not prescribe how social workers should handle such dilemmas, it does permit social workers to engage in organized action, including formation of and participation in labor unions, to improve services to clients and working conditions. The code states that "reasonable differences of opinion exist among social workers concerning their primary obligation as professionals during an actual or threatened labor strike or job action" (standard 3.10(b), p. 22).

Ethical Responsibilities as Professionals

This section of the code focuses on issues primarily related to social workers' professional integrity. Standards pertain to social workers' competence, obligation to avoid any behavior that discriminates against others, private conduct, honesty, personal impairment, misrepresentation, solicitation of clients, and acknowledging credit.

In addition to emphasizing social workers' obligation to be proficient, the code exhorts social workers to routinely review and critique the professional literature; participate in continuing education; and base their work on recognized knowledge, including empirically based knowledge, relevant to social work practice and ethics.

Several standards address social workers' values and personal behavior. The code states that social workers should not practice, condone, facilitate, or collaborate with any form of discrimination and should not permit their private conduct to interfere with their ability to fulfill their professional responsibilities. Thus, for example, it would be unethical for a social worker to campaign for political office while simultaneously publicizing his or her social work credentials and publicly espousing explicitly racist social policies; this would violate the code's standard on discrimination. In addition, this private conduct would likely interfere with the social worker's ability to fulfill his or her professional responsibilities, assuming that the social worker's racist views became well known among clients and professional colleagues and reflected on his or her professional work. The code further obligates social workers to make clear distinctions between statements and actions engaged in as a private individual and those engaged in as a social worker.

A prominent theme in the code concerns social workers' obligation to be honest in their relationships with all parties, including accurately representing their professional qualifications, credentials, education, competence, and affiliations. Hence, social workers should not exaggerate or falsify their qualifications and credentials and should claim only those *relevant* professional credentials that they actually possess. For example, a social worker who has a doctorate in physics should not claim to have, or create the impression that he or she has, a doctorate that is relevant to clinical social work. Also, social workers are obligated to take responsibility and credit, including authorship credit, only for work they have actually performed and to which they have contributed. For example, social workers should not claim to have had a prominent role in a research project to which they contributed minimally. Also, social workers should honestly acknowledge the work of and contributions made by others. Therefore, it would be unethical for a social worker to draw or benefit from a colleague's work without acknowledging the source or contribution.

The code also requires that social workers not engage in uninvited solicitation of potential clients who, because of their circumstances, are vulnerable to undue influence, manipulation, or coercion. Thus, social workers are not permitted to approach vulnerable people in distress (for example, victims of a natural disaster or serious accident) and actively solicit them to become clients. Furthermore,

social workers must not solicit testimonial endorsements (for example, for advertising or marketing purposes) from current clients or from other persons who, because of their particular circumstances, are vulnerable to undue influence.

One of the most important standards in the code concerns social workers' personal impairment. Like all professionals, social workers sometimes encounter personal problems. This is a normal part of life. The code mandates, however, that social workers must not allow their personal problems, psychosocial distress, legal problems, substance abuse, or mental health difficulties to interfere with their professional judgment and performance or jeopardize others for whom they have a professional responsibility. In instances where social workers find that their personal difficulties interfere with their professional judgment and performance, they are obligated to seek professional help, make adjustments in their workload, terminate their practice, or take other steps necessary to protect clients and others.

Ethical Responsibilities to the Profession
Social workers' ethical responsibilities are not limited to clients, colleagues, and the public at large; they also include the social work profession itself. Standards in this section of the *NASW Code of Ethics* focus on the profession's integrity and social work evaluation and research. The principal theme concerning the profession's integrity pertains to social workers' obligation to maintain and promote high standards of practice by engaging in appropriate study and research, teaching, publication, presentations at professional conferences, consultation, service to the community and professional organizations, and legislative testimony.

In recent years social workers have strengthened their appreciation of the role of evaluation and research. Relevant activities include needs assessments, program evaluations, clinical research and evaluations, and the use of empirically based literature to guide practice. The 1996 code includes a substantially new series of standards concerning evaluation and research. The standards emphasize social workers' obligation to monitor and evaluate policies, implementation of programs, and practice interventions. In addition, the code requires social workers to critically examine and keep current with emerging knowledge relevant to social work and to use evaluation and research evidence in their professional practice.

The code also requires social workers involved in evaluation and research to follow widely accepted guidelines concerning the protection of evaluation and research participants. Standards focus specifically on the role of informed consent procedures in evaluation and research, the need to ensure that evaluation and research participants have access to appropriate supportive services, the confidentiality and anonymity of information obtained during the course of evaluation and research, the obligation to report results accurately, and the handling of potential or real conflicts of interest and dual relationships involving evaluation and research participants.

Ethical Responsibilities to Society at Large
The social work profession has always been committed to social justice. This commitment is clearly reflected in the *NASW Code of Ethics*' preamble and in the final section of the code's standards. The standards explicitly highlight social workers' obligation to engage in activities that promote social justice and the general welfare of society "from local to global levels" (standard 6.01, p. 26). These activities may include facilitating public discussion of social policy issues; providing professional services in public emergencies; engaging in social and political action (for example, lobbying and legislative activity) to address basic human needs; promoting conditions that encourage respect for the diversity of cultures and social diversity; and acting to prevent and eliminate domination, exploitation, and discrimination against any person, group, or class of people.

CONCLUSION

Ethical standards in social work, particularly as reflected in the *NASW Code of Ethics*, have changed dramatically during the profession's history. During the late 19th and early 20th centuries, social work's ethical standards were sparse and generally vague.

Along with all other professions, and largely as a result of the emergence of the applied and professional ethics field beginning in the 1970s, social work's ethical standards have matured considerably in recent years. The current *NASW Code of Ethics* (NASW, 1996) reflects social workers' increased understand-ing of ethical issues in the profession and the need for comprehensive ethical standards.

Ethical standards in social work cannot guarantee ethical behavior, however. Ethical standards can certainly guide practioners who encounter ethical challenges and establish norms by which social workers' actions can be judged. However, in the final analysis, ethical standards in general, and a code of ethics in particular, are only one tool in social workers' ethical arsenal. In addition to specific ethical standards, social workers must draw on ethical theory and decision-making guidelines; social work theory and practice principles; and relevant laws, regulations, and agency policies. Most of all, social workers must consider ethical standards within the context of their own values and ethics. As the *NASW Code of Ethics* states, ethical principles and standards "must be applied by individuals of good character who discern moral questions and, in good faith, seek to make reliable ethical judgments" (p. 4).

REFERENCES

Bayles, M. (1986). Professional power and self-regulation. *Business and Professional Ethics Journal, 5,* 26–46.

Council on Social Work Education. (1992). *Curriculum policy statement for master's degree programs in social work education.* Alexandria, VA: Author.

Greenwood, E. (1957). Attributes of a profession. *Social Work, 2,* 44–55.

Hall, R. H. (1968). Professionalization and bureaucratization. *American Sociological Review, 33*(1), 92–104.

Jamal, K., & Bowie, N. (1995). Theoretical considerations for a meaningful code of ethics. *Journal of Business Ethics, 14,* 703–714.

Johnson, A. (1955). Educating professional social workers for ethical practice. *Social Service Review, 29,* 125–136.

Kultgen, J. (1982). The ideological use of professional codes. *Business and Professional Ethics Journal, 1,* 53–69.

Lindeman, E. (1947). *Social work matures in a confused world.* Albany: New York State Conference on Social Workers.

Loewenberg, F., & Dolgoff, R. (1992). *Ethical decisions for social work practice* (4th ed.). Itasca, IL: F. E. Peacock.

McCann, C. W., & Cutler, J. P. (1979). Ethics and the alleged unethical. *Social Work, 24,* 5–8.

National Association of Social Workers. (1960). *NASW code of ethics.* Washington, DC: Author.

National Association of Social Workers. (1979). *NASW code of ethics*. Silver Spring, MD: Author.

National Association of Social Workers. (1990). *NASW code of ethics*. Silver Spring, MD: Author.

National Association of Social Workers. (1993). *NASW code of ethics*. Washington, DC: Author.

National Association of Social Workers. (1996). *NASW code of ethics*. Washington, DC: Author.

Pumphrey, M. W. (1959). *The teaching of values and ethics in social work education*. New York: Council on Social Work Education.

Reamer, F. G. (1990). *Ethical dilemmas in social service* (2nd ed.). New York: Columbia University Press.

Reamer, F. G. (1994). *Social work malpractice and liability*. New York: Columbia University Press.

Reamer, F. G. (1995). *Social work values and ethics*. New York: Columbia University Press.

Rhodes, M. L. (1986). *Ethical dilemmas in social work practice*. London: Routledge & Kegan Paul.

Frederic G. Reamer, PhD, is professor, School of Social Work, Rhode Island College, Providence, RI 02908.

For further information see

Clinical Social Work; Direct Practice Overview; Ethical Issues in Research; Ethics and Values; Legal Issues: Confidentiality and Privileged Communication; **Legal Issues: Recent Developments in Confidentiality and Privilege;** Licensing, Regulation, and Certification; National Association of Social Workers; Professional Conduct; Professional Liability and Malpractice; Social Work Practice: History and Evolution; Social Work Practice: Theoretical Base; Social Work Profession Overview.

Key Words

code of ethics	standards
ethics	values
NASW	

F

Federal Social Legislation from 1994 to 1997
Nancy S. Dickinson

Between 1961 and 1980 federal social legislation played a broad and active role in effecting change. The election of President Ronald Reagan in 1980 began a new era of retrenchment and reformation of 50 years of liberal social policies in the federal government, with a concentration on lowered taxes, cuts in social spending, and devolution of power from a central federal role to states and localities. Bill Clinton was elected president in 1992 on the promise of an active role for government in social and economic change. By the time of his re-election campaign in 1996, however, President Clinton had moved to a centralist platform of fiscal restraint, targeted social spending, and legislative compromise. These changes reflect increased pressures from Republican conservatives and illustrate the fragility of the American welfare state.

In 1992 Bill Clinton was elected president on the promise of an active role for government in social and economic change. Although he enjoyed such successes as the Family and Medical Leave Act of 1993 (P.L. 103-3) and the Violent Crime Control and Law Enforcement Act of 1994 (P.L. 103-322), it was clear that political leaders and the public alike were doubtful that government could or should be used to solve social problems, even when unmet needs were obvious. This perception was reinforced by the president's early failure to bring about national health care reform. It was also clear when Congress passed the Omnibus Budget Reconciliation Act of 1993 that President Clinton's initial goals of social investment and stimulus spending were modified by the deficit-reduction mood of Congress and the Republican party. At the time of Clinton's fiscal 1995 budget proposals, his increased support of deficit reduction was apparent, and he favored considerable social spending cuts to meet budgetary targets (Social Legislation Information Service, 1994).

THE REPUBLICAN CONTRACT WITH AMERICA
In the November 1994 congressional elections, Republicans gained majority status in both houses of Congress, the first time in 40 years that Democrats did not control at least one house (Jansson, 1997). This devastating blow to the Democratic Party and administration had been planned for some time, under the leadership of Republican Representative Newt Gingrich of Georgia. Gingrich used his posi-

tions of minority whip in 1989 and minority leader in early 1994 to forge a conservative takeover, first of the leadership of the Republican party and then of the congressional campaigns and elections.

The intent of these new and extremely conservative House Republicans was to dismantle the Great Society. To do so, Republicans vowed to pass 10 complex pieces of legislation with immense societal implications, which they called the Contract with America. The National Association of Social Workers' Office of Government Relations (1994, November 18) noted that specific provisions of the contract called for legislation to

- enact a balanced budget amendment
- increase punishments as an approach to combatting crime
- radically change the welfare system
- strengthen the family through more strict child support enforcement, a $5,000 tax credit for adoption, strict enforcement of child pornography laws, and a tax credit for those caring for elderly parents or grandparents
- overhaul the tax structure by a $500 per child tax credit for families with incomes up to $200,000 and creation of "American Dream Savings Accounts" to provide additional tax breaks for retirement income, purchase of a first home, education expenses, or medical costs
- strengthen national defense
- aid senior citizens by canceling the 1993 tax on 85 percent of upper-income taxpayers'

social security benefits and allowing older adults to earn more in regular income without losing their social security benefits

* terminate unfunded mandates and cut capital gains tax to stimulate investment
* curb excessive litigation by reforming certain laws
* enact term limits.

House Republicans dominated policy discussions and decisions in early 1995, enacting most items of the Contract with America within their promised 100 days. The Senate, however, did not approve some of the provisions.

WELFARE REFORM

President Clinton had campaigned on the pledge to "end welfare as we know it" (Lochhead, 1996, p. A8). Early in his first term he formed an administration task force to develop proposals for welfare reform, and in June 1994 he proposed the Work and Responsibility Act of 1994 (H.R. 4277). The proposal focused on time limits and work requirements and also included money for educational, training, and social services necessary to make a universal work requirement effective rather than punitive.

In March 1995 House Republicans offered their version of welfare reform that conformed with the Contract with America. Essentially the bill proposed to end the federal guarantee of cash assistance to low-income children and families and use block grants to states to replace Aid to Families with Dependent Children (AFDC), food stamps, child care, child protection programs, school meals, and nutritional programs for low-income pregnant women and children. State funding for such programs was optional. Other restrictions included eliminating benefits to minor mothers and denying higher payments to mothers who have additional children while they are receiving aid. The proposal established a lifetime limit of five years on cash assistance and a two-year time limit before most recipients would be required to work. The bill also provided that most legal immigrants would be ineligible for Supplemental Security Income (SSI), cash benefits, social services, Medicaid, and food stamps, and made it more difficult for disabled children to qualify for SSI.

The Senate enacted welfare reform legislation in September 1995 that softened the House version by requiring states to

spend at least 80 percent of their 1993 and 1994 expenditures, raising the level of exemptions from 10 percent of recipients to 15 percent, and retaining child welfare programs as separate entitlement programs. Consequently, the Senate's bill was supported by many Democratic senators who were hoping to steer conference committee legislation away from the harsh House version of welfare reform. Nevertheless, the welfare reform bill that emerged from conference agreement in November, entitled the Personal Responsibility and Work Opportunity Reconcilliation Act of 1995 (H.R. 4/conference report 104-430), retained many House provisions. In contrast to the Senate version, it provided much less money for jobs and child care and severely cut SSI for elderly and poor people with disabilities, the Food Stamp Program, and social services for legal immigrants.

On January 9, 1996, President Clinton vetoed the congressional welfare agreement. Although he cited the need for welfare reform, the president said that the bill as presented

> is burdened with deep budget cuts and structural changes that fall short of real reform. . . . Making $60 billion in budget cuts and massive structural changes in a variety of programs, including foster care and adoption assistance, help for disabled children, legal immigrants, food stamps, and school lunch is not welfare reform. . . . We must demand responsibility from young mothers and young fathers, not penalize children for their parents' mistakes. I am deeply committed to working with the Congress to reach bipartisan agreement on an acceptable welfare reform bill that addresses these and other concerns. (Clinton, 1996, pp. 2–3)

On February 6, 1996, the National Governors' Association (NGA) unanimously approved bipartisan agreement for changes in the nation's welfare programs (American Public Welfare Association, 1996). Although this legislation was based on the bill that the president had vetoed, including ending the federal guarantee of cash aid to all eligible low-income mothers and children, the governors' proposals called for easing the bill's work requirements and many of its proposed restrictions on social services. NGA also asked for more federal child care money to help welfare recipients get jobs and proposed maintaining the open-ended entitlement for foster care and adoption assistance and reauthorizing the Food Stamp Program in its current uncapped entitlement form (Social Legislation Information Service, 1996a).

On May 22, 1996, a new, revised Republican welfare reform bill, the Personal Responsibility and Work Opportunity Act of 1996, was introduced. Throughout the spring and early summer, congressional committees held hearings on the House and Senate versions of the welfare reform bill (which was modeled after the NGA proposal) and recommended slight changes in various provisions of the legislation. The House of Representatives passed its version of welfare reform (H.R. 3507) on July 18; the Senate passed its version (S. 1956) on July 23. A conference committee quickly convened and agreed on a conference bill. Spurred on by President Clinton's announcement that he would sign the bill, the House passed the conference bill on July 31 and the Senate voted for the bill on August 1. Welfare reform became a reality on August 22, 1996, when President Clinton signed into law the Personal Responsibility and Work Opportunity Reconciliation Act of 1996 (P.L. 104-193).

KEY ELEMENTS OF THE PERSONAL RESPONSIBILITY AND WORK OPPORTUNITY RECONCILIATION ACT

The 1996 act—

- replaces AFDC, the federal guarantee of cash aid to all eligible low-income mothers and children, with a block grant to states for Temporary Assistance for Needy Families (TANF).
- requires a 75 percent reduction in employment at federal agencies replaced by the block grants.
- requires the head of a family receiving welfare assistance to find work within two years and sets a five-year lifetime limit on assistance. States must have half of their clients employed by 2002 or face a 5 percent penalty on their block grant. States may exempt 20 percent of their caseloads and may use their own money to provide benefits after the federal cutoff.
- prohibits a single parent with a child older than age five from claiming lack of child care as a reason for not working.
- continues Medicaid coverage for families on welfare and extends Medicaid for one year

after the head of the family has obtained a job.
- prohibits future legal immigrants from receiving most federal benefits during their first five years in the United States. Most legal immigrants already are barred from receiving food stamps and SSI, unless they are veterans of the U.S. military or have worked and paid U.S. taxes for at least 10 years.
- requires able-bodied recipients with no dependents to work part-time after they have received food stamps for three months. Laid-off workers can get an additional three months of benefits if they are looking for work.
- tightens eligibility for SSI for children with disabilities, eliminating behavioral problems as a disabling mental impairment.
- requires states to help establish paternity, maintain automated tracking systems to enforce child support orders, and provide a W-4 tax form to child support enforcement offices from all newly hired employees.
- provides $22 billion in child care financing over the next six years, an increase of more than $3 billion, and consolidates seven federal programs into one block grant to states.
- requires states to continue spending 75 percent of what they now spend on welfare.
- allows states to decide whether to deny added benefits for women who have additional children while on welfare.

The act proposes to reduce federal spending by $2.9 billion in 1997 and by $54.2 billion over the period from 1997 to 2002, as well as increase revenues by $60 million and $394 million over these respective periods. Most of the savings comes from reductions in programs other than AFDC, with especially large reductions in the Food Stamp Program, SSI for elderly people and poor people with disabilities, and assistance to legal immigrants. The particularly harsh food stamp provisions affect poor, unemployed individuals between the ages of 18 and 50 who are not raising children. These individuals will generally be limited to receiving just three months of food stamps while they are unemployed in any three-year period. The Congressional Budget Office estimates that this provision will each month deny food stamp benefits to an average of 1 million people who are willing to work but cannot find a job and are not offered a workfare or training slot (Super, Parrott, Steinmetz, & Mann, 1996). In all, food stamp reductions would cut benefits by 20 percent, the equivalent of reducing the average food stamp benefit from its current level of 80 cents per person per meal to about 66 cents per person per meal (Center on Budget and Policy Priorities, 1996).

Not surprisingly, predictions about the impact of the act fall into two ideological camps. Liberals and advocates predict that it will push 2.6 million persons—including 1.1 million children—into poverty (Super et al., 1996). Conservatives such as Republican Representative Clay Shaw of Florida expressed joy that the day of the bill's signing "has got to go down as independence day for those who have been trapped in a system that has created . . . layers of intergenerational welfare which has corrupted their souls and stolen their future" (Lochhead, 1996, p. A8).

CHANGES IN SOCIAL SECURITY
Significant changes in Social Security and Supplemental Security Income programs occurred when President Clinton signed the Contract with America Advancement Act of 1996 (P.L. 104-121) on March 29, 1996 (Social Legislation Information Service, 1996b). For those receiving disability benefits based on drug addiction or alcoholism, cash benefits, Medicare, and Medicaid coverage ended on January 1, 1997. New applicants for benefits must meet the disability requirements on the basis of an impairment other than drug addiction or alcoholism.

Social security beneficiaries who work and are age 65 or older, but younger than 70, are now allowed to earn more money without a reduction in social security payments. The earnings limit for workers younger than age 65 remains the same, and there is no limit for beneficiaries age 70 and older. The annual earnings limit will gradually rise from $12,500 in 1996 to $30,000 in 2002. After 2002, the annual amount will be indexed to growth in average wages.

HEALTH CARE LEGISLATION
The Health Insurance Portability and Accountability Act of 1996 (P.L. 104-191), known as the Kennedy–Kassebaum Act, was signed into law on August 21, 1996. The intent of the law was to increase the availability of health insurance by guaranteeing the availability and renewability

of health insurance coverage for employees and individuals and limiting the use of restrictions on pre-existing condition (American Public Welfare Association, 1997b). The law also includes stipulations that affect Medicaid-funded managed care programs. For example, Medicaid serves as prior creditable coverage, helping beneficiaries to gain access to full employer-covered health insurance benefits. The law also provides a mental health parity provision, stipulating that there can be no lifetime or annual limits on mental health benefits when a plan does not place such limits on medical and surgical benefits. Moreover, beneficiaries, including Medicaid recipients, are entitled to longer hospital stays for newborns and their mothers. Finally, long-term care and accelerated death benefit provisions are more likely to prevent or delay reliance on Medicaid and thus to save money for the Medicaid program.

The Kennedy–Kassebaum Act is typical of the future of health care reform, in which incremental changes and state-by-state initiatives will be preferred to a major overhaul of the country's health care system. For example, one Democratic health initiative likely to occur during the 105th Congress will be legislation to ensure that all children have access to health care by helping working families purchase health insurance for their children (American Public Welfare Association, 1997a).

FEDERAL SOCIAL LEGISLATION AND THE BUDGETARY PROCESS
A stated Republican motive for overhauling welfare was to help balance the federal budget within seven years. House Speaker Gingrich intended to use the budget process to implement his conservative social agenda to downsize government by cutting social programs or returning them to states (Jansson, 1997). Philosophical differences between the two political parties have increasingly been reflected in the budgetary process and have to do with the size of government and what it should do. President Clinton's use of the budgetary process, however, defied these traditional distinctions.

In May 1995 the House and Senate approved similar budget resolutions that included parts of a welfare bill and major changes in Medicare and Medicaid. Other entitlement cuts were proposed, including cuts in the earned income tax credit (EITC), federal pensions, veterans benefits, farm subsidies, and student loans.

President Clinton had criticized Republicans for seeking to balance the budget on the backs of poor people, and on June 13, 1995, he presented his own plan to balance the budget within 10 years. The president's budget also proposed significant cuts in Medicare and Medicaid and savings from poverty programs, EITC, and benefits for immigrants. He exempted programs he favored, such as education and national service (Hager, 1995).

Congressional Democrats were furious with the president's budget and criticized the proposed Medicare cuts, even though they were far less than the Medicare cuts in Republican proposals. Some accused President Clinton of abandoning his commitment to a strong, socially active government, and others saw his behavior as politically expedient. President Clinton had appeared to be liberal during his first two years in office, when he promoted social investments and worked for health care reform. Some influential advisers warned the president that he could not win re-election in 1996 if he did not appear to be more centrist (Jansson, 1997).

In November 1995 Congress passed the fiscal 1996 Omnibus Budget Reconciliation bill (H.R. 2491; H. Rept. 104-350, S135), which replaced the existing Medicaid program with a block grant with extensive state flexibility and no individual entitlement. Trying to force the president to sign the reconciliation bill, Republicans refused to increase the national debt limit, a move necessary to pay government expenses and keep government agencies operating. President Clinton refused to sign the bill, and many agencies shut down in November and again in late December, for a total of 43 days (Jansson, 1997). The president's refusal to accede to Republican demands was fueled by polls showing that Speaker Gingrich's popularity had plummeted in late 1995 and early 1996 and that many citizens blamed the Republicans for the government shutdown (Hager, 1996). Moreover, many Americans supported some of the programs the Republican budget threatened, including environmental, education, and health programs, and they disagreed with Republican proposals for deep tax cuts that would aid wealthy Americans and be funded by cuts in social programs that benefit less affluent citizens.

Social programs were at the mercy of the continuing debates about the budget throughout March and April 1996. Ten continuing resolutions were signed during fiscal year 1996, and Republicans were able to inflict severe cuts in social programs by including only partial funding for them in the resolutions. On April 25, Congress and the White House finally agreed on a budget for fiscal year 1996. Republicans got $23 billion in cuts, and the president got $5 billion added for education, job training, and the environment (Jansson, 1997).

To avoid the contentious budget stalemates of the previous year, Congress completed at the last minute, and President Clinton signed into law, the Omnibus Consolidation Appropriations Act of 1997 (P.L. 104-208), which made significant concessions to the president (Child Welfare League of America, 1996). Unlike earlier attempts to slash social spending, this bill increased funding for many social programs, including Title IV-B Child Welfare Services, Family Violence Prevention, Child Care and Development Block Grants, Head Start, Children's Mental Health, Family Planning, Pediatric AIDS, Juvenile Justice and Delinquency Prevention Act State Grants, and the Title XX Social Services Block Grant.

PRESIDENT CLINTON'S SECOND TERM
On November 5, 1996, President Clinton easily won re-election to a second term, defeating the Republican challenger, Bob Dole, the former Senate Majority Leader. The president had campaigned on a centrist platform of fiscal restraint, targeted social spending, and legislative compromise.

On February 6, 1997, Clinton sent his fiscal year 1998 budget to Congress—a proposal to spend $1.69 trillion and save enough from Medicare, defense, and other programs over time to produce a $17 billion surplus in 2002. In addition, there would be $76 billion in tax increases, mostly for corporations and airline travelers (Chronicle News Services, 1997).

President Clinton's education-friendly budget proposes to increase the U.S. Department of Education's budget from $28 billion in 1997 to $32 billion in 1998. Specific educational proposals include $1,500 scholarships for the first two years of college, $10,000 deductions for college expenses, penalty-free withdrawals from individual retirement accounts to cover education expenses, increases in the maximum Pell grants for low-income students, and increased spending for school technology support and reading programs.

The new budget also proposes tax credits of up to $500 per child, which would be phased out for families with incomes exceeding $75,000. The president also proposed expanded health care coverage for children and jobless workers and restoring welfare benefits for legal immigrants and many disabled citizens. Medicaid savings would be achieved by capping the amount spent on each recipient, and Medicare savings would be attained by freezing reimbursements to health maintenance organizations, hospitals, and doctors (Associated Press, 1997).

THE FUTURE OF AMERICA'S WELFARE STATE

Political leaders and the public alike remain skeptical about government's ability to solve problems, even when unmet needs are so apparent. Health and welfare reform initiatives have devolved responsibility for social programs away from a central federal role to states and localities. Some say that President Clinton's difficulty in achieving a more active role for government is a result of former President Ronald Reagan's success in creating the notion that government is the problem and that most federal programs, taxes, and spending are bad (Apple, 1993). Others criticize the president for failing to reorient the nation's priorities toward domestic needs and, instead, becoming defensive in the face of Republican conservative pressures (Jansson, 1997). These arguments illustrate the fragility of the American welfare state and the increasingly polarized political debate about the role of the federal government in protecting its neediest citizens.

REFERENCES

American Public Welfare Association. (1996). Governors approve welfare, Medicaid compromise. *This Week in Washington, 17*(6), 1.

American Public Welfare Association. (1997a). Democrats announce goals for a child health initiative. *This Week in Washington, 18*(3), 1.

American Public Welfare Association. (1997b). The Health Insurance Portability and Accountability Act of 1996: Guidance for Medicaid programs. *W Memo, 9*(1), 3–7.

Apple, R. W., Jr. (1993, August 1). Reagan curse on Clinton. *New York Times*, pp. 1, 15.

Associated Press. (1997, February 6). Highlights of Clinton's 1997–98 budget. *San Francisco Chronicle*, p. A15.

Center on Budget and Policy Priorities. (1996, August 12). *The depth of the Food Stamp cuts in the final welfare bill* [press release], p. 1.

Child Welfare League of America. (1996). Congress passes spending bill. *Children's Voice, 6*(1), 30.

Chronicle News Services. (1997, February 6). President's budget focus is on health. *San Francisco Chronicle*, pp. A1, A15.

Clinton, W. J. (1996, January 9). *To the House of Representatives*. Washington, DC: The White House, Office of the Press Secretary.

Contract with America Advancement Act of 1996. P.L. 104-121, 110 Stat. 847.

Family and Medical Leave Act of 1993. P.L. 103-3, 107 Stat. 6.

Hager, G. (1995, June 17). Clinton shifts tactics, projects erasing deficit in ten years. *Congressional Quarterly Weekly*, 1715–1720.

Hager, G. (1996, January 6). A battered GOP calls workers back to the job. *Congressional Quarterly Weekly*, 53–57.

Health Insurance Portability and Accountability Act of 1996. P.L. 104–191, 110 Stat. 1936.

Jansson, B. S. (1997). *The reluctant welfare state: American social policies—Past, present, and future (3rd ed.)*. Pacific Grove, CA: Brooks/Cole.

Lochhead, C. (1996, August 1). Clinton backs welfare overhaul: GOP joyful, liberals glum as House approves bill. *San Francisco Chronicle*, pp. A1, A.8.

Office of Government Relations. (1994, November 18). *Position paper: Republican Contract with America* (pp. 1–2). Washington, DC: National Association of Social Workers.

Omnibus Budget Reconciliation Act of 1993. P.L. 103-66, 107 Stat. 31.

Omnibus Consolidation Appropriations Act of 1997. P.L. 104-208, 110 Stat. 3001.

Personal Responsibility and Work Opportunity Reconciliation Act of 1996. P.L. 104-193, 110 Stat. 2105.

Social Legislation Information Service. (1994). The president's FY 1995 budget proposals. *Washington Social Legislation Bulletin, 33*(27), 105–108.

Social Legislation Information Service. (1996a). National Governors' Association plans for welfare and Medicaid. *Washington Social Legislation Bulletin, 34*(27), 105–108.

Social Legislation Information Service. (1996b). P.L. 104-121 Social Security changes. *Washington Social Legislation Bulletin, 34*(36), 141–142.

Super, D. A., Parrott, S., Steinmetz, S., & Mann, C. (1996, August 14). *The new welfare law* [Monograph]. Washington, DC: Center on Budget and Policy Priorities.

Violent Crime Control and Law Enforcement Act of 1994. P.L. 103-322, 108 Stat. 1797.

Nancy S. Dickinson, PhD, is executive director, California Social Work Education Center, School of Social Welfare, University of California, Berkeley, CA 94720.

For further information see

Advocacy; Aid to Families with Dependent Children; Child Welfare Overview; Civil Rights; Disability; Families Overview; Federal Legislation and Administrative Rule Making; Federal Social Legislation from 1961 to 1994; **Health Care: Policy Development;** Health Care: Reform Initiatives; Health Services Systems Policy; Income Security Overview; JOBS Program; Poverty; Public Health Services; Public Social Services; Social Security; Social Welfare Expenditures: Public; Social Welfare History; Social Welfare Policy; Social Work Profession Overview; Supplemental Security Income; **Temporary Assistance to Needy Families;** Welfare Employment Programs: Evaluation.

Key Words

American welfare state	social welfare policy
history of social welfare legislation	welfare reform

H

Health Care: Policy Development

Terry Mizrahi

The concept of health care reform must be redefined as the second term of President Clinton, the last president of the 20th century, begins. This entry examines the reasons for the failure in 1994 of the Clinton administration and other government-initiated health care reform proposals to be enacted into law by the 103rd Congress. *Health care reform* is defined as federal legislation to cover the costs of comprehensive health and mental health care for the people of the United States. The cautious optimism of 1994 quickly eroded with intensive organized opposition from many quarters. This was the fourth major failure to achieve universal health insurance in the 20th century (Mizrahi, 1995). To clarify the prospects and problems for future proposals, a detailed analysis of why the movement for health care reform collapsed is provided. This entry also includes a discussion of the developments in health care financing and organization that occurred in 1995 and 1996. These developments include government attempts to reform Medicare and Medicaid, as well as the proliferation of market-driven changes, most commonly characterized as managed care.

OVERVIEW

With the election of the conservative, Republican-majority 104th Congress in November 1994, the concept of health care reform was redefined within the context of federal government downsizing, deregulation, and devolution. Reform in this political climate has meant cutting or shifting costs, lowering expectations about government's responsibility to meet human needs, and generally doing less. At the same time, the public and private leaders who oppose government's role in ensuring a right to health care have allowed or even encouraged market forces to expand and take control of an increasingly privatized American health care system. Unrestrained by government regulation, corporate-dominated, for-profit managed care has burgeoned since 1994, although the transformation of the health care system in that direction began before then (Eckholm, 1994; Salmon, 1995; Sherrill, 1995; Starr, 1982). Both the executive and the legislative branches of the federal government have focused their attention primarily on reforming the existing health care entitlements, limiting growth, and changing the direction of Medicare for elderly people and people with disabilities (Title XVIII) and Medicaid for very poor people (Title XIX).

It was not until near the end of the 104th Congress, in the summer of 1996, that a modest bipartisan health insurance proposal, the Health Insurance Reform Act (P.L. 104-191),

was passed and signed into law by President Clinton. Sponsored by Senators Edward Kennedy of Massachusetts, a liberal Democrat and long-time proponent of universal federal health insurance, and Nancy Landon Kassebaum of Kansas, a moderate Republican, the law was also designed to demonstrate that Congress could get something done after a year of government shutdowns and bitter partisan struggles. As 1997 began, other incremental health reform measures to protect patients and expand coverage were suggested, especially as the excesses of market-driven health care adversely affected the middle class. Nevertheless, as the Republican-majority 105th Congress opened, the prospect for a comprehensive national health care program for all Americans remained dim.

FAILURE OF CONGRESSIONAL HEALTH CARE REFORM IN 1994

President Clinton suffered what many believe to be his most serious and even devastating political defeat during his first term when Congress in 1994 rejected his plan (and all others) to guarantee health insurance for all Americans (Johnson & Broder, 1996; Navarro, 1995; Skocpol, 1996). It is also believed that this defeat contributed to the Republican victories in both houses of Congress in the November 1994 elections—bringing about a Republican majority for the first time in 40 years—and to the Republicans maintaining that control in the 1996 elections, despite President Clinton's re-election.

Various critics offer myriad reasons for the failure of even a modest bill to increase health coverage and moderate costs, let alone a comprehensive, publicly administered, single-payer bill such as the one supported by the National Association of Social Workers (NASW) and other progressive groups (Mizrahi, 1995). Given this outcome, the critical question is, Why was health care reform the major domestic policy agenda for President Clinton in 1992, only to be totally repudiated two years later?

By 1992 a confluence of forces was working for national health care reform. The costs of overall, and especially publicly funded, health care were skyrocketing, but the health status of Americans continued to be relatively poor compared with other industrialized countries, especially given the percentage of the gross domestic product spent on health (then approaching 14 percent). The business community, especially big business, believed that expenditures for fringe benefits, which included health insurance for workers and their families, were too large and were, therefore, lessening U.S. ability to compete in world markets. Labor unions were losing power in collective bargaining for health benefits. Millions of Americans remained without health care coverage or were beginning to lose it, as progressive health consumer, professional, and advocacy groups increased their mobilization efforts and large majorities of Americans polled said major health care reform was needed (Mizrahi, 1995).

As President Clinton and the 103rd Congress began their new terms in 1993, nearly everyone agreed that something had to be done, but there were great differences among the various constituencies as to what was to be done and how. Ultimately, public opinion was divided so intensely that coalitions and compromises were doomed (Baumgartner & Talbert, 1995; Hacker, 1997; Smith, 1995). Those opposing any change included the Speaker of the House, Newt Gingrich of Georgia, and the House Republican leadership; conservative, organized political and religious groups; and the health insurance industry and small business organizations (Johnson & Border, 1996; Skocpol, 1996; Steinmo & Watts, 1995).

A detailed analysis of the failure of health care reform must scrutinize the operation of the American political system and, in particular, the role of well-financed special interest groups and the media. Responsibility—if not blame—has been placed on various sectors, including the president and the American people themselves. Although there may not be ultimate agreement on a single cause of the demise of health insurance legislation, it is evident that the interaction among the various groups to defeat any health care reform was based on economic, ideological, and political grounds (Martin, 1995). In hindsight, any comprehensive proposal seems to have been doomed from the beginning, despite several compelling reasons to cooperate to bring about change (Peterson, 1995).

Lobbying and Media Effort against Reform

The Center for Public Integrity (1995a, 1995b) was among the many "watchdog" organizations that investigated the decision-making processes of the congressional leaders and the president and the forces that influenced them. The results suggest that health care reform was the most heavily lobbied legislative initiative in recent U.S. history. More than $100 million was spent to influence the outcome of this public policy issue (Podhorzer, 1995; Watzman & Woodall, 1995). These funds were spent to influence individual members of Congress directly, through campaign contributions, and indirectly, through public media campaigns and grassroots lobbying efforts that would turn public opinion against the Health Security Act (also known as the Clinton plan), and ultimately against any legislative reform. The most famous advertising campaign used television commercials featuring the characters "Harry and Louise": At least $10 million in paid advertisements were placed by the Health Insurance Association of America, the trade association of all but the largest U.S. insurance companies. In addition, the five largest insurance companies, including Aetna (Hartford, CT), Travelers (Hartford, CT), Cigna (Hartford, CT), Prudential Insurance Company of America (Newark, NJ), and Metropolitan Life Insurance Company (New York, NY) (Center for Public Integrity, 1995b); the National Federation of Independent Business; the Business Roundtable; the National Restaurant Association; the American Medical Association; the tobacco industry; the pharmaceutical companies; and many other industrial groups lobbied against the Clinton plan.

At stake was an almost trillion-dollar health enterprise often referred to as the "medical–industrial–insurance complex"; health care had become one-seventh of the U.S. economy. The collaboration between political and economic leaders has been documented by examining the relationship of lobbyists for these groups with the various congressional committees and members of Congress (Navarro, 1995). Added to these connections was the network of organized, behind-the-scenes activity of conservative organizations such as the Christian Coalition, the National Taxpayers Union, and the National Rifle Association, among others, who vehemently opposed any proposals that expanded the federal government's role in or responsibility for health care. These groups worked with conservative radio talk show hosts, including the widely popular Rush Limbaugh, to flood the airwaves with anti-Clinton and antigovernment sentiment. With the active support of Speaker Gingrich and other conservative Republican leaders, this opposition was carefully translated into a mobilization of grassroots demonstrations and actions aimed at Congress (Johnson & Broder, 1996).

By 1994 it was clear that Robert Dole of Kansas, the Senate Minority (and, later, Majority) Leader, wanted to run for president in 1996, and he was vacillating as to whether to work for a compromise health insurance bill. He was finally influenced by the conservative members of his party and obstructed any progress by threatening filibusters toward the production of moderate, compromise legislation (Johnson & Broder, 1996).

Labor unions also made large contributions to political campaigns, but they and consumer groups such as the American Association of Retired Persons and Families USA supported the Clinton proposals only reluctantly and ambivalently. No additional backing came from the more liberal sector, which supported a single-payer system in the form of a bill introduced by Senator Paul Wellstone of Minnesota and Representative Jim McDermott of Washington State. (NASW supported that bill, and also had its own version of a single-payer bill introduced into the Senate and House.)

President Clinton rejected the simpler, government-funded and publicly regulated, single-payer system because he believed politically, if not ideologically, in the private

sector. His plan was based on a regulated, managed-competition model that would use market forces to promote efficiency and lower prices but guarantee universal access to a minimum benefit package through employer contributions (rather than direct taxation). Nevertheless, the complexity of the Clinton bill (more than 1,300 pages long) and the proposed creation of new federal and state bureaucracies were abhorrent to conservative, and some liberal, forces. These perceptions of increased government control and higher taxes, along with the projected loss of Americans' freedom to choose their physician (although this is already the case for millions of Americans), ultimately fueled an already growing distrust by the American people of the government—especially the federal government (Skocpol, 1996). The public was confused; at worst, it was manipulated (Brodie & Blendon, 1995; Jacobs, 1995). Consensus building was almost impossible (Hacker, 1997).

Government Disunity and Fragmentation of Political Power

Because of the division of political power among the three branches of government, American politics historically has faced difficulties in achieving any major domestic policy initiative, barring a national catastrophe. Added to this structural uniqueness of the U.S. political system is the changing nature and reduced power of political parties, especially the fragmentation of the Democratic party in recent times (Steinmo & Watts, 1995; White, 1995).

This fragmentation meant that the Democrats could not unify around a single bill, even when they held a majority in both houses of Congress and in spite of leadership by Senator Jay Rockefeller of West Virginia and the Health Care Reform Project. There was disagreement and division among the Democratic leaders of the 10 House and Senate committees and subcommittees with jurisdiction over health care bills. At best, some gave lukewarm support to Clinton's bill (Senator George Mitchell of Maine and Representative John Dingell of Michigan), and at worst, a few, such as Senator Daniel Patrick Moynihan of New York, opposed it and all major reform measures. Still others vied with the president by offering alternative and even contradictory proposals to his (Representatives Pete Stark of California and Jim Cooper of Tennessee). During this time the powerful chairman of the

House Ways and Means Committee, Dan Rostenkowski of Illinois, was under indictment and then forced to resign his position, so there was no one Democratic congressional leader powerful and supportive enough to unify the Democrats around the president's bill or any other bill. With no groundswell to counter the intensive lobbying and grassroots campaign that was opposing reform, not one bill was ever fully debated and voted on by either body of the 103rd Congress.

Role of President Clinton, Hillary Rodham Clinton, and the Clinton Administration

There are differing opinions as to whether the strategies used by the president and his administration directly contributed to the failure of health care reform. The administration made admitted strategic mistakes at several critical junctures (Johnson & Broder, 1996). Hillary Rodham Clinton was appointed by the president to organize and lead the campaign, and many of the large group of policy professionals she involved in the development of the plan were outsiders to the political process. The task force she formed met secretly for a year; the bill that emerged was extraordinarily complex and confusing to most Americans. Although the first lady was praised as a highly effective and powerful spokesperson, she was also increasingly the target of criticism and condemned by the political opponents of reform. Moreover, the White House staff assigned to move the bill along were, for the most part, also inexperienced, and they alienated many potential allies along the way.

Also during this period, the Clintons were surrounded by allegations of unethical, if not illegal, conduct in what has become known as "Whitewater" and alleged abuses of presidential power. Most critics agree that the credibility of the White House was weakened at this time. Given the scale of the reform, the president ultimately failed to recognize the limits of his authority, which were imposed upon him by his election by only 43 percent of those Americans who voted. He did not have the political capital to overcome opposition (Johnson & Broder, 1996).

Medicare and Medicaid Reform

The Gingrich-led Republican Congress came into power promoting their *Contract with America* (Gillespie & Schellhas, 1994), a series of proposals to eliminate entitlements, limit government spending and oversight, and allow the states and corporations freedom to control the economy and former government functions. In this climate, reforming Medicare and Medicaid were the only major health issues placed on the national political agenda in 1995 and 1996, and debates about the future of these two programs affected the presidential campaign of 1996.

Medicaid covers more than 37 million people (up from 21 million in 1989), more than 12 million of whom are now enrolled in health maintenance organizations (HMOs). Another 38 million Americans are covered by Medicare (up from 31.5 million in 1989), more than 5 million of whom are in HMOs, and these figures are growing (Pear, 1996d).

Both President Clinton and the Republican leadership offered proposals to cut the growth of Medicare and Medicaid, and to reorganize the delivery system toward managed care, in the context of balancing the federal budget soon after the year 2000 (Iglehart, 1996). However, the Republican proposal was much more drastic in its proposed cuts: They wanted a $270 billion reduction in Medicare alone—to be achieved primarily by reducing payments to physicians, hospitals, and medical equipment suppliers and, to a lesser extent, by increasing premiums paid by beneficiaries. Republicans also wanted to impose an absolute cap on Medicare spending, and they favored the increased use of HMOs by eliminating many of the restrictions on HMO marketing. They also promoted the development of private medical savings accounts to attract the well-to-do and healthy segment of the population. On the Medicaid side, in addition to substantially cutting the total federal contribution, the Republican plan included the elimination of Medicaid as a federal entitlement and proposed substituting limited block grants to the states, with few standards and mandates, for health care for poor people. President Clinton opposed most of these proposals, and he vetoed the Balanced Budget Act of 1995, which contained these Medicaid and Medicare reforms.

Nevertheless, there continues to be bipartisan agreement that slowing the rate of growth and restructuring these entitlements is needed. There is also growing concern that the Hospital Insurance Trust Fund (also known as the Medicare Trust Fund) will become insolvent sometime before the first baby boomers reach age 65 in the year 2011. As part of his 1997 budget strategy, President Clinton (as of early 1997) was not planning to propose any increase in costs for Medicare beneficiaries, but his administration will attempt to reduce payments to hospitals, physicians, and others who provide health care to elderly people (Pear, 1997d). The Clinton administration is also considering proposals by the American Medical Association and the American Hospital Association to enable providers, grouped in community-based delivery networks that they control, to contract directly with Medicare.

ATTEMPTS TO CONTROL MANAGED CARE

Managed care is a more general term for HMOs or prepaid, capitated arrangements whereby providers (or provider organizations) are paid a fixed sum per patient for taking care of all the agreed-on health care needs of that patient. As a model for the organization of health services, HMOs offer the promise of concentrating on preventive and early intervention measures, which are also less costly to the system and to the patient. The traditional method of health provider reimbursement, on a fee-for-service, per visit, or per procedure basis, was blamed for its inflationary excesses (that is, providing too many or even unnecessary services), but the tendency with capitated arrangements, if they are unregulated, is to limit access to needed services.

By the end of 1996, more than 60 million Americans were enrolled in managed care plans; three in four physicians participated in at least one managed care program (Belkin, 1996). Seventy-four percent of workers who receive health benefits through their employers now use some form of managed care, up from 29 percent in 1988 and 55 percent in 1992. The growth in managed care is believed to be responsible for the slowed growth in health costs: In 1996 employers' premiums rose less than 1 percent, whereas in 1991 the increase was 11.5 percent (Samuelson, 1996). However, serious questions have been raised in many quarters about the quality, access to services, and consumer satisfaction that are provided by commercial managed care.

The impact of managed care on various patient populations has received mixed reviews. One national poll conducted in June 1996 documented consumer dissatisfaction: 32 percent thought their health care had gotten worse since 1992 compared with 12 percent

who thought it had improved (Belkin, 1996). Other reports show that Americans are confused or uninformed, if not totally dissatisfied (Toner, 1996). Some studies are demonstrating that managed care works well for healthy people (based on patient perceptions as well as health status and outcomes) and less satisfactorily for those with chronic and catastrophic illnesses (Noble, 1995).

Although consumer advocacy is increasing, consumer problems or unhappiness with HMOs do not automatically translate into public action to limit the authority and autonomy of the commercial conglomerates. Managed care corporations and their trade associations continue to spend millions of dollars on public advertising campaigns—for example, in California, where in November 1996 voters rejected a ballot measure to impose tough new regulations on HMOs. Nevertheless, the need for patient and even provider protections under managed care has gotten public attention after numerous negative reports in the media from consumers, advocacy groups, and professional associations of health care providers.

An increasing number of reports are concentrating on the cost-conscious and profit-driven managed care companies' systematic diminishment of the quality of medicine, preventing those in need of complex treatment from obtaining it (Anders, 1996; Belkin, 1996). More and more commercial companies are competing for their perceived market share, and many may be committing illegal acts in the process such as deliberately misinforming patients, submitting fraudulent claims, and secretly paying specialists for expenses not incurred (Eisler, 1996; Gottleib & Eichenwald, 1997; Pear, 1997c). Even the once publicly regulated, not-for-profit Blue Cross plans in certain states are converting to profit-making corporations.

There have been complaints about the way managed care companies do business, including accusations of potential or actual fraudulent practices. For example, in New York State, in response to a sharp rise in complaints about sales tactics used by companies to recruit Medicaid recipients, the state health department prohibited them from directly marketing to Medicaid patients (Fisher, 1995).

Serious allegations of attempts to limit access to and quality of health care are often accompanied by reports about the amount and percentage of profits being made by managed care companies. Concerns have been raised about the percentage of return on investments and the percentage of income going to pay the salaries and benefits of executives of these corporations. (Profits are estimated to be as high as $200 billion of the nearly trillion-dollar U.S. health care enterprise.) Commercial health insurers and managed care companies expend as little as 75 percent (some, even less) of their premium income (including federal and state payments) for patient care, compared with more than 90 percent spent by not-for-profit organizations ("Health Care: Profitization," 1996). It has been projected that, without any controls on their income and outlays, these companies will continue to provide multimillion-dollar annual incomes and other financial benefits for their top executives, incur much higher administrative costs than those of Medicare, and provide generous returns to their investors (Eckholm, 1994; "Health Care: Profitization," 1996; Nudelman & Andrews, 1996). The relevant question is whether the companies making these large profits are reducing costs (if costs continue to be reduced) at the expense of patient access and the delivery of comprehensive, quality care.

Regulatory, Judicial, and Statutory Safeguards on HMOs

Some states are becoming active in managed care reform by introducing regulatory measures to monitor and contain the activities of commercial managed care and insurance companies. For example, after much pressure from health consumer and advocacy groups and in spite of resistance from HMO trade organizations, New York State passed compromise legislation in 1996 to establish some protections for patients (Dao, 1996). By the end of 1996, 16 states, including California and now the federal government, had adopted laws or regulations banning so-called "gag clauses" in contracts between physicians (and other health care providers) and managed care firms (Pear, 1996a).

The Health Care Financing Administration (HCFA) has ruled that Medicare patients have a right to full information about treatment options, meaning that HMOs and other health plans cannot limit what doctors tell Medicare patients. This ruling is directed at clauses that discourage or prohibit doctors from telling patients about alternative treatments not covered by the HMO, which are often expensive

options. HCFA will be issuing a similar policy for HMOs serving Medicaid patients in 1997. Congress is expected to pass a similar bill covering private insurance HMOs (Pear, 1996d).

There are also new federal and state regulations that prohibit gag clauses that restrict physicians from revealing information about their financial arrangements with HMOs, including contracts that reward doctors for controlling health costs and limiting the use of medical specialists (Pear, 1996e). HCFA's new policy limits (but does not prohibit) the types of bonuses that can be paid to doctors as a reward for controlling the cost of services for Medicaid and Medicare patients. This could set a standard for the commercial insurance industry. The 105th Congress is expected to focus more attention on the negative effects on access and quality caused by private managed care's policies, and will likely pass some laws monitoring and restricting the autonomy of managed care corporations (Pear, 1997c).

Federal judges are also becoming involved as lawsuits are brought on behalf of individuals and classes of patients and providers. The judicial trend seems to be in the direction of limiting the autonomy and increasing the accountability of the private managed care corporations and insurance companies. For example, several federal court rulings in late 1996 stated that Medicare patients in HMOs are entitled to immediate hearings whenever they are denied medical services (Pear, 1996b). The Clinton administration opposed such rulings, stating, as the industry did, that HMOs were private entities and the government should not be held responsible for their decisions.

To accelerate market-influenced reform, many states—and, in some instances, even the federal government—are also deregulating the overall hospital and health care system. This move may actually increase the role of corporate-controlled health care and decrease access to services for poor and uninsured people. Many states have lifted the regulated rate-setting mandates on hospitals, causing not-for-profit teaching, community, and public hospitals to act more like their proprietary counterparts. These not-for-profit hospitals are attempting to compete for privately and publicly insured patients and are cutting costs by merging and downsizing, through the elimination of beds, positions, and services. Professionally educated social workers are considered to be health care providers, and hospital social work departments are among the structures being reorganized and controlled, if not eliminated. The proprietary hospitals and managed care conglomerates may have an edge in the long term: They have had more freedom from the constraints that were a by-product of the mission of the once-charitable, tax-exempt health care institutions, and of the teaching and research mission of major medical centers.

In 1996 HCFA made several proposals to lessen the regulations governing providers who are reimbursed by Medicare and Medicaid (known as "conditions of participation"). These proposals include downgrading the definitions and qualifications of social workers providing services through Medicare's Home Health, Hospice, and End Stage Renal Disease Programs. The current conditions of participation governing Medicare include professional standards and other requirements that have been used as a norm for social work practice in health care. Social workers have been active in urging the maintenance of these standards. To date, mounting opposition to lowering standards by consumer and professional groups has prevailed.

CURRENT STATE OF HEALTH CARE REFORM

The Health Insurance Reform Act of 1996 (P.L. 104-191), also known as the Kennedy–Kassebaum bill, was passed almost unanimously at the end of the 104th Congress after much debate and compromise. It allows workers to maintain health insurance coverage if they change or lose their jobs (known as "portability"), and it bars insurance companies from denying coverage to people who have pre-existing medical conditions. It also makes it easier for self-employed workers to afford their own insurance by increasing the share they can deduct from their income tax, and it toughens penalties for Medicaid and Medicare fraud.

However, in the view of social workers and others interested in more comprehensive reform, this law is extremely limited and deficient in many areas. It does not prescribe a standard benefits package, nor does it require employers to offer health insurance coverage. Moreover, because the act does not set price limits on how much such insurance would cost, insurance will continue to be inaccessible to many consumers because of prohibitive costs. As part of the compromise that ensured passage, the bill also included the introduction of medical savings accounts, which allow

people working for small businesses or who are self-employed to set aside their own funds, before taxes, for routine or long-term care. This opens the door for a privatized insurance model for healthy and well-off people, leaving sick and poor people in the traditional insurance pool—with presumably higher premiums. The bill also omitted parity for mental health and substance abuse benefits (Keigher, 1996).

At the close of the 104th Congress, the Departments of Veterans Affairs and Housing and Urban Development, and Independent Agencies Appropriations Act (P.L. 104-204) became the vehicle to require insurance companies to offer comparable coverage for mental and physical illnesses and to guarantee coverage for mothers of at least 48 hours of hospital care after childbirth. The mental health parity provision is historic in its attempt to equalize annual payment limits and lifetime caps for coverage of physical and mental illness and to end discriminatory treatment in coverage of mental health services.

The law does not mandate the provision of a mental health benefit, however, so employers can still limit what they offer or can even drop current benefits without legal penalty. There are additional loopholes in the mental health provision: It excludes substance abuse treatment, and it exempts employers with 50 or fewer employees and even larger employers, if they can demonstrate that expanded mental health coverage raised their premium costs by just 1 percent.

FUTURE OF HEALTH CARE REFORM

Clearly, the Clinton administration is opening the door to increasing health care coverage incrementally rather than proposing a plan to redesign the health care system. The proposals announced by President Clinton just before the 105th Congress convened in January 1997 include coverage for some of the nation's 10 million uninsured children and assistance in paying premiums for workers who are between jobs. These initiatives presumably will build upon both the success of the Kennedy–Kassebaum bill and the slowing of health care inflation and Medicaid costs—the latter is down from 17 percent a year in the period from 1990 to 1995, to 3 percent in fiscal year 1996 (Pear, 1996c).

In early 1997 President Clinton appointed a federal advisory commission (the Presidential Commission on Quality and Consumer

Protection in the Health Industry) to draft a bill of rights for health care consumers and assess the need for the federal government to regulate private health insurance plans (Pear, 1997a). This commission will also lay the foundation for other health policy initiatives and legislative proposals. Although it is not likely that the commission will mandate health coverage by employers, it probably will begin to specify what should be covered by employers who do provide health coverage. For example, after complaints from across the country by privately insured consumers, Congress required insurers to extend hospital care for new mothers and their babies and it will probably prohibit mastectomies and certain other medical treatments as outpatient procedures (Pear, 1996c).

The outlook remains bleak for uninsured people and those with chronic illnesses. The current number of uninsured people is estimated to be 43.4 million—18.7 percent of those under age 65, up from 40 million in 1992 (Bradsher, 1995). This figure is growing at a rate of about 1.2 million people a year as companies reduce or eliminate their health care benefits. In addition, the number of people living in poverty continues to grow, and the gap between rich and poor people is widening. Many poor people with incomes slightly above the national poverty level (approximately $15,000 for family of four) are not eligible for current benefits.

When the Personal Responsibility and Work Opportunity Reconciliation Act of 1996 was passed, Aid to Families with Dependent Children, which had been in effect for more than 60 years, was repealed. This new legislation may force many more people into poverty, without any or lasting health care benefits. In particular, the number of uninsured children, which in 1994 reached 10 million (14.2 percent)—the highest level since 1987—will no doubt rise again (Pear, 1996c).

Millions more people are believed to be underinsured, that is, not sufficiently covered for chronic or catastrophic illnesses. In this context a Republican proposal to cut Medicaid spending over the next several years is conservatively estimated to leave 9 million additional Americans uninsured by 2002 (Bradsher, 1995). Some members of the 105th Congress have expressed concern about coverage of some aspects of children's health. In early 1997, for example, Senator Kennedy

and Senator Orrin G. Hatch of Utah, a conservative Republican, backed a proposal to cover about half of the 10 million uninsured children (Pear, 1997b).

As part of welfare reform, the Clinton administration bowed to pressure to limit the definition of disability, thereby reducing the benefit payment to physically and mentally disabled Americans. This action has threatened the income of millions of recipients of Supplemental Security Income and Social Security Disability insurance and is projected to adversely affect more than 100,000 children across the country.

ROLE OF SOCIAL WORK
Social workers around the country are feeling the ill effects of sentiments against the government, human services, and entitlements. The political center has been redefined: What once was considered to be conservative is now the mainstream of the new political center in the United States, as defined by the president's policies. Social workers in health care are particularly threatened by the shifts to privatization and corporatization of health and mental health services and the accompanying emphasis on cutting costs and increasing profits. Downsizing has brought about the reduction of supervisory and managerial social work positions (Berger et al., 1996), which has been accompanied in many institutions by the takeover of social work functions by other professionals and even less skilled personnel. With renewed emphasis on outpatient care, social work jobs in hospital inpatient services are disappearing. The challenge for social work will be to reconfigure its roles without giving up its core values.

The 1996 Delegate Assembly of NASW adopted a policy statement supporting the role of government, social work, and social policy and a program priority to promote a positive role of government in meeting human needs (NASW, 1997). NASW and other social work organizations are working to ensure that social work and social services will be an integral part of any managed care package and that such services will be provided by professionally qualified social workers. Social workers have also joined consumer and health advocacy organizations to protect all patients' access to quality health and mental health services in public and private insurance plans.

As moves to privatize, deregulate, defund, and deprofessionalize health and human services continue, social workers must remain proactive and participate as advocates and providers of needed professional services. They will need to make their case effectively in the political and policy arenas as well as the agency administrative, program, and practice arenas, where reorganization is taking place.

The vertical and horizontal integration of services delivery systems accompanying managed care seems imminent. These developments place responsibility on those systems for providing complete health care to an identified population. As a result, there are opportunities for developing consumer-dedicated and community-based models of public health, prevention, behavioral health, and primary care services. As professional and consumer groups organize and advocate for making these systems publicly accountable, affordable, and accessible, social work can emerge with stronger roles and expanded functions.

REFERENCES

Anders, G. (1996). *Health against wealth: HMOs and the breakdown of medical trust.* Boston: Houghton Mifflin.

Baumgartner, F. R., & Talbert, J. C. (1995). From setting a national agenda on health care to making decisions in Congress. *Journal of Health Policy, Politics and Law, 20,* 437–445.

Belkin, L. (1996, December 8). The Ellwoods and the price of reform: But what about quality? *New York Times Magazine,* pp. 68, 70–71, 101, 106.

Berger, C. S., Cayner, J., Jensen, G., Mizrahi, T., Scesny, A., & Trachtenberg, J. (1996). The changing scene of social work in hospitals: A report of a national study by the Society of Social Work Administrators in Health Care and NASW. *Health & Social Work, 21,* 167–177.

Bradsher, K. (1995, August 27). Rise in uninsured becomes an issue in Medicaid fight. *New York Times,* pp. A1, A20.

Brodie, M., & Blendon, R. J. (1995). The public's contribution to congressional gridlock on health care reform. *Journal of Health Politics, Policy and Law, 2,* 403–410.

Center for Public Integrity. (1995a). Well-healed: Inside lobbying for health care reform—Part I. *International Journal of Health Services, 24,* 593–632.

Center for Public Integrity. (1995b). Well-healed: Inside lobbying for health care reform—Part II. *International Journal of Health Services, 24,* 593–632.

Dao, J. (1996, May 9). New Pataki bill offers protection to H.M.O. clients. *New York Times,* pp. A1, B6.

Departments of Veterans Affairs and Housing and Urban Development, and Independent Agencies Appropriations Act. (1996). P.L. 104-204, 110 Stat. 2874.

Eckholm, E. (1994, December 18). While Congress remains silent, health care transforms itself. *New York Times,* pp. A1, A34.

Eisler, P. (1996, November 11). Home health care opens door to abuses. *USA Today,* pp. 11B–13B.

Fisher, I. (1995, June 24). New York acts to curb fraud in managed care for the poor. *New York Times,* pp. A1, A24.

Gillespie, R., & Schellhas, B. (Eds.). (1994). *Contract with America: The bold plan.* New York: Times Books.

Gottlieb, M., & Eichenwald, K. (1997, March 28). Biggest hospital operator attracts federal inquiries. *New York Times,* pp. A1, D15.

Hacker, J. S. (1997). *The road to nowhere: The genesis of President Clinton's plan for health security.* Princeton, NJ: Princeton University Press.

Health care: Profitization. (1996). *Health Letter, 12*(8), 10–11.

Health Insurance Portability and Accountability Act of 1996. P.L. 104-191, 110 Stat. 1936.

Iglehart, J. K. (1996). The struggle to reform Medicare. *New England Journal of Medicine, 334,* 1071–1075.

Jacobs, L. R. (1995). Don't blame the public for failed health care reform. *Journal of Health Politics, Policy and Law, 20,* 411–423.

Johnson, H., & Broder, D. S. (1996). *The system: The American way of politics at the breaking point.* Boston: Little, Brown.

Keigher, S. M. (1996). Speaking of personal responsibility and individual accountability [National Health Line]. *Health & Social Work, 21,* 304–311.

Martin, C. J. (1995). Stuck in neutral: Big business and the politics of national health reform. *Journal of Health Politics, Policy and Law, 20,* 431–436.

Mizrahi, T. (1995). Health care: Reform initiatives. In R. L. Edwards (Ed.-in-Chief), *Encyclopedia of social work* (19th ed., Vol. 2, pp. 1185–1198). Washington, DC: NASW Press.

National Association of Social Workers. (1997). The role of government, social policy, and social work. In *Social work speaks: NASW policy statements* (4th ed., pp. 267–271). Washington, DC: NASW Press.

Navarro, V. (1995). The politics of health care reform in the United States, 1992–1994: A historic review. *International Journal of Health Services, 25,* 185–201.

Noble, H. B. (1995, November 8). H.M.O. quality called equal, at less cost. *New York Times,* p. A6.

Nudelman, P. M., & Andrews, L. M. (1996). The "value added" of not-for-profit health plans. *New England Journal of Medicine, 334,* 1057–1059.

Pear, R. (1996a, September 17). Laws won't let H.M.O.'s tell doctors what to say. *New York Times,* p. A12.

Pear, R. (1996b, October 31). Medicare patients in H.M.O.'s win a case. *New York Times,* p. B15.

Pear, R. (1996c, November 11). New approach to overhauling health insurance: Step by step. *New York Times,* pp. A1, A12.

Pear, R. (1996d, December 7). U.S. bans limits on H.M.O. advice within Medicare. *New York Times,* pp. A1, A12.

Pear, R. (1996e, December 25). U.S. limits H.M.O.'s linking bonuses to cost controls. *New York Times,* pp. A1, A24.

Pear, R. (1997a, March 27). Clinton names panel to draft health consumer bill of rights. *New York Times,* p. B11.

Pear, R. (1997b, March 14). Hatch joins Kennedy to back a health program. *New York Times,* p. A24.

Pear, R. (1997c, March 18). H.M.O.'s limiting Medicare appeals, U.S. inquiry finds. *New York Times,* pp. A1, A17.

Pear, R. (1997d, January 5). Premium rise on Medicare seen as unlikely. *New York Times,* pp. A1, A14.

Peterson, M. A. (1995). The health care debate: All heat and no light. *Journal of Health Politics, Policy and Law, 20,* 399–402.

Podhorzer, M. (1995). Unhealthy money: Health reform and the 1994 elections. *International Journal of Health Services, 25,* 393–401.

Salmon, J. W. (1995). A perspective on the corporate transformation of health care. *International Journal of Health Services, 25,* 11–42.

Samuelson, R. J. (1996, November 24). [Review of *Mismanaged care*]. *New York Times Book Review,* p. 13.

Sherrill, R. (1995, January 9/16). The madness of the market. *Nation,* pp. 45–71.

Skocpol, T. (1996). *Boomerang: Clinton's health security effort and the turn against government in U.S. politics.* New York: W. W. Norton.

Smith, S. R. (1995). The role of institutions and ideas in health care policy. *Journal of Health Politics, Policy and Law, 20,* 385–389.

Starr, P. (1982). *The social transformation of American medicine.* New York: Basic Books.

Steinmo, S., & Watts, J. (1995). It's the institutions, stupid! Why comprehensive national insurance always fails in America. *Journal of Health Politics, Policy and Law, 20,* 329–372.

Toner, R. (1996, November 24). Health care. Harry and Louise were right, sort of. *New York Times Week in Review,* section 4, pp. 1, 4.

Watzman, N., & Woodall, P. (1995). Managed health care companies' lobbying frenzy. *International Journal of Health Services, 25,* 403–410.

White, J. (1995). The horses and the jumps: Comments on the health care reform steeplechase. *Journal of Health Politics, Policy and Law, 20,* 373–383.

Terry Mizrahi, PhD, is professor, School of Social Work, Hunter College, 129 East 79th Street, New York, NY 10021.

For further information see

Advocacy; Federal and Administrative Rule Making; Federal Social Legislation from 1961 to 1994; **Federal Social Legislation from 1994 to 1997;** Health Care: Direct Practice; Health Care: Reform Initiatives; **Health Care Practice Overview;** Health Services Systems Policy; Managed Care Overview; **Managed Care: Implications for Social Work Practice; Managed Care: A Review of Recent Research;** Mental Health Overview; Public Health Services; Social Security; Social Welfare Expenditures: Public; Social Welfare Policy.

Key Words	
health financing	Medicaid
health policy	Medicare
managed care	

Health Care Practice Overview

Barbara Berkman

Patricia Volland

Contemporary health care problems are complex, even for the most sophisticated and knowledgeable professionals. Technological advances within pharmacology and biomedicine now are enabling patients with certain complex, chronic conditions to live longer. As managed care organizations take an increasing role in the administration of health care benefits, patients and family members must deal with situations of greater uncertainty, which creates new practice roles and tensions for social workers (Pawlson, 1994). The challenge for social work practice is to meet the need for continually changing roles and practices in physical and mental health (Berkman, 1990).

DEMOGRAPHIC AND ECONOMIC CHANGES IN HEALTH CARE

Modern health care is skillful in providing high-quality, technologically advanced, acute care treatment, but its ability to meet chronic care needs is limited because the system is complex and fragmented. Individuals and families need help to use these systems effectively. Health care is beginning to respond to these needs by addressing continuity-of-care issues through reorganizing and restructuring services away from hospital-based inpatient services to community-based health care services (Abel et al., 1995). The average number of hospital inpatient days has fallen from 95,427 in 1980 to 89,109 in 1993, and the average length of hospital stays has decreased from 8.1 days to 7.0 days (National Public Health and Hospital Institute, 1995). These decreases have resulted in significantly reduced occupancy rates from 78.3 percent to 69.2 percent (National Public Health and Hospital Institute, 1995). This reduction of inpatient services has been made possible by advanced biomedical and pharmacological technologies, as well as by gains in financial incentives brought about by managed care's introduction of cost savings and cost-effectiveness into health care delivery. In addition, new community-based networks are linking providers of services to a continuum of health care that includes long-term care, home care, and community social services (Kenney, 1990).

Social workers are needed throughout the continuum of care to address complex mental health needs, assist individuals and families in using services more effectively, and develop preventive and health promotion programs (Ibrahim, House, & Levine, 1995). Once found practicing primarily in hospitals, health care social workers are now practicing in ambula-

tory primary care settings, home health care, long-term care, public health departments, community health care clinics, school-based health clinics, and associations focused on specific illnesses (such as the Multiple Sclerosis Society and HIV and AIDS consortia).

Challenges to Health Care and Social Work

A significant challenge to health care and to social work is the increased incidence of socially related diseases, especially in cities. In New York City, for example, "by March 1996, the city had registered 83,874 cumulative cases of adult AIDS, and 1,645 cases of pediatric AIDS" (Office of AIDS Surveillance, 1996). "It is estimated that as many as 5,000-10,000 New Yorkers are acquiring HIV infection each year" (New York City Department of Health, 1994). "New York City reported 2,995 cases of tuberculosis, the highest in the United States" (New York City Department of Health, 1995). Not only do these conditions present enormous financial burdens to city, state, and federal governments, they present overwhelming social and situational problems in addition to the medical problems, particularly for urban-based health care professionals (Hellinger, 1993). Providers are challenged daily to find solutions to these chronic medical and social problems within a system of care that is not prepared to provide effective interventions. The need to manage the duality of medical and social problems requires a new emphasis on both medical and behavioral health interventions (Volland, 1996).

Another challenge of significance to health care delivery and to social work is that individuals are expecting and often demanding more participation in their own care. All 50 states have legislated, and the medical profession has recognized, the patient's right to choose in advance his or her medical treatment options in the event of a critical or terminal illness (New York State Task Force on Life and the Law, 1996). This legislated choice, and the growing empowerment of individuals who wish to participate in decisions about their own health and treatment, are shifting the decision-making role away from the physician and to the patient. In addition, when patients are no longer capable of making autonomous choices, families and other appointed individuals are asked to act as surrogates in making these critical health care decisions. The complexity of medical decision making includes decisions that concern providing or withholding treatment, organ donations, complex or risky surgical and other innovative medical procedures, and the many ethical decisions related to newly emerging knowledge about genetic diseases, which present individuals with options and choices of genetic screening and testing that have never before been available. As individuals and their families become more responsible for decision making, they will need additional education and support. Social workers can provide the assistance needed in these critical decision-making processes.

Challenges to social work are also presented by the situation of families who are increasingly expected to be responsible for a patient's transition to home care. With the number of beneficiaries of the Medicare home health program rising from 1,682,139 in 1989 to 2,836,912 in 1993, a 69 percent increase in just four years, this pressure on families has been increasing (Special Committee on Aging, 1996). These families may not have the psychological or financial resources they need to provide such care. As sicker patients are being discharged from the hospital earlier, resources must be immediately available to facilitate this transition and support both the patient and the family caregivers (National Public Health and Hospital Institute, 1995). When the system of care demands that the patient be "managed" so that services are provided in the most cost-effective way, social workers must be available to advocate on behalf of patients and family members. Individuals without identifiable families will be at particular risk if their return to the community depends on this support. Social work services will be needed to ensure that problems in transition to home- and community-based care are met.

Measuring the outcomes of practice interventions for all health care professionals is increasingly necessary and a challenge to all health professionals (Corcoran & Gingerich, 1994). The changing health care marketplace demands that health care providers better meet the needs and preferences of the patients they serve. For hospitals, this means "increased competition for a shrinking inpatient market, rising consumerism, greater focus on the quality of medical care, and concerns about its cost-effectiveness and appropriateness. To survive in this new environment, hospitals must pay greater attention to their basic mission: caring for patients" (Rogut, 1995). In this environment, evaluating the effectiveness of interventions becomes especially necessary. Professionals are already expected to respond to institutional and systemic requirements. They will now be expected to demonstrate effectiveness through an evaluative process based on clinical practice guidelines (Shueman & Troy, 1994). This process should consider the impact of social supports on recovery and the important role of the family in facilitating an effective transition back to the community (Caroff & Mailick, 1985).

Assessment and Intervention

Social work practice has been an important component of health care since the early 1900s. It was initially conceived as a service for poor and needy dispensary patients. Today the diversity of individuals, both culturally and in terms of health status, who require social work services has expanded dramatically. The psychological components that make up a person's character are based on multiple levels of development: physical, social, psychological, cognitive, cultural, and moral (Berkman et al., 1996). The framework of social work practice in health care includes an understanding of the interaction between these dimensions. These dynamic challenges to health care delivery and to social work forecast the increasing needs that individuals and families will have for sophisticated, compassionate, and accessible psychosocial care and guidance. They may also forecast the need for increasing education of staff about the patient's and the family's cultural beliefs regarding health, illness, and disability.

In practice, social workers use biopsychosocial assessments to understand how individuals adjust to illness and medical treatment and to define what social health care needs must be addressed. The profession's ability to view the individual within his or her social environment is essential in the emerging health care environment. The social worker understands how the psychological and the biological interact physiologically and behaviorally. A social worker in health care must develop sophisticated knowledge specific to diseases or populations at risk, including knowledge of various types of diseases, treatments and their outcomes, prognoses, the course of illness, and issues related to disease recurrence and survival. It is equally important to understand the patient's and the family's perception of the disease, its causes, and its cures: The social worker must be able to identify common and uncommon psychosocial needs of patients and families, as well as understand how they will cope with the stress of illness. The social worker is a member of the health care team who has the knowledge and skills to identify patients in need of psychosocial help (Berkman et al., 1996).

Many modes of intervention in health care are available to the social worker. These are based on assessment of the problems facing an individual or family within the specific context of the disease or disability—for example, mobilizing external resources (through advocacy, provision of concrete services, involvement of familial and community resources, and the like) or strengthening internal resources (through clarifying, educating the individual and the family about the illness and its implications, helping set priorities, regulating the tempo of the coping activity, and so forth) (Berkman et al., 1996).

The patient's family plays important roles in terms of the onset of stress-related or psychosomatic illness, the course and management of any illness, and the impact that episodes of illness have on patient and family roles. Because much of what social workers do involves helping patients and families cope with and adapt to changes brought about by illness and hospitalization, family therapy can be an effective framework for intervention. In addition to work with the individual and the family, there is growing recognition of the importance of groups in helping patients and families cope with illness (Glassman, 1991). Group work has become an increasingly significant method of social work intervention

in health care settings, particularly with the advent of managed care (Winegar, Bistline, & Sheridan, 1992). Much of the available literature describes groups or group programs for patients and families who are coping with the psychosocial effects of a particular disease (for example, cancer), life crisis (such as aging), or role change (as when institutionalization occurs) (Rutchick, 1990).

SOCIAL WORK IN HEALTH CARE'S NEW CONTEXT

The health care system is in a period of rapid change, motivated primarily by efforts to contain the rising cost of health care services. These efforts have had direct implications for the organization of health care services: New types of organizational structures have been created, and there is continuing concern about access to health care services. New methods of cost control have been introduced, and the community responsibility aspect of health care is being replaced by the corporate profit motive (Robinson, 1994; Shortell, Gillies, & Devers, 1995).

Social workers and all health care professionals need an appreciation of the organizational dimension—and the conflicts inherent in this new corporate approach. The social worker must be sensitive to these issues of the organizational setting and the concerns they pose to the patient. At the same time, the nature of social work practice calls for much system-related activity. Practice in health settings demands frequent interdisciplinary collaboration, team meetings, and interorganizational relations (Berkman et al., 1988). Thus, an area of increasing importance to social work practice in health care is an understanding of the evolving integrated services delivery networks. Efficiency in interdisciplinary collaboration for effective patient care within the institution, in ambulatory care settings, and in the community at large is a necessary skill. Collaboration with community agencies and programs for patients with particular diseases, including nursing and home care services, local community programs, hospices, and support groups, is essential. The social worker's role as care coordinator or case manager will probably be brief and intensive, with the goal of creating and strengthening support systems that will enhance and maintain social functioning (Williams, Warrick, Christianson, & Netting,

1993). A social worker in health care must be able to cope with organizational complexities, have sophisticated knowledge of state-of-the-art medical care, be comfortable with ethical decision making, and be a flexible, creative leader in services delivery both in the hospital and in care settings in the community.

Social Work in Health Care Policy Making

Social work practice is also dramatically affected by changing public policy priorities and the advent of new health care policies that concern such health crises as AIDS. Most health care services are financed by public funds and private insurers, with the latter financed largely by employers. Policy decisions determine the availability, length, and type of services provided to patients. Social workers in the health care setting are a natural source of policy information for patients and families, as well as for other health care professionals. They are confronted by questions about eligibility for entitlement programs such as Medicaid, insurance coverage of services by programs such as Medicare, and the availability of community services such as home health care. The social worker must know the eligibility standards for financial assistance and be able to provide referrals to sources of assistance or services. The social worker must also understand the process by which policies are developed, approved, implemented, and ultimately experienced, which demonstrates the need for social workers to know and effectively participate in policy development. Social work's expertise in the relationship between social systems and individuals and populations can be a major contribution to the policy process (Berkman et al., 1988).

To be effective in health care policy making, the social worker must be well versed in the particulars of a policy question and skilled in policy analysis and intervention. The ability of the social worker to articulate the impact of policy on patients is an essential element in policy development. Many policy issues deserve special attention—for example, health care finance as it affects availability, quality, and nature of services; Medicare and Medicaid questions of entitlement, eligibility, and implementation; long-term health care and quality of services, alternative services, and appropriateness of services; primary health care for special populations such as children,

elderly people, disabled people, and people with HIV/AIDS; and funding to support social work services, education, and research.

BIOPSYCHOSOCIAL APPROACH

Social work professionals in the emerging health care environment do not have the luxury of limiting the number of variables they will face in their practice. If social work's goal is to maintain and support the social functioning and physical health of individuals and their families, there cannot be a narrow basis for practice. Social workers must be careful to avoid a dogmatic, single-factor, causality-based way of thinking that has too frequently directed both biomedically based and psychodynamically based practitioners. Although in the past social work placed greater emphasis on the psychological and interpersonal elements of social functioning, there is a growing substantive argument for the inclusion of biomedical, social, cultural, and environmental knowledge in social work practice.

Social work's biopsychosocial approach provides a carefully balanced perspective, which takes into account the entire person in his or her environment and helps social workers in screening and assessing the needs of an individual from a multidimensional point of view. Social work practice often focuses on helping a person cope with a particular difficulty or episode of illness. Now, however, social work is also increasingly concerned with health promotion and disease prevention programs to prevent the occurrence of a condition or disease in a population, or to reduce the risk of particular problems occurring in a population, and in which individuals take responsibility for their own health behaviors (Ibrahim et al., 1995).

A primary preventive approach is not merely a matter of early intervention. Prevention in social work requires, for example, screening protocols that have been effective in identifying people at risk who might benefit from early intervention. Screening protocols result from epidemiological studies that have identified risk factors in particular populations. Although a number of clinical screening tools for nonmedical services needs have been developed and implemented in inpatient settings, there are few clinical tools specifically developed to help social workers screen ambulatory clients for potential psychosocial and environmental risk.

The scope of screening for individuals and populations at risk must be broad enough to encompass multidimensional factors, particularly those that are likely to be overlooked by primary care physicians. Dimensions of such an instrument should assess

- physical functioning (the ability to perform activities of daily living [ADLs] and instrumental ADLs [IADLs])
- psychological functioning (the presence of depression or other mental disorders)
- cognitive functioning
- availability of social support, both formal and informal
- environmental resources
- financial resources.

Because social health care factors have interrelated effects, a screening tool that focuses on difficulties patients have with ADLs and IADLs may serve as a reasonably accurate tool in identifying those patients who may be having difficulty in other areas as well. Theoretically, if physiological functioning is bolstered through early identification of risk and supportive intervention, it is likely that improved psychological or environmental functioning will also be achieved.

Biopsychosocial assessments will play an increasingly important role in public policy debates, health planning, and clinical practice. The goals of maintaining patients' viability in independent settings and enhancing quality of life emphasize the need for standardized screening tools that include assessment factors to predict which patients are at risk for social health care needs.

Conclusion

Although practicing in a less autonomous system (Munson, 1996), social workers in health care now have the opportunity to shift their frame of reference to support the changing needs of individuals and families. Social work can reclaim its early focus on community health and continue to develop its expertise in the provision of clinical services for individuals and families facing complex decisions about values and lifestyles driven by advances in health-related technology (Rosenberg & Holden, 1995). The new social worker will work with a more empowered individual and family and assume a more supportive advocacy role: A fundamental tenet would be acceptance of the increased participation of individuals in making their own health care choices. The family will be active participants with multiple roles, including—but not limited to—caregiving (Bergman et al., 1993). The community will be the laboratory where social workers shift their emphasis and develop expertise in helping to improve the community's health. It will be essential to evaluate the effectiveness of these interventions. This outcome-directed practice will need to demonstrate the value of interventions that are supportive of individual, family, and community needs. As such, this process will strengthen the ability of the social worker to advocate for the interests of individuals and families. Evaluating the interests of the individual and assessing the capacity of the family to cope will be equally important to the systemwide goal of maximizing resources.

Social work practice in health care is distinct from other health professions because it redefines patients as clients. The focus of practice is on the psychosocial effects of illness, not the physiological dimensions of disease; the identification and treatment plan is dependent on clear understanding of psychosocial and environmental causation. In practice, social workers use the process of biopsychosocial assessment to describe how individuals adjust to illness and medical treatment and to explain and define how health care resources are organized to meet social health care needs. Social work's specialized ability to focus on individuals and their social environment is fundamental and has been an increasing focus of the profession. This focus is essential in the changing health care delivery system. As health care moves into community-based care, social work can and will expand its focus of concern.

References

Abel, A., Boland M., Durand, B. A., Geolot, D. H., Goodson, J. D., Isham, G. J., & Steele, L.G.F. (1995). Work force and community health care needs: A model to link service, education, and the community. *Family and Community Health, 18*(1), 75–79.

Bergman, A., Wells, L., Bogo, M., Abbey, S., Chandler, V., Emberton, L., Cuirgis, S., Huot, A., McNeill, T., Prentice, L., Stapleton, D., Shekter-Wolfson, L., & Urman, S. (1993). High-risk indicators for family involvement in social work in health care: A review of the literature. *Social Work, 38,* 281–288.

Berkman, B. (1990). Bridging biomedical and psychosocial perspectives in health. In *Building on our history: Bridges to the 21st century.* Philadelphia: University of Pennsylvania Press.

Berkman, B., Bonander, E., Kemler, E., Isaacson-Rubinger, M. J., Rutchick, I., & Silverman, P. (1996). Social work in the academic medical center: Advanced training a necessity. *Social Work in Health Care, 24*(1), 115–135.

Berkman, B., Bonander, E., Kemler, E., Marcus, L., Isaacson-Rubinger, M. J., Rutchick, R., & Silverman, P. (1988). *Social work in health care: A review of the literature.* Chicago: American Hospital Association, Society of Hospital Social Work Directors.

Caroff, P., & Mailick, M. (1985). The patient has a family: Reaffirming social work domain. *Social Work in Health Care, 10*(4), 17–34.

Corcoran, K., & Gingerich, W. J. (1994). Practice evaluation in the context of managed care: Case-recording methods for quality assurance reviews. *Research on Social Work Practice, 4,* 326–337.

Glassman, U. (1991). The social work group and its distinct qualities in the health care setting. *Health & Social Work, 16*(3), 203–212.

Hellinger, F. (1993). The lifetime cost of treating a person with HIV. *JAMA, 270,* 474–478.

Ibrahim M. A., House, R. M., & Levine, R. H. (1995). Educating the public health work force for the 21st century. *Family and Community Health, 18*(3), 17–25.

Kenney, J. J. (1990). Social work management in emerging health care systems. *Health & Social Work, 15,* 22–31.

Munson, C. E. (1996). Autonomy and managed care in clinical social work practice. *Smith College Studies in Social Work, 66,* 241–260.

National Public Health and Hospital Institute. (1995). *Urban social health.* Washington, DC: Author.

New York City Department of Health. (1994). *Annual summary.* New York: Author.

New York City Department of Health. (1995, September-December). *Annual report* (Vol. 14, No. 4). New York: Author.

New York State Task Force on Life and the Law. (1996). *When death is sought: Assisted suicide and euthanasia in the medical context.* New York: Author.

Office of AIDS Surveillance, New York City Department of Health. (1996, April). *AIDS Surveillance update, first quarter 1996.* New York: Author.

Pawlson, L. G. (1994). Chronic illness: Implications of a new paradigm for health care. *Joint Commission Journal on Quality Improvement, 20*(1), 33–39.

Robinson, J. C. (1994). The changing boundaries of the American hospital. *Milbank Quarterly, 72,* 259–275.

Rogut, L. (1995, November). *Meeting patients' needs: Quality care in a changing environment.* New York: United Hospital Fund.

Rosenberg, G., & Holden, G. (1995, January). *The role of social work in improving quality of life in the community.* Keynote address at the First International Conference on Social Work in Health and Mental Health Care, Jerusalem, Israel.

Rutchick, I. (1990). Research on practice with groups in health care settings. *Social Work in Health Care, 15*(1), 97–114.

Shortell, S. M., Gillies, R. R., & Devers, K. J. (1995). Reinventing the American hospital. *Milbank Quarterly, 73,* 131–160.

Shueman, S. A., & Troy, W. G. (1994). The use of practice guidelines in behavioral health programs. In S. A. Shueman, W. G. Troy, & S. L. Mayhugh (Eds.), *Managed behavioral health care: An industry perspective* (pp. 149–164). Springfield, IL: Charles C Thomas.

Special Committee on Aging. (1996). *GAO report to the chairman.*

Volland, P. J. (1996). Social work practice in health care: Looking to the future with a different lens. *Social Work in Health Care, 24*(1/2), 35–51.

Williams, F. G., Warrick, L. H., Christianson, J. B., & Netting, F. E. (1993). Critical factors for successful hospital-based case management. *Health Care Management Review, 18,* 63–70.

Winegar, N., Bistline, J. L., & Sheridan, S. (1992). At the agency: Implementing a group therapy program in a managed care setting—Combining cost effectiveness and quality care. *Families in Society, 73*(1), 56–58.

Barbara Berkman, DSW, is Helen Rehr/Ruth Fizdale Professor, Columbia University School of Social Work, 622 West 113th Street, New York, NY 10025. **Patricia Volland, MSW, MBA,** is senior vice president, New York Academy of Medicine, 1216 Fifth Avenue, New York, NY 10029.

For further information see

Bioethical Issues; Clinical Social Work; Disability; End-of-Life Decisions; Ethics and Values; Families: Direct Practice; Family Caregiving; Goal Setting and Intervention Planning; Health Care: Direct Practice; Health Care: Financing; **Health Care: Policy Development;** Health Care: Reform Initiatives; Health Planning; Health Services Systems Policy; HIV/AIDS: Direct Practice; Hospice; Hospital Social Work; Long-Term Care; Managed Care Overview; **Managed Care: Implications for Social Work Practice;** Patient Rights; Prevention and Wellness; Primary Health Care; Primary Prevention Overview; Public Health

Services; Social Work Practice: History and Evolution; Social Work Practice: Theoretical Base; Substance Abuse: Direct Practice; Women and Health Care.

Key Words

biopsychosocial   health care delivery
approach   interdisciplinary
chronic care   approach

I

The Internet: Accessing the World of Information

William H. Butterfield

Dick Schoech

Social workers are using the Internet as a communication and information management tool to enhance their ability to perform many tasks. Social workers and agencies are using the Internet as a communication tool for client advocacy and to influence legislative and regulatory policy. They are using the Internet to establish community networks that allow clients or agencies to set up the equivalent of an interactive community newspaper. Like newspapers, these community networks convey news and information as well as advertise projects of interest, jobs, and services. Community networks also are used as forums to discuss community issues in much the same way as town meetings performed this function in the past. Agencies and social workers are using the Internet to get needed information and to consult with others on how to provide the services their communities and clients need. They are also using the electronic mail (e-mail) capability of the Internet to communicate with each other and, in some instances, with clients. They are adapting Internet tools to internal agency networks, called intranets, to manage client and agency data. Intranets make it possible for social workers to record or access client data in the field and easily add data to their database. Even therapy and support groups are now being offered via the Internet. Of course, social workers were accomplishing all these tasks long before the Internet existed. What distinguishes the Internet is the ease, speed, and flexibility of communication it provides. Like the automobile and the telephone before it, the Internet has vastly expanded the ability of social workers to deliver services.

What Is the Internet?

The term "Internet" has become almost mythical. Everyone is talking about it, and many people are using it without a basic understanding of what it is or how it was developed. There is nothing magical about the Internet: It is a powerful and versatile tool, but nevertheless a tool. Shorn of all its mythical trappings, the Internet is a communication network—a medium for exchanging information. Rather like the telephone network, the Internet consists of wire lines, radio relay towers, and communication satellites that connect computers all over the world. Some have called it the world's largest computer network, with all its subnets freely exchanging information—but the Internet is more than just a medium for exchanging information. Earlier technologies such as the telegraph, telephone, and facsimile (fax) machine were effective for transmitting information over long distances. The Internet adds information storage, searching, and manipulation to the existing information exchange capabilities of these earlier technologies.

The many types of computers connected to the Internet belong to all kinds of companies and individuals. They range from simple, low-power computers to large mainframe computers. Normally, computers of such diverse makeup can exchange only limited information. However, any computer connected to the Internet potentially has access to all the information and the information manipulation capacity of all the other computers connected to the Internet. The Internet overcomes the previous communication barrier with a universal set of communication rules or commands called a "computer protocol." The protocol used by all computers connected to the Internet is called TCP/IP (transmission control protocol/Internet protocol).

The Internet is a global connection of the information in millions of computers that is easily accessible by anyone from his or her home with just an inexpensive computer, a modem, and standard telephone lines. It is a network that links people and information processing, storage, retrieval, and transmission capacities as never before. This linking of capacities is important to social workers because social work is a profession based on the communication of complex information.

Analogies aid understanding of the Internet. One familiar analogy is the term "information superhighway." Table 1 presents several analogies between a transportation network and the Internet.

Historical Perspective

The Internet has been in existence since 1982. Like the interstate highway system, it was developed by the U.S. Department of Defense to create a decentralized network that would function even if one or many of the computers on the network were disabled or destroyed by nuclear war. The original Internet commands and programs were developed by computer experts and were not easily used by others.

The development of the World Wide Web (WWW) and Web browsers has made it possible for almost anyone to use the Internet. WWW is a network of Internet sites that use a common site identification system and a common language to display information. The common addressing system results in each site having its own uniform resource locator (URL), which is analogous to each house having its own street address. The common language— hypertext markup language (HTML)—allows a graphical user interface similar to that used in Macintosh- and Windows-based computers. The software that provides users with a graphical interface to WWW is called a "browser." Just as paved highways and the mass-produced model T Ford spurred our use of the highway system, WWW and graphical

browsers have opened the Internet to people with limited computer ability and spurred the development of WWW sites.

Intranets

Intranets use Internet tools and communication protocols within organizations. That is, rather than connecting to networks outside the organization, intranets operate within the confines of a single organization. With that exception, an intranet functions in the same way as the Internet. An intranet could consist of a single internal network, or large organizations may have several subnets tied together through an intranet. Looked at another way, the Internet connects an agency or person to the universe of information that exists in the world. An intranet makes internal information available to members of an organization. With intranets, agencies that have an Internet service provider (ISP) but little networking expertise can develop networks by having the ISP manage the intranet. This places much of the burden of managing the network on the ISP. This is especially useful for small consortia of agencies or dispersed partnerships of social work practitioners, such as those organized for managed care purposes. Another alternative is for the agency to use commercial Internet software and protocols to create a stand-alone system apart from the Internet. This approach requires that the agency devote substantial resources to the management of the intranet.

The central uses of an intranet may be different from those of the Internet. Finding and transmitting information and files would be common on both, but on intranets one would expect to see more sharing of common documents and tasks. For example, many social workers might receive e-mail, enter client data, and review internal memos and

---

TABLE 1
Transportation Network and Internet Analogies

Transportation Network	"Information Superhighway" Network
All interconnected roads in the system	The Internet
Interstate highway system	World Wide Web (WWW)
Car that lets people travel on a highway	Browser that lets people use the Internet
Your home	An Internet site
The street address of your home	Uniform resource locator (URL)
The entrance of your home	Home page
The roads from your home to other houses	Links from one WWW site to another WWW site
Traffic jams and gridlock	Traffic jams and gridlock
Traveler's terms and road-sign symbols	Hypertext markup language (HTML)

policies on an intranet. The distinction between the Internet and intranets is becoming less important because many software products are being made Internet capable. That is, they can seamlessly interact with the Internet without starting a separate program. Intranets can still be problematic for social workers, however, because internal agency information must be kept private and confidential. Internet security and confidentiality are not yet well developed, so social services agencies should pay special attention to maintaining intranet security and confidentiality.

WHAT YOU NEED TO SEARCH THE INTERNET

Hardware

The Internet can be accessed by a wide variety of computers. The most common personal computers on the Internet are IBM compatible. For use on the Internet, IBM compatibles should use a version of Microsoft Windows and a graphical browser. Better yet is a computer that can support the latest version of Windows: Although a computer with an Intel 386 central processing unit and a graphics board that will support a color monitor with video graphics array (VGA) resolution (640 x 480 pixels) (Lowe, 1994) can access the Internet, it is preferable to use the best multimedia personal computer you can reasonably afford. Users of Apple computers will need to use the latest version of the TCP/IP connection for the Macintosh (MacTCP). Installing MacTCP is a little difficult, so it may be best to call on a local Mac expert for help. Local ISPs can offer names of people who can help you use other kinds of computers.

Most people access the Internet by use of a modem to send signals over a standard telephone line. Although internal modems (installed inside the computer) are less expensive and work as well as external ones, some knowledgeable computer users prefer external modems because the modems may have lights indicating various modem operations and can be reset without turning off the computer when the communication link between the computer and another modem is disrupted. Resetting the modem without turning off the computer is not always possible with internal modems. Many Internet users also find that a separate telephone line is desirable but not essential. The higher the speed of the modem, the less time is spent waiting for text, images, and files. A modem that operates at at least a 14,400 bits per second (bps) transfer rate is required, but one that operates at 56,000 bps is desirable. Modems with even higher speed are now becoming available, as are modems that allow a simultaneous voice and Internet connection. To return to the transportation system analogy, the pleasure of driving on a superhighway is enhanced by the car you drive. Driving a small, rough-riding car with limited horsepower can make the traveling unpleasant. Similarly, an unreliable connection to the Internet with a slow computer capable of running only limited graphics will result in an unpleasant Internet experience.

The Internet Connection

Most people connect to the Internet by use of a commercial ISP. (Also, most telephone companies are now ISPs.) Check with others to learn what ISP they use and how satisfied they are with the service. It is also possible for some people to get an Internet connection through their employer or an educational institution. Features to consider when choosing an ISP are

- unlimited Internet access time at a reasonable price
- a high-quality connection available at peak hours without a busy signal
- a reliable connection that does not frequently disconnect
- dial-up access from where you work and live. (If you travel frequently or live in a remote area, an ISP with a toll-free telephone number is best)
- quick response with technical support
- a short host address
- free provision for developing your own home page or WWW site.

There are several ways to physically connect to the Internet, including direct connection ("hard wired"), telephone or cable television line and modem, and specialized telephone lines called integrated services digital networks (ISDN) and T1. (For an explanation of ISDN and T1 lines, see Appendix B.) Some are for specialized uses and can be very expensive. Before you decide how to connect, contact a computer expert to help you choose the kind of connectivity that best suits your needs.

Your connection source will assign you an Internet address. (See Appendix A for a discussion of Internet addressing.) Install and configure your computer and Internet software. Typically, your ISP will supply Internet software and instructions. First, provide the computer software with the information it needs to communicate between your computer and the computer that connects to the Internet. If you are connected on a network by wire or by fiberoptic line, the person who runs the network will do this configuration for you. If you are connected by a modem, you will probably have to enter the information provided by your ISP. Typically, you will have to configure the mail, newsgroups, and file transfer parts of your Internet browser. This is the most difficult part of connecting to the Internet because configuration files are sometimes difficult to understand and find. If you do not understand how to configure software, your ISP's technical support staff should be able to help you. Newer software that is now being developed will be much more Internet ready and eliminate many of the configuration tasks. In addition, a few other pieces of information have to be entered in several places. Consult with your ISP or a computer store if you are not sure what to enter or where to enter it.

The most common method for connecting to the Internet is a modem or network connection to a host computer that allows Internet programs to be stored on your computer. A remote host is connected to the Internet, and the Internet programs are on a local computer. The host computer acts as a gateway to the Internet. Files copied from the Internet are generally saved on the local computer, and new Internet programs can be loaded and run from the local computer. At one time this level of connectivity was limited to people whose computers were connected to the host by a local area network (LAN) or a wide area network (WAN) and was not available to people who connected to the host through a modem. Point to point (PPP) and serial line Internet protocol (SLIP) software now make it possible for computers connected to the host by a telephone line to have the same full access to the Internet as those connected through LANs. This kind of Internet access is available through subsidized access through agencies, educational institutions, community organizations, or freenets; fee-for-service access through ISPs; and fee-for-service access through added-content proprietary ISPs.

Subsidized access through agencies and educational institutions. Agencies and educational institutions often make Internet access available to their employees, students, and members, who may use the computers in the facility at little or no cost. They may also use their home computers to connect to the agency or educational host through a modem.

Subsidized access through community organizations. One of the concerns about the growth of the Internet is that it will not be available to those who cannot afford their own computers. In response to this concern, a number of communities have made access available through libraries and other public institutions. Some communities have decided to place public-access computers in other locations, such as street kiosks or business areas. A few have also made available "neighborhood computers." These computers are placed in private homes where the owners have agreed to provide access to people in the neighborhood. For discussion of some aspects of community access, see http://www.rand.org/publications/MR/MR650/index.html.

Subsidized access through freenets. Other communities have taken a different approach. They have not provided computers but instead have provided free connections—called "freenets"—to people who own their own computers by allowing them to dial into an ISP at no cost. Since freenets were developed at Case Western Reserve University in Cleveland, Ohio, they have spread to many other regions of the United States. More information on freenets can be found at many sites on the Internet (such as http://www.nslsilus.org/freenet.html or http://excite.com/Subject/Computing/Internet/Freenet/s-index.l.html).

Fee-for-service access through ISPs. Many users prefer Internet services provided by one of the two types of commercial providers. ISPs operate in the same manner as telephone companies do for telephone services. These companies' business is providing Internet access services. Unlimited access to the Internet from these sources usually costs about $20 per month. Lower rates are sometimes available in areas where there is substantial competition between providers. Some of the more common ISPs include telephone companies, cable television companies, and other businesses whose only purpose is to provide commercial Internet access. Sources of this type of service can be found under "Computers" in the Yellow Pages. These companies also advertise frequently in newspapers and on television.

Fee-for-service access through added-content proprietary ISPs. These services were in business before the ISP services described above became available. Prodigy and CompuServe are examples of this type of Internet provider. They provide many specialized, extra services that are not usually available to Internet users who use other ways to connect, so they are called "value-added" or "added-content." Examples of value-added services include discussion groups, interactive chat rooms, and interactive multiplayer games. Although most services now offer full Internet access, a few may still restrict the level of Internet connectivity available to their customers. Also, they often charge hourly access fees rather than a flat monthly rate for access to the Internet. The type of access these companies offer is changing rapidly, however. Pressures from other services and pricing structures offered by other types of Internet providers make it likely that these services will have to provide full dial-up connectivity to survive. America Online (AOL) and American Telephone and Telegraph (ATT), for example, have removed all restrictions on the Internet access they provide and have changed their pricing structure so that it is competitive with other ISPs.

HOW TO USE THE INTERNET
The best way to use the Internet is to use a graphical browser. When activated, the browser automatically connects to the Internet. The rest of the operations can be accomplished, for the most part, by mouse clicking to activate functions that use buttons, scroll bars, and other icons on the screen. A number of browsers exist for use on the Internet. The best known are Microsoft's Internet Explorer and Netscape Navigator. Netscape is currently the most popular, but product popularity on the Internet changes quickly.

Once a browser is installed and configured on the computer, you can use its built-in tutorial, which is a good guide to how to use the Internet. Among other things, it tells you how to use the various menus, toolbars, and buttons that appear on the screen. It also tells you how to use the bookmark function and the e-mail address book to save Internet addresses for later use. (Other applications are described elsewhere in this entry.) The easiest way to access the tutorial is to click on the Help option of the browser's menu bar. It is also a good idea to print out the browser's tutorial for reference as you learn how to use the Internet.

Home Pages and WWW Sites
Documents used by Netscape and other browsers are stored in page format. A special page is the home page—an on-line screen of information designed by an individual or organization as a gateway to all other information the page designer wants the user to access. It usually contains introductory information or graphics that help the user understand what information is available through the home page, and it almost always has links to other home pages. When users select one of these links, called "hyperlinks," they may be transferred to

- another part of the same page
- another page of the same site
- another site
- a specific file or other source of information.

Users of the Internet quickly become familiar with home pages because almost every location they visit will have one. Until recently, developing a home page was a challenge best left to professionals. It is now common, though, for almost anyone to set up a home page with pictures, an agency logo, and other useful and important information, and many vendors have developed easy-to-use tools for creating home pages. Most of the popular word processing software also has HTML capabilities for designing WWW pages. The latest version of Netscape, for example, provides many authoring tools and a wizard that takes the user through the process of constructing a simple home page.

WHAT TO DO ON THE INTERNET
The most commonly used applications available through the Internet are

- e-mail to send and receive messages
- listserv e-mail
- newsgroups e-mail or Usenet
- database access

- transfer of files from a remote location
- chat, conferences, and Internet telephone.

E-Mail

E-mail is written and sent electronically over the Internet from one individual to another. When it arrives, it remains in the computer's mail box until it is retrieved by the recipient. You can also use it to

- include a copy of the original message in your reply
- attach (transfer) copies of files or other information without copying the documents to your e-mail document
- send the address of another Internet site or page (the e-mail recipient can then connect to the site by simply clicking the mouse on the address)
- send copies of e-mail to many others.

The last facility listed above, called "broadcasting," is one of the most powerful e-mail features. Broadcasting electronically is much easier than it would be manually. When E-mail addresses have been entered into the computer, broadcasting is simply a matter of selecting the addresses and sending the e-mail. One can even create a group address and then broadcast mail to all members of the group by simply sending a message to the group address. Common uses of this process include scheduling meetings, sending agendas or minutes to committee members, or notifying employees of policy changes. Newer mailing software allows the user to send embedded computer programs in e-mail, which make it possible to send forms and surveys that are easily completed and returned. Remember, however, that the broadcasting function is very powerful and must be used carefully, with regard for privacy and confidentiality. Choosing a group e-mail address rather than a private one could send your message all over the United States or all over the world. Before you send e-mail, check to be sure where it is going.

E-mail usually reaches its destination within minutes of being sent. On occasion, however, it is lost or delayed—just like regular mail from the post office. If timely delivery is important, ask for verification of delivery from the recipient. This is especially important because a person may have more than one e-mail address but not check all of them regularly.

Listservs

Listservs are useful because they offer an easy way to manage communications among a group wanting to discuss a common topic. The e-mail sent to the listserv group is duplicated and sent to all subscribers. When a topic of wide or especially important interest is discussed, the volume of messages that arrive from a listserv can be overwhelming. Although the quality of discussion on listservs can sometimes be erratic, if not trivial, many people find the application useful. Listservs are especially useful to groups who want to disseminate information or mobilize people and organizations. For example, during the 1996 congressional debate on social welfare policy, much useful information was distributed on the SOCWORK listserv, a list for social workers who want to discuss issues of professional relevance.

Listservs can be a little confusing to some users because they have both an e-mail address and a command address. The e-mail address is where all e-mail to the subscribers is sent. The command address is where e-mail telling the listserv to change the subscriber's status is sent. For example, the SOCWORK listserv's e-mail address is SOCWORK@ UWRF.EDU, and its server address is majordomo@uwrf.edu. To subscribe to SOCWORK, send an e-mail to majordomo @uwrf.edu with only the words "subscribe socwork" in the body of the message. To unsubscribe, follow the same procedure but substitute the word "unsubscribe."

The commands for SOCWORK may differ slightly from those needed to use other listservs—for example, some listservs require users to subscribe and unsubscribe by using the above commands followed by the user's first and last name. There are also dozens of other commands that listservs will recognize. As is often the case when working with computers, more than one program is available for listserv operations. In addition to majordomo, some other listservs are listserv, Bitnet, LISTPROC, MAILBASE, and mailserv. Each uses a slightly different set of commands. Typically, when you subscribe, the listserv computer will automatically send you a list of commands that will work with that listserv. Also, you can usually get the information you need by sending a message with the command "help."

To obtain a list of the more than 30,000 listservs available on the Internet, send the command "list global" to the command address of a listserv server. (A complete list of listservs can also be found at http://www.lsoft.com/lists/listref.html.) A better strategy, however, is to limit your search with key words. For example, to obtain a list of all social work listservs available on the Internet, send the command "list global/social work" to a listserv command server. You can also find lists of social work listservs at http://www.rit.edu/~694www/lists.htm or http://www.sc.edu/swan/listserv.html.

Usenet

Usenet is another type of mail program. It is actually a completely separate network from the Internet, but it is well integrated into most Internet browsers. Usenet is also called "Internet news," "newsgroups," or "News Net."

News Net works like a newspaper's classified advertisement section. With News Net, e-mail messages are sent to and stored in a single computer, where anyone who contacts that computer can read the messages. News Net messages are stored according to the type of information they contain. All social work messages can be found in several groups with a primary focus on the profession. As is the case with listservs, the messages contained in News Net vary in quality.

Web Search Tools

The ability to conduct key word searches of all the many Internet sites in the world is the most powerful aspect of the Internet. Extensive, valuable information about Internet search programs (including subject catalogues, indexes, reviews and ratings sites, metaindexes, and other tools) is available from an Internet tutorial (http://wwwmedlib.med.utah.edu/travel/srchtool.html) created by Nancy Lombardo, systems librarian at the Eccles Health Sciences Library, University of Utah, Salt Lake City. Some of the most widely used search tools—often called "search engines"—are AltaVista, Excite, HotBot, InfoSeek, Lycos, Magellan, and Yahoo, software programs that continually travel WWW, record the contents of each Web site, and create an index of site contents. Site searching and indexing go on 24 hours a day, every day of the year, so it is possible to quickly find up-to-date links to any information. For example, thousands of Internet sites may contain the term "social work." With an index, there will be only one entry for the words

"social work." That one entry has already been linked to all WWW sites containing the term, so the search program can quickly display the list of social work–related sites. The search tools do not actually contact the sites for the user: They present a clickable list of sites and let the user decide which ones to examine. Different search programs use different indexing and updating methods, so you may want to duplicate your search on more than one search program.

Information accessed on the Internet is especially useful because it can be

- printed out
- saved to a file
- bookmarked to be easily found later
- e-mailed to yourself or others.

Remember, however, that although Internet information is easily copied, it is considered to be copyrighted under U.S. copyright law unless stated otherwise.

Some WWW sites offer a convenient way to use many search engines at once. Search.com (http://www.search.com) is a well-designed Internet site dedicated to making Internet searches easy. It allows the user to choose a search engine or do simultaneous searches of several search engines. It also has prepackaged search categories, such as sports, stock quotes, jobs, weather information, and news.

Using the Internet for Database Access

The Internet can be used to access large data files that are maintained by many organizations. This function differs from standard Internet access, through which the user views specific pages of information. Internet databases provide interactive access to the information they contain: The user enters the specific information requested, and the program then displays the latest information in its database that is related to the specified search criteria. An excellent example can be found at the searchable database maintained by the National Center for Missing and Exploited Children (http://www.missingkids.org/criteria.html). Some Internet databases allow the user to enter as well as search for information. These databases are already in use for such tasks as entering case notes on clients or getting specific information about clients. For example, the New Mexico Department of Children and Youth is transferring 60,000 case records on adults and children to a computerized client tracking system that will provide social workers with the latest information on each of their clients. Connecticut, Rhode Island, and Alaska have similar programs ("Better Case Scenarios," 1996).

Transferring Files
Web browsers make it easy to transfer files on the Internet by use of file transfer protocol (FTP). On most WWW sites, transferring a file is as easy as clicking the mouse on a command such as "download software." Unlike most other parts of the Internet, many FTP sites use an older, text-based technology—called "gopher"—that gives the reader an index of file names. Usually the first file on the list is a "readme" file or an index file that displays the descriptions of the other files when clicked.

The Washington University Archive (http://wuarchive.wustl.edu) is a good example of a download site. It stores nearly 72 billion bytes of information—the equivalent of the information contained in 150 copies of the *Encyclopaedia Britannica*—and is a good place to experiment with the file transfer function. The archive also gives instructions on how to get files through e-mail. Another useful download site is the Software Connection at Virtual CUSSN (Computer Use in Social Services Network at http://www.uta.edu/cussn/cussn.html). This site has human services shareware, freeware, and demos available for downloading. Note that many downloadable products from WWW are shareware—that is, you are expected to buy them if you use them after a trial period (typically 30 days).

FTP is an increasingly important way to upgrade to the latest versions of software. With the pace of new software developments increasing, it is sometimes desirable to download the latest copy of your browser several times a year. Also, most companies have the latest versions of their software (and ways to fix "bugs" in their software) on the Internet. Software upgrades can be found by use of a search engine.

Chat, Conferences, and Internet Telephone
Chat software lets users interact in writing or by voice in real time over the Internet. The chat function allows for either private or public conversations, and several people can send messages to each other at nearly the same time. Chat software is rapidly becoming much easier to use, so the function has become one of the

fastest growing features of the Internet. Many chat sites include self-help groups. Although games, socializing, and self-help have long been popular chat activities, human services professionals are just discovering the value of chat for client support and educational purposes. Many social workers providing help over the Internet have an open chat room and specific hours posted when they will be in the chat room interacting with clients. In contrast to face-to-face groups, however, chat groups are not used for therapy. Most courses offered over the Internet have a weekly teacher–student chat session. For a list of social work courses offered over the Internet, see The World Lecture Hall (http://microlib.cc.utexas.edu/world/lecture).

Text-based chat is limited because most people cannot type as fast as they can think or talk. However, technology now allows the transfer of audio over the Internet, as well as video. Unfortunately, video is often transmitted at a few frames per second, making the picture jumpy, as a very old film. The latest versions of browsers have tools designed to hold audio-based meetings over the Internet. As corporations rapidly develop intranets, these conferencing tools are in great demand and are maturing rapidly. However, to converse by voice over the Internet at acceptable quality still requires special hardware and software. In certain circumstances, this hardware and software can be cost-effective because they provide the capacity to make long-distance calls to colleagues, even in other countries, at no additional cost.

Chat and game tools are combined on the Internet to create virtual worlds and three-dimensional environments. Virtual worlds can be used for social work purposes, too. For example, the social work department at the virtual campus of Diversity University (http://www.du.org) offers courses and workshops.

Important Issues in Use of the Internet

Privacy and confidentiality. The Internet is so new that many users assume that Internet communication is as private as regular mail. Unfortunately, this is not true: Internet users should always operate on the assumption that all communications, including e-mail, on the Internet are public.

In most states, employers have a legal right to read employees' e-mail, even though they do not have a right to open mail sent through the U.S. Postal Service. They also have the right to install computer programs that record all work done on their computers. When you access any Internet site, your computer and the host you contact both record the connection. The pattern of your computer usage is often marketed to many businesses. Stephen Wildstrom (1996) described this situation well:

> Information about current and potential customers is gold to marketers. Most magazines including *Business Week* use questionnaires to learn as much as they can about subscribers, including such things as family income. Some may even rent data for use in tightly targeted campaigns. However, the World Wide Web is different. Site operators can link questionnaires to observed behavior. For example, they can compile the names of high income 50-year-olds with an interest in fly fishing. In addition, email provides an instant path back to the potential customer. This capacity is possible because when you visit a Web site, the log files can record what site you came from and everything you do while you're visiting. There is no requirement that you be notified that this information is being gathered and almost no restrictions on its use or sale. (p. 19)

It is very difficult to totally erase e-mail or other computer activity records. Even when computer files are erased or deleted, it may still be possible for technical experts to retrieve them.

The limits on computer privacy evolve on the basis of consensus because laws concerning the issue do not currently exist. For example, a Web site could send your computer a short program, called a "cookie" in Internet jargon. A cookie program could record your Internet use and then upload the record to a remote site the next time you access the Internet. Information collected via cookies has great marketing value for the companies wanting to target potential customers on the Internet. Such questionable practices generate hate mail to the companies using the cookies, and hackers often punish the offending site by breaking into it and altering its contents.

Privacy is a two-way street on the Internet. ISPs have a difficult time protecting information on any computer connected to the Internet. Even the U.S. Central Intelligence Agency's WWW site has been hacked into, and

pornographic links were added to it. Although this lack of privacy should not stop you from using the Internet, the safe operating rule is to assume that everything you do on the Internet can become public knowledge. However, encryption programs can be used to increase the security of data and communications on the Internet. Social workers who transmit data on clients or other sensitive information should consult a knowledgeable computer consultant to set up a secure communications system that uses encryption.

Security of Internet commerce. The current systems for guaranteeing financial transactions, including banking and security of credit card numbers, transmitted over the Internet are suspect. Hackers have penetrated many sites where security is lax. Although the theft of bank or credit card numbers is infrequent, one incident can involve hundreds of thousands of numbers, which can instantly be transmitted worldwide. Users must be very cautious, despite the convenience of being able to order products, read on-line bank statements, make financial transfers, and pay bills electronically from home or office.

Offensive material. Hate groups, pedophiles, and pornographers also use the Internet. However, downloadable software exists to block objectionable sites, and some Internet providers cater to users with children by blocking such sites. Still, adults should treat the Internet as they do cable television, and discuss and monitor their children's use of it.

Viruses. Computer viruses can be transmitted over the Internet, although not as easily as by the sharing of floppy disks. To date, Internet viruses have not been a large problem, but a virus can be crippling to an individual or agency by making one or many files unusable. A virus can arrive in a computer attached to an e-mail, for example, but virus-scanning software will notify the user of the virus. An Internet search engine can then be used to find a site that explains the virus, its destructive potential, and how to remove it from the system. In large computer systems, such as in a university, hundreds of computers can be infected by a single virus. There are many sites where Internet virus scanning software can be downloaded, such as the popular http://www.mcafee.com. You can find downloadable software by using one of the search engines mentioned earlier or by going to almost any store that sells software.

Internet culture and "netiquette." Internet culture is fast paced and terse. Information in messages is often poorly written and formatted, with few emotional cues. New users often do not understand this culture and are treated harshly if they transgress Internet social norms. New members of newsgroups, lists, or chat sessions often "lurk" (read messages without taking part in the conversation) for a while to discover the rules

TABLE 2
Netiquette (Internet Etiquette)

Advice	Rationale
Keep your mail box clean and up to date	If the messages in your mail box take up more space than your ISP allows, the sender will receive an error message. Most lists allow users to suspend messages by sending a simple command.
Do not use all capital letters	Text typed in all capital letters is hard to read, and capital letters are used on the Internet to simulate shouting.
Be aware of FAQs (frequently asked questions) and read and keep instructions	When you join a conference, see if a FAQ file exists so you do not ask questions that have been answered over and over by others. Keep instructions for quitting the conference so you do not have to send a message to all conference participants asking how to exit.
Separate personal e-mail from conferences	Sending personal e-mail to someone via a conference is rude and may cost some conference members who pay for Internet access by the amount of mail they receive. Also, always get permission to forward a personal e-mail message to someone else or to a conference.
Keep lines to 60 characters or less	Some mailers do not handle lines longer than 70 characters. Long lines may cause formatting problems for some users. Often portions of the original message are quoted to make the reply more meaningful. Short line lengths help avoid the line wrapping of these quotes.
Make messages meaningful	Messages such as "me too" typically do not add anything to the conversation, are unnecessary, and require others to do extra work to read and delete them.
Warn of long messages	Readers should be warned if a post is over several paragraphs (for example, "long message" or "20 pages follow"). This allows users to download the message and read it later.
Warn of cross-posting	If you post a message to several conferences, indicate at the beginning which conferences will receive the post so that readers will know to avoid the message on the other conferences once they read it.
Identify requests for information	Identify messages seeking information by preceding the subject field with two ?? so that mailers can automatically identify these requests and store them in a mailbox for answering when the reader has more time.
Avoid flaming	E-mail carries few emotional cues. People can easily become offended by misinterpreting e-mail. Try to state positions without attacking positions different from yours. Be very clear if you are using sarcasm or irony.
Be careful if advertising	Special conferences exist for advertising. Check the norms of groups before submitting self-promotional or advertising materials.
Use formatting to enhance readability	Terminal screens read differently from the printed text. Help readability by formatting. For example, separate paragraphs with a blank line.
Personalize your e-mail to help identify you to the receiver	People who belong to many lists may get hundreds of e-mail messages a day. Put something in the subject field or place their name or your name in an obvious location on a message to ensure that they do not delete the message while quickly skimming through their e-mail.
Sign your e-mail message with your e-mail address	Often it is difficult to identify the sender from the message header. Signing all e-mail with your e-mail address allows people to contact you, no matter where your message is forwarded.
Have only one subject per message and use subject titles on your messages	Subject titles on messages help users skim through the volume of mail they receive. To keep conference discussions on track, use the same subject title of the original message, unless you change the topic significantly. Also, limit each message to the subject specified in the title.
Download large files during off hours	Downloading takes away resources from those performing more interactive tasks. Downloading during evening or night hours is more courteous to others.

SOURCE: Adapted with permission from: Schoech, D & Smith, K. K. (1996) How to use the Internet and electronic bulletin boards. In T. Trabin (Ed.), *The computerization of behavioral healthcare*. San Francisco: Jossey-Bass.

and social norms, which are not always immediately obvious. The term "flaming" was coined to describe an unexpected and unwarranted attack by someone who feels offended by an action or message on the Internet.

Over time, ways to emphasize text and express emotions—called "emoticons"—have been invented on the Internet. When viewed sideways, emoticons resemble facial expressions:

:-) happy or joking
:-(sad
;-) wink or sarcasm
:-o shouting or shocked

See Table 2 for more points of Internet etiquette (netiquette).

INTERNET SEARCH SITES

There are many Internet search programs. Table 3 lists information about numerous Internet resources. The information is largely taken from an Internet tutorial that can be found at http://www-medlib.med.utah.edu/travel/srchtool.html. We want to thank Nancy Lombardo (nancy.lombardo@m.cc.utah.edu), who produced the table. It is reproduced here with her permission.

CONCLUSION

The technology of the Internet is constantly changing. Some of the information in this entry may have already become outdated. You cannot rely solely on the printed word to learn about the Internet. To return to the highway analogy, it is very difficult to learn to drive by reading articles. The best way to learn to drive is to get in a car and practice, and having an adviser close by who can answer questions when things do not go as expected is important. Similarly, the best way to learn about the Internet is to

TABLE 3
Internet Resources

Name of Site (URL)	Search Methods	Types of Information	Other Features
Internet Directories or Subject Catalogs			
YAHOO http://www.yahoo.com/	Browsable menus, keyword, partial Boolean	Web, Usenet, e-mail addresses	Well-organized, easy to browse
Excite http://www.excite.com/	Browsable menus, keyword, concept	Web, Usenet, newswire	Includes reviews
A2Z http://a2z.lycos.com/	Browsable menus, keyword, Boolean, truncation	Web, graphics, sound	Links to Lycos Index and Point Reviews; can search for multimedia
Galaxy http://galaxy.einet.net/	Browsable menus, keyword, titles, links, Boolean	Web, gopher, Telnet	Provides links to other reference tools and directories
Internet Indexes			
HotBot http://www.hotbot.com/	Keyword, summary, title, headings, URLs, Boolean, proximity	Web, graphics, sound	Good tool for specific searches. More relevant sites appear first on list. Allows searching of multimedia.
AltaVista http://www.altavista.digital.com/	Keyword, phrases, date, type, location, Boolean, truncation	Web, Usenet, graphics	Excellent tool for specific searches. Various search strategies available. Good online help file.
Lycos http://www.lycos.com/	Keyword, Boolean, truncation	Web, graphics, sound	Very large database. Links to A2Z Directory and Point Reviews of Web sites. Can search for multimedia
Ultra InfoSeek http://ultra.infoseek.com/	Keyword, phrases, Boolean (+,−), proximity	Web, Usenet, news, e-mail, addresses	Link to InfoSeek Directory. Click "Special" for links to many reference tools (dictionary, thesaurus, news)

Continued

TABLE 3 *(continued)*

Name of Site (URL)	Search Methods	Types of Information	Other Features
Internet Reviews or Rating Sites			
MAGELLAN McKinley's Internet Directory http://www.mckinley.com/	Browsable menus, keywords, Boolean, proximity	Web reviews	On-line directory of reviewed and rated sites. Provides some evaluation based on depth, organization, and appeal of the site. Excellent on-line help files.
POINT Communications http://www.pointcom.com/	Browsable menus, keyword, Boolean	Web-rated	Point indexes only the "top 5 percent" of Web sites based on content, presentation, and Web experience. Includes link to Lycos for Internet-wide searches.
WebCrawler Select http://webcrawler.com/select/	Browsable subject categories	Web	Indexes only "the best" sites on the Internet. Looks for frequent updates, effective design, Web culture, and no cost.
Meta-Indexes			
MetaCrawler http://metacrawler.cs.washington.edu/	Keywords, partial Boolean, phrases	Web, news, FTP, e-mail	Queries nine different services: Open Text, Lycos, WebCrawler, InfoSeek, Excite, Inktomi, Alta Vista, Yahoo, and Galaxy. Can limit by geographic region and type of site (edu, gov).
Savvy Search http://guaraldi.cs.colostate.edu:2000/	Keywords, partial Boolean, phrases	Web, news, FTP, e-mail	Queries more than two dozen databases.
Starting Point http://www.stpt.com/	Keywords	Web, news, FTP, e-mail	Queries more than a dozen databases.
Other Internet Searching Tools			
DejaNews http://www.dejanews.com/	Keywords, specific newsgroups, authors, dates	Usenet	Index to Usenet newsgroups only. Good tool if you want to communicate with others on the Internet.
TileNet http://www.tile.net/	Browsable menus, keyword, concept	Mailing lists Usenet newsgroups, FTP sites	Index to mailing lists and Usenet news. Good tool for finding electronic discussion groups on a topic.
Mailing Lists http://www.nova.edu/Inter-links/LISTSERV.html	Varies	Mailing lists	Index to mailing lists only. Links to many directories of electronic discussion groups.
Four11 http://www.four11.com/	Name, host	E-mail addresses	Index to e-mail addresses only. Not comprehensive but worth a try. Register to enlarge the database.
Switchboard http://www.switchboard.com/	Name (people and businesses)	Addresses and telephone numbers	Large national directory of residential and business addresses.
Shareware.Com http://www.shareware.com/	Searchable by platform	Shareware or free software	Great site for finding software from archives on the Internet.
WhoWhere http://query1.whowhere.com/	Name, city, state, country, business name	Addresses, names, group affiliation, personal interests	Not comprehensive, but worth a try. Register to enlarge the database.

connect to it and use it. Inexpensive technical consultation can be obtained by contacting the many other Internet users. Getting connected and exploring the Internet can be time consuming and even frustrating at times; however, the rewards are well worth the effort, and the services social workers can use the Internet to provide will be expanded and improved.

REFERENCES

Better case scenarios. (1996, July 6). *CIO, 9,* 21–23.

Lowe, D. (1994). *Networking for dummies.* Foster City, CA: IDG Books.

Wildstrom, S. (1996, November 11). They're watching you online. *Business Week,* p. 19.

FURTHER READING

Gilster, P. (1994). *The Internet navigator* (2nd ed.). New York: John Wiley & Sons, Inc.

Levine, J. R., & Baroudi, C. (1994). *The Internet for dummies* (2nd ed.). Foster City, CA: IDG Books Worldwide, Inc.

Schoech, D., & Smith, K. K. (1996). How to use the Internet and electronic bulletin boards. In T. Trabin (Ed.), *The computerization of behavioral healthcare.* San Francisco: Jossey-Bass.

Appendix A: Internet Addressing

E-MAIL ADDRESSES

Internet e-mail addresses are like street addresses. They have a personal section, a host section, a type of organization section, and a country section. For example, in an address such as billb@en.com the first section ("billb") is the personal section of the address. It is separated from the host section by an "@" symbol. The next section is the host location ("en" for "exchange net"). The final section tells the reader what kind of organization is the host. The country section is missing from this example because it is in the United States.

Note that the first (personal) section uses a name or an acronym. The preferred form is to use the last name, but often that is not possible, because e-mail names must be unique for each host location. For example, there may be many Smiths or Joneses who use the same host, but there can be only one smith@ or jones@ on a given host. Most people use acronyms that are a combination of their first and last names. The second section is treated similarly, but sometimes this section must be expanded to more subsections because more than one host may exist within a single organization. The third section tells what type of organization operates the hosts: *com* (a commercial company—for example, "ATT.com" for American Telephone and Telegraph), *edu* (an educational institution—for example, "uta.edu" for University of Texas at Arlington), *gov* (a U.S. government host—for example, "nih.gov" for the National Institutes of Health), *mil* (a U.S. military site—for example, "stl.army.mil" for the U.S. Army Aviation Troop Command), *net* (an administrative organization for a network—for example, "internic.net"

for the Internet Information Center), and *org* (any Internet site that does not fit into one of the other categories—for example, "isoc.org" for the Internet Society). The last section, the country section, consists of address designations for all countries that have Internet sites. For example, the country code for New Zealand is *nz* and for the Netherlands *nl.* (Country codes are rarely used in the United States.)

Every Internet e-mail address (domain name) also has a numerical equivalent: an IP address. This numerical address is what the Internet uses to locate an Internet site. An IP address contains four sets of numbers separated by periods. For example, the numerical address for billb@encom is 207.78.12.36. This form is rarely used, but either the IP address or the domain address can be used to contact an Internet site.

URLs

The uniform resource locators (URLs) are extensions of Internet addresses used to provide addresses for the information stored on the computer. The Internet can store information in a variety of formats. For example, it can store text, still pictures (called "images" in Internet parlance), video, and audio. All this information is presented to the computer as a screen page. Screen pages are dynamic. That is, they do not simply display the contents of a single document but may also access files and images from several locations and combine them into what the viewer sees on the screen or hears over the computer's speakers. Screen pages can be of any length, and they are multimedia in composition. The screen of the computer can display a picture, a text document, or a video clip while the attached computer plays the sound clip through its speakers. Because these pages can be very complex and can display information from many different places, the computer displaying the information needs to know where on all of the world's computers to look for the information. URLs are simply the addresses of specific screen pages. Screen pages may also contain URLs that pull in information for use on the page. Screen pages are the similar to an 800 or 888 telephone number that can serve many people simultaneously by an answering machine. The answering machine gives you a menu of choices that take you to different place in the telephone system, just as the URL can take you to various places on the Internet system.

Here is a sample URL: http://www.nytimes.com/subscribe/help/index.html. Slashes are used to separate the sections of the address. The middle portion of the address—nytimes.com—is the address of the computer where the screen page is located. The first section (http:) tells the Internet program how to access the data—what communication protocol to use as it transfers data to the user's computer. The most common is http, which stands for hypertext transfer protocol and is the protocol used to for many data transfers on the Internet. Other protocols include:

- FTP: File transfer protocol, for copying files to and from the user's computer
- File: exactly the same as FTP
- News: for transferring text and other information from newsgroups
- Telenet: for connecting the user to a remote computer and allowing the user to run programs on the remote computer.

The protocol section of a URL always ends with a colon. The two forward slashes (//) that follow the protocol section tell the computer that the section to the right of the slashes is the address of the computer system on which the information is located. The last section, which is called the "path name," tells where to look on the computer for the information and the format of the document. The format is listed in the last section of the path name. For most documents it will be html (hypertext markup language), which is a language used to format documents for viewing on the Internet.

Appendix B: A Compendium of Internet Terms

ARCHIE: An Internet tool for searching a database of anonymous FTP sites for specific file names or directories.

ARPA (Advanced Research Projects Agency): This agency funded the original research that resulted in ARPANET, the network that validated the concept of packet switching through TCP/IP.

ARPANET: Funded by ARPA to study how to make computer networks secure in the event of nuclear war, this network later split its functions, with MILNET breaking off in 1983 for military networking. ARPANET, which was retired in 1990, is important, as it represents the root source of today's Internet.

backbone: The system of high-speed connections that routes long-haul Internet traffic, connecting to slower regional and local data paths.

bandwidth: The amount of information that can be transmitted over a communications link. Common computer modems can transfer data at different rates starting at 300 bps up to 56 kbps. The higher the bandwidth of the communications link, the faster you can receive a file over the computer network.

baud rate: A measurement of data transmission speed. Baud rate is sometimes measured in bits per second. Your modem may have a baud rate of 14.4 kB (kilobytes). This translates to 14,400 bits per second.

BBS (bulletin board system): Networks that your computer can dial into through your modem. You communicate with other people by exchanging messages and files. You can also take files of information that the bulletin board operator (SYSOP for system operator) makes available for public use and download these to your computer for subsequent use.

Bitnet: An academic network containing mailing lists on a wide variety of subjects, often populated by scholars and experts in their various fields. Bitnet used a different protocol than the Internet to move its data. Bitnet traffic now moves almost entirely over the Internet.

bookmarks: Markers that allow you to mark a gopher menu or World Wide Web page that you like so you can return to that menu or page whenever you want. All of your bookmarks are kept in a booklist that acts just like your own personal menu.

browser: A generic term often used to refer to programs that allow a user to "point-and-click" through gopherspace or the Web (for example, Netscape, Mosaic, or Internet Explorer).

chat: An on-line chat is a lot like talking to someone on the telephone in real time, only you type out your words on your computer rather than speak out loud.

CGI (common gateways interface): A standard method that allows Web documents to use programs that are locally resident on the host computer system. This capability allows Web documents to be created on the fly.

client: Software that requests services from another computer (called the "server"). This model is known as client–server computing.

compression: The process of squeezing data to eliminate redundancies and allow files to be stored in less disk space.

cyberspace: That place where people and computers meet. Cyberspace is where you go when you go on-line. It's the universe that exists inside computer networks. You cannot see cyberspace, but you can visit it.

domain name: Part of the Internet addressing scheme that allows messages to be sent to the correct company or organization that has registered on the Internet. An example of a domain name is "westbury.com," which refers to an organization called Westbury that is registered as a commercial organization. Other types of classifications of organization include ".edu" (educational), ".gov" (government), ".mil" (military), ".net" (administration), and ".org" (for all others).

downloading: The process of transferring a file of information from another computer to your computer via modem.

EDI (electronic data interchange): EDI supports paperless business transactions between cooperating companies. Business is transacted using electronic forms and computer-to-computer communication.

e-mail (electronic mail): Electronic mail involves sending and receiving messages over the network. You use a mail program like Eudora, Pine, or Elm to compose and read your messages. E-mail is one of the most popular uses of the Internet today.

encryption: The scrambling of a message or file to prevent unauthorized viewing. The message or file may be unscrambled using a password or "key."

E-ZINE (electronic magazine): An electronic version of a magazine found on the World Wide Web.

FAQ (Frequently Asked Questions): An FAQ list is a document that covers basic information from a particular Usenet newsgroup or mailing list.

firewall: A method of protecting your computer system from unauthorized intrusions when connected to the Internet. A necessary precaution if you are connecting your business's computer network to the Internet.

flaming: Attacking someone in cyberspace for saying something you consider wrong or inappropriate, without being reasonable.

freenet: A community-based, volunteer-built network. Freenets are springing up in cities around the world, as citizens work to provide free access to selected network resources and to make local information available on-line.

freeware: Software that can be used and distributed without charge.

FTP (file transfer protocol): Allows and expedites the transfer of files throughout the world. Anonymous FTP is a common method for allowing any Internet user using an FTP tool to obtain files from another computer on the Internet without having to be a registered user on that computer. A guest user may log into a computer using the log-in name "anonymous," and access any files that the system administrator has made public.

GIF (graphic interchange format): A format developed for use in storing photo-quality graphic images on computers.

gopher: A tool developed at the University of Minnesota that creates menus that allow you to access network resources by moving an on-screen pointer. The idea behind gopher is to simplify the process of using network information. Gopher can point to text files, Telnet sites, WAIS databases, and a wide range of other data.

gopherspace: Anywhere on the Internet to which a gopher program can go.

handshake: The process that two modems do to connect and agree on how to transfer data.

home page: A top-level (that is, starting point) Web page for a company, organization, or individual. For this location, you can telescope down to get further information or travel to other sites if the appropriate hypertext links are in place.

host: Usually a synonym for either computer or IP address, which often does not matter, as there is typically one IP address per computer.

host name: A name that can be resolved (using a name server) into an IP address.

hypertext: A set of highlighted data in readable text that allows a user to point and click on a particular word to find out more information on the subject. This is a popular method used by computerized help systems that allow the user to create links between information on the system at the user's convenience.

HTML (hypertext markup language): Generally considered to be the language for writing Web documents. Special sequences of characters and letters allow the user to include references to graphics, sound, images, or other Internet resources that then may be accessed using a browser by pointing and clicking.

HTTP (hypertext transfer protocol): The standard protocol that a Web browser uses to communicate with a Web site (that is, Web server). HTTP supports the multimedia capabilities of the Web.

HYTELNET: A hypertextual program that offers a database of Telnet sites.

Internet: The worldwide matrix of connecting computers using the TCP/IP protocols.

interrelay chat: A chat function that allows real-time teleconferencing with friends and business associates around the world over the Internet.

intranet: An internal Internet that has been established and limited to the confines of a single organization. For example, a government or business may set up its own intranet within the various offices where its employees conduct everyday business operations. It may include development and maintenance of an internal miniweb. Employees may use graphical browsers for accessing hypertext information contained within various organizational databases. E-mail represents a significant component as well. Intranets are a recent phenomenon, taking on increasing significance within the realm of technological innovation.

IP (internal protocol): Defines the packet structure of a datagram. It functions at the network layer of the protocol stack. IP also defines the addressing mechanism used to deliver data to its destination.

IP address: A set of four numbers (each between 0 and 255, with some restrictions) separated by periods that uniquely identifies an address on a network.

ISDN (integrated services digital network): Basic rate ISDN service provides up to 128 kB per second dial-up or dedicated connection between computer systems. ISDN requires special telephone service connections to your home or business in addition to a special ISDN modem.

ISP (Internet service provider): A company that offers access to the Internet. Dial-up users obtain an account on the service provider's system and use its computers to log onto the Internet.

jughead: A tool that allows a user to search for information accessible using gopher.

LAN (local area network): A local area network connecting several computers that are located near to each other, either in the same room or building, allowing them to share files and devices such as printers.

listserv: A program that automatically sends and receives e-mail to and from a particular group of subscribers. A listserv mailing list is like a subscription to an on-line magazine. When you join up, you can get information on whatever subject you have chosen, and you receive updates usually every day. These mailing lists are designed for many people to use who share similar interests and want to exchange messages with each other.

LYNX: A character-based World Wide Web browser that allows access to the World Wide Web for people with shell accounts.

modem: Modem stands for modulator–demodulator and acts as a link between computers via the telephone line. Running communications software makes your computer emulate a terminal and allows you to communicate with a variety of individuals, organizations, and services regardless of the type of computer on the other end.

multimedia: A combination, or integration, of various media, such as graphics, video, audio, and text.

name server: A machine on the network that allows you to resolve host names into IP addresses.

netiquette: The proper way to behave when you are surfing the Internet, such as respecting the rights and opinions of others and treating others the way you want to be treated.

netizens: Persons who actively use the Internet on a regular basis.

network: A group of computers joined by data-carrying links. A network may be as small as two or three personal computers tied together by telephone lines in the same building. Or, it may be a vast complex of computers spread across the world, whose data links include telephone lines, satellite relays, fiber optic cables, or radio links.

newbie: A neophyte. Classically, a new poster to Usenet or one of the local on-line services.

newsgroup: A discussion group on Usenet devoted to a particular topic. Some 11,000 newsgroups now exist.

NSF (National Science Foundation): The organization that managed the Internet backbone in the United States until 1995.

packet: The basic unit of Internet data. A message sent across the Internet is broken into packets, each marked with the address and other pertinent information, such as error-checking data. The TCP/IP protocols see to it that the packets are rebuilt at their destination.

packet switching: The process of sending packets through the network, allowing for alternate routing if a particular network link fails.

PDF (portable document format): A standard file format that allows documents to be viewed and printed on a large variety of different computer types, for example, Macintoshes and PCs.

PKZIP: A utility that allows you to decompress a file.

POP (post office protocol): Allows electronic mail messages to be stored on your service provider's computer until you log in to retrieve them. The protocol then downloads the messages to your computer. You use a client program like Eudora or Pegasus Mail to read and reply to messages.

PPP (point to point protocol): One of two methods (the other being SLIP) for exchanging data packets with the Internet over a telephone line. PPP offers data compression and error corrections and remains under active development.

protocol: A protocol defines how computers communicate; it is an agreement between different systems on how they will work together. The set of TCP/IP protocols defines how computers on the Internet exchange information (a set of protocols is commonly called a "suite").

router: A computer system that makes decisions about which path Internet traffic will take to reach its destination.

search engines: Programs that are designed to go out onto the Internet and search for the information you requested. Think of them as librarians who give you a list of possible books to read to find out what you want to know, then help you find the books.

server: A computer that provides a resource on the network. Client programs access servers to obtain data.

shareware: A method of software distribution in which the software may be freely distributed, and you may try it before paying. If you decide to keep and use the program, you send your payment directly to the shareware author.

shell account: A dial-up account to a UNIX-based service provider's machine. Using a shell account, you use whatever resources the provider has made available on his or her machine but do not exchange data packets directly with the Internet. You cannot run client programs like Netscape and Eudora over a shell account; they demand a SLIP/PPP connection.

signature (or .sig): A short note (3 to 6 lines) usually attached to the end of an e-mail or newsgroup message that contains your name, address, and other information about you or your business.

SLIP (serial line Internet protocol): As opposed to regular dial-up accounts, a SLIP account allows your computer to receive an IP address. FTP sessions are thus handled directly between remote computers and your system, without going through your service provider's computer first. A SLIP account also allows you to run graphical browsers like Mosaic or Netscape.

smiley: Facial expressions used to enhance the spoken word. In e-mail smileys, otherwise known as "emoticons," are used to enhance the words written in a similar fashion. For example, :) or :(or :-p

SMTP (simple mail transfer protocol): The Internet standard protocol for handling electronic messages between computers.

snail mail: Traditional mail as sent in envelopes with stamps as opposed to electronic mail.

spamming: Posting advertising or off-topic messages to one or more unrelated Usenet newsgroups.

surfing: Traveling from site to site on the Internet's World Wide Web via your computer.

T1: 1,544 Megabits per second data transfer over a leased line.

T3: 45 Megabits per second data transfer over a leased line.

TCP/IP (transmission control protocol/ Internet protocol): This is the set of protocols that drives the Internet, regulating how data are transferred between computers.

Telnet: An Internet tool that allows you to log into another computer system on the Internet without having to dial up the system.

UNIX: A widely used operating system on the Internet. UNIX is generally more complex to set up and maintain than PC operating systems such as DOS and Windows NT.

uploading: The process of transferring a file from your computer to another one.

URL (uniform or universal resource locator): A standard method of specifying the address of a resource on the Internet that a user wants to access.

Usenet (user network): A large conferencing system that uses the Internet to distribute its newsgroups. Usenet consists of more than 10,000 newsgroups. Newsgroups are the equivalent of special-interest groups. A user may select any newsgroup and view all messages that have been posted. Users may also post messages to newsgroups.

Veronica: A program that allows you to search gopher menus for particular keywords.

WAIS (wide area information server): A system that allows you to search databases by keyword and refine your search through relevance feedback techniques.

WAN (wide area network): Any network whose components are geographically dispersed.

Web site: A collection of Web pages that are linked to each other via hypertext links typically from the home page.

WHOIS: A program that allows you to search a database for people or network addresses.

WWW (World Wide Web): A series of protocols that work through hypertext links to data, allowing you to explore network resources from multiple entry points.

Compendium Sources

Engst, A. C. (1993). *Internet starter kit for MacIntosh.* Indianapolis: Hayden Books.

Gilster, P. (1996). *Finding it on the Internet.* New York: John Wiley & Sons.

Hurley, B., & Birkwood, P. (1996). *A small business guide to doing big business on the Internet.* Vancouver: Self-Counsel Press.

Pedersen, T., & Moss, F. (1995). *Internet for kids.* New York: Price Stern Sloan.

Richards, L. (1995). *Using the Internet.* Toronto: Self-Counsel Press.

Stout, R. (1996). *The World Wide Web complete reference.* New York: McGraw-Hill.

NOTE: This compendium was prepared by Bruce Tudin Information Technologies, (http://www.inasec.ca/com/btudin/tudmain.htm) for use by Internet trainers. It may be freely copied and distributed.

William H. Butterfield, PhD, is professor emeritus, George Warren Brown School of Social Work, Washington University, One Brookings Drive, St. Louis, MO 63130. **Dick Schoech, PhD,** is professor, School of Social Work, University of Texas at Arlington, Arlington, TX 76019.

For further information see

Computer Utilization; Expert Systems; Information Systems; Research Overview; **Social Work Education: Electronic Technologies.**

Key Words	
browser	intranet
e-mail	World Wide Web
Internet	

J

Jewish Communal Services

Sheldon R. Gelman
David J. Schnall

T he form and character of communal services provided under Jewish auspices has been shaped by religious teachings and tradition developed over a 5,000-year period. Righteousness is achieved by fulfilling obligations to those less fortunate or in need. Acts of *tzedakah,* translated as justice, are the hallmark of Jewish philanthropy. The evolution, role, functions, and organizational structure of services are reflective of these obligations. Preservation and continuity of Jewish ideals and the Jewish people are the centerpiece of refugee assistance programs; educational, family, and vocational programs; services for the frail and elderly; and training for Jewish communal professionals. While changing funding patterns and managed care have blurred the sectarian nature of many communal agencies, these agencies remain as key elements in the voluntary social services network of this country.

Contemporary Jewish communal service emerges from a religious and social tradition rooted in Scripture, the Talmud, and rabbinic dicta. Jewish religious practice is defined by *mitzvot,* which literally means commandments. These are broadly separated into those that are largely ritual and ecclesiastical and those that define a vast array of social relations, including marriage; economic pursuits; child rearing; and care for the widow, the orphan, and the stranger. Thus, Judaism views personal charity as part of a systematic network of social obligations, rather than a voluntary act of kindness (Bernstein, 1965).

As an example, the Bible enjoins that crops forgotten in the field or inadvertently left standing after the harvest remain for poor people. In addition, a corner of a farmer's field must be purposefully left uncut so that needy people might glean in private. Such prescriptions stand side by side with those that require employers to pay workers punctually and those that restrict creditors in their demands on debtors (Schnall, 1993).

Overall, two themes have remained constant over the years: First, one who extends a hand for assistance must never be turned away, and second, in helping someone else, the benefactor follows in the paths of righteousness and sanctity that characterize the Lord. In sum, although numerous Hebrew terms connote philanthropy and voluntary service,

tzedakah, the most popular term used, derives from a term that is more accurately translated as justice. This epitomizes the classic Jewish attitude toward such an undertaking.

Fundamental sources regarding personal obligations to needy people gave rise to discussions of the organization and structure of community services. This became especially important as largely autonomous Jewish communities emerged, first as part of a centralized monarchy in ancient Israel and later as Jews were dispersed throughout the Near East, North Africa, and Europe. By Talmudic times (that is, during the first centuries of the Common Era), Jewish communities were required to maintain systems of assessment and collection, with detailed prescriptions for the oversight and accountability of those who were trustees and administrators. Food was disbursed through the "tamhuy" or community kitchen, and cash was available from a community fund known as a "kupah."

The dignity and self-respect of those who were recipients of communal beneficence were given primacy. Thus, the highest form of *tzedakah,* according to Maimonides (1965), a 12th century Jewish philosopher and jurist, is that which provides poor people with the wherewithal to become productive and self-sufficient (for example, extending loans or providing assistance in finding a job or beginning a business). Second is a system of completely anonymous philanthropy in which neither recipient nor donor can be directly identified. This reduces embarrassment on one side, and arrogance on the other. Maimonides suggested that the goal is best facilitated through a central "kupah," in which the process of donation is separated from disbursement.

Given the heavy emphasis on religious education as equivalent to all other *mitzvot* combined, it is no surprise to find that public education was an area of special concern to early Jewish communities. The Talmud warns that a town in which no facilities for primary education are provided deserves to be destroyed. Medieval authorities established detailed principles regarding educational method, curriculum structure, teacher training and certification, and appropriate remuneration. These were included as part of the basic documents of local governance in Jewish communities throughout the Middle Ages and the early modern era.

In addition to caring for the needy and seeing to public education, Jewish sources established the communal obligation to create local structures of governance and to provide for refugee aid, hospitality for wayfarers, funeral and bereavement assistance, and mediation of civil and domestic disputes (Schnall, 1995). The scholarly literature of the period recorded active debates about public participation and the scope of the franchise in communal decisions, including the choice of leadership.

Communities typically had a board of governors, known as *parnassim,* who worked alongside the rabbi and other religious functionaries to oversee the social and spiritual needs of their constituents. Beyond their local bounds, they represented their people before gentile overlords and at meetings of loose confederations of Jewish communities that were established during the early modern era. By the Middle Ages, these boards were invested with quasi-judicial authority. They established tribunals for mediation, assessed taxes in support of public services, placed liens on private property, and used a variety of bans and social sanctions to enforce their decisions.

It is against this backdrop that Jewish communities were founded in the New World, as early as the mid-17th century. From the first, they attempted to maintain linkages with these religious and social obligations while integrating new patterns of democracy and voluntary association. This dynamic continues to inform much of what they have established in the United States over the past 350 years (Elazar, 1995).

The pattern of Jewish welfare organizations, although rooted in Scripture, is distinctively different from that of other sectarian groups. For the most part, Jewish social services have developed apart from the synagogue. They have been the response of the Jewish community to the special needs of its members. Although the beginning of American Jewish philanthropy took place in the synagogue, the sudden and massive influx of Jewish immigrants created needs for which a synagogue alone could not provide (Reid & Stimpson, 1987). Jewish immigrants formed literary societies for recreation and "landsmanchaften" for mutual aid and self-help. These organizations facilitated the acculturation of emigrés to their new land and assisted in caring for those in need, facilitating their independence and self-sufficiency.

It is estimated that 5.8 million Jews currently live in the United States (Kosmin et al., 1991). Just as their numbers have increased since the original 23 Jews debarked in New Amsterdam in 1654 with special permission from the Dutch West India Company, as long as "the poor among them shall be supported by their own nation," so too have the social organizations that provide for their health, welfare, recreational, and spiritual needs (Berger, 1980).

Although there is a perception that poverty does not exist among Jews, it is a very real problem. In New York City, the city with the largest Jewish population in the United States, 51,000 Jewish households—13 percent of all Jewish households in the city—have incomes that fall below 150 percent of the federal poverty standard. The majority of these 145,000 individuals are older women and children. Although one-third of those who are considered to be of working age work full- or part-time, their incomes are insufficient to meet basic needs. More than half of these individuals have no education beyond the high school level (Metropolitan New York Coordinating Council on Jewish Poverty, 1993).

Demographic changes and the complexity and scope of service needs required by those identifying themselves as Jews have, over time, resulted in the development of a comprehensive, coordinated, and evolving service network that currently provides a wide array of services to the Jewish and general communities.

THE ROLE OF COMMUNAL SERVICE AGENCIES

According to Steinitz (1995–1996), Jewish communal agencies through much of their history have focused on four primary goals:

1. delivering basic social services to indigent members of the Jewish community
2. resettling refugees and helping Americanize both the immigrant and second generations
3. responding to international crises
4. fighting anti-Semitism.

However, beginning in the 1960s, because of changing demographics, identification with the developing state of Israel, newly established governmental funding streams designed to expand service options and opportunities, and interest in specialized therapeutic interventions delivered by highly trained professional personnel led to a reordering of organizational priorities. The overview provided by Berger (1980) is enlightening:

> The headlong shift to seek government support for sectarian agencies was marked by some of these factors: (1) Agencies, unhappy with the modest increases received annually from Jewish federations, saw an opportunity for dramatically enriching and widening their services. (2) Federations unable to meet the demands of their societies encouraged their affiliates to seek such help. (3) Agencies had become enamored of "big" business attitudes; planning, expansion, computerization, executive suites, use of government consultants, and so forth. There was a definite power shift toward the professional with expertise in government contacts. (4) There was a widespread acceptance of the rationalized social welfare principle which mixed public and private welfare as a boon to experimentation, efficiency, economy, and expansion. (5) New services in mental health, in work with the retarded, the aged, those in need of rehabilitation, in drug addiction, in research, and, of course, service to the poor could now be funded in a way undreamed of by private Jewish philanthropy. (p. 77)

These changes not only resulted in the dramatic expansion of social services provided under Jewish auspices (Blum & Naparstek, 1987; Gibelman, 1995; Smith & Lipsky, 1993) but also led to a real blurring of what had been the historical distinction between sectarian and nonsectarian agencies (Levine, in press; Ortiz, 1995). Jewish agencies currently exhibit a great degree of autonomy from religious authority and are largely nonsectarian in intake.

THE JEWISH FEDERATIONS

The 200 Jewish federations in the United States are autonomous, voluntary organizations that engage in or provide a series of functions for communal affiliates that include

- joint or coordinated fundraising
- allocations and central budgeting
- centralized research and community planning
- leadership development and training services
- initiation of new services.

Federations developed in the United States beginning in 1895 and currently exist in communities where there is a significant Jewish presence. The Council of Jewish Federations (CJF), founded in 1932, represents the local Jewish federations of the United States and Canada on issues of public social policy nationally and internationally.

Currently, the federations and the United Jewish Appeal (UJA) are the central fundraising organizations within the Jewish community, raising and distributing hundreds of millions of dollars to local community agencies and Jewish communities around the world and in Israel.

According to Dubin (1994), Jewish communal agencies have historically been dependent on federation and United Way allocations for significant support. The federations were the conduit and authority for the planning, initiation, and, in some instances, initial operation of needed community services. Increasingly, the support and development of expanded service commitments abroad, particularly the rescue and resettlement of refugees and declines in campaign growth, have affected the level of support available to a range of communal service agencies. This phenomenon has resulted in the need to identify other funding streams (for example, membership dues, contributions, and fee-for-service and government contacts), thereby blurring the Jewish identity of many agencies.

On average, federation network agencies receive more than 41 percent of their total budget, an amount exceeding $3.67 billion (CJF, 1995), from federal, state, and local government sources. UJA–Federation of New York, which conducts the largest federation campaign, raising more than $200 million annually, received $2.45 billion, or approximately 62 percent of its budget in 1993, from government sources (UJA–Federation, 1994).

Jewish agencies have learned to apply for, receive, and use public funding for the benefit of the Jewish and general community. Although one can debate the nature of the change created by the acceptance of public funds by these historically sectarian agencies, it is clear that the number of units of services delivered to the Jewish community, as well as the general community, has increased dramatically as a result of the acceptance of this support (Solomon, 1995–1996).

The following examples of Jewish communal service agencies are presented to provide a sense of the mission, scope, and involvement of such agencies. The examples are not all-inclusive, and the authors apologize in advance for not providing a more extensive listing of Jewish communal agencies that play important roles in the community with youths, families, college students, and volunteer and specialized health and research programs. It should be noted that the several branches of Judaism also have affiliated agencies and programs that provide education, youth services, and gerontological care for their membership.

INTERNATIONAL AND REFUGEE SERVICES

The primary mission of the Hebrew Immigrant Aid Society (HIAS) is to help Jews whose lives and freedom are endangered. Since 1880, HIAS has been the worldwide arm of the American Jewish community for rescue, relocation, family reunification, and resettlement of refugees and other migrants. Its mission is derived from the Biblical teaching "Kol Yisrael Arevim Ze Ba Ze," which means "all Jews are responsible, one for the other."

During 1995 HIAS resettled 21,967 migrants, including 21,659 Jewish refugees from the former Soviet Union, into 125 communities throughout the United States. Its annual budget exceeds $37 million, with more than 80 percent of its funding coming from contracts with the U.S. government. Since the mid-1970s, when barriers to immigration were eased in the

former Soviet Union, HIAS has assisted in the resettlement of almost 400,000 Jewish refugees in the United States (HIAS, 1996).

The American Joint Distribution Committee (JDC) was formed as a merger of three agencies in 1914. Over the course of its history, it has assisted hundreds of thousands of Jews and non-Jews in Europe, Israel, the former Soviet Union, the Middle East, Asia, and Africa through humanitarian and development efforts. Its goal is "to develop systematic solutions to social problems through research and development, pilot demonstration projects and strategic interventions" (Schneider, 1994, p. 1). The JDC's activities take place in various areas of the world where war or natural disasters occur and where populations have been displaced. It is currently training social workers in former Soviet bloc countries and has formed a coalition with 35 other Jewish agencies to mobilize emergency relief in response to the Rwandan tragedy. They work collaboratively with the United Nations, the U.S. Agency for International Development, the U.S Department of Agriculture, and the World Bank.

COMMUNITY CENTERS

Jewish community centers and Young Men's and Women's Hebrew Associations provide cultural, recreational, educational, and social opportunities for members of the community. Although under Jewish auspices, these community-based centers serve populations that are ethnically diverse, fall along a continuum of religious observance, and vary by age from nursery school to senior citizens. The centers embody in their mission and functioning the notions of "citizenship responsibility," "social concern," and "community relatedness" (Dubin, 1987; Linzer, 1987). They are group work–focused agencies that employ a range of programs designed to facilitate the socialization of their members. The centers are affiliated with the Jewish Community Center Association (JCCA), the successor organization to the Jewish Welfare Board, which came into being during World War I to provide welfare, morale, and religious services to men and women in the armed forces.

The continuing group work focus of these agencies is reflected in a set of model standards for social group work student internships in Jewish community centers that were developed and field tested by a working committee of the JCCA and the Wurzweiler

School of Social Work, Yeshiva University. The standards represent a series of expectations and obligations for agencies, students, and schools of social work and serve as a model of cooperation and professional development (Aronowitz & Birnbaum, 1992). Unlike the services provided by Jewish family services agencies, which have a sliding fee scale for services, the centers are membership agencies.

FAMILY SERVICE

Jewish family service (JFS) agencies have been a mainstay of the Jewish communal network since the 19th century. They are affiliated with the Association of Jewish Family and Children's Agencies and employ trained social workers and other professional personnel who specialize in clinical work and case management. JFS agencies are recognized for their clinical expertise and innovative approaches to current challenging mental health issues (Abramson, 1994). Many of these agencies provide adoption services, foster care, group homes for people with developmental disabilities, and geriatric services under contract with government agencies. Services address individual and family concerns, including the mental health needs of recent immigrants. JFS agencies provide the Jewish and non-Jewish communities with high-quality mental health services sanctioned by the Jewish community. The New York–based Jewish Board of Family and Children's Services, a UJA–Federation network agency, is reputedly the largest nonprofit mental health and social services organization in the nation and has an annual budget in excess of $80 million, 82 percent of which is provided by the government (CJF, 1995). This agency has taken a leadership role in responding to the managed care environment.

HOSPITALS AND SERVICES FOR ELDERLY PEOPLE

The development of sectarian hospitals, nursing homes, and specialized geriatric facilities in American communities is a tradition that dates back to the 19th century. Homes for elderly people have been the primary source of service to Jewish older people since the early 20th century. Since the 1930s, Jewish geriatric facilities have been innovative in providing a range of community-based services. According to Shore (1995/1996), these innovations include the provision of meals to shut-ins; independent and assisted

living arrangements; and health services and the introduction of outpatient physical, occupational, and speech therapies. The Jewish community has also been instrumental in the development of hospice-based care for patients in the final stages of terminal illness. In addition to serving a humanitarian purpose, these facilities were established to provide kosher food for patients or residents who observe traditional dietary laws. Although these facilities have historically received support from benefactors, self-pay and third-party sources, and federation subsidies, they are increasingly dependent on government Medicare and Medicaid reimbursement for the services they provide. More than $2.5 billion was provided to Jewish-supported hospitals by Medicare and Medicaid in 1994 (CJF, 1995); an additional $500 million a year of Medicare and Medicaid funds went to support Jewish geriatric facilities (CJF, 1995). It should be noted that the services of these organizations are available to all people, regardless of race, ethnicity, or religious identification.

VOCATIONAL SERVICES

Jewish vocational services (JVS) agencies were founded by federations to address specific communal needs in the areas of employment. "Founded on the concept of 'parnosah,' JVS agencies had an obligation to help Jews secure a source of income so they could raise a family, remain independent, live in dignity, and continue to be a vital and productive part of the Jewish community" (Miller, 1995–1996, p. 88). They supplement the efforts of public employment services, with special assistance being provided to physically and mentally handicapped individuals and to recent emigrés who are in need of retraining. Services include vocational testing; individual and group counseling; job placement; educational support; training programs for people with developmental disabilities, mental illness, and dual diagnoses; and economic development services. These programs are designed to assist individuals in becoming self-sufficient. Federation-supported JVS agencies receive approximately 77 percent of their $180 million annual budget from government funding (CJF, 1995).

COMMUNITY RELATIONS

Community relations are an integral part of the Jewish communal service agenda, something that is reflected in the work of the Anti-

Defamation League, the American Jewish Committee, the American Jewish Congress, and the national and local community relations councils. These agencies are concerned with issues of church-state separation, anti-Semitism, human and civil rights, immigration, equality of women, cultural relations, and relationships among various religious and ethnic groups.

JEWISH COMMUNAL SERVICE ASSOCIATION

The current Jewish Communal Service Association was founded in 1899 as the National Conference of Jewish Communal Service. It is the primary professional association for a wide range of professionals employed in Jewish communal agencies, and it publishes the major quarterly journal in the field, the *Journal of Jewish Communal Service*. Affiliated professional associations include the following:

- Association of Jewish Center Professionals
- Association of Jewish Community Organization Personnel
- Association of Jewish Community Relations Workers
- Association of Jewish Vocational Service Professionals
- Council for Jewish Education
- Jewish Family and Children's Professional's Association
- North American Association of Jewish Homes and Housing for the Aging.

In addition to these groups, whose primary concern is Jewish communal service, in recent years a group of Jewish social work educators has come together under the auspices of the Council on Social Work Education to address issues of curriculum, anti-Semitism, and ethnic understanding.

EDUCATION FOR JEWISH COMMUNAL SERVICE

According to Teicher (1996), efforts to educate professional personnel for Jewish communal service began in 1890, when scholarships were offered to college graduates expressing a desire to prepare for service in Jewish agencies. In 1902 the National Conference of Jewish Charities made three such scholarship grants available. Lack of interest quickly led to the program's demise. During the ensuing 10 years, "earn-while-you-learn" courses were provided in Baltimore, Chicago, and New York, where, under the auspices of the Jewish Chautauqua

Society, communal workers took courses to improve their skills.

The first Jewish school of social work was formally established in 1913 by the Jewish Settlement, a social agency affiliated with the Federation of Jewish Charities in Cincinnati. This pioneering institution was abandoned 18 months later because it was unable to attract students. The New York Kehillah, which opened its offices in the spring of 1909, organized a school for Jewish communal work in October 1916. This school closed in its third year, partly because military conscription for World War I made it difficult to find students. The Graduate School for Jewish Social Work, sponsored by the National Conference of Jewish Charities, opened in 1925. It operated until 1940, when lack of funds caused it to close its doors.

The Training Bureau for Jewish Communal Service was launched in 1947 by five major agencies: the American Association for Jewish Education, the National Community Relations Advisory Council, the National Jewish Welfare Board, the American Jewish Joint Distribution Committee, and the Council of Jewish Federations and Welfare Funds. The training bureau closed in 1951. The first attempt to prepare Jewish communal workers in a university setting occurred at Yeshiva University in 1957, with the founding of what was to become the Wurzweiler School of Social Work. Wurzweiler has continued to serve the Jewish and general communities in the preparation of master's-level and doctoral-level social workers.

There has been a continuing dialogue since the early 1970s as to whether Jewish communal service is a field (Pins & Ginsburg, 1971), a profession (Reisman, 1972), or both (Bubis, 1976, 1994; Bubis & Reisman, 1995/1996). Currently there are 11 different programs in North America that specifically train individuals for careers in Jewish communal service agencies; nine of these are linked to the Federation Executive Recruitment and Education Program of the Council of Jewish Federations. Several are housed in or affiliated with schools of social work that grant the master's degree in social work plus a certificate in Jewish communal service; others award a master's degree in Jewish communal service, reflecting the belief that Jewish communal service is a distinct profession, separate from social work, which formerly had provided requisite professional preparation to the

Jewish community (Reisman, 1972). Jewish communal service is not a unitary profession, but a field of practice bound by a series of shared attributes in which workers are personally committed and responsible for the following:

- developing and deepening Jewish conscious-ness based on knowledge and emotional commitment
- excellence in professional competence, management, interpretation, and planning
- leadership through initiative and service as educators and models for emulation and inspiration
- participation of laypeople
- effective use of human and financial commu-nity resources (Goldman, 1981).

THE JEWISH POPULATION SURVEY

Since the 1960s, Jewish communal organiza-tions have attempted to better understand their constituencies, evaluate their services, and plan for future needs through a series of systematic statistical profiles and community surveys. The most ambitious and influential of these surveys to date is the 1990 National Jewish Population Survey (NJPS), sponsored by the Council of Jewish Federations, through the North American Jewish Data Bank housed at the City University of New York.

The 1990 NJPS yielded important findings about how American Jews live, what they think and believe, and how they behave both as Jews and as Americans. Despite limitations in definition and sampling procedure, NJPS data are the most comprehensive and authoritative gathered to date (Kosmin et al., 1991).

The study served as a testament to the geographic mobility of the American Jewish community. It confirmed social patterns with which American Jews have long been associ-ated. It also found that Jewish marital and fertility rates had declined. Most significant of all the findings were data regarding Jewish identity, ritual behavior, and patterns of intermarriage. Rates of intermarriage have increased by generation, with some 90 percent of those married before 1965 choosing a born or converted Jew as a marital partner, as compared to only 48 percent of those married between 1985 and 1990. Data regarding strength of identification and ritual behavior indicated high levels of secularism and indifference to Jewish affiliations and creed

(Medding, Tobin, Fishman, & Rimor, 1992). Similar findings were also evident with regard to patterns of communal affiliation (Goldstein, 1992; Rimor & Katz, 1993).

JEWISH CONTINUITY

Against the backdrop of the 1990 NJPS and its evidence of waning levels of Jewish affiliation and dramatic increases in intermarriage rates, the delegates to the 1992 General Assembly of the Council of Jewish Federations declared "Jewish continuity" to be the primary and foremost mission of Jewish communal and social services efforts. The call was to "re-invent" community and create a strategic vision of Jewish life that accounted for the realities of its constituents, both actual and potential. The 1990 NJPS made it clear that most Jews in the United States considered themselves well accepted in the general society and operated within a largely secular arena. The community would have to prove "worthy" of their support by providing initiatives that instill a sense of belonging and affiliation independent from those of their ancestors.

In response, local Jewish federations, especially those from larger cities with a substantial Jewish population, established continuity commissions. These undertook to establish goals and objectives for this mission, with particular focus on Jewish education, the vitality of the Jewish community, and indi-vidual Jewish identity (Dashefsky & Bacon, 1994). Community endowments have been created to support new programs of outreach, family education, professional training, and study or travel to Israel. Collaborations have been encouraged between local institutions already involved in such activities, and efforts have been made to win support from donors and activists for this redirection of communal priorities (Dashefsky & Bacon, 1994).

In addition to the issues raised by the NJPS, other issues have become a focus of concern and service of Jewish communal agencies; these include spousal and child battering; substance abuse; the changing role of women; serving intermarried couples; abortion; and serving populations at risk, including people with the human immunodefi-ciency virus (HIV) or acquired immune deficiency syndrome (AIDS) (Bayme & Rosen, 1994; Dubin, 1996; Linzer, 1996; Linzer, Levitz, & Schnall, 1995). Although some of these concerns relate specifically to the Jewish community, they are similar, if not identical, to concerns being addressed by other sectarian organizations and by social services agencies in general.

TRENDS IN JEWISH COMMUNAL SERVICE

The future of Jewish communal service is intertwined with efforts to ensure Jewish continuity in the United States. In addition to the growth in formal Jewish day school education, alternatives for enhancing Jewish social and religious culture are being developed. In particular, various programs of informal Jewish education have been launched.

For example, Jewish summer camps and touring programs have been designed to create a "total environment" for young people to explore their heritage with carefully trained advisers and staff. Linkage is maintained through campus and youth programs that support these objectives during the course of the school year.

Jewish community centers have undertaken early childhood, after-school, and weekend programs of family education. These engage parents and children in religious ritual and tradition through family and community participation. These programs have also focused on outreach to special client groups (for example, recent immigrants from Eastern Europe or the Middle East, single-parent families, or intermarried couples).

Some communities have created a "Jewish communal campus" (that is, one large facility housing the community center, day school, museum and cultural agency, home for older adults, and other arms of the organized Jewish community). This allows intergenerational and multidisciplinary activities and coordinated efforts at fundraising and planned change. However, it presumes the physical stability of a community known for its demographic and residential mobility.

Much has also been done with study tours to Israel. Aside from generating political and fiscal support for the Jewish homeland, these are intended to spark and reinforce Jewish identity. Family tours, bar or bat mitzvah celebrations, summer courses, archaeological digs, accredited academic programs, and study at religious academies—all have been promoted as ancillaries to synagogue or community center activities. The March of the Living is an international program designed for high school students. Comprising a week-long visit to the remains of the death camps in Poland, followed by a week in Jerusalem, it is timed to coincide with Holocaust Memorial Day and Israel Independence Day.

CONCLUSION

As evidenced in the preceding description, Jewish communal services have emerged from and been supported by a set of social obligations that have as their root the concept of tzedakah, or justice. Although these services and the agencies that provide them are sectarian and derive ongoing support from the Jewish community, their specialized services are available to members of both the Jewish and the general communities. Currently the Jewish community and Jewish communal agencies are struggling with the specific issue of Jewish continuity and the broader issues raised by the emerging managed care environment in which all social services operate.

REFERENCES

Abramson, G. (1994). Doing the job in difficult times: An appreciation of Jewish family service. *Journal of Jewish Communal Service, 70,* 248–252.

Aronowitz, E., & Birnbaum, M. (1992). *Field work standards for group work students in Jewish community centers.* New York: Association of Jewish Center Professionals—Eastern Region.

Bayme, S., & Rosen, G. (1994). *The Jewish family and Jewish continuity.* Hoboken, NJ: KTAV Publishing House.

Berger, G. (1980). *The turbulent decades.* New York: Conference of Jewish Communal Service.

Bernstein, P. (1965). Jewish social services. In H. L. Lurie (Ed.), *Encyclopedia of social work* (15th ed., pp. 418–428). New York: National Association of Social Workers.

Blum, A., & Naparstek, A. J. (1987). The changing environment and Jewish communal services. *Journal of Jewish Communal Service, 63,* 204–211.

Bubis, G. (1976). Professional education for the Jewish component in casework practice. *Journal of Jewish Communal Service, 52,* 270–277.

Bubis, G. (1994). Jewish communal service today: Paradoxes and problems. *Journal of Jewish Communal Service, 71,* 6–12.

Bubis, G., & Reisman, B. (1995/1996). Jewish communal service training programs and the federation system. *Journal of Jewish Communal Service, 72,* 102–109.

Council of Jewish Federations. (1995). *Government funding for human services in the Jewish community* (revised working draft). New York: Council of Jewish Federations.

Dashefsky, A., & Bacon, A. (1994). The meaning of Jewish continuity in the North American community: A preliminary assessment. *Agenda: Jewish Education, 4*, 22–28.

Dubin, D. (1987). Ethical dilemmas in the Jewish community center. *Journal of Jewish Communal Service, 64*, 23–31.

Dubin, D. (1994). The liberation of the constituent agency. *Journal of Jewish Communal Service, 70*, 226–231.

Dubin, D. (1996). *"I witness": Comments on continuity by a Jewish communal professional.* Floral Park, NJ: Association of Jewish Center Professionals and the Jewish Community Centers Association.

Elazar, D. (1995). *Community and polity.* Philadelphia: Jewish Publication Society.

Gibelman, M. (1995). Purchasing social services. In R. L. Edwards (Ed.-in-Chief), *Encyclopedia of social work* (19th ed., Vol. 3, pp. 1998–2007). Washington, DC: NASW Press.

Goldman, R. (1981). The role of the professional in developing and shaping Jewish communal policies and strategies. *Proceedings of the International Conference of Jewish Communal Service, Jerusalem,* pp. 5–36.

Goldstein, S. (1992). Profile of American Jewry: Insights from the 1990 National Jewish Population Survey. *American Jewish Yearbook, 92*, 77–173.

Hebrew Immigrant Aid Society. (1996). *Rescue, hope, freedom.* New York: Author.

Kosmin, B. A., Goldstein, S., Waksberg, J., Lerer, N., Keysar, A., & Scheckner, J. (1991). *Highlights of the CJF 1990 National Jewish Population Survey.* New York: Council of Jewish Federations.

Levine, E. M. (in press). Church, state and social welfare: Purchase of service and the sectarian agency. In M. Gibelman & H. Demore (Eds.), *Cases in the privatization of human services: Perspectives and experiences in contacting.* New York: Springer.

Linzer, N. (1987). Resolving ethical dilemmas in the Jewish community center. *Journal of Jewish Communal Service, 64*, 145–155.

Linzer, N. (1996). *Ethical dilemmas in Jewish communal service.* Hoboken, NJ: KTAV Publishing House.

Linzer, N., Levitz, I., & Schnall, D. (1995). *Crisis and continuity: The Jewish family in the 21st century.* Hoboken, NJ: KTAV Publishing House.

Maimonides, M. (1965). *Yad Hahazakah: Hilchot Matanot Le Aniyim.* New York: Monzaim Press.

Medding, P., Tobin, G. A., Fishman, S. B., & Rimor, M. (1992). Jewish identity in conversionary and mixed marriages. In D. Singer (Ed.), *The American Jewish yearbook 1992* (pp. 3–76). New York: American Jewish Committee.

Metropolitan New York Coordinating Council on Jewish Poverty. (1993). *Jewish poverty in New York City in the 1990s.* New York: Nova Institute.

Miller, A. P. (1995–1996). Jewish vocational service and the federations. *Journal of Jewish Communal Service, 72*, 87–90.

Ortiz, L. P. (1995). Sectarian agencies. In R. L. Edwards (Ed.-in-Chief), *Encyclopedia of social work* (19th ed., Vol. 3, pp. 2109–2116). Washington, DC: NASW Press.

Pins, A. M., & Ginsburg, L. (1971). New developments in social work and their impact on Jewish center and communal service workers. *Journal of Jewish Communal Service, 48*, 60–71.

Reid, W. J., & Stimpson, P. K. (1987). Sectarian agencies. In A. Minahan (Ed.-in-Chief), *Encyclopedia of social work* (18th ed., Vol. 2, pp. 545–556). Silver Spring, MD: National Association of Social Workers.

Reisman, B. (1972). Social work education and Jewish communal service and JCCs: Time for a change. *Journal of Jewish Communal Service, 48*, 384–395.

Rimor, M., & Katz, E. (1993). United States National Jewish Population Survey: A first report. *American Jewish Yearbook, 73*, 264–306.

Schnall, D. J. (1993). Exploratory notes on employee productivity and accountability in classic Jewish sources. *Journal of Business Ethics, 12*, 485–491.

Schnall, D. J. (1995). Faithfully occupied with the public need. *Journal of Jewish Communal Service, 71*, 315–324.

Schneider, M. (1994, July 28). *Weathering the storms of a changing world.* Speech given at Wurzweiler School of Social Work, Block Commencement, Yeshiva University, New York.

Shore, H. (1995–1996). Jewish homes and housing for the aging: Relating to the federation. *Journal of Jewish Communal Service, 72*, 91–95.

Smith, R., & Lipsky, M. (1993). *Nonprofits for hire: The welfare state in the age of contracting.* Cambridge, MA: Harvard University Press.

Solomon, J. R. (1995–1996). Evolving models of federation-agency cooperation. *Journal of Jewish Communal Service, 72*, 60–65.

Steinitz, L. Y. (1995–1996). It's all in the family: Jewish family services and the federation. *Journal of Jewish Communal Service, 72*, 70–76.

Teicher, M. (1996). Letter to the editor. *Journal of Jewish Communal Service, 73*, 91–92.

United Jewish Appeal—Federation of New York. (1994). *Report to the community 1993–1994.* New York: UJA–Federation of New York.

Sheldon R. Gelman, PhD, is Schachne dean and professor, and **David J. Schnall, PhD,** holds the Schiff Chair in Management and Administration, Wurzweiler School of Social Work, Yeshiva University, 2495 Amsterdam Avenue, New York, NY 10033-3299.

For further information see
Advocacy; **Christian Social Work;** Church Social Work; Citizen Participation; **Community Building;** Community Organization; Ecological Perspective; Ethnic-Sensitive Practice; Families Overview; Mutual Aid Societies; Natural Helping Networks; Organizations: Context for Social Services Delivery; Sectarian Agencies; Self-Help Groups; Settlements and Neighborhood Centers; Social Welfare History; Social Work Practice: History and Evolution.

Key Words	
charity	nonprofit
Jewish	sectarian
mutual aid	

L

Legal Issues: Recent Developments in Confidentiality and Privilege

Carolyn I. Polowy
Carol Gorenberg

Confidentiality of client communications is one of the ethical foundations of the social work profession and has become a legal obligation in most states. Recognition that the client will gain greater benefits from treatment and consultation without fear of disclosure in judicial proceedings has led most states to recognize some form of privilege to protect confidential client communications in legal proceedings. The 1979 *NASW Code of Ethics* specifically outlined the concept of a commitment to client confidentiality, and the 1996 revised *Code* greatly expanded the provisions regarding privacy and confidentiality. In 1996 the federal law of evidence was clarified by the U.S. Supreme Court's decision in *Jaffee v. Redmond* to confirm that clients' communications with licensed social workers in the context of psychotherapy are privileged communications under the federal rules of evidence.

Many problems arise in the application of the principles of confidentiality and privilege to the professional services provided by social workers. Numerous states have yet to address the issue of privileged communications for social workers, and a few have accorded communications with social workers different treatment than that for other mental health providers. Three states—Alaska, North Dakota, and Oklahoma—have yet to recognize that communications with social workers are as valuable and private as those with psychologists or psychiatrists. This entry discusses the concepts of client confidentiality and privileged communications and outlines some of the exceptions applicable to them, particularly in the context of clinical social work practice.

HISTORY OF CONFIDENTIALITY AND PRIVILEGE

As members of a profession involved with the implementation of the Social Security Act of 1935 and allied with the medical and mental health fields, social workers have traditionally incorporated adherence to the principles of client privacy and confidentiality into their work (National Association of Social Workers [NASW], 1997).

The concept of a commitment to client confidentiality was specifically outlined in the *NASW Code of Ethics* in 1979 (NASW, 1979). The provisions regarding privacy and confidential-ity are greatly expanded in the recently revised *Code* (NASW, 1996). Where previously there were five subsections (NASW, 1994), there are now 18.

Although the issue of confidentiality often arises in the context of communications between the clinical social worker and the client, it applies to all areas in which the social worker provides professional services. For example, under § 5.01(l) of the 1996 *Code of Ethics*, social workers who are engaged in evaluations or research must "assure the anonymity or confidentiality of participants and of the data obtained from them." Participants also must be advised of any limits on this confidentiality. The duty of the social worker to keep the confidences of a client is reinforced by the fact that a violation of the *Code of Ethics* can be based on the social worker's failure to do so. In addition, inappropriate disclosure of a client's confidences can be grounds for a malpractice suit for breach of confidentiality (*Cutter v. Brownbridge*, 1986) or a civil action for invasion of privacy.

IMPORTANCE OF CONFIDENTIALITY

There is general agreement that confidentiality is a critical underpinning to the provision of mental health services and in particular to the establishment of a beneficial therapeutic relationship:

Without the promise of confidentiality, provided primarily through the clinician's professional ethics but also the law, many individuals in need of treatment would be afraid to seek it. It is even clearer that once in treatment, clients would be affected by the absence of confidentiality. Research has shown that clients expect confidentiality in treatment and wish to be informed of its extent and limits. Every client, however well motivated, has to overcome the resistance to therapeutic exploration. These resistances seek support from every possible source, including the possibility of unwanted disclosure outside the treatment setting. (Weiner & Wettstein, 1993, pp. 201-202)

When a specific situation arises that requires the possible or necessary revelation of a client's records or communications, clear guidance often is not available. Moreover, many social workers are not trained in the intricacies of law or ethics and find themselves in conflict about loyalty to their clients, concerns about meeting ethical and legal responsibilities, and worries about their own potential liability. Applying the concepts of confidentiality and privilege requires a basic understanding of the meaning of the terms and the trend of legal developments around each term.

SCOPE OF CONFIDENTIALITY

The generally accepted definition of *confidentiality* of client information, as described by Weiner and Wettstein (1993), is quite broad:

Any information related to the fact that an individual has sought mental health services is generally considered confidential. The fact that the person is, or has been, in treatment is confidential. Communications by the client during treatment, observations by the therapist, the results of psychological testing and laboratory testing, diagnosis, and prognosis are confidential. Even the fact that someone had a one session consultation with a therapist is confidential. (p. 203)

Confidential communications must occur in a setting in which privacy is reasonably expected. This would generally be in the course of consultation, diagnosis, or treatment and would also include eligibility determinations, referral information, and chart reviews.

Some state statutes specifically define the scope of confidentiality for social work records (Perlman, 1988). These statutes may be incorporated in licensing acts, licensing board regulations for social workers, or evidence laws applying the rules of privilege. Medical records statutes in many states define what an inpatient medical record is, what it should contain, and to whom it may be made available with or without the consent of the patient or client. Outpatient, primary care, and private-practice therapy records may be less well defined, and access to social work records may or may not be clearly delineated. From a professional ethical standpoint, all documentation and information related to or obtained from a client or patient should be viewed as confidential, whether or not a specific law or regulation defines it as a confidential medical record.

OBTAINING THE CLIENT'S CONSENT

In an ethical sense, a breach of confidentiality involves the release of confidential information about a client without that client's informed written or oral consent. In a legal sense, a breach of confidentiality involves the violation of a statutory, regulatory, or common law requirement to maintain the confidentiality of a client's information and records.

There is no breach of confidentiality if the client has consented to the release of information within the specific circumstances. An appropriate release may be implemented at the commencement of treatment to permit records or reports to be sent to an insurance company, referring physicians, or other likely third-party requesters who have a professional need to know the information. The client should be made aware of the scope and intent of the release.

Weiner and Wettstein (1993) indicated that within the specific limitations of state law, consent to release information can be obtained from

- a legally competent adult
- the legal guardian of an adult found to be legally incompetent
- an emancipated minor as defined under state law
- the parent or legal guardian of an unemancipated minor
- the executor or administrator of the estate of a deceased person.

A release form should also describe situations in which it is ethically or legally necessary to provide access to a client's information or records. (See Figure 1; also see

NASW, 1989, p. 9.) When in doubt about whether such information should be provided, the social worker should not divulge information or release records without a written release or court order. This caveat is generally true for all confidential information a social worker maintains about a client. When no release has been provided and the client refuses to provide one or is not available, social workers should consider consulting an attorney about alternatives. The attorney may be the social worker's own counsel or the attorney for the agency with which he or she has a contractual relationship or worked for at the time the matter at issue arose. Some alternatives to consider and discuss include

- preparing a letter to the requester advising that the information is confidential and privileged and that, absent the client's consent or a court order, the requested material cannot be released. Copies of any correspondence should be maintained in the file, and it may be necessary to present them in a hearing on the matter.
- filing a motion to quash or objections to the subpoena based on the privileged nature of

the communication between the client and the social worker. A request for a protective order may also be filed seeking to limit access to the records.

After writing a letter to the relevant parties in the case, advising that the requested materials are confidential and privileged, it may be necessary to follow such a letter with written objections that would be filed with the court or with a motion for a protective order that asks the court to deny access to the file because it contains privileged information about the client. Finally, a motion to quash the subpoena could also be filed.

SITUATIONS REQUIRING OR PERMITTING DISCLOSURE OF A CLIENT'S CONFIDENTIAL INFORMATION

Many states have legislated or developed through case law certain exceptions to the rule of confidentiality. Whenever a situation requires the nonconsensual release of information about a client, the social worker should document the factual circumstances that require the release and the ethical and legal bases supporting a professional judgment

FIGURE 1

Sample Draft Release

(Review under applicable state or federal laws)

I, _____, hereby agree to the release of information by _____ about my treatment or my treatment records under the following circumstances:

- If required for insurance coverage, third-party payer, or utilization review.
- If professionally necessary for consultation with other mental health or medical professionals or as required for review with my supervisors or with other professionals.
- If required by any agreement that I may have with an employer and only to the extent required by that agreement.
- If required to prevent serious harm to me or others.
- If required by state or federal laws or court order.

This agreement remains in effect during my treatment and subsequent to my treatment within any time limits imposed by state or federal law. I have been provided an opportunity to discuss the effect of each point noted above that permits release of my records.

_____
Client Signature

_____
Date

compelling release of information or records without the client's consent.

Duty to Control or Warn about a Dangerous Patient or Client

In the landmark case *Tarasoff v. The Regents of the University of California* (1976), California was the first state to recognize the duty of a psychotherapist to protect a third party from the foreseeable harm of a client. In that case, a student in an outpatient clinic told his therapist of his intent to take the life of a young woman who had stopped seeing him. Because of the seriousness of the threat, the campus police were contacted, and they briefly detained the patient but released him on his promise not to hurt the woman. About two months later, the patient killed her. When the woman's parents sued the psychotherapists for failure to warn the woman of the potential harm, the California Supreme Court decided that the relationship between a psychotherapist and a client in the outpatient setting was "special" so as to trigger the duty to take protective action by releasing confidential information about the client to those who are capable of preventing the threatened harm. In the psychotherapy setting, controlling the client can include warning an outpatient's caregiver or family, involving the police, warning the potential victim, or involuntarily committing the client.

Four years after the *Tarasoff* decision, the California Supreme Court clarified the outside limits of the duty to warn or take preventive action. In *Thompson v. County of Alameda* (1980), the court held that when a juvenile offender had issued a general intent to take the life of a child, the parole officer and county were not liable to the parents of a child who was killed because the killer had not indicated with any particularity whom he intended to hurt. The court concluded that a duty to warn the public at large of the presence of a potentially dangerous person was neither practical nor likely to be effective.

The *Tarasoff* and *Thompson* cases breathed life into a California statute that had been codified in 1966 but apparently had little impact until the court decisions were handed down. California Evidence Code § 1024 (1966) allows disclosure of confidential communications "if the psychotherapist has reasonable cause to believe that, as a result of a mental or emotional condition, the patient is dangerous to the person or property of himself or another, and that only through disclosure can the threatened danger be prevented." A psychotherapist, as defined for the purpose of this statute, includes social workers and other mental health care providers [California Evidence Code, 1966 (amended 1970)].

The *Tarasoff* and *Thompson* decisions brought into focus a difficult public policy dilemma. Once a state recognizes the duty of a therapist to breach a patient's or client's confidentiality to protect third parties from a potentially dangerous client, what is the extent of that duty? Is the duty triggered only when there is a clearly identified and specifically threatened victim, or does that duty extend to the general public and more amorphous threats? State laws today reflect this policy debate and fall into roughly three groups. Some states (for example, Arizona, Delaware, and Washington) recognize a duty to warn when there is a general threat or a threat against the public at large. Other states (for example, Colorado, Massachusetts, Nebraska, and New Jersey) recognize the duty only against a specific threat to a readily identifiable victim. The remaining states have yet to address the issue or have not recognized any such duty at all (for example, North Dakota) or, although ostensibly recognizing such a duty, have yet to encounter a situation in which they are willing to impose it (for example, Alabama and Hawaii).

States that follow the first approach are willing to sacrifice confidentiality at a low threshold of certainty, thus placing the greatest emphasis on protection of the public. They leave the most discretion to the mental health professional. For example, in Illinois the social worker may disclose confidential communications to "protect any person from a clear, imminent risk of serious mental or physical harm or injury, or to forestall a serious threat to the public safety." There is no requirement under this formulation that the identity of the victim be known. The threat can be a harm to the general public and need not be as dire as death or even involve physical injury. Although these statutes tend to be permissive, *allowing* but not *requiring* disclosure, some courts are inclined to read "may" as "must" and impose a duty to warn.

Massachusetts, however, takes the second approach and maintains that confidentiality should be breached only in cases where there is great certainty of harm. The duty exists only when the client communicates "an explicit threat to kill or inflict serious bodily injury upon a reasonably identified victim or victims and the client has the apparent intent and ability to carry out the threat or has a history of physical violence which is known to the social worker" (Massachusetts General Laws Annotated, 1991). There is great particularity required in this formulation: specificity in knowing the identity of the victim, the severity of the harm threatened, and the likelihood that the patient will carry out the threat.

In the third group of states, the law does not impose a duty on any mental heath professional to warn of a patient's dangerous inclinations, either because the courts have rejected such a duty as unreasonable (*Boynton v. Burglass*, 1991), because the courts have not had occasion to address the issue (as in North Dakota), or because although ostensibly recognizing the duty, no actual situation has been presented that triggers the duty (Idaho Code, 1995).

Duty to Report Past Criminal Acts

Most states do not require social workers to report a client's prior criminal acts or harmful acts unless the victim is a child or, in some states, an elderly or vulnerable adult. However, some states permit but do not require the disclosure of a client's confidences that reveal past commission of other crimes. In the Idaho Code (1995), for example, a social worker may breach confidentiality when a client's communication "reveals the contemplation or execution of a crime or harmful act" (Ca. 32 Section 54-3213 [2]). The Kansas licensing of social workers statute, article 53, § 65-6315(a)(1) (1990), is even more vague: Confidentiality is not required when a client communicates information that "pertains to criminal acts or violations of the law." Even though some states permit disclosure of prior criminal acts, many factors should enter into a social worker's decision about whether to take such a step. The ethical rule should be observed that a compelling professional reason would provide the prime motivation, and all facts and ethical or legal principles supporting the decision should be documented.

Child Abuse or Neglect

All states require a mental health professional to report known or suspected cases of child abuse or neglect. The now-universal requirement that child abuse and neglect be reported to appropriate authorities reflects the national concern about this problem as well as the federal role in funding programs to stem child abuse. The plurality of cases dealing with disclosure of confidential or privileged communications are cases involving children (for example, *People v. Bowman*, 1991; *N.H. v. District of Columbia*, 1990; *Young v. Arkansas Children's Hospital*, 1989; *L.A.R. v. Ludwig*, 1991; *M. v. K.*, 1982; *Matter of Jeanne T.T.*, 1992). These laws reflect the policy that protection of children supersedes the preservation of the privacy of individuals. Reporting child abuse and neglect is generally protected by immunity from suit under state law (for example, California Penal Code §11172, 1995).

Some states have also enacted reporting laws designed to protect the interests of elderly, mentally or physically ill, or other classes of vulnerable or dependent adults (Massachusetts General Laws Annotated, 1991). Social workers should be familiar with the reporting requirements mandated by the statutes in their own states.

Preventing Harm to the Client

It is ethically understood, and confirmed by statute in a few states, that a therapist or social worker would ordinarily act to prevent harm to the client (Connecticut General Statutes, 1992; Massachusetts General Laws Annotated, 1991). The client's disclosure of suicidal intent, for example, may require contact with other professionals or the client's family or action for involuntary commitment. Such action must be reasonable, professionally appropriate, and taken in consideration of the client's particular circumstances.

If the client's situation requires involuntary commitment, it may be necessary to breach the client's confidentiality in the commitment process or during the commitment hearing (Massachusetts General Laws Annotated, 1991). This is generally allowed because release of information about a client protects the client or society from harm and is necessary because of the serious nature of the client's condition.

HIV and AIDS Reporting

The advent of the acquired immune deficiency syndrome (AIDS) epidemic created numerous problems related to confidentiality and reporting requirements (Labowitz, 1990; Reamer, 1991). Advocates for people with AIDS and those testing positive for the human immunodeficiency virus (HIV) fought against use of traditional reporting procedures established for other contagious diseases because such disclosure was likely to result in the loss of civil rights, employment, or health insurance for those with the disease (*Chalk v. U.S. District Court,* 1988). The dual public policy objectives of reducing the spread of the disease and maintaining the privacy rights and economic independence of people with AIDS and HIV have sometimes seemed diametrically opposed.

An extensive body of jurisprudence has been developed around the many legal issues involving AIDS. However, confidentiality requirements remain inconsistent among the states. Although all states now have some legislation relating to AIDS, many do not directly address the issue of whether it is mandatory or permissible to report a client's HIV-positive or AIDS status to sexual or needle-sharing partners ("contacts"). Emerging themes among the states are as follows:

- Disclosure to the client's contacts should be made only after counseling the client and determining that he or she is unlikely to make the disclosure (New York Public Health Law § 2782.4[a][3], 1994).
- Many states require that the disclosure be made through the public health department, which has procedures in place or provides guidance for notifying the contacts (New York Public Health Law § 2782, 1994).
- Disclosure of statistical and epidemiological information for research (New Hampshire Revised Statutes Annotated § 141-C:10, 1994), government-mandated reporting (New York Public Health Law § 2782.1[g], 1994), or news collection (New Hampshire 1987 Opinions of the Attorney General 96) is not barred as long as no information that identifies the individual is included.
- Medical personnel are mandated in certain situations to report a patient's HIV status to other medical personnel to ensure appropriate treatment of the person and precautions for those who will be exposed. Disclosure is not permitted for the purpose of discriminating against the individual (New York Public Health Law § 2782.1[d], 1994).

When state laws regarding social services or mental health providers are absent or unclear, the social worker should look to laws mandating a duty or permission to warn a client who would pose a serious threat of harm to others. As with all such protective measures, the client should be counseled, the case well documented, and action taken to balance the third party's safety against the client's right to privacy. In addition, the case should be discussed with the client's treating physician or other appropriate medical personnel to determine who is in the best position to discuss the matter with the client and the person at risk. Consultation with the public health department is highly recommended before any disclosure is made, because there may be a protocol in place for such notifications.

Alcohol and Drug Rehabilitation Programs Receiving Federal Funds

The Code of Federal Regulations 42 CFR 2.31 (1994), contains specific rules outlining federal law that provide limited circumstances for the release of information from alcohol and drug treatment programs that receive federal funds. Such treatment programs should promulgate guidelines to protect the client's confidentiality that are based on current federal law and regulations. The following issues should be addressed:

- Release of a client's records and information including identification of the client should be restricted unless permitted under a specific exception.
- Release would normally be based on the written consent of the client. The consent form must identify the person or organization to whom the records will be released, the content of information released, and the purpose for the disclosure. The consent form must be specific to the situation, state that it can be revoked, and be signed and dated (42 CFR § 2.31, 1994).
- Records may be released without the consent of the client for a bona fide medical emergency or for research purposes that will not include identifying data. When a client commits a crime on the agency's premises, threatens to do so, or threatens program personnel, records may also be released without the client's consent to law enforcement agencies.

- In all other circumstances, records may be released only with a specific court order. Federal law limits the circumstances under which the court can order the release of records. These circumstances include cases in which release would protect against serious injury, disclosure is necessary to investigate or prosecute a serious crime, or the client has raised an issue related to his or her treatment in legal proceedings.

PRIVILEGE AND THE RELEASE OF A CLIENT'S INFORMATION IN LEGAL PROCEEDINGS

Privileged communication is an important subcategory or characteristic of confidential communications. The *privilege* is the client's legal right to keep certain communications with the social worker private and not available as evidence in legal proceedings, including subpoenas of records, pretrial depositions or affidavits, and testimony at trial. It parallels other evidentiary privileges, such as the common law spousal privilege ("Developments in the Law," 1985) and the Fifth Amendment to the U.S. Constitution, that guarantee privilege against self-incrimination. Privilege serves to prevent the social worker from being a witness against a client's wishes or best therapeutic interests.

The privilege against disclosure of confidential communications in legal proceedings is a matter of public policy. It is grounded in the community value that the client should be confident that his or her innermost thoughts can be revealed in confidence, without being subject to public exposure (*Jaffee v. Redmond*, 1996), and is intended to protect the client from humiliation, embarrassment, or disgrace and to promote mental health treatment. As such, it is a right of the client, not of the social worker. Although the social worker is obligated to assert the client's privilege when records or testimony are demanded, if the client waives the privilege, the social worker must accede (*In re Lifschutz*, 1970).

By definition, privilege keeps information out of the knowledge of those who are called on to resolve disputes and vindicate rights. There is a conflict between the client's privacy rights and the need to promote use of therapy, on the one hand, and, on the other hand, the search for truth and justice. The balance of the two sets of competing values and the establishment of ground rules by which to be guided are essential to the well-being of society. The result is a number of exceptional situations in which courts or legislatures have determined that privilege should not apply or that a client, by bringing a certain type of legal action, has waived his or her right to privilege.

The most widely accepted group of exceptions is again in the area of protection of children. Most states make exceptions to privilege in matters of child custody, adoption, and termination of parental rights. However, when, to protect a child, a social worker has an obligation to report cases of child abuse learned from a client, courts will not necessarily allow that same information in the criminal proceeding against the perpetrator (*People v. Wood*, 1993). In weighing the importance of admitting confidential communications, courts will consider whether there are other sources for similar evidence that would make the confidential communications reported in the clinical setting duplicative.

A number of actions on the part of the client are considered to be effective waivers of the privilege. Some of these are generally accepted, but acceptance of others varies from state to state. A written waiver or release signed by a competent person in the context of a legal proceeding is generally accepted as an effective waiver. Independent disclosure by a client to a third party may or may not constitute a waiver, depending on the circumstances and state law. Most states consider that the client has waived the privilege when his or her mental health is made an issue in either a civil or criminal case. For example, in a civil case, if a patient is suing a third party for pain and suffering or emotional distress, or suing a social worker for malpractice, the client's records will not be held to be privileged because the content of the records is central to the claim being adjudicated (*Caesar v. Mountanos*, 1976, 542 F. 2d 1064 [Cal. App 1976; cert denied, 97 St. Ct. 1598]). In a criminal case in which a client is pleading a defense of insanity or diminished capacity, access to mental health records will also be granted. Such disclosure will be limited, however, to the client's mental or emotional condition and may not be used as evidence of whether he or she committed the crime (*McMunn v. Florida*, 1972).

Although it is possible to make the distinction between confidentiality and privilege, many state statutes use the two terms interchangeably; sometimes the intent of

TABLE 1
Social Worker–Client Privilege Laws

State	Social Worker Privilege Recognized		Social Worker Privilege Not Recognized	
	Generic Privilege Statute for All Mental Health Professionals	Specific Privilege Statute for Social Workers	Statute or Case Specifically Excludes Social Workers	Silence on Social Workers—No Statutes or Cases
Alabama				yes
Alaska			Alaska R. Evid. § 08.95.300(a)(3); Allred v. Alaska, 554 P.2d 411 (1976)	
Arizona	Ariz. Rev. Stat. § 32-3283			
Arkansas		Ala. Code Ann. § 17-39-107		
California	Cal. Evid. Code § 1012			
Colorado	Colo. Rev. Stat. § 12-43-218			
Connecticut		Conn. Gen. Stat. Ann. § 52-146q		
Delaware		24 Del. Code § 3913		
District of Columbia	D.C. Code § 14-307			
Florida	Fla. Stat. Ann. § 90.503			
Georgia	Ga. Code § 24-9-21			
Hawaii				Haw. Rev. Stats. § 626-1, Rule 504.1[a]
Idaho		Idaho Code § 54-3213		
Illinois		225 I.L.C.S. § 20/16		
Indiana		Ind. Code Ann. § 25-23.6-6-1		
Iowa	Iowa Code Ann. § 622.10			
Kansas		Kan. Stat. Ann. § 65-6315		
Kentucky	Ky. R. Evid., Rule 507			
Louisiana	La. Stat. Ann.- Code Evid. Art. 510			
Maine		32 Me. Rev. Stat. Ann. § 7005		
Maryland		Md. Code, Cts. & Jud. Proc. § 9-121		
Massachusetts		Mass. Gen. Laws C112 - § 135B		
Michigan		Mich.Comp. Laws § 339.1610		
Minnesota	Minn. Stat. Ann. § 595.02 (g)			
Mississippi		Miss. Code Ann. § 73-53-29		
Missouri	Mo. Rev. Stats. § 337.636			
Montana		Mont. Code Ann. § 37-22-401		
Nebraska	Neb. Rev. Stat. § 71-1,335			
Nevada	Nev. Rev. Stat. §§ 49.215 -49.245			
New Hampshire	N.H.Rev.Stat.Ann. § 330-A:19; Rules of Evid., Rule 503			

State	Statute / Citation	
New Jersey	N.J. Stat. Ann. § 45:15BB-13	
New Mexico	N.M. Stat. Ann. § 61-31-24	
New York	N.Y. Civ. Prac. L. & R. § 4508	
North Carolina	N.C. Gen. Stat. § 8-53.7	
North Dakota		N.D. v. Copeland, 448 N.W.2d 611 (1989)
Ohio	Ohio Rev. Code Ann. § 2317.02(G)	
Oklahoma	59 Okl. St. Ann. § 1261.6	Peninger v. Okla., 811 P.2d 609 (Okla. Crim. App. 1991)[b]
Oregon	Or. Rev. Stat. § 40.250 Rule 504-4	
Pennsylvania		
Rhode Island	R.I. Gen. Laws § 5-37.3-3[d]	
South Carolina	S.C. Code § 19-11-95[e]	
South Dakota	S.D. Codified Laws § 36-26-30	
Tennessee	Tenn. Code Ann. § 63-11-213	
Texas	Tex. R. Civ. Evid., Rule 510[f]	
Utah	Utah Code Ann. § 58-60-114	
Vermont	Vt. R. Evid., Rule 503[g]	
Virginia	Va. Code § 8.01-400.2	
Washington	Wash. Rev. Code Ann. § 18.19.180	
West Virginia	W. Va. Code § 30-30-12	
Wisconsin	Wis. Stat. Ann. § 905.04	
Wyoming	Wyo. R. Evid., Rule 501[h]	

[a] Rule 504.1 grants privilege to psychologist–patient communications, and the definition of psychologists does not refer to social workers. Communications with all counselors, including social workers who are counselors to sexual assault victims or domestic violence victims are privileged under Haw. Rev. Stats. § 626-1, Rule 505.5

[b] But see Okla. Stat. Ann. § 1261.6. The court's reading of the statute in *Penninger* ignores a key phrase. The statute seems to provide a privilege to social workers, but includes an exception that "no information shall be treated as privileged and there shall be no privilege created by this act as to any information. . . . *when such information pertains to criminal acts or violations of any law*" (at 611, italics added). The discussion in *Penninger* made no mention of this and appears to negate the intent of the statute, leaving it to be clarified by the legislature or a case overruling *Penninger*.

[c] Some Pennsylvania social workers are covered by privileges relating to specific client groups, for example, sexual assault victims (Knapp, Vandecreek, & Zirkel, 1987).

[d] This privilege statute applies to "psychiatric social workers," defined by the statute as a "person holding a Master's or further advanced degree from a school of social work accredited by the council of social work education" [R. I. Gen. Laws § 5-37.3-3(l)].

[e] The title of this statute is "Communications with Mental Health Professionals Privileged," and it includes a nonexclusive list of mental health practitioners who would be covered in this role. The law is presented in terms of the rights of the patient. It is an unusual and reasonable approach, which focuses on the holder of the privilege, rather than the professional degree or the mental health practitioner providing the service.

[f] This rule does not name any professions covered by the privilege. It applies to communications with any "professionals," defined as "any person (A) authorized to practice medicine. . . ; or (B) licensed or certified by the State of Texas in the diagnosis, evaluation or treatment of any mental or emotional disorder; or (C) involved in the treatment or examination of drug abusers; or (D) reasonably believed by the patient to be included in any of the preceding categories" (West's Texas Rules of Court, Texas Rules of Civil Evidence, Article II, 1995).

[g] The statute is titled "Patient Privilege." See comment in note e.

[h] Wyoming has adopted Rule 501 of the Federal Rules of Evidence, which gives the court discretion to determine on a case-by-case basis whether there is a privilege, according to the "principles of the common law as they may be interpreted. . . in the light of reason and experience" (Wyoming Court Rules Annotated, Wyoming Review of Evidence, V. Privilege, 1982–83). The federal rule has been criticized for being too vague and leaving too much discretion to the court (Baylton, 1995). There is no case law to indicate how the Wyoming courts would interpret the existence of a psychotherapist–patient privilege or a social worker—client privilege.

the law to either create a privilege or mandate confidentiality must be inferred from the context. Because privilege arises when determining whether evidence is admissible in a judicial proceeding, privilege rules are most logically found within a state's evidence code. However, with the increasing recognition of the social work profession as a significant provider of mental health treatment and evaluation, many legislatures have grafted privilege rules onto social work professional licensing codes. When the privilege appears in the professional code rather than the evidence code, it may not be clear whether exceptions to privilege that have been established for other professions (for example, psychology or medicine) within the evidence code are equally applicable to the social work profession.

FEDERAL AND STATE TREATMENT OF PRIVILEGE

The federal law of evidence was recently clarified by the U.S. Supreme Court's decision in *Jaffee v. Redmond* (1996) to confirm that clients' communications with licensed social workers in the context of psychotherapy are privileged communications under the federal rules of evidence. Therefore these communications are generally not subject to disclosure as evidence in the federal courts. The Supreme Court's majority opinion accorded much weight to the fact that the "psychotherapist privilege is rooted in the imperative need for confidence and trust" (Jaffee at p. 1928 citing *Tramel v. U.S.,* 445 U.S. 40 [1980]). The Court contrasted the physician's need for medical facts with the psychotherapist's dependence on "an atmosphere of confidence and trust in which the patient is willing to make a frank and complete disclosure of facts, emotions, memories and fears" (Jaffee, p. 1928).

This need for frank and open discussion and revelation of innermost thoughts in psychotherapy requires protection from public disclosure. The Court concluded that both private and public interests would be served by treating communications between psychotherapist and client as privileged. The public interest to be protected was defined by the Court as "the provision of appropriate treatment for individuals suffering the effects of a mental or emotional problem" (Jaffee, p. 1929). The Court concluded that the "mental health of our citizenry, no less than its physical health, is a public good of transcendent importance" (Jaffee, p. 1929). The Court viewed the eviden-

tiary benefit to be gained by revelation of communications during psychotherapy as limited and the negative or chilling effect on treatment as great. In its decision in *Jaffee,* the Supreme Court's majority opinion also concluded "without hesitation" that the federal psychotherapy privilege should extend to clients of licensed social workers.

Although the *Jaffee* ruling is not automatically applicable to cases brought in state courts, the holding could greatly influence decision making in state courts. A state court would find ample support to confirm a state law's grant of privilege in situations that might have otherwise been questionable. For example, in *Commonwealth v. Fuller* (1996), an accused rapist sought production of a victim's records from the rape crisis center at which she had been counseled. The rape crisis center refused to provide the records on the grounds that the records were absolutely privileged under a Massachusetts statute that protects from disclosure a victim's sexual assault counseling records. The Massachusetts court cited *Jaffee v. Redmond* in support of the existence of "psychotherapist privilege" as a part of federal common law, which buttressed the court's conclusion that a constitutional basis is not necessary for an application of privilege.

Statutes in 22 states and the District of Columbia grant privilege to communications between clients and mental health professionals. These "generic" privilege laws generally consider communications with psychiatrists, psychologists, social workers, and any other listed professionals to have equivalent importance and rights to privacy. In 21 states, privilege is granted to social workers as a profession, and separate statutes identify the privilege granted to other mental health professions. In Alaska, North Dakota, and Oklahoma, courts or legislatures have explicitly denied any privilege to communications with social workers; and in Alabama, Hawaii, Pennsylvania, and Wyoming, it is unclear whether all such communications are privileged, because there is no general statutory provision or the courts have had no opportunity to adjudicate the issue. The specific state-by-state breakdown is shown in Table 1.

The generic privilege laws applicable to the mental health professions in a state offer the best protection to the client, who may not be familiar with the varying educational and licensing requirements among the many mental health care providers. Moreover, a generic privilege focuses on the services provided because privilege is accorded to clients' communications with all licensed mental health professionals who provide similar services.

The privilege statutes specific to social workers provide considerable protection to the client but have one shortcoming: If they are worded differently from the privilege statutes applicable to psychotherapists or other privilege statutes, courts may assume that the legislature intended the social worker's privilege to be different in scope from that of the other mental health professions and may give unequal treatment to similar fact situations that involve mental health professionals who hold other licenses. To avoid this problem, legislatures should include social workers in the definition of "psychotherapist" for the purpose of privilege (as in the California Evidence Code [1994] and the Wisconsin Act 160, Chapter 457. 01[9] [1991]), provide that the privilege granted to social workers will be the same as that for other psychotherapists (as in the Tennessee Code Annotated, Chapter 63, Section 23-107 [1992]), or grant the privilege in terms of the right of the client to confidential mental health treatment and include the professional titles of all appropriate licensed providers (as in the Vermont Rules of Evidence [1993]).

In the three states where there is clearly no privilege for social workers, courts or legislatures have declared that communications with social workers do not warrant the same protection as communications with psychiatrists or psychologists. Because social workers are the major providers of mental health care in the United States, this minority view is a disservice to the clients who are the recipients of social work services in those states and is contrary to the professional standards accepted in most states.

CONCLUSION

The social work profession must work toward increasing the universality and uniformity of state laws protecting client confidentiality and privilege. The different uses of the terms and lack of common agreement on meanings create confusion in applying general rules to specific situations. Now that the Supreme Court has provided guidance to the federal courts, state legislatures should recognize that the disparity in the protection of social worker-client communications in particular, and

psychotherapist-patient privilege in general, is detrimental to the treatment process. Thus, all state laws should follow the federal sector in granting privileged status to communications between clients and their social worker psychotherapists.

Awareness of the requirements of the state laws pertaining to social workers and efforts toward consistent treatment of licensed mental health professionals, based on the nature of the services provided, will enable social workers to better serve the needs of clients and further the advancement of the profession.

REFERENCES

Baytion, C. M., (1995). Toward uniform application of a federal psychotherapist–patient privilege [Note & Comment]. *Washington Law Review, 70,* 153–175.

Boynton v. Burglass, 590 So. 2d 446 (Fla. Dist. Ct. App. 1991).

Caesar v. Mountanos, 542 F.2d 1064 (Cal. App. 1976) *cert. denied,* 97 S.Ct. 1598.

California Evidence Code § 1010(c) (1966) (amended 1970).

California Evidence Code § 1024 (1996).

California Penal Code § 11172 (1995).

Chalk v. U.S. District Court, 840 F.2d 701 (9th Cir. 1988).

Commonwealth v. Fuller, 423 Mass. 216 (1996).

Connecticut General Statutes, § 52-146(c)(2) (1992).

Cutter v. Brownbridge, 228 Cal. Rptr. 545 (Ct. App. 1986).

Developments in the law: Privileged communications. (1985). *Harvard Law Review, 98,* 1450-1666.

Idaho Code, § 54-3213 (1995).

In re Lifschutz 467 P.2d 557 (Cal. 1970).

Jaffee v. Redmond, 116 S.Ct. 1923 (1996).

Knapp, S. J., VandeCreek, L., & Zirkel, P. A. (1987). Privileged communications for psychotherapists in Pennsylvania: A time for statutory reform. *Temple Law Quarterly, 60,* 267–292.

Labowitz, K. E. (1990). Beyond *Tarasoff*: AIDS and the obligation to breach confidentiality. *St. Louis University Public Law Review, 9,* 495–517.

L.A.R. v. Ludwig, 821 P.2d 291 (Ariz. App. 1991).

M. v. K., 452 A.2d 704 (N.J. Ch. 1982).

Massachusetts General Laws Annotated, Ch. 112 § 135A (c)(1) (1991).

Matter of Jeanne T.T., 585 N.Y.S.2d 552 (3 Dept. 1992).

McMunn v. Florida, 264 So. 2d 868 (Fla. App 1 Dist 1972).

National Association of Social Workers. (1989). *NASW standards for the practice of clinical social work.* Silver Spring, MD: Author.

National Association of Social Workers. (1997). *Social work speaks: NASW policy statements* (4th ed.). Washington, DC: NASW Press.

New Hampshire 1987 Opinions of the Attorney General 96 (1987).

New Hampshire Revised Statutes Annotated, § 141-C:10 (1993).

N.H. v. District of Columbia, 569 A.2d 1179 (D.C. App. 1990).

New York Public Health Law §§ 2782.1(d), 2782.1(g), 2782.4(a)(3)

People v. Bowman, 812 P.2d (Colo. App. 1991).

People v. Wood, 505 N.W.2d (Mich. App. 1993).

Perlman, G. L. (1988). Mastering the law of privileged communication: A guide for social workers. *Social Work, 33,* 425–429.

Reamer, F. (1991). *AIDS & Ethics.* New York: Columbia University Press.

Social Security Act of 1935. ch. 351, 49 Stat. 620.

Tarasoff v. Regents of Univ. of Cal., 551 P.2d 334 (Cal. 1976).

Thompson v. County of Alameda, 614 P.2d 728 (Cal. 1980).

Vermont Rules of Evidence, § 503 (1993).

Weiner, B. A., & Wettstein, R. M. (1993). *Legal issues in mental health care.* New York: Plenum Press.

West's Texas Rules of Court, Texas Rules of Civil Evidence, Article II (1995).

Wyoming Court Rules Annotated, Wyoming Review of Evidence, V. Privilege (1982–83).

Young v. Arkansas Children's Hospital, 721 Federal Supplement 197 (Eastern District of Arkansas, 1989).

Further Reading

Abt, C. C., & Hardy, K. M. (Eds.). (1990). *AIDS and the courts.* Cambridge, MA: Abt Books.

AIDS and the law. (2nd ed.). (1992). New York: John Wiley & Sons.

Austin, K. M. (1990). *Confronting malpractice.* Newbury Park, CA: Sage Publications.

Burris, S., Dalton, H. L., & Miller, J. L. (Eds.). (1993). *AIDS law today: A new guide for the public.* New Haven, CT: Yale University Press.

Coco, A. (1982). *Finding the law: A workbook on legal research for lay persons, prepared for Bureau of Land Management.* Washington, DC: U.S. Government Printing Office.

Conidaris, M. G., Ely, D. F., Erikson, J. T., & Levin, S. M. (1989). *California laws for psychotherapists.* Gardena, CA: Harcourt Brace Jovanovich.

Elias, S. (1986). *Legal research: How to find and understand the law* (3rd ed.). Berkeley, CA: Nolo Press.

Knapp, S., & VandeCreek, L. (1987). *Privileged communications in the mental health professions.* New York: Van Nostrand Reinhold.

Monahan, J. (1981). *Predicting violent behavior.* Beverly Hills, CA: Sage Publications.

Rennert, S. (1991). *AIDS/HIV and confidentiality: Model policy and procedures.* Washington, DC: American Bar Association.

Shroeder, L. O. (1995). *The legal environment of social work.* Washington, DC: NASW Press.

Strama, B. T. (Ed.). (1993). *AIDS and governmental liability: State and local government guide to legislation, legal issues, and liability.* Chicago: American Bar Association.

Carolyn I. Polowy, JD, is general counsel, National Association of Social Workers, 750 First Street, NE, Suite 700, Washington, DC 20002-4241. **Carol Gorenberg** was a student, George Washington University School of Law, Washington, DC, and a law clerk to the NASW general counsel at the time this entry was written.

For further information see

Bioethical Issues; Civil Rights; Clinical Social Work; **Ethical Standards in Social Work: The *NASW Code of Ethics;*** Ethics and Values; Human Rights; Legal Issues: Confidentiality and Privileged Communication; Peace and Social Justice; Professional Conduct; Professional Liability and Malpractice.

Key Words

client confidentiality	privileged
Jaffee v. Redmond	communication
privilege	psychotherapy

M

Managed Care: Implications for Social Work Practice

Kevin Corcoran

Managed care has become an integral aspect of social work practice in many settings. The term is often used to refer to any effort to control the costs of services while—at least ostensibly—ensuring the quality of care. Although originally it was concerned with health and mental health care costs and quality, managed care has begun to influence other social services, including family services, child welfare services, and a variety of public programs. This entry will consider social work practice in managed care settings. Emphasis is given to managed care in health and mental health settings, including programs in which costs are contained by controlling the services delivery system and the managed care procedures that control the actual services delivered. Some of the apparent value conflicts between managed care and both the new *NASW Code of Ethics* and the new roles for social work practice in an era of managed care are also reviewed.

COST OF CARE AND NEED FOR CONTROL

Managed care is often considered a recent entry into the health and mental health services marketplace, but its rich history extends back to the early health maintenance organizations' (HMOs') prepaid plans (Edinburg & Cottler, 1995). This includes an early form of the HMO model that dates back to 1939 in a small farming community in Oklahoma, where a physician sold shares in a health organization for $1.00 and then offered services at a discount rate (Corcoran & Vandiver, 1996). Significant impetus for HMOs occurred with President Richard Nixon's support of the HMO Act of 1973, which was designed as an alternative to the Democratic proposal for national health care. It was intended to promote HMO development by, among other things, offering tax incentives and federal grants. The bill did not require inpatient stays for mental health but did mandate emergency care and crisis intervention and allowed up to 20 outpatient visits. The restrictions on HMOs, however, outweighed the incentives, and after five years only 183 plans covering only 7 million persons had been developed (Bittker, 1992). Managed care received another historic step forward with the development of the Medicare prospective payment system. This occurred in the form of diagnostic-related groups (DRGs), which pay a fixed price for all services for specific diagnoses, regardless of the level of care. A prospective payment system contrasts sharply with the traditional retrospective fee-for-service model originally found in most insurance policies.

The current need to control the costs of health and mental health services is responsible for much of managed care's prevalence. This need to control costs is the result of three factors. First, the availability of third-party reimbursement, including government programs and private insurance, has insulated the service provider and client from much of the pecuniary burden of service utilization. Such a system is guaranteed to facilitate unbridled acceleration of costs. This includes the well-known entitlement programs of Medicaid and Medicare, in which expenditures are increasing at a rate of 10 percent a year; the programs are expected to go bankrupt by the year 2002 and to run a $126 billion deficit by 2004. Coverage for the costs of care is not limited to these two major programs, even though Medicare pays more than 25 percent of all hospital costs and Medicaid covers about 36 million Americans. Third-party payment by the government also includes many other federal and state services; examples include more than 6 million federal employees and their dependents who are covered by Civilian Health and Medical Program of Uniformed Services (CHAMPUS), the 172 Veterans Affairs hospitals and almost as many military hospitals, the 29,000 state-run mental health programs, and other examples too numerous to mention (Corcoran & Vandiver, 1996).

The second factor influencing the cost of care has been the expansion of private insurance to include mental health services and substance abuse treatment. Before the advent of psychotropic medications, much of the care for people with mental illness was custodial and of questionable effectiveness; from the perspective of the insurance industry, the high cost of care, the relative ineffectiveness of treatment, and the meager financial support provided by state revenue made mental health coverage an unwarranted benefit. Psychotropic medication changed much of this. Not only did phenothiazine, for example, successfully control symptomatology, but medication had traditionally been seen as a legitimate health care service covered by an insurance policy. Typically this type of third-party coverage is provided as a benefit of full-time employment. Consequently, this source of escalation excludes the nearly 45 million Americans who are underinsured or uninsured and rely on high-cost emergency departments for much of their health care coverage. Of particular concern to social workers, these people are disproportionately women and children, people of color, and people with low incomes (that is, working poor people). However, more than 211 million citizens are fortunate enough to have some form of private health insurance, which covers about 31 percent of the total health care cost in the country (Corcoran & Vandiver, 1996).

The third factor facilitating the crisis over the cost of care has been the development of new technology. As noted by Eisenberg et al. (1989), many examples of medical technology do not replace older and more basic ones but are primarily supplemental; consequently, because the basic technology is used before the more advanced ones, the costs are increased by much of the new, effective, and expensive equipment.

In general these factors have produced an escalating cost of health and mental health care that far outpaces other sectors of the economy, with the notable exception of higher education. The need to control the cost of health and mental health services cannot be overstated. The problem is a serious one. For example, when Medicaid began in 1966, it was a fee-for-service system much like Medicare. In 1988 Medicaid costs represented only 8 percent of a given state's budget, but by 1994 it had grown to 20 percent. Similarly, the per capita cost of the Supplemental Medical

Insurance program of Medicare was about $800 in 1970, but more than $1,600 in 1994 (Corcoran & Vandiver, 1996). Even care that is managed by prospective payment has not always been successfully controlled. The most recent and troubling example seems to be subacute care, which is exempt from much of the prospective payment schedules. Consequently, Medicare can be billed twice: once for the cost of a hip replacement, for example, at approximately $10,500 and then again for the subacute care, which can easily exceed $500 per day; this second type of payment is in the form of fee for service for therapy, tests, and laboratory work (Anders, 1996). The result of this "loophole" is that Medicare payments for subacute care increased from less than $3 billion in 1990 to $10.3 billion in 1995. This same inflationary price escalation has occurred for private third-party payers as well. For example, the cost of private insurance benefits obtained through employment is currently approximately $4,000 per employee; the cost of such benefits is expected to exceed the current average salary by the year 2030 (Harris, 1994).

The problem of escalating health and mental health care costs is so severe that it is increasingly consuming more and more of the gross national product (GNP). In 1990, for example, 12 percent of the total GNP (approximately $660 billion) went to health care. This figure increased to $838 billion in 1993, or about 14 percent of the GNP (Harris, 1994). At the current rate, by 2000 health care costs will exceed 20 percent of the GNP (Resnick & DeLeon, 1995). The consequence of this acceleration is that less money is available in the economy for other goods and services, including social work services. At the current rate of inflation, by 2030 the entire GNP will be dedicated to health care. This, of course, is simply not possible and therefore necessitates cost containment while ensuring that quality of care is not adversely affected.

DEFINING MANAGED CARE

As stated earlier, "managed care" is a nebulous term that is carelessly used to describe a wide range of programs and procedures designed to contain costs and ensure quality. In reality it is the administration and oversight of health and mental health services by someone other than the client and provider, someone who most likely works for the third-party payer; consequently, most managed care organizations are technically a fourth party in the client-provider relationship. As Austad and Hoyt (1992) have observed, managed care refers to anything that attempts to regulate the cost, utilization, or site of services. This may include an agent of the third-party payer, regardless of whether that payer is the government, an insurance company, an employee assistance program, or someone in a self-insured company's department of human resources.

Managed care programs and procedures may be categorized as control over the service delivery system or regulation of the actual services. This distinction is more a matter of convenience than authority, as managed care is a complex and changing aspect of service delivery in which no single definition or model exists (Edinburg & Cottler, 1995). It is also changing so rapidly that its future is unlikely to resemble its current structure. This is evidenced in the recent increase in state legislative initiatives (Families USA Foundation, 1996) and the federal and state legislative debate about mandating a set number of hours of maternity care (for example, the Newborn's and Mother's Health Protection Act of 1996, P.L. 104-204).

Controlling the Service Delivery System

Costs are more likely contained—and, ideally, quality is monitored—when managed care controls the actual service delivery system. There are numerous examples of situations in which the payer of the services also provides those services; these include the historic ship's physician and the company nurse, but currently the most familiar ones are probably HMOs and employee assistance programs (EAPs). These types of managed care systems are fairly self-contained organizations that provide in-house services whenever possible. When it is not possible to provide the services, the self-contained managed care system coordinates other necessary services. The need for services is based on the concept of medical necessity, and interestingly it is often the organization committed to controlling costs that determines whether the client's problem warrants treatment.

The funding for these and other managed care programs is often based on a capitation model. A capitation model provides a lump sum of money to cover whatever services are required and not a fee for all services provided. Funds for services rendered may have a cap on how much will be paid for a group of clients or how much will be spent per person.

Under a capitation model all or most of the services are provided by the managed care program or are contracted out to a provider in a network of programs. For example, an EAP may provide a limited number of sessions to assess and treat a work-related problem such as stress, but may refer the client to a member of a panel of providers if there is a dual diagnosis that includes dysthymia or substance abuse. In essence, capitation programs attempt to control costs by providing services at a reduced rate and contracting with those providers who agree to deliver the services at a lower cost. Capitation may also control costs by restricting services to those conditions that are clinically necessary to treat conditions that are within the range of coverage of the plan; many problems, such as some DSM-IV VCodes and attention deficit and hyperactive disorder, often are not covered by an insurance policy or a managed care program.

This approach to cost containment includes public health and mental health services, both of which are traditional auspices of social work practice. For mental health services, this has resulted in part from block grants for such services and the phasing out of federal funding for community mental health centers (Cutler, 1992). Most community mental health centers have become community mental health organizations that may provide particular services for people with severe and persistent mental illness (for example, medication and assertive case management) and contract with other providers for additional necessary services (for example, supportive housing). Costs are frequently contained by vertical integration of services (V. H. Jackson, 1996), which keeps people with a mental disorder in the community, where care is less expensive than inpatient hospitalization.

There are a number of different managed care structures that attempt to control costs by controlling the service delivery system. The two mentioned earlier (that is, HMOs and EAPs) may actually provide the services. Control of the service delivery system may also include controlling who provides those services, such as which health or mental health professional is authorized to deliver services in a network of programs. Examples include preferred provider organizations (which are similar to, if not the same as, independent provider organizations), exclusive provider organizations (which are also known as "closed panels" of providers), and point-of-service plans (Edinburg & Cottler, 1995; V. H. Jackson, 1995, 1996).

In the public sector managed care is often seen in the form of a community mental health organization, which includes networks of providers. Often brokerage of services, in which providers agree to a reduced rate of payment in exchange for an assurance that there will be a certain number of referrals, is the most effective means of controlling costs. Quality is partially ensured through the preauthorization of providers in the network. This brokerage role illustrates another way in which managed care may indirectly control the service delivery system by determining who will provide the services and at what predetermined cost.

Controlling Service Utilization

Costs are also contained by regulating the services that clients receive, especially what specific services will be provided and at what cost. The most common examples are DRGs. The DRG system, initiated by Medicare in an effort to control hospital costs, is a prospective payment system that determines in advance how much a physician or hospital will be reimbursed for all necessary procedures used for different diagnoses. Based on more than 460 diagnostic groups, patient demographics, and complicating factors, a specific amount of money is paid to the provider independent of what services are provided (for example, $10,500 for a hip replacement, as mentioned earlier; Anders, 1996). Prospective payment systems sharply contrast with the retrospective payment for all services provided, and they shift the risk of providing superfluous services to the provider. Psychiatric diagnoses and psychiatric wards in general hospitals were excluded from the DRG prospective payment system; however, they were not exempt from federal efforts to control costs (Bittker, 1992).

Utilization Reviews

Probably the most common procedures for controlling services, and therefore controlling costs, are found in utilization reviews (Corcoran & Vandiver, 1996; J. A. Jackson, 1987). Utilization reviews are designed to determine the medical necessity for treatment and whether the services are covered under the managed care contract. The determination of treatment necessity is an assessment commonly used by both public community mental health networks and private insurers;

among commonly denied services are, for example, those provided by marriage and family therapists (Ridgewood Finance Institute, 1995). Utilization reviews also monitor the course of treatment, including the ongoing need for additional services, a function similar to that provided by case management. Finally, utilization reviews evaluate outcomes of services; in fact, the original utilization review procedure may be traced to retrospective utilization reviews in which payment was denied or reduced for outcomes that were ineffective or less than expected. Utilization reviews include prospective utilization reviews, concurrent utilization reviews, and retrospective utilization reviews (Corcoran & Vandiver, 1996).

Prospective utilization reviews. A familiar example of a prospective utilization review is the second-opinion mandate, in which a corroborating opinion that treatment is indeed necessary is required before authorizing payment for services. Although it may sound like semantics, prospective utilization reviews only authorize the payment for services based on treatment necessity. Actual authorization of the need for services is within the purview of the provider and is probably tantamount to practicing medicine or clinical mental health treatment without a license (*Wickline v. California,* 1986). It is important to note that the provider of the second opinion does not actually work for the client, unless the assessment would reasonably lead to treatment. In fact, the provider of the second opinion is an agent of the managed care organization and not necessarily of the potential client; thus, the legal duty of this provider is to the cost-conscious managed care company. A second-opinion mandate is most often required in cases necessitating hospitalization for both health and mental health patients alike.

As a cost containment procedure, second-opinion mandates are a risky business for a managed care organization. If the second opinion supports the assessment by the original provider, then the cost of the second opinion is not only needless, it is also wasteful. In such circumstances future savings must then offset the cost of the superfluous second opinion. Over time the financial risk increases. As managed care changes, it is likely that second-opinion mandates as a means of controlling the costs of services will be used more cost-effectively. The need for a second opinion will probably be waived for preferred providers or others providers with proven track records.

Prospective utilization reviews may also assess and determine the actual services that are to be provided before those services are implemented. The apparent need to control the type of services used resulted from studies showing relatively equal outcomes regardless of whether the interventions used were short term or long term (Lambert & Bergin, 1994), even though clinicians continue to prefer to rely on long-term, insight-oriented psychotherapy (Rabinowitz & Lufkoff, 1995). Consequently, for pecuniary reasons managed care sought to authorize short-term treatment as a preferred modality, especially when balanced against the minimal added benefit of long-term interventions. Needless to say, the goal is for the managed care organization to approve the most effective health and mental health procedures at the lowest cost. The intent is to ensure that important aspects of sound practice are up to date and potentially effective when implemented completely and in accordance with professional standards. To clarify, this preauthorization does not approve what might work for a given individual case, but what seems to work best for most cases or the typical case.

The preauthorization of services is seen by many as interference with the client's autonomy and the professional's clinical judgment, topics discussed later in this entry. It is also a matter of sound social work practice, which defines the treatment as a logical consequence of the presenting problem and then implements a planned and systematic goal-directed intervention, including components that are identifiable, replicable, and subject to evaluation. In some respects prospective utilization reviews fulfill both the cost-containment and quality assurance goals of managed care. Quality is ensured by assessing what is and is not more likely to be effective treatment and increasing the likelihood that these preferred practices are implemented in a systematic and effective manner.

Concurrent utilization reviews. Concurrent utilization reviews are often used in conjunction with prospective utilization reviews. This is especially true for high-cost clients, such as those with severe and persistent mental illness or chronic health conditions. Costs are potentially contained by monitoring the ongoing use of services and authorizing continuous use only if medically necessary. A concurrent utilization review might also serve the purpose of a retrospective utilization review by determining whether services warrant reimbursement. Similarly, quality is ensured by changing the course of treatment or service delivery when sufficient progress is not observed.

Retrospective utilization reviews. The third type of utilization review is done after the completion of treatment. Retrospective utilization reviews were one of the original managed care procedures used in early cost-containment attempts by the federal government. In 1977 CHAMPUS contracted with the American Psychiatric Association to review cases in an effort to control costs and ensure that treatment was sufficiently effective. Much of the concern was similar to those concerns addressed by prospective and concurrent utilization reviews—namely determining the necessity for treatment and ensuring that the most effective treatment was implemented efficiently. The reviews, however, are performed "after the fact" and may include the inspection of a social worker's records. Because of its retrospective nature, much discontent emerged. Practitioners and clients alike found it unfair to assess cost and quality after services were received. Consequently, managed care organizations may use retrospective utilization reviews alone or in conjunction with prospective and concurrent reviews.

Managed Care and Medicare and Medicaid

Although much of the prospective payment system began with Medicare and DRGs, recent years have witnessed continued penetration by managed care (that is, HMOs) into both Medicare and Medicaid. This is changing quite rapidly. For example, as late as 1992, 22 of 56 programs in the individual states and territories had no HMO contracts for Medicaid beneficiaries, and only 200 HMOs had contracts with Medicaid programs (Harris, 1994). By 1994, 43 states and the District of Columbia had some Medicaid managed care initiative (Gold, Sparer, & Chu, 1996). By 1996, 32 percent of Medicaid beneficiaries were enrolled in some form of managed care (Rawland & Hanson, 1996). In some states the enrollment is much higher; in Oregon, for example, more than 80 percent of the Medicaid population is enrolled in prepaid health plans, including recipients of Aid to Families with Dependent Children, people eligible for

Supplemental Security Income, and citizens with low incomes eligible for the Oregon Health Plan (Kitzhaber, 1996).

As for Medicare, the proportion of beneficiaries enrolled in HMOs more than doubled between the late 1980s and the mid-1990s. However, this is only about 8 percent of Medicare beneficiaries (Welch, 1996). The Congressional Budget Office predicts an increase to about 17 percent of Medicare beneficiaries enrolled in some form of managed care by 2002 (Welch, 1996), even without efforts to reform the system.

The percentage of the Medicare market penetrated by HMOs varies tremendously across the county. In only 15 states are more than 3 percent of Medicare beneficiaries enrolled in HMOs, with California (26.3 percent), Arizona (26.0), and Oregon (20.6) having the highest percentages. The national average, greatly influenced by these extreme cases, is just over 6 percent of beneficiaries enrolled in HMOs by 1994; among people eligible for both Medicare and Medicaid, the percentage enrolled in HMOs was only 2 percent (Welch, 1996). Similarly, there is considerable variability in the percentage of the market share within different states. For example, the highest market share is found in California; in San Francisco the market share is only 21.6 percent, whereas in Riverside and San Bernardino, more than 47 percent of Medicare beneficiaries are enrolled in HMOs.

These figures illustrate three aspects of managed care and its role in the two largest federal health care programs. First, the rate of increase is staggering and is likely to continue to grow. Second, it is difficult to say exactly how managed care will affect social workers involved in Medicare and Medicaid, because there is such variability among states and even within a single state; what is true for Amarillo, Texas, may not be the case for Athens, Georgia. Finally, and most important, in light of the increased enrollment and anticipated savings, managed Medicare and Medicaid could provide additional resources, resources that will be available for redistribution to other needy members of society. If managed care affords any promise, it is not simply in its designed cost containment, but in the fact that resources will become available to redistribute to others in an effort to promote an agenda of social justice and access to resources, a role ideally designed for social work involvement.

Social Work Values and Managed Care

The changes in health and mental health service delivery brought about by managed care have resulted in several ethical challenges (Corcoran & Vandiver, 1996; Rodwin, 1995). This is especially so in light of the new NASW code of ethics, which was approved in August 1996 (NASW, 1996). These ethical challenges include potential conflicts between the gatekeeping role of some managed care organizations and client self-determination, informed consent, confidentiality, and conflicts of interest.

No longer does the client in need of services select a physician for scambosis or a social worker for treatment of depression. The selection of who will provide the services is no longer an autonomous decision between the client and providers; instead, it is likely to be determined by a utilization reviewer or a case manager performing triage. In many instances this fourth party is outside the social worker-client relationship. Consequently, there can be little doubt that some managed care procedures undermine the bioethic principle of autonomy, which in social work is called self-determination (NASW, 1996, Ethical Standard 1.02).

Client self-determination interfaces with Ethical Standard 1.03, informed consent, which is also contrary to some procedures of managed care. Informed consent requires that the client know in advance the clinical procedures, the risk of those procedures, and the available alternative procedures. Managed care may destroy informed consent by restricting the available procedures to a limited number. For example, a managed care company may determine the preferred practice and the preferred providers, with little consideration or disclosure of alternative procedures. The standard on informed consent does not speak to the potential requirement that the client consent to the disclosure of information to a managed care organization; this is addressed in another standard and may be implied in terms of obtaining consent before "permitting third party observation of clients." This is predicated, of course, on the idea that reviewing a client's records or utilization review forms are vicarious observations of the client. As such, Ethical Standard 1.03(f) would seen to require permission from clients before disclosing information about the client to a managed care organization.

However, loopholes exist with the ethical principle of privacy and confidentiality, in which confidential information may be disclosed when "regulations require disclosure without a client's consent" (Ethical Standard 1.07(c)), and the social worker should inform the client of the disclosure "to the extent possible" (Ethical Standard 1.07(d)). In the view of most managed care organizations, nonconsensual disclosure is just such a regulation. Eventually guidelines will be needed to decide what is meant by the phrase "to the extent possible" and whether this is determined by the social worker or the managed care organization. Moreover, almost every state has provisions for nonconsensual disclosure based on insurance law, which few clients would understand and fewer yet would approve (Winslade, 1982). Even though the code of ethics avers that only the minimal amount of information be disclosed, the conflict remains if the client has not given permission in advance of the disclosure.

The issues of self-determination and informed consent give rise to a particularly difficult value conflict with confidentiality. Confidentiality is the result of once-private information known only to the client having been disclosed to someone else—namely, the social worker. As such, the code's first approach is to protect such private information by establishing that social workers should respect the right to privacy and not solicit information unless it is essential to service delivery, research, or evaluation (Ethical Standard 1.07(a)). Furthermore, social workers are not to disclose this confidential information without the client's consent (Ethical Standard 1.07(b)). This requirement, however, is waived because of a legal duty to protect the client or others from foreseeable and imminent harm or as required by regulations; third-party payers—and, thus, managed care—would provide these regulations (Corcoran & Winslade, 1994; Winslade, 1982).

The provision of nonconsensual disclosure clearly conflicts with Section 1.07(h), which requires client authorization to reveal information to a third-party payer. Even though the code of ethics requires client consent for disclosure to third-party payers and managed care organizations, most state statutes do not (Winslade, 1982). Thus the value conflict: Social workers are held to a standard in the code not found in state law, and compliance with the code may result in the inability to secure authorization or payment for services addressing client needs. A client in need of

services that require preauthorization from a managed care organization may not receive them if disclosure is not authorized; this choice—authorizing the disclosure or having to find alternative means of funding the service—clearly is a coercive one. Such a choice breaches confidentiality and does not constitute truly informed consent.

Managed care, then, frustrates the public policy of protecting confidentiality so that those in need of services will be encouraged to seek them and presents an ethical dilemma for social workers. Although NASW may facilitate a resolution of this conflict by revising Ethical Standard 1.07(h), a more promising and legally binding approach is to link managed care with the confidential relationship between the client and social worker; this approach expands the burden of protecting confidential information to a managed care company (Corcoran & Vandiver, 1996; Corcoran & Winslade, 1994).

One of the most pressing value conflicts between social work and managed care concerns nondisclosure clauses frequently found in some managed care contracts. A nondisclosure clause essentially requires that the social worker not discuss certain aspects of managed care's influence on the social worker-client relationship. Nondisclosure clauses are also called "gag orders." From the view of managed care, these clauses are designed to prevent discontent among the enrolled members and are often defined as "antidisparagement clauses." The required silence, however, has been interpreted as restricting discussion of recommendations and interventions that are alternatives to those preauthorized by a managed care organization (Families USA Foundation, 1996).

An agreement with a managed care company to restrict the information disclosed to a client potentially conflicts with the client's right to self-determination, informed consent, and privacy and confidentiality. Nondisclosure clauses also conflict with the value of "integrity" and the ethical principle encouraging social workers to behave in a "trustworthy manner." Compliance with a nondisclosure clause clearly challenges the requirements of honesty and fiduciary duty to the client.

The new code of ethics attacks nondisclosure clauses head-on in its standard on informed consent (Ethical Standard 1.03(a)). This standard requires that social workers inform clients about "limits to service because of the requirements of a third-party payor" (NASW, 1996). The language of this standard is clear; it is a transgression of ethics for a member of NASW to agree to or comply with a nondisclosure clause.

The problems created by nondisclosure clauses have not gone unnoticed by others outside of social work. Such clauses may not necessarily be unlawful and in many respects are legally binding once agreed to (*Varol v. Blue Cross/Blue Shield,* 1987). As a consequence of the adverse effects of nondisclosure clauses, 17 states have introduced legislation prohibiting gag rules; 16 of these (California, Colorado, Georgia, Indiana, Maine, Maryland, Massachusetts, New Hampshire, New York, Oregon, Rhode Island, Tennessee, Texas, Virginia, Vermont, and Washington) enacted anti-gag order legislation between 1995 and the first half of 1996. These state statutes establish up to three restrictions:

1. They prohibit a nondisclosure clause pursuant to discussing treatment options.
2. They prohibit restricting advocacy on behalf of a client.
3. They prohibit outlawing restrictions on disclosures of financial arrangements and incentives.

Some states (for example, Massachusetts, New Hampshire, and Tennessee) have prohibitions only against gag orders for disclosing treatment options. Others (California and Texas) prohibit only gag orders against advocacy. Still others prohibit two or more of the above gag orders, and Washington and Virginia prohibit all three domains. The states with the best protection are Colorado, California, Maine, Maryland, New York, Virginia, and Washington; these states prohibit gag orders dealing with treatment alternatives and advocacy (Families USA Foundation, 1996).

Another ethical conflict faced by social workers in managed care settings concerns conflicts of interest. This is probably the most apparent, and most general, conflict between managed care and social work. A conflict of interest occurs between two legitimate and competing duties. In managed care this occurs between the duty to provide quality care (that is, the bioethical principle of beneficence) and the duty to contain costs with a managed care organization (a contractual duty) and not to waste limited societal resources (the bioethical principle of social justice). The social worker is an agent of the client but concomitantly is an agent of the managed care company and the provider of

scarce and valuable societal resources; in some respects the social worker is a double agent, although nondisclosure clauses many render him or her a "secret agent" as well. Sabin (1994) considered this a conflict with society in which scare and limited resources are bought and sold in a regulated marketplace. The dilemma is between the best interest of the client and the cost of that interest. As Sabin stated, in the United States, only the NASW code of ethics addresses this issue (Ethical Standard 6.01). Sabin, a psychiatrist, recommended that other professional organizations also attempt to balance the best interest of the client against the social justice issue of costs and distribution of services.

As advanced in the new code, conflicts of interest should be avoided when at all possible. In an era of managed care, this is increasingly difficult. Consequently, the guidance provided by the code suggests that reasonable steps be taken to resolve the conflict in a way that it is in the best interest of the client, and not necessarily in the pecuniary interest of the managed care company.

Value Compatibility

Needless to say, managed care is not completely at odds with social work values. In fact, the goal of cost containment runs parallel to social work's commitment to the social welfare of all people and social justice. The missing element, of course, is the redistribution of any resources that might be freed up as a result of managed care's effectiveness. When costs are contained, savings must be redistributed to those in need of other services and not necessarily to cooperative stockholders, executives, or benefits administrators.

Managed care also promotes the value of a commitment to competent social work practice through prospective utilization reviews, which are mandated for goal-directed clinical practice (Wells, 1994) and the selection of assessment tools to monitor and evaluate practice (Corcoran & Gingerich, 1994). These interventions are to be planned and implemented in a systematic manner that enhances the likelihood of successful outcomes. Practice guidelines and treatment protocols are increasingly becoming available from professional organizations (American Psychiatric Association, 1994) and managed care organizations (Giles, 1993). Sources are available for developing treatment protocols, including protocols for various mental health interventions for adults, children, and adolescents (Corcoran & Vandiver, 1996).

The reliance on goal-oriented interventions provides for an open-ended treatment model in which change is targeted to specific impairments over the life cycle (Austad & Hoyt, 1992). This contrasts sharply with more traditional, open-ended, insight-oriented interventions, which rely heavily on the therapeutic relationship and strive to resolve conflicts. In a managed mental health care setting, the emphasis of social work treatment is on performance and rehabilitation, and insight and resolution of intrapersonal conflict is left for outside supports.

Conclusion

The two purposes of managed care are to contain costs and ensure quality. It has been suggested in this entry that quality assurance has been overshadowed by cost containment. Many have argued that costs are contained only by reducing services (that is, by deciding whether or not a service will be provided or for how long and at what cost it is provided) (Woolsey, 1993). This is especially true when the actual costs of managed care are factored into the cost of service delivery; although estimates vary, the costs of managed care may make up as much as 22 percent of a health benefit budget (Wagner & Gartner, 1996). Consequently, any true cost containment must exceed the cost of the managed care program.

Finally, just as managed care came on the health and mental health care scenes with unpredicted swiftness, so, too, it is changing. Most expects agree that managed care will look quite different within the next few years. The merger-and-acquisition mentality of corporate America is leading to bigger firms buying smaller ones, and smaller firms are merging into more competitive ones. Similarly, providers are forming alliances among themselves and bypassing managed care organizations altogether by contracting directly with third-party payers. These efforts are often financially risky, may be economically ineffective, and may provide for even fewer resources for the promotion of health and well-being of individuals in society.

References

American Psychiatric Association. (1994). Practice guidelines for the treatment of patients with bipolar disorders. *American Journal of Psychiatry, 151*(Suppl.), 1-36.

Anders, G. (1996, October 3). Pricey operation: A plan to cut back on Medicare expenses goes awry; costs soar. *Wall Street Journal,* pp. A1, A6.

Austad, M. F., & Hoyt, C. S. (1992). The managed care movement and the future of psychotherapy. *Psychotherapy, 29,* 109-118.

Bittker, T. E. (1992). The emergence of prepaid psychiatry. In J. L. Feldman & R. J. Fitzpatrick (Eds.), *Managed mental health care: Administrative and clinical issues* (pp. 3-10). Washington, DC: American Psychiatric Press.

Corcoran, K., & Gingerich, W. (1994). Practice evaluation in the context of managed care: Case recording methods for quality assurance review. *Research on Social Work Practice, 4,* 326-337.

Corcoran, K., & Vandiver, V. (1996). *Maneuvering the maze of managed care: Skills for mental health practitioners.* New York: Free Press.

Corcoran, K., & Winslade, W. J. (1994). Eavesdropping on the 50-minute hour: Confidentiality and managed mental health care. *Behavioral Sciences and the Law, 12,* 351-365.

Cutler, D. (1992). A historical overview of community mental health centers in the United States. In S. Cooper & T. Lantner (Eds.), *Innovations in community mental health* (pp. 1-22). Miami: Professional Resource Press.

Edinburg, G. M., & Cottler, J. M. (1995). Managed care. In R. L. Edwards (Ed.-in-Chief), *Encyclopedia of social work* (19th ed., Vol. 2, pp. 1635-1642). Washington, DC: NASW Press.

Eisenberg, J. M., Schwartz, J. S., McCaslin, F. C., Kaufman, R., Glick, H., & Kroch, E. (1989). Substituting diagnostic services: New tests only partially replace older ones. *JAMA, 262,* 1196-1200.

Families USA Foundation. (1996). *HMO consumers at risk: States to the rescue.* Washington, DC: Author.

Giles, T. R. (1993). *Managed mental health care: A guide for practitioners, and hospital administrators.* Needham Heights, MA: Allyn & Bacon.

Gold, M., Sparer, M., & Chu, K. (1996). Medicaid managed care: Lessons from five states. *Health Affairs, 15,* 153-165.

Harris, J. S. (1994). *Strategic health management: A guide for employers, employees, and policy makers.* San Francisco: Jossey-Bass.

HMO Act of 1973. P.L. 93-222.

Jackson, J. A. (1987). Clinical social work and peer review: A professional leap ahead. *Social Work, 32,* 213-220.

Jackson, V. H. (Ed.). (1995). *Managed care resource guide for social workers in agency settings.* Washington, DC: NASW Press.

Jackson, V. H. (Ed.). (1996). *Managed care resource guide for social workers in private practice.* Washington, DC: NASW Press.

Kitzhaber, J. A. (1996). The governor of Oregon on Medicaid managed care. *Health Affairs, 15,* 107-109.

Lambert, M. J., & Bergin, A. E. (1994). The effectiveness of psychotherapy. In A. E. Bergin & S. L. Garfield (Eds.), *Handbook of psychotherapy and behavior change* (4th ed., pp. 143-189). New York: John Wiley & Sons.

National Association of Social Workers. (1996). *Code of ethics.* Washington, DC: NASW Press.

Newborn's and Mother's Health Protection Act of 1996, P.L. 104-204, 42 U.S.C.S. §201.

Rabinowitz, J., & Lufkoff, I. (1995). Clinical decision making of short- versus long-term treatment. *Research on Social Work Practice, 5,* 62-79.

Rawland, D., & Hanson, K. (1996). Medicaid: Moving to managed care. *Health Affairs, 15,* 150-152.

Resnick, R. J., & DeLeon, P. H. (1995). The future of health care reform: Implications for 1994 elections. *Professional Psychology: Research and Practice, 26,* 3-4.

Ridgewood Finance Institute. (1995). Survey report. *Psychotherapy Finances, 21,* 1-8.

Rodwin, M. C. (1995). Conflicts in managed care. *New England Journal of Medicine, 332,* 604-607.

Sabin, J. E. (1994). Care about patients and caring about money: The American Psychiatric Association Code of Ethics meets managed care. *Behavioral Sciences and the Law, 12,* 317-330.

Varol v. Blue Cross/Blue Shield, 708 F. Supp. 826 (1987).

Wagner, J., & Gartner, C. G. (1996). Issues in managed care: Highlights of the 1995 Institute on Psychiatric Services. *Psychiatric Services, 47,* 15-20.

Welch, W. P. (1996). Growth in HMO share of the Medicare market, 1989-1994. *Health Affairs, 15,* 201-214.

Wells, R. A. (1994). *Planned short-term treatment.* New York: Free Press.

Wickline v. California, 228 Cal. 661 (1986).

Winslade, W. J. (1982). Confidentiality and medical records. *Journal of Legal Medicine, 3,* 497-525.

Woolsey, S. L. (1993). Managed care and mental health: The silencing of a profession. *International Journal of Eating Disorders, 14,* 387-401.

Kevin Corcoran, PhD, JD, is professor, Graduate School of Social Work, Portland State University, P.O. Box 751, Portland, OR 97201-0751.

For further information see

Aging Overview; Federal Social Legislation from 1961 to 1994; **Federal Social Legislation from 1994 to 1997;** Health Care: Direct Practice; Health Care: Financing; **Health Care: Policy Development;** Health Care: Reform Initiatives; **Health Care Practice Overview;** Health Services Systems Policy; Hospital Social Work; Income Security Overview; Long-Term Care; Managed Care Overview; **Managed Care: A Review of Recent Research;** Mental Health Overview; Primary Health Care; Primary Prevention Overview; Public Health Services; Social Security; Social Welfare Expenditures: Public; Social Work Profession Overview; Women and Health Care.

Key Words

health care reform	mental health
managed care	financing reform

Managed Care: A Review of Recent Research
Roger A. Lohmann

Managed care is a generic label for a broad and constantly changing mix of health insurance, assistance, and payment programs that seek to retain quality and access while controlling the cost of physical and mental health services. One essential feature of virtually all managed care regimens is protection of reimbursement decisions from the economic incentives affecting both patient and care provider. Under managed care, such decisions are routinely placed in the hands of neutral third parties with a presumed incentive for enhancing cost-effective delivery of services. Words such as "capitation," "co-insurance" and "co-payment," "deductibles," "fee-for-service," "formularies," "HMO," "PPO," "risk contracts," and "utilization review" are increasingly part of the social work vocabulary. Cynics may be forgiven for mistaking managed care for bureaucratic medicine or for suspecting that the central dynamic of managed care involves a massive realignment of power in the health industry away from medical and other professional care providers and toward legal and financial professionals.

To date, the movement toward managed care in the public mental health system has surpassed efforts to develop a systematic literature concerning its theory, practice, and outcome (Cuffel, Snowden, Masland, & Piccagli, 1996). The remainder of this article is concerned with a selective review of the recent literature on managed care as it affects social work and related professional services in health and mental health. Coverage is by no means exhaustive or comprehensive. (Additional articles, letters to the editor, and editorial comments are listed in the supplementary bibliography.) Discussion is not limited to articles appearing in social work publications but includes articles throughout the literature for the health care industry and other professions.

The present implications of managed care for social work practice can be distinguished programmatically. Health care social workers, like all other professionals in health and mental health services, have already seen the nature of professional decision making transformed. Decreased professional autonomy and the redefinition of service delivery as a commercial transaction are two of the central dynamics of that transformation. For social workers practicing in all other venues, managed care may also soon be synonymous with public support (Mordock, 1996).

MANAGED CARE TRANSFORMS PRACTICE

The introduction of managed care fundamentally transformed the traditional "agency" relationships on which modern social work was built. In the agency model, social workers provided service free from the practical burdens of finance, which were isolated as separate administrative responsibilities. Administrators in this model served as intermediaries who explained the actions of social workers to funding agencies and negotiated continued support for services, usually in the forms of grants or open-ended "purchase-of-service" contracts.

Managed care introduced an utterly new division of labor in which, like it or not, financial management sophistication is an assumed characteristic of social worker and client alike. Such a fundamental transformation has already been under way for some time and will obviously take longer to complete. Again, cynics may be forgiven for suggesting that managed care will ultimately mean the complete demise of traditionally recognizable forms of social

work practice. Indeed, long-term therapy, most forms of group work, and virtually all types of community practice have already proved equally difficult to justify under managed care rubrics and have been seriously curtailed.

The stakes in the managed care arena are tremendous. In 1992 the United States spent an estimated $820 billion on health care, while as many as 15 percent of the U.S. population, approximately 43 million people, were uninsured. As costs continue to rise, the number of people able to afford even basic health service continues to decline, while the indirect costs of health care bureaucracies continue to rise (French, Dunlap, Galinis, Rachal, & Zarkin, 1996; Geller, 1996). A key issue in the health reform debate is whether insurance coverage to the uninsured should be voluntary or mandatory (Madden et al., 1995).

Lambrew, Defriese, Carey, Ricketts, and Biddle (1996) claimed, based on analysis of more than 30,000 cases, that policies that promote the physician–patient relationship will increase access to health care, although the gains may be negligible for individuals who use mainstream primary care sites (physician's offices, clinics, or health maintenance organizations [HMOs]) versus sites such as walk-in clinics or emergency departments. Because many traditional social work clients do precisely that, it is quite plausible that negligible gains from managed care for social work clients can be anticipated.

"Managed care" is the current label in health and mental health for an interrelated set of contractual, accounting, and management assumptions and expectations for practitioners ("providers") and clients ("consumers"). Managed care plans and HMOs in particular rely on a variety of financial incentive systems to induce providers to control health care expenditures (Kwon, 1996). However, concern is evident in many parts of the current health care delivery system as to whether cost savings attributed to managed care are real and whether the unintended effects on health care may be adverse (Kovner, 1996). Despite these concerns, nearly every state currently encourages or requires its Medicaid beneficiaries to enroll in managed care (Sparer, 1996).

At least part of the scramble for the adoption of managed care plans may be explained by the shield established by the federal Employee Retirement Income Security Act (ERISA), which protects managed care organizations from liability when they are part of an employee group health plan governed by ERISA. Unlike patients with other types of insurance, patients in ERISA health plans do not have a malpractice remedy for a managed care organization's negligence (Mariner, 1996).

At any rate, managed care is changing the health care system in the United States in fundamental ways (Landry & Knox, 1996). It has the potential to completely refashion the relationship between social workers and their clients, as well as social workers' relations to agencies and communities, by reshaping the traditional "powers of the purse." Kwon (1996) claimed, for example, in an analysis based on the theory of incentive contracts, that the group incentive scheme on which HMOs are based provides an essential control over the perverse incentives associated with excessive referrals by primary care physicians.

The effects are not just limited to social work. The managed care model is having a similar impact across the entire range of health and mental health professions (Brayman, 1996; Broskowski & Eaddy, 1994; Elias & Navon, 1996). Furthermore, the effects may not be limited to health and mental health. For example, Mordock (1996) argued that success-ful operation of agencies serving children and families will increasingly depend on the ability of those agencies to market their services in a managed care environment.

The traditional basis on which social work services were delivered was an uneasy blend of "social liberalism," built up over decades of experience and practice. (For an attempt to bring financial and programmatic concerns together, see chapter 1 of Lohmann, 1980.) This practice model recognized as real the rights of agencies and individuals but also such social collectivities as families, neighborhoods, agencies, and communities. "Systems theory" in social work has been an ongoing effort to regularize and integrate the diverse and somewhat inconsistent understandings of these phenomena into something resembling a unified whole.

With financial management, these concerns have always been partial, at best. Social work systems approaches since the 1970s assumed (although seldom explicitly discussed) the role of financial management as a necessary, if uninteresting, technical support service far removed from the central relation between worker and client. There is no attempt in the DSM-IV, for example, to link cost considerations to any substantial aspect of client diagnosis and assessment. Managed care is likely to change that by bringing considerations of cost directly into the worker–client relationship and by strengthening the case for the private or independent practice of social work.

Independent practice association (IPA) model HMOs represent one of the fastest growing segments of managed care in the United States (Johnstone, 1995). Wolf and Gorman (1996) and Zarabozo, Taylor, and Hicks (1996) discussed some of the "cutting edge" financial management practices emerg-ing in the managed care environment.

Thus, for social workers in health and mental health care settings, the rise of managed care represents the complete (and seemingly sudden) triumph of financial management concerns over virtually all other professional considerations. The seeming suddenness is more apparent than real, however, because managed care represents the culmination (so far) of nearly three decades of gradually accelerating efforts to transform health care delivery in the United States and introduce effective cost controls.

Managed health and mental health care represents a highly individualistic and laissez-faire "reform strategy" embraced by lawyers, cost accountants, politicians, and insurance companies. It is being imposed on the interdisci-plinary, multiprofessional community of health and mental health providers, which includes social workers, physicians, psychiatrists, nurses, and others. The managed care practice model is at the opposite end of the communitarian spectrum from the systems approaches most familiar in social work: It recognizes only individuals (providers and consumers) and the "fictive individuals" of contract law (corporations and partnerships) that employ them.

Managed care is zealously liberal (in the original meaning of that word) in that it explicitly allows no place for social systems or other "social fictions," whether families, groups, agencies, neighborhoods, or communi-ties. Its apparent sole purpose is to improve the aggregate "bottom line" cost of public health and mental health care in the United States, regardless of the social cost in lives, "inconvenience," pain and suffering, or any other nonfiscal consideration. Managed care is the latest in a growing list of signs that, in the long-term struggle between profession and bureaucracy noted decades ago in the social work literature, the latter is emerging supreme

(Vinter, 1959). The apparent success of managed care is premised directly on practice models in which the activities of psychotherapists are being micromanaged by insurance companies (Chipman, 1995).

Schlesinger, Dorwart, and Epstein (1996) concluded that the increasing involvement of insurers and hospitals in monitoring patient care is encroaching on psychiatrists' autonomy in making clinical decisions. The same might be (and undoubtedly will be) said for social workers. In a survey of 2,500 psychiatrists, these authors found that more than three-fourths of those surveyed reported pressure from insurers for early discharge. Nearly two-thirds of respondents said hospitals limited length of stay; and about half said they had been discouraged from admitting severely ill patients, the uninsured, or Medicaid recipients. These basic findings square with the anecdotal experiences of many social workers.

This is occurring on top of the "procedural revolution" in policy (Sandel, 1996), in which substantial degrees of professional autonomy have already been yielded to legal "advisers." It is possible to "paper over," obfuscate, and qualify this fundamental, unpleasant truth in a variety of ways, but it would be nearly impossible at present to refute it directly.

SOCIAL WORK RESEARCH IS LIMITED

The managed care revolution is still so new and unfolding so swiftly that little research regarding its impact on social services is currently available. Social work contributions to the managed care discussion have been relatively few in number and on relatively tangential issues (Alperin, 1994; Corcoran & Gingerich, 1994; Kanter, 1996; Munson, 1996; Weimer, 1996). More to the main point are works by F. Brown (1994), Cornelius (1994), Elias and Navon (1996), Geller (1996), Katz (1994), and Trugerman (1996). As of this writing, there are no empirical studies of managed care's impact or its implications in the social work literature.

UNTESTED MANAGED CARE MODEL RAISES CONCERNS

It is both interesting and disturbing to note that despite managed care's revolutionary impact, the assumptions underlying the managed care model are largely untested and perhaps not yet even standardized. In this it bears a certain uncanny resemblance to "supply-side" ("voodoo") economics, which was similarly untested when undertaken by the Reagan administration and subsequently shown to be without substance.

There is, however, a growing body of literature expressing concerns of various types (Morreim, 1995a, 1995b; Pipal, 1995; Rutman, 1995; Sabin, 1994a, 1994b, 1994c, 1995a, 1995b, 1996). Boyle and Callahan (1995) pointed to allegations that managed care may adversely affect quality of care, access to care, provider–patient relationships, and informed patient choice. Watanabe (1996) argued that managed care could also undermine the research enterprises that undergird professional practice. Academic scientists are worried that managed care organizations' refusal to pay for ancillary tests and procedures performed in the course of clinical trials will lead to decreased patient participation in these studies. Butcher and Rouse (1996) raised similar concerns about the future of research in clinical psychology. Any concerns one might have for basic biomedical research are likely to hold as well for research in social work, where research support is already even more tentative and elusive.

Sumerall, Oehlert, and Trent (1995) concluded that reorganizations of the type associated with managed care have the potential to adversely affect psychological practices in organizations. They recommended that psychologists—and the advice seems to extend to social workers and other professionals as well—take a proactive stance in the rapidly changing health care landscape: Research regarding empirically validated treatments and effects of psychological interventions on overall health care costs should be disseminated to health care administrators and other decision makers.

Not all of the evidence about managed care is negative by any means. Callahan, Shepard, Beinecke, Larson, and Cavanaugh (1995) found, in a study of the Massachusetts Medicaid program for mental health services, that over a one-year period, expenditures were reduced by 22 percent, without any overall reduction in access or relative quality, primarily because of reduced lengths of stay, lower prices, and fewer inpatient admissions. Summerfelt, Foster, and Saunders (1996) found that a managed care demonstration served more than three times as many children as the traditional (Civilian Health and Medical Program of the Uniformed Services, CHAMPUS) comparison service. In addition to serving more children, the managed care project also provided more and different types of services to each child treated. Finally, the demonstration delivered services in a more timely fashion and made a seemingly greater effort to match children's and families' needs with services.

Despite a growing body of evidence supporting its effectiveness, managed care has raised a large number of value questions and ethical concerns (Boyle & Callahan, 1995; G.S.J. Brown & Kornmayer, 1996; Bursztajn & Brodsky, 1994; Christensen, 1995; Emanuel, 1995; Gosfield, 1995; Howe, 1995; Johnson, 1995; Mariner, 1995; Miles & Koepp, 1995; Morreim, 1995a; Munson, 1996; Orentlicher, 1995; Pellegrino, 1995; Petrila, 1995; Pipal, 1995; Plows, 1995; Rimler & Morrison, 1993; Sabin, 1994b; Sulmasy, 1995; Surles, 1995; Zolothdorfman & Rubin, 1995). In one of the most interesting of these articles, Petrila (1995) laid out six strategies for dealing with the dilemma posed by insurers' unwillingness to pay for civil commitment services, which providers are legally obligated to provide. There are also at least a few pioneering studies pointing to the financial and professional impact of the managed care model (Rissmiller, Steer, Ranieri, Rissmiller, & Hogate 1994; Robinson, 1993).

There is also little current understanding of how managed care strategies affect hospital inpatient psychiatric care for mentally ill patients. There is a need for careful study of the effects of managed care on outcomes and quality of psychiatric care (Wickizer, Lessler, & Travis, 1996).

Trugerman (1996) reminded readers that not all managed care systems are identical. Sparer (1996) detected great variation among state managed care plans in mental health. Noting the untested nature of managed care, Wickizer and Feldstein (1995) set out to test the model. They analyzed the competitive effects of HMOs on the growth of fee-for-service indemnity insurance premiums over the period from 1985 through 1992, using premium data on 95 groups that had policies with a single, large, private insurance carrier. Their conclusion was that "competitive strategies, relying on managed care, have *significant potential* to reduce health insurance premium growth rates, thereby resulting in substantial cost savings over time" (italics added) (p. 251).

M. Brown (1996) argued that these relentless pressures to build regional systems of health services have transformed the health care industry from a charitable, community orientation to one of business, market shares,

and profits. Weil (1995) explored the possibility that the geographically linked health networks of integrated HMOs that are currently gaining tremendous market penetration and fiscal power, together with projected cutbacks in Medicare and Medicaid reimbursement, could conceivably set the stage for the kind of financial machinations that led to the savings and loan debacle in the late 1980s.

SHOULD WE EXPECT REAL SAVINGS IN THE COST OF CARE?

One of the real ironies is that, for all the emphasis on cost reduction, several early studies have found that quality can be maintained under managed care, but costs may not be reduced. The most massive evaluative effort of managed care to date, according to its investigators, is the Fort Bragg Managed Care Experiment, a five-year, $80 million effort to evaluate the cost-effectiveness of a full continuum of mental health services for children and adolescents (Bickman, 1996a; Breda, 1996; Lambert & Guthrie, 1996). In a study of cost-effectiveness, Bickman, Summerfelt, and Bryant (1996) also sought to evaluate two aspects of the quality of services provided: intake assessment and case management. They concluded that these two components of care were implemented with sufficient quality to have the theoretically predicted effects on mental health. The bottom line on the Fort Bragg experiment was that the continuum of care provided a high-quality system of care but was more expensive and produced no better clinical outcomes than traditional services (Bickman, 1996b).

In a review of the Massachusetts Mental Health/Substance Abuse Program from the viewpoints of the providers, Beinecke, Callahan, Shepard, Cavanaugh, and Larson (1996) found that even though the severity of illness of most clients in the program was greater than that before managed care, most providers believed that the quality of care and access to services for these clients was the same or better than before managed care. The providers interviewed were also concerned because savings in a managed care program occur primarily during its initial stages and because future reductions have greater potential for negative effects on clients and providers.

A randomized trial of the Florida Program for Prepaid Managed Care established that the HMO was able to limit members' utilization. Thus, cost savings were in the form of lower likelihood of using care. The amount of services received, once care was initiated, was the same in both fee-for-service Medicaid and HMOs (Buchanan, Leibowitz, & Keesey, 1996).

Given the generally poor track record of cost monitoring in mental health and other social services, it may be well to keep in mind that other strategies may also prove effective. Thus, in a comparative cost-effectiveness study, Jerrell (1995) found that a Program of Assertive Community Treatment (PACT) model for delivering care to chronically mentally ill patients was not significantly more expensive in terms of the costs of providing supportive services than the clinical team approach and the intensive broker model of care.

METHODOLOGY

A small portion of the managed care literature speaks directly to issues of research and financial analysis methodology. For example, Fedorowicz and Kim (1995) examined the impact of data analysis as a critical tool for tracking costs, allowing managers to set priorities and develop strategies to manage and contain costs. Boles and Fleming (1996) addressed the issue of break-even analysis as applied to managed care under capitation by expanding the traditional two-dimensional break-even analysis into a three-dimensional graphic analysis using cost, enroll-ment, and utilization.

G.S.J. Brown and Kornmayer (1996) reported on the development of computerized decision support technologies for the manage-ment of patient care. They told of being in the midst of implementing a computerized deci-sion support system for care management in their managed care organization. Glazer and Gray (1996) reported on the psychometric properties (reliability and validity) of a decision support scale designed to evaluate the level of care needed for patients requiring psychiatric treatment in an HMO setting.

CONCLUSION

Regardless of the cases that can be made for and against the managed care model, three things are clear:

1. Managed care has arrived. Although the buzzwords may shift in the next few years, the age of brokered decision making in care provision has arrived and is not likely to leave soon.
2. Managed care is and will continue to trans-form the practice of social work, particularly by bringing the formerly specialized cost

considerations of financial management directly into the worker–client transaction.
3. The managed care model, with its distinctive external patterns of accountability, raises serious questions about the continuing viability of the "social agency" model of practice to which social work has been committed for most of this century.

REFERENCES

Alperin, R. M. (1994). Managed care versus psycho-analytic psychotherapy—Conflicting ideologies. *Clinical Social Work Journal, 22,* 137–148.

Beinecke, R. H., Callahan, J. J., Shepard, D. S., Cavanaugh, D. A., & Larson, M. J. (1996). The Massachusetts mental health/substance abuse managed care program: The providers' view. *Administration and Policy in Mental Health, 23,* 379–391.

Bickman, L. (1996a). The evaluation of a children's mental health managed care demonstration. *Journal of Mental Health Administration, 23,* 7–15.

Bickman, L. (1996b). Implications of a children's mental health managed care demonstration evaluation. *Journal of Mental Health Administration, 23,* 107–117.

Bickman, L., Summerfelt, W. T., & Bryant, D. (1996). The quality of services in a children's mental health managed care demonstration. *Journal of Mental Health Administration, 23,* 30–39.

Boles, K. E., & Fleming, S. T. (1996). Break even under capitation: Pure and simple? *Health Care Manage-ment Review, 21,* 38–47.

Boyle, P. J., & Callahan, D. (1995). Managed care in mental health: The ethical issues. *Health Affairs, 14,* 7–22.

Brayman, S. J. (1996). Managing the occupational environment of managed care. *American Journal of Occupational Therapy, 50,* 442–446.

Breda, C. S. (1996). Methodological issues in evaluating mental health outcomes of a children's mental health managed care demonstration. *Journal of Mental Health Administration, 23,* 40–50.

Broskowski, A., & Eaddy, M. (1994). Community mental health centers in a managed care environ-ment. *Administration and Policy in Mental Health, 21,* 335–352.

Brown, F. (1994). Resisting the pull of the health insurance tar-baby—An organizational model for surviving managed care. *Clinical Social Work Journal, 22,* 59–71.

Brown, G. S. J., & Kornmayer, K. (1996). Expert systems restructure managed care practice: Implementation and ethics. *Behavioral Healthcare Tomorrow, 5*(1), 31–34.

Brown, M. (1996). Mergers, networking, and vertical integration: Managed care and investor-owned hospitals. *Health Care Management Review, 21,* 29–37.

Buchanan, J. L., Leibowitz, A., & Keesey, J. (1996). Medicaid health maintenance organizations: Can they reduce program spending? *Medical Care, 34,* 249–263.

Bursztajn, H. J., & Brodsky, A. (1994). Authenticity and autonomy in the managed-care era—Forensic psychiatric perspectives. *Journal of Clinical Ethics, 5,* 237–242.

Butcher, J. N., & Rouse, S. V. (1996). Personality: Individual differences and clinical assessment. *Annual Review of Psychology, 47,* 87–111.

Callahan, J. J., Shepard, D. S., Beinecke, R. H., Larson, M. J., & Cavanaugh, D. (1995). Mental health/ substance abuse treatment in managed care: The Massachusetts Medicaid experience. *Health Affairs, 14,* 173–184.

Chipman, A. (1995). Meeting managed care: An identity and value crisis for therapists. *American Journal of Psychotherapy, 49,* 558–567.

Christensen, K. T. (1995). Ethically important distinctions among managed care organizations. *Journal of Law, Medicine & Ethics, 23,* 223–229.

Corcoran, K., & Gingerich, W. J. (1994). Practice evaluation in the context of managed care—Case-recording methods for quality assurance reviews. *Research on Social Work Practice, 4,* 326–337.

Cornelius, D. S. (1994). Managed care and social work—Constructing a context and a response. *Social Work in Health Care, 20,* 47–63.

Cuffel, B. J., Snowden, L., Masland, M., & Piccagli, G. (1996). Managed care in the public mental health system. *Community Mental Health Journal, 32,* 109–124.

Elias, E., & Navon, M. (1996). Implementing managed care in a state mental health authority: Implications for organizational change. *Smith College Studies in Social Work, 66,* 269–292.

Emanuel, E. J. (1995). Medical ethics in the era of managed care: The need for institutional structures instead of principles for individual cases. *Journal of Clinical Ethics, 6,* 335–338.

Fedorowicz, J., & Kim, C. (1995). Information technology: Managed care's critical tool. *International Journal of Technology Management, 1* (Special Issue), 175–185.

French, M. T., Dunlap, L. J., Galinis, D. N., Rachal, J. V., & Zarkin, G. A. (1996). Health care reforms and managed care for substance abuse services: Findings from eleven case studies. *Journal of Public Health Policy, 17,* 181–203.

Geller, J. L. (1996). Mental health services of the future: Managed care, unmanaged care, mismanaged care.

Smith College Studies in Social Work, 66, 223–239.

Glazer, W. M., & Gray, G. V. (1996). Psychometric properties of a decision-support tool for the era of managed care. *Journal of Mental Health Administration, 23,* 226–233.

Gosfield, A. G. (1995). The legal subtext of the managed care environment: A practitioner's perspective. *Journal of Law, Medicine & Ethics, 23,* 230–235.

Howe, E. G. (1995). Managed care: "New moves," moral uncertainty, and a radical attitude. *Journal of Clinical Ethics, 6,* 290–305.

Jerrell, J. M. (1995). Toward managed care for persons with severe mental illness: Implications from a cost-effectiveness study. *Health Affairs, 14,* 197–207.

Johnson, S. H. (1995). Managed care as regulation: Functional ethics for a regulated environment. *Journal of Law, Medicine & Ethics, 23,* 266–272.

Johnstone, P. M. (1995). A glimpse of an IPA as a living system. *Behavioral Science, 40,* 304–313.

Kanter, J. (1996). Depression, diabetes and despair: Clinical case management in a managed care context. *Smith College Studies in Social Work, 66,* 358–369.

Katz, A. H. (1994). [Review of the book *Managing managed care—A mental health practitioner's survival guide*]. *Health & Social Work, 19,* 78–79.

Kovner, A. R. (1996). Assessing Medicaid managed care in eastern states. *Journal of Policy Analysis and Management, 15,* 276–284.

Kwon, S. (1996). Structure of financial incentive systems for providers in managed care plans. *Medical Care Research and Review, 53*(2), 149–161.

Lambert, E. W., & Guthrie, P. R. (1996). Clinical outcomes of a children's mental health managed care demonstration. *Journal of Mental Health Administration, 23,* 51–68.

Lambrew, J. M., Defriese, G. H., Carey, T. S., Ricketts, T. C., & Biddle, A. K. (1996). The effects of having a regular doctor on access to primary care. *Medical Care, 34,* 138–151.

Landry, C., & Knox, J. (1996). Managed care fundamentals: Implications for health care organizations and health care professionals. *American Journal of Occupational Therapy, 50,* 413–416.

Lohmann, R. A. (1980). *Breaking even: Financial management in human services.* Philadelphia: Temple University Press.

Madden, C. W., Cheadle, A., Diehr, P., Martin, D. L., Patrick, D. L., & Skillman, S. M. (1995). Voluntary public health insurance for low-income families: The decision to enroll. *Journal of Health Politics, Policy and Law, 20,* 955–972.

Mariner, W. K. (1995). Business vs. medical ethics: Conflicting standards for managed care. *Journal of Law, Medicine & Ethics, 23,* 236–246.

Mariner, W. K. (1996). Liability for managed care decisions: The Employee Retirement Income Security Act (ERISA) and the uneven playing field. *American Journal of Public Health, 86,* 863–869.

Miles, S. H., & Koepp, R. (1995). Ethical issues in managed care—Comment. *Journal of Clinical Ethics, 6,* 306–311.

Mordock, J. B. (1996, May). The road to survival revisited: Organizational adaptation to the managed care environment. *Child Welfare, 75,* 195–218.

Morreim, E. H. (1995a). Lifestyles of the risky and infamous—From managed care to managed lives. *Hastings Center Report, 25*(6), 5–12.

Morreim, E. H. (1995b). Moral justice and legal justice in managed care: The ascent of contributive justice. *Journal of Law, Medicine & Ethics, 23,* 247–265.

Munson, C. E. (1996). Autonomy and managed care in critical social work practice. *Smith College Studies in Social Work, 66,* 241–260.

Orentlicher, D. (1995). Physician advocacy for patients under managed care. *Journal of Clinical Ethics, 6,* 333–334.

Pellegrino, E. D. (1995). Interests, obligations, and justice: Some notes toward an ethic of managed care. *Journal of Clinical Ethics, 6,* 312–317.

Petrila, J. (1995). Who will pay for involuntary civil commitment under capitated managed care? An emerging dilemma. *Psychiatric Services, 46,* 1045–1048.

Pipal, J. E. (1995). Managed care: Is it the corpse in the living room? An exposé. *Psychotherapy, 32,* 323–332.

Plows, C. W. (1995). Ethical issues in managed care—Response. *Journal of Clinical Ethics, 6,* 318–319.

Rimler, G. W., & Morrison, R. D. (1993). The ethical impacts of managed care. *Journal of Business Ethics, 12,* 493–501.

Rissmiller, D. J., Steer, R., Ranieri, W. F., Rissmiller, F., & Hogate, P. (1994). Factors complicating cost containment in the treatment of suicidal patients. *Hospital and Community Psychiatry, 45,* 782–788.

Robinson, J. C. (1993). Payment mechanisms, nonprice incentives, and organizational innovation in health care. *Inquiry, 30,* 328–333.

Rutman, I. D. (1995). Managed care: Let the buyers beware [Editorial]. *Psychiatric Rehabilitation Journal, 19*(2), 1–2.

Sabin, J. E. (1994a). Caring about patients and caring about money—The American Psychiatric Association Code of Ethics meets managed care. *Behavioral Sciences & the Law, 12,* 317–330.

Sabin, J. E. (1994b). Managed care—A credo for ethical managed care in mental health practice. *Hospital and Community Psychiatry, 45,* 859.

Sabin, J. E. (1994c). The moral myopia of academia and the big chill of managed care—Reply [Letter]. *Academic Psychiatry, 18,* 164–165.

Sabin, J. E. (1995a). Managed care: Lessons for US managed care from the British National Health Service: 1. "The vision thing." *Psychiatric Services, 46,* 993–994.

Sabin, J. E. (1995b). Perspectives: Organized psychiatry and managed care: Quality improvement or holy war? *Health Affairs, 14,* 32–33.

Sabin, J. E. (1996). Managed care: Getting managed care organizations to cover extended psychotherapy for patients with personality disorders [Editorial]. *Psychiatric Services, 47,* 365–366.

Sandel, M. J. (1996). *Democracy's discontent: America in search of a public philosophy.* Cambridge, MA: Harvard University Press, Belknap Press.

Schlesinger, M., Dorwart, R. A., & Epstein, S. S. (1996). Managed care constraints on psychiatrists' hospital practices: Bargaining power and professional autonomy. *American Journal of Psychiatry, 153,* 256–260.

Sparer, M. S. (1996). Medicaid managed care and the health reform debate: Lessons from New York and California. *Journal of Health Politics, Policy and Law, 21,* 433–460.

Sulmasy, D. P. (1995). Managed care and the new medical paternalism. *Journal of Clinical Ethics, 6,* 324–326.

Sumerall, S. W., Oehlert, M. E., & Trent, D. D. (1995). Vertical integration in medical settings: A brief introduction to its potential effects on professional psychology. *Journal of Clinical Psychology in Medical Settings, 2,* 399–406.

Summerfelt, W. T., Foster, E. M., & Saunders, R. C. (1996). Mental health services utilization in a children's mental health managed care demonstration. *Journal of Mental Health Administration, 23,* 80–91.

Surles, R. C. (1995). Perspectives: Broadening the ethical analysis of managed care. *Health Affairs, 14*(3), 29–31.

Trugerman, A. (1996). All managed care is not equal. *Smith College Studies in Social Work, 66,* 261–267.

Vinter, R. (1959). The social structure of service. In A. J. Kahn (Ed.), *Issues in American social work* (pp. 242–269). New York: Columbia University Press.

Watanabe, M. E. (1996). Bottom line, culture clash impeding cooperation of managed-care organizations in clinical trials. *Scientist, 10*(13), 1.

Weil, T. P. (1995). Any possibility of an S&L-type debacle occurring in the health industry? *Health Care Management Review, 20*(4), 34–41.

Weimer, S. E. (1996). The development of self-love and managed care—Or, reflections on being a tutor. *Smith College Studies in Social Work, 66,* 342–348.

Wickizer, T. M., & Feldstein, P. J. (1995). The impact of HMO competition on private health insurance premiums, 1985–1992. *Inquiry, 32,* 241–251.

Wickizer, T. M., Lessler, D., & Travis, K. M. (1996). Controlling inpatient psychiatric utilization through managed care. *American Journal of Psychiatry, 153*, 339–345.

Wolf, L. F., & Gorman, J. K. (1996). New directions and developments in managed care financing. *Health Care Financing Review, 17*, 1–5.

Zarabozo, C., Taylor, C., & Hicks, J. (1996). Medicare managed care: Numbers and trends. *Health Care Financing Review, 17*, 243–261.

Zolothdorfman, L., & Rubin, S. (1995). The patient as commodity: Managed care and the question of ethics. *Journal of Clinical Ethics, 6*, 339–357.

FURTHER READING

Abreu, B. C. (1996). Guest editorial: Occupational therapy in a managed care environment. *American Journal of Occupational Therapy, 50*, 407–408.

Acklin, M. W. (1996). Personality assessment and managed care. *Journal of Personality Assessment, 66*, 194–201.

Allred, C. A., Arford, P. H., & Michel, Y. (1995). Coordination as a critical element of managed care. *Journal of Nursing Administration, 25*(12), 21–28.

Anderson, P. A. (1993). Making it in the managed care environment. *Journal of Nursing Administration, 23*(12), 7.

Anthony, W. A. (1993). Managed care—A misnomer [Letter]. *Hospital and Community Psychiatry, 44*, 794–795.

Anthony, W. A. (1995). Managed care outcomes— "Places to be and symptom free." *Psychiatric Rehabilitation Journal, 19*(2), 73.

Anthony, W. (1996). Managed care case management for people with serious mental illness. *Behavioral Healthcare Tomorrow, 5*(2), 67–69.

APA outlines principles of psychiatric practice and obligations to patients under managed care. (1996). *Psychiatric Services, 47*, 101.

Apolone, G., & Mosconi, P. (1996). Health status assessment and managed care competition: Are we on target? *International Journal for Quality in Health Care, 8*, 105–106.

Appelbaum, P. S. (1993). Economic grand rounds: Modifying the impact of managed care. *Hospital and Community Psychiatry, 44*, 525–527.

Appelbaum, P. S. (1993). Legal liability and managed care. *American Psychologist, 48*, 251–257.

Appelbaum, P. S. (1996). Law & psychiatry: Managed care and the next generation of mental health law. *Psychiatric Services, 47*, 27.

Appelbaum, P. S. (1996). Managed care and mental health law—Reply [Letter]. *Psychiatric Services, 47*, 765.

Bachrach, L. L. (1995). The chronic patient: Managed care. 1. Delimiting the concept. *Psychiatric Services, 46*, 1229.

Bachrach, L. L. (1996). The chronic patient: Managed care. 2. Some "latent functions." *Psychiatric Services, 47*, 243–244.

Bachrach, L. L. (1996). The chronic patient: Managed care. 3. Whose business is patient care? *Psychiatric Services, 47*, 567.

Baker, L. C., & Cantor, J. C. (1993). Physician satisfaction under managed care. *Health Affairs, 12*(Suppl.), 258–270.

Balon, R. (1994). The moral myopia of academia and the big chill of managed care [Letter]. *Academic Psychiatry, 18*, 163.

Bartman, B. A. (1996). Women's access to appropriate providers within managed care: Implications for the quality of primary care. *Womens Health Issues, 6*, 45–50.

Bartman, B., Yancy, C., Rios, E., & Dunn, L. J. (1996). Women's access to appropriate providers within managed care settings. *Womens Health Issues, 6*, 11–15.

Benson, P. R. (1994). Deinstitutionalization and family caretaking of the seriously mentally ill—The policy context. *International Journal of Law and Psychiatry, 17*, 119–138.

Bergman, R. (1994). Are patients happy—Managed care plans want to know. *Hospitals & Health Networks, 68*(23), 68.

Bergman, R. (1994). No accreditation, no contract, say most managed care plans. *Hospitals & Health Networks, 68*(21), 64.

Birenbaum, A. (1995). Managed care and the future of primary care for adults with mental retardation. *Mental Retardation, 33*, 334–337.

Blendon, R. J., Knox, R. A., Brodie, M., Benson, J. M., & Chervinsky, G. (1994). Americans compare managed care, Medicare, and fee-for-service. *Journal of American Health Policy, 4*(3), 42–47.

Broskowski, A., & Eaddy, M. (1994). Community mental health centers in a managed care environment. *Administration and Policy in Mental Health, 21*, 335–352.

Budman, S. H. (1996). Introduction to special section on group therapy and managed care. *International Journal of Group Psychotherapy, 46*, 293–295.

Budman, S. H., & Armstrong, E. (1992). Training for managed care settings—How to make it happen. *Psychotherapy, 29*, 416–421.

Caper, P. (1995). Commentary: The next shift: Managed care. *Public Health Reports, 110*, 682–683.

Cerne, F. (1994). Atlanta—Managed care heats up competition among payers and providers. *Hospitals & Health Networks, 68*(8), 56–57.

Cerne, F. (1994). Lowering the boom on workers' comp—Rising employer costs spark a shift to managed care and even capitation. *Hospitals & Health Networks, 68*(16), 50.

Cerne, F. (1994). New Jersey university system forms managed care network to assure future survival. *Hospitals & Health Networks, 68*(10), 76.

Cerne, F. (1994). Comment on New Jersey university system forms managed care network to assure future survival (Vol. 68, p. 76). *Hospitals & Health Networks, 68*(16), 6.

Cerne, F. (1994). Tampa, Florida—Battles are won and lost as managed care gradually moves in. *Hospitals & Health Networks, 68*(10), 82–83.

Christiansen, C. (1996). Nationally speaking: Managed care: Opportunities and challenges for occupational therapy in the emerging systems of the 21st century. *American Journal of Occupational Therapy, 50,* 409–412.

Chung, R., & Filstead, W. J. (1995). Inside outcomes: Substance abuse treatment: Outcomes of managed care techniques. *Behavioral Healthcare Tomorrow, 4*(6), 78.

Chung, R. S. (1995). Clinician update: Managed care: Customizing networks through provider profiling. *Behavioral Healthcare Tomorrow, 4*(5), 61–62.

Cohen, G. D. (1996). Put the reimbursement with the rhetoric—Medicare, managed care, and mental health. *American Journal of Geriatric Psychiatry, 4,* 93–95.

Cohen, G. D. (1996). Time, managed care, and mental health. *American Journal of Geriatric Psychiatry, 4,* 185–187.

Coleman, P. G., & Shellow, R. A. (1995). Privacy and autonomy in the physician–patient relationship—Independent contracting under Medicare and implications for expansion into managed care. *Journal of Legal Medicine, 16,* 509–543.

Collins, K. S., Katz, R., & Thompson, J. (1996). Women's experiences in managed care systems. *Womens Health Issues, 6,* 4–7.

Collins, K. S., & Simon, L. J. (1996). Women's health and managed care: Promises and challenges. *Womens Health Issues, 6,* 39–44.

Crosby, G., & Sabin, J. E. (1996). Managed care: A planning checklist for establishing time-limited psychotherapy groups. *Psychiatric Services, 47,* 25–26.

Crow, M. R., Smith, H. L., McNamee, A. H., & Piland, N. F. (1994). Considerations in predicting mental health care use—Implications for managed care plans. *Journal of Mental Health Administration, 21,* 5–23.

Davis, K., Collins, K. S., & Morris, C. (1994). Managed care—Promise and concerns. *Health Affairs, 13,* 178–185.

Deekelly, P. A., Heller, S., & Sibley, M. (1994). Managed care—An opportunity for home care agencies. *Nursing Clinics of North America, 29,* 471–481.

Dowd, B., Moscovice, I., Feldman, R., Finch, M., Wisner, C., & Hillson, S. (1994). Health plan choice in the Twin Cities Medicare market. *Medical Care, 32,* 1019–1039.

Durham, M. L. (1994). Health care's greatest challenge—Providing services for people with severe mental illness in managed-care. *Behavioral Sciences & the Law, 12,* 331–349.

Durham, M. L. (1994). Prospects and problems in using data from HMOs for the study of aging populations and their health care needs. *Gerontologist, 34,* 481–485.

Dwore, R. B., & Murray, B. P. (1996). A comparison of Utah hospital CEO turnover between 1973–1987 and 1988–1992. *Health Care Management Review, 21*(2), 62–73.

Dyer, A. R. (1996). Managed care or managed costs? *Australian and New Zealand Journal of Psychiatry, 30,* 317–318.

Eckert, P. A. (1993). Acceleration of change—Catalysts in brief therapy. *Clinical Psychology Review, 13,* 241–253.

Eckert, P. A. (1994). Cost control through quality improvement—The new challenge for psychology. *Professional Psychology: Research and Practice, 25,* 3–8.

Enthoven, A. C. (1993). Why managed care has failed to contain health costs. *Health Affairs, 12,* 27–43.

Fensterheim, H., & Raw, S. D. (1996). Psychotherapy research is not psychotherapy practice. *Clinical Psychology—Science and Practice, 3,* 168–171.

Fink, P. J. (1993). Economic grand rounds: Psychiatrists' roles in managed care programs. *Hospital and Community Psychiatry, 44,* 723–724.

Finkel, M. L. (1993). Managed care is not the answer. *Journal of Health Politics, Policy and Law, 18,* 105–112.

Fitzgerald, M. (1996). Emergency psychiatry: Structuring psychiatric emergency services for smaller communities in response to managed care. *Psychiatric Services, 47,* 233–234.

Foti, S. K. (1995). One hospital's managed care makeover. *Hospitals & Health Networks, 69*(24), 79.

Fox, P. D., & Wasserman, J. (1993). Commentary: Academic medical centers and managed care—Uneasy partners. *Health Affairs, 12,* 85–93.

Frederick, J. (1996). Perspective: Implications of managed care on early intervention services for infants and toddlers. *Infants and Young Children, 8*(3), 136–138.

Freeborn, D. K., & Hooker, R. S. (1995). Satisfaction of physician assistants and other nonphysician providers in a managed care setting. *Public Health Reports, 110,* 714–719.

Frisch, J. A. (1996). [Review of the book *Marketing mental health services to managed care*]. *Psychiatric Rehabilitation Journal, 19*(3), 104.

The "frisson" benefits of managed care. (1995). *Professional Psychology: Research and Practice, 26,* 629.

Garnick, D. W., Hendricks, A. M., Dulski, J. D., Thorpe, K. E., & Horgan, C. (1994). Characteristics of private-sector managed care for mental health and substance abuse treatment. *Hospital and Community Psychiatry, 45,* 1201–1205.

Goldberg, R. J., & Stoudemire, A. (1996). The future of consultation–liaison psychiatry in medical–psychiatric units in the era of managed care (Vol. 17, p. 268). *General Hospital Psychiatry, 18,* 209.

Goodman, G. S. K. (1995). [Review of the book *Marketing mental health services to managed care.*] *Australian Psychologist, 30,* 224.

Goplerud, E. (1996). Managed care in the public sector: The federal role. *Behavioral Healthcare Tomorrow, 5*(2), 71–73.

Gordon, R. L., Baker, E. L., Roper, W. L., & Omenn, G. S. (1996). Prevention and the reforming US health care system: Changing roles and responsibilities for public health. *Annual Review of Public Health, 17,* 489–509.

Groner, P. N. (1996). Observations regarding the Brown–Johnson debate. *Health Care Management Review, 21*(1), 61–64.

Grossman, J. H. (1993). AMCs—Committed to managed care [Letter]. *Health Affairs, 12,* 275.

Guralnickbernstein, B. (1993). Improving managed care. *Hospital and Community Psychiatry, 44,* 1194–1195.

Hagland, M. (1996). Making managed care second nature. *Hospitals & Health Networks, 70*(8), 88.

Hall, L. L. (1996). Impact of managed care on severe mental illness: The role of report cards, consumers, and family members. *Behavioral Healthcare Tomorrow, 5*(3), 57.

Hall, R. C. W. (1994). Legal precedents affecting managed care—The physicians responsibilities to patients. *Psychosomatics, 35,* 105–117.

Hall, R. C. W. (1994). Social and legal implications of managed care in psychiatry. *Psychosomatics, 35,* 150–158.

Hampton, D. C. (1993). Implementing a managed care framework through care maps. *Journal of Nursing Administration, 23*(5), 21–27.

Hampton, D. C. (1994). King's theory of goal attainment as a framework for managed care implementation in a hospital setting. *Nursing Science Quarterly, 7,* 170–173.

Harper, G., & Walzer, S. (1994). Resident training in the 90s—Professional development and managed care. *Harvard Review of Psychiatry, 2,* 228–230.

Heflinger, C. A., Sonnichsen, S. E., & Brannan, A. M. (1996). Parent satisfaction with children's mental health services in a children's mental health managed care demonstration. *Journal of Mental Health Administration, 23,* 69–79.

Herron, W. G., Eisenstadt, E. N., Javier, R. A., Primavera, L. H., & Schultz, C. L. (1994). Session effects, comparability, and managed care in the psychotherapies. *Psychotherapy, 31,* 279–285.

Herron, W. G., Javier, R. A., Primavera, L. H., & Schultz, C. L. (1994). The cost of psychotherapy. *Professional Psychology: Research and Practice, 25,* 106–110.

Hicks, L. L., & Bopp, K. D. (1996). Integrated pathways for managing rural health services. *Health Care Management Review, 21*(1), 65–72.

Hiebertwhite, J. (1995). From the editor: Managed care and the new economics of mental health. *Health Affairs, 14,* 5–6.

Ho, S. (1996). Managing health risks within managed care systems. *Womens Health Issues, 6,* 7–11.

Hoffman, J. A., Eckert, M. A., Koman, J. J., & Mayo, D. W. (1996). Profiles of clients in government-funded drug user treatment settings. *Substance Use & Misuse, 31,* 453–477.

Hoge, M. A., Davidson, L., Griffith, E. E. H., Sledge, W. H., & Howenstine, R. A. (1994). Defining managed care in public-sector psychiatry. *Hospital and Community Psychiatry, 45,* 1085–1089.

Horton, E. (1995). Special report: A provider to managed care. *Behavioral Healthcare Tomorrow, 4*(6), 22.

Hudson, T. (1994). Providers beware—Managed care contracts can be tricky. *Hospitals & Health Networks, 68*(3), 72.

Hughes, J. J. (1996). Managed care, university hospitals, and the doctor–nurse division of labor. In J. J. Kronenfeld (Ed.), *Research in the sociology of health care* (Vol. 13, pt. A and pt. B, pp. 63–92). Greenwich, CT: Jai Press.

Hunter, R. B., Ross, C. E., Dennis, R. P., Shaffer, I., & Cochrane, T. (1994). Building strategic partnerships between employers and managed care firms to enhance quality of care. *Behavioral Healthcare Tomorrow, 3*(5), 39–43.

Hurley, R. E. (1995). [Review of the book *Promise and performance in managed care: The prepaid group practice model.*] *Journal of Health Politics, Policy and Law, 20,* 1061–1064.

In the courts—Managing managed care. (1993). *Hastings Center Report, 23*(5), 4.

Jellinek, M. S. (1994). Managed care—Good or bad news for children. *Journal of Developmental and Behavioral Pediatrics, 15,* 273–274.

Joel, L. A. (1996). The scapegoating of managed care. *American Journal of Nursing, 96*(6), 7.

Kanter, J., & Silva, M. (1996). Managed care: Case management and managed care: Investing in recovery. *Psychiatric Services, 47,* 699–701.

Keepers, G. A., & Bloom, J. D. (1994). The moral myopia of academia and the big chill of managed care [Letter]. *Academic Psychiatry, 18,* 163–164.

Kelleher, W. J., Talcott, G. W., Haddock, C. K., & Freeman, R. K. (1996). Military psychology in the age of managed care: The Wilford Hall model. *Applied & Preventive Psychology, 5,* 101–110.

Kent, C. (1994). Chronically ill clash with managed care's cost controls [Editorial]. *Journal of American Health Care, 4*(5), 8–9.

Kerstein, J., Pauly, M. V., & Hillman, A. (1994). Primary care physician turnover in HMOs. *Health Services Research, 29,* 17–37.

Kirkmanliff, B. (1995). [Review of the book *Promise and performance in managed care.*] *International Journal of Health Planning and Management, 10,* 321–324.

Knuth, K. M. (1996). Student anxious about role of the occupational therapist under managed care [Letter]. *American Journal of Occupational Therapy, 50,* 462.

Koocher, G. P. (1995). Managed care: Hidden benefits or delusional thinking? [Editorial]. *Professional Psychology: Research and Practice, 26,* 630–631.

Kuhl, V. (1994). The managed care revolution—Implications for humanistic psychotherapy. *Journal of Humanistic Psychology, 34,* 62–81.

Larocca, F. E. F. (1994). [Review of the book *Managing managed care—A mental health practitioner's survival guide.*] *Journal of Clinical Psychiatry, 55,* 419.

Lazarus, A. (1993). Improving psychiatric services in managed care programs. *Hospital and Community Psychiatry, 44,* 709.

Lazarus, A. (1994). Economic grand rounds—Dumping psychiatric patients in the managed care sector [Editorial]. *Hospital and Community Psychiatry, 45,* 529–530.

Lazarus, A. (1994). Managed care—Lessons from community mental health. *Hospital and Community Psychiatry, 45,* 301.

Lazarus, A. (1994). Opportunities for psychiatrists in managed care organizations. *Hospital and Community Psychiatry, 45,* 1206–1210.

Lazarus, A. (1994). A proposal for psychiatric collaboration in managed care. *American Journal of Psychotherapy, 48,* 600–609.

Leong, G. B., & Silva, J. A. (1996). Civil commitment and managed care [Letter]. *Psychiatric Services, 47,* 432.

Levant, R. F. (1996). The psychological physician: Onward to the future. *Journal of Clinical Psychology in Medical Settings, 3,* 167–172.

Lewis, J. B. (1992). [Review of the book *Introduction to managed care—Health maintenance organizations, preferred provider organizations, and competitive medical plans.*] *Inquiry, 29,* 477.

Lindeman, C. (1994). The dangers in managed care [Editorial]. *Nursing & Health Care, 15,* 376.

Luft, H. S. (1995). [Review of the book *Promise and performance in managed care: The prepaid group practice model.*] *Inquiry, 32,* 363.

Lumsdon, K. (1994). Home care prepares to catch wave of managed care, networking. *Hospitals & Health Networks, 68*(7), 58.

Lumsdon, K. (1994). Ready for more managed care—Home care execs discuss their strategies. *Hospitals & Health Networks, 68*(19), 48.

Lundberg, G. D. (1995). Managed care in *JAMA* and the *Archives* journals—A call for papers for coordinated theme issues [Editorial]. *Archives of General Psychiatry, 52,* 967.

Madden, M. J., & Ponte, P. R. (1994). Advanced practice roles in the managed care environment. *Journal of Nursing Administration, 24,* 56–62.

Malcolm, L., & Barnett, P. (1994). New Zealand's health providers in an emerging market. *Health Policy, 29,* 85–100.

Manton, K. G., Newcomer, R., Vertrees, J. C., Lowrimore, G. R., & Harrington, C. (1994). A method for adjusting capitation payments to managed care plans using multivariate patterns of health and functioning—The experience of social/health maintenance organizations. *Medical Care, 32,* 277–297.

Mark, J. C. (1995). Prisoner of managed care? [Editorial]. *Professional Psychology: Research and Practice, 26,* 629.

McCallperez, F. (1993). What employers want in managed care programs. *Hospital and Community Psychiatry, 44,* 682–683.

McCullough, L. B. (1994). Should we create a health care system in the United States. *Journal of Medicine and Philosophy, 19,* 483–490.

McFarland, B. H. (1994). Health maintenance organizations and persons with severe mental illness. *Community Mental Health Journal, 30,* 221–242.

Mechanic, D. (1994). Managed care—Rhetoric and realities [Editorial]. *Inquiry, 31,* 124–128.

Meyer, R. E., & Sotsky, S. M. (1995). Managed care and the role and training of psychiatrists. *Health Affairs, 14,* 65–77.

Miller, S. I. (1995). Managed care survival manual—Adapting to change. *American Journal on Addictions, 4,* 279–284.

Minkoff, K. (1994). Community mental health in the nineties—Public sector managed care. *Community Mental Health Journal, 30,* 317–321.

Moffic, H. S. (1996). Life, liberty, happiness, and managed care [Editorial]. *Psychiatric Services, 47,* 223.

Moffic, H. S., Krieg, K., & Prosen, H. (1993). Managed care and academic psychiatry. *Journal of Mental Health Administration, 20,* 172–177.

Mone, I., C, (1994). Managed care cost effectiveness—Fantasy or reality. *International Journal of Group Psychotherapy, 44,* 437–445.

Montague, J. (1994). Joining the race—State medical societies try to beat managed care integrators to the punch. *Hospitals & Health Networks, 68*(17), 50.

Montague, J. (1994). MDs in the middle—Managed care and looming reform put the squeeze on many middle-aged physicians. *Hospitals & Health Networks, 68*(6), 52.

Moore, P., Fenlon, N., & Hepworth, J. T. (1996). Indicators of differences in immunization rates of Mexican American and white non-Hispanic infants in a Medicaid managed care system. *Public Health Nursing, 13,* 21–30.

Morehart, T. B. (1994). [Review of the book *Introduction to managed care.*] *Journal of Risk and Insurance, 61,* 155–156.

Moss, M. T. (1996). Preparing nurse managers for a managed care future [Editorial]. *Nursing Economics, 14,* 132–133.

Murphy, A. M. (1995). Listening to the knock on the door—Provider strategies for managed care initiatives under Medicaid and other programs. *Behavioral Healthcare Tomorrow, 4*(6), 30–35.

O'Malley, F. (1993). Short-term residential treatment of disturbed adolescents in a continuum of care. *Children and Youth Services Review, 15,* 245–260.

Patricelli, R. E. (1994). Managed care industry perspectives: Why do we need health alliances? *Health Affairs, 13,* 239–242.

Peloquin, S. M. (1996). The issue is: Now that we have managed care, shall we inspire it? [Editorial]. *American Journal of Occupational Therapy, 50,* 455–459.

Perneger, T. V., Etter, J. F., & Rougemont, A. (1996). Switching Swiss enrollees from indemnity health insurance to managed care: The effect on health status and satisfaction with care. *American Journal of Public Health, 86,* 388–393.

Petrila, J. (1995). Legal briefing: Outpatient civil commitment and managed care: Issues for providers. *Behavioral Healthcare Tomorrow, 4*(6), 73.

Petrila, J. (1996). Civil commitment and managed care—Reply [Letter]. *Psychiatric Services, 47,* 432.

Pierce, S. F., & Luikart, C. (1996). Managed care: Will the healthcare needs of rural citizens be met? *Journal of Nursing Administration, 26*(4), 28–32.

Platform for action—Consumer managed care network. (1996). *Behavioral Healthcare Tomorrow, 5*(2), 36.

Pomerantz, J. M. (1996). [Review of the book *Brief therapy and managed care: Readings for contemporary practice.*] *Psychiatric Services, 47,* 95.

Ponte, P. R., Higgins, J. M., James, J. R., Fay, M., & Madden, M. J. (1993). Development needs of advance practice nurses in a managed care environment. *Journal of Nursing Administration, 23*(11), 13–19.

Principles of patients' rights, responsibilities under managed care endorsed by health groups [Editorial]. (1996). *Psychiatric Services, 47,* 102.

Reader, G. G. (1995). [Review of the book *Promise and performance in managed care.*] *Journal of Public Health Policy, 16,* 372–373.

Rosenbaum, S., Schofield, L., Roseff, J., & Chavkin, W. (1996). Women at risk: Integrating reproductive health services into public systems of managed care. *Womens Health Issues, 6,* 15–17.

Rutman, I. D. (1996). Managed care: What's happening out there? [Editorial]. *Psychiatric Rehabilitation Journal, 19*(3), 1–2.

Sandrick, K. (1995). Managing managed care. *Hospitals & Health Networks, 68*(20), 58.

Savitch, L. A., & Brown, H. W. (1994). Will managed care succeed in rural areas? *Hospitals & Health Networks, 68*(1), 13.

Schouten, R. (1993). Legal liability and managed care. *Harvard Review of Psychiatry, 1,* 189–190.

Schreter, R. K. (1993). Economic grand rounds: 10 trends in managed care and their impact on biopsychosocial model. *Hospital and Community Psychiatry, 44,* 325–327.

Schreter, R. K. (1995). Economic grand rounds: Earning a living: A blueprint for psychiatrists. *Psychiatric Services, 46,* 1233–1235.

Selden, D. R. (1995). Case management in the managed care environment: Keystone to integrated service delivery. *Behavioral Healthcare Tomorrow, 4*(6), 36.

Shamansky, S. L. (1996). Yet another treatise on managed care [Editorial]. *Public Health Nursing, 13,* 161–162.

Sharfstein, S. S. (1993). My fears about managed care—Response [Letter]. *Harvard Review of Psychiatry, 1,* 124–125.

Sharfstein, S. S. (1995). Funding, 3rd-party payers, and managed care. In H. S. Ghuman & R. M. Sarles (Eds.), *Handbook of adolescent inpatient psychiatric treatment* (pp. 293–301). New York: Brunner/Mazel.

Sherer, J. L. (1993). Will college nursing education include managed care? [Editorial]. *Hospitals & Health Networks, 67*(13), 47.

Sherer, J. L. (1994). Providers organize to deal with managed care demands [Editorial]. *Hospitals & Health Networks, 68*(1), 55.

Shore, M. F. (1993). One tentative cheer for managed care [Editorial]. *Harvard Review of Psychiatry, 1,* 123–124.

Slay, J. D., & Glazer, W. M. (1995). Best practices: "Carving in," and keeping in, mental health care in the managed care setting. *Psychiatric Services, 46,* 1119.

Staines, V. S. (1993). Potential impact of managed care on national health spending. *Health Affairs, 12*(Suppl.), 248–257.

Stauffer, M. (1996). States update: Minnesota pioneers managed care for chemical dependency clients [Editorial]. *Behavioral Healthcare Tomorrow, 5*(1), 21–23.

Stern, S. (1993). Managed care, brief therapy, and therapeutic integrity. *Psychotherapy, 30,* 162–175.

Stone, A. A. (1995). Paradigms, pre-emptions, and stages: Understanding the transformation of American psychiatry by managed care. *International Journal of Law and Psychiatry, 18,* 353–387.

Talbott, J. A. (1996). Must managed care dominate the scene? [Editorial]. *Psychiatric Services, 47,* 455.

Tanenbaum, S. J., & Hurley, R. E. (1995). Disability and the managed care frenzy: A cautionary note [Editorial]. *Health Affairs, 14*(4), 213–219.

Taylor, K. S. (1993). Clinical contracting—Moves into managed care. *Hospitals & Health Networks, 67*(24), 32.

Taylor, K. S. (1993). A dose of pharmaco-economics—Can health networks learn from the drug policies of managed care plans? *Hospitals & Health Networks, 67*(13), 33–36.

Taylor, K. S. (1994). Survey—Oncologists frustrated with managed care hurdles. *Hospitals & Health Networks, 68*(22), 78.

Taylor, K. S. (1994). Transplants flourish under managed care. *Hospitals & Health Networks, 68*(6), 64.

Tiffany, B. A. (1994). Legal briefing: Structural alternatives for providers to increase managed care business and service integration. *Behavioral Healthcare Tomorrow, 3*(5), 79–81.

Uzych, L. (1996). Managed care and mental health law [Letter]. *Psychiatric Services, 47,* 765.

Wagner, J., & Gartner, C. G. (1996). Issues in managed care: Highlights of the 1995 Institute on Psychiatric Services. *Psychiatric Services, 47,* 15–20.

Weilitz, P. B., & Potter, P. A. (1993). A managed care system—Financial and clinical evaluation. *Journal of Nursing Administration, 23,* 51–57.

Weiner, J. P., & Delissovoy, G. (1993). Razing a tower of Babel—A taxonomy for managed care and health insurance plans. *Journal of Health Politics, Policy and Law, 18,* 75–103.

Weisman, C. S. (1996). Proceedings of women's health and managed care: Balancing cost, access, and quality. *Womens Health Issues, 6,* 1–4.

Whiting, F. (1996). The association: AOTA and managed care [Editorial]. *American Journal of Occupational Therapy, 50,* 460–461.

Wholey, D. R., & Christianson, J. B. (1994). Product differentiation among health maintenance organizations—Causes and consequences of offering open-ended products. *Inquiry, 31,* 25–39.

Wiens, A. N. (1993). [Review of the book *Managing managed care—A mental health practitioner's survival guide.*] *Contemporary Psychology, 38,* 1107–1108.

Wooley, S. C. (1993). Managed care and mental health—The silencing of a profession. *International Journal of Eating Disorders, 14,* 387–401.

Zwanziger, J., Melnick, G. A., & Simonson, L. (1996). Differentiation and specialization in the California hospital industry 1983 to 1988. *Medical Care, 34,* 361–372.

Roger A. Lohmann, PhD, is professor of social work and director, Nonprofit Management Academy, West Virginia University, P.O. Box 6830, Morgantown, WV 26506-6830.

For further information see
Health Care: Direct Practice; **Health Care: Policy Development;** Health Care: Reform Initiatives; **Health Care Practice Overview;** Health Services Systems Policy; Managed Care Overview; **Managed Care: Implications for Social Work Practice;** Mental Health Overview; Primary Health Care; Primary Prevention Overview; Public Health Services; **Social Welfare Expenditures: Private;** Social Welfare Expenditures: Public; **Working Poor.**

Key Words

cost-effectiveness	managed care
health insurance	service delivery

Management: Cost Measurement

Roger A. Lohmann
Nancy L. Lohmann

Cost is one of the most useful, and at the same time one of the trickiest, notions with which the financial manager in social services has traditionally had to contend. Its usefulness arises out of the manner in which "unit cost" has come to take a place in the nonprofit universe that is roughly comparable to "price" in the market/for-profit arena. Its trickiness arises ultimately out of hundreds of years of commercial usage of the concept of cost in determination of "bottom-line" profits. With the advent of managed care, all social workers—not just those who are administrators—must now contend with some of the arcane and esoteric ideas associated with cost. Therefore, this entry is presented as a means of helping social work administrators and other social workers who may be struggling to understand cost concepts in managed care and other contexts.

The concept of cost is simple to define, at least in a general way: The cost of an activity, program, or service (or anything else) consists of what must be given up to obtain it. The actual determination of costs in a particular situation, however, leads to a number of critically important complexities.

This brief introduction will be concerned primarily with presenting some of these complexities, along with some of the important terms found commonly in discussions of the cost of personal care and other social services.

Social services are well along in a "cost revolution" that has come about since the 1960s, largely through the influence of two important cost concepts. The idea of unit cost has gradually come into widespread use by public and other funding authorities, as a summary measure of service performance stated in terms of the volume of resource use. In roughly the same time period, the idea of associating costs (a financial measure) with benefits as a measure of effectiveness has also gained a strong following. In both instances, serious methodological and computational problems still remain in the meaningful and consistent application of these ideas to the social services context. Despite these remaining problems, the gradual transformation of social services to a fully accountable, cost-conscious activity continues unabated.

All of the concepts discussed in this entry have been used in the business arena for decades and are presently more completely developed in the health care and education arenas than in social services. It is only in recent years that they have begun to enter into widespread, general use in the evaluation of social services. In all cases the measure of the market prevails here: Wide adoption and general use, and not the isolated proclamations of academic or professional writers, are the true tests of the importance of concepts such as these.

Cost Elaborated

Perhaps the most intuitive conception of costs for the typical social work administrator or managed care provider is the concept of outlay costs, usually indicated by an expenditure or an obligation. Thus, photocopies that one purchases from a local copy center for $0.10 each cost exactly that, whether they are paid for immediately or charged and paid for later. This basic idea is simple and intuitive and part of everyday language.

However, there are several difficulties with the seemingly straightforward notion of assessing costs by outlay: First and most important, there is the problem of equating the cost of an object with the price paid for it. Generally, this leaves out of consideration relevant but unmeasured costs of purchasing, transporting, storing, or using the item. If it takes an hour to walk or drive to the copy center and back, for example, the real cost of those copies is actually much greater than a dime, because an hour of time has been used in the process. If the hour spent walking to and from the copy center is unpaid leisure time, then its cost may not be a consideration. However, if that hour constitutes work time (that is, occurs during paid employment), then its cost is a relevant overall expense of the employing organization, regardless of whether it is tracked or monitored.

There are also the problems associated with accruals of various types. All of the elements contributing to a particular cost measurement may not be paid for, or expenses may not be reported in the same period as their actual use. If that is so, when is the cost actually incurred? If something is purchased on credit on the last day of the old fiscal year and paid for a month later (say, on the first day of the second month of the new fiscal year), was the cost incurred in? In the old fiscal year? In the first month of the new fiscal year? Or in the second month of the new fiscal year?

In most instances there are no general answers to such questions. We can rely only on certain conventions and our own ad hoc assumptions, which must be spelled out to make any cost analysis meaningful. Consistency of measurements becomes a major issue in establishing the comparability of different cost measurements.

In social services there is the additional problem that many actual costs involve donated goods and services that are never "expenses" as such. Does this mean that they involve no costs? If these are left out of cost calculations, aren't costs actually understated? What if volunteers or donations suddenly disappeared and equivalent resources had to be purchased? Would this mean that the cost of your service had actually risen, or only that you were obtaining the same resources in a different way?

OPPORTUNITY COST

Because of these and other limitations, economists seldom use outlay costs. They typically use the more sophisticated concept of "opportunity cost," which is generally a comparative measure in which the cost of an alternative is measured in terms of foregoing the next most likely alternative. For example, the cost of applying for a grant may be the inability to carry out some other activity that is almost as desirable, such as a training session.

However, there are also problems with opportunity cost. First and foremost, because of its definition, opportunity cost is useful only for anticipated or planned actions and not for the evaluation of actual events. Opportunity cost is not applicable to measurement of actual events, because it requires that one second-guess what might have been. Even if one overlooks this considerable obstacle, however, there are other difficulties with applying opportunity cost notions to social services, simply because of the large areas of uncertainty and large range of options growing out of almost any decision.

Although there are regular calls for the use of opportunity costs in social services, practi-

tioners have shown a marked reluctance to apply this concept. Generally speaking, however, the most widespread applications of cost measurement in the social services context grow out of the outlays notion. Curiously (some might argue, perversely), the issue of outlays versus opportunity costs seldom arises in public policy debates associated with cost containment and managed care.

COST MEASUREMENT

All types of cost measurement assume the existence of some type of cost center (or "cost magnet") to which a particular series of outlays are attached for measurement purposes. There are two principal approaches to cost measurement of interest to the social services agency: Cost accounting is a way of capturing, recording, and reporting information on activities and expenditures that generate cost data directly from the accounting system. Cost accounting is most fully developed in commercial manufacturing, where two systems of accounting—job costing and process costing—are frequently found. In job costing, costs are associated with a particular job, project, or discrete activity, such as organizing a particular neighborhood or implementing a program. In process costing, costs are attached to a particular process, such as intake or discharge interviews. Within social services settings, contemporary hospital accounting is probably the most advanced form of cost accounting, with the patient episode from admission to discharge constituting a "job"-type cost center. When patients receive the familiar detailed printout of all charges incurred as part of their discharge, for example, that printout is generated directly from a cost accounting data system.

Cost analysis (also known as "cost study" or "cost finding") involves special secondary analysis of financial and case records and other relevant research techniques to recover cost information. Because of the general absence of cost accounting techniques in most of the social services, most cost data outside of hospitals are gathered through the use of cost analysis techniques. One of the implications of managed care is that this situation may have to change rapidly. However, the profession of social work has never before been called on to deal with cost accounting and cost analysis in sophisticated ways.

MORE COST TERMINOLOGY

Two underlying questions are useful for organizing various cost terms and concepts: "What type of costs are there?" and "Which costs do we count?" Types of costs are usually identified by attaching an adjective in front of the word "cost": For example, we speak of direct and indirect cost; true or full cost; contract or reimbursable cost; and fixed, semifixed, semivariable, step-variable, and variable costs. Within the manufacturing world, cost terminology arose slowly and directly out of experience, only gradually achieving its current levels of standardization through the medium of cost accounting. Movement toward a standardized vocabulary of cost in the public and nonprofit sectors has come much more quickly, largely through the efforts of the federal government's Office of Management and Budget (OMB), which imposed standardized cost vocabulary on all federal grantees and contractors. In particular, three OMB circulars—A-21 (education), A-87 (state and local government), and A-122 (nonprofit organizations)—seek to spell out a uniform set of cost principles applicable to all public and nonprofit grantees and contractors (Office of Management and Budget, 1980, 1995, 1996). Anyone who is serious about understanding the position of the U.S. government on service costs should consult these three documents and the other OMB circulars listed in Table 1.

In many cases the adjectives of the cost vocabulary clearly describe the types of costs involved. For example, *joint* costs are those shared by two or more cost centers. *Budgeted* costs are projected costs for which financial consideration has already been made or planned. *Standard* costs are those that are determined by close, careful scrutiny to be typical or conventional for a particular cost element or cost center. Standard costs usually refer to the type or category, whereas *average* cost usually refers to a typical amount. Thus, across all social agencies in a particular community, office rental—a standard cost—may be an average cost of $1,500 per month.

The question of which costs to consider and which to ignore in any given case is in part a question of distinguishing controllable and uncontrollable costs. A controllable cost is one that can be influenced or determined by a particular decision maker. An uncontrollable cost is one that is beyond that decision maker's authority, responsibility, or ability to influence or determine. Many types of commodities purchased from commercial vendors, from food supplies to office supplies, may be partly to fully uncontrollable costs for the social services program or managed care provider.

Which costs to consider also requires distinguishing relevant (or related) and irrelevant costs. In any situation costs determined to be relevant will be those related to a particular decision or planned action, whereas irrelevant costs will be those "in the background" and unrelated to the particular decision or action. The problem of determining relevance is usually approached through applying conventions and ad hoc assumptions to a defined cost center (or apportioning costs among several cost centers). A cost center (sometimes also called a "cost objective" or "cost pool") may thus be thought of as a conceptual device (or "container") for distilling costs by associating purposes, expenditures, and other relevant value estimates. In other words, cost centers are general, abstract objects for bringing together and linking costs that are related in some way. Uniform definition, consistently applied conventions, and consistent assumptions are also fundamental to the comparability of cost measurements.

Any notion of comparability of cost measurements is squarely at odds with assumptions of case uniqueness and client individuality. If each case, each situation, and each person served is truly unique, then there is apparently no basis for comparing the costs involved in doing so, because the resulting comparisons will be largely meaningless.

Comparability and individuality in most instances can be reconciled through applications of concepts of statistical distribution. In particular, where individual differences result in large differences in cost, the concept of mean, or average, cost becomes very important. In social services it is vitally important to recognize that any cost figure cited for a program or service is, by definition, the mean cost summarizing a distribution of individual costs both above and below the mean. Where there are wide discrepancies, it may be important to look also at other descriptive statistics, such as the mode (the most frequently occurring value) and the median (the value that separates the top 50 percent from the bottom 50 percent) of the distribution and significant outliers (that is, very-high-cost and very-low-cost cases).

DIRECT AND INDIRECT COSTS

Carefully defined cost centers are one of the two most fundamental and useful distinctions when considering costs; the other is the distinction between direct cost and indirect cost. No meaningful cost analysis is possible unless clearly defined cost centers, or "units of analysis," are spelled out, and all relevant direct and indirect costs are assigned to those centers. When a cost center is defined, it will nearly always have both direct and indirect costs attached to it.

According to the OMB (1980), "Direct costs are those that can be identified specifically with a particular final cost objective; i.e., a particular final award, project, service, or other direct activity of an organization. Indirect costs are those a) incurred for a common or joint objectives, and cannot be readily identified with a particular final cost objective" (p. 46025). In an effort to reflect the meaning of indirect cost more clearly, the recently revised OMB circular A-21 drops the use of the term "indirect" completely and relabels such costs as "facilities and administration." Indirect costs (or "F&A," as they are already becoming known) can be thought of, then, as temporary calculations or determinations that exist only to be assigned to more final or permanent direct cost centers. Making those assignments is one of the key steps in any cost analysis.

The direct/indirect distinction commonly arises, for example, in an agency with two or more programs that are funded separately and with a central management, even if this "management" consists exclusively of a single secretary shared by the programs. In writing the grants for these separate programs, the question of how much of that secretary's time to include in the budget of each grant (that is, how much to allocate to each separate cost center) becomes important. For the managed care provider, a central cost issue may be the proper assignment of indirect costs, such as continued training, which may be of benefit to several clients but not clearly assignable to any one client.

In the past, the definition of cost centers in social services has been largely an ad hoc—and consequently highly variable—process. However, in light of the development of accounting standards for nonprofit organizations and the federal definition of cost principles referred to in the OMB circulars, cost analysis of virtually any nonprofit program or service should begin with at least three such centers: program costs

(direct), administrative costs (indirect), and fundraising costs (indirect).

DISTRIBUTION OF INDIRECT COSTS

OMB circular A-122 says that using these three cost centers—program costs, administrative costs, and fundraising costs—in what it terms "the direct allocation method" (discussed below) is compatible with the *Standards of Accounting and Financial Reporting for Voluntary Health and Welfare Organizations,* issued jointly by the National Health Council, Inc., the National Assembly of Voluntary Health and Welfare Organizations, and the United Way of America (referred to below as the "coalition standards"). These voluntary standards were subsequently updated by the American Institute of Certified Public Accountants (AICPA) and National Accounting Standards Board standards (referred to below as "generally accepted principles of accounting") beginning in the mid-1970s, even though the OMB apparently continues not to recognize them (OMB, 1980, p. 46026).

The Simplified Allocation Method

"Where a nonprofit organization has only one major function, or where all of its major functions benefit from its indirect costs to approximately the same degree, the allocation of indirect costs and the computation of an indirect cost rate may be accomplished through simplified allocation procedures" (OMB, 1980, p. 46025). The simplified method itself involves "(i) separating the organization's total costs for the base period as either direct or indirect, and (ii) dividing the total allowable indirect costs (net of applicable credits) by an equitable distribution base. The result of this process is an indirect cost rate which is used to distribute indirect costs to individual awards" (OMB, 1980, p. 46025). Although this may sound complex, it really is quite simple: Center City Services, for example, in applying step (i), may determine that it has $75,000 in direct costs and $25,000 in indirect costs. Applying step (ii) results in determination of an indirect cost ratio of 75/25, or 0.333. In subsequent actions, this 1:3 ratio may be used to project, for example, that an additional project with $150,000 in direct costs should be expected to have $50,000 in indirect costs.

The Multiple Allocation Base Method

Reality is seldom this simple, however. Thus, for example, an agency may rent offices,

---

TABLE 1
OMB Financial Management Circulars[a]

A-21	Cost Principles for Educational Institutions
A-50	Audit Followup
A-87	Cost Principles for State, Local and Indian Tribal Governments
A-102	Grants and Cooperative Agreements with State and Local Governments
A-110	Uniform Administrative Regulations for Grants and Other Agreements
A-122	Cost Principles for Nonprofit Organizations
A-123	Management Accountability and Control
A-125	Prompt Payment
A-127	Policies and Standards for Financial Management Systems
A-128	Audits of State and Local Governments
A-129	Managing Federal Audit Programs
A-133	Audits of Institutions of Higher Education and Other Nonprofit Institutions
A-134	Financial Accounting Principles and Standards

[a]All of these circulars were available at the OMB web site (http://www.whitehouse.gov/WH/EOP/OMB/html/index-ffm.html) at the time of publication.

---

operate vehicles, and rent post office boxes or have other indirect costs that benefit its programs to different degrees. (One program, for example, may monopolize the staff car, whereas other programs almost never use it. Similarly, two programs may get lots of mail and others very little.) By OMB definition, the multiple allocation base method is a procedure for allocating indirect costs where such discernible inequities exist. "Where an organization's indirect costs benefit its major functions in varying degrees, such costs shall be accumulated into separate cost groupings. Each grouping shall then be allocated individually to benefiting functions by means of a base which best measures the relative benefits" (OMB, 1980, p. 46025). Thus, using separate calculations similar to those in the simplified method, one may determine, using the multiple allocation base method, that one program should pay 50 percent of the office rent, 30 percent of the staff car expenses, and 90 percent of the post office box rental.

The Direct Allocation Method

Finally, OMB circular A-122 also allowed use of what it termed the "direct allocation method," in which costs may be allocated to "program" and "general management" categories (for example, F&A or management and fundraising) as allowed by the coalition standards and generally accepted principles of accounting—in effect using the multiple base allocation method in a slightly different way. For those nonprofit organizations that "treat all costs as direct costs except general management and general expenses" (OMB, 1980), the direct allocation method is acceptable, "provided each joint cost is prorated using a base which accurately measures the benefits provided to each award or other activity" (OMB, 1980, p. 46026).

Commentary

The simplified allocation method is what cost accountants term a "direct distribution method." The principal weakness of direct distribution, however, is that it ignores the cost implications of activity between indirect cost centers (for example, the support provided to fundraising by general management) and, as a result, in many cases it may tend to distort the outcome. Generally, the greater the volume of such "unmeasured" activity, the larger the error resulting from this method.

Although not mentioned in OMB circular A-122, both the multiple allocation base method and the direct allocation method may require that the agency involved give some thought to the implications of the order in which calculations are made. (The indirect cost of general management will vary, for example, before and after the indirect support provided to general management by specific program managers is factored in. This in turn will raise or lower indirect cost calculations for each of those programs.) Because of this, it is frequently necessary to give some consideration to "step-down" methods, in which indirect cost centers are "closed out" (that is, computed) in a particular sequence, with costs assigned both to other (open) indirect cost centers and to direct cost centers, as appropriate. Because of the general lack of agreed-on step-down procedures in human services, some consistency in the actual procedures used is the most important consideration to ensure maximum comparability of cost figures over time.

In the worst-case scenario, the order of calculation or closing can actually result in a failure to produce unique solutions, as the order in which indirect cost centers are closed out affects the outcome. As such, it is most useful in cases where rules or procedures are established specifying the order of closeouts, at least in those cases where indirect costs are large enough to materially affect the resulting final cost figures. (Variances of hundredths or thousandths of a cent are not ordinarily worth considering—or even determining—in non-profit human services settings.)

FULL COSTS

When all of the direct and indirect costs associated with a cost center or cost objective have been assigned and other necessary adjustments made, the resulting measurements may be called "full," "total," or "true" cost. Full or true cost, in this sense, is the best estimate or measurement of all relevant costs associated with a cost center, based on the conventions and assumptions of the cost assessment model used. OMB circular A-122 defined total cost as "the sum of all allowable direct and allocable indirect costs less any applicable credits" (OMB, 1980, p. 46024).

Although determination of full costs is important in some contexts, one may not always need to make this particular measurement. Cost analysis always occurs in a particular context and for a particular reason, and recognizing context and reason is an essential step in the process of interpreting cost measurements. From this vantage point, one can find at least two important general approaches that in turn serve to distinguish full or true costs from contract costs, discussed in the next section.

In many cases one is genuinely interested in knowing the full costs associated with a center: Is the budget sufficient to cover all the costs of the program? Does the funding source provide resources consistent with the program it expects or demands?

If one's interest is in determining the true or full cost of an activity, program, or any other cost center, then the way in which the cost model allocates indirect cost becomes an issue of fidelity—that is, the pattern of direct and indirect costs should accurately reflect, or model, the actual activities involved. Thus, if the secretary works four days a week for one program and one day a week for another, assigning 80 percent of her "costs" (for example, salary and fringe benefits) to the first grant and 20 percent to the second would be a reasonable thing to do.

It is important to remember that completely accurate determination of the full costs of any cost center, applying the allocation methods discussed above, can be an expensive, time-consuming, and often frustrating experience. For example, distinguishing the portions of expendable supplies, such as paper and pencils that are consumed by different staff members, can be extremely difficult and time consuming. Thus, as a practical matter, one often is concerned only with tolerably accurate full-cost data. What is "tolerable," of course, varies widely by circumstances, although certain general rules, such as mathematical rules of rounding, should be heeded.

As an example, the question of how to allocate secretarial costs as an administrative (indirect) cost center is usually an interesting one: This would probably involve at least salary and fringe benefits for the secretarial position. It might also involve equipment and supplies and other costs, to the extent these can be associated with different programs or cost centers. The greater one's desire to establish the "full" cost of a center, the more necessary it becomes to delve into such definitional issues.

An important consideration in all cases, but particularly with small, low-budget programs and services, is the important issue of the feasibility of highly precise measures. In particular, when the costs of determining full costs outweigh any possible benefits that might accrue from increased accuracy, questions of feasibility should arise.

A convenient way to think of this problem is to mentally arrange all possible costs in decreasing rank order, with the largest cost items at the top of the list. One proceeds down the list, assigning costs to direct or indirect categories until the point of indifference (that is, the point at which it no longer matters) is reached. As a general guide, cost elements of less than one-tenth of 1 percent of total costs ($100 of a $100,000 budget) will ordinarily have a negligible effect on the final result and can usually be ignored unless one is extremely concerned with accuracy. (For example, if differences in reimbursement rates of one or two cents per hour are important, then obviously precision must be greater than that required if one is interested in accuracy to the nearest 10 cents per unit.)

CONTRACT COSTS

Ordinarily, one of the important limits on considerations of full, total, or true cost in the social services program or service is established by the alternative concept of contract or reimbursable cost. Contract costs (also known as "allowable" or "allocable" costs) are those that are recognized and accepted by a funding source or contractor. (Thus, in the case of federal grants and contracts, for example, the OMB definition of total costs noted above becomes a contract cost consideration.)

Federal grants and contracts operate within an environment of explicitly defined and recognized contract costs set forth by the OMB financial management circulars listed in Table 1. Federal OMB circulars A-21, A-122, and A-87, for example, spelled out a variety of distinct and different contract costs within two very general categories of allowable (that is, allocable) and unallowable principles applicable to all federal grants and contracts (OMB, 1980, 1995, 1996). Each of these circulars listed 50 or more categories, from advertising to travel, in which what is allowable and allocable to federal grants and contracts was detailed.

PROPOSAL COSTS
Proposal costs are an especially appropriate way to illustrate the general differences between full cost and contract cost approaches, for they reveal a conflict—only partially resolved by OMB circular A-122 (OMB, 1980)—between the cost standards of the federal government and the generally accepted nonprofit accounting procedures of the accounting profession and the coalition standards . AICPA standards for health and welfare organizations distinguish three types of recognizable costs, as noted above: Program costs would ordinarily be considered direct costs, and both administrative and fundraising costs would be indirect (or what some organizations call "overhead") (Lohmann, 1980).

Determination of all three categories of cost would, in a particular instance, presumably result in a determination of full cost. However, federal grants and contracts explicitly disallow (that is, forbid) recognition of the costs of proposal preparation as a legitimate contract cost; in other words, the federal government cannot be charged for the cost of writing federal grants. Many funding sources for managed care providers may also disallow the costs of proposal development, training, and other expenses in an effort to curtail costs or limit cost increases. In the case of nonprofit service agencies and service providers, this amounts to nonrecognition of fundraising costs as a legitimate cost category when federal grant funds are involved.

Whether it would be better to resolve this conflict (1) by amending accounting standards to acknowledge the exception in the case of public (and some private) funding or (2) by changing U.S. Department of Health and Human Services (DHHS) rules to allow recognition of proposal development costs is not a concern here. What is of interest, however, is the disagreement over whether federally supported programs have fundraising costs. If one adopts a contract cost posture (and the viewpoint of the OMB), the answer is no— only administrative and program costs are typically acknowledged. If one takes an agency-based "true cost" perspective, however (which is the intent behind the AICPA approach), the answer would be yes, but they are hidden in administrative and program cost categories.

The reasons a public funding authority might choose to hide fundraising or proposal development costs are not difficult to see, and the more extensive (and thus more costly) the funding authority's mandated proposal development procedures, the greater its interest in hiding those costs would presumably be. The ability of funders to hide these costs by failing to acknowledge their existence does not mean that the agency or the provider does not experience them.

This issue is of great practical interest when comparing administrative costs or unit costs of service for publicly funded and privately funded services. One should be careful to establish whether fundraising costs are either included or excluded from both types of services before reaching any conclusions about comparable costs.

UNALLOWABLE COSTS
The final category of the federal cost standards is unallowable costs. In some cases only costs explicitly allowed in the contract are acceptable. In the case of federal funds, there are also certain categories of costs that are uniformly disallowed in all grants and contracts.

According to OMB circular A-122 (OMB, 1980), unallowable costs include bad debts, contingency funds, reimbursements for contributions and donations, entertainment expenses, fines and penalties (including traffic tickets), governor's or legislative expenses, interest and other financial costs, and underrecovery of costs under other grant agreements. The circular also spelled out conditions under which certain other allowable expenses may be unallowable. Grantees and contractors may not ever use federal funds for any of these particular items.

FIXED AND VARIABLE COSTS

Yet another fundamental cost distinction in social services, but one not mentioned in the federal standards, is the distinction between fixed and variable costs. A fixed cost is one that remains constant over a budget period (usually a quarter or a fiscal year), despite any fluctuations in levels of service that may occur. A *variable* cost, by contrast, is one that changes with variations in level of service. (There is also a third possibility, random costs, which fluctuate for no predictable or understandable reasons, but there is not much that can be done with this idea in cost analysis.)

Everything discussed above, for example, implicitly assumes that costs are fixed for the period of the analysis. (Reminder: It is the average, or mean, cost that is assumed to remain constant during the budget period.) As an example, for most social services, wages and salaries of full-time employees are a fixed cost, because they tend to remain constant over an entire fiscal year (and sometimes longer). By contrast, total wages and salaries of part-time employees are a variable cost, not only because they are adjustable but also, and more important, because adjustments tend to be correlated with service "output": the more hours people work, the more service that can be delivered.

Several types of cost "behaviors" (or patterns of cost fluctuation) that fall in between the limits of fixed and variable have also been identified. In general, cost measurement in social services is not sufficiently advanced at present to allow identification of most of them.

Step-variable (or semifixed) costs are those in which cost increases and decreases occur not in gradual or continuous increments, but in discrete "steps." For example, a program that uses only full-time staff members will experience step-variable costs, regardless of whether they are recognized as such (and most small social services presently do not recognize them). Assume, for simplification purposes only, that each worker can accommodate up to 20 cases and no more, and the need or demand for the service is such that any worker will always have a full caseload. In this case, total program costs will follow a step-variable pattern, and unit costs will remain fixed (primarily as a result of the second assumption).

Semivariable costs, on the other hand, are those that are variable under some conditions and fixed under others. For example, whenever there are quantity discounts on expenditures,

one can suspect that semivariable costs may result, although many different patterns may be observed. Thus, agency letterhead or forms, for example, whose price decreases as the quantity of orders increases, is likely to create semivariable cost patterns. Ordinarily, however, semivariable costs are not too common in social services, because the major cost elements (personnel, fringe benefits, rent, travel) do not behave in a semivariable manner (or at least they are, it is not currently recognized as doing so).

Regardless of the patterns of variability, the important point with variable costs, as opposed to randomly fluctuating costs, is that variability is associated directly with levels of service delivered. Close determination of such variability, for example, is a factor in determination of optimal staff workloads and a host of other management issues and problems.

UNIT COST ANALYSIS

The second of the most fundamental forms of cost study, after cost determination (discussed earlier), is unit cost analysis, in which full or contract costs are compared, usually in ratio form, with some nonmonetary quantitative indicator of program activity. Hospital and nursing home costs are often presented on a cost-per-bed or cost-per-bed-day basis.

There is, in principle, no reason why unit cost data cannot be developed for outcome measures rather than process or activity measures. Thus, the cost of higher education can be presented as easily in terms of numbers of graduates as in numbers of attendees. Doing so, however, requires establishing quantitative measures of outcomes rather than processes (analogous to college graduation as opposed to attendance). This has proved to be a major stumbling block in social services. Two highly sophisticated techniques—cost-benefit analysis and cost-effectiveness analysis—have often been suggested as ways of dealing with the measurement of the cost of outcomes.

Cost-Benefit Analysis

The idea of cost-benefit analysis is one of the most misused concepts in modern social services management. The intuitive idea of cost-benefit analysis is a simultaneous determination of the cost and the benefits of a service or activity, but there are tremendously complicated issues associated with defining and measuring benefits. Cost-benefit analysis is also the name of a set of economic planning techniques for measuring opportunity costs and comparing them with future economic benefits, measured in discounted present dollars.

With the exception of programs in employment and training and some health programs in which it is possible to precisely estimate future effects on earnings, health care costs, and so on, cost-benefit analysis is of little practical value in social services cost measurement. Even so, the idea continues to exercise a strong hold over federal, foundation, state, and other officials seeking to ensure greater accountability for funds under their discretion.

Cost-Effectiveness Analysis

The idea of cost-effectiveness analysis, on the other hand, has substantial unrealized possibilities in social services. One way to think of it is as unit cost analysis focused on outcome rather than process measures. In other words, the quantitative units that serve as the denominators to full or contract cost numerators are outcomes or results rather than activities or processes.

Thus, for example, the general cost-effectiveness formula for prevention programs is the full (or contract) cost of the program divided by the number of problems prevented. Infant mortality rates, for example, can be compared with total maternal and infant services costs in this way to determine the cost-effectiveness of those services (that is, the cost per live birth improvement in the infant mortality rate).

Only in a relatively few instances, however, is it possible to establish adequate levels of precision in observation and measurement to make cost-effectiveness measurements useful and meaningful.

Scale and Scope Economies

Two related concepts whose meaning is dependent on the costs concepts outlined above and whose applications (and misapplications) to contemporary practice have been widespread are scale and scope economies. *Scale economies* can be said to involve variable costs that decrease in proportion to increases in output. Thus, the more of something that is produced, the lower the cost of producing a single unit. *Scope economies* are decreases in costs that result from coproduction of different types of services. Scale economies are a long-recognized phenomenon, whereas scope economies have generally been recognized only recently.

The clearest, although not necessarily the easiest, cases of scale economies in social situations are likely to be associated with underutilization of staff. The unit cost of a program in which each worker has only a single client are likely to be considerably higher, for example, than the unit costs of a comparable program in which each worker has a number of clients.

In theory, considerable economies of scale (that is, reductions in the unit cost of services) could be achieved in such a case without affecting the quality of services simply by bringing each worker's workload up to, but not exceeding, full utilization. The difficulty is that such "open-and-shut" cases seldom occur in reality, and determination of the difference between full utilization and overloading of staff is no simple matter. Nonetheless, the intuitive notion of scale economies is an important one to keep in mind when conducting cost studies.

Scope economies may occur in social services in any of several areas. For example, although few social agencies need or can afford full-time legal counsel on staff, an agency with its own legal aid staff may realize considerable scope economies (for example, in reduced legal fees) over the agency that has to hire attorneys on a case basis. Likewise, a staff family therapist may also consult with protective services staff or a staff accountant may provide backup technical assistance to a consumer counseling program to achieve scope economies.

Scope economies of this type are generally treated in an ad hoc manner in most contemporary agencies, and little or no knowledge exists about particular combinations of programs or skills likely to result in such economies. Nevertheless, in the contemporary cost-conscious environment, the idea of scope economies appears to be a fruitful area for further work.

The U-Shaped Curve: Is Small Beautiful?

One of the strongest arguments in defense of services delivered in the small agency comes in the form of various possibilities that the cost curves of scale and scope economies in social services may generally be "U-shaped"—that is, there may be a "point of diminishing returns" beyond which increasing the number of units of output results in no further scale economies and actually begins to push up unit costs. In other words, beyond that point, rather paradoxically, increases in service output produce higher unit costs rather than lower ones.

It is highly likely, for example, that the unit costs of supervision continue to diminish as additional workers are assigned to a pool of supervisors; at the point where the number of new workers exceeds the combined ability of existing supervisors and a new supervisor must be added, the average unit cost of supervision will increase, at least temporarily. If communication problems among supervisors requires the addition of a higher-level supervisor-of-supervisors, nearly the average cost of all supervision will increase irreversibly.

Every worker intuitively grasps this idea. The difficulty with applying this insight to social services, however, is that we almost never know with any precision where and when such changes in direction (called "saddle points," or "cusps") can be expected to occur. Consequently, it is extremely easy to suggest that there should be a way to deal with this issue, but enormously difficult to come up with one.

PROBLEMS IN CALCULATION

Closely related to these definitional issues are problems in the actual calculation of costs. At least three highly questionable cost measurement strategies are widely used in social services contexts today.

The first of these is the concept of cost reduction as efficiency improvement. This is a stance commonly and widely taken by local government officials, as well as a number of state and federal officials. The suggestion, in effect, is that cost cutting leads to improved efficiency. The absurdity of this view is well summed up in the conclusion that results from its consistent application: If reducing costs alone increases efficiency, then spending nothing should produce the greatest efficiency. Although this is an obvious absurdity, advocates of cost reduction approaches to efficiency (of which there are many) have yet to point out the theoretical or actual "breaking point" at which this concept of efficiency ceases to govern.

One unexplored possibility is that the relation between cost and efficiency is also U-shaped, with a saddle point beyond which further cost reductions may actually produce decreases in efficiency. Although many service workers and not a few administrators may be tempted to argue that they are at or near that point, the fact remains that actual measurement of "efficiency" is such a primitive and inexact art in social services that no one can say with any certainty when or if such a point is ever reached.

A second equally questionable application of cost concepts that has been very popular in recent years is the application of the criterion of least cost. Whenever several alternative ways of doing things exist, it is commonly assumed in many quarters that the least expensive one is the most desirable. The general weak point in this criterion as it relates to social services concerns the comparability of the alternatives (the "apples and oranges" problem). It is anything but self-evident that several service programs with the same label or title are actually doing the same things or providing the same services. Until such comparability is established, any cost comparisons that result should be treated as completely meaningless; programmatic decisions made on the basis of such comparisons are on a par with rolling dice or random numbers tables.

A third questionable application of cost concepts is the view of cost containment as an adequate management strategy. Certainly every administrator should be concerned about costs and should strive to keep costs as low as possible. However, the substitution of cost containment for goal attainment is virtually guaranteed to produce long-term program disaster.

It is one thing, however, to suggest caution in the use of cost concepts. It is quite another to negate or overcome the effects of a political economy built on the (mis)application of these same concepts. The 1980s saw the growth and maturity of just such a political economy, and Americans continue to live under its spell in the late 1990s. The long-term effects on the social services system have yet to be determined.

THE ELUSIVE "MEASURABLE UNIT" OF SERVICE

Although we are not yet there, we have been gradually moving toward improved cost measurement capability in social services for many years. One area with great potential for improvement would appear to be the establishment of some type of uniform outcome measures. Although it is not yet possible to clearly identify the exact specifications of a widely agreed-on unit of service for any of the social services, it is possible to identify some of the main specifications that such units must meet to be useful in the measurement of costs. The most important of these specifications might be called the "integrity" of the cost measure. Integrity consists of five separate considerations: homogeneity, intersubjectivity, stability, established variance, and generalizability.

Homogeneity means that any unit that is selected as a cost measure should be practically identical with any other service unit whose cost it is measuring. *Intersubjectivity* refers to the likelihood that independent observers will report the same thing under the same circumstances. *Stability* in this sense is the opposite of variability; it means that each unit should remain approximately the same over a reasonable period of time as it was when it was first measured. *Established variance* refers to the possibility that variations in units themselves or observations over time should fall within limits that can be identified or determined. Finally, *generalizability* can be measured only when it is clearly and explicitly stated and understood, when there is some type of comparison or reference group with which to compare. Ideally, such comparability should be established across programs and agencies. Unless cost measurements can meet these criteria, the likelihood is not very great that they will prove useful at all.

Most of the service units in use for measurement purposes in social services—whether measures of inputs, outputs, efficiency, or something else—fail miserably on one or more of these criteria. A program, for example, is seldom an explicitly identified or a consistent thing; for example, it may be a two-hour entertainment put on by an ensemble or a permanent, ongoing endeavor. A case may be an individual, a family, or an organization, involved for a single incident or episode or enduring across a lifetime. A client contact may vary from a telephone call to a trip involving many miles and hours or even days. Likewise, terms such as "interview" and "episode," as well as many others, are susceptible to the same vagaries.

The situation is not entirely bleak, however. Some progress has been made in establishing standard program structures and definitions, even though great variations, as well as several overlapping and competing taxonomies, exist.

Considerable progress has also been made in the standardization of expense items; OMB circular A-21 (OMB, 1996) contains a particularly detailed listing of such elements in the context of higher education grants. In addition, there has been some recognition of the functional cost categories of administrative, fundraising, and program costs. The next leap

forward in this area may be for federal grant agencies and other funding sources to begin to recognize the true costs of fundraising as a legitimate expense, rather than the current practice of simply burying such expenses in general administrative expenses. One way to do this would be to disallow the use of federal funds for such purposes (something that has already been done), but to require reporting of fundraising costs as a part of the local match.

Another area of progress might be to further simplify and standardize line-item budgets, relegating some of the tedious details of such documents to backup sheets. Thus, for example, a summary budget might report all expenditures by program, summarized as services (personnel costs), current expenses (everything else), and capital expenses, with subcategories for administrative, program, and fundraising costs. The point here is not to eliminate the reporting of proposed and actual line-item expenditures, but to back such detail further down the line in the budget justification.

THE DAY AS A MEASUREMENT UNIT

Time is a centrally important measurement unit (perhaps *the* central measure) in social services cost measurement. The general importance of days as measurable, cost-relevant units of the volume of service delivered in hospitals, nursing homes, and residential treatment facilities is already well established. Within the clinical arena, the traditional "therapeutic hour" is in itself a kind of tribute to cost measurement. This "hour" typically consists of 50 minutes of service provision with an additional 10 minutes for support activities of one sort or another (for example, coffee refills, restroom breaks, and returning telephone calls). As such, it is a clear reflection, in professional jargon and practice, of the distinction between direct and indirect costs discussed above. In a similar vein, nursing homes, hospitals, day care services, and residential care facilities have gone a long way toward standardizing service units based on time.

The "day" of day care and hospital and nursing home "bed-days" are widely recognized units that offer remarkably stable "natural" cost centers. Any time there is a tangible good that figures prominently in a service—for example, the patient's bed or room in hospitals and nursing homes, and the meal served by food programs (or the meal materials provided by food banks)—there is a tangible base for establishing a potentially valid and reliable cost measure.

In other cases mere usage or convention is sufficient to establish an indicator. For example, some years ago the national continuing education body established the continuing education unit (CEU) as a standard measure of service provided. One CEU is said to equal 10 hours of instruction. That measure is now sufficiently universal to allow certain limited cost comparisons per CEU (for example, in licensure considerations).

Many problems still remain. There are, for example, a great many remaining unidentified sources of variability in service units. Furthermore, the importance of consistency and variability over time is largely discounted. We might, for example, usefully be examining for period and cohort effects in many types of services. We know, for example, that many people experience depression associated with holidays. Consequently, demand for service is likely to increase and effectiveness may prove more challenging during such periods.

Finally, the duration-of-service effect as it relates to cost is a virtually unstudied topic. Is it more cost-effective, for example, to administer a low-cost treatment repeatedly, or a more costly treatment once? The present preoccupation with "least-cost" criteria has often meant the reemergence of the old problem of the revolving door. In such cases, although a single episode of treatment may be highly efficient, the long-term costs of repeated application may far exceed the costs of a more expensive but less frequently needed intervention.

CONCLUSION

The rapidly rising importance of cost concepts in the world of managed care, combined with the traditional social work posture of leaving cost considerations to management alone, are likely to prove increasingly problematic in social work over the next few years. In the real world of today, the unit cost of a service episode may be as critically important as more traditional concerns. Current professionals generally are not well equipped to understand the sometimes arcane jargon of cost accountability and measurement, and few mechanisms are in place for aiding professionals with this or other important transitions to the new order of managed care, independent practice, and contracting. Even more important, most professional social workers are not ready to deal with the kinds of issues and questions

raised by cost considerations, and even those social agency managers who are prepared to deal with them often find themselves somewhat stymied in efforts to explain and interpet cost considerations to service professionals, boards, and publics. Clearly, new approaches to this important topic are needed in social work education and practice.

REFERENCES
Lohmann, R. (1980). *Breaking even: Financial management in human services.* Philadelphia: Temple University Press.

Office of Management and Budget. (1980, July 8). *OMB circular A-122: Cost principles for non-profit organizations.* Washington, DC: U.S. Government Printing Office.

Office of Management and Budget. (1995, May 17). *OMB circular A-87: Cost principles for state, local, and Indian tribal governments.* Washington, DC: U.S. Government Printing Office.

Office of Management and Budget. (1996, April 26). *OMB circular A-21: Cost principles for educational institutions.* Washington, DC: U.S. Government Printing Office.

FURTHER READING
Babu, A. J. G., & Suresh, N. (1991). Project management with time, cost, and quality considerations. *European Journal of Operational Research, 88,* 320–327.

Beaudin, C. L., & Chambre, S. M. (1996). HIV/AIDS as a chronic disease—Emergence from the plague model. *American Behavioral Scientist, 39,* 684–706.

Beigel, A., & Shore, M. F. (1996). Adapting to the realities of managed care. *Harvard Review of Psychiatry, 4,* 221–224.

Bertram, D. A., Thompson, M. C., Giordano, D., Perla, J., & Rosenthal, T. C. (1996). Implementation of an inpatient case management program in rural hospitals. *Journal of Rural Health, 12*(1), 54–66.

Borooah, V. K. (1995). [Review of the book *Paying for inequality: The economic cost of social injustice,* by A. Glyn, D. Miliband]. *Economic Journal, 105,* 1649–1651.

Bradley, C. J., & Zarkin, G. A. (1996). Inpatient stays for patients diagnosed with severe psychiatric disorders and substance abuse. *Health Services Research, 31,* 387–408.

Brown, C., & Schulberg, H. C. (1995). The efficacy of psychosocial treatments in primary care—A review of randomized clinical trials. *General Hospital Psychiatry, 17,* 414–424.

Buchanan, J. L., Leibowitz, A., & Keesey, J. (1996). Medicaid health maintenance organizations: Can they reduce program spending? *Medical Care, 34,* 249–263.

Buchanan, R. J. (1995). Medicaid policies for the nursing facility care provided to Medicaid recipients with AIDS. *AIDS & Public Policy Journal, 10,* 94–103.

Carroll, B. T., Goforth, H. W., Kennedy, J. C., & Dueno, O. R. (1996). Mania due to general medical conditions: Frequency, treatment, and cost. *International Journal of Psychiatry in Medicine, 26*(1), 5–13.

Christ, G. H. (1996). School and agency collaboration in a cost conscious health care environment. *Social Work in Health Care, 24*(1-2), 53–72.

Clark, R. E. (1996). Searching for cost-effective mental health care. *Harvard Review of Psychiatry, 4,* 45–48.

Cockerill, R., Scott, E., & Wright, M. (1996). Interest among occupational therapy managers in measuring workload for case costing. *American Journal of Occupational Therapy, 50,* 447–451.

Cohen, M. B. (1979). Long-term care and cost control: A critical analysis. *Health & Social Work, 4,* 60–88.

Davidson, T., & Davidson, J. R. (1995). Cost-containment, computers and confidentiality. *Clinical Social Work Journal, 23,* 453–464.

Dickey, B., Cannon, N., & McGuire, T. (1986). Mental health cost studies: Some observations on methodology. *Administration in Mental Health, 13,* 189–201.

Dmello, D. A., Finkbeiner, D. S., & Kocher, K. N. (1995). The cost of antidepressant overdose. *General Hospital Psychiatry, 17,* 454–455.

Ellis, R. P., & Ash, A. (1995). Refinements to the diagnostic cost group (DCG) model. *Inquiry, 32,* 418–429.

Experton, B., Ozminkowski, R. J., Branch, L. G., & Li, Z. L. (1996). A comparison by payor/provider type of the cost of dying among frail older adults. *Journal of the American Geriatrics Society, 44,* 1098–1107.

Feldman, P. H., Latimer, E., & Davidson, H. (1996). Medicaid-funded home care for the frail elderly and disabled: Evaluating the cost savings and outcomes of a service delivery reform. *Health Services Research, 31,* 489–508.

Finney, J. W., & Monahan, S. C. (1996). The cost-effectiveness of treatment for alcoholism: A second approximation. *Journal of Studies on Alcohol, 57,* 229–243.

Geiger, D. R., & Ittner, C. D. (1996). The influence of funding source and legislative requirements on government cost accounting practices. *Accounting Organizations and Society, 21,* 549–567.

Goldberg, D., Jackson, G., Gater, R., Campbell, M., & Jennett, N. (1996). The treatment of common mental disorders by a community team based in primary care: A cost-effectiveness study. *Psychological Medicine, 26,* 487–492.

Goldberg, R. J., Daly, J., & Backstrom, D. (1996). Psychiatric complications and comorbidities in medical inpatients—The inadequacy of attestation at discharge. *General Hospital Psychiatry, 18,* 102–105.

Grundy, T. (1996). Cost is a strategic issue. *Long Range Planning, 29*(1), 58–68.

Gudex, C. (1996). Measuring patient benefit in mental illness. *European Psychiatry, 11,* 155–158.

Hadley, J., Zuckerman, S., & Iezzoni, L. I. (1996). Financial pressure and competition—Changes in hospital efficiency and cost-shifting behavior. *Medical Care, 34,* 205–219.

Hartwell, T. D., Steele, P., French, M. T., Potter, F. J., Rodman, N. F., & Zarkin, G. A. (1996). Aiding troubled employees: The prevalence, cost, and characteristics of employee assistance programs in the United States. *American Journal of Public Health, 86,* 804–808.

Helburn, S. W., & Howes, C. (1996). Child care cost and quality. *Future of Children, 6,* 62–82.

Hoerger, T. J., Picone, G. A., & Sloan, F. A. (1996). Public subsidies, private provision of care and living arrangements of the elderly. *Review of Economics and Statistics, 78,* 428–440.

Holmes, J. (1996). Psychiatric illness and length of stay in elderly patients with hip fracture. *International Journal of Geriatric Psychiatry, 11,* 607–611.

House, A. (1995). Psychiatric disorders, inappropriate health service utilization and the role of consultation-liaison psychiatry. *Journal of Psychosomatic Research, 39,* 799–802.

Hu, T. W., Cuffel, B. J., & Masland, M. C. (1996). State health care reform: The effect of contracting on the cost of public mental health services in California. *Psychiatric Services, 47,* 32–34.

Hughes, S. L. (1995). Evaluation and quality assurance for in-home services. *Journal of Gerontological Social Work, 24,* 117–131.

Hwang, G. H., & Aspinwall, E. M. (1996). Quality cost models and their application: A review. *Total Quality Management, 7,* 267–281.

Jerrell, J. M., & Hu, T. W. (1996). Estimating the cost impact of three dual diagnosis treatment programs. *Evaluation Review, 20,* 160–180.

Jha, R. (1996). True cost of public expenditure. *Economic and Political Weekly, 30,* 29–33.

Jones, N. F., & Holden, M. S. (1995). Mental health treatment and medical utilization: First pilot study in the military. *Journal of Clinical Psychology in Medical Settings, 2,* 269–274.

Knapp, M. (1991). Cost. *Administration in Social Work, 15*(1-2), 45–63.

Knapp, M. R. J. (1996). Cost-effectiveness in the treatment of schizophrenia. *European Psychiatry, 11,* 137–143.

Lazarus, A. (1996). Cost-shifting and managed care. *Psychiatric Services, 47,* 1063–1064.

Li, L. X., & Benton, W. C. (1996). Performance measurement criteria in health care organizations: Review and future research directions. *European Journal of Operational Research, 93*, 449–468.

Lobianco, M. S., Mills, M. E., & Moore, H. W. (1996). A model for case management of high cost Medicaid users. *Nursing Economics, 14*, 303.

Mansell, J. (1996). [Review of the book *The cost and quality of community residential care*, by N. V. Raynes, K. Wright, A. Shiell, & C. Pettipher]. *Journal of Intellectual Disability Research, 40*, 482–483.

Marks, I. (1996). Clinical computing: A computerized system to measure treatment outcomes and cost. *Psychiatric Services, 47*, 811–812.

Martin, B. C., & McMillan, J. A. (1996). The impact of implementing a more restrictive prescription limit on Medicaid recipients:Effects on cost, therapy, and out-of-pocket expenditures. *Medical Care, 34*, 686–701.

McFarlane, W. R., Dushay, R. A., Stastny, P., Deakins, S. M., & Link, B. (1996). A comparison of two levels of family-aided assertive community treatment. *Psychiatric Services, 47*, 744–750.

Merson, S., Tyrer, P., Carlen, D., & Johnson, T. (1996). The cost of treatment of psychiatric emergencies: A comparison of hospital and community services. *Psychological Medicine, 26*, 727–734.

Miller, L. L., Hornbrook, M. C., Archbold, P. G., & Stewart, B. J. (1996). Development of use and cost measures in a nursing intervention for family caregivers and frail elderly patients. *Research in Nursing & Health, 19*, 273–285.

Monahan, S. C., & Finney, J. W. (1996). Explaining abstinence rates following treatment for alcohol abuse: A quantitative synthesis of patient, research design and treatment effects. *Addiction, 91*, 787–805.

Moos, R. H., & Mertens, J. R. (1996). Patterns of diagnoses, comorbidities, and treatment in late-middle-aged and older affective disorder patients: Comparison of mental health and medical sectors. *Journal of the American Geriatrics Society, 44*, 682–688.

Mordock, J. B. (1993). Hidden cost of children's outpatient mental health services—Lessons from New York State. *Administration and Policy in Mental Health, 20*, 215–229.

Oakes, L. S., & Miranti, P. J. (1996). Louis D. Brandeis and standard cost accounting: A study of the construction of historical agency. *Accounting Organizations and Society, 21*, 569–586.

Pelletier, K. R. (1996). A review and analysis of the health and cost-effective outcome studies of comprehensive health promotion and disease prevention programs at the worksite, 1993-1995 update. *American Journal of Health Promotion, 10*, 380–388.

Peters, D. A., & Hays, B. J. (1995). Measuring the essence of nursing: A guide for future practice. *Journal of Professional Nursing, 11*, 358–363.

Posnett, J., & Jan, S. (1996). Indirect cost in economic evaluation: The opportunity cost of unpaid inputs. *Health Economics, 5*, 13–23.

Powe, N. R., Weiner, J. P., Starfield, B., Stuart, M., Baker, A., & Steinwachs, D. M. (1996). Systemwide provider performance in a Medicaid program—Profiling the care of patients with chronic illnesses. *Medical Care, 34*, 798–810.

Powell, J., & Goddard, A. (1996). Cost and stake-holder views: A combined approach to evaluating services. *British Journal of Social Work, 26*, 93–108.

Priebe, S., Hoffmann, K., Isermann, M., & Kaiser, W. (1996). Clinical characteristics of long-term hospitalized patients—Part of the Berlin Deinstitutionalization Study. *Psychiatrische Praxis, 23*(1), 15–20.

Prochniak, A. L. (1996). Does your fund cost too much? *Fortune, 132*, 145–146.

Quinlivan, R., & McWhirter, D. P. (1996). Best practices: Designing a comprehensive care program for high cost clients in a managed care environment. *Psychiatric Services, 47*, 813–815.

Reschovsky, J. D. (1996). Demand for and access to institutional long-term care: The role of Medicaid in nursing home markets. *Inquiry, 33*, 15–29.

Robins, A. G., & Board, G. (1996). Assessing mental health care policy: Pennsylvania's Health Care Cost Containment Council. *Administration and Policy in Mental Health, 24*, 85–90.

Ross, P., & West, D. J. (1995). Advance directives: The price of life. *Nursing Economics, 13*, 355–361.

Rydman, R. J. (1995). Evaluating the cost effectiveness of case management. In G. L. Albrecht (Ed.), *Advances in medical sociology* (Vol. 6, pp. 341–361). Greenwich, CT: Jai Press.

Salize, H. J., & Rossler, W. (1996). The cost of comprehensive care of people with schizophrenia living in the community—A cost evaluation from a German catchment area. *British Journal of Psychiatry, 169*, 42–48.

Saur, C. D., & Ford, S. M. (1995). Quality, cost-effective psychiatric treatment: A CNS-MD collaborative practice model. *Archives of Psychiatric Nursing, 9*, 332–337.

Schlenker, R. E., Shaughnessy, P. W., & Hittle, D. F. (1995). Patient-level cost of home health care under capitated and fee-for-service payment. *Inquiry, 32*, 252–270.

Schneiderbraus, K. (1996). Exploring the ethics of cost containment in psychiatric training. *Academic Psychiatry, 20*, 158–164.

Sederer, L. I., & Bennett, M. J. (1996). Managed mental health care in the United States: A status report. *Administration and Policy in Mental Health, 23,* 289–306.

Shah, A. (1996). Cost of transportation to a psychogeriatric day hospital: Minibus versus taxi service. *International Journal of Geriatric Psychiatry, 11,* 555–558.

Stessman, J., Ginsberg, G., Hammermanrozenberg, R., Friedman, R., Ronen, D., Israeli, A., & Cohen, A. (1996). Decreased hospital utilization by older adults attributable to a home hospitalization program. *Journal of the American Geriatrics Society, 44,* 591–598.

St. Pierre, R. G., Layzer, J. I., & Barnes, H. V. (1995). Two-generation programs: Design, cost, and short term effectiveness. *Future of Children, 5,* 76–93.

Svensson, M., Edebalk, P. G., & Persson, U. (1996). Group living for elderly patients with dementia—A cost analysis. *Health Policy, 38,* 83–100.

Swaney, J. A. (1995). Social economics and risk analysis. *Review of Social Economy, 53,* 575–594.

Szeto, K. L., & Devlin, N. J. (1996). The cost-effectiveness of mammography screening: Evidence from a microsimulation model for New Zealand. *Health Policy, 38,* 101–115.

Tengs, T. O. (1996). An evaluation of Oregon's Medicaid rationing algorithms. *Health Economics, 5,* 171–181.

Vandeven, W. P. M. (1996). Market-oriented health care reforms: Trends and future options. *Social Science & Medicine, 43,* 655–666.

Vaz, F. J., & Salcedo, M. S. (1996). A model for evaluating the impact of consultation-liaison psychiatry activities on referral patterns. *Psychosomatics, 37,* 289–298.

Weisman, C. S. (1996). Proceedings of women's health and managed care: Balancing cost, access, and quality. *Womens Health Issues, 6*(1), 1–4.

Whitemeans, S., & Chollet, D. (1996). Opportunity wages and workforce adjustments: Understanding the cost of in-home elder care. *Journals of Gerontology. Series B, Psychological Sciences and Social Sciences, 51,* S82–S90.

Wholey, D., Christianson, J., & Peterson, M. (1996). Organization of mental health care in HMOs. *Administration and Policy in Mental Health, 23,* 307–328.

Wickizer, T. M., Lessler, D., & Travis, K. M. (1996). Controlling inpatient psychiatric utilization through managed care. *American Journal of Psychiatry, 153,* 339–345.

Yates, B. T. (1995). Cost-effectiveness analysis, cost-benefit analysis, and beyond: Evolving models for the scientist-manager-practitioner. *Clinical Psychology—Science and Practice, 2,* 385–398.

Yuen, E. J., Gerdes, J. L., & Gonzales, J. J. (1996). Patterns of rural mental health care—An exploratory study. *General Hospital Psychiatry, 18*(1), 14–21.

Roger A. Lohmann, PhD, is professor of social work and director, Nonprofit Management Academy, West Virginia University, P.O. Box 6830, Morgantown, WV 26506-6830. **Nancy L. Lohmann, PhD,** is senior associate provost and professor of social work, West Virginia University, P.O. Box 6203, Morgantown, WV 26506-6203.

For further information see

Boards of Directors; Financial Management; Income Distribution; Management Overview; **Management: New Developments and Directions;** Nonprofit Management Issues; Public Services Management; Purchasing Social Services; **Social Welfare Expenditures: Private;** Social Welfare Expenditures: Public; Social Welfare History; Social Welfare Policy; Strategic Planning; Vendorship.

Key Words	
cost	financial management
cost allocation	planning
cost analysis	managed care

Management: New Developments and Directions

Philip W. Cooke

P. Nelson Reid

Richard L. Edwards

$\mathbf{S}$ocial work managers continue to be buffeted and challenged by rapidly changing global, domestic, and local environments that are mandating changes in the ways that human services are sponsored, organized, financed, delivered, and judged to be effective. Economic and political imperatives have shifted, and a new "marketplace" culture is shaping the management of health and human services organizations. Within this context of rapid technological and social change, there are several themes that are both affecting the delivery of social and human services and having a direct impact on social work management. These include marketization, the "devolution revolution," performance- or outcome-based accountability, and rapid change. Together, these themes are causing social work managers to search for appropriate strategic responses and new management paradigms. This entry explores these themes and their impact on the practice of social work management.

WINDS OF CHANGE

Social workers are approaching the 21st century with more than 100 years of experience in the large-scale provision of human services (Edwards, Cooke, & Reid, 1996). Throughout the early part of the 20th century, the progressive movement promoted a rational, public, social science—based government response to social problems that emphasized economic regulation, meritocracy, social insurance, and other protections, as well as the "professionalization" of human services. During this period, social work emerged as a distinct profession, and social science in general expanded rapidly.

The impact of the progressive movement continued in the 1930s and beyond. The 1930s brought the Great Depression, Roosevelt's New Deal, and the effective federalization of many progressive movement–initiated social programs that had previously been implemented in various states. The passage of the Social Security Act of 1935 created a national system of social insurance and a funding and regulatory mechanism for state programs and services. These developments, together with legislation related to labor and public works, created America's version of the welfare state. However, in contrast to many European countries, the American welfare state was more diverse, pragmatic, and limited. Without the class politics that characterized European nations, the United States was unable to sustain the necessary political support for growth of

the welfare state after the crisis of the Great Depression waned, and the 1940s and 1950s were characterized by slow evolution of the social insurance programs under the Social Security Act (Reid, 1996).

The 1960s brought another surge of public support and public funding for social programs. This occurred in part because of a major shift of direction in social policy, which was increasingly driven by the issues of race and poverty. As a result, there was a new wave of social programming and a recasting of social policy to promote inclusion, participation, and social equality. These goals were pursued through efforts to create new opportunities through social reform, programs, and services focused on expanding opportunities related to education and work and use of government regulatory powers to expand civil rights.

By the 1970s, the United States was approaching European levels of social welfare expenditures as a percentage of the gross domestic product (GDP), a major feat for a nation without a national health care program. However, the human services policy and service delivery framework in the United States differed dramatically from those in the European model, with its emphasis on universalism and citizen-based, non–means-tested benefits. The American policy configuration, which was embodied in the War on Poverty efforts of the late 1960s, emphasized community-level initiatives, activism of the poor, continuation of means-tested income supports, and an "opportunity" construct of poverty reduction with services that reflected those purposes (Dobelstein, 1996).

This policy shift was accompanied by specific initiatives that altered the character of social services and created a new context for their management. Before the 1960s, social and human services were generally conceived of as essentially nonmarket, publicly provided professional services to individuals and families who met income requirements or had other defined special needs. These services related to rehabilitation, child welfare and protection, mental health, and care and advice under the auspices of religious, secular nonprofit, or government organizations. Recipients were called "clients" or "patients," not "consumers," and the problems of nonmarket, functional monopoly provision were rarely considered. The idea was to provide professionally defined services to people whom the providers, whether public or private, deemed to be in need.

Social work or human services managers were involved primarily in organizing the delivery of services, accounting for the dollars spent, and relating to the funding sources. Accountability was upward and internal, from social worker to supervisor to director to board or legislative authority. Social workers were essentially not accountable to clients, who were given little choice in consumption and little real voice in program design or operations. Funding at both the federal and state levels was categorical (that is, specific to a particular service in a specific problem context). The manager's job in this context was comparatively simple. All of the important actors were both visible and relatively close at hand, continuity was pretty much ensured from year to year, and the system was largely closed to competitors and comparative cost-effectiveness evaluation.

However, by the mid-1960s, change began to be reflected in policy and law. In 1967 Congress included in its amendments to the Social Security Act a provision that allowed states to contract for delivery of services and for the carrying out of certain administrative tasks. In 1974 the Nixon administration was successful in getting Congress to consolidate four previous titles of the Social Security Act that had provided for federal funding of some categorical services into one social service funding stream (Plotnick & Skidmore, 1975).

This new title provided for a block of federal funds to be used in ways determined by state governments and requiring a state match (25 percent). Furthermore, and most important, Title XX required the states to devote half of the funds to services for poor people. These provisions, along with others, greatly increased state latitude as well as state cost and at the same time expanded typical services to include day care for children and adults, transportation, home health and homemaker services, job training and education, mental health counseling, and referral services.

The Omnibus Budget Reconciliation Act, enacted by Congress in 1981, compressed 57 social programs funded by categorical grants into seven block grants. These new block grants covered social services; community services; alcohol, drug abuse, and mental health services; maternal and child health services; community development services; primary health services; and preventive health services (Dickinson, 1996).

Significantly, the newer service areas that emerged during the 1970s and early 1980s were not specific to poor people; virtually all had parallels in the private market, which was producing services for paying consumers or for third-party reimbursement (Edwards et al., 1996). Inevitably, questions arose as to whether such services for individual consumption might be produced more efficiently and effectively in competitive markets, something that was typical for the health, legal, financial, and self-development services being consumed by nonpoor people. Once the overlap of services between poor people and nonpoor was apparent, and the social control aspect of social services was rendered less important by cultural and legal changes, the stage was set for marketization of social services.

MARKETIZATION OF SOCIAL AND HUMAN SERVICES

Definition
The term "marketization" is used here to refer to a reliance in public policy on natural trade exchange practices (for example, competition, privatization, commercialization, decentralization, and entrepreneurialism). Although its impact was felt first in the health and mental health sectors, marketization is currently affecting child welfare and other sectors as well. Marketization is the key to understanding

the changing environment of social work management.

Marketization, based on a presumption of the desirability of competition and market allocation, depends on a diversity of available providers (Jackson & Biesbrouck, 1995). Among other things, marketization changes the roles of public agencies from those of provider and manager to broker and contract administrator, and it places nonprofit organizations in a situation of much greater competition with other nonprofit and for-profit organizations.

Experience in the health services sector suggests that there is no necessary connection between personal income and service consumption in a private provider market. As long as insurance exists, whether public or private, people can be supported in consumption and given access to existing markets for services. In such a situation, the need for government to produce services is eliminated or greatly diminished. The health service arena has rapidly become the model that is being extended to the entire human services field.

Perhaps the logic of marketization would have taken hold regardless of circumstances in an American context that has always valued both the market and the individual, but its popularity has undoubtedly been aided both by real reductions in available government funds and the rapid and far-reaching technological changes that have occurred since the 1970s. Nevertheless, since the 1970s the context within which social work managers must work has been subject to a transformation that is more dramatic than at any other comparable period in its history. This transformation, which has been accompanied by progressively diminishing federal responsibility and control, has been profound and wrenching. Furthermore, it is requiring a wholesale reconceptualization of the role and character of both the human services enterprise and its management.

Management Implications

The increased economic imperative associated with the political and economic changes identified earlier has defined a "market culture" in which competitive markets—in contrast to public monopoly provision—have increasingly become the basis for public policy and planned social intervention. Markets represent a means to allow voluntary exchange between consumers or users of a service or commodity and

those who produce it. In their pure form markets allow consumers to express interests precisely and producers to incorporate those interests while consistently testing consumer preferences against price constraints. If such "natural" economic exchanges could be captured in the pursuit of public policy objectives, there would likely be advantages in terms of cost, effectiveness, and citizen satisfaction. In contrast, government nonmarket provision is associated with organizational bloat, service objectives that reflect producer interests, high cost, and low levels of individual user satisfaction.

According to Fisher (1995), market-based public policy produces privatization of public services, utilization of user fees rather than taxes to finance public services, deregulation in place of universal service, government competition, capital mobility, welfare reform, and a new federalism that forces local communities to adopt "market discipline." As stated earlier, marketization refers to the trend in public policy to rely on natural trade exchange practices and principles (for example, competition and privatization) as the basis for generating goods and services.

Hasenfeld (1996) described the outcome of human services marketization as "commercialization." He pointed out that traditional public services are increasingly being provided by nonprofit and for-profit providers and that human services vendors are having to "sell" their services in an environment that is rapidly assuming the characteristics of a marketplace. Citizens and users of services more often are being addressed as "customers," and managers must increasingly assume the role of entrepreneur. Those who have traditionally relied on government to provide them with a fair and equitable distribution of services are more often expected to become informed consumers. An evident by-product of this trend, according to Hasenfeld, is the "bifurcation and segmentation of services along income lines" and the erosion of "universal" services (p. 193). Gilbert and Gilbert (1989) and Stoesz (1986) also argued that a market transformation has occurred in American social services and that a corporate, health care–based model is the probable future of all human services provision.

However, an examination of the health care context also reveals some of the limitations of economic markets where there is a substantial public and government interest. The presence of insurance, whether private or public, changes market transactions in fundamental ways that reduce the incentive of both consumers and producers to control costs. Consequently, "managed competition" and other concepts have emerged in health care, along with devices to substitute for the loss of market forces.

The most evident of these devices is managed care, an effort to administer health services to individuals through constant case management and cost assessment. A sizable industry has developed in recent years in an effort to manage resources and redefine how health services can be provided more efficiently while holding service providers more accountable for cost and outcome. The managed care approach is designed to provide health, mental health, and other services at predictable costs by monitoring the work of, and predetermining the rate of reimbursement to, professionals or vendors who deliver the services.

Managed care encompasses a variety of methods used to affect the financing and delivery of health services. Edinburg and Cottler (1995) pointed out that managed care has a long history as an approach with different models designed to contain the cost of service delivery while maintaining quality. Leukefeld and Welsh (1995) presented an in-depth overview of health care financing that included a discussion of unwanted consequences of the managed care approach. Berkman (1996) referred to managed care as a new paradigm that will require new training for social workers to become effective players.

The capitation practices of some managed care health companies provide one example of a managed care approach that is currently fairly common (Berkman, 1996). In this approach physicians or provider systems are reimbursed a fixed amount over a period of time on a per-capita basis for each patient or family and encouraged to be both innovative and cost conscious in their practice. The capitation approach represents a manipulation of the reward structure, with the goal of stimulating the creation of new and alternative infrastructures and technologies that presumably will be an incentive to practitioners and provider systems to find more responsive and efficient ways to treat patients. It is presumed that these incentives will result in more preventive care designed to keep patients

healthy, thus controlling costs by avoiding more costly types of care.

As managed care has become more widespread as a mechanism for financing health services, there has been growing interest in transferring the model or approach to other human services arenas. A recent survey by the Child Welfare League of America found that 82 percent of states are considering applying elements of the managed care approach to child welfare services (Field, 1996). Congressional action to expand health insurance coverage for mental health further increases the demand for health maintenance organizations and other health plans that control costs by managing care.

Employers, both public and private, have been confronted for a number of years with rapidly and dramatically increasing costs for health insurance coverage for their employees and their dependents. In response to these escalating costs, employers are being encouraged to make greater use of a managed care approach while the market strives to provide ways to meet their employees' needs and control costs. Of course, not everyone sees the move toward managed care as positive. Adams and Krauth (1995) argued that managed care as a market mechanism for controlling cost will eventually influence the quality of health care because of the increased paperwork and reduced incentives for physicians and health care organizations to be proactive in providing care to citizens and in developing community partnerships and networks.

The "managed competition via managed care" approach to cost containment is redefining the products and practices of both public and nonprofit human services organizations, as well as those of individual practitioners. Managed care is also restructuring how services are delivered and by whom. Individual practitioners are adjusting their practices to comply with managed care reimbursement requirements. Lower-cost service vendors are replacing those requiring higher rates of reimbursement, and managed care companies are dictating what kinds of interventions and service providers will be reimbursed. Professionals and service provider organizations are having to become more aggressive in identifying managed care systems and gaining entry into managed care networks.

The managed competition approach is also being adopted by the private nonprofit sector, as illustrated by the informed and selective "investment" approach being adopted by local human services sponsors and funders, such as foundations and United Way organizations. Many foundations have been re-examining their missions and focusing on ways to have a more targeted impact on the communities or regions they serve. Similarly, many United Way groups are redefining their roles as "community investment brokers" for community investing in human services. This redefinition of roles, in turn, is placing more demands on member agencies to demonstrate a return on investment in terms of improved productivity, increased cost efficiency, responsible fiscal management, and results- or outcome-oriented performance.

At the same time these market-oriented approaches to funding and investing in human services are reshaping professional practices and organizational operations, they are stimulating increased management competition among professionals from various fields. They are creating a merit-based management selection process rather than a credential-based or political-based selection approach. Social workers in general—who traditionally have been selected for management on the basis of credentials, program knowledge, and experience—are faced with having to learn a new set of survival skills that include negotiating among competing values in market-driven environments. One of the implications of this is that social work education programs will have to modify their curricula to include additional content on system productivity, cost, and effectiveness. In addition, there is a need for postgraduate continuing education programs emphasizing practice principles and tools that are associated with managing in a market-driven environment.

In response to the impact of marketization on the human services sector, social work managers increasingly must play by the rules created by a marketplace arena. They are being challenged to become "market oriented" by acquiring new competition and conflict management skills while providing leadership in developing more streamlined, efficient governance models (Edwards et al., 1996). This suggests a value challenge, in that entrepreneurship is often associated with aggressive and competitive behaviors and attributes that may not be consonant with traditional social work values.

In the context of marketization, it is little wonder that managers of social work and other types of human services organizations are often urged by policymakers, board members, or the public to adopt the latest management fad or fancy that is sweeping the for-profit business sector. Many managers feel compelled, even in the absence of sufficient evidence of applicability, to adopt the newest, most popular management approach. Consequently, one of the key tasks for the social work manager is to try to sort through the various bits of management information and literature to determine which of the new approaches have real promise in terms of their application to the human services arena.

Marketplace dynamics also suggest a number of new developments in the area of human resource management, such as managing a career-resilient workforce in which employees must learn to embrace continuous change while steadily reinventing their careers and skills. Furthermore, the management of human resources currently requires increased skill in the management of diversity. In the public sector human resource management is undergoing fundamental changes from a civil service, union-oriented management environment to an environment increasingly characterized by the management of private employment contracts, flexible employee arrangements, and part-time workers.

DEVOLUTION REVOLUTION
In recent years a component and a consequence of the marketization of human services is a major public policy change in the United States. The embodiment of this change—labeled the "devolution revolution"—is the shifting of many federal government responsibilities to state and local government entities (Nathan, 1995). The devolution revolution involves the decentralization of service control; the geographic and demographic "localizing" of the provision of services; and, usually, greater consumer sovereignty through providing consumers with more choices.

To a large extent the devolution revolution was reflected in many of the provisions of the Republican party's "Contract with America" (Gingrich, Armey, & the House Republicans, 1994), and the term became a kind of mantra that was repeated by the presidential nominees of both major political parties throughout the 1996 election season. The devolution revolution is a response by political leaders of both major parties "to a common set of economic and social forces and assumptions . . . that are driving them to seek solutions to the federal budget deficit, rampant increases in expenditures for various entitlement programs, and decades of growth in federal regulations that affect almost every aspect of Americans' lives" (Edwards et al., 1996, p. 469).

The Personal Responsibility and Work Opportunity Reconciliation Act of 1996, which ushered in welfare reform, eliminated the entitlement basis to many services and gave states more policy and management responsibilities for public social services. With its emphasis on several areas of reform, as well as a reduction in federal funding to the states, the legislation represented a benchmark in the localization trend. In addition, the legislation included a new set of federal requirements that demand localized results-oriented reporting and accountability.

With this new legislative framework, state and local government units, as well as local nonprofit organizations, are being confronted with having to redesign their local human services infrastructures and delivery systems. Generally, existing local administrative and program delivery structures and technologies are no longer adequate for the new localization challenges. Citizens increasingly are being expected both to play stronger roles in advocating for needed services and to become more informed consumers. This increased expectation for individual action and responsibility is taking place at a time when there seems to be a general trend for people to withdraw from traditional community participation. As a result, local human services vendors are having to learn and apply the fundamentals of competitive marketing (that is, product, promotion, placement, pricing, and performance) to individual consumers.

This is not to say that community, in the sense of groups of similar stakeholders or consumers, is irrelevant. Rather, communities of stakeholders are extremely relevant, and social work managers are expected to provide the leadership needed by human services organizations and the various stakeholder groups during the devolution transformation process. Increasingly, social work managers will have to understand and represent the interests of the various "communities" they serve, as well as the interests of their programs or organizations. Fortunately, social work managers can turn to a growing body of literature that advocates for a definition of social work practice that includes community perspectives and technology (Adams & Nelson, 1995; Fisher & Karger, 1997; Weil, 1996).

The increasing localization of human services effectively reduces, if not eliminates, the distinction between management as a program/organization practice and management as community practice. Social workers who manage human services programs and organizations already live a "dicey" existence, having to negotiate the demands and competing values of various interest and stakeholder groups (Edwards & Austin, 1991). The pluralistic, and often competing, multiple-stakeholder environment frequently casts social work managers in roles that make it inevitable that some adversarial elements will be introduced into management practice.

PERFORMANCE- OR OUTCOME-BASED ACCOUNTABILITY

In addition to being effective players in the marketplace, social work managers are having to address changes in the way fiscal and program performance is monitored and evaluated. Human services programs, organizations, and systems are being confronted with demands from political leaders and the general public for changes in accountability and performance expectations, revolutionary changes that Sepic (1996) suggested involve paradigm shifts that require reinventing existing resources and finding new ways to manage change.

A reflection of this changing environment is the Government Performance and Results Act of 1993 (GPRA, or Public Law 103-62). This law, which began implementation in 1997, requires government or public agencies and programs, as well as nonprofit organizations that contract with public agencies, to develop performance plans for each activity. These plans must include "performance indicators" and "objective, quantifiable and measurable goals." In a parallel movement, the Governmental Accounting Standards Board (GASB) has been developing standards for performance auditing of state and local governments—and their contractees (GASB, 1994).

These shifts in performance measurement and fiscal auditing are a part of a fundamental historical change in the practice of planning and budgeting. This strategy of performance- or outcome-based accountability involves shifting the emphasis from organizational/ system inputs and processes (that is, efforts) to an emphasis on the outcomes produced.

The mandates of the outcome-based strategy suggest that any public service initiative, whether public or nonprofit, should involve identification of outcomes, selection of outcome measures, development of outcome-based performance standards, implementation of appropriate monitoring and reporting systems, and application of outcome information to a continuous quality or product improvement process. It is assumed that if these steps are followed by public and non-profit entities such as human services organizations, a results-oriented accountability system will be created that will be honored by various public and private funders, political and business leaders, and the general public.

Although many may regard performance- or outcome-based accountability simply as another "fad" in the long history of efforts to renew or improve organizations, the current sociopolitical and economic environment augurs for a different picture. Human services, in the historical welfare state model of government, existed in a noncompetitive marketplace that measured outcome effectiveness by the budget size and number of persons served. In a market environment involving competition, profitability and cost efficiency are the primary indicators of success. Performance-based accountability is also being driven by the expansion and increasing sophistication of evaluation technology. Schools of social work, for example, increasingly are providing program evaluation as a key product of their community service activities.

In the human services sector, organizational survival or other less tangible measures have typically been regarded as indicators of profitability or success. In the absence of ways to empirically measure the effectiveness of human services, communities and political systems demonstrated their support through a strategy of resource maximization (Hagglund & Stymne, 1996). In essence support was provided through regular expansion of the amounts and kinds of resources for services. Managers tended to exploit this strategy by emphasizing the indispensability of the services provided by their organizations and documenting the ever-increasing demands for those services. This resulted in a constant expansion and growth of programs. Recently, however, this scenario has been undergoing dramatic change, with funding decisions increasingly aimed at fostering a smaller, reinvented, privatized, more localized, and more market-oriented approach to addressing social problems and measuring their effectiveness (Edwards et al., 1996).

Responses to the new outcome-based performance mandates include widespread experimentation with and efforts to operationalize outcome-oriented measurement systems at the program, organization, and community levels. Public entities at the local, state, and federal levels, as well as nonprofit organizations and local community human services networks, increasingly are involved in defining measurable outcomes and having to confront the arduous task of developing performance measurement and accountability systems that effectively document the results of human services expenditures.

This is a new milieu for social work managers that requires new skills and attitudes. Historically the attention to performance management in the human services sector has largely been concerned with (1) individual professional behavior by practitioners or managers; (2) accessibility and availability of services to clients; and (3) compatibility with, or adherence to, applicable law and policy. The outcome performance of programs, organizations, and systems received less emphasis, because it was assumed that organizational and system performance was contingent on the professionalization and "best-practice" behavior of the individual professionals. However, recently there has been more consideration of the significance of the relationship between individual professional performance and organizational performance (Weiner, 1991). Furthermore, the relationship between individual professional behavior and organizational/system performance and its management is implied in much of the recent social work literature on total quality management (Gummer & McCallion, 1995).

An inherent challenge for social work managers in the new marketplace and outcome-based performance measurement milieu is redefining the ways in which their organizations relate to their various customers or constituencies. Managers must become "arbitrators" between the capacities of their programs or organizations and the demands and expectations of their various customers. Meeting this challenge effectively requires that managers be firmly grounded in experiential reality and have the ability to successfully represent that reality in the marketplace.

The renewed preoccupation with the measurement of organizational and system outcomes within marketplace environments has resulted in the exploration of new approaches to and definitions of accountability. Traditionally accountability in government-sponsored social and human services was mainly a matter of accounting for fiscal expenditures and policy (legal and administrative) compliance. Managers of those services were responsible for how public money was spent and on what, and for whether their programs met federal or state requirements. In the nonprofit arena accountability has primarily involved a "tax status" oversight infrastructure with a loose connection to the notion of public good.

In the current environment accountability is not so simple. A study of the federal government's efforts to monitor itself through the development of offices of inspector general identified three approaches to accountability: compliance accountability, performance accountability, and capacity building (Light, 1993). Efforts to ensure conformity with rules and regulations are considered compliance accountability, which relies on correcting problems after they occur to avoid potential punishment. Traditionally this has been the accountability approach used in most government initiatives. The general consequences of compliance accountability are the rewarding of short-term outputs instead of long-term capacity building, and the proliferation of regulations that deal with exceptions and variances. The role of the manager in compliance accountability is one of supervision and discipline.

In contrast, performance accountability relies on the establishment of incentives and rewards for desired outcomes. Performance accountability has an impact before something happens; it emphasizes continuous evaluation and benchmarking and is more complex than compliance accountability. The manager's role in performance accountability involves a greater emphasis on planning, goal setting, and reinforcement (Light, 1993).

The capacity building approach, which represents a broader definition of accountability than either the compliance or performance accountability approaches, refers to efforts at longer-term capital investing in technologies, performance pay, merit bonuses, and positive sanctions. The manager's role in capacity building accountability involves a greater emphasis on advocacy and stewardship. Light (1993) pointed out that although these approaches have distinctive features, the choice of one approach does not rule out the need for one or both of the other approaches.

Kearns (1996) argued that a new accountability environment for both public and nonprofit organizations has been spurred by the publicity surrounding scandals such as those involving William Aramony of United Way of America (Dundjerski, 1995). He developed a strategic approach to accountability that incorporated a public trust orientation, the inclusion of stakeholder expectations, and an emphasis on accountability standards as a part of an organization's strategic environment and planning process that involves proactive and anticipatory accountability management. According to Kearns, specifically this involves (1) anticipating explicit accountability standards (for example, laws and regulations); (2) scanning the environments and stakeholders for implicit accountability standards (for example, professional norms and social values); and (3) a sustained commitment of resources to develop objective, valid, and reliable accountability systems.

Most discussions of social work management recognize the many "hats" that must be worn, the many publics to which the manager is accountable, and the competing values that have to be negotiated (Edwards & Austin, 1991). Effectively negotiating these roles and stakeholders—pleasing some without offending most—has become a hallmark of successful management practice. Selecting a prime beneficiary to whom to be accountable in a field of competing players and values is usually difficult and absorbs much of the manager's time and energy (Weinbach, 1994). Added to this challenge is the reality that most human services agencies and community initiatives have had difficulty in producing evidence of their effectiveness in terms of business performance criteria that are generally accepted by the public at large. Furthermore, it is often difficult to clearly define the customers, or primary stakeholders, for human services organizations. This creates a dilemma for social work managers that is addressed in much of the total quality management literature (Gummer & McCallion, 1995; Gunther & Hawkins, 1996).

The changing definitions of accountability, although they make the job of the social work manager more complex, also provide some organizational opportunities. Social work managers can use the changing accountability environment as a catalyst to engage critical stakeholders in defining how, on what basis, and by whom the success or failure of their organizations, programs, and initiatives are to be measured. This process is characteristic of virtually any "self-learning," market-oriented enterprise. Social work managers can seize the opportunity presented by the demands of the new outcome-based accountability environment to engage their various customer or stakeholder groups in a serious effort to identify the desired organizational outcomes and to develop a consensus about how these outcomes will be evaluated.

ACCELERATED CHANGE AND THE "INSTANT" MARKETPLACE ENVIRONMENT

In addition to marketization, the devolution revolution, and outcome-based accountability, another important and dynamic theme shaping social work management is the rapid pace of change and its behavioral consequences. Social work managers are being challenged to "survive" in environments that are changing at an increasingly accelerated pace. Although social work managers have always operated within a context of constant change, at no point in recent history has the pace of change been as accelerated, been experienced by so many people in so many areas, and had such a pervasive influence on daily behavior.

Technology transformation, social and demographic changes, and the increasing realities of a competitive global community have combined to create a sense of immediacy and urgency in Americans' daily lives and in their ways of doing business. Personal computers, the Internet, e-mail, fax machines, cellular telephones, and the like have contributed to a technological environment in which instant response has become the norm. Television, with its penchant for reducing major news events to 15- and 30-second sound bites and its dramatic portrayals of serious interpersonal or social problems being solved in 30 minutes or an hour,

has also contributed to the sense that life is a series of short-term, rapidly changing events.

Becoming "lean, quick, and mean" has become a guiding principle for many organizations. In the for-profit corporate sector, news of mergers, acquisitions, restructuring, and downsizing is virtually a daily occurrence. In terms of information technology, the life cycle of products grows shorter as technological change accelerates, and at the same time demand increases and competition intensifies (Oberlin, 1996). In the political environment, new human services programs that address complex social situations often appear to have a life cycle coexistent with the tenure of the incumbent politician or political party. For social work managers, handling the rapid and pervasive changes associated with the dramatically evolving role of information in society is a key issue (Schoech, 1996).

The traditional view of social work management, based on an assumption of incremental changes and stable organizations with normative patterns of behavior, no longer captures the realities of management practice. Managers no longer have the luxury of extended time periods in which to build relationships, transform work groups into teams, and achieve community stakeholder consensus on desired outcomes. Increasingly, interventions and programs are expected to be implemented instantly and have immediate measurable consequences. Latting (1996) argued that because of the rapid pace of change, human services organizations and managers "may no longer be able to study and learn before acting . . . " (p. 225). As a consequence, "organizational members will become more sophisticated in making leaps of faith, committing to some action and then learning from their failures and successes" (p. 225). Overman (1995) observed that modern managers perceive their environments as chaotic because things happen "too quickly all at once, and seemingly out of control and incomprehensible . . . when everything seems on the verge of collapse" (p. 487).

Creating organizational strategies and systems to cope with and survive accelerated change has become another critical task in the panoply of leadership challenges confronting social work managers. Accelerated change, and the numerous proposed coping strategies, have produced a climate of skepticism among rank-and-file human services workers. It has also created a culture in which innovations and transformations have a low survival rate (Light, 1993). Sepic (1996) argued that "when organizational members continue to be forced to adopt strategies that are not of their own and not guided by what they think is possible, there is bound to be emotional exhaustion and feelings of low personal accomplishment by depersonalization (i.e., burnout)" (p. 9).

The management literature suggests numerous managerial techniques and approaches for dealing with accelerated change and its consequences, including individual, organizational, and community "burnout" and low innovation success rates (Eadie, 1997; Quinn, 1995). The common thread underlying most of the suggestions is that it is important for managers to have a method or plan for managing change.

SEARCH FOR STRATEGIC RESPONSES

When considering how social work management is being affected by the themes described here, it is worth noting that there is an identifiable culture of management that is American in character (Hampden-Turner & Trompenaars, 1994). The U.S. economy has prospered by emphasizing standardization and production control, with such companies as the "big three" auto makers, McDonalds, and IBM as prime examples. A passion for rules, job descriptions, the devaluation of personal individual characteristics as "immaterial" to productive work, and the undermining of personal relationships among workers have all characterized American corporations and organizations for decades. "Scientific management," management by objectives, and other popular management theories and practices have reflected these emphases. A discussion of the larger cultural sources of these qualities is beyond the scope of this entry, but failure to recognize that the United States has a distinctive, relatively consistent quality to its management style is a failure to understand a major source of America's economic success, and of its current vulnerability.

Our nation has relied heavily on a notion of management that is heroic and short term in nature, emphasizing the correct organizational diagnosis and treatment carried out by brave and insightful individuals with management authority. The focus has been on "fixing" what is not working and on looking for the "bottom line," in terms of either price or productivity.

Organizations, including those in the human services sector, have tended to be viewed as variations of an assembly line, and there has been a willingness to move the human and nonhuman pieces of the line around to effect some momentary desired outcome. However, much of the world does not work like this, and as a nation America is currently beginning to recognize a need to adapt and reform.

However, finding appropriate and effective responses to deal with the environmental realities of marketization, devolution, outcome-based accountability, and accelerated change is hardly easy. The search dominates much of the current management literature, which is rich with discussions of proposed new approaches, techniques, organizational structures, and community processes that offer potential survival benefits in an era of mandated change and marketplace dynamics (Adams & Nelson, 1995; Asamoah, 1995; Eadie, 1997; Edwards et al., 1996; Edwards & Eadie, 1994; Ginsberg & Keys, 1995; Gummer & McCallion, 1995; Gunther & Hawkins, 1996; Healy, Havens, & Pine, 1995; Linden, 1994; Raffoul & McNeece, 1996). In recent years many public and nonprofit human services organizations have been experimenting with a variety of specific management innovation techniques, including total quality management, re-engineering, strategic planning, strategic change management, benchmarking, privatization, diversity management, commercialization, rapid assessment procedures, and seamless government, among a host of others.

The above references are but a sample of the search for answers to managerial coping with new realities that require more localized and rapid responses, greater flexibility, enhanced creativity and innovation, and nonbureaucratic relationships with multiple stakeholders. The search also seeks to find formulas and techniques that allow for the maintenance of professional integrity and values while managing in the face of an unknown and unpredictable future.

Research on the strategic choices made by nonprofit human services agencies in response to changing environments reveals that such agencies tend to follow an identifiable pattern of four strategies (McMurtry, Netting, & Kettner, 1990):

1. They first try productivity enhancement or slack utilization strategies.

2. They proceed to try power enhancement strategies.
3. They then use cutback strategies.
4. Finally, they implement efforts to restructure the agency.

Those strategies involving internal agency adjustments (that is, productivity enhancement, slack utilization, and service cutbacks) and efforts to gain control over external revenue sources (power enhancement strategies) were significantly associated with declining revenues. When strategies to acquire power within the environment failed or were not sufficient, the managers of the nonprofit organizations studied resorted to cutting back services before acting to restructure their organizations (McMurtry et al., 1990). This research suggested that social work managers must be prepared to deal with a number of issues and attempt a variety of strategies as they try to lead their organizations though the kind of transformation required by the current environment. The research also suggests that the more radical responses, such as restructuring or re-engineering, are more likely to be the most difficult strategies to implement.

Although both for-profit business and public and nonprofit human services organizations are confronted with the same turbulent environment, those who manage in the human services arena are confronted with a significantly different task environment (for example, multiple constituents with conflicting values and goals and products that are defined by funders instead of customers). As a result, a different set of practice competencies is required for those who manage in the human services arena. For example, whereas managers of for-profit business organizations may readily use cutbacks, downsizing, or other restructuring strategies, the same is not as true for the managers of human services organizations. Human services managers, guided by ideological values, historically tended to regard cutbacks as a retreat from their primary "mission." The tendency of human services organizations to avoid restructuring strategies reflects an effort not only to avoid personal disruption and loss of control and identity but also to preserve professional solutions, technology, and an economic base—all of which are constraints to effective efforts at reform, re-engineering, and reinvention.

The search for strategic responses to the themes identified earlier has stimulated a quest for new paradigms that will enable organizations to effectively adapt to environments that are rapidly changing, unpredictable, and chaotic. The more traditional linear, orderly approaches to organizational change are no longer appropriate, nor is the traditional Newtonian view of systems as machines that can be reduced to their parts for understanding and manipulation. Fresh new approaches are needed that will enable organizations to survive and prosper in the complex environments currently confronting them.

Social work managers increasingly must attempt to distinguish substantive trends from fads in finding a managerial "model which provides for an effective transition of organizational structure and culture to fit the changing realities" (Edwards et al., 1996, p. 475). Gummer and McCallion (1995) compared the faddish nature of management practice with that of psychiatric practices and argued for a more substantive base for practice. Ginsberg (1995) alluded to the need to avoid fads by defining "new management" in social work as being based on "systematic, scientific observation of what . . . 'is' . . . rather than . . . what . . . 'should' be" (p. 3).

Management practice is basically defined by responses to particular situations and by approaches or techniques to negotiate changing organizational environments. Effective management practice, in human services or elsewhere, involves doing the "right thing" at the "right time" for the "right reasons" to produce the "right result" in the "right environment." Theoretically, effective management practice entails the application of strategies and techniques that are appropriate to particular situations, within a particular environmental context, and lead to the survival or success of an enterprise. Given that situations and contexts constantly change, effective managers, therefore, are those who are able to accurately "read" environments, discern changes in those environments, and distinguish those changes that represent critical developments from those that are faddish in nature.

CONCLUSION

Historically America's culture favored an active government role in regulating the human services marketplace and valued collaboration over competition. In this context social work managers have tended to place greater emphasis on the "how" of practice rather than on the results or outcomes of practice. Until recently, not much emphasis was placed on developing the knowledge and technological base for identifying and measuring or evaluating outcomes.

Current environmental changes are having a profound impact on social work management. Social work managers increasingly must understand and be able to effectively address a range of issues confronting their organizations, including marketization, devolution and localization, outcome-based accountability, and rapid and constant change.

What characteristics or attributes do social work managers have that will enable them to be effective players in the new marketplace environment? As both key players and stakeholders in the new marketplaces, social work managers have a number of attributes that represent real strengths. These include a strong value base; proven interpersonal competencies; an appreciation and commitment to workplace and community diversity; a history of planning and managing both government and nonprofit human services; and skills in facilitating participation by a wide range of stakeholders at individual, organizational, and community levels, to name just a few. Social work managers typically are predisposed to facilitating and doing things to empower others, competencies that are very important in the current organizational environments.

Nevertheless, there are a number of knowledge and skill areas that social workers must further develop to compete effectively in the marketplace. These include skills in reading sociopolitical and economic environments, the trends and forces shaping them, and the ideological/technological orientations of potential allies. The economic imperatives of changing environments call for competencies in managing cutbacks, creative budgeting, identifying new resources, and providing leadership in developing and implementing new fundraising strategies (Edwards, Benefield, Edwards, & Yankey, 1997).

Increasingly social work managers are being expected to provide leadership in managing environmental relationships, such as effective agency or program representation and positioning, networking, coalition building, negotiating hostile environments, and dealing with multiple customer and stakeholder groups. Social work managers increasingly are confronted with the task of selling and negotiating the actual and symbolic value of their organizations' services or products to funders in a highly politicized environment. They are challenged to create and orchestrate the visions, processes, measurements, technologies, and organizational cultures that will make the provision of human services more efficient, productive, and results oriented. Finally, social work managers must find appropriate approaches to manage the change and transformation that is taking place in American communities and in the human services arena.

REFERENCES

Adams, P., & Krauth, K. (1995). Working with families and communities. In P. Adams & K. Nelson (Eds.), *Reinventing human services*. New York: Aldine de Gruyter.

Adams, P., & Nelson, K. (Eds.). (1995). *Reinventing human services*. New York: Aldine de Gruyter.

Asamoah, Y. (1995). Managing the new multicultural workplace. In L. Ginsberg & P. R. Keys (Eds.), *New management in human services* (2nd ed., pp. 115–127). Washington, DC: NASW Press.

Berkman, B. (1996). The emerging health care world: Implications for social work practice and education. *Social Work, 41,* 541–551.

Dickinson, N. S. (1996). Federal social legislation from 1961 to 1994. In R. L. Edwards (Ed.-in-Chief), *Encyclopedia of social work* (19th ed., Vol. 2, pp. 1005–1013). Washington, DC: NASW Press.

Dobelstein, A. W. (1996). *Social welfare policy and analysis*. Chicago: Nelson-Hall.

Dundjerski, M. (1995). United Way: 1 percent increase in gifts. *Chronicle of Philanthropy, 7*(22), 27–29.

Eadie, D. C. (1997). *Changing by design*. San Francisco: Jossey-Bass.

Edinburg, G. M., & Cottler, J. M. (1995). Managed care. In R. L. Edwards (Ed.-in-Chief), *Encyclopedia of social work* (19th ed., Vol. 2, pp. 1635–1642). Washington, DC: NASW Press.

Edwards, R. L., & Austin, D. M. (1991). Managing effectively in an environment of competing values. In R. L. Edwards & J. A. Yankey (Eds.), *Skills for effective human services management* (pp. 5–22). Washington, DC: NASW Press.

Edwards, R. L., Benefield, E.A.S., Edwards, J. A., & Yankey, J. A. (1997). *Building a strong foundation: Fundraising for nonprofits*. Washington, DC: NASW Press.

Edwards, R. L., Cooke, P. W., & Reid, P. N. (1996). Social work management in an era of diminishing federal responsibility. *Social Work, 41,* 468–479.

Edwards, R. L., & Eadie, D. C. (1994). Meeting the change challenge: Managing growth in the nonprofit and public human services sectors. *Administration in Social Work, 18,* 107–123.

Field, T. (1996). Changes in the child welfare system and role of the public sector casework under child welfare managed care. *Georgia Academy Journal, IV*(1), 13–15.

Fisher, P. S. (1995). The economic context of community-centered practice: Markets, communities, and social policy. In P. Adams & K. Nelson (Eds.), *Reinventing human services.* New York: Aldine de Gruyter.

Fisher, R., & Karger, H. (1997). *Social work and community in a private world.* White Plains, NY: Longman.

Gilbert, N., & Gilbert, B. (1989). *The enabling state: Modern welfare capitalism in America.* New York: Oxford University Press.

Gingrich, N., Armey, D., & the House Republicans. (1994). *Contract with America.* Washington, DC: U.S. House of Representatives, Committees, and House Organizations. Also available online at http://www.house.gov/org.pubs.htmc.

Ginsberg, L. (1995). Concepts of new management. In L. Ginsberg & P. R. Keys (Eds.), *New management in human services* (2nd ed., pp. 1–37). Washington, DC: NASW Press.

Ginsberg, L., & Keys, P. R. (Eds.). (1995). *New management in human services* (2nd ed.). Washington, DC: NASW Press.

Government Accounting Standards Board. (1994). *Concepts statement no. 2: On concepts related to service efforts and accomplishments reporting.* Norwalk, CT: Author.

Government Performance and Results Act of 1993. P.L. 103-62, 107 Stat. 285.

Gummer, B., & McCallion, P. (Eds.). (1995). *Total quality management in the social services.* Albany, NY: Rockefeller College of Public Affairs and Policy.

Gunther, J., & Hawkins, F. (1996). *Total quality management in human service organizations.* New York: Springer.

Hagglund, P. B., & Stymne, B. (1996). The speedy government. *Public Productivity & Management Review, 20*(1), 45–55.

Hampden-Turner, C., & Trompenaars, F. (1994). *The seven cultures of capitalism.* London: Piatkus.

Hasenfeld, Y. (1996). The administration of human services—What lies ahead? In R. Raffoul & C. A. McNeece (Eds.), *Future issues for social work practice* (pp. 191–202). Needham Heights, MA: Allyn & Bacon.

Healy, L. M., Havens, C. M., & Pine, B. A. (1995). Women in social work management. In L. Ginsberg & P. R. Keys (Eds.), *New management in human services* (2nd ed., pp. 128–150). Washington, DC: NASW Press.

Jackson, M., & Biesbrouck, W. (Eds.). (1995). *Marketization, restructuring, and competition in transition industries of central and eastern Europe.* Brookfield, VT: Avebury.

Kearns, K. P. (1996). *Managing for accountability.* San Francisco: Jossey-Bass.

Latting, J. K. (1996). Human service organizations of the future. In R. Raffoul & C. A. McNeece (Eds.), *Future issues for social work practice* (pp. 214–226). Needham Heights, MA: Allyn & Bacon.

Leukefeld, C. G., & Welsh, R. (1995). Health services systems policy. In R. L. Edwards (Ed.-in-Chief), *Encyclopedia of social work* (19th ed., Vol. 2, pp. 1206–1213). Washington, DC: NASW Press.

Light, P. C. (1993). *Monitoring government.* Washington, DC: Brookings Institution.

Linden, R. (1994). *Seamless government.* San Francisco: Jossey-Bass.

McMurtry, S. L., Netting, F. E., & Kettner, P. M. (1990). Critical inputs and strategic choice in non-profit human service agencies. *Administration in Social Work, 14*(3), 67–82.

Nathan, A. P. (1995). *Hardroad ahead: Block grants and the "devolution revolution."* Albany, NY: Nelson A. Rockefeller Institute of Government.

Oberlin, J. L. (1996). The financial mythology of information technology: Developing a new financial game plan. *Cause/Effect, 19*(2), 10–17.

Omnibus Budget Reconciliation Act of 1981, P.L. 97-35, 95 Stat. 357.

Overman, E. S. (1995). Privatization in China, Mexico, and Russia. *Public Productivity & Management Review, 19*(1), 46–59.

Personal Responsibility and Work Opportunity Reconciliation Act of 1996. Title IV, P.L. 104-193, 110 Stat. 2105.

Plotnick, R., & Skidmore, F. (1975). *Progress against poverty: A review of the 1964–1974 decade.* New York: Academic Press.

Quinn, W. H. (1995). Expanding the focus of intervention: The importance of family/community relations. In P. Adams & K. Nelson (Eds.), *Reinventing human services* (pp. 245–260). New York: Aldine de Gruyter.

Raffoul, R., & McNeece, C. A. (Eds.). (1996). *Future issues for social work practice.* Needham Heights, MA: Allyn & Bacon.

Reid, P. N. (1996). Social welfare history. In R. L. Edwards (Ed.-in-Chief), *Encyclopedia of social work*

(19th ed., Vol. 3, pp. 2206–2225). Washington, DC: NASW Press.

Schoech, D. (1996). Information systems. In R. L. Edwards (Ed.-in-Chief), *Encyclopedia of social work* (19th ed., Vol. 2, pp. 1470–1479). Washington, DC: NASW Press.

Sepic, F. T. (1996). Public change strategies. *Public Productivity & Management Review, 20*(1), 5–10.

Social Security Act of 1935. Ch. 351, 49 Stat. 620.

Social Security Act Amendments of 1967, P.L. 90-248, 81 Stat. 821.

Stoesz, D. (1986). Corporate welfare: The third stage of welfare in the United States. *Social Work, 31,* 245–250.

Weil, M. O. (1996). Community building: Building community practice. *Social Work, 41,* 481–499.

Weinbach, R. (1994). *The social worker as manager* (2nd ed.). Needham Heights, MA: Allyn & Bacon.

Weiner, M. E. (1991). Motivating employees to achieve. In R. L. Edwards & J. A. Yankey (Eds.), *Skills for effective human services management* (pp. 302–316). Washington, DC: NASW Press.

Philip W. Cooke, DSW, is professor and chair, management concentration, School of Social Work, University of North Carolina at Chapel Hill, 301 Pittsboro Street, Chapel Hill, NC 27599-3550.
P. Nelson Reid, PhD, is professor and director, Social Work Department, North Carolina State University, Rm 231 A 1911 Bldg, Raleigh, NC 27695-7639. **Richard L. Edwards, PhD, ACSW,** is dean and professor, School of Social Work, University of North Carolina at Chapel Hill, 301 Pittsboro Street, Chapel Hill, NC 27599-3550.

For further information see

Clinical Social Work; Ethics and Values; Interdisciplinary and Interorganizational Collaboration; Managed Care Overview; **Managed Care: Implications for Social Work Practice; Managed Care: A Review of Recent Research;** Management Overview; **Management: Cost Measurement;** Management: Diverse Workplaces; Nonprofit Management Issues; Planning and Management Professions; Public Services Management; Purchasing Social Services; Quality Assurance; Quality Management; Social Work Education Overview; Social Work Profession Overview; Strategic Planning; Supervision and Consultation; Unions; Vendorship; Volunteer Management.

Key Words

devolution	outcome quality
marketization	privatization
nonprofit management	

Mental Illness

See **Serious Mental Illness: A Biopsychosocial Perspective**

O

Oppression

Kathryn G. Wambach
Dorothy Van Soest

Because of social work's commitment to promoting social and economic justice, a firm grasp of the dynamics of power and oppression is necessary to avoid unintended collusion with these pervasive systems. A discussion of the varying conceptualizations of oppression includes consideration of institutional, psychological, and cultural aspects. The subtle dynamics of power and oppression in American society are examined, demonstrating that all people in an oppressive system experience both victim and perpetrator roles. In terms of social work education, the painfulness of acknowledging both professional and personal culpability and privilege is examined. Suggestions for social work research and practice emphasize that there is no neutral position for opposing oppression. Without a continual commitment to social action and social change, the professional activities risk reinforcing oppressive systems. Active opposition to oppression may be fostered by strengths and empowerment approaches that explicitly acknowledge power differentials, the coping strategies through which individuals and groups seek to thrive, and the need to advocate for social change.

The social work profession has a historical commitment to oppose oppression. This commitment—usually stated in terms of promoting social and economic justice—is made official in professional documents such as the *NASW Code of Ethics* (National Association of Social Workers, 1996) and the *Curriculum Policy Statement* for social work education (Council on Social Work Education [CSWE], 1994). Included in this entry are (1) an overview of the concept of oppression, (2) an examination of its dynamics, and (3) a discussion of the implications for the social work profession.

KEY CONCEPTS AND DEFINITIONS

Oppression Defined

Definitions of oppression tend to focus on distinct themes. Lipman-Blumen (1984, 1994) focused primarily on the institutional qualities of the concept by defining oppression as the act of molding, immobilizing, or reducing opportunities, which thereby restrains, restricts, or prevents social, psychological, or economic movement of an individual or a group. Similarly, Pinderhughes (1973) defined oppression as a relatively constant pattern of prejudice and discrimination between one party (who is idealized, favored, and given privileges on the basis of favored status) and another (who is devalued, exploited, and deprived of privileges chiefly because he or she is a member of a devalued group). Simply stated, oppression is an institutionalized, unequal power relationship—prejudice plus power (Rothenberg, 1988).

In contrast, Smith (1991) emphasized the result of oppression, rather than its process, when asserting that oppressive conditions delimit a person's ability to fulfill his or her potential. Frye (1995) also focused on the experience of oppression: "living . . . one's life . . . confined and shaped by forces and barriers which are not accidental or occasional and hence avoidable, but are systematically related to each other in such a way as to catch one between and among them and restrict or penalize motion in any direction" (p. 39).

Prilleltensky and Gonick (1994) captured more clearly that oppression involves both internal and external forces. They defined oppression as "a state of asymmetric power relations characterized by domination, subordination, and resistance, where the dominating people exercise their power by restricting access to material resources and by implanting in the subordinated people self-deprecating views about themselves" (p. 153). Brittan and Maynard (1984) reflected the same inclusiveness of internal and external forces by conceptualizing oppression as encompassing primary and secondary processes. Primary processes involve institutional forces of unequal economic, cultural, and social resources, whereas secondary processes include personal effects and internal forces generated within the subordinate groups.

Along with these forms of individual and institutional oppression, there is another level of oppression called "cultural oppression," in which the norms and values of the dominant group are deemed superior and serve as the standards for judging all other groups (Griffin, 1991). In contrast to institutional oppression, which carries the force of law and formal government, cultural oppression involves issues of "taste," such as music, art, literature, language, religion, or standards of physical beauty.

Oppression and Power

All definitions of oppression have an underlying theme related to the use and misuse of power in human relationships (Alderfer, 1994). Although recognizing the wide variety of definitions of power, this discussion draws heavily on the work of Lipman-Blumen (1984, 1994) for both content and structure. Power is thus defined as processes whereby one party (for example, individuals, groups, institutions, or states) can gain or maintain the capacity to impose its will repeatedly on another, despite any opposition, through invoking or threatening punishment or through offering or withholding rewards based on its control of critical resources.

Documentation of power relationships throughout human history raises questions regarding the existence of a universal human need for power. Smith (1991) suggested, in fact, that human capacities to label and differentiate make it virtually inevitable that status inequality will develop in social systems. The universality of hierarchically organized social systems is explained in purely functional terms by social dominance theory (Sidanius & Pratto, 1993). Specifically, group-based dominance systems have proved useful historically for establishing principles of scarce resource allocation, reducing internal social conflict, and providing a competitive advantage over systems that are not hierarchically organized.

Lipman-Blumen (1984, 1994) suggested that the universality of dominance is based on an existential issue: the uncertainty of human life. Specifically, people are essentially helpless and lack control over their lives, and this inherent powerlessness produces an existential sense of anxiety that people seek to manage by creating the illusion of control. Several strategies are used to relieve the anxiety of inherent powerlessness. First, people rely on the existence of an all-powerful, unseen (and thus irrefutable)

force (for example, religion) with which to align so that, although they remain powerless, they are assured of protection and access to power through their relationship with this force. Second, people align themselves with institutions or human leaders through which they seek protection or access to power (for example, nationalism).

The final human strategy—one that has been employed throughout history—is to seek control of something, or preferably someone, else. When successful, this strategy essentially redirects one's attention from one's own powerlessness and focuses it on the powerlessness of others, thereby obscuring one's anxiety about lack of control. It is from this last strategy that oppression results.

DYNAMICS AND MECHANISMS OF OPPRESSION

Well-established oppressive relationships, propelled by internal and external forces, are characterized by a particularly insidious nature. Frye (1995) created a metaphor to convey the difficulty in recognizing these forces in action, which likens oppression to a birdcage that is invisible to microscopic scrutiny but starkly apparent from a macroscopic view:

> It is now possible to grasp one of the reasons why oppression can be hard to see and recognize: one can study the elements of an oppressive structure with great care and some good will without seeing the structure as a whole, and hence without seeing or being able to understand that one is looking at a cage and there are people there who are caged, whose motion and mobility are restricted, whose lives are shaped and reduced. (p. 40)

Frye's depiction of the nature of oppression illustrates that its operation depends on both microlevel processes ("the wires") and their structural linkages in macrolevel processes ("the cage"). Thus, a clear understanding of oppression can be derived only from a firm grasp of its dynamics and mechanisms. The following discussion of several considerations that are particularly important to recognizing and understanding oppressive relationships draws heavily again on the work of Lipman-Blumen (1984, 1994).

Violence and the Threat of Violence Undergird Oppression

Most oppressive relationships are instituted through the use of, or the threat of the use of, force or punishment. Because maintaining superior force (that is, controlling punishment) requires a substantial commitment of resources, it is impractical to use constant force to maintain an unequal relationship once that relationship is established. However, "random" violence serves as an effective means of social control, at least partially through reminding subordinate groups that the use of force for punishment remains possible. Pheterson (1995) described this use of force as "a warning against insubordination rather than as a strategy of annihilation" (p. 189). Richard Wright (1937) described, in his autobiographical novel, how his behavior was thoroughly controlled by a pervasive fear that violence by whites could strike at any time: "The things that influenced my conduct as a Negro did not have to happen to me directly; I needed but to hear of them to feel their full effects in the deepest layers of my consciousness. Indeed the white brutality that I had not seen was a more effective control of my behavior than that which I knew" (p. 65).

Maintaining Oppression through Invisibility

A strategy for maintaining power that is preferable to the use of physical violence, however, is the controlling and monopolizing of rewards and resources available to the subordinate group. Over time, the resulting inequitable structures are taken for granted, and the basis of the unequal relationships (that is, control of resources) becomes less visible. Instead, unequal access to resources is seen as resulting from innate abilities or predispositions. When an oppressive arrangement is fully accomplished, success in a particular society is seen as resulting from competence or individual talent rather than being accurately linked to institutional arrangements (for example, laws, customs, and practices) that favor the oppressors. Consequently, the rules of the competition for resources are "rigged," but these arrangements are as invisible or unacknowledged as possible.

Such invisibility of the underlying oppressive structure ensures that neither party—subordinate or powerful—in the unequal power relationship will question the arrangement. First, people in the subordinate group may view their situation as being the result of their own weakness (that is, internalized oppression). Thus, their motivation to revolt is suppressed, and the potential targets of revolt are obscured. Numerous authors have discussed this process

of psychological internalization that occurs when people are forced to adapt to an inferior status for any period of time (Smith, 1985). Hershel (1995) explained how the need for subordinate group members to maintain dual identities—one appropriate for interactions within the subordinate group and a separate one appropriate for interactions with the dominant group—can generate self-doubt, hypervigilance, heightened self-consciousness, and self-alienation, depending on the extent to which the separate identities are inconsistent. In contrast, Candib (1994) focused on the unique set of developmental problems that create self-doubt and despair within individuals (women, for example, experience problems such as sexual abuse, date rape, wife battering, chronically reduced educational and occupational opportunities, and excessive household and caregiving responsibilities). Carby (1987) highlighted the results of internalization: an increased likelihood of blaming one's self and engaging in self-destructive behavior when encountering discriminatory barriers.

Second, people in the more powerful group lose sight of their advantage, and thus the invisibility of oppressive structures serves to distort their reality. McIntosh (1995) discussed this dynamic as failure to recognize privilege. Instead, members of the dominant group are likely to feel that they bear a great burden for society through protecting and managing the subordinate group. Not only does this situation alleviate potential guilt but, more important, it engenders a sense of power balanced with a sense of responsibility or burden. Carby (1987) discussed the purpose of stereotypes as an additional mechanism to relieve the dominant group's guilt by justifying disparate power relationships. In sum, all parties in the unequal power relationship are less likely to question the arrangement.

Frequently the invisibility of unequal advantage is further reinforced by some degree of "ghettoization." Specifically, dominant and subordinate groups work and live separately, obscuring the discrepancies between the groups. Disparate sexist power relationships are an exception to this arrangement, however, because men and women have generally coexisted in intimate relationships. For women, then, ghettoization has been focused rather exclusively on work arrangements through job segregation and the redefinition of unpaid labor.

The dynamics of cultural oppression also aid in obscuring the imbalances in power arrangements (Griffin, 1991), particularly in a highly technical society. For example, the relative absence of people belonging to various subordinate groups in mass media presentations encourages "forgetfulness" on the part of the dominant group while clearly communicating their own unimportance to members of subordinate groups. When there are portrayals of subordinate group members, they are typically structured either to reinforce existing stereotypes or to depict a thoroughly assimilated subordinate group member. Assimilation, one of the mechanisms underlying cultural oppression, is the process through which subordinate group members are encouraged (and sometimes forced) to adopt the norms of the dominant group (Pharr, 1988). For example, skin color concerns among some African Americans reflects internalization of dominant group standards of physical beauty (Harvey, 1995); and pretending to be heterosexual keeps the sexual orientation of gay men and lesbians— and, consequently, their oppression—invisible.

Rationalizing Oppression

When imbalances in power relationships are visible, an acceptable rationale for continuation must be in place. Stated in the terminology of social learning theory, for generally moral people to engage in culpable acts, they must disengage evaluative self-reactions (Bandura, 1978). This disengagement may proceed through a number of mechanisms, including relabeling oppression as serving some moral purpose, placing responsibility for oppression on another entity, choosing not to see the effects, and stereotyping and assigning the blame for oppression on its victims (Bandura, 1990).

Certain facts and beliefs also serve to maintain dominance, even when disparity is visible. The following lead the subordinate group to view their domination as inevitable, as resulting from their own inadequacies, and as the best available situation under the circumstances:

- the belief that the more powerful are more knowledgeable and capable (ideally, these differences are viewed as inevitable, genetically based, or the "natural order")
- the belief that the more powerful have the interest of the subordinate group at heart (ideally, the oppressors are viewed as "protectors")

- the fact that the more powerful group controls valuable and otherwise unattainable resources
- the fact or belief that the disparity in resources is so overwhelming that efforts to disrupt the power relationships are inevitably doomed
- the fact or belief that the subordinate group can have access to resources if it behaves in a manner prescribed by the more powerful group.

Unification of Oppressed Groups

In modern multicultural societies, the major threat to the dominant group is the unification of subordinate groups. In the United States, a plethora of "-isms" exist: racism, classism, sexism, heterosexism (homophobia), ageism, adultism, ableism, and anti-Semitism, for example. In addition, prejudices have evolved around innumerable other distinctions (for example, religious beliefs, physical attributes, national origin, ethnic group identity, and occupational status), and each may constitute an oppressive situation when the prejudice is held by a person in a position of institutional power. When many oppressive systems are operative, the numeric majority of the dominant group is maintained only through avoiding unification of subordinate groups.

This possibility of unification of subordinate groups is forestalled by strategies such as

- convincing subordinate groups through stereotypes that other disenfranchised groups are unworthy of consideration for alignment
- setting various subordinate groups against each other in competition for scare resources
- co-opting any emergent leaders from subordinate groups by giving them individual power in unimportant domains.

IMPLICATIONS FOR THE SOCIAL WORK PROFESSION

The above discussion reveals that all parties in an oppressive system are participants in the reproduction of the disparate power arrangements. For example, humiliation is a powerful, microlevel dynamic used to oppress stigmatized groups. Klein (cited in Griffin, 1991), in his conceptualization of the humiliation dynamic, proposed that three roles—perpetrator, victim, and witness—are necessary for humiliation to occur. The perpetrator typically gains or maintains power in the transaction. The victim may be enraged and suffer damage to his or her sense of self and identity. Witnesses, by their presence, increase the humiliation potential in the interaction but also support the process, whether actively or passively, consciously or unconsciously. More generally, Swigonski (1995) pointed out that nearly everyone participates on a day-to-day basis in some system of privilege, leaving only actions that explicitly work to transform or sabotage the oppressive system as alternatives to actively supporting the continuation of such a system.

The reality of collusion in oppressive systems has significant implications in terms of social workers' responsibility to oppose oppression. As should be evident from examining the dynamics of oppression, aspects of its operation permeate all structures and members of society. Thus, simple suggestions or solutions are of limited utility. The following discussion is consequently meant to be suggestive rather than exhaustive.

Social Work Education
The most important implication for social work education is related to the need to include content on oppression and social justice in the education of professional social workers, as mandated in the most recent curriculum policy statement (CSWE, 1994). Content about human diversity is inextricably linked to oppression; the term "minority" is based less on shared culture than on the shared context of oppression (Watts, Trickett, & Birman, 1994).

A key consideration in teaching and learning about oppression is the awareness that the enlightenment process will be painful and is likely to meet with resistance. To develop an awareness of the behaviors and attitudes related to various forms of oppression, it is helpful (if not necessary) to understand oneself as both a victim and a perpetrator of oppression (Swigonski, 1995). Because of society's "either/or" orientation, such understanding does not come easily. However, it is critical that students come to recognize ways in which each person oppresses others, both intentionally and unintentionally. Some research indicates that students, as they learn about distinctions based on individual and social power, privilege versus constraint, and entitlement versus vigilance, experience strong

affect (for example, self-censure, distress, anger, or despair) as they struggle with personal and professional meanings of oppression on a deeper level (Garcia & Van Soest, 1997; Van Soest, 1994, 1996).

Although personal exploration and awareness are critical, it is also important (and may help keep personal awareness less painful and in perspective) to acknowledge the culpability of the profession in terms of oppression. As social workers have sought social sanction for their activities, they have become involved in social control activities that directly and indirectly further oppressive structures. For example, Solomon (1976) regarded the history of social welfare as an example of institutional racism against African Americans; Blanchard (1982) provided incisive criticism of social workers from the viewpoint of Native American women; Horejsi, Craig, and Pablo (1992) justified the suspiciousness and resistance of Native American parents toward child protection agencies; and McMahon and Allen-Meares (1992) described the profession's treatment of minorities in its literature as "naive and superficial" (p. 537).

In pursuing both personal and professional awareness, it is particularly critical to bring attention and focus to contemporary issues and debates (for example, anti-immigrant sentiment, affirmative action, and the U.S. English movement). Although historical context is essential to understanding particular oppressive systems, failing to grapple with current issues can allow students to view oppression as something that happened "back then," for which they are (perhaps unjustly) expected to redress now. Furthermore, engaging students in more contemporary considerations allows them clear awareness of the difficulties involved for all parties, thereby minimizing feelings of personal inadequacy. The *Journal of Social Work Education's* Point/Counterpoint debates and the recent "Controversial Issues" series are particularly good examples of honest disagreements among social workers struggling with complex issues. For example, recent foci have included multiculturalism (Wambach, Grant, & Chatterjee, 1997), institutional nondiscrimination related to sexual preference (Parr & Jones, 1996), and affirmative action (Peebles-Wilkins & Chestang, 1996).

Although personal and professional awareness are necessary steps in developing multicultural competence, students must also acquire knowledge about groups with whom they will practice (Pederson, 1988). Ideally, such knowledge should reach the level of empathic understanding, a real shift in viewpoint in which one begins to see reality through the eyes of others. Such a dual perspective helps students become aware of their own culturally learned assumptions. Lugones (1990) presented a powerful description of this process focused on lesbians of color. This type of knowledge development is unlikely to result from reading academic accounts of various oppressed groups; literature written from the standpoint of members of the specific group is a more powerful source of information. Furthermore, interactions with subordinate group members are particularly useful, although students cannot absorb such knowledge passively— they must ask to be challenged in the process.

A final step in developing multicultural competence involves skill acquisition (Pederson, 1988). Although the interpersonal skills associated with generalist practice provide a foundation, students must learn to form effective alliances with client groups. Alliance work attempts to balance power relationships through explicit acknowledgment of each party's identity and the terms of the tasks to be undertaken (Anzaldua, 1990). The goal of such alliances is to undermine and subvert the system of domination and subordination that is present. A second, less forcefully stated formulation of this approach is labeled as "empowerment" by Solomon (1976), who suggested that the goals include helping the client perceive

- self as a causal agent in achieving a solution to one's own problems
- the practitioner as having knowledge and skills that the client can use
- the practitioner as peer–collaborator or partner in the problem-solving effort
- the "power structure" as multipolar, demonstrating varying degrees of commitment to the status quo and therefore open to influence.

The difference between the alliance and empowerment formulations, although subtle, is the extent to which oppressive social structures are challenged. This distinction will serve as the unifying theme in discussing implications for social work practice.

Social Work Practice

Despite the profession's stated commitment to social and economic justice, social work practice has been criticized as assimilationist, treating oppression and its dynamics as "isolated abnormalities in an otherwise sound society" (Montiel & Wong, 1983, p. 116). In a content analysis of social work journals, McMahon and Allen-Meares (1992) found empirical support for this contention. In a review of a decade of articles in four social work journals, only 117 of 1,965 articles (5.95 percent) dealt with social work intervention with racial minorities. More than three-fourths (77.8 percent) of the articles suggested some form of individually oriented intervention aimed at helping the client adjust to an oppressive environment or emphasized the social worker's awareness of the client's minority status. Only one article made concrete suggestions for achieving institutional change.

In reality, there can be no neutral social work practice position for opposing oppression. Encouraging clients to adapt successfully to oppressive conditions supports the continuation of those conditions unless such action is explicitly combined with efforts to change them. The distinction made between the empowerment approach (Solomon, 1976) and alliance approach (Anzaldua, 1990) is in the degree of commitment to social activism and social change. To avoid assimilationism, social work practice must focus more on advocacy and proactive interventions, regardless of what size system is involved.

In intervening with small systems (for example, individual or family), a strengths perspective (Saleebey, 1992; Weick, Rapp, Sullivan, & Kisthrardt, 1989)—in which workers seek to understand and confirm the adaptive abilities of clients—provides a model for enhancing balance in the helping relationship. To resist the "witness" role in the process of humiliation and oppression, social workers must explicitly acknowledge oppression and its dynamics when interacting with clients (Griffin, 1991). In group interventions, the worker must be aware of both diversity issues and associated structural inequalities and act to equalize the power position of group members (Brown & Mistry, 1994). Within any intervention strategy, the goal of developing or enhancing positive self-esteem should be included to address client wounds resulting from internalizing oppressive structures. One means of enhancing self-esteem is to participate in social activism. Whether applied at a personal or a political level, assertiveness and advocacy skills are important tools for clients to develop to confront oppression and enhance their self-esteem.

Social work practice with larger systems (for example, administration, policy, advocacy) must be scrutinized carefully for evidence that it may support oppressive structures. Cross, Bazron, Dennis, and Isaacs (1989) proposed a cultural competence continuum that may be used to assess individuals or organizations in terms of performance with human diversity. In their formulation, treating everyone the same— labeled "cultural blindness"—is the midpoint on the continuum. Self-awareness, knowledge about relevant cultures, and inclusionary tactics are necessary to move into competent practice. Three values seem particularly relevant to challenging oppression in macro practice (Prilleltensky & Gonick, 1994):

1. The value of self-determination suggests that uniqueness should be celebrated and diverse identities affirmed, with subordinate groups ultimately having the power to define their own identities.
2. The value of distributive justice demands equal access to opportunity and fair allocation of available resources.
3. The value of collaboration and democratic participation encourages inclusion in decision making and conscious pursuit of "voiceless" groups in any process.

Research

Social work research, like other research in the social sciences, is being increasingly challenged by scholars who address ways in which sexism, racism, heterosexism, and ageism, for example, appear throughout the research process. They maintain that this creates bias, perpetuates stereotypes, and serves to maintain the status quo—that is, the effect of research can be to reinforce oppression (Callaway, 1981; Cambell, 1981; Davis, 1986; McHugh, Koeske, & Frieze, 1986; Morin, 1977; Schaie, 1988; Westkott, 1979).

Perhaps the most pervasive problem encountered in social work research involves ignoring the societal context of the client (McMahon & Allen-Meares, 1992). Little attention is given to clients' experience of day-to-day oppression or the degree of internalized oppression present. Indeed, reports of gross demographic categories of research subjects represent the extent to which societal position variables are generally considered. Furthermore, the strengths perspective seems not to have penetrated social work research; consideration of personal characteristics and abilities is generally limited to a deficit focus.

Most discussions of context stripping in social work research emphasize the use of qualitative research methods to combat the problem (Brekke, 1986; Pieper, 1985; Witkin & Gottschalk, 1988). Certainly approaches using grounded theory, ethnography, and participatory methods offer richer data and give voice to the subjects of research. Such approaches to social work research should receive equal recognition both in doctoral education and in publishing decisions.

At the same time, the power of quantitative research must be preserved. Dealing with the problem of context-stripping in quantitative research may be regarded as a measurement problem. Researchers are urged to begin to identify means of quantifying important indicators of client context. The body of literature dealing with life stress and social support may well provide a starting place for operationalizing context. In addition, scale development is needed to measure internalized oppression and exposure to humiliation and other oppressive dynamics. Finally, assessment approaches that delineate strengths as well as problems should be incorporated into research protocols.

CONCLUSION

Although the discussion in this entry about the dynamics and mechanisms of oppression at times may have implied purposeful intent on the part of the dominant group, the main point is that in well-established oppressive relationships, such structures are invisible to both the subordinate party and the more powerful party. In well-established disparate power relationships, the "sources" of oppressive structures are embedded within the psychological makeup of all parties, thereby obscuring the realities of the relationships. The greatest challenge for social work professionals is to uncover, make visible, expose, and oppose oppressive relationships and systemic power arrangements that give undue advantage to one group over another.

REFERENCES

Alderfer, C. P. (1994). A white man's perspective on the unconscious processes within black–white relations in the United States. In E. J. Trickett, R. J. Watts, & D. Birman (Eds.), *Human diversity: Perspectives on people in context* (pp. 201–229). San Francisco: Jossey-Bass.

Anzaldua, G. (1990). Bridge, drawbridge, sandbar or island. In L. Albrecht & R. M. Brewer (Eds.), *Bridges of power: Women's multicultural alliances* (pp. 216–231). Santa Cruz, CA: New Society Publishers.

Bandura, A. (1978). Social learning theory of aggression. *Journal of Communication, 28*(3), 12–29.

Bandura, A. (1990). Selective activation and disengagement of moral control. *Journal of Social Issues, 46*(1), 27–46.

Blanchard, E. L. (1982). Observations on social work with American Indian women. In A. Weick & S. Vandiver (Eds.), *Women, power, and change* (pp. 96–103). New York: National Association of Social Workers.

Brekke, J. S. (1986). Scientific imperatives in social work research: Pluralism is not skepticism. *Social Service Review, 60*, 538–544.

Brittan, A., & Maynard, M. (1984). *Sexism, racism, and oppression.* Oxford, England: Basil Blackwell.

Brown, A., & Mistry, T. (1994). Group work with "mixed membership" groups: Issues of race and gender. *Social Work with Groups, 17*(3), 5–21.

Callaway, H. (1981). Women's perspectives: Research as re-vision. In P. Reason & I. Rowan (Eds.), *Human inquiry* (pp. 457–471). New York: John Wiley & Sons.

Cambell, P. B. (1981). Was research, is research, "objective": An overview. *Interracial Books for Children Bulletin, 12*(3), 7–10.

Candib, L. M. (1994). Self-in-relation theory: Implications for women's health. In A. J. Dan (Ed.), *Reframing women's health: Multidisciplinary research and practice* (pp. 67–78). Thousand Oaks, CA: Sage Publications.

Carby, H. (1987). *Reconstructing womanhood: The emergence of the African-American woman novelist.* New York: Oxford University Press.

Council on Social Work Education. (1994). *Handbook of accreditation standards.* Alexandria, VA: Author.

Cross, T., Bazron, G., Dennis, K., & Isaacs, M. (1989). *Toward a culturally competent system of care.* Washington, DC: George Washington University Child Development Center. Child and Adolescent Service System Program, Technical Assistance Center.

Davis, L. V. (1986). A feminist approach to social work research. *Affilia, 1*(1), 32–47.

Frye, M. (1995). Oppression. In M. L. Andersen & P. H. Collins (Eds.), *Race, class, and gender: An anthology* (2nd ed., pp. 37–41). Belmont, CA: Wadsworth.

Garcia, B., & Van Soest, D. (1997). Changing perceptions of diversity and oppression: MSW students discuss the effects of a required course. *Journal of Social Work Education, 33*, 119–129.

Griffin, J. T. (1991). Racism and humiliation in the African-American community. *Journal of Primary Prevention, 12*, 149–167.

Harvey, A. R. (1995). The issue of skin color in psychotherapy with African Americans. *Families in Society, 76*, 3–10.

Hershel, H. J. (1995). Therapeutic perspectives on biracial identity formation and internalized oppression. In N. Zack (Ed.), *American mixed race: The culture of microdiversity* (pp. 169–181). Lanham, MD: Rowman & Littlefield.

Horejsi, C., Craig, B.H.R., & Pablo, J. (1992). Reactions by Native American parents to child protection agencies: Cultural and community factors. *Child Welfare, 71*, 329–342.

Klein, D. (1989, April). *The humiliation dynamic.* Paper presented at the Twelfth Annual Erich Lindemann Memorial Lecture, Harvard Medical School, Boston, MA.

Lipman-Blumen, J. (1984). *Gender roles and power.* Englewood Cliffs, NJ: Prentice Hall.

Lipman-Blumen, J. (1994). The existential bases of power relationships: The gender role case. In H. L. Radtke & H. J. Stam (Eds.), *Power/gender: Social relations in theory and practice* (pp. 108–135). Thousand Oaks, CA: Sage Publications.

Lugones, M. (1990). Playfulness, "world" traveling, and loving perception. In G. Anzaldua (Ed.), *Making face, making soul/haciendo cara: Creative and critical perspectives by women of color* (pp. 390–402). San Francisco: Aunt Lute Foundation.

McHugh, M. C., Koeske, R. D., & Frieze, I. H. (1986). Issues to consider in conducting nonsexist psychological research: A guide for researchers. *American Psychologist, 41*, 879–890.

McIntosh, P. (1995). White privilege and male privilege: A personal account of coming to see correspondences through work in women's studies. In M. L. Anderson & P. H. Collins (Eds.), *Race, class and gender* (2nd ed., pp. 76–87). Belmont, CA: Wadsworth.

McMahon, A., & Allen-Meares, P. (1992). Is social work racist? A content analysis of recent literature. *Social Work, 37*, 533–539.

Montiel, M., & Wong, P. (1983). A theoretical critique of the minority perspective. *Social Casework, 64*, 112–117.

Morin, S. F. (1977). Heterosexual bias in psychological research on lesbianism and male homosexuality. *American Psychologist, 32,* 629–637.

National Association of Social Workers. (1996). *NASW code of ethics.* Washington, DC: Author.

Parr, R. G., & Jones, L. E. (1996). Should CSWE allow social work programs in religious institutions an exemption from the accreditation nondiscrimination standard related to sexual preference? *Journal of Social Work Education, 32,* 297–313.

Pederson, P. (1988). *A handbook for developing multicultural awareness.* Alexandria, VA: American Association for Counseling and Development.

Peebles-Wilkins, W., & Chestang, L. W. (1996). Is it time to rethink affirmative action? *Journal of Social Work Education, 32,* 5–18.

Pharr, S. (1988). *Homophobia: A weapon of sexism.* Inverness, CA: Chardon Press.

Pheterson, G. (1995). Historical and material determinants of psychodynamic development. In J. Adleman & G. M. Enguidanos (Eds.), *Racism in the lives of women: Testimony, theory, and guides to antiracist practice* (pp. 181–205). New York: Haworth Press.

Pieper, M. H. (1985). The future of social work research. *Social Work Research & Abstracts, 21*(4), 3–11.

Pinderhughes, C. A. (1973). Racism and psychotherapy. In C. Willie, B. Kramer, & B. Brown (Eds.), *Racism and mental health* (pp. 61–121). Pittsburgh: University of Pittsburgh Press.

Prilleltensky, I., & Gonick, L. S. (1994). The discourse of oppression in the social sciences: Past, present, and future. In E. J. Trickett, R. J. Watts, & D. Birman (Eds.), *Human diversity: Perspectives on people in context* (pp. 145–177). San Francisco: Jossey-Bass.

Rothenberg, P. (1988). *Racism and sexism: An integrated study.* New York: St. Martin's Press.

Saleebey, D. (Ed.). (1992). *The strengths perspective in social work practice.* New York: Longman.

Schaie, K. W. (1988). Ageism in psychological research. *American Psychologist, 43,* 179–183.

Sidanius, J., & Pratto, F. (1993). The inevitability of oppression and the dynamics of social dominance. In P. M. Sniderman, P. E. Tetlock, & E. G. Carmines (Eds.), *Prejudice, politics, and the American dilemma* (pp. 173–211). Stanford, CA: Stanford University Press.

Smith, E. J. (1985). Ethnic minorities: Life stress, social support, and mental health issues. *Counseling Psychologist, 17,* 277–288.

Smith, E. J. (1991). Ethnic identity development: Toward the development of a theory within the context of majority/minority status. *Journal of Counseling & Development, 70,* 181–188.

Solomon, B. B. (1976). *Black empowerment: Social work in oppressed communities.* New York: Columbia University Press.

Swigonski, M. E. (1995). For the white social worker who wants to know how to work with lesbians of color. *Journal of Gay & Lesbian Social Services, 3*(2), 7–21.

Van Soest, D. (1994). Social work education for multicultural practice and social justice advocacy: A field study of how students experience the learning process. *Journal of Multicultural Social Work, 3*(1), 17–28.

Van Soest, D. (1996). Impact of social work education on student attitudes and behavior concerning oppression. *Journal of Social Work Education, 32,* 191–202.

Wambach, K. G., Grant, D., & Chatterjee, P. (1997). Can HBSE classes discuss socially sensitive topics wihout being labeled "politically incorrect?" In M. Bloom & W. C. Klein (Eds.), *Controversial issues in human behavior in the social environment* (pp. 214–227). Boston: Allyn & Bacon.

Watts, R. J., Trickett, E., & Birman, D. (1994). Convergence and divergence in human diversity. In E. Trickett, R. Watts, & D. Birman (Eds.), *Human diversity: Perspectives on people in context* (pp. 452–464). San Francisco: Jossey-Bass.

Weick, A., Rapp, C., Sullivan, P., & Kisthardt, W. (1989). A strengths perspective for social work practice. *Social Work, 34,* 350–354.

Westkott, M. (1979). Feminist criticism of the social sciences. *Harvard Educational Review, 49,* 422–430.

Witkin, S. L., & Gottschalk, S. (1988). Alternative criteria for theory evaluation. *Social Service Review, 62,* 211–224.

Wright, R. (1937). *Black boy.* New York: Harper & Row.

FURTHER READING

Adelman, J., & Enguidanos, G. M. (1995). *Racism in the lives of women: Testimony, theory, and guides to antiracist practice.* New York: Haworth Press.

Aguirre, A., Jr., & Turner, J. H. (1995). *American ethnicity: The dynamics and consequences of discrimination.* New York: McGraw-Hill.

Belenky, M. F., Clinchy, B. M., Goldberger, N. R., & Tarule, J. M. (1986). *Women's ways of knowing: The development of self, voice, and mind.* New York: Basic Books.

Bulhan, H. A. (1985). *Frantz Fanon and the psychology of oppression.* New York: Plenum Press.

Bushnell, D. E. (Ed.). (1995). *"Nagging" questions: Feminist ethics in everyday life.* Lanham, MD: Rowman & Littlefield.

DeCrescenzo, T. (Ed.). (1994). *Helping gay and lesbian youth: New policies, new programs, new practice.* Binghamton, NY: Harrington Park.

Essed, P. (1990). *Everyday racism: Reports from women of two cultures.* Alameda, CA: Hunter House.

Feagin, J. R., & Vera, H. (1994). *White racism.* New York: Routledge.

Morrison, T. (Ed.). (1992). *Race-ing justice, en-gendering power.* New York: Pantheon Books.

Pharr, S. (1988). *Homophobia: A weapon of sexism.* Inverness, CA: Chardon Press.

Radtke, H. L., & Stam, J. (Eds.). (1994). *Power/gender: Social relations in theory and practice.* Thousand Oaks, CA: Sage Publications.

Trickett, E. J., Watts, R. J., & Birman, D. (Eds.). (1994). *Human diversity: Perspectives on people in context.* San Francisco: Jossey-Bass.

Turner, J. H., Singleton, R., Jr., & Musick, D. (1986). *Oppression: A socio-history of black–white relations in America.* Chicago: Nelson-Hall.

West, C. (1993). *Beyond eurocentrism and multiculturalism: Prophetic reflections—Notes on race and power in America (Vol. 1 & 2).* Monroe, ME: Common Courage Press.

Kathryn G. Wambach, PhD, ACSW, is assistant professor, and **Dorothy Van Soest, DSW, LMSW-AP,** is associate dean and associate professor, School of Social Work, University of Texas at Austin, 1925 San Jacinto Boulevard, Austin, TX 78712.

For further information see

Advocacy; African Americans Overview; Aging Overview; American Indians; Asian Americans Overview; Civil Rights; Criminal Justice: Class, Race, and Gender Issues; Deaf Community; **Ethical Standards in Social Work: The *NASW Code of Ethics*;** Ethics and Values; Ethnic-Sensitive Practice; Federal Social Legislation from 1961 to 1994; **Federal Social Legislation from 1994 to 1997;** Gay Men Overview; Hispanics Overview; Homelessness; Human Rights; International and Comparative Social Welfare; Legal Issues: Low-Income and Dependent People; Lesbians Overview; Peace and Social Justice; Poverty; Progressive Social Work; Social Planning; Social Welfare History; Social Welfare Policy; Social Work Practice: History and Evolution; Social Work Profession: History; Social Workers in Politics; Victim Services and Victim/Witness Assistance Programs; Victims of Torture and Trauma; Violence Overview; Women Overview; **World Social Situation.**

Key Words

discrimination	power
diversity	

P

Privileged Communication

See Legal Issues: Confidentiality and Privileged Communication; **Legal Issues: Recent Developments in Confidentiality and Privilege**

Prostitution

Adele Weiner

> The prostitute is not the only one to engage in acts of prostitution.
> —S. Day, 1988

Social workers often come in contact with women, men, and teenagers who use prostitution as a means of income and survival. Individuals may earn their entire income in this manner; they may use it to supplement low earnings or welfare benefits; or they may trade sex for drugs, shelter, or the safety of pimps. Violence, drug use, arrest, and transmission of the human immunodeficiency virus (HIV) are constant risks for those who engage in prostitution. Those who engage in prostitution, whether as prostitutes or as clients, represent the entire spectrum of American society.

DEFINING AND ESTIMATING PROSTITUTION

It is very difficult to estimate the number of people engaging in prostitution because of the illegal nature of the activity and disagreement on the definition. The National Task Force on Prostitution estimated that more than 1 million people work as prostitutes in the United States annually (Alexander, 1987). The Prostitutes Education Network (PENet, 1996) has estimated that approximately 100,000 arrests for prostitution are made annually. Of those arrested, 70 percent are female prostitutes, 20 percent are male prostitutes, and 10 percent are customers. Women of color are disproportionately represented among the arrestees and are more likely to serve jail time. Approximately 85 percent to 90 percent of those arrested are streetwalkers, although street work accounts for only about 20 percent of all prostitution. It is estimated that in larger cities, 20 percent to 30 percent of prostitutes are male. Drug abuse varies widely among various prostitute populations, with streetwalkers more likely than those who work off the streets to be using illegal substances. In larger cities, as many as 25 percent of female prostitutes may be transgender (PENet, 1996). Those who work in off-street settings may have somewhat more protection but may be controlled by an "employer," "madam," or "pimp."

Because prostitution is illegal in 49 states and only brothel prostitution is legal in certain localities in Nevada, most prostitutes make efforts to hide their activities. In addition, definitions of prostitution vary widely. In its broadest definition prostitution includes the exchange of sex for money, drugs, shelter, or some other commodity. Goldstein, Ouellet, and Fendrich (1992) reported on women who exchanged sex for dental work, furniture, automobile repairs and tires, television sets, clothes, and professional services of both physicians and lawyers. The definition of "sex" for prostitution has often been limited to acts involving physical contact. Those who work with prostitutes indicate that there is a very fine line between actual intercourse and manual or oral stimulation and a number of activities that may all result in orgasm, such as lap dancing, erotic dancing, massage, or sadomasochistic activities. Exotic dancers may deep-kiss men in the audience (Shedlin, 1990). A number of legal activities may in fact be closely aligned with activities that are legally defined as prostitution. This widened definition implies that many more people are engaged in exchanging sex for a commodity than might be assumed if one looks only at the number of people involved in what is legally defined as prostitution.

SOCIOCULTURAL ISSUES AND CONCERNS

Prostitution has existed throughout recorded history and has been more or less accepted at various times and in different cultures. As with any other social institution, its endurance is a reflection of the social needs that it meets. Shedlin (1990) found that prostitutes "perceived their most important sexual function as providing what other women, 'straight women,' do not like or refuse to provide" (p. 140). She also found that men used prostitutes because they can be sexually gratified without investing energy in building a relationship, maintaining an image, or pleasing their partner.

Poor drug-using women often exchange sex for drugs, whereas poor drug-using men have other options such as theft or drug dealing. Some of these women identify themselves as prostitutes and even walk the streets and act like traditional prostitutes; the money they earn is used to purchase drugs. Other women, however, may trade sex for drugs without walking the streets like traditional prostitutes and do not identify themselves as such (Goldstein et al., 1992). Such women may establish long-term relationships with one or two drug dealers and have sex only with them. Other women may engage in sex with any man who has access to drugs. Factors that tend to influence women's decisions to barter sex for drugs include the availability of men who are willing and able to enter into such a transaction, whether the woman has any alternative criminal skills (for example, shoplifting or forgery), and how afraid the woman is of engaging in prostitution or other illegal activities. In Goldstein et al.'s study, there were women who only bartered drugs for sex, and those who engaged in both bartering and more traditional forms of prostitution. How the participants perceived their activities involved a complex network of social and economic variables.

Day (1988) suggested that there are three general issues involved in understanding the social dynamics of prostitution. First, the practices associated with prostitution vary with time and place. Second, in some geographic areas there are no clear boundaries between prostitution and other forms of sexual union, such as marriage. Finally, the practices linked with prostitution are determined by societal factors, such as the nature of labor and how children are legitimized and incorporated in a wider kin group. Thus, the activities that are defined as prostitution and society's views toward the women (or men) who engage in these activities vary according to culture and time. Throughout history, societies have ritualized and legitimized activities that might

be considered prostitution by current Western standards. Day also noted that "professional prostitutes tend to create a marked distance between their working and private lives" (p. 421). Of course, the woman who uses heroin and trades sex for drugs may distinguish between her boyfriend and the men she has sex with to get drugs, but she may not necessarily define herself as a professional prostitute. Such a woman may be arrested and not legally defined as a prostitute because she is charged with drug possession or some other crime she may have engaged in to support her drug use.

Shedlin (1990) categorized the social hierarchy of female prostitutes. The better escort or call services recruit younger, prettier, better educated women who are less likely to be drug users. Topless bars and massage parlors occupy the next level. At such establishments workers obtain customers through the business and usually pay a percentage of their earnings to their employer or are paid directly by the owners for their sexual services. "Street girls" "occupy the bottom rung in the hierarchy; however, individuals on the street represent a huge range in age, education, ethnicity, drug involvement and price" (p. 138). At the bottom of the street scale are the throwaway children—children who are unwanted by parents or family. Some may actually be initiated into prostitution by their parents. Their home life is such that they may be "pushed out" or "forced" to run away. Prostitution becomes their means of survival, and they may seek the protection of pimps or older prostitutes. Relationships with pimps are complicated and may be based on a combination of fear; the need for drugs, affection, sexual attention, or safety; or the fathering and control of the prostitute's children.

VULNERABLE POPULATIONS AND DIFFERING NEEDS

Prostitution, as it is most broadly defined, is engaged in by differing populations and in different settings. Although all prostitutes are vulnerable to arrest, sexually transmitted diseases (STDs), and violence, the settings in which they engage in their trade may provide more or less protection, offer norms for acceptable behavior, and provide resources to meet basic needs. In the United States, the brothels of Nevada offer more protection than other settings, and the women who are employed make a good income, have institutional support for safer sex practices, and work in an environment that provides security. Illegal brothels may also provide employees with similar environments and a rarefied clientele. Other organizations for off-street sex work may offer a continuum of safety and security services. Prostitutes who are on call and must go to a location of the client's choosing may place themselves at greater risk than those who work in a known environment.

Those who engage in street work are usually the most vulnerable and have fewer resources to protect themselves. Weiner (1996) found that female streetwalkers are likely to be homeless or live in an arrangement that might be considered unstable (for example, with relatives, in a residential hotel, with a boyfriend, or on the street). Virtually half (49.7 percent) had not finished high school. This population used a wide variety of drugs, and many used more than one. They had an extensive history of STDs, including HIV, and lacked resources to obtain medical care. Women of color were disproportionately represented; 52.5 percent were non-Hispanic black women, 26.8 percent were Hispanic, and 20.7 percent were non-Hispanic white women. Hispanic women had more children, on average, than women in the other ethnic categories and the lowest level of education. Non-Hispanic black women were also more likely to be living on the street.

Adolescent runaways are likely to engage in prostitution as a means of survival (Weiner & Pollack, 1996). Many young people are escaping violence at home, and the dangers they face on the street may be less dire than those they face in their homes (San Francisco Task Force on Prostitution, 1996). The relationship between childhood sexual abuse and adolescent prostitution is not direct but may involve runaway behavior as an intervening variable (Seng, 1989). Because of fear, inexperience, and ignorance, the adolescent prostitute may be more easily coerced into unsafe sexual practices that may result in generally higher payments (Markos, Wade, & Walzman, 1992).

Child prostitution raises different issues. Although many adolescents below the age of consent engage in survival prostitution, child prostitution often involves a parent or some other caretaker who forces the child to participate. In extreme cases the child may actually be traded or sold for money or drugs. In such situations the child's caretakers obviously are not suitable, and the social and emotional damage to the child is immeasurable. As with other situations involving child abuse, the child may be unable to acknowledge the problem, unable to communicate it to other responsible adults, or afraid of the consequences of telling.

The threat of deportation or denial of citizenship makes immigrants who engage in sex work particularly vulnerable (San Francisco Task Force on Prostitution, 1996). "Trafficking" refers to the illegal transport of women for the purposes of prostitution. Many women enter this country illegally, only to find themselves held captive and forced to engage in prostitution until they or their families provide a sizable ransom for their release. Some are arrested and deported prior to obtaining their freedom. Women may be promised legitimate jobs by recruiters, but when they enter this country, they are told that the original job is no longer available and the only work is for stripteasers and exotic dancers. They are required to mix drinks and socialize with customers (Cao, 1987).

Migrant workers are particularly susceptible to prostitution. The crew boss may hire women, many of who have developmental disabilities or are emotionally disturbed, who are forced to serve as labor camp prostitutes (Cao, 1987). Such women are unable to call the police to file charges against those who abuse or exploit them.

Prejudice and poverty make women of color more vulnerable as prostitutes. In many circumstances, when discussing streetwalkers, labor camp prostitutes, and immigrant prostitutes, the factors that make them particularly vulnerable are intertwined with race. Racism creates discriminatory conditions in the sex industry as it does in the rest of society (PENet, 1996). White or Asian women may be able to choose to work in upscale settings (such as hotels or escort services), but street work may be the only option for black or Hispanic women. Street workers earn less money than women in off-the-street establishments, have less control over the conditions in which they work, and are at greater risk of violence or arrest.

Transgender sex workers are likely to be stigmatized by nontransvestite male and female prostitutes, law enforcement personnel, and the population at large (Boles & Elifson, 1994). They are also more likely than other prostitutes to be the object of ridicule and verbal abuse when arrested (San Francisco Task Force on Prostitution, 1996). Within the status hierarchy of prostitution, transgender prostitutes have the lowest status, work in the least desirable locations, and make the least money. They prefer to engage in oral sex to minimize the risk of the customer discovering they are not female (Boles & Elifson, 1994), and they are frequently victims of violence when a customer makes such a discovery. In larger cities there may be transvestite "strolls" or clubs, where customers purposefully seek out transgender prostitutes. Boles and Elifson (1994) found that transgender prostitutes perceived the outside world as hostile and threatening and lived in a restricted social environment. They were afraid of getting sick and having to go to the hospital.

Male prostitutes present another set of issues and dynamics. In fact, they use a different language, identifying themselves as "hustlers" rather than prostitutes. Simon, Morse, Osofsky, Balson, and Gaumer (1992) found that male prostitutes exhibited a higher level of psychopathology than normal, nonhospitalized populations. Male prostitutes reported using various substances to self-medicate in "response to depression, loneliness and a sense of hopelessness as they realize how much they are locked into a deviant career" (Simon et al., 1992, p. 43). Trouble with police, lack of job skills, unstable employment histories, and the threat of a fatal STD all lead to a chaotic lifestyle. Cates and Markley (1992) made the distinction between men who are forced into prostitution for survival and those who engage in this behavior by choice. Men involved by choice held regular jobs and used prostitution to supplement their incomes. As a group they were more likely to use drugs and to have been abused as children. They were not more likely to report themselves as being homosexual. Browne and Minichiello (1995) found that the way in which the male sex worker constructs the meaning of the sex act has implications for the worker's ability to negotiate safer sex.

Drug Use

Drug use is relatively high among prostitutes (Weiner, 1996) and is greater among female prostitutes than among other female arrestees (Kuhns, Heide, & Silverman, 1992). The frequency and choice of drugs used vary among different populations of prostitutes. Alexander (1987) found that drug abuse was common among streetwalkers (approximately 50 percent) but relatively rare among women who worked off the street. Goldstein et al. (1992) determined differing drug use patterns for what they defined as "high-class prostitutes" (for example, call girls and madams) and "low-class prostitutes" (for example, streetwalkers and barterers). The low-class prostitutes regularly used heroin (96 percent) and cocaine (64 percent), whereas the drugs of choice among high-class prostitutes were stimulants (61 percent). Addicted women who engage in prostitution are more likely to report use of injectable drugs, and those who trade sex for drugs are more likely to engage in risky behaviors (Kail, Watson, & Ray, 1995). Prostitutes who inject drugs face multiple threats of HIV infection: from sharing HIV-infected syringes and needles, drug-cooking implements, and rinse water or from multiple unprotected sex contacts (Bellis, 1993).

This relationship between illicit drugs, particularly cocaine, and prostitution has been well documented. Rolfs, Goldberg, and Sharrar (1990) found that women who used cocaine were more likely to engage in prostitution than women who did not use cocaine. Cocaine use is a risk factor in the transmission of STDs such as syphilis (Gunn et al., 1995; Rolfs et al., 1990) and HIV (Chiasson et al., 1991; Weiner, Wallace, Steinberg, & Hoffman, 1992). According to Goldstein et al. (1992), women who traded sex for drugs reported working more days as a prostitute than those who did not trade sex for drugs. In addition, those who traded were also more likely to use heroin or cocaine as their drug of choice. Women who traded for drugs reported using cocaine almost twice as often as those who did not trade for drugs. For many of these women, the drug dealer has replaced the pimp as the protector.

Crack-related prostitution usually involves a high number of anonymous sex partners, and sex is exchanged directly for drugs, often in locations where drugs are used or sold (Gunn et al., 1995). Under such circumstances, drug use increases the number of high-risk sex encounters. Kuhns et al. (1992) found that prostitutes reported using crack or freebase cocaine one to four times a day.

HIV Status

Street workers have higher rates of HIV infection than the general population. The rate of HIV infection among a large sample of New York City streetwalkers ($N = 3,050$) was 31.4 percent for the period 1989 through 1996.

Among those who had ever used intravenous (IV) drugs, the HIV infection rate was higher— 51.4 percent (Wallace & Weiner, 1996). There is some evidence that transgender (Boles & Elifson, 1994) and male (Bloor, McKeganey, Finlay, & Barnard, 1992) prostitutes may have higher rates of HIV infection than female prostitutes.

Much of the research on prostitutes and HIV transmission has focused on the working lives of prostitutes. Prostitutes' private sexual relations, however, may be important to understanding the transmission of HIV, especially when boyfriends or husbands are at other risk of infection (Day, 1988). Weiner (1996) found that streetwalkers more consistently used condoms for sex with clients, but were less consistent in using them with their boyfriends or husbands. This occurred even when the boyfriend or husband had a history of IV drug use.

In addition, concern about the spread of HIV has focused on prostitutes as disease vectors, with little concern for the health of prostitutes at risk of HIV (King, 1990). Gender-neutral language reinforces the notion that female-to-male heterosexual transmission is prevalent. In reality, the behaviors that female prostitutes engage in with clients tend to place them at risk of being infected with the HIV virus and less likely to transmit it to the male client (Wallace, Mann, & Beatrice, 1988). Condom use among male prostitutes is well below that reported by female prostitutes (Bloor et al., 1992).

The interrelationships among drug use, sex, and HIV transmission are complex. Although some studies have indicated that drug use is a leading route for the transmission of HIV infection (Centers for Disease Control, 1987), other investigations have suggested that heterosexual sex rather than drug use is the predominant route of HIV transmission among prostitutes (DeMeis, DeVasconellos, Linhares, & Andrada-Serpa, 1991; Piot et al., 1987). As with other heterosexual transmission, it is more likely that women are infected by men, rather than that prostitutes infect male clients (Wallace et al., 1988). Among female prostitutes in the developed world who are not using crack or IV drugs, the rates of HIV infection are low and reported use of condoms is high. This is not the case with male prostitutes (Bloor et al., 1992), however. Although male prostitutes did not intend to engage in unsafe sex, when it did occur, it was under the control of the client.

Shedlin (1990) indicated that accurate information about safe sex and needle cleaning has reached the street, yet streetwalkers continue to engage in unprotected sex and share IV drug equipment ("works"). Shedlin suggested that the nature of drug addiction, poverty, low education levels, lack of self-esteem, hopelessness, and a lack of appropriate information and supporting services all operate to prevent risk-reduction behaviors.

VIOLENCE

Prostitutes are afraid to call the police when they are crime victims. Current patterns of prosecution and law enforcement further marginalize the most vulnerable individuals. Immigrants engaged in the sex trade are reluctant to report abuses such as rape, robbery, and illegal curtailment of their freedom of movement (San Francisco Task Force on Prostitution, 1996).

A project funded by the San Francisco Bay Homeless Project surveyed homeless people who had engaged in some amount of sex trade (San Francisco Task Force on Prostitution, 1996). Eighty percent reported that they had been physically assaulted since entering prostitution, 54 percent had been attacked by clients, 66 percent had been raped, and 78 percent had been threatened with a weapon. Of particular concern is the development of a system of barter in crack-for-sex exchanges, in which women experience the dual effects of addiction and trauma (San Francisco Task Force on Prostitution, 1996). The use of illegal substances in a criminalized environment among an already marginalized population of users leads to an increase in violence-related trauma.

PROSTITUTES' RIGHTS

Because of social stigma and financial factors, it is extremely difficult for prostitutes to leave the business and find and hold legitimate jobs. The criminalization of prostitution, particularly the use and exchange of illegal drugs for sex, forces practitioners "underground" and into associations with criminals. Once in such settings they accumulate an arrest history and develop a criminal record. This criminal history may preclude them from participating in some rehabilitation and education programs or, after training, from qualifying for licenses that would allow them to earn a legitimate income.

The San Francisco Task Force on Prostitution (1996) noted that law enforcement was uneven and that street workers, those who were visible, and especially black, transgender, and immigrant women were more likely to be arrested. Even with an increase in law enforcement, there was no evidence that it did anything more than force street workers to move from one place to another. In fact, police enforcement may keep women trapped in a system of debt bondage (Cao, 1987). Once a pimp has paid a prostitute's bail or fine, the pimp may force her (or him) into more acts of prostitution or other criminal activities until the debt is paid.

In 1949 the United Nations adopted a resolution in favor of the decriminalization of prostitution; this resolution has been ratified by 50 countries but not by the United States. Although there is no uniform definition of decriminalization, the term usually refers to the repeal of laws against consensual adult sex in both commercial and noncommercial contexts. Legalization of prostitution would set in place a system of regulation and control that would allow prostitutes to work in specific and limited ways. Cooper (1989) has suggested additional benefits in reconceptualizing prostitution, in that "prostitution affords women—especially those from economically deprived backgrounds—the opportunity to earn a living, support themselves and exercise some control over their own sexuality" (p. 112).

COYOTE (Call Off Your Old Tired Ethics) is a grassroots organization of prostitutes and others that has tried to redefine the public perception of prostitution (Jenness, 1990). "COYOTE advocates the repeal of all existing prostitution laws, the recognition of prostitution as a credible service occupation and the protection of prostitutes' rights as legitimate workers" (Jenness, 1990, p. 403). COYOTE has suggested that prostitution as a form of work should replace the conceptualization of this activity as criminal; such a conceptualization recognizes that people may choose this kind of work, and occupational safety protections should be instituted. The San Francisco Task Force on Prostitution (1996) noted that strip clubs, erotic performance theaters, erotic film and video production, pornographic magazine publishing, telephone sex switchboards, commercial parties, and sex clubs are all part of the legal sex industry in San Francisco. Employees in these workplaces are accorded

the full protection of the law, and their complaints are investigated by the California Occupational Safety and Health Administration (OSHA) and Labor Commission.

The National Task Force on Prostitution was formed to act as an umbrella organization to support the rights of prostitutes and other sex workers. It has five overriding goals:

1. to repeal the existing prostitution laws
2. to ensure the rights of sex workers to bargain with their employers to improve working conditions
3. to provide public education on issues related to prostitution
4. to promote support services, including services involving HIV, the acquired immune deficiency syndrome (AIDS), and STDs; violence prevention; and health and social services
5. to end public stigma associated with sex work.

The PENet, a service providing information about legislation and cultural issues from organizations throughout the United States, maintains a web page on the Internet (http://www.bayswan.org/penet.html).

IMPLICATIONS FOR SOCIAL WORKERS
There is some evidence that people resort to prostitution when other means of meeting their basic needs are unavailable. The San Francisco Task on Prostitution (1996) actually found that the rise in enforcement and prosecution of prostitutes coincided with a decrease in funding for social services. Thus, those prostitutes who come to the attention of social workers may be the most vulnerable and have the least resources to meet their own needs.

To provide appropriate services, social workers must understand the life circumstances of this vulnerable and disenfranchised population. The social dynamics of prostitution highlight discrimination on the basis of sex, race, sexual orientation, age, citizenship status, and socioeconomic status, which places prostitutes in jeopardy of not meeting their basic human needs. Given the life circumstances of many of these individuals, prostitution is an alternative that may provide prostitutes and their families with needed resources. Workers must appreciate and understand both the strengths and vulnerabilities of such families and offer services in a way that supports their strengths while not placing them at further risk.

Those engaging in prostitution may legitimately fear loss of benefits, arrest, or both. The role of social workers relative to mandated child protection services also significantly impedes disclosure. Prostitutes have reported that "their greatest fear is that of being investigated by social service agencies and having their children taken away" (Shedlin, 1990, p. 138). The status of prostitute places women in a vulnerable position, which may result in loss of social services, removal of children from their care and termination of parental rights, rape or other violence, or arrest. The stigma associated with the identification of a woman as a prostitute may also lead to expulsion from social support systems such as family or church (Weiner, 1996).

The reported rates of multiple drug use and risk of STDs and HIV infection point to the need for medical attention and referral to detoxification programs. Access to drug and alcohol treatment is problematic. Not only may prostitutes lack proper documentation or medical insurance, they may have learned a variety of survival tactics on the street that may be dysfunctional in a treatment setting. Agencies may believe that such individuals will continue to trade sex for money or favors and that such behavior would undermine their programs. For women who are mothers, treatment may be difficult unless they can find adequate child care arrangements.

Drug use practices, risky sexual practices, and multiple sex partners—who themselves may be HIV infected—increase the spread of HIV and other STDs. Public health efforts must address the testing needs of this population through public clinics or outreach vans. Such programs must be prepared to offer treatment when diagnosis is positive.

The homeless, streetwalking, runaway, and illegal alien population is not easily accessible through normal agency service delivery. They are unlikely to approach agencies for help because of their lifestyles and realistic fear of arrest. Thus, social workers and agencies must develop outreach programs that are sensitive to cultural differences and vulnerabilities. It is important to recognize that although many prostitutes have been excluded from some social support networks (for example, family, church, or community), they have often created their own alternative networks or families. These societies may have developed their own values and norms, which may or may not coincide with those of the larger society.

Runaways and illegal immigrants may require legal services to protect their rights. Those who are homeless must have help in securing stable living arrangements. The nature of this population is such that often they do not always present themselves as "acceptable" clients for agencies. As is often the case in social services, those who need the services the most may not be accepted in programs because they are "difficult" or "undesirable" or lack the necessary resources (that is, Medicaid) to receive services. In addition, homeless people are not easily contacted when services are available. Agencies may have to establish a mail drop for homeless individuals so that they can be contacted by mail and have a mailing address for applying for public assistance. The lack of a secure mailbox is often cited as the cause for failure to get a Medicaid card or to receive notification of a certification meeting to receive public assistance.

Drop-in centers and shelters are needed specifically for homeless streetwalkers. Although general drop-in centers and shelters for the homeless exist, women often do not use such facilities because of their realistic fear of violence. When they do approach shelters, these women may be excluded from them by the staff because of the stigma associated with prostitutes. Such centers might offer meals, showers, clothing, lockers for belongings, mailboxes, social work services, and medical treatment. Although some might suggest that this encourages prostitution, this opportunity to have contact with women who might otherwise be "invisible" provides social workers with a chance to help reintegrate them into society.

This brief description of the lives of prostitutes may encourage social workers to look for creative ways to provide outreach and develop relationships with a vulnerable population that has invested much effort in remaining concealed. Help should be offered in such a way as to support the strengths of these clients without compromising them. Working with such individuals "stretches" workers to operationalize their values about self-determination and acceptance.

REFERENCES

Alexander, P. (1987). Prostitution: A difficult issue for feminists. In F. Delacoste & P. Alexander (Eds.), *Sex work: Writings by women in the sex industry.* San Francisco: Cleis Press.

Bellis, D. J. (1993). Reduction of AIDS risk among 41 heroin addicted female street prostitutes: Effects of free methadone maintenance. *Journal of Addictive Diseases, 12*(1), 7–23.

Bloor, M. J., McKeganey, N. P., Finlay, A., & Barnard, M. A. (1992). The inappropriateness of psychosocial models of risk behaviour for understanding HIV-related risk practices among Glasgow male prostitutes. *AIDS Care, 4,* 131–137.

Boles, J., & Elifson, K. W. (1994). The social organization of transvestite prostitution and AIDS. *Social Science and Medicine, 39,* 85–93.

Browne, J., & Minichiello, V. (1995). The social meanings behind male sex work: Implications for sexual interactions. *British Journal of Sociology, 46,* 598–622.

Cao, L. (1987). Illegal traffic in women: A civil RICO proposal. *Yale Law Journal, 96,* 1297–1322.

Cates, J. A., & Markley, J. (1992). Demographic, clinical and personality variables associated with male prostitution by choice. *Adolescence, 27,* 695–706.

Centers for Disease Control. (1987). Antibody to human immunodeficiency virus in female prostitutes. *Morbidity and Mortality Weekly Report, 36*(1), 157–161.

Chiasson, M. A., Stonebruner, R. L., Hildebrandt, D. S., Ewing, W. E., Telzak, E. E., & Jaffe, H. W. (1991). Heterosexual transmission of HIV-1 associated with the use of smokable freebase cocaine (crack). *AIDS, 5,* 1121–1126.

Cooper, B. (1989). Prostitution: A feminist analysis. *Women's Rights Law Reporter, 11*(2), 99–119.

Day, S. (1988). Prostitute women and AIDS: Anthropology. *AIDS, 2,* 421–428.

DeMeis, C., DeVasconellos, A. C., Linhares, D., & Andrada-Serpa, M. J. (1991). HIV infection among prostitutes in Rio de Janeiro, Brazil. *AIDS, 2,* 236–237.

Goldstein, P. J., Ouellet, L. J., & Fendrich, M. (1992). From bag brides to skeezers: A historical perspective on sex-for-drugs behavior. *Journal of Psychoactive Drugs, 24,* 349–361.

Gunn, R. A., Montes, J. M., Toomey, K. E., Rolfs, R. T., Greenspan, J. R., Spitters, C. E., & Waterman, S. H. (1995). Syphilis in San Diego County 1983–1992: Crack cocaine, prostitution, and the limitations of partner notification. *Sexually Transmitted Diseases, 22*(1), 60–66.

Jenness, V. (1990). From sex as sin to sex as work: COYOTE and the reorganization of prostitution as social problem. *Social Problems, 17,* 403–419.

Kail, B. L., Watson, D. D., & Ray, S. (1995). Needle using practices within the sex industry. *American Journal of Drug and Alcohol Abuse, 21,* 241–255.

King, D. (1990). Prostitutes as pariah in the age of AIDS. A content analysis of coverage of women prostitutes in *The New York Times* and the *Washington Post,* September 1985–April 1988. *Women and Health, 16,* 155–176.

Kuhns, J.B.D., Heide, K. M., & Silverman, I. (1992). Substance use/misuse among female prostitutes and female arrestees. *International Journal of the Addictions, 27,* 1283–1292.

Markos, A. R., Wade, A. A., & Walzman, M. (1992). The adolescent female prostitute and sexually transmitted diseases [Editorial]. *International Journal of STD & AIDS, 3,* 92–95.

PENet. (1996). *Prostitution in the United States—The statistics.* Available online at http://www.bayswan.org/penet.html.

Piot, P., Plummer, F. A., Rey, M. A., Ngugi, E. N., Rouzioux, C., Ndinya-Achola, J. O., Veracauteren, G., D'Costa, L. J., Laga, M., Nszanza, H., Fransea, L., Haase, D., Vander Green, G., Brunham, R. C., Robnald, A. R., & Burn-Vézinet, F. (1987). Retrospective seroepidemiology of AIDS virus infection in Nairobi populations. *Journal of Infectious Disease, 155,* 1108–1112.

Rolfs, R. T., Goldberg, M., & Sharrar, R. G. (1990). Risk factors for syphilis: Cocaine use and prostitution. *American Journal of Public Health, 80,* 853–857.

San Francisco Task Force on Prostitution. (1996). *Final Report.* San Francisco: Author.

Seng, M. J. (1989). Child sexual abuse and adolescent prostitution: A comparative analysis. *Adolescence, 24,* 665–675.

Shedlin, M. G. (1990). An ethnographic approach to understanding HIV high-risk behaviors: Prostitution and drug abuse. *NIDA Research Monograph, 93,* 134–149.

Simon, P. M., Morse, E. V., Osofsky, H. J., Balson, P. M., & Gaumer, H. R. (1992). Psychological characteristics of a sample of male street prostitutes. *Archives of Sexual Behavior, 21*(1), 33–44.

Wallace, J. I., Mann, J., & Beatrice, S. (1988, July). *HIV-1 exposure among clients of prostitutes.* Paper presented at the Fourth International AIDS Conference, Stockholm.

Wallace, J. I., & Weiner, A. P. (1996). Unpublished data. New York: Foundation for Research on Sexually Transmitted Diseases.

Weiner, A. (1996). Understanding the social needs of streetwalking prostitutes. *Social Work, 41,* 97–105.

Weiner, A., & Pollack, D. (1996). Urban runaway children: Sex, drugs and HIV. In N. Phillips & L. Straussner (Eds.), *Children in the urban environ-*

ment: Linking social policy and clinical practice. Springfield, IL: Charles C Thomas.

Weiner, A., Wallace, J. I., Steinberg, A., & Hoffman, B. (1992, July). Intravenous drug use, inconsistent condom use and fellatio practiced by crack using streetwalking prostitutes are risky behaviors for acquiring AIDS. In *Abstracts of VII International Conference on AIDS.* Amsterdam.

Adele Weiner, PhD, is associate dean, Wurzweiler School of Social Work, Yeshiva University, 50 West 185th Street, New York, NY 10033.

For further information see

Adolescence Overview; Adult Corrections; Adult Courts; Child Sexual Abuse Overview; Community-Based Corrections; Criminal Justice: Class, Race, and Gender Issues; Drug Abuse; Families Overview; Female Criminal Offenders; HIV/AIDS Overview; HIV/AIDS: Women; Homelessness; Human Sexuality; Juvenile Corrections; Poverty; Rehabilitation of Criminal Offenders; Runaways and Homeless Youths; Sentencing of Criminal Offenders; Substance Abuse: Direct Practice; Violence Overview.

Key Words

HIV/AIDS	women
prostitution	work
substance abuse	

S

Serious Mental Illness: A Biopsychosocial Perspective

Edward H. Taylor

This entry reviews mental disorders that are primarily related to neurobiological abnormalities. It includes a historical overview of methods used for labeling and diagnosing schizophrenia and bipolar disorders as well as an outline of neurological disorders and a discussion of their biological foundation. A short section describing how social work moved toward a neurobiological perspective of severe mental illness is also provided.

The social work profession has always participated in treating and helping people with serious mental illness. In the late 1980s, however, the profession's commitment to serving this population gained momentum, clarity, and direction, with social workers and social work educators adopting bioecological models rather than psychoanalytic methods for helping clients and families who experience serious and persistent mental illness (SPMI). Initiatives for improving social work interventions and research with SPMI populations were sponsored by clinical treatment facilities, academia, the National Institute of Mental Health (NIMH), and NASW. The entry briefly documents significant events that have contributed to social work's mental health knowledge base, practice methods, and research. In addition, the neurobiology of SPMI, along with a review of the profession's movement toward bioecological practice interventions, is outlined.

Many people suffer from "real" mental or emotional pain created by trauma, poverty, discrimination, social injustice, community chaos, destructive interpersonal relationships, and other nonbiological forces. These human issues are critical social work practice and policy concerns. Furthermore, they represent serious mental health issues. Social work has a long history of providing specialized mental health services and support to individuals who are in crisis, traumatized, or experiencing long-term psychosocial problems. This entry reviews disorders that are known to stem principally from neurobiological abnormalities.

SPMI: A Social Work Priority

In 1988 NIMH funded and provided guidance for a planning committee to develop recommendations for increasing social work's knowledge, involvement, and research with SPMI populations. David Austin, an internationally recognized social work researcher and educator, chaired the committee, which was composed of distinguished social workers in academia, clinical settings, and research. Their work resulted in a series of federally sponsored training seminars and financial assistance for developing research centers within selected schools of social work. To date, schools of social work at the following institutions have been awarded NIMH grants for SPMI research centers: Washington University (St. Louis), University of Tennessee, University of Michigan, Portland State University, and University of Washington (Seattle). This represents a federal investment of between $4 million and $6 million in social work mental health research.

It is also significant that in 1989 the elected delegates for the NASW Assembly unanimously supported a proposition directing the association to recognize serious mental illness as a group of neurobiological brain diseases. Two years earlier, several articles published in *Social Work* had—for the first time in the journal's history—both advocated for and explained the biology of schizophrenia. Additionally, at its 1988 national conference, NASW sponsored a half-day training seminar on the brain and schizophrenia. Meanwhile, the School of Social Work, University of North Carolina at Chapel Hill was commissioned to provide in-service training on serious mental illness to allied mental health workers throughout their state. The state government supported the faculty in creating two comprehensive mental health training curriculums. One series of demonstrations, lectures, and seminars focused on adults with SPMI and their families, and a completely separate program introduced professionals to case management theories and methods with children in need of community mental health services. The profession's endorsement of serious mental illness as a biological disease was further underscored by Bentley and Walsh (1996). These professors from the school of social work at the University of Virginia published the first textbook dedicated solely to educating social work practitioners about psychotropic medications.

HISTORICAL PERSPECTIVE

Throughout recorded history, researchers in science, philosophy, and religion have attempted to define and understand serious mental disorders. Scholars from the time of Hippocrates described symptoms resembling schizophrenia and theorized that the illness was a form of organic dementia. As Western civilization struggled to develop, these early insights were largely lost or replaced by myths, religious hypothesis, and dehumanizing conceptualizations. Not until the late 1800s, with the advent of European psychiatry, was the organic nature of serious mental illness again emphasized.

Emil Kraepelin (1856–1926) borrowed Benedict Morel's (1809–1873) term "dementia praecox" for describing schizophrenia-like symptoms. *Dementia* symbolizes a distinct form of cognitive dysfunction, and *praecox* defined the illness as having an early onset. More important, however, Kraepelin was the first to delineate a difference between patients with long-term psychoses (dementia praecox) from those with manic-depressive psychoses or paranoia. Dementia praecox was categorized as an organic neurological deterioration that caused hallucinations and delusions. A *manic-depressive psychosis* was defined as an episodic illness that caused normal functioning to be disrupted and then restored. Kraepelin further defined *paranoia* as persecutory delusions without the neurological deterioration seen in dementia praecox, but occurring persistently rather than episodically, as with a manic-depressive psychosis.

Eugen Bleuler (1857–1939) used the term "schizophrenia" instead of dementia praecox after conceptualizing the illness as a schism between thought, emotion, and behavior. Bleuler also introduced the idea that schizophrenia does not always result in an ever-increasing state of neurological deterioration. That is, he observed that the illness could improve, remain fixed, intensify and then plateau, or continue to grow worse. Although the term "schizophrenia" has gained international acceptance, Bleuler's criteria for diagnosing the illness were extremely broad and inclusive. For many years most European researchers used Kraepelin's criteria for diagnosing schizophrenia, while Bleuler's ideas became the American standard. Consequently, nearly twice as many people in the United States were diagnosed with schizophrenia as were in Europe. The introduction and acceptance of the *Diagnostic and Statistical Manual of Mental Disorders* (DSM) by the American mental health community largely resolved the diagnostic disparity between the two continents. Today, both Europe and the United States have similar standards for diagnosing severe mental illness.

The early pioneers established general agreement on the symptoms of severe illness but failed to explain their pathogenesis or physiological components. As a result, treatment for severe mental illness throughout much of this century remained an unhappy marriage between medicine and psychology. That is, the illness was framed by most mental health professionals as psychological disruptions within the control and will of the individual. Yet, the symptoms yielded not to psychotherapies, social training, family manipulations, motivational exercises, or environmental changes but solely to neuroleptic medications. This confused perspective on schizophrenia did not change until a series of studies of monozygotic twins (from the same egg) appeared in the 1970s, and the computed tomography scan allowed scientists a look into the living brain. Table 1 provides a biological overview and definitions that are helpful for understanding neurobiological illnesses.

BIOLOGY OF SPMI

Swedish researchers studied twins who were separated at birth and documented a strong association between genetics and mental illness (Gottesman, 1993; Kaplan, Sadock, & Grebb,

TABLE 1
Neurobiological Terms and Definitions

Term	Definition
Brain atrophy	Atrophy means that sections of the brain have shrunk in size. This is often seen in the thalamus, cerebral cortex, and hippocampus of people who have schizophrenia.
Brain structure	The brain's physical components, size, shape, weight, and cellular tissue.
Brain functioning	The brain's chemical activities. Studies have shown that key areas of the brain function differently when people have any of the neurobiological illnesses.
Dopamine hypothesis of schizophrenia	Studies have shown that blocking dopamine receptors with neuroleptic drugs decreases psychosis. It is also thought that dopamine may be a factor in causing mood disorders. During periods of depression, dopamine may decrease or be low and greatly increase when a manic episode is experienced (see also the definition of serotonin).
Frontal cortex	The frontal cortex of the brain is often conceptualized as the mind's filter and coordinator. It is directly involved in motor activation, social intellectual skills, conceptualizing and conceptual planning, and components of personality expression. There is evidence that prefrontal cortex blood flow and glucose metabolism are altered in people who have schizophrenia.
Glucose metabolism	When brain structures are activated (working) and require energy, the cells metabolize glucose. This allows neuroscientists to measure levels and locations of brain activity when an individual performs a mental task or is at rest.
Hippocampus	The hippocampus is part of the brain's limbic system. This structure plays a critical role along with the amygdala (another limbic structure) and temporal cortex in learning and memory. Damage in these areas is thought to cause memory distortions that are linked to hallucinations and delusions.
Limbic system	The limbic system is a group of interconnecting brain structures, which among other things, regulates motivated and emotional behaviors, including eating, drinking, sexuality, anxiety, and aggression. Individuals with severe mental illness often exhibit symptoms relating to limbic system functions. Physical damage to major limbic structures has been documented in clients with SPMI classifications.
Magnetic resonance imaging (MRI)	MRI uses powerful magnets to create sectional images of the living brain. It does not expose the client to radiation, and unlike the older computed tomography scan, the MRI can distinguish between the brain's white and gray matter.
Neurons	Neurons are specialized brain cells used for transmitting and receiving "messages" that are encoded in electrochemical signals. By sending and receiving neurochemicals, neurons serve as the brain's information-processing units.
Neurotransmitters or neurotransmission	Neurotransimission is the process used by the brain for sending information from one neuron to another. The message is chemically encoded and transmitted to the receiving or binding site of another neuron. Almost all psychiatric medications act on neurotransmitters. For example, psychosis is often reduced or controlled by neuroleptic medications (such as haloperidol) that block the dopamine receptors.
Positron-emission tomography (PET)	PET is currently the most powerful instrument available for imaging the living brain.
Serotonin	Serotonin is a neurochemical that influences mood. When the brain has too little serotonin, depression is experienced; manic episodes can occur when serotonin levels are too high (see also the definition of dopamine hypothesis of schizophrenia).
Temporal cortex and temporal lobe	The temporal cortex is part of the temporal lobe structure and is involved in the formation and maintenance of language, memory, and emotion. Studies have shown that this structure is often damaged in a person with schizophrenia.
Ventricles	Ventricles are interconnecting chambers within the brain that produce and transport cerebrospinal fluid. MRI imaging indicates that many people with schizophrenia have enlarged ventricles.

1994; Torrey, Taylor, et al., 1994). In addition, longitudinal studies of children of mentally ill parents have documented a genetic link to neurobiological illnesses (Fish, Marcus, Hans, Auerbach, & Perdue, 1992). The most convincing evidence that SPMI is a biological illness, however, has come from the technological ability to image neurological structures and measure the brain's metabolic rate. Numerous differences in the brain's structure and functioning between individuals with and without serious mental illness have been documented. For example, advanced brain-imaging technology was used in a recent American study of monozygotic twins, one whom had either schizophrenia or bipolar illness and the other of whom had no DSM-IV (American Psychiatric Association [APA], 1994) diagnosis. This is the largest study ever conducted of monozygotic twins discordant for schizophrenia.

Biological, developmental, educational, and behavioral differences between the well and ill twins were explored, and significant differences in brain structure and functioning were documented. Specifically, the hippocampus, frontal cortex, temporal lobe, and ventricles differed in size and shape between the well and ill twins. In addition, electronic frontal cortex measurements showed that ill twins, when compared with those with no mental illness, showed less activation (glucose metabolism) during problem solving or reasoning tasks. Identical twins used as controls (neither sibling had a disorder categorized in DSM-IV) had no significant differences in their brain structures or chemical–electrical functioning (Torrey, Bowler, Taylor, & Gottesman, 1994). Comprehensive biopsychosocial developmental studies were also conducted with the same sample. It was discovered that almost 30 percent of the twins who as young adults developed mental illness had significant neurological, social learning, or behavioral symptoms before reaching their sixth birthday. These early deficits did not appear in the twin siblings who developed no brain disorders (Torrey, Taylor, et al., 1994). Similar findings have also been reported by Fish and associates (1992).

Most scientists currently believe that schizophrenia occurs from the interaction of multiple genes and environmental factors, rather than from a single gene. Environmental notions, however, are conceived and researched much differently today than in the past. Families and communities are no longer hypothesized as causing schizophrenia, yet if an individual's brain incorrectly processes information, the environment may appear for that person to be frightening, or chaotic, and punishing. In addition, concrete environmental elements such as pollutants, viruses, or unidentified physical health problems, rather than psychological perceptions, may interact with genes to cause schizophrenia. Furthermore, genetics as a single or interacting stimulus may not account for all cases of schizophrenia. New evidence suggests that some people may develop schizophrenia from a neurovirus contracted as a fetus during the second trimester of pregnancy (Torrey, Bowler, et al., 1994).

Although the exact cause of schizophrenia remains unknown, the biological factors responsible for symptoms are rapidly being discovered. Damage or alterations to the limbic system, temporal lobe, and frontal cortex can now be identified in many people with schizophrenia. It is also known that the neurotransmitter dopamine does not correctly or efficiently bind to the five different types of dopamine receptors found in the brain. This may be caused by an overproductive dopamine system, a reduced number of neuroreceptors, or other neurodevelopmental problems. We do know that the frontal cortex chemically reacts differently to cognitive stimulation in people with and without a history of schizophrenia, most likely because of an interaction between the brain's structural damage and a chemical imbalance (Andreasen, 1994; Austrain, 1995; Taylor, 1987; Torrey, Bowler, et al., 1994).

Neurobiological factors determine, in addition to schizophrenia, whether a person develops major mood disorders, schizoaffective disorder, pervasive developmental disorders, and some anxiety disorders. Almost 5 percent of Americans suffer from a serious debilitating illness known as "major depressive episodes." Women are twice as likely as men to develop severe depression, which most often appears in a person's late 20s and recurs, on average, five or six times throughout the life span. Untreated, a major depressive episode can last six months or longer. Fortunately, 75 percent to 80 percent of clients who are treated with psychotherapy, medications, or a combination of both experience substantial improvement or symptom relief within three or four months.

Many people, however, continue to report depressive symptoms a year after treatment begins, and 5 percent to 10 percent of those who have a major depressive episode will be depressed after being treated for two years. In addition, another 3 percent to 6 percent of the U.S. population has dysthymia, or chronic mild depression, and an additional .08 percent to 1 percent have a bipolar disorder. Dysthymia occurs two or three times more often in women than in men; bipolar disorders appear to develop at an equal rate in both sexes (APA, 1994; Hales & Hales, 1995; Kaplan et al., 1994).

Bipolar disorders (comprising bipolar I, bipolar II, and cyclothymia) account for approximately 20 percent of all reported depressive disorders. These three illnesses are highly responsive to biopsychosocial treatments (medications and psychotherapy), but, unfortunately, they are often misdiagnosed and underdiagnosed (APA, 1994; Hales & Hales, 1995; Goodwin & Jamison, 1990). A person with bipolar I disorder experiences extreme highs and lows in mood. During a manic episode, a person may feel more inspired, exuberant, powerful, creative, energized, or invincible than at any other time in his or her life, yet the ability for self-efficacy, social judgment, and problem solving greatly deteriorates. People with bipolar illness therefore often make poor decisions and place themselves in physical, economic, or social danger. For example, during a manic episode they may (with no history of sexual promiscuity) have sex with multiple strangers or spend large sums of money on illogical projects and personal items. Then, after the bipolar "high" dissolves, the person sinks into a major depressive episode. During this phase, simple personal hygiene tasks, daily routines, interpersonal relationships, or even getting out of bed can appear monumental and impossible to accomplish. The internal psychic pain is intense, and cognitive self-messages of hopelessness abound. Furthermore, it is not unusual for people with bipolar I disorder to experience periods of psychoses that require neuroleptic medications.

Science has yet to find a specific genetic marker for mood disorders. It is known that bipolar disorders appear concurrently in monozygotic twins six or seven times more often than in fraternal twins (from two eggs). That is, the disorder has a much higher probability of occurring in a pair of identical twins, who share the same genes, than in a pair of fraternal twins, who do not share identical genetic codes. In severe depression, the concurrent rate for identical twins is twice that of fraternal twins (Kaplan et al., 1994; McGuffin & Katz, 1993). Furthermore, several different brain chemicals appear to play important roles in mood disorders. Antidepressant medication, for example, is thought to reduce symptoms by changing levels of norepinephrine and serotonin. These are neurotransmitters that permit or conduct communications between different brain cells. In addition, researchers are finding that one's hormonal system also plays a role in depression. Many people suffering with severe depression have unusually high levels of cortisol (adrenocorticotropin), a hormone produced by the adrenal glands. Cortisol is a steroid that appears in the blood when the brain senses external stress. It is hypothesized that a depressed person's brain fails to stop the chemical signals for physiological stress reactions even after the environmental stimulus has been removed or resolved. As a result, depressive episodes may result in part from a prolonged activation of the brain's stress system (Chrousos & Gold, 1992).

Suicide can be a tragic side effect of serious mental illness, both schizophrenia and mood disorders. Approximately 10 percent to 15 percent of all people with schizophrenia will end their lives by suicide, usually within a few weeks after discharge from an inpatient hospitalization. Some clinicians and researchers believe these people develop a sense of hopelessness and fear that they will again slip into a painful state of anxiety and chaotic psychoses. The apprehension of helplessness, hopelessness, and never-ending cycles of psychosis requiring rehospitalizations may limit the person's perceived choices and increase suicidal thoughts. In addition, some people with schizophrenia commit suicide because of command hallucinations and beliefs that stem from an internal delusional system. For example, a person may have an auditory hallucination that God or the devil is commanding that the soul to be cleansed by death, or delusions of grandeur may cause a person to believe that, through death, rebirth and power will be gained. Furthermore, separating suicide from a fatal accident can be extremely difficult: How does one determine whether stepping in front of a speeding car or falling from a bridge occurs from deficits in attention and concentration or from a drive for self-destruction?

A person who has a mood disorder, whether severe or not, must be screened continuously for suicidal thoughts and behavioral indicators. Life will end by suicide for 15 percent of all people who suffer from any mood disorder. Although most people with depression do not have a psychosis, their problem-solving skills and information-processing capacities are diminished. These temporary social cognitive deficits, along with decreased physical energy, isolation, and a decaying sense of self-worth, can create extreme emotional pain and a belief that there are no answers—only anguish, hopelessness, and a wish for death. Moreover, depressed people must often face family members, communities, and sometimes even mental health professionals who interpret their lack of activity as willful defiance and a considered decision to remain incapacitated. This is particularly true when depressive symptoms are viewed as psychological choices, not biologically driven signs of illness. Unvoiced suicidal thoughts can be validated by social interactions that, directly or indirectly,

- blame the individual for not improving
- provide little empathy for emotional pain
- deny that some family, social, or work tasks cannot be performed
- fail to acknowledge persuasively that the accomplishment of any routine task requires deliberate physical energy and painfully difficult or slow cognitive processing.

Suicide prevention strategies therefore need to include periodic screening of both the individual's and the family's interpersonal perceptions, interaction behaviors, communication styles, and beliefs. Biopsychosocial education, support, and coordinated services also are usually therapeutic for families who are experiencing serious mental illness (Hales & Hales, 1995).

People with a bipolar disorder are at risk not only for suicide but also for victimization by criminals and rapists; during a manic episode, they are in danger also of being involved in life-threatening accidents. A manic high can cause people to unknowingly, or with little concern, place themselves in dangerous environments and increase their risk-taking behaviors to precarious levels.

Epidemiologists report that between 2 percent and 3 percent of the U.S. population have obsessive-compulsive disorder (OCD). It is the fourth most common mental problem in the United States, following phobias, substance abuse, and depression. The disorder is characterized by high anxiety, recurring (obsessional) thoughts, and compulsive behaviors. People with OCD are aware that their repetitive behaviors are irrational and embarrassing. Nonetheless, awareness and social pressures do not serve as a stimulus for ending the redundant thoughts or behaviors. The problem often starts in childhood, but it may not appear until adolescence or early adulthood. Females and males are equally affected by this disorder. However, the age of onset differs by gender. Boys have a higher risk for developing OCD early, between the ages of six and 15, whereas females generally get OCD as young women between the ages of 20 and 29 (Hales & Hales, 1995; Kaplan et al., 1994).

Researchers believe that OCD is caused primarily by biological abnormalities in the brain's basal ganglia region. Damage in this area can cause a person to doubt information gathered from sight, past knowledge, or experience. As a result, that person is biologically driven to repeat behavior sequences (such as hand washing), revisit a cognitive set, or do countless re-examinations or "checks" of familiar environments. Positron-emission tomography and magnetic resonance imaging (MRI) show differences in specific brain regions and metabolic patterns between people with OCD and normal control subjects. For example, for people with OCD, the metabolic and blood flow rates in the brain's frontal cortex, caudate, and cingulum are faster than for those with no mental illness. Interestingly, the opposite (a slowed metabolism) is the case in the frontal cortex of people with schizophrenia. Additionally, MRI studies have shown that the brains of individuals with OCD have smaller caudate (bilaterally) than found in normal control subjects. It is not known whether defective neurotransmitters are involved in the cause of OCD, but the illness often responds positively to medications that reduce the brain's serotonin levels. Studies have also linked heredity and OCD. About 25 percent of people with OCD report having relatives who also have obsessions and compulsive behaviors. An identical rate is also found for people who suffer from panic attacks.

Studies of monozygotic twins also support a genetic hypothesis for both OCD and panic disorder (APA, 1994; Hales & Hales, 1995; Kaplan et al., 1994).

Panic disorder is a form of extreme anxiety (panic attacks) that can overwhelm an individual, even when no stimulus or stressor is present. The intense anxiety usually occurs spontaneously and generally lasts less than an hour. It occurs in women twice as often as in men, and most often symptoms are first experienced during late adolescence or young adulthood, although panic attacks can appear at any age. Approximately 1.5 percent to 3.5 percent of the population are reported to have the disorder. Neurological studies have found temporal lobe abnormalities and cerebral vasoconstriction in people who have panic attacks. The dysregulation of cerebral blood flow or vasoconstriction may be responsible for the physical symptoms of dizziness and hyperventilation associated with panic attacks.

CHILDREN WITH NEUROBIOLOGICAL DISORDERS

Although children and young adolescents are not as vulnerable as adults to the illnesses discussed above, major mood disorders, schizophrenia, and pervasive developmental disorders (PDDs) are nonetheless reported across the youthful age spectrum (Asarnow, Thompson, & Goldstein, 1994; Fleming & Offord, 1990; Gordon et al., 1994; Kafantaris, 1995). Because all children have limited language skills, few life experiences, and incomplete social knowledge and skills, and because they encounter rapid biopsychosocial developmental changes, the diagnosis of serious neuropsychiatric problems can be very difficult. Furthermore, the diagnostic criteria for most severe disorders were developed by researching adult clients, yet children often manifest major psychiatric symptoms differently than do older adolescents and adults. Depression in children, for example, may cause behavioral aggression or agitation rather than the adult symptoms of withdrawal and sadness (Fleming & Offord, 1990; Geller, Fox, & Clark, 1994; Kaplan et al., 1994). Moreover, the rich fantasy life experienced by most children confounds the adult criteria for identifying delusional systems and hallucinations. Specific diagnostic information for PDDs, which is founded on child research, is provided in DSM-IV. Nonetheless, even this category, which is specifically aimed at youths, does not classify many children who

experience atypical social, language, cognitive, or motor neurobiological symptoms.

Early-Onset Schizophrenia

Childhood and adult-onset schizophrenia are currently thought to be identical neurobiological illnesses. Approximately 61 percent of children diagnosed with schizophrenia will have similar symptoms throughout their life cycle, and less than 25 percent will recover fully (Asarnow et al., 1994). Children, more so than adults, experience a progressive mental deterioration that evolves into psychotic symptoms. Before classical DSM-IV symptoms occur, parents have often requested help for behavioral disturbances, developmental lags, neuromotor problems, and socialization difficulties. A rapid onset preceded by no visible symptoms is reported in a few children (Russell, 1994); these children respond better to treatment and have a more positive prognosis than those who experience a series of evolving symptoms. Unfortunately, whether the onset was rapid or progressive, a child's prognosis is most often poorer when schizophrenia appears before the 10th birthday rather than later (Taylor, in press).

Pervasive Developmental Disorders

PDDs include autism, Rett's disorder, childhood disintegrative disorder (CDD), and Asperger's disorder. Children who do not meet the specific requirements for a PDD category but appear significantly impaired and have similar symptoms are given the diagnosis "pervasive developmental disorder not otherwise specified" (APA, 1994). These neurodevelopmental illnesses usually occur before the child is three years old, and they have a devastating impact on the child's social, language, and behavioral development (APA, 1994; Rutter, Bailey, Bolton, & Couteur, 1993). It is therefore important to make ongoing parental training part of the bioecological treatment. Parents need behavioral management skills, along with instruction in methods for encouraging socialization, language, and motor skills. Family members also need to be taught how to observe and measure the child's symptoms across social climates. Medication and behavioral–cognitive treatment approaches must constantly be shifted as the child develops and environmental reactions change. Strategies for training parents, modifying the environment, and directly intervening with children who have PDD have been detailed by Schreibman and Koegel (1996); Koegel and Koegel (1996); and Strain, Kohler, and Goldstein (1996).

Autism

Autism is the most commonly diagnosed PDD; it occurs in two to five individuals per 10,000 children (under 12 years of age). Boys are three to four times more likely than girls to have autism, but girls with autism often have more serious impairment. Results from genetic studies suggest that girls disabled by autism will more often than boys have neurobiological illnesses in their family histories (Kaplan et al., 1994; Young, Newcorn, & Leven, 1989).

Autism limits the child's reciprocal social interaction skills, creates unusual or restricted communication patterns, and often causes unique behaviors that are frequently repeated. Transitions from one setting to another or changes in a setting's physical appearance (how furniture is arranged, for example) can be intolerable for the child. Early age-appropriate exploratory play (even as an infant) will quickly disappear or never occur; when these children play, they will appear rigid and seemingly lack imagination. Autism also makes it nearly impossible for children with the disorder to imitate positive behaviors from modeling and logically process abstract social or environmental cues. Stereotypical or ritualistic behaviors, such as grimacing, spinning, banging, or placing objects in a specific order, are also routinely reported by parents and clinicians.

The sensory skills (response to pain, sounds, sights, and so on) of some children with autism are either over- or underdeveloped. Furthermore, autism causes many children to appear hyperactive, have unexplained temper tantrums, and engage in self-injurious behaviors (head banging, biting, hitting, hair pulling, and so on). Autism may also create ongoing problems in sleeping, eating, toilet care, attention, or concentration (Kaplan et al., 1994; Kassari, Sigman, & Yirmiya, 1993; Ozonoff & McEvoy, 1994).

Rett's Disorder

Rett's disorder almost exclusively strikes girls between the ages of six months and two years. The prenatal and perinatal life stages are usually symptom free and provide no hint of the coming tragedy. It is estimated that out of every 100,000 girls, six to seven will be dramati-

cally disabled for life by this illness. Besides severely damaging language skills and ending the development of most social skills, this illness also interferes with normal body and muscle development (head growth slows) and often causes seizures.

Childhood Disintegrative Disorder

CDD is diagnosed when a child two years of age or older with no previous neurodevelopmental problems acquires several symptoms of autism. Typically, children with CDD will incur some of the following characteristics: inability to make transitions and adapt behaviorally; stereotyped movements; reduction of social interaction and problem-solving skills; compulsive behaviors; decreased language skills; impaired coordination; and lack of bowel or bladder control. The symptoms generally occur between the ages of three and four years. Although rarely, the illness can mysteriously appear in children who are nine to ten years old.

A CDD diagnosis cannot be given if the symptoms are observed before the child is 24 months old. Boys are reported with CDD more often than girls (four times more often according to some estimates, and eight times more often according to others); CDD is thought to afflict one in 100,000 boys. Although the course and prognosis for CDD is variable, most children with this disorder experience at least moderate mental retardation and language difficulties throughout their remaining life cycle.

Asperger's Disorder

Asperger's disorder is characterized by poorly developed social and interpersonal skills, limited alternatives for routine behaviors, little curiosity or interest in the environment, and indifference toward peer or other sociable activities. The illness does not disrupt the child's language development, however. These children often isolate themselves and cannot independently modify their behaviors to contextually fit with the environment.

A child with this disorder cannot use language for linking with others or for pragmatic problem solving. Parents may complain that their child cannot initiate and maintain social conversations or that the child speaks in a tangential manner with a lack of voice inflections (or inappropriate inflection) and cannot provide meaningful information about an observed event. In addition, children with Asperger's disorder may develop obsessive-compulsive behaviors at a very early age. Unlike people with an obsessive-compulsive disorder or Tourette's syndrome, the child with Asperger's disorder does not experience rituals and compulsions as repugnant or unwanted. Conversely, discomfort over repetitive behaviors is an important diagnostic indicator for children with obsessive-compulsive or Tourettes disorder.

The epidemiology of Asperger's disorder is unknown. It is thought, however, to occur more often in males. Symptoms are usually first observed in preschoolers and during the early elementary grades. Fortunately, the disorder is not highly associated with mental retardation. Although Asperger's disorder is a lifelong illness, rehabilitation varies with each client. People who have higher social skills (as a child) and no mental retardation are thought to have fewer disabilities as adolescents and adults. Generally, these children appear to function throughout the life cycle at a higher level than individuals with autism (APA, 1994; Kaplan et al., 1994; Szatmari, 1991).

SOCIAL WORK AND NEUROBIOLOGICAL RESEARCH

Professional social workers are not intuitively pictured as active scientific participants in researching the neurobiology of serious mental illness. Nevertheless, individual social workers have, both individually and in collaboration with others, made a number of valuable contributions to the field. For example, Gerald Hogarty, MSW, has over 100 professional publications relating to the biology, cognition, and treatment of schizophrenia. He has conducted neurodevelopmental studies, medication and social skills efficacy trials, and cognitive intervention evaluation research (Hogarty, 1993; Hogarty & Flesher, 1992). Moreover, Hogarty and colleagues have researched relationships among the brain's limbic system, frontal cortex, and social cognitive skills. Hogarty was recently awarded a multimillion-dollar NIMH grant to determine whether specific social cognitive interventions will improve problem-solving and community living skills for participants who have schizophrenia. Other social workers, who seldom receive much publicity, are also involved in biopsychosocial and neurologically oriented research. Some of these social workers have published articles or made presentations at professional conferences. Others have been involved in designing data collection methods, and yet others conduct clinical interviewing, provide specialized treatment, or recruit and screen volunteers for biological research.

A social worker designed all of the biological and genetic developmental histories, as well as the psychosocial, educational, and interpersonal research, conducted with the previously mentioned monozygotic twins discordant for schizophrenia. Findings drawn from data concerning the twins' prenatal histories have been published in the United States and Sweden. Furthermore, it was the social worker's biopsychosocial and ecological perspective that led the NIMH research team to discover that up to 30 percent of people who develop schizophrenia as adults had social cognitive, neuromotor, problem-solving, or behavioral problems by the time they had reached five years of age.

Other NIMH social workers have also contributed to neurobiological research. For example, Edward Turner, MSW, has helped design and conduct research on the neurobiological and social factors related to suicide by people with schizophrenia. He has also worked on studies of early atypical child development and researched how biological, environmental, and maternal factors influence the development of infants found to be physically at risk. Carol Rodifer, MSW, has participated in studies focused on a specific biological dysfunction that causes some individuals with schizophrenia to obsessively consume water. This can be a life-threatening behavioral problem that is directly linked to specific brain abnormalities. Additionally, she has studied biosocial treatment methods with mentally ill patients requiring institutional care; she is currently researching stress perceptions of SPMI clients who volunteer for biological research. Cathy O'Leary, MSW, has spent a large portion of her career researching the biopsychosocial components of borderline personality disorder. Denise Juliano, MSW, and Sue Bell, MSW, have been part of the NIMH team researching the biology of depression. Rina Segal, MSW, is presently working with NIMH neuroscientists on a longitudinal study of siblings with schizophrenia; this research is designed to investigate whether and when brain structures and functions change in people at risk for schizophrenia. Linda Nee, MSW, has made international presentations on her genetic research on movement disorders and Alzheimer's disease (Higgins, Morton, Patronas, & Nee, in press; Nee & Higgins, in press). Rosemary Farmer,

PhD, who trained at the NIMH Neuroscience Hospital and is now a university professor, is studying how neurobiological abnormalities affect specific social skills required for community living. These individuals are representative of social workers who are directly involved in researching SPMI from a biopsychosocial perspective, but they are not the only ones so involved. Indeed, an impressive number of social workers have made and continue to make meaningful contributions in the areas of mental health treatment, evaluation, research, and policy analysis.

SOCIAL WORK INTERVENTIONS

Although the specific causes of SPMI remain unknown, science has successfully shown that biological rather than psychological or social factors best explain how serious mental illness starts and progresses. In response, social work education and practice have shifted mental health training to emphasize interventions, policy, and research founded on biopsychosocial theories. Social workers thus are among the most highly trained nonmedical professionals who perform clinical interventions with people with SPMI and their families. It is often the social worker's responsibility to provide families with education about mental illness; develop interventions for helping clients cope; and continue helpful medication, rehabilitation, and psychosocial treatments. In addition, professional social workers are trained to conduct a variety of individual, group, and family problem-solving therapies. Within the community, social work has developed or adopted several case management and support models, and many social workers provide ecological, behavioral, cognitive, and support treatments for clients in both outpatient and inpatient settings. Community programs are designed to enhance the quality of life of people with SPMI, maintain or coordinate outpatient and rehabilitative commitments, and prevent illness relapses that require hospitalization.To that end, social work skills are often used in psychosocial clubhouses, group homes, clinics for clients with dual diagnoses, part- and full-day hospitals, and homeless shelters. The discovery that SPMI is related to neurobiological abnormalities has created new treatment roles for social work and, for the first time, hope for our clients and their families.

REFERENCES

American Psychiatric Association. (1994). *Diagnostic and statistical manual of mental disorders* (4th ed.). Washington, DC: Author.

Andreasen, N. C. (1994). *Schizophrenia: From mind to molecule.* Washington, DC: American Psychiatric Press.

Asarnow, J. R., Thompson, M. C., & Goldstein, M. J. (1994). Childhood-onset schizophrenia: A follow-up study. *Schizophrenia Bulletin, 20,* 599–617.

Austrain, S. G. (1995). *Mental disorders, medications, and clinical social work.* New York: Columbia University Press,

Bentley, K. J., & Walsh, J. (1996). *The social worker and psychotropic medication.* Pacific Grove, CA: Brooks/Cole.

Chrousos, G. P., & Gold, P. W. (1992). The concepts of stress and stress system disorders: Overview of physical and behavioral homeostasis. *JAMA, 267,* 1244–1252.

Fish, B., Marcus, J., Hans, S. L., Auerbach, J. G., & Perdue, S. (1992). Infants at risk for schizophrenia: Sequelae of a genetic neurointegrative defect. *Archives of General Psychiatry, 49,* 221–235.

Fleming, J. E., & Offord, D. R. (1990). Epidemiology of childhood depressive disorders: A critical review. *Journal of the American Academy of Child and Adolescent Psychiatry, 29,* 571–580.

Geller, B., Fox, L. W., & Clark, K. A. (1994). Rates and predictors of prepubertal bipolarity during follow-up of 6- to 12-year-old depressed children. *Journal of the American Academy of Child and Adolescent Psychiatry, 33,* 461–468.

Goodwin, F. K., & Jamison, K. R. (1990). *Manic depressive illness.* New York: Oxford University Press.

Gordon, C. T., Frazier, J. A., McKenna, K., Giedd, J., Zametkin, A., Hommer, D., Hong, W., Kaysen, D., Albus, K. E., & Rappoport, J. L. (1994). Childhood-onset schizophrenia: An NIMH study in progress. *Schizophrenia Bulletin, 20,* 697–712.

Gottesman, I. (1993). Origins of schizophrenia: Past as prologue. In R. Plomin & G. E. McClearn (Eds.), *Nature nurture and psychology* (pp. 231–244). Washington, DC: American Psychological Association.

Hales, D., & Hales, R. E. (1995). *Caring for the mind: The comprehensive guide to mental health.* New York: Bantam Books.

Higgins, J. J., Morton, D. H., Patronas, N., & Nee, L. E. (in press). An autosomal recessive genetic disorder with posterior column ataxia and retinitis pigmentosa. *Neurology.*

Hogarty, G. E. (1993). Prevention of relapse in chronic schizophrenic patients. *Journal of Clinical Psychiatry, 54*(Suppl.), 18–23.

Hogarty, G. E., & Flesher, S. (1992). Cognitive remediation in schizophrenia: Proceed . . . with caution! *Schizophrenia Bulletin, 18,* 51–57.

Kafantaris, V. (1995). Treatment of bipolar disorder in children and adolescents. *Journal of the American Academy of Child and Adolescent Psychiatry, 34,* 732–741.

Kaplan, H. I., Sadock, B. J., & Grebb, J. A. (1994). *Synopsis of psychiatry* (7th ed.). Baltimore: Williams & Wilkins.

Kassari, C., Sigman, M., & Yirmiya, N. (1993). Focused and social attention of autistic children in interactions with familiar and unfamiliar adults: A comparison of autistic, mentally retarded, and normal children. *Development and Psychopathology, 5,* 403–414.

Koegel, L. K., & Koegel, R. L. (1996). The child with autism as an active communicative partner: Communication and reducing behavior problems. In E. D. Hibbs & P. S. Jensen (Eds.), *Child and adolescent disorders* (pp. 553–572). Washington, DC: American Psychological Association.

McGuffin, P., & Katz, R. (1993). Genes, adversity, and depression. In R. Plomin & G. E. McClearn (Eds.), *Nature nurture and psychology* (pp. 217–230). Washington, DC: American Psychological Association.

Nee, L. E., & Higgins, J. J. (in press). Should spinocerebellar ataxia type 5 be called Lincoln ataxia? *Neurology.*

Ozonoff, S., & McEvoy, R. E. (1994). A longitudinal study of executive function and theory of mind development in autism. *Development and Psychopathology, 6,* 415–431.

Russell, A. T. (1994). The clinical presentation of childhood-onset schizophrenia. *Schizophrenia Bulletin, 20,* 599–617.

Rutter, M., Bailey, A., Bolton, P., & Couteur, A. L. (1993). Autism: Syndrome definition and possible genetic mechanisms. In R. Plomin & G. E. McClearn (Eds.), *Nature nurture and psychology* (pp. 269–284). Washington, DC: American Psychological Association.

Schreibman, L., & Koegel, R. (1996). Fostering self-management: Parent-delivered pivotal response training for children with autistic disorder. In E. D. Hibbs & P. S. Jensen (Eds.), *Child and adolescent disorders* (pp. 525–552). Washington, DC: American Psychological Association.

Strain, P. S., Kohler, F. W., & Goldstein, H. (1996). Learning experiences . . . An alternative program: Peer-mediated interventions for young children with autism. In E. D. Hibbs & P. S. Jensen (Eds), *Child and adolescent disorders* (pp. 573–587). Washington, DC: American Psychological Association.

Szatmari, P. (1991). Asperger's syndrome: Diagnosis, treatment, and outcome. *Psychiatric Clinics of North America, 14,* 81–93.

Taylor, E. H. (1987). The biological basis of schizophrenia. *Social Work, 32,* 115–121.

Taylor, E. H. (in press). Advances in the diagnosis and treatment of children with serious mental illness. *Child Welfare.*

Torrey, E. F., Bowler, A. E., Taylor, E. H., & Gottesman, I. I. (1994). *Schizophrenia and manic-depressive disorder: The biological roots of mental illness as revealed by the landmark study of identical twins.* New York: Basic Books.

Torrey, E. F., Taylor, E. H., Bracha, S., Bowler, A. E., McNeil, T. F., Rawlings, R. R., Quinn, P. O., Bigelow, L. B., Rickler, K., Sjostrom, K., Higgins, E. S., & Gottesman, I. I. (1994). Prenatal origin of schizophrenia in a subgroup of discordant monozygotic twins. *Schizophrenia Bulletin, 20,* 423–432.

Young, G., Newcorn, H. H., & Leven, L. I. (1989). Pervasive developmental disorders. In H. I. Kaplan & B. J. Sadock (Eds.), *Comprehensive textbook of psychiatry* (5th ed., Vol. 2, pp. 1772–1787). Baltimore: Williams & Wilkins.

Edward H. Taylor, PhD, ACSW, is associate professor, School of Social Work, University of Illinois at Urbana–Champaign, 1207 West Oregon Street, Urbana, IL 61801.

For further information see

Aging: Alzheimer's Disease and Other Disabilities; Assessment; Children: Mental Health; Clinical Social Work; Cognitive Treatment; Deinstitutionalization; Diagnostic and Statistical Manual of Mental Disorders; Direct Practice Overview; Genetics; Goal Setting and Intervention Planning; Interviewing; **Managed Care: Implications for Social Work Practice;** Mental Health Overview; Psychosocial Approach; Psychosocial Rehabilitation; Psychotropic Medications; Substance Abuse: Direct Practice; Suicide; Victims of Torture and Trauma.

Key Words

child mental disorders	schizophrenia
mood disorders	severe and persistent
neurobiological	mental illness
illnesses	

Social Welfare Expenditures: Private

Richard Hoefer
Ira C. Colby

Changes in public, governmental expenditures for social welfare get a lot of attention, but changes in private spending for social welfare receive little. This neglect ignores a very important way Americans provide for human needs. Private social welfare spending equals about two-thirds of public social welfare spending. This translates to a very large amount of money—approximately $825 billion in 1992, or 14 percent of that year's gross domestic product. Data detailing private social welfare indicate that the sector plays a critical role in the overall financing of the nation's social welfare system (Kerns & Glanz, 1991). This entry examines the history of private spending for social welfare, discusses its uses and magnitude, and considers the implications of this information for the social work profession and social welfare in general.

HISTORY

The history of American social welfare is largely a history of private social welfare (Axinn & Levin, 1992; Trattner, 1989). Founded on the principles of individualism and limited government, the American welfare system traditionally has relied on the market, family, and churches and other charitable welfare institutions to satisfy people's basic needs (Jansson, 1997). Only in the 1930s did public spending for social welfare become significant at the national level, but even though the 1930s and the 1960s saw the enactment of many proactive governmental social programs, the American welfare state is still best characterized as weak, with little orchestration, coordination, or planning.

Moreover, public programs have never supplanted private initiatives. McInnis-Dittrich (1993) argued that a pervading national ambivalence about the government's role in helping those in need has led to a national fragmentation of public policy. Public welfare policies, guided by the tenets of rugged individualism, have produced short-term, emergency-based program structures (McInnis-Dittrich, 1993). In this public policy model, social welfare is not a governmental function but a province of the private sector. Indeed, because of the long period before there was a significant national governmental presence in the area of social welfare, the American system consists of overlapping public and private welfare systems. As Kerns (1994) argued, knowledge of both public and private welfare spending is "necessary for a comprehensive understanding of spending trends in social welfare" (p. 87).

Social welfare is usually thought of as public social services and income maintenance programs directed toward poor people. This conception is incorrect, however, because it posits that poor people are the primary recipients of governmental aid, and it ignores the role of nongovernmental actors in providing for human need. In the "shadow welfare state" identified by Abramovitz (1983), it is the middle and upper classes that are able to accrue the majority of public benefits through tax policies (credit for home loan interest, child care costs, and business expenses, for example), social security pensions, and federal subsidies for agriculture and large corporations. And the voluntary, independent sector—what Karger and Stoesz (1994) call the "forgotten sector"—is only one part of the world of nongovernmental social welfare. The corporate presence in social welfare has been growing in importance (Karger & Stoesz, 1994). Individuals have also been spending more on their own social welfare by paying for schooling and funding personal pension plans.

Just as there is a shadow welfare state and a forgotten sector, there is also a "mirror welfare state" that benefits primarily the middle and upper classes. The mirror welfare state, like public social welfare services, is usually narrowly conceived as activities for poor people. It is most often thought to consist of private expenditures, based on individual tax-deductible contributions, that provide services for poor individuals and families. But just as the shadow welfare state and forgotten sector include significant activities that spread their benefits through all economic groups, so too does the mirror social welfare system. Significant mirror welfare supports are aimed at the middle and upper-middle classes, primarily through programs in health care, insurance, retirement, and education. The mirror welfare system furnishes meaningful resources and benefits to specific categorical groups as an entitlement based on individual or corporate fiscal contributions.

MEASUREMENT ISSUES

Data on private welfare expenditures are collected annually by the Social Security Administration and published in the *Social Security Bulletin,* although the series of data was not published from 1979 to 1986, presumably because of the difficulties in estimating private spending. As Kerns (1994) noted, "Data on private social welfare expenditures are more difficult to collect than is information on public expenditures" (p. 87). Moreover, public social welfare expenditures are traditionally presented in the federal fiscal year budget, October 1 through September 30, and data for private welfare expenditures are collected on a calendar-year basis (Kerns & Glanz, 1991). The results of attempts to make these data comparable are available from 1988 onward (Kerns, 1994), but continuing revisions to procedures mean that there can be significant changes in estimated expenditures for the same category of spending from one year to the next (personal communication with W. Kerns, Office of Research and Statistics, Division of Program Analysis, Social Security Administration, January 7, 1997). These revisions make it imperative to use the latest information available.

CATEGORIES AND SPENDING LEVELS OF PRIVATE SOCIAL WELFARE SPENDING

In 1992 total private social welfare spending reached $852 billion, an 800 percent increase over the preceding two decades, rising from less than $100 billion in 1972 (Kerns, 1995). Another way to look at the growth is as a percentage of the gross domestic product (GDP). In 1972 private social welfare spending was only 8 percent of GDP; by 1992, it had increased to nearly 14 percent (Kerns, 1995) (see Table 1).

A comparison of private and public spending for social welfare shows three significant periods between 1972 and 1992. From 1972 to 1976, private social welfare spending decreased from 48 percent to 43 percent of public spending. The trend reversed

from 1977 to 1989: Private spending, as a percentage of public spending, increased from 43 percent to 70 percent. In 1990 the direction reversed again, and private spending had decreased to 64 percent of public social welfare spending by 1992 (Kerns, 1995).

Such data would seem to indicate that the private welfare system is a large counterpart to the public system. A superficial analysis might even suggest that the combination of private and public welfare expenditures, $1.9 trillion in 1991 (Kerns, 1995), illustrates a strong and vibrant national commitment to welfare matters. A more thorough analysis of private welfare expenditures, however, leads to the conclusion that the welfare commitment is made to people who are not poor.

Private-sector welfare, according to the federal government, includes these components: health, income maintenance, education, and welfare services. Expenditures for each of these categories have grown at a rapid pace, although income maintenance and welfare services grew the most quickly between 1972 and 1992.

Health

More than half of all private social welfare expenditures made since 1972 have gone to health care, and the amount of spending has been steadily rising. Between 1972 and 1992, private health care spending grew by more than 800 percent, from $57.2 billion to $462.9 billion. For most of this period, private expenditures ranged from 58 percent to 59 percent of all health expenditures, although the percentage dipped to just 56.6 percent in 1992; in absolute figures, 1992 private health care expenditures outstripped government health expenditures, $462.9 billion to $357.5 billion (Kerns, 1995).

Private health care spending comprises three broad areas: (1) health services and supplies, (2) noncommercial medical research, and (3) research and construction of medical facilities. Of these, the largest and most costly by far is services and supplies, for which almost $452 billion—97.5 percent of health expenditures—was spent in 1992, more than eight times as much as in 1972 and more than double the amount spent in 1982 (Kerns, 1995). Expenditures in 1992 for hospital care, physician services, and drugs and other medical nondurables—major components of the category "services and supplies"—totaled $305

TABLE 1

Private Social Welfare Expenditures by Category, 1972–92 (in millions of current dollars, except where noted)

Year	Total	Private Expenditures				% GDP
		Health	Income Maintenance	Education	Welfare Services	
1972	97,024	57,200	17,123	15,156	7,545	8.0
1973	105,852	63,100	18,063	16,392	8,297	7.8
1974	115,922	69,300	19,660	17,992	8,970	7.9
1975	131,200	77,500	23,336	20,297	10,067	8.3
1976	148,484	89,300	25,004	22,432	11,748	8.4
1977	170,353	102,200	30,662	23,956	13,535	8.6
1978	193,510	113,400	36,743	26,777	16,590	8.7
1979	221,279	127,800	44,703	29,236	19,540	8.9
1980	255,279	145,800	53,519	33,180	22,776	9.4
1981	290,061	168,500	58,741	37,092	25,728	9.6
1982	333,017	191,300	72,445	41,205	28,067	10.6
1983	374,064	212,700	84,652	45,343	31,369	11.0
1984	414,877	235,200	95,759	49,219	34,699	11.0
1985	471,223	259,400	118,871	54,038	38,914	11.7
1986	520,597	275,300	143,670	58,541	43,086	12.2
1987	555,036	298,600	143,509	65,498	47,429	12.2
1988	610,313	336,100	148,858	72,137	53,218	12.5
1989	677,809	370,700	167,260	80,383	59,466	12.9
1990	727,622	410,000	164,772	87,864	64,887	13.1
1991	767,622	432,900	172,010	93,813	68,899	13.4
1992	824,871	462,900	185,724	100,491	75,756	13.7

SOURCE: Kerns, W. (1995). Role of the private sector in financing social welfare programs. *Social Security Bulletin, 58,* 66.

billion, or 65.9 percent, of all private health expenses. Private costs for medical research were $1.2 billion in 1992, six times the amount spent in 1972, while expenditures for construction in 1992 were more than three times that of 1972 ($9.9 billion in 1992, $3.1 billion in 1972).

Income Maintenance

According to the Social Security Administration, "Private income maintenance expenditures are payments made under employee benefit plans in the private sector" (Kerns, 1995, p. 67). Such payments cover private pension plans, group life insurance, accidental death and dismemberment insurance, cash disability insurance, paid sick leave, supplemental unemployment benefits, and sickness and disability insurance. This component of private spending grew more than 1,000 percent between 1972 and 1992, reaching $185.7 billion in 1992. Income maintenance expenditures accounted for 22.5 percent of all private expenditures. Reflecting the growth in the number of people over the age of 65, the vast majority of this spending was for pension plan benefits; these expenses accounted for 85 percent of income maintenance costs in 1992

(the figure was 57 percent in 1972), excluding spending for individual savings plans (such as individual retirement accounts, or IRAs) and retirement plans for self-employed people (Keogh plans, for example).

Because of doubts regarding the future solvency of the federal social security system, two changes in the scope and nature of private pension plans are especially important to note. First, the amount of money involved is growing rapidly. In 1991, $1.96 trillion was held by private pension plans, a 17 percent increase from the 1990 level of holdings (Kerns, 1995). Second, the type of pension plans in force is changing. Three basic approaches exist: (1) defined benefit plans, (2) defined contribution plans, and (3) employee stock ownership plans (ESOPs). Under a defined benefit plan, recipients receive a specified pension benefit. With a defined contribution plan, such as a 401(k) plan, recipients contribute a specified amount of their salary, with or without employer contributions, into a variety of investment options. The level of pension payment received is determined by the performance of the investments made. In an ESOP, employees purchase stock in the company for which they work. Once again, pension benefits are not guaranteed. If the company were to fail, all retirement assets could be lost.

Defined benefit plans are decreasing in number, an emerging trend since the 1970s (Kerns, 1995), while defined contribution and ESOPs are increasing. The effects of this trend are to increase the level of knowledge needed to plan adequately for retirement, increase the uncertainty associated with planning for retirement, and to decrease the financial security of elderly Americans. The ultimate effect of these changes in private pensions may be to increase inequality between financially savvy elderly people and less knowledgeable, but equally deserving, elderly people.

Education

The third component of private social welfare spending is education. Typical expenditures are for education and research (both public and private); student tuition and fees, gifts, and grants; and fees paid to business, trade, and correspondence schools.

Around $100.4 billion was spent for such items in 1992, an increase of 663 percent from 1972 spending (Kerns, 1995). More than half of this amount, $51.2 billion, was spent on higher education; approximately 25 percent, $27.8 billion, was spent for elementary and secondary education; and 14 percent, $16.8 billion, was spent on commercial and vocational schools. The remainder, $4.6 billion, went for private construction costs (Kerns, 1995).

Compared with 1972 figures, spending for commercial and vocational schools increased the most, 956 percent. Spending for higher education and elementary and secondary education increased about the same amount during this period, 656 percent and 604 percent, respectively. Private spending on construction rose by 475 percent.

Welfare and Other Services

Private expenditures for welfare and other services increased by more than 1,000 percent between 1972 and 1992, to $75.8 billion. Although the dollar amount of private spending for welfare has increased steadily over time, the percentage of total private expenditures for welfare and other services has ranged between 8 and 9 percent over the 20-year period.

Included in this component of overall private social welfare costs are six categories of expenditures, based on Standard Industrial Classification definitions of the approximately 106,000 social services agencies and establishments found by the Census Bureau in 1989: (1) individual and family social services; (2) residential care; (3) civic and social/fraternal organizations; (4) child day care; (5) job training and vocational rehabilitation services; and (6) social services not elsewhere classified (Kerns, 1995). Table 2 shows the percentage of total private spending for each category.

Three of the classifications are roughly equal in size: (1) social services for individuals and families, (2) residential care, and (3) civic and social/fraternal organizations. Child day care and job training and vocational rehabilitation services are each about half the size of the other categories.

This area of private social welfare spending is somewhat different in nature from the other three overall components. Welfare and other services are funded in large part by charitable donations. The other components—health, education, and income maintenance—are tied to private spending for self-benefit. It is therefore worthwhile to look at trends in charitable giving to better understand this part of private spending.

Nonprofit organizations established for educational and charitable purposes receive much of their funding from governmental sources, but government cutbacks have forced them in recent years to rely on charitable donations to a greater extent, a trend examined in the early 1980s by the Urban Institute (see, for example, Salamon & Abramson, 1982).

TABLE 2
Expenditures for Welfare and Other Services, 1992

Type of Service	Total Private Social Welfare Expenditures (%)
Individual and family social services	19.6
Residential care	18.2
Civic and social/fraternal organization	18.1
Child day care	10.9
Job training and vocational rehabilitation services	9.4
Social services not elsewhere classified	23.9
Total	100.1

SOURCE: Kerns, W. (1995). Role of the private sector in financing social welfare programs. Social Security Bulletin, 58, 69.
NOTE: Total does not add to 100 percent because of rounding.

Several key findings emerge from a recent study of charitable contributions in America. First, nearly 27 percent of all households gave money to human services in 1993, a slight decrease from 1991, when almost 28 percent of households gave (Hodgkinson, Gorski, Noga, & Knauft, 1995). Second, the average contribution dropped from a high of $263 in 1989 to $208 in 1993 (Hodgkinson et al., 1995). "Human services' share of total contributions increased in 1991, but in 1993 it dropped back to its 1987 level" (Hodgkinson et al., 1995, p. 137). In addition, the percentage of survey respondents volunteering their time in human services settings has declined steadily from 14 percent in 1989 to 10 percent in 1993 (Hodgkinson et al., 1995).

One of the underlying themes of the so-called Reagan revolution of the 1980s was that the private sector would replace the federal government's role in social welfare. Through tax reform initiatives and a rediscovered social responsibility, the public would take an active role in private philanthropy. The Bush administration, through its "1,000 Points of Light" program, honored local, nonprofit volunteer efforts. Certainly, the theme of social responsibility is time honored, but private welfare data indicate that the expectation that the American people are willing to replace decreased government spending is probably wrong.

ADVANTAGES AND DISADVANTAGES OF PRIVATE FUNDING FOR SOCIAL WELFARE

Various arguments have been made for additional private funding of individual programs in each of the four areas of social welfare expenditure discussed earlier. Individual retirement accounts, for example, have served as a prototype for individual health accounts and individual education accounts. A recent law provides tax incentives for people to purchase insurance to cover the cost of long-term care (Quinn, 1996).

Privatization of all government welfare programs has also been a consistent theme of the conservative wing of the Republican party. The creative political "Contract with America" called for reducing welfare spending as well as capping the number of years a person can participate in a public program (Gillespie & Schellas, 1994). The contract also called for reducing the capital gains tax by 50 percent and implementing indexation to control for inflation on investments.

The two most noted advantages to private spending are increased choice for consumers and better programs. The advantages are closely related to the ideological position of economic individualism, one of the two major competing ideologies in America (McClosky & Zaller, 1984). Economic individualism argues that people are responsible for their own welfare and that economic security is achieved by people's own hard work and thrift. The advantages of increased choice for individuals and better programs come about because people are allowed to allocate their own resources, whether for health care, retirement, human services, or education. The impetus for an increasing reliance on the ideas of economic individualism came about during the Reagan years. Economic individualism requires that citizens invest in themselves regarding their own welfare, using personal rather than governmental resources to implement their decisions. To make this personal responsibility possible, government must "get off people's backs" and create policies to increase people's choices.

Increased choice for citizens is perhaps the key advantage of private social welfare expenditures. Rather than being limited to choices put forward by a government entity—the social security system, for example—the marketplace can provide multiple alternatives, each with different characteristics. Although it is conceivable that government funding could secure this variety of choices, proponents of this view argue that private spending in the marketplace spurs greater entry of service providers than does government spending (Butler, 1985; Carleson & Hopkins, 1981; Savas, 1982).

According to this argument, choice spurs competition, and competition creates better programs. Privately funded programs are better because they are more efficient in using resources (Struyk, 1985); they better meet the needs of their users (their market), and they have a greater ability to innovate (Savas, 1982). Although there is little empirical evidence to support the view that these outcomes are an inevitable outcome of competition, advocates for private funding argue that they will automatically occur if the market is left alone.

An important disadvantage cited frequently by critics of private spending revolves around equality and inequality. The corollary to economic individualism is collective responsibility (McClosky & Zaller, 1984). This approach argues that government has a major role in providing equal economic opportunities and in ensuring that each resident has a minimally adequate quality of life.

The primary problem with a stronger reliance on the market and private funding of social welfare is that such an approach will increase inequality. The beneficiaries of private social welfare spending are those who are likely to have high-paying jobs with health, pension, and other benefits, which are often supplemented by employer contributions. Moreover, people with ample financial resources are able to purchase better-quality human services (health, education, counseling, child care, and so on) than are people with little or no money.

The role of government spending, according to this view, is to offset the advantages that well-paid and educated people have in the marketplace by ensuring that less advantaged people also have access to adequate human services. This perspective is in line with social work ethics regarding the importance of social justice and the profession's special concern for individuals and groups who are disadvantaged or oppressed (National Association of Social Workers, 1996).

IMPLICATIONS AND CONCLUSION

Abramowitz's (1983) analysis of public welfare documented that most programs and services benefited the middle and upper classes and corporations. Analysis of private welfare also illustrates that program services and benefits are targeted at the nonpoor population: 90.8 percent of private welfare expenditures covers health, income maintenance, and education programs, while the remaining 9.2 percent goes toward welfare programs. This analysis leads to two conclusions. First, private welfare is closely tied to employment, which benefits middle- and higher-income people more than it does poor people. Private health insurance and pension plans are the two largest subcategories of private welfare expenditures, and these are closely tied to well-paying jobs. People with jobs that provide these benefits are the main beneficiaries of private welfare expenditures.

Second, further privatization of social welfare spending will increase the gap between the middle and upper classes, on the one hand, and poorer people, on the other hand. This is clear in several areas. Individuals will be required to manage their pension assets more actively, to spend more of their own funds to purchase higher education, and to pay higher fees for social services formerly subsidized by government. Middle-class and upper-class people will be able to increase their advantages over poor people through superior access to information, better education at all levels, and the ability to rely on their own resources to pay for potentially higher quality services of all types.

The U.S. economy has strengthened in the 1990s: Unemployment decreased, employment rose among most groups, the stock market increased in both volume and value, and inflation decreased. But the economic gulf between rich and poor people continues to broaden (Hoechstetter, 1996; Phillips, 1991; Stoesz, 1996). Haynes and Michelson (1997) argue that the Republican party's Contract with America ensures not that economic parity progress will be achieved, but that the gap between classes will further increase.

The 1980s, according to Phillips (1991) was "a second Gilded Age" in which inequality was further intensified, with the gap between poor and wealthy people dramatically increasing (p. xviii). According to Phillips, Ronald Reagan's legacy included the reduction of taxes, minimization of public intrusion in the lives of people, and deregulation of constraining policies. Merger laws were weakened, many taxes were reduced or eliminated, funding for discretionary federal programs was diminished, and the influence of many federal regulatory bodies was lessened. The Clinton presidential campaign in 1992 promised to "end welfare as we know it." In fact, the 104th Congress's passage of the Personal Responsibility and Work Opportunity Reconciliation Act of 1996 (P.L. 104-193), which was signed by Clinton, did end the federal government's welfare commitment to poor people. For example, federal cash entitlements to poor families were eliminated, states now determine eligibility criteria and set benefit levels, time limits were placed on clients, and categorical programs were replaced by block grants. Public welfare reform under the Clinton administration carries distinctive elements of the Reagan, conservative agenda.

Hoechstetter (1996) recommended that the social work profession become more active in the political process and work toward reversing the trend of resources going to wealthy people. In addition, she argued that redirecting resources to poor people and to the middle class will create more opportunities for these more vulnerable population groups (Hoechstetter, 1996). Jansson and Smith (1997) imply that change in the future is both possible and probable. A "new nationalism" will evolve, contrary to the conservative political philosophy, that will encourage and expect the public to participate in a global economy (Jansson & Smith, 1997). The government will be required to provide public services with increased financial support in job training, child care, and education. Stoesz (1996) predicted that the philosophies of the two major political parties will change as society evolves from an industrial to a postindustrial stage. Such philosophical changes may provide the needed political contextual support for the evolution to a new nationalism.

While public social welfare continues to be in a state of flux, the private system grows and becomes an even stronger haven for wealthy people. It continues to provide opportunities for tax-free investments; additional protections against threats to income insecurity; and a separate and unequal system of health, education, and economic provisions. The "mirror welfare state" will continue to grow as the governmental sector decreases in size and policy and services devolve to states and localities. Public policy targeted at reducing the size of the federal government will require individuals to accept greater burdens to provide for themselves and to care for those who cannot provide for themselves. These burdens will include increased out-of-pocket costs—increased taxes and donations, for example—as well as more time devoted to learning about options and to providing direct care. The increased pressure on people and the higher levels of inequality may mean that, in the end, we will not like what the mirror reveals about us as a society.

REFERENCES

Abramovitz, M. (1983). Everyone is on welfare: "The role of redistribution in social policy" revisited. *Social Work, 28,* 440-445.

Axinn, J., & Levin, H. (1992). *Social welfare: A history of the American response to need* (3rd ed.). New York: Harper & Row.

Butler, S. M. (1985). *Privatizing federal spending.* New York: University Books.

Carleson, R. B., & Hopkins, K. R. (1981). The Reagan rationale. *Public Welfare, 39,* 8-17.

Gillespie, E., & Schellas, B. (Eds.). (1994). *Contract with America: The bold plan by Rep. Newt Gingrich, Rep. Dick Armey and the House Republicans to change the nation.* New York: Random House.

Haynes, K., & Michelson, I. (1997). *Affecting change* (3rd ed.). New York: Longman.

Hodgkinson, V. A., Gorski, H. A., Noga, S. M., & Knauft, E. B. (1995). *Giving and volunteering in the United States: Volume 2. Trends in giving and volunteering by type of charity.* Washington, DC: Independent Sector.

Hoechstetter, S. (1996). Taking new directions to improve public policy. *Social Work, 41,* pp. 343-346.

Jansson, B. S. (1997). *The reluctant welfare state.* Pacific Grove, CA: Brooks/Cole.

Jansson, B. S., & Smith, S. (1997). A "new nationalism in American social policy." In P. Ewalt, E. Freeman, S. Kirk, & D. Poole (Eds.), *Social policy, reform, research, and practice* (pp. 5-19). Washington, DC: NASW Press.

Karger, H. J., & Stoesz, D. (1994). *American social welfare policy: A pluralist approach* (2nd ed.). New York: Longman.

Kerns, W. (1994). Private social welfare expenditures, 1972-91. *Social Security Bulletin, 57,* 87-95.

Kerns, W. (1995). Role of the private sector in financing social welfare programs. *Social Security Bulletin, 58,* 66-73.

Kerns, W., & Glanz, M. (1991). Private social welfare expenditures, 1972-88. *Social Security Bulletin, 54,* 2-11.

McClosky, H., & Zaller, J. (1984). *The American ethos: Public attitudes toward capitalism and democracy..* Cambridge, MA: Harvard University Press.

McInnis-Dittrich, K. (1993). *Integrating social welfare policy & social work practice.* Pacific Grove, CA: Brooks/Cole.

National Association of Social Workers. (1996). *NASW code of ethics.* Washington, DC: Author.

Personal Responsibility and Work Opportunity Reconcilliation Act of 1996. P.L. 104-193, 110 Stat. 2105.

Phillips, K. (1991). *The politics of the rich and poor.* New York: First HarperPerennial Edition.

Quinn, J. B. (1996, October 12). Elderly care insurance is tax deduction. *Arlington Star-Telegram,* p. 13B.

Salamon, L. M., & Abramson, A. J. (1982). *The federal budget and the nonprofit sector.* Washington, DC: Urban Institute.

Savas, E. S. (1982). *Privatizing the public sector.* Chatham, NJ: Chatham House.

Stoesz, D. (1996). *Small change: Domestic policy under the Clinton presidency.* New York: Longman.

Struyk, R. J. (1985). Administering social welfare: The Reagan record. *Journal of Policy Analysis and Management, 4*(4), 481-500.

Trattner, W. (1989). *From poor law to welfare state: A history of social welfare in America* (4th ed.). New York: Free Press.

Richard Hoefer, PhD, is associate professor, School of Social Work, University of Texas at Arlington, Arlington, TX 76019. **Ira C. Colby, DSW,** is professor and director, School of Social Work, University of Central Florida, Orlando, FL 32816.

For further information see

Aging: Public Policy Issues and Trends; Baby Boomers; Charitable Foundations and Social Welfare; Economic Analysis; Employee Assistance Programs; **Health Care: Policy Development;** Income Distribution; Income Security Overview; Jobs and Earnings; Managed Care Overview; **Managed Care: A Review of Recent Research;** Poverty; Social Welfare Expenditures: Public; Retirement and Pension Programs; Social Planning; Social Security; Social Welfare History; Social Welfare Policy; Unemployment Compensation and Workers' Compensation; **Working Poor.**

Key Words

education	privatization
health	welfare
income maintenance	

Social Work Education: Electronic Technologies

Frank B. Raymond III

Cathy K. Pike

Recent developments in technology have had a significant impact on higher education, including social work education. One of the primary functions of higher education is the transmission of knowledge to others. For years the primary tools available to teachers to assist them in transferring information were books, papers, and the chalkboard. It was not until the mid-20th century that educators had at their disposal other means of communicating information, such as slides, films, and recordings. More recently, however, rapid technological advancement has provided educators with an extremely wide variety of electronic tools to assist them in transmitting knowledge to others. Indeed, the end of the 20th century has been called the "information revolution," an era that has encompassed other radical and pervasive changes variously called the "electronic and micro-electronic revolution," the "telecommunications revolution," and the "computer revolution" (Geiss & Viswanathan, 1986, p. 8).

When compared with other institutions, higher education in general—and social work education in particular—have been slow to take advantage of the technological developments that have occurred during the information revolution (J. P. Flynn, 1994; Seabury, 1994). Nonetheless, in recent years most schools of social work have responded to these technological developments (Buckles, 1989; Caputo & Cnaan, 1990; Pittman, 1994). First, schools have responded by including in their curricula content related to information technology, such as the use of computers for research purposes, in agency administration, and in client assessment. This content has been taught through electives, through required courses, and through integration into other courses. Computer education in social work is tending to shift from an orientation that is primarily technological to one that is application and social work focused (Cnaan, 1989; Geiss & Viswanathan, 1986; Nurius, Richey, & Nicoll, 1988). Increasingly, schools of social work are treating information technology skills and concepts as an integral part of the curriculum and a built-in component of core courses, including practice. The incorporation of course content on information technology and the use of computers in practice has been the primary way schools of social work have responded to the information revolution in the United States and in other countries (Steyaert, Colombi, & Rafferty, 1996).

The second way schools of social work have responded to the information revolution is by using new technologies to facilitate and enhance teaching. Schools have been less inclined to *use* technology in this way, however, than to *teach* technology. Perhaps this response has been slow because the use of developing technologies for teaching purposes requires paradigm shifts. Educators rather quickly adopt technologies that support the teacher-student relationship inherent in traditional pedagogical models. For example, educators have readily accepted educational technology such as overhead projectors and video players. These teaching aids pose no threat to existing teaching methods because the teacher remains in control and the same physical spaces are used. However, technologies that have become available during the information revolution, such as interactive television systems, multimedia courseware, and the Internet, have not been as readily adapted by educators to facilitate the teaching and learning processes. The use of such technologies necessitates a fundamental rethinking of the nature of higher education, the roles of teachers and students, the physical environment, and the ownership of intellectual property (Buckles, 1989; Frans, 1993; Mandel, 1989; Pittman, 1994; Steyaert et al., 1996). With the use of this type of technology, the educator becomes less a purveyor of information and more a facilitator. The student becomes a more active participant in the learning process and more accountable for the learning outcomes. The teacher and student may be separated from each other during the learning process, in both time and space.

Yet, although social work education, like other academic disciplines, has often adopted a "minimalist approach" to implementing new technology, rather than re-evaluating and restructuring practices and procedures (Hammond & Trapp, 1992, and Henry & Rafferty, 1995, cited in Steyaert et al., 1996), there is little doubt that the use of these developing technologies in social work education will expand significantly in future years. Furthermore, the rapidity of new developments in information technology will challenge schools of social work to find new ways to use and to teach this new knowledge.

One of the difficulties in understanding developing information technology is that there is not a commonly agreed-on typology to help differentiate among the technologies. There is a further problem in that some terms do not have universally accepted meanings; some writers differentiate among terms that other writers use synonymously. This chapter will attempt to address these problems by organizing technologies into three groups—computer applications, computer networks, and distance education technologies—and indicating where words are used inconsistently in the literature.

Computer Applications

Computer applications are an integral feature of the information revolution of the 20th century and have had a significant impact on the delivery of social work education. During the early history of computers, computer applications were written for existing hardware. In effect, computer applications kept in step with what computers offered with regard to memory, storage, speed, and visual developments. Programming technologies did not exceed computer equipment capacities. However, an interesting reversal has taken place in recent years, in that innovations in software development programs are now guiding the development of state-of-the-art computers. As developers of computer applications began to incorporate text, sound, graphics, and video that were only minimally supported by computer equipment, the demand for high-speed, technologically advanced computer equipment increased substantially.

Object-Oriented Programs

Early computer applications were text-based, linearly structured programs. Users opened the applications and then moved through them in the format deemed best by the developer. Function keys and menus were used to select and initiate certain aspects of a program, and users relied heavily on written manuals to obtain the codes to initiate options within these applications. Early computer applications sometimes were experienced by learners as difficult and discouraging. In spite of these difficulties, however, social work educators were able to use these applications to locate information for teaching and research purposes and to instruct students in the use of the computer for data gathering. These tasks became easier for students and faculty with the development of object-oriented computer applications, which represented a major technological breakthrough in computer programming and solved many of the difficulties that learners had experienced with earlier versions of programs. Object-oriented applications use links to access program functions and options. Users open these types of programs with the click of a mouse and then point and click to access options. Most of the object-oriented programs contain help manuals within programs that users can easily access. Questions that arise while working in a program can be answered without leaving the application or using written manuals.

Object-oriented programs enable users to accomplish a wide variety of tasks relevant to social work education, such as word processing, statistical analysis, budget writing, and database development. These general programs, or "tools," that facilitate learning provide useful platforms for educating social work students (Heerman, 1988). For example, teachers can use word processing applications, (for example, WordPerfect or Microsoft Word) to help students learn how to write assessments and reports for course assignments. Students can submit assessments and reports on disk or on paper for evaluation and comments by the teacher. Having students submit assignments on disks is especially useful for content that is unfamiliar or involves the development of complex skills. For example, learning how to complete assessments often involves an iterative process of submission, evaluation, and resubmission. Assessments that are submitted on disks allow the teacher to provide extensive comments that guide students to develop thoughtful, strengths-oriented, and comprehensive assessment skills.

A second example of the use of object-oriented programs for teaching and learning purposes in social work education is the use of statistical packages. These programs are enormously time-saving devices for statistics teachers, and they simplify the learning process for students in statistics courses. The earlier types of text-based statistical packages required that students learn not only the statistics taught in their course but also the intricate details of program and syntax codes for a given statistics package. An error in entering any of these codes often resulted in a vague reference to an error by the statistics package and failure of the program to analyze the data. Students frequently required the

teacher's assistance to determine the nature and location of the program or syntax error. In the case of multiple errors in one data set, the process quickly became both time consuming for the teacher and disheartening to the student. Students in statistics courses were challenged by the unfamiliar statistics content and the tools used in a course to analyze data. The inherent difficulty of learning the statistics packages meant that many statistics teachers spent hours before class developing error-free models of the program to be used in analyzing each data set. The Statistical Package for the Social Sciences (SPSS) currently uses object-oriented programming for both Macintosh and IBM-compatible machines that allows students to analyze data without complicated directions from the teacher about program and syntax codes. At this writing, Statistical Analysis System (SAS) is completing the programming to move to an object-oriented platform. Statistical packages less expensive than SPSS and SAS are also being developed as object-oriented programs. For example, Statistical Package for the Personal Computer, a statistics package developed by WALMYR Publishing, currently is under development as an object-oriented program (W. W. Hudson, WALMYR, personal communication, October 11, 1996). These object-oriented tools represent remarkable innovations in making statistics more accessible and less threatening to social work students.

A third example of how object-oriented programs can facilitate the social work education process is the use of object-oriented spreadsheets and database programs. These programs can be used to help students develop skills in administrative, planning, and practice-related tasks. Students in administration courses can learn how to develop budgets and databases that are used for program evaluation, administrative planning, and agency accountability. Teachers can use database programs (for example, Microsoft Excel) to teach students how to maintain current information about client characteristics and progress, types and extent of field agency services provided to clients, and other types of service information. Such packages can be used by teachers in practice evaluation courses to teach students how to track client progress and develop graphs that depict progress in interventions. Students can then use these graphs as aids in computing statistics and developing conclusions about the statistical, visual, and practical significance of single-system designs for client interventions and formative program evaluation (Bloom, Fischer, & Orme, 1995; Gabor & Grinnell, 1994).

Interactive Computer Applications

Interactive computer applications, a fairly recent technological development, provide extremely useful tools to facilitate the teaching and learning process in social work education. These programs are especially useful as aids in teaching course-specific knowledge, skills, or values content. Types of interactive computer applications include hypertext, hypermedia, multimedia, and interactive video discs. All of these programs allow the user to select a variety of functions within the program, but they have the further advantage of interacting with users. Components of the program and information can be accessed in nonlinear ways. Depending on the application, users also can obtain feedback about their performance from the application. Because the technology is new, universally agreed-on definitions do not yet exist to describe interactive applications, and each of the four types of interactive computer applications listed above will be defined.

Hypertext programming is the basis of interactive computer applications (Patterson & Yaffe, 1994). Hypertext as a programming function underlies interactive computer applications. Programs that are written in hypertext use nonsequential links to information (Dyson, 1994; Patterson & Yaffe, 1994). However, when a specific application is described as "hypertext," the term usually refers to a program that not only uses text and graphics but also incorporates nonsequential linking capabilities for the information contained in the program. This is the definition of hypertext that will be used here. Computer applications that use hypertext allow users to learn by association rather than in the linearly structured content presentation that was typical of earlier programs. These text-based programs allow users to let their curiosity guide them through a program. In addition to being able to access information in the order users prefer, hypertext programs can be written to provide immediate feedback to students about their progress.

"Hypermedia" and "multimedia" both refer to interactive programs that have not only text and graphics but also sound or video clips that are accessed within an application. The two terms are often used interchangeably. Macintosh users tend to use the term "hypermedia," because a popular Macintosh program, HyperCard, that is used to write these applications incorporates the prefix "hyper" in its name. The term multimedia has been used more often to describe IBM-compatible applications. There is one functional distinction between hypermedia and multimedia, however, and this is the underlying structure of an application. When an application that incorporates text, graphics, sound, and video is unstructured (that is, the user can freely move from one concept or topic to another), the term "hypermedia" is usually used to describe this type of application (Dyson, 1994). When an application has an underlying structure (that is, the content is presented from concrete to abstract levels in a teaching program), multimedia is the term often used to describe the application (Dyson, 1994). The specific way that hypermedia and multimedia are used for a given application can usually be derived from the description of the application. The functional distinction between multimedia and hypermedia will be used here to differentiate between structured and unstructured interactive computer applications.

Interactive video discs (IVDs) were the first type of interactive computer applications to be developed (Falk & Carlson, 1995). They are described last in this section because these interactive programs combine computers, computer programs, and external devices in their production and use. IVD programs developed in the past used the text-based computer programming languages that were then available, but recently upgraded and new IVD programs use interactive computer programs to manage the structure and presentation of the IVD. A team of specialists is required to produce an IVD program. For instance, the production of an IVD on counseling techniques required, in addition to the professor and doctoral student who acted as content specialists, additional specialists in software development, design, video, and production (Engen, Finken, Luschei, & Kenney, 1994). The equipment that is needed to use an IVD can vary, depending on how the developers structured it. Most IVD applications require a computer; a computer monitor or television; a keyboard, touch pad, or touch-screen computer monitor; and a laser disc player. IVD programs can be used in classroom teaching to facilitate discussion or provide modeling of techniques or in laboratories as single-user or small-group tutorial programs. In the classroom setting the IVD is projected onto a screen, which allows the class members to view video segments of the program, discuss the problems or challenges raised by the segment, and select an option in response to the prompt. Students in a laboratory setting can move through the program at their own pace. Most IVD programs developed for social work teaching purposes provide the user with three or four selections, with each choice initiating various video segments. Depending on the student's choice (either individually in a laboratory setting or as part of a group decision in the classroom), the videotape will continue, remedial instruction will be provided, or feedback will be given about the option selected.

All of the types of interactive computer applications discussed earlier can be used to teach social work students course-specific knowledge, skills, and values content. These applications can be used to present or enhance didactic presentations, provide structured observation, simulate role plays, aid in teaching assessment skills and decision making, and allow free exploration of a topic area (Falk & Carlson, 1995). A variety of methods can be incorporated to teach course-specific content; these include drill and practice, tutorials, gaming, simulations, discovery, and problem solving (Verduin & Clark, 1991). Most interactive applications combine two or more of these types of content presentations and methods to teach course-specific knowledge, skills, and values. For example, a program used to teach statistics incorporates a blend of multiple teaching methods. This IVD application on statistics teaches content on the principles of evaluation, evaluation techniques, and simple statistical analyses used in program evaluation. The IVD application incorporates didactic presentations, tutorials, structured observation, and drill-and-practice methods (Falk, Shepard, Campbell, & Maypole, 1992). Several programs have been developed to help students learn problem solving with course content, assessment, and decision-making skills. An IVD program on social policy, for example, incorporates knowledge and content about social policy, problem solving, a game involving social policy, and drill-and-practice exercises (M. Flynn, 1987). Another computer

program incorporates information from DSM-IIIR and is used to improve students' accuracy in making Axis II diagnoses. This program includes didactic clinical information on a variety of personality disorders, case examples that illustrate how someone with a given diagnosis may behave or think, and tests of diagnostic decision making that include feedback (Patterson & Yaffe, 1993).

IVD programs, because they allow for a great deal of video-intensive content, are often used for applications that involve simulated role plays. Several IVD applications have been developed to teach direct practice skills in social work and other helping professions. These include simulations to assist students in developing communications skills and problem-solving, assessment, and counseling techniques (Engen et al., 1994; Falk et al., 1992; Maple, 1994; Seabury, 1994); in acquiring knowledge and skills in human diversity and ethnic-sensitive practice (Falk et al., 1992); in assessing and intervening at group and organizational levels (Falk et al., 1992; Seabury, 1994); and in developing knowledge and skills in applying a specific intervention (for example, crisis counseling) (Seabury & Maple, 1993). All of these applications include didactic presentations of knowledge and skills content, structured observation, and interviews or interventions with videotaped case enactments.

Virtual reality computer programs have substantial potential for social work education, particularly as pre-field placement experiences. Students could use these programs in simulated role plays with clients to enhance interviewing and assessment skills. To date, however, there has been little development of virtual reality computer programs for education. One authoring program, developed by Calgari, Inc., is currently available for use in creating virtual reality programs. This software uses object-oriented language to write virtual reality programs, and educators who already have experience in this type of language can write virtual reality programs without an additional substantial investment in training.

Extent of Use

Schools of social work have been rather slow to use computer applications to facilitate the teaching and learning process. Before 1990 relatively few social work educators had incorporated computer applications in their courses (Finnegan & Ivanoff, 1991; J. P. Flynn,

1990; Green, 1988; Hudson, 1985; LaMendola, 1987). The use of computer applications among social work educators appears to be increasing, however, especially in certain courses. In a 1993 survey of graduate social work educators (330 respondents from a randomly selected sample of 1,025), it was found that the computer application most commonly used for instructional purposes was statistical packages (Pittman, 1994). Forty percent of the respondents used this application. The other applications most commonly used by the respondents were as follows: spreadsheets (19 percent), tutorial programs (13 percent), clinical software (11 percent), games and simulations (6 percent), drill and practice (5 percent), and video interactive (4 percent). This study also revealed that there were no significant relationships among the number of applications adopted and faculty rank, years of experience, area of specialization, gender, age, ethnicity, level of education, type of institution, number of students, and resource availability (Pittman, 1994).

Effectiveness and Cost Considerations

The effectiveness of using computer applications in the delivery of social work education can be assessed in terms of the extent to which a given computer application is useful in helping students master the knowledge, skills, or values content presented by the application. Additional effectiveness considerations include the quality and consistency of instruction, the flexibility and ease of use of the application in meeting differing learning needs, and the amount of time needed to learn the content.

A literature of effectiveness studies on computer-assisted learning is building gradually across the academic disciplines. Research reports on computer-assisted learning in other disciplines have indicated that students benefit from the use of computer applications to learn course content. Repeated meta-analyses of effectiveness studies for computer-assisted learning consistently point to the effectiveness of computer applications in student learning outcomes (J. A. Kulik, 1983; J. A. Kulik & Kulik, 1986, 1987; C. C. Kulik & Kulik, 1991). A second consistent finding from these meta-analyses is that students view the quality of computer-assisted learning as higher than that acquired by traditional methods. In addition, several studies have found that students participating in computer-assisted learning master the content more quickly than those receiving traditional training (Dossett & Konczak, 1985; Hartig, 1985; Madlin, 1987; Orlansky, 1983).

Research on the effectiveness of computer applications in social work education has yielded results similar to those reported for other disciplines. Objective tests of learning outcomes in social work education have found equally effective learning outcomes for both computer-assisted learning groups and comparison groups (M. Flynn, 1987; Patterson & Yaffe, 1993). However, student reports about the effectiveness of computer-assisted learning in mastering course content were positive, almost without exception (Falk et al., 1992; Forte, Healey, & Campbell, 1994; Seabury & Maple, 1993). Several reports in social work have found positive student affective learning from computer-assisted coursework (Finnegan & Ivanoff, 1991; M. Flynn, 1987; Forte et al., 1994; Patterson & Yaffe, 1993; Seabury & Maple, 1993).

Several cautions should be noted regarding the applicability and quality of research on computer-assisted learning. Because effectiveness studies are often based on specific applications within academic disciplines, educators may find no reports dealing with the effectiveness of a particular application under consideration. As a result, conclusions about the effectiveness of an application may be delayed until educators conduct their own trial of the application. In addition, most of the effectiveness studies in social work have been conducted with one class or have used a comparison of two or more classes in one institution. There is a need for collaborative research across schools of social work that examines the effectiveness of computer-assisted learning for students in comparable courses. This would provide useful information about the generalizability of findings regarding the effectiveness of a given computer application. The studies in social work and other disciplines regarding computer-assisted learning reflect several other problems related to the quality of research designs, data analyses, and reporting of results. Some research reports poorly specified how the interventions in comparison studies were implemented, used only descriptive statistics in comparison studies, conducted multiple bivariate tests without controlling for the resulting increase in Type I error, and provided only anecdotal information about the results.

Costs related to implementing computer applications in social work education can vary considerably. General object-oriented programs are usually the least expensive type of computer-assisted learning applications. These programs often are available as free services to students in laboratories supported by universities or schools of social work. General applications also require less time for educators to develop and implement than other applications and are flexible with regard to the modifications needed to enhance teaching design.

Content-specific interactive applications can range in cost from less expensive general applications to very expensive specific applications. Schools of social work incur some expense in purchasing interactive computer programs "off the shelf," and faculty may need more time to implement these applications than they do to implement those general applications with which they are already familiar. Modifications to commercial interactive computer applications are usually not possible. Developing interactive computer applications for a specific course is more expensive than purchasing commercially available applications. In determining the costs of developing an interactive computer application, one should consider not only the purchase price of the authoring platform but also the investment of time and money required to develop, pilot, and implement the application.

IVD applications are the most expensive type of computer-assisted learning to develop, and there are advantages and disadvantages that should be considered in weighing the relative costs of using them (Engen et al., 1994; Falk et al., 1992; Maple, 1994; Reinoehl & Shapiro, 1986; Resnick, 1994; Seabury, 1994; Seabury & Maple, 1993; Wodarski, Bricout, & Smokowski, 1996). Every IVD application reported herein was funded by external sources, the university involved, or both. In addition to social work educators, media production specialists were involved in developing these applications. For course content that changes frequently, such as social policy, an IVD can quickly become obsolete. Video modifications are impossible with IVD applications. IVD applications are most useful in presenting course content that relies heavily on visual learning (for example, nonverbal client behaviors and interviewing skills in practice courses). On the other hand, for presenting didactic information, for drill-and-

practice exercises, for developing assessment and diagnostic skills, and for brief video simulations, CD-ROM is more cost-effective than IVD, given the recent improvements in CD-ROM technology. Virtual reality programs are not currently used in social work education, and the costs associated with developing and using such programs may preclude the use of virtual reality in the near future. These costs are substantial, particularly with regard to the type of equipment required to use these programs.

COMPUTER NETWORKS

Computer networks are a collection of computers that are electronically linked and allow information to flow among different computers (Dyson, 1994). They have revolutionized the way information is delivered in government, business, and academic institutions, including schools of social work. Communications channels, which provide the means of linking these computer networks, can range from a coaxial cable that links a monitor and keyboard with a large computer located elsewhere within a university to the use of a certain frequency that moves along a larger and more advanced channel to sources outside the university. Computers can be linked in a small work environment as "peer-to-peer" networks or as local area networks (LANs). Computer networks require software to manage the information flow within the network, ensure that security is maintained, administer the system, and share resources (Dyson, 1994). In a peer-to-peer network, the computers in the network share the operating system software, sometimes with one computer having the greatest portion of this software without actually being solely dedicated to monitoring the network. An example of a peer-to-peer network is a small office or department that uses Windows for Workgroups to manage and provide information sharing among a small number of computers.

A LAN can include an academic department, a college, or an entire university. For example, a school of social work can have a LAN that connects all the computers within the school and then connects these to a university LAN. In this type of network arrangement, the university LAN manages the LANs of numerous other colleges and departments. LANs require a computer, referred to as a "server," that is dedicated solely to maintaining operations, storing programs and other information, and managing communications within and among its network and other networks. A Wide Area Network (WAN) is an extension of a LAN and connects computers within large geographic areas. A WAN can include several cities, counties, and states in a large regional network.

The Internet is the largest computer network in the world (Dyson, 1994). This mammoth network connects many of the world's LANs and WANs. As of July 1996, the Internet connected 134,365 of the world's networks (Zakon, 1996). In addition, there were 12,881,000 hosts, or controlling computers, for smaller networks that make up these larger networks. Estimates of the number of Internet users vary but have ranged as high as 5 billion (Zakon, 1996).

The beauty of the Internet is its ability to accommodate a wide variety of different operating systems used by LANs. The connectivity of the Internet means that a multitude of diverse communications systems can transfer information flawlessly within the Internet environment (Cerf, 1993). This ability to make communication viable among differing types of computers that use different operating systems has made immediate, worldwide computer-linked communication a reality.

The 1990s have brought a proliferation of new Internet developments, including menu-based search mechanisms (for example, Gopher), Internet telephone services, and the World Wide Web (WWW) (Zakon, 1996). The WWW can be used with hypertext documents, with interactive computer programs, and for teaching on-line courses in real time (Zakon, 1996). The WWW is so flexible and heavily used that it is currently experiencing "traffic jams" from the number of users and the variety of resources that can be used with it. The heavy use of WWW resources is causing slow-downs or "crashes" of the system. This proliferation of applications on the WWW was unanticipated during its development and is a source of embarrassment for the developers of the WWW (Cerf, 1993). However, future enhancements in routing and management of the WWW should improve its performance (Cerf, 1993).

Current directions in computer networks point to the establishment of a second Internet that will handle very high speed transmissions for research universities and the government (DeLoughry, 1996). The "Internet II" will work at speeds that are several times faster than the National Science Foundation's Very High Speed Backbone Network Service (VBNS), which currently operates at 155 megabits per second. Actually, the VBNS is about three times as fast as the fastest portion of the current Internet (DeLoughry, 1996). Internet II is expected to work alongside the current Internet but will be used for resource-intensive uses (for example, collaborative research conducted on-line, digital libraries, and courses taught on-line) (DeLoughry, 1996).

Databases and Other Information Resources

It has been only a short while since social work students and faculty physically went to the library to obtain information from databases and other information resources. Hours passed while dusty, bound sets of journals were combed for information for a research project or paper. Currently, much of the information from databases and other resources can be accessed from the home or office. University card catalogues have been placed on-line so that students and faculty can use computer networks to access the library and obtain information about the texts carried by the library for a given topic. Many universities also provide journal indexes on-line. PsychLit and the Social Science Index, two databases of journal articles and research in the social sciences, can be accessed from the office or home. *Social Work Abstracts* and the *Encyclopedia of Social Work* are both available on CD-ROM. Many universities and schools of social work have made these social work resources available through networked computers.

Other information resources relevant for social work education are available through the Internet. Gopher, a text-based network on the Internet, contains many useful types of information for social work students and faculty. Samples of information resources on Gopher that may be used in course-specific learning are the University of Michigan Institute for Public Policy Studies, the University of Maryland's Women's Studies and Diversity resources, the Centre for Women's Studies in Education at Ontario Institute for Studies in Education, the Social Science Computing Cooperative, and the Institute for Research on Poverty (Holden, Rosenberg, & Weissman, 1995).

The WWW provides a multitude of databases and information resources and includes a variety of indexes, reference lists, government resources, on-line journals, and searching capabilities (called "search engines") (Holden,

Rosenberg, & Weissman, 1996). Students can access WWW government sources to obtain information from such entities as the Centers for Disease Control and Prevention, the U.S. Census Bureau, U.S. Department of Health and Human Services, the Social Security Administration, and the White House. Information on instruments used to measure client progress and a variety of client problems can be accessed through the WWW (Holden et al., 1996).

The Social Work Access Network (SWAN) is owned and maintained by the University of South Carolina College of Social Work. This resource, located on the WWW, functions as a sort of electronic yellow pages for social work and contains a wide variety of resources that are catalogued by topic area (University of South Carolina, 1996). A brief sample of these information resources includes aging, child abuse, human immunodeficiency virus (HIV) and acquired immune deficiency syndrome (AIDS), adoption, and health care. Users simply click on highlighted text to go to the WWW resource. A database of social workers with interests in specific areas will soon be included on SWAN to facilitate research, advocacy, and other professional endeavors among social workers having common interests and areas of expertise.

Social work educators can use databases and other information resources as generic information retrieval tools or as aids in course-specific exercises. For instance, teachers can routinely schedule a class session in the computer laboratory at the beginning of students' enrollment to demonstrate how to access a variety of databases and information resources from the library and Internet for their use in writing papers and completing assignments. Course-specific exercises that use databases and information resources can be used for any type of social work course. The resources available for use in social work span the entire social work curriculum. In some schools of social work, it is becoming standard practice for teachers to include references to databases and other information resources on their course syllabi reading lists.

Teaching about databases and other information resources also can help social work students learn how to make distinctions about the quality of resources they encounter. Although a key value of the Internet is its openness of information, because of this openness, there is a great deal of information that is inaccurate or useless to students. Thus, an important component in teaching students about databases and information resources is helping them learn how to assess the validity and usefulness of information. A comparative approach in the computer laboratory, using examples of both superbly documented and poorly documented resources, is an excellent way to help students further develop their skills in evaluating the quality of information.

Electronic Mail

Electronic mail, often called "e-mail," provides another means of using computer networks in teaching social work education. E-mail is the use of computer networks to write and forward messages, papers, reports, assignments, or other text-based information. In the past e-mail services were available most often for use on university mainframe computers. These computers used text-based operating environments similar to the early text-based computer applications for personal computers. Users mastered a complicated array of instructions, function keys, and computer commands to use e-mail services on university mainframe computers. In addition to the continued availability of e-mail on university mainframe computers, e-mail is used on peer-to-peer networks, LANs, and the WWW. Learning to use e-mail on LANs and the WWW typically is a much easier and less time-consuming task for students than learning to use e-mail on a university mainframe computer. LANs and the WWW use object-oriented or hypertext-based e-mail programs. These types of programs do not require users to be familiar with the operating language or the commands used by a program.

E-mail can enhance teaching and learning in a variety of ways. Social work authors have noted the benefits of using e-mail in managing the learning environment and improving class cohesiveness and participation (Finn, 1995; Folaron, 1995). Although e-mail is a generic tool, it can be used for course-specific exercises. For example, course exercises can be submitted to the teacher via e-mail, and the teacher can provide feedback to the student via this medium. As another example, students in a policy or community development course can send an e-mail to government officials and advocate a policy change or the need for a community service.

Listserve Servers

Listserve servers (commonly called "listservs") provide a means of transferring ongoing information among people with a common interest. E-mail is used to send and receive messages from other people who are members of the listserv. The listserv distributes entire texts of messages or brief digests of messages to all members. To enroll in a listserv, one sends an e-mail message to a central computer requesting membership. Upon the computer's successful receipt and enrollment of the individual in a listserv, the central computer for the listserv relays a set of instructions and tips about how members can use the listserv to send messages, access information about the listserv and the membership list, and accomplish other options that are available through the listserv.

A wide variety of listservs are useful in social work education. The best-known listserv for social workers is SOCWORK. This listserv was developed to provide social workers a forum through which to effectively communicate professional concerns and share information across wide geographic boundaries. A current effort in social work is the establishment of a social work listserv in every state, often with the state chapter of the National Association of Social Workers (NASW) operating and maintaining that state's listserv (S. Marson, Pembroke State University, personal communication, October 19, 1996). At the time of this writing, about half the states either had a listserv in place or were developing one. Many other types of listservs are useful in social work education. For instance, there are listservs for advocacy and groups dealing with diversity. Other listservs have been formed for individuals who share a common life experience, such as a chronic illness or psychiatric diagnosis. SWAN (University of South Carolina, 1996) provides a compilation of many of the listservs that are relevant to social workers, social work educators, and students and provides users with information on how to become a member of the listservs.

In addition to encouraging social work students to use listservs that are already in existence, teachers can develop listservs specifically for the members of their classes. Listservs can be based in either mainframe university computers or the WWW. A teacher can plan the listserv so that it can either allow or prohibit access by individuals not enrolled in the class. Sometimes access is prohibited to preserve the confidentiality of students who might disclose private information about themselves to the others on the listserv. Prohibiting access is accomplished by establishing user identifications and passwords for the members in a class.

Listservs that are developed for a specific social work class have an advantage over the simple use of e-mail among members of a class. Messages, notices, and assignments can be posted simultaneously to the entire membership list. Discussions of course material and issues related to learning can also be posted to the list. Used in this manner, the listserv ensures that all members of a class receive the same information, directions, and suggestions from the teacher. Furthermore, use of a listserve can facilitate more active participation among the class members. In addition to general postings on the listserv, class members can send private messages to each other or to the teacher regarding the issue under study.

Additional Uses of the WWW

Because of its flexibility, the WWW provides social work educators many additional educational tools. Teachers can use the WWW to manage courses in the following ways, to note a few examples. A teacher can develop a home page for a specific course and include a syllabus that has hypertext links to information relevant to the course. A syllabus with hypertext links to WWW topics related to the course can be much more interesting and stimulating to students than the more traditional paper syllabus (Polyson, Saltzberg, & Godwin-Jones, 1996). Notices and assignments can be posted to the class members over the WWW, and a listserv for class members can facilitate ongoing discussion of class topics. Teachers can post outlines and course notes for students to use in preparing for class. Social work educators can also use the WWW to develop and implement course-specific interactive computer programs. The WWW can accommodate hypertext documents and hypermedia and multimedia computer applications. These applications can include the same range of teaching methods used in interactive computer applications, such as drill and practice, simulations, exploration, and problem solving. Teachers can use these applications to teach course content, help students assess their understanding of course content, or evaluate student progress. Students can submit written assignments over the WWW and receive feedback, including their grades, in private messages from the teacher.

It appears that social work educators are beginning to use computer networks for instructional purposes, although the numbers are not large. One study of graduate social work faculty found that 31 percent of the respondents used databases or information retrieval for instructional purposes. Twenty percent of the respondents reported that they use e-mail, networks, and communications for instruction (Pittman, 1994). This study did not separate WWW use from use of other types of computer networks, and no information is available that addresses differential usage of networks in social work education.

Effectiveness and Cost Considerations

Research outside of social work suggests that the use of computer networks can facilitate effective student learning (Haile & Richards, 1984; J. Siegel, Dubrovsky, & Kiesler, 1986). It has been shown that the use of e-mail can improve the level of participation among class members (J. Siegel et al., 1986). It has also been demonstrated that when e-mail is used in independent study courses, students drop out of these courses at rates that are no higher than those for courses taught in the traditional classroom format (Haile & Richards, 1984). These findings suggest that the increased interpersonal communication afforded by the use of e-mail may facilitate student motivation and prevent class members from feeling isolated.

Research concerning the use of computer networks in social work education has yielded results similar to those found in studies reported earlier, but it should be noted that most of these are case studies reporting anecdotal information. The use of e-mail has been shown to increase student involvement, ensure full class participation, improve students' level of comprehension of the course content, and actually increase verbal interaction among students during class time (Folaron, 1995). Another study that focused primarily on the practical issues of using e-mail in teaching social work content found that the use of e-mail increased students' levels of personal and intellectual involvement in the course content and made them become more active learners (Finn, 1995). It has been also

been found that students in a course taught by e-mail scored significantly higher on tests and assignments than students receiving instruction through traditional means (D'Souza, 1991). Furthermore, it has been reported that the use of e-mail in teaching allows teachers to individualize their courses more effectively to meet different students' learning needs (D'Souza, 1991; Finn, 1995). Although a different study reported more negative results with the use of e-mail in a course, issues related to course planning and faculty interactions with class members may have affected the outcomes (Latting, 1994).

The costs associated with using computer networks are generally low. Because the academic institution typically funds the costs associated with establishing and maintaining computer networks, it is relatively inexpensive for educators and students to use these teaching tools. Although some universities still allocate certain hours of usage to students who take courses that use computer networks, many universities now issue student identification numbers and passwords to all students on registration. Relatively little time is required by faculty to instruct students on the use of network resources such as databases and information resources, e-mail, and the WWW. Because a variety of the resources available through LANs and the WWW can be used intuitively, these resources do not require extensive written instructions to teach students to use them. However, the costs associated with purchasing an authoring program, learning to use it, and developing a course that will be accessed on the WWW are similar to those associated with developing course-specific computer applications. Teachers should be aware that a fully developed WWW course home page with hypertext links to WWW resources, interactive testing, interactive computer applications, or any combination of these requires dedication and a substantial investment of time.

An additional cost in using computers that come into contact with data obtained over communications networks is the potential of acquiring computer viruses. Many current computer viruses are stealthy in nature—that is, computer users are not aware of the virus until after it has been installed in machines and is activated. The most direct costs associated with protecting against viruses are related to purchasing and frequently upgrading computer virus software. Many universities provide this software to schools of social work as a free service or at a minimal cost. A greater cost, however, can occur when students or even an entire class lose data because of a computer virus. This requires that educators carefully plan how data will be protected against a potential virus when students work collaboratively on course projects.

DISTANCE EDUCATION TECHNOLOGIES

Whereas the traditional mode of education in social work has involved the teacher and the learner interacting within the same classroom, recent developments in telecommunications technology have made it possible for the two to be miles apart. The student can engage in "live" interaction with the teacher and with other students through a variety of telecommunications systems. Furthermore, with the advances that have been made in computer technology, such as computer-assisted learning programs and IVDs, it is now possible for the teacher to provide an educational experience that does not require real-time interaction with the student. Hence, the traditional teaching-learning model is no longer essential, and effective education can be achieved even though the teacher and learner interact while apart from each other in time and location.

Developments in telecommunications technology have greatly enhanced the potential for social work to provide what is known as "distance education." Distance education refers to "any formal approach to learning in which a majority of the instruction occurs while educator and learner are at a distance from one another" (Verduin & Clark, 1991, p. 8). This term has existed for many years and may have first appeared in the 1892 catalog of the University of Wisconsin (Rumble, 1986). It was popularized by the German educator Otto Peters (1968) in the 1960s and became commonly used in the United States in the 1980s. The earliest distance education consisted of printed and written correspondence by mail. Later, the print materials were supported by audio tapes, video tapes, or both. As this evolutionary process continued, the print materials used in correspondence study were supported by radio or television broadcast signals, but with no direct real-time communication between the teacher and learner. In all of these approaches to distance education, the teacher-learner interactivity was minimal, feedback from teacher to student was delayed, and the interaction among students was virtually nonexistent (Barker, Frisbie, & Patrick, 1989). These problems have been resolved by recent innovations in computer technology and audio and video communications technology.

Computer-Assisted and Computer-Mediated Distance Education

The uses of computer applications for social work education purposes, as discussed earlier in this article, can be applied to distance education. When computer applications are used in this way, the computer becomes a teaching machine to deliver social work education to learners in remote locations. The advent of computer-assisted distance education has enhanced the interactivity of the learning process. Although there is no real-time interaction with the faculty member, the student interacts with the instructional units presented through the computer. The level of interaction can range from low to high, depending on the type of computer application used, as discussed earlier. There are six modes of computer-assisted instruction that can be used effectively for distance education purposes: drill and practice, tutorial, gaming, simulation, discovery, and problem solving (Heinich, Molenda, & Russell, 1985).

Computer-assisted distance education has obvious advantages. The use of computer applications for teaching students in remote locations facilitates self-paced, individualized learning. Furthermore, students in distance education receive immediate positive reinforcement and feedback when computer applications are used. Through IVDs the distance learner can be exposed to a wide variety of information, including graphics, electronic print, and sound, and can control the time and length of study of each learning unit until mastery is achieved. Computer-assisted distance education thus makes it possible to provide individualized learning on a large scale to students in many diverse sites. A disadvantage of computer-assisted distance education, however, is the tremendous cost that may be involved in developing the software, as discussed earlier.

Distance education has also been enhanced through the development of computer-mediated education technologies that facilitate learning rather than provide instruction. Distance education can be delivered through the use of facsimile, networks, electronic mail, computer conferencing, and other electronic delivery systems. These technologies allow for interactivity between the teacher and learner, and this interactivity can occur in real time. The discussion of the use of computer networks to deliver social work education, as described in an earlier section of this entry, applies to distance education. Another use of the computer to deliver distance education, interactive compressed video, is described in the following section.

Audio and Video Communications Systems

Recent developments in audio and video communications (AVC) technology have also made it possible for students at remote locations to engage in live interaction with the teacher and with other students in real time. This interaction can be achieved in one of several ways, depending on the type of AVC equipment used. First, there can be a two-way audio system with no video. This arrangement is similar to an audio teleconference or conference call but includes more participants. Students located at various sites interact with the instructor by using a speakerphone or comparable technology.

A second type of AVC system entails two-way audio and one-way video. Students at remote sites can see the professor and can speak with the professor and other students. The signals can be delivered by a number of means, including telephone lines, satellite, cable television, and closed-circuit television. Often multiple technologies are used as an integrated system of signal delivery (Conklin & Osterndorf, 1995).

A third type of telecommunications system makes possible two-way audio and two-way video interaction. This system enables the teacher to see, hear, and interact with the students while allowing the students to see, hear, and interact with the teacher and one another. Multiple technologies can be used to produce this level of interaction, including satellite, cable television, closed-circuit television, and interactive compressed video (ICV) systems. Although ICV technically is a computer-mediated system, because it involves real-time transmission of sound and video, it is included in the AVC section of this entry. ICV systems, which combine computers with telephone lines to transmit signals, are being increasingly used because of their relatively low cost. This technology involves the use of codecs (devices that compress or decompress the signal) on both ends of a digital phone line. Depending on the type of equipment that is used, there may be a slight delay of sound and some impairment in video quality (Conklin & Osterndorf, 1995; Freddolino, 1996).

Extent of Use

There has been little use of computer-assisted education in social work distance education programs. Furthermore, social work has made minimal use of computer-mediated technologies for distance education purposes. Although some schools of social work have experimented in using these technologies to support learning in distance education programs, no schools are known to have used computer-assisted or computer-mediated education (other than ICV) as the sole means of providing education to students in remote locations.

In recent years, however, schools of social work have increasingly used AVC systems (including ICV) to provide distance education. Although the first use of this medium was as early as 1981 (Raymond, 1988; Weinbach, Gandy, & Tartaglia, 1984), most schools of social work did not have the technology to offer this type of distance education until more recent years. The number of schools using this modality is now growing rapidly. In 1993 27 of 238 respondents (11 percent) to a national survey of undergraduate, graduate, and combined undergraduate-graduate social work education programs indicated that they were providing curricula through distance education via AVC (Conklin, Jennings, & Siegel, 1994). When this study was repeated in 1996, 41 of 259 respondents (15.8 percent) indicated that they were offering courses through AVC. Thirty-three percent of the responding schools had been providing education through AVC for less than one year (E. Siegel, Conklin, Jennings, & Napolitano, 1996). Because of the growing number of schools offering coursework through AVC, the Commission on Accreditation of the Council on Social Work Education developed guidelines for schools to follow in developing accreditable distance education programs (Council on Social Work Education, 1995).

In addition to undergraduate- and graduate-level coursework, schools of social work are now offering continuing education through AVC. In 1993 seven programs reported that they provided continuing education through AVC; by 1996 this number had increased to 20 (Conklin et al., 1994). As the availability of communications technology expands in schools and agencies, it is likely that this modality will be increasingly used as a cost-effective way of delivering continuing education to social workers. This increased use by academia (and others) poses some risks related to "overcrowding." Schools of social work must not only compete for Internet and AVC systems with which to deliver education, they must also develop contingency plans to implement in the event of equipment failure.

Effectiveness and Cost Considerations

The effectiveness of teaching through distance education technologies has been documented by numerous studies. As reported earlier, research has shown that both computer applications and computer networks are effective means of facilitating student learning (Haile & Richards, 1984; J. A. Kulik, 1983; J. A. Kulik & Kulik, 1986, 1987; C. C. 1991; J. Siegel et al., 1986). It should be noted that these studies do not necessarily address the issue of distance education—that is, in some of these studies the teacher may have been present in the environment instead of physically apart from the student, as is true in distance education. However, there has been research that demonstrates that when computer-assisted instruction is used for distance education purposes, the cognitive learning outcomes of remotely based students are equal or superior to those of students in the conventional classroom (Broussard, 1983).

As early as 1975, a meta-analysis examined a number of research reports that compared courses taught via AVC with equivalent courses taught in the conventional classroom, looking at all academic levels (Chu & Schramm, 1975). This secondary data analysis found that most courses can be taught successfully by AVC and that in most cases there are not significant differences in the cognitive outcomes of AVC teaching and conventional teaching. Later meta-analyses of studies of AVC teaching versus conventional teaching revealed that in practically all of these studies, students who took courses through telecommunications showed cognitive outcomes comparable to or better than those of students who took traditional classroom courses (Verduin & Clark, 1991; Whittington, 1987). Social work programs using AVC to deliver education have also demonstrated the effectiveness of this medium as measured by factors such as student learning, grades, graduation rates, and student retention (Elliot, Coe, & Mayadas,1996; Kelley, 1993; Raymond, 1988, 1996; Weinbach et al., 1984).

A question often raised by social work educators with regard to teaching courses through distance education technologies is whether students will experience affective growth and professional socialization. Some educators believe that changes in values, attitudes, and beliefs can occur only in a social context such as the traditional classroom. Nevertheless, although only a few studies have dealt with the socialization question, research indicates that affective development also occurs successfully when AVC is used as the medium of education (Verduin & Clark, 1991). Because it has not been well documented that adequate socialization occurs when social work courses are offered via AVC, most schools that use this technology have made structural program arrangements to address this issue. For example, some schools require that the students who take AVC classes also take other classes offered through the traditional format. Other schools require on-site facilitators to meet with students in groups at remote locations to facilitate professional socialization (and to achieve other purposes).

The previous discussion of the costs related to computer applications and computer networks is applicable to the use of these technologies for the purpose of distance education. The cost of offering AVC courses varies, depending on the type of equipment used. Offering courses by satellite or microwave is generally very expensive. Most schools of social work have found that teaching courses through compressed video is the most efficient approach to AVC instruction. The initial equipment cost has diminished significantly in recent years, making it affordable to social work programs. Furthermore, many universities now have AVC systems in place that can be used by their schools of social work. In addition to equipment costs, there are expenses for technical personnel and rental of communication lines during broadcast time, costs that are sometimes offset by charging special fees.

Faculty who teach courses through AVC need special training to use the medium effectively. This includes technical training by the production staff regarding use of the equipment and other technical matters. Faculty who teach courses via AVC must also learn how to prepare appropriate audiovisual material, how to gauge their time correctly, and how to involve students in on-line discussion. This training is often made available through orientation sessions led by experienced telecommunications teachers or through mentoring arrangements. Most faculty who teach AVC courses report a high level of satisfaction with the use of this medium, in spite of initial concerns they may have had (Dillion, 1989; Weinbach et al., 1984).

Students who take courses taught through AVC also must learn to make optimal use of this medium. Primarily this involves becoming able to interact with faculty and other students freely and easily. To facilitate this purpose, most schools offer new students an orientation session, led by the teacher or on-site facilitator.

CONCLUSION

The technological developments that have occurred in recent years have had a significant impact on social work education. Although social work educators have been somewhat slow to take advantage of the new technologies, they have recently begun to use these new tools with increasing frequency. The studies cited previously have demonstrated that growing numbers of social work faculty are adopting technological innovations to facilitate their teaching. The fact that more than 40 percent of the respondents to a recent survey of graduate faculty are using some type of computing applications in teaching underscores this point (Pittman, 1994).

Research has shown also that the new technologies are effective means of providing social work education. Cognitive learning and affective development do occur successfully when computer applications, computer networks, and distance education technologies are used to provide or support education. The findings are less conclusive about the effectiveness of these technologies in promoting socialization of social work students. The socialization issue should be seen from a larger perspective, however, given other developments that have occurred in social work education in recent years. With the large

percentage of current students who study part time, there is less exposure to faculty and other students than in traditional classroom settings, regardless of the technology that may be used to facilitate the educational process. Furthermore, research has not demonstrated conclusively whether social work values and beliefs are "caught" (as opposed to taught), as the socialization proposition suggests. If they are caught, perhaps this occurs most successfully in field placement rather than in the classroom.

It is likely that the speed of technological development will not only continue but will increase. Continuing innovations in computer applications, computer networks, and distance education technologies will present new challenges for social work educators. Educators must remain abreast of new technological developments and must recognize the potential of these emerging technologies to support the educational process. They must consider these technologies as adjuncts, rather than threats, to the instructional process.

The biggest challenge facing social work educators will be defining their roles in terms of a new pedagogical philosophy. No longer will the role of the instructor be that of giving information to students in a traditional classroom setting. The educator and the student may be apart from each other in both time and location during the teaching-learning process. In the new educational era, the role of the social work teacher will include (1) acting as a facilitator to suggest actions and research implications, (2) updating information to make current research findings and literature available to the students, (3) identifying and discussing with the students new technological possibilities and obstacles, and (4) serving as an "information navigator" to help students in their search for information through computer applications and networks (Resnick, 1996).

In this new educational paradigm, students will also take on a more proactive role, assuming increasing responsibility for their own learning. Students will use electronically supported instruction to access information independently, establish educational goals and objectives, and measure learning achievements. They will view the teacher-student relationship as egalitarian in nature, with the educator serving as a facilitator or enabler rather than a purveyor of information.

However, along with the potential for advances that can be made in social work education through the use of developing technologies, there may be barriers to such progress. First, there may be reluctance on the part of faculty and administrators to use new approaches to education. Such change requires not only new learning but also a willingness to shift from the traditional, time-honored modes of social work education. Second, a tremendous amount of time must be committed to becoming knowledgeable about these new technologies and their uses in the educational process. More than 50 percent of social work educators in a recent study stated that they do not have access to technical training (Pittman, 1994). Courses, workshops, and mentoring activities must be implemented to deal with this problem. Third, the cost of developing, acquiring, or adapting new technologies can be exorbitant. However, as discussed herein, relatively inexpensive technologies are available, and computer resource availability is not a problem for most social work educators (Pittman, 1994). Nonetheless, technology costs can be a problem for small, underfunded social work programs, and such programs may struggle to maintain adequate resources and to be competitive with schools that have better support.

Fourth, the traditional methods of evaluating faculty cannot be used to assess faculty accomplishments in developing, adapting, or applying technological innovations. As the traditional teaching role changes, new methods for measuring teaching effectiveness must be designed. University policies and standards must be modified to give credit for faculty accomplishments in technology and to consider these as scholarly achievements for purposes such as tenure, promotion, and merit raises. Fifth, the use of technological innovations in delivering education raises a number of new legal questions and policy issues. For example, when a faculty member develops software or video modules for use in distance education, the issues of ownership, financial rewards, and public domain must be addressed. When an entire course is offered via the Internet, consideration must be given to who owns the course. Also, the potential for schools to offer these academic programs virtually anywhere through the use of distance education technology raises questions of geographic domain. New interinstitutional,

interstate, and even international agreements may be needed to protect territorial academic prerogatives. Finally, the expanding use of technology may require schools to reexamine their policies regarding matters such as matriculation requirements, as the traditional time and space constraints need not apply when social work education courses are delivered through electronic media.

In spite of these barriers, however, it is likely that social work education will continue to progress in its use of developing technologies. Many younger social work educators have grown up during the information revolution and are very comfortable with technology and appreciate its potential. Most of the students in social work education programs, as "children" of the information revolution, also have positive attitudes regarding technology. This technology orientation of social work faculty and students, coupled with the inevitability of continuing and profound technological development, holds promise for an exciting future for social work education.

References

Barker, B., Frisbie, A., & Patrick, K. (1989). Broadening the definition of distance education in light of the new telecommunications technologies. *American Journal of Distance Education, 3*(1), 20–29.

Bloom, M., Fischer, J., & Orme, J. G. (1995). *Evaluating practice: Guidelines for the accountable professional.* Needham Heights: Allyn & Bacon.

Broussard, R. L. (1983). *Homebased computer assisted adult education project—Phase III.* Unpublished manuscript, University of Southwestern Louisiana, Lafayette, ERIC Document Retrieval Service No. ED 234 181.

Buckles, B. J. (1989). Identification of variables influencing readiness-to-implement information technology by social work faculty (Doctoral dissertation, Adelphi University, 1989). *Dissertation Abstracts International, 52,* 3652.

Caputo, R. K., & Cnaan, R. A. (1990). Information technology availability in schools of social work. *Journal of Social Work Education, 26,* 187–198.

Cerf, V. (1993). How the Internet came to be. In B. Abdon (Ed.), *The online user's encyclopedia.* Reading, MA: Addison-Wesley. (Available on-line at http://info.org/guest/zakon/Internet/History/How_the_Internet_came_to_Be.)

Chu, G., & Schramm, W. (1975). *Learning from television: What does the research say?* Stanford, CA: Stanford University Press.

Cnaan, R. A. (1989). Social work education and direct practice in the computer age. *Journal of Social Work Education, 25,* 235–243.

Conklin, J., Jennings, J., & Siegel, E. (1994, March). *The use of technology as an enhancement to teaching distance education.* Paper presented at Faculty Development Institute, Council on Social Work Education Annual Program Meeting, Atlanta.

Conklin, J., & Osterndorf, W. (1995). Distance learning in continuing social work education: Promise of the year 2000. *Journal of Continuing Social Work Education, 6*(3), 13–17.

Council on Social Work Education. (1995). *Guidelines for distance education proposals in social work.* Alexandria, VA: Author.

DeLoughry, T. J. (1996, October 11). Computing officials at 34 universities seek to create a network for higher education. *Chronicle of Higher Education, 42,* A29–A30.

Dillion, C. (1989). Faculty rewards and instructional telecommunications: A view from the telecourse facility. *American Journal of Distance Education, 3*(2), 35–43.

Dossett, D., & Konczak, L. (1985). New and improved, or just new? *Training and Development Journal, 5,* 41–44.

D'Souza, P. V. (1991). The use of electronic mail as an instructional aid: An exploratory study. *Journal of Computer-Based Instruction, 18*(3), 106–110.

Dyson, P. (1994). *The PC user's pocket dictionary.* San Francisco: Sybex.

Elliot, D., Coe, J. A., & Mayadas, N. (1996, July). *Distance education: A social development perspective on outreach programs for women and special groups.* Paper presented at the Ninth International Symposium of the Inter-University Consortium for International Social Development, Oporto, Portugal.

Engen, H. B., Finken, L. J., Luschei, N. S., & Kenney, D. (1994). Counseling simulations: An interactive videodisc approach. In H. Resnick (Ed.), *Electronic tools for social work practice and education* (pp. 283–298). New York: Haworth Press.

Falk, D. R., & Carlson, H. L. (1995). *Multimedia in higher education: A practical guide to new tools for interactive teaching and learning.* Medford, NJ: Learned Information.

Falk, D. R., Shepard, M. F., Campbell, J. A., & Maypole, D. E. (1992). Current and potential applications of interactive videodiscs in social work education. *Journal of Teaching in Social Work, 6,* 117–136.

Finn, J. (1995). Use of electronic mail to promote computer literacy in social work undergraduates. *Journal of Teaching in Social Work, 12*(12), 73–83.

Finnegan, D. J., & Ivanoff, A. (1991). Effects of brief computer training on attitudes toward computer use in practice: An educational experiment. *Journal of Teaching in Social Work, 5*(1/2), 73–81.

Flynn, J. P. (1990). Using the computer to teach and learn social policy: A report from the classroom and the field. *Computers in Human Services, 4*(3/4), 199–209.

Flynn, J. P. (1994). Practical issues for newcomers to computer-based education. In H. Resnick (Ed.), *Electronic tools for social work practice and education* (pp. 359–375). New York: Haworth Press.

Flynn, M. (1987). Computer-based instruction in social policy: A one-year trial. *Journal of Social Work Education, 13*(1), 52–59.

Folaron, G. (1995). Enhancing learning with E-mail. *Journal of Teaching in Social Work, 12*(1/2), 3–18.

Forte, J. A., Healey, J., & Campbell, M. H. (1994). Does microcase statistical software package increase the statistical competence and comfort of undergraduate social work and social science majors? *Journal of Teaching in Social Work, 10*(1/2), 99–115.

Frans, D. J. (1993). Computer diffusion and worker empowerment. *Computers in Human Services, 10*(1), 15–34.

Freddolino, P. P. (1996). Maintaining quality in graduate school social work programs delivered to distance sites using electronic instruction technology. In E. Torre Reck (Ed.), *Modes of professional education II: The electronic social work curriculum in the twenty-first century* (Tulane studies in social welfare, Vol. 20, pp. 48–63). New Orleans: Tulane University.

Gabor, P. A., & Grinnell, R. M., Jr. (1994). *Evaluation and quality improvement in the human services.* Needham Heights: Allyn & Bacon.

Geiss, G. R., & Viswanathan, N. (1986). *The human edge: Information technology and helping people.* New York: Haworth Press.

Green, M. M. (1988). Computer assisted instruction in social work. *Dissertation Abstracts International, 49,* 07A.

Haile, P. J., & Richards, A. J. (1984, October). *Supporting the distance learner with computer teleconferencing.* Paper presented at the 15th Annual Convocation of the Northeastern Educational Research Association, Ellenville, New York. ERIC Document Reproduction Service No. ED 256 293.

Hammond, N., & Trapp, A. (1992). CAL as a Trojan horse for educational change: The case of psychology. *Computers and Education, 19*(1/2).

Hartig, G. (1985). *Students are capable of assessing the effectiveness of computer-assisted instruction.* Unpublished manuscript, Indiana University, Independent Study Program, School of Continuing Studies, Indianapolis. ERIC Document Reproduction Service No. ED 270 098.

Heerman, B. (1988). *Teaching and learning with computers: A guide for college faculty and adminis-trators.* San Francisco: Jossey-Bass.

Heinich, R., Molenda, M., & Russell, J. D. (1985). *Instructional media and the new technologies of instruction* (2nd ed.). New York: John Wiley & Sons.

Henry, M. S., & Rafferty, J. (1995). Equality and CAL in higher education. *Journal of Computer Assisted Learning, 11*(2), 72–78.

Holden, G., Rosenberg, G., & Weissman, A. (1995). Gopher accessible resources related to research on social work practice. *Research on Social Work Practice, 5,* 235–245.

Holden, G., Rosenberg, G., & Weissman, A. (1996). World Wide Web accessible resources related to research on social work practice. *Research in Social Work Practice, 6,* 236–262.

Hudson, W. W. (1985). Computer managed instruc-tion: An application in teaching introductory statistics. *Computers in Human Services, 1*(1), 117–123.

Kelley, P. (1993). Teaching through telecommunica-tions. *Journal of Teaching in Social Work, 7,* 63–74.

Kulik, C. C., & Kulik, J. A. (1991). Effectiveness of computer-based education: An updated analysis. *Computers in Human Behavior, 7*(2), 75–94.

Kulik, J. A. (1983). Synthesis of research on com-puter-based instruction. *Educational Leadership, 41,* 19–21.

Kulik, J. A., & Kulik, C. C. (1986). Effectiveness of computer based education in colleges. *AEDS Journal, 19*(2/3), 81–108.

Kulik, J. A., & Kulik, C. C. (1987). Review of recent literature on computer-based instruction. *Contemporary Educational Psychology, 12,* 222–230.

LaMendola, W. (1987). Teaching information technology to social workers. *Journal of Teaching in Social Work, 1,* 53–69.

Latting, J. K. (1994). Diffusion of computer-mediated communication in a graduate social work class: Lessons from "the class from hell." *Computers in Human Services, 10*(3), 21–45.

Madlin, N. (1987, November). Computer-based training comes of age. *Personnel, 64,* 64–65.

Mandel, S. F. (1989). Resistance and power: The perceived effect that computerization has on a social agency's power relationships. In W. LaMendola, B. Glastonbury, & S. Toole (Eds.), *A casebook of computer applications in the social and human services* (pp. 29–40). Binghamton, NY: Haworth.

Maple, F. F. (1994). The development of goal-focused interactive videodiscs to enhance student learning in interpersonal practice methods classes. In H. Resnick (Ed.), *Electronic tools for social work*

practice and education (pp. 333–346). Binghamton, NY: Haworth.

Nurius, P. S., & Nicoll, A. E. (1989). Computer literacy preparation: Conundrums and opportunities for the social work educator. *Journal of Teaching in Social Work, 3,* 65–81.

Nurius, P. S., Richey, C. A., & Nicoll, A. E. (1988). Preparation for computer usage in social work: Student consumer variables. *Journal of Social Work Education, 24,* 60–69.

Orlansky, J. (1983). Effectiveness of CAI: A different finding. *Electronic Learning, 3,* 58–60.

Patterson, D. A., & Yaffe, J. (1993). Using computer-assisted instruction to teach axis-II of the DSM-III-R to social work students. *Research on Social Work Practice, 3,* 343–357.

Patterson, D. A., & Yaffe, J. (1994). Hypermedia computer-based education in social work education. *Journal of Social Work Education, 30,* 267–277.

Peters, O. (1968). New perspectives in correspon-dence study in Europe. In O. MacKenzie & E. L. Christensen (Eds.), *The changing world of correspondence study.* University Park: Pennsylva-nia State University Press.

Pittman, S. W. (1994). An exploratory study of the diffusion of instructional computing innovation among social work faculty. *Dissertation Abstracts International, 55,* 152.

Polyson, S., Saltzberg, S., & Godwin-Jones, R. (1996). A practical guide to teaching with the World Wide Web. *Syllabus 10*(2), 12–16.

Raymond, F. B. (1988, July). *Providing social work education and training in rural areas through interactive television.* Paper presented at Annual Institute on Social Work and Human Services in Rural Areas, Fort Collins, CO. ERIC Document Reproduction Service No. ED 309 910.

Raymond, F. B. (1996). Delivering the MSW curricu-lum to non-traditional students through interactive television. In E. Torre Reck (Ed.), *Modes of professional education II: The electronic social work curriculum in the twenty-first century* (Tulane studies in social welfare, Vol. 20, pp. 18–31). New Orleans: Tulane University.

Reinoehl, R., & Shapiro, C. H. (1986). Interactive videodiscs: A linkage tool for social work educa-tion. *Journal of Social Work Education, 22*(3), 61–67.

Resnick, H. (Ed.). (1994). *Electronic tools for social work practice and education.* Binghamton, NY: Haworth.

Resnick, H. (1996). IMM in the future social work classroom. In E. Torre Reck (Ed.), *Modes of professional education II: The electronic social work curriculum in the twenty-first century* (Tulane studies in social welfare, Vol. 20, pp. 53-62). New Orleans: Tulane University.

Rumble, G. (1986). *The planning and management of distance education.* London: Croom Helm.

Seabury, B. A., (1994). Interactive video disc programs in social work education: "Crisis counseling" and "organizational assessment." In H. Resnick (Ed.), *Electronic tools for social work practice and education* (pp. 299-316). Binghamton, NY: Haworth.

Seabury, B. A., & Maple, F. F., Jr. (1993). Using computers to teach practice skills. *Social Work, 38,* 430–439.

Siegel, E., Conklin, J., Jennings, J., & Napolitano, S. (1996). *National survey on distance learning in social work education, preliminary data.* Manuscript in preparation, Southern Connecticut University, Department of Social Work, New Haven.

Siegel, J., Dubrovsky, V., & Kiesler, S. (1986). Group processes in computer-mediated communication. *Organizational Behavior and Human Decision Processes, 37,* 157–187.

Steyaert, J., Colombi, D., & Rafferty, J. (Eds.). (1996). *Human services and information technology: An international perspective.* Aldershot, England: Arena, Ashgate Publishing.

University of South Carolina. (1996). Social work access network. Available on-line at http://www.csd.sc.edu/swan.

Verduin, J. R., & Clark, T. A. (1991). *Distance education: The foundation of effective practice.* San Francisco: Jossey-Bass.

Weinbach, R., Gandy, J., & Tartaglia, L. (1984). Addressing the needs of the part-time student through interactive closed circuit television: An evaluation. *Arete, 9*(2), 12–20.

Whittington, N. (1987). Is instructional television educationally effective? A researcher review. *American Journal of Distance Education, 1*(1), 47–57.

Wodarski, J. S., Bricout, J. C., & Smokowski, P. R. (1996). Making interactive videodisc computer simulation accessible and practice relevant. *Journal of Teaching in Social Work, 13*(1/2), 15–26.

Zakon, R. H. (1996). Hobbes' Internet timeline v2.5. Available on-line at http//www.info.isoc.org/guest/zakon/Internet/History/HIT.html.

Frank B. Raymond III, DSW, is professor and dean, and **Cathy K. Pike, PhD,** is assistant professor, College of Social Work, University of South Carolina, Columbia, SC 29208.

For further information see
Computer Utilization; Continuing Education; Council on Social Work Education; Expert Systems; Information Systems; **The Internet: Accessing the World of Information;** Recording; Social Work Education Overview; Social Work Profession Overview.

Key Words

computers	information systems
distance education	technology
electronics	

Spirituality

Edward R. Canda

This entry addresses four topics. First, it gives an overview of the history of connections between spirituality and social work, from sectarian beginnings through secularization to current reconnections. Second, it presents various definitions in the social work literature of spirituality and related terms such as religion, transpersonal experience, mysticism, and religiosity. Third, adverse religious and nonreligious expressions of spirituality are discussed, including their relation to cultural variation. Fourth, current trends and issues for social work practice are summarized. In general, the discussion suggests that there is a trend of rapidly increasing interest in this topic, especially in relation to an expanded person-in-environment conception of effective practice with culturally and spiritually diverse people. Spiritually sensitive practice is described as a helping relationship in which the worker links personal and professional growth, engages in dialogue with clients about their frameworks for meaning and morality, appreciates diverse religious and nonreligious expressions of spirituality, supports creative resolutions of life crises, and connects with a variety of spiritual resources as relevant to the client.

The topics of spirituality and religion often raise lively debate within the profession of social work. They have been central to our heritage and yet are often rejected as legitimate domains for social workers in education and practice. Social work in the United States developed with significant influences from religious institutions and spiritual perspectives. Over the course of the 20th century until the 1980s, the profession tended to distance itself from its religious origins. However, from the 1980s to the present, interest in spirituality and religion has increased. The current challenge is how to address spirituality in a manner that is consistent with professional ethics and respectful of spirituality's diverse religious and nonreligious expressions. This entry examines these professional historical trends, definitions of spirituality, diversity of spiritual perspectives and related controversies, and relevancy to practice. The focus is on spirituality as understood from a nonsectarian vantage point within the profession of social work.

HISTORICAL TRENDS
There have been three historical phases in the relationship between spirituality and professional social work in the United States: sectarian origins (beginning with the establishment of the American colonies through the first few decades of the 1900s), professionalization and secularization (1920s through 1970s), and resurgence of interest in spirituality (1980s through the present). In addition, before European immigration, hundreds of indigenous cultures extant throughout North America had their own systems of providing for individual and community welfare that were deeply involved with spirituality. Social welfare developments with a strong Catholic orientation had existed in French and Spanish territories in North America since the 1400s. Furthermore, during the period of slavery, people of African descent mobilized mutual support and liberation systems inspired by traditional African spirituality and Christian principles under extremely adverse conditions. Unfortunately, there is little published information about the impact of these various developments on the formation of professional social work.

During phase 1, *sectarian origins,* social work in the United States arose to a great extent out of sectarian institutions and ideologies pertaining to charity and commu-

nity service (Axinn & Levin, 1982; Brower, 1984; Bullis, 1996; Canda, 1988b; Garland, 1992; Leiby, 1977; Loewenberg, 1988; Marty, 1980; Niebuhr, 1932; Reid & Popple, 1992). The most influential religious perspectives were Christian and Jewish. This was reflected in the importance of the Charity Organization Society, the Settlement House movement for immigrants, and Jewish communal services in the foundation of social work. However, the process of professionalization included a movement away from these sectarian roots.

During the second phase, *professionalization and secularization,* problems with sectarian affiliation of the emerging profession were expressed. As Canda (1997) put it, "Although charitable efforts to assist the poor and distressed may be praiseworthy, the biblical concept of charity (unconditional love) has been too often distorted into condescending pity and love 'with strings attached'" (p. 174). As the Charity Organization Society and Settlement House movement vied to form a profession in competition with others, such as medicine and the law, acceptance by the larger, increasingly pluralistic society, the government, and academia became more important. The rapid rate of increased immigration from all regions of the world during this time meant that the religious composition of American society changed dramatically. It became increasingly obvious that Jewish and Christian religious beliefs could not be applied to all Americans. Many social work practitioners and educators became concerned about the harmful effects of attaching service to proselytization. Religiously based moralistic judgmentalism stimulated objections, for example, in the victim-blaming and condescending connotations of the distinctions between "worthy" and "unworthy" poor and in condemnations of people with substance abuse disorders. Especially as social work education shifted to an academic approach within secular universities and colleges, social work educators turned more to the latest trends of scientific and quasi-scientific explanations and interventions for personal and social problems, ranging from Freudianism to Marxism to behaviorism, none of which were sympathetic to religious or spiritual matters. Furthermore, as social work and social welfare were increasingly being administered or funded by government agencies, concerns about separation between church and state grew (Ressler, in press).

This shift toward a secular view of social work has been reflected in the development of the Council on Social Work Education (CSWE) curriculum policy guidelines. Early statements during the 1950s and 1960s referred to the importance of the spiritual needs of people (Marshall, 1991; Russel, in press). The statements developed in the 1970s and 1980s eliminated references to religious and spiritual issues. During this period some social workers advocated for a return of attention to religion and spirituality (Canda, 1988a; Joseph, 1987; Siporin, 1982, 1985), but this was not reflected in the predominant approaches to education, practice, or policy.

The third phase, *resurgence of interest in spirituality*, began to emerge in the late 1970s and has gained momentum rapidly since the 1980s (Canda, 1995; Russel, in press). This phase paralleled general social trends of public interest and debate concerning religious and spiritual issues pertaining to public policy, war, civil rights, increasing religious diversity, the rise of religiously conservative political movements, and the New Age popular culture movement (Lippy & Williams, 1988; Melton, 1993; Williamson, 1992). In this phase advocates called for ways to address spirituality that would respect diversity and avoid the pitfalls of sectarian exclusivism and proselytization. This was not so much an attempt to return to the profession's sectarian roots as an effort to restore attention to the spiritual aspect of human experience while learning from the difficulties of the past. This trend was initiated with a few books about spiritual perspectives on social work that went beyond the Judeo-Christian tradition, such as Brandon's *Zen in the Art of Helping* (1976) and Krill's *Existential Social Work* (1978). During the 1980s, many more publications called for attention to spirituality in an inclusive manner (Brower, 1984; Canda, 1988a, 1988b, 1989; Constable, 1983; Joseph, 1987, 1988; Loewenberg, 1988; Marty, 1980; Meystedt, 1984; Siporin, 1982, 1985). During the 1990s, research on spirituality and social work continued to grow, focusing more on specific practice and education issues (Canda & Phaobtong, 1992; Cowley, 1993; Cowley & Derezotes, 1994; Denton, 1990; Derezotes & Evans, 1995; Dudley & Helfgott, 1990; Furman, 1994; Sermabeikian, 1994; Sheridan, Bullis, Adcock, Berlin, & Miller, 1992; Sheridan,

Wilmer, & Atcheson, 1994). The first social work practice textbook focusing on spirituality from a nonsectarian perspective was published recently (Bullis, 1996). The first human behavior theory textbook systematically addressing spirituality will be published soon (Robbins, Chatterjee, & Canda, in press).

This publication activity has been accompanied by growing numbers of presentations on spirituality and religious diversity at national conferences and professional networking through the National Association of Social Workers (NASW), CSWE, and other organizations from the mid-1980s to the present. The first national conference dedicated to the theme of religion and spirituality in a nonsectarian manner was the Conference on the Impact of Religious Fundamentalism on Social Work Education and Practice, held in Cleveland during 1985. Participants expressed many different perspectives, including Jewish, fundamentalist Christian, liberal Christian, humanist, and nonsectarian spirituality. In 1989, Edward Canda, then of the University of Iowa, began organizing the Spirituality and Social Work Network to bring together scholars and practitioners from many different spiritual perspectives to advocate for further innovation in research, teaching, and practice. In 1990, after Canda moved to the University of Kansas, this became the Society for Spirituality and Social Work. Since 1994 it has been directed by Robin Russel at the University of Nebraska at Omaha. It continues to publish a newsletter and to network nationally and internationally. Since 1995 this society has organized annual national conferences on spirituality and social work.

All of these professional networking attempts, as well as most of the research in the 1990s, were initiated from state-sponsored universities, which further reinforced the spiritually inclusive, nonsectarian orientation. The 1995 version of the CSWE's *Handbook of Accreditation Standards and Procedures* serves as a clear indicator of this professional shift. Belief systems, religion, and spirituality are mentioned as important areas of curriculum content, especially with regard to diversity among clients (Russel, in press).

In addition to these nonsectarian efforts, religiously affiliated groups have also encouraged greater attention to matters of religion and spirituality in social work. See related entries on Christian social work, church social work, and sectarian agencies.

DEFINITIONS OF SPIRITUALITY

There have been many difficulties defining spirituality for social work purposes, which is an indication of the professional quandaries as well as the limitations inherent in the term. Attempts to define spirituality in social work did not begin in earnest until the late 1970s and early 1980s. During historical phases 1 and 2, the term "spirituality" was not used as commonly as the term "religion," and when it was used, it was usually given a religion-specific meaning, with Jewish or Christian theological assumptions. Some people attempted to develop Christian values and concern into general, nonsectarian themes relevant to most social workers, recognizing the religious diversity among social work students, faculty, and clients.

One of the earliest attempts to do this was by Charlotte Towle (1965), in *Common Human Needs,* written primarily for social workers in public settings in the 1940s. She insisted that the "spiritual needs of the individual must be recognized" (p. 11). She did not define spirituality precisely, but she referred to the needs for church attendance, use of church resources, respect for religious convictions, search for a sense of life purpose, development of ethics and values, and formation of social responsibility. Similarly, Spencer (1956) pointed out that social work should address religious concerns in a way that accommodated religious heterogeneity and the requirements of public settings. She took a liberal Christian ecumenical view that Christian values of human freedom, creativity, love, and service can be extended to all without explicit use of theological language or sectarian settings for service. In fact, in 1952, she was instrumental in keeping reference to "the spiritual" in the education accreditation standards (Russel, in press). However, the distinction between religion and spirituality is unclear in her writing. For both Towle and Spencer, there was a distinction between sectarian and nonsectarian approaches to religious themes that became highlighted in future work.

Formal attempts to develop a nonsectarian definition of spirituality grew in the late 1970s through the mid-1980s with existential and humanistic writings in social work (Edwards, 1982; Krill, 1979). They alluded to the human quest for a sense of meaning and purpose as a spiritual process. In 1984 Brower referred to the "spiritual dimension" (p. 2) as involving an immaterial human spirit, a process of integrating all aspects of the person, and an awareness of and relationship with the "spirit/energy source of the creation" (p. 2). Siporin (1985) said that the spiritual is a moral aspect of the person, called the soul, which is concerned about striving for transcendental values, a sense of meaning, knowledge of ultimate reality, and relatedness with other people and supernatural powers. He pointed out that spirituality may be expressed within or outside religious institutions. Later Siporin (1990) clarified that the concept of spirituality should not be limited to beliefs in God or the soul. Joseph (1987) defined spirituality as "the underlying dimension of consciousness which strives for meaning, union with the universe, and with all things; it extends to the experience of the transcendent or a power beyond us" (p. 14).

Guided by these insights, Canda (1986, 1988a, 1988b, 1990c) developed a comprehensive conceptualization of spirituality, taking into account its diverse expressions in the full range of English social work writings and the personal views of 18 social work educators who were advocates of spirituality. These educators expressed atheist, Christian, humanist, existentialist, Jewish, shamanic, and Zen Buddhist perspectives. The variety of perspectives required a formulation of spirituality that avoided particular religious images or assumptions. Canda (1990a) summarized his definition of spirituality as follows:

> I conceptualize spirituality as the gestalt of the total process of human life and development, encompassing biological, mental, social, and spiritual aspects. It is not reducible to any of these components; rather, it is the wholeness of what it is to be human. This is the most broad meaning of the term. Of course, a person's spirituality is concerned significantly with the spiritual aspect of experience. In the narrow sense of the term spirituality, it relates to the spiritual component of an individual or group's experience. The *spiritual* relates to the person's search for a sense of meaning and morally fulfilling relationships between oneself, other people, the encompassing universe, and the ontological ground of existence, whether a person understands this in terms that are theistic, atheistic, nontheistic, or any combination of these. (p. 13)

In this conceptualization, spirituality is distinguished from religion. Canda (1997) said that "religion involves the patterning of spiritual beliefs and practices into social institutions, with community support and traditions maintained over time" (p. 173). Institutional religion also involves economic, political, social support, psychological, and social control functions, but these are addressed in terms that are heavily laden with spiritually oriented symbols and rituals. The closely related definitions of spirituality and religion established by Siporin (1985), Joseph (1987), and Canda (1988a) in the 1980s are most commonly used in current social work writing.

Carroll (in press) has reviewed the various definitions of spirituality used in social work and concluded that there are three common features. First, spirituality is understood to be an *essential or wholistic quality* of the human being that cannot be reduced to any parts. Sometimes this is described as the essence, soul, life force, or wholeness of the person. The importance of a holistic view of spirituality, which does not create dichotomies between matter and spirit, or between material and spiritual needs, has been widely affirmed (Constable, 1990; Logan, 1990; Siporin, 1990). Second, spirituality is also understood as an *aspect* of the person concerned with the development of meaning and morality and establishment of a relationship with a transcendent, divine, or ultimate reality. Finally, spiritual development may involve experiences of a *transpersonal* nature that expand one's sense of identity beyond the personal ego and social roles. These include peak experiences inspiring visions and revelations; and experiences of profound unity with other people, aspects of nature, divinity, or cosmic consciousness (Canda, 1991; Cowley, 1993; Cowley & Derezotes, 1994; Smith, 1995; Smith & Gray, 1995).

Two of these themes are reflected commonly in definitions given by practitioners in response to recent surveys (Derezotes & Evans, 1995; Sheridan & Bullis, 1991). First, spirituality is recognized as a natural part or capacity of all people involving a search for meaning. Second, spirituality as a basic aspect of human nature is distinguished from religion as an institution.

Despite this attention to defining spirituality, there remain problems with use of the concept in social work. One problem is the lack of consensus on precise meanings. One reason for this may be that many academics and practitioners are still unaware of the existing literature on the topic. For example, definitions offered by Sermabeikian (1994) and Barker (1995) barely used the relevant literature in social work. Some practitioners have indicated that their social work education has not prepared them in either theory or practice to deal with spirituality, even though they and their clients recognize its importance (Derezotes & Evans, 1995; Sheridan et al., 1992). Another reason may relate to inconsistency of use even by a single author, thus adding to confusion. For example, Bullis (1996) defined spirituality in ways consistent with Carroll's (in press) observations. However, he also gave inconsistent and limiting definitions, such as "inner feelings and experiences of the immediacy of a higher power" (p. 2), which is narrowly linked to 12-step program language; the "the relationship of the human person to something or someone who transcends themselves" (p. 2), which does not account for the experience of sacredness within oneself and the world; and "divinely focused altered states of consciousness" (p. 3), which is biased toward theistic religious beliefs and reduces spirituality from a holistic quality to a particular state of consciousness.

Canda (1990a) summarized the advantages and disadvantages of his own conceptualization of spirituality. The merits are that it is inclusive of diverse beliefs and behaviors without judgmentalism; it addresses the holistic nature of the person in relationship with the environment; it does not imply dichotomies "such as spirit versus nature, individual versus community, immanent versus transcendent, or soul versus body" (p. 13); it appreciates religious institutions and commitments but does not restrict spirituality to them; and it expands the person-in-environment concept to include "the wholeness of the person in the context of cosmological and ontological understandings of the environment, such as beliefs and experiences pertaining to a soul, spirit powers, God, demons, or cosmic consciousness"; furthermore, it does not limit recognition of spirituality to any of these particular beliefs or experiences.

However, problems remain with this conceptualization. First, the word "spirituality" is derived from the concept of spirit, which denotes a nonphysical entity or force.

Canda (1990a) gave the concept of spirituality a broader use than such beliefs, but the terminology may not be comfortable for atheists, agnostics, and members of nontheistic traditions such as Buddhism. Second, a challenge inherent in an inclusive conceptualization is that it must *include* exclusive understandings of spirituality, such as in some fundamentalist religions. This is fine for inclusivists but may be objected to by exclusivists. Third, the notion of spirituality as the wholeness of the person is so encompassing that it may be difficult to operationalize for research purposes or to distinguish it in practice from other aspects of human experience. Fourth, this definition is congruent with current use in popular culture, but it is not accepted in many particular religious traditions or in the academic field of religious studies (Pals, 1996).

Difficulties in defining spirituality arise also from the mystical quality of many of the phenomena it encompasses. The term "mystical" means going beyond the limitations of concepts and reason to direct experience of the ground of our being on forces considered to be sacred. Drawing on the classic work of the psychologist of religion, William James, Dupres (1987) described five characteristics of mystical experience:

1. It is ineffable—that is, deeply private and incommunicable except by symbols or metaphor.
2. It is noetic—that is, infusing life with a sense of all-encompassing order and integration.
3. It is often experienced passively, as an undeserved gift, even if prepared for by disciplines.
4. The experience usually has a transient and fluctuating course.
5. Finally, the experience may result in a sense of profound, transpersonal communion with a higher, deeper, or more complete level of reality than one has in ordinary experience.

For these reasons, communication about the mystical aspects of spirituality are often indirect, metaphorical, imprecise, and even paradoxical. Mystical experience is not irrational, but rather transrational and transpersonal.

Despite these various problems, the concept of spirituality is playing a useful role in expanding social work practice, research, and teaching into the arenas of individual meaning systems and collective world views, religious support systems and religiously derived helping activities, moral development, and experiences of a transpersonal nature. O'Brien (1992) suggested that it is not necessary to arrive at universal agreement about a precise definition as long as a cluster of related themes are evoked by use of the concept. Some of his themes of spirituality included morality; the meaning and purpose of life; integration and wholeness; creativity and intuition; altruistic service; mystery; traditions, rituals, and myths; virtues; transpersonal states of consciousness and experiences; openness, willingness, surrender, and receptivity; freedom and responsibility; wisdom or revealed knowledge; prayer, meditation, and contemplation; understandings about suffering and death; relation to ultimate reality; relations with nonphysical reality; the path to enlightenment or salvation; and a sensitive awareness of the earth and nonhuman world.

SPIRITUAL DIVERSITY IN SOCIAL WORK AND RELATED CONTROVERSIES

The spiritual themes mentioned previously are addressed in all religions and cultures in a wide variety of ways. Some beliefs and moral positions contradict one another. There is often conflict between people of different religious traditions. This diversity poses a major challenge for finding common terms and meanings related to spirituality, as we have seen. It also poses a major challenge in the arenas of social work practice and policy-making. Social workers must develop sensitivity and competence in dealing with spiritual diversity, just as in dealing with cultural diversity (Canda, 1997; Lum, 1996; Raines, 1996).

Spiritual diversity in the United States has increased tremendously during American history, especially because of various waves of immigration of Europeans and people of color (Melton, 1993). Before European immigration, there were hundreds of distinct indigenous cultures with their own flourishing spiritual traditions. Those who practiced these indigenous spiritual ways were often denigrated and persecuted by European immigrants through individual behavior, the conduct of religious institutions, and government policy (Bullis, 1996). Although hundreds of these indigenous spiritual traditions have continued and experienced a revitalization since the 1970s, government protection for freedom of religious practice for native peoples was not provided in law until the 1970s and had to be reinforced by the Religious Freedom Restoration Act in 1993 (Bullis, 1996). Spirituality, in various forms for diverse native communities, is an important resource for healing, resiliency, and empowered responses to oppression (Chenault, 1990; Nabigon & Mawhiney, 1996; Yellow Bird, 1995).

Forced removal of African peoples brought a wide variety of African religious beliefs and practices, but the slavery system generally prohibited the preservation of traditional African religions in the United States. During the period of slavery and emancipation, many African Americans merged African religious patterns with Christianity and also used the liberating symbols and beliefs of Christianity. Since that time churches, mosques, and other religious support systems have been very important in African American communities (Corbett, 1997; Logan, 1996; Logan, Freeman, & McRoy, 1990).

Before the 1880s there was little political and economic competition to the predominance of Christianity, which had the support of the Euro-American majority and the federal government; but many of the masses were indifferent to organized religion (Melton, 1993). At the time of the American Revolution, church-state relations were cut. In the American colonies and states, various forms of Protestant Christianity prevailed. From the beginning of the 19th century to the present, there has been a tremendous increase in formal *religiosity*—that is, participation in religious institutions. The national population increased 350 percent while church membership increased 700 percent. However, the role and varieties of religions changed significantly as church—state separation was enacted and the population composition changed. For example, in 1800 there were only 20 Christian denominations; in 1988 there were more than 900. Competition with non-Christian religions also increased exponentially, including more recent immigrant religions from the Middle East and Asia and new spiritual movements such as American Spiritualism, Latter Day Saints, Theosophy, Christian Science, and New Age. In the past few decades, many people have disaffiliated from formal religions and developed private and small support group approaches to spiritual belief and practice.

The numbers of adherents to major religious denominations can be estimated from surveys and self-reports by religious organizations (Famighetti, 1995; Lippy & Williams, 1988; Melton, 1993; Williamson, 1992). The following figures indicate the tremendous variety of religious affiliations. The largest organizational membership is in the Roman Catholic Church, with nearly 60 million. The next largest group is the Southern Baptist Convention, with about 16 million members; there are about 20 million more members of other Baptist denominations. There are about 9 million United Methodists and 5 million members in two African Methodist denominations. There are about 4 million members of Reform, Orthodox, and Conservative Jewish congregations. Some of the fastest growing religious traditions are not Christian or Jewish; these include Islam, Hinduism, and Buddhism. There are at least 6 million members of Moslem and related groups, including Sunnis, Shiites, Ismaelis, members of the Nation of Islam, and Sufi practitioners. Figures for Hindus and Buddhists are most difficult to estimate. Estimates for Hindus range from 1 million to 5 million in more than 100 denominations, and for Buddhists, from 1 million to 5 million in more than 75 organizations. Of course there are numerous other Protestant and Eastern Orthodox Christians, participants in Native American spiritual traditions, Latter Day Saints, Wiccans, Baha'is, Zoroastrians, Sikhs, and Taoists. Indeed, virtually any religion or spiritual perspective in the world is likely to be represented in the United States to some degree. A search of the Internet using the term "spirituality" will produce links to thousands of sites dealing with religious and nonreligious spiritual perspectives and their relation to issues of health, mental health, and social justice.

Social workers and their clients reflect this diversity, but precise figures are not available. Bibliographies compiled by the Society for Spirituality and Social Work show the following spiritual perspectives discussed by social work authors: Buddhist; Christian; Confucian; existentialist, in both religious and nonreligious forms; Hindu; Islamic; Jewish; shamanistic and spiritistic; Taoist; and various nonsectarian perspectives on spirituality, such as humanistic and transpersonal. Each of these involve distinct theories about human behavior, ideals of human service, and service programs and practices to support human well-being and social justice. The many religious and spiritual perspectives intersect with cultural diversity, producing great variety and complexity. Some religious forms are closely tied to particular American ethnic groups (for example, Judaism, Hispanic Catholicism, Eastern Orthodox Christianity, African American Baptist and Methodist churches and the Nation of Islam, traditional indigenous spiritualities, Islam among immigrants from the Middle East, Hinduism, and Buddhism) (Corbett, 1997). Some of these variations are discussed in other entries.

Interaction between social workers and clients across different spiritual perspectives results in many value tensions, dilemmas, and controversies, as well as opportunities for mutual spiritual learning and support (Canda, 1990a). Some current controversies in the profession relate to areas of value conflict between conservative religious positions and social work values, such as support for a client's right to decide whether to have an abortion or for gay rights (Faver, 1987; Holland, 1989; Parr & Jones, 1996); whether and when it may be appropriate to pray with clients or to collaborate with religious support systems (Canda, 1990b); how to evaluate the helpful or harmful impact of participation in religious or spiritual groups, including so-called cults (Lewandowski & Canda, 1995); perceived threats to separation of church and state (Ressler, in press); and cross-cultural cooperation between workers and clients who may be unfamiliar or uncomfortable with each others' spiritual practices (Bullis, 1996).

SPIRITUALITY AND SOCIAL WORK PRACTICE

The studies cited in this entry address numerous social work practice issues. Interviews with clinical practitioners (Derezotes & Evans, 1995; Sheridan & Bullis, 1991) have identified their views of the relevance of spirituality to practice. Practitioners identified the importance of linking their own spiritual growth with professional development, so that they can apply themselves in an empathic, respectful, and self-aware manner in work with clients. This included working through practitioners' own unresolved negative religious experiences or discomfort toward clients with unfamiliar or contrasting spiritual beliefs and practices. Workers also expressed a need to deal with

referrals from religious or spiritual groups. Spirituality often comes into play when clients are coping with doubt about religious faith, conversion experiences, or crises of meaning. Developmental assessment of life cycle crises and frameworks for morality and faith were also mentioned. Practitioners suggested that positive and negative influences from spiritual beliefs, practices, and policies must be examined. When clients bring up explicitly religious or spiritual matters, workers are faced with a decision of whether to deal with this directly or to refer the client to or collaborate with a specialist in the client's religious or spiritual tradition. Many practice skills and techniques explicitly related to spirituality were used by some social workers in these studies, including prayer, meditation, ritual, guided visualization, reading of scriptures and spiritual texts, and cooperation with religious community–based support systems.

The fields of practice of substance abuse recovery (Krill, 1990; Morell, 1996) and hospice (Ita, 1995–1996; Millison & Dudley, 1990; Nakashima, 1995) especially emphasize the importance of spirituality. Transpersonally oriented social workers attempt to address the whole person, with a focus on spirituality (Cowley & Derezotes, 1994; Robbins et al., in press). There are also many church and sectarian settings for social work practice (see entries on Christian social work, church social work, and sectarian agencies). There have also been attempts to develop guidelines for macro-level social work practice and policy formulation (Netting, 1984), especially drawing on the spiritual activist movements of Martin Luther King, Mohandas Gandhi, and liberation theology (Breton, 1989; Canda & Chambers, 1994; Walz, Sharma, & Birnbaum, 1990). Culturally competent social work practice requires cooperation with religious community–based support systems and culture-specific forms of healing (Lum, 1996).

Canda (1988b) emphasized that spiritually sensitive practice should be founded on continual self-inquiry and personal growth of workers, respectful dialogue with clients about their ways of making meaning and moral frameworks, appreciation of spiritual diversity, creative support of transformational possibilities in life crises, and familiarity with a variety of spiritual resources for personal and community support.

REFERENCES

Axinn, J., & Levin, H. (1982). *Social welfare: A history of the American response to need* (2nd ed.). New York: Harper & Row.

Barker, R. L. (1995). *The social work dictionary* (3rd ed.). Washington, DC: NASW Press.

Brandon, D. (1976). *Zen in the art of helping.* New York: Delta/Seymour Lawrence.

Breton, M. (1989). Liberation theology, group work, and the right of the poor and oppressed to participate in the life of the community. *Social Work with Groups, 12*(3), 5–18.

Brower, I. C. (1984). *The 4th ear of the spiritual-sensitive social worker.* Doctoral dissertation, Union for Experimenting Colleges and Universities, Ann Arbor, MI: University Microfilms International, 8500785.

Bullis, R. K. (1996). *Spirituality in social work practice.* Washington, DC: Taylor & Francis.

Canda, E. R. (1986). *A conceptualization of spirituality for social work: Its issues and implications.* Doctoral dissertation, Ohio State University, Columbus. Ann Arbor, MI: University Microfilms International, 8625190.

Canda, E. R. (1988a). Conceptualizing spirituality for social work: Insights from diverse perspectives. *Social Thought, 14*(1), 30–46.

Canda, E. R. (1988b). Spirituality, religious diversity, and social work practice. *Social Casework, 69,* 238–247.

Canda, E. R. (1989). Religious content in social work education: A comparative approach. *Journal of Social Work Education, 25,* 36–45.

Canda, E. R. (1990a). Afterword: Spirituality re-examined. *Spirituality and Social Work Communicator, 1*(1), 13–14.

Canda, E. R. (1990b). An holistic approach to prayer for social work practice. *Social Thought, 16*(3), 3–13.

Canda, E. R. (1990c). Spiritual diversity and social work values. In J. J. Kattakayam (Ed.), *Contemporary social issues.* Trivandrum, India: University of Kerala.

Canda, E. R. (1991). East/west philosophical synthesis in transpersonal theory. *Journal of Sociology and Social Welfare, 18*(4), 137-152.

Canda, E. R. (1995). Retrieving the soul of social work. *Society for Spirituality and Social Work Newsletter, 2*(2), 5–8.

Canda, E. R. (1997). Does religion and spirituality have a significant place in the core HBSE curriculum? Yes. In M. Bloom & W. C. Klein (Eds.), *Controversial issues in human behavior in the social environment* (pp. 172–177, 183–184). Boston: Allyn & Bacon.

Canda, E. R., & Chambers, D. (1994). Should spiritual principles guide social policy? Yes. In H. J. Karger & J. Midgley (Eds.), *Controversial issues in social policy* (pp. 64-69, 74-78). Boston: Allyn & Bacon.

Canda, E. R., & Phaobtong, T. (1992). Buddhism as a support system for Southeast Asian refugees. *Social Work, 37,* 61–67.

Carroll, M. (in press). Social work's conceptualization of spirituality. *Social Thought.*

Chenault, V. (1990). A Native American practice framework. *Spirituality and Social Work Communicator, 1*(2), 5–7.

Constable, R. (1983). Values, religion, and social work practice. *Social Thought, 9*(4), 29–41.

Constable, R. (1990). Spirituality and social work: Issues to be addressed. *Spirituality and Social Work Communicator, 1*(1), 4–6.

Corbett, J. M. (1997). *Religion in America* (3rd ed.). Englewood Cliffs, NJ: Prentice Hall.

Council on Social Work Education, Commission on Accreditation. (1995). *Handbook of accreditation standards and procedures.* Alexandria, VA: Author.

Cowley, A. S. (1993). Transpersonal social work: A theory for the 1990s. *Social Work, 38,* 527–534.

Cowley, A. S., & Derezotes, D. (1994). Transpersonal psychology and social work education. *Journal of Social Work Education, 30,* 32–41.

Denton, R. T. (1990). The religiously fundamentalist family: Training for assessment and treatment. *Journal of Social Work Education, 26,* 6–14.

Derezotes, D. S., & Evans, K. E. (1995). Spirituality and religiosity in practice: In-depth interviews of social work practitioners. *Social Thought,18*(1), 39–56.

Dudley, J. R., & Helfgott, C. (1990). Exploring a place for spirituality in the social work curriculum. *Journal of Social Work Education, 26,* 287–294.

Dupres, L. (1987), Mysticism. In M. Eliade (Ed.), *The encyclopedia of religion* (pp. 245–261). New York: Macmillan.

Edwards, D. G. (1982). *Existential psychotherapy: The process of caring.* New York: Gardner Press.

Famighetti, R. (Ed.). (1995). *The world almanac and book of facts, 1996.* New York: World Almanac Books.

Faver, C. A. (1987). Religious beliefs, professional values, and social work. *Journal of Applied Social Sciences, 11,* 206–219.

Furman, L. E. (1994). Religion and spirituality in social work education: Preparing the culturally sensitive practitioner for the future. *Social Work and Christianity, 21,* 103–115.

Garland, D.S.R. (Ed.). (1992). *Church social work: Helping the whole person in the context of the church.* St. Davids, PA: North American Association of Christians in Social Work.

Holland, T. P. (1989). Values, faith, and professional practice. *Social Thought, 15*(1), 28–40.

Ita, D. (1995–1996). Testing of a causal model: Acceptance of death in hospice patients. *Omega: Journal of Death and Dying, 32,* 81–92.

Joseph, M. V. (1987). The religious and spiritual aspects of clinical practice: A neglected dimension of social work. *Social Thought, 13*(1), 12–23.

Joseph, M. V. (1988). Religion and social work practice. *Social Casework, 60,* 443–452.

Krill, D. (1978). *Existential social work.* New York: Free Press.

Krill, D. (1979). Existential social work. In F. J. Turner (Ed.), *Social work treatment: Interlocking theoretical perspectives* (pp. 147–176). New York: Free Press.

Krill, D. F. (1990). Reflections on teenage suicide and adult addictions. *Spirituality and Social Work Communicator, 1*(1), 10–11.

Leiby, J. (1977). Social welfare: History of basic ideas. In J. B. Turner (Ed.), *Encyclopedia of social work* (17th ed., pp. 1513–1518). Washington, DC: National Association of Social Workers.

Lewandowski, C. A., & Canda, E. R. (1995). A typological model for the assessment of religious groups. *Social Thought, 18*(1), 17–38.

Lippy, C. H., & Williams, P. W. (Eds.). (1988). *Encyclopedia of American religious experience: Studies of traditions and movements.* New York: Charles Scribner's Sons.

Loewenberg, F. M. (1988). *Religion and social work practice in contemporary American society.* New York: Columbia University Press.

Logan, S. L. (1990). Critical issues in operationalizing the spiritual dimension of social work practice. *Spirituality and Social Work Communicator, 1*(1), 7–9.

Logan, S. L. (Ed.). (1996). *The black family: Strengths, self-help, and positive change.* Boulder, CO: Westview Press.

Logan, S. L., Freeman, E. M., & McRoy, R. G. (1990). *Social work practice with black families: A culturally specific perspective.* New York: Longman.

Lum, D. (1996). *Social work practice and people of color: A process-stage approach* (3rd ed.). Pacific Grove, CA: Brooks/Cole.

Marshall, J. (1991). The spiritual dimension in social work education. *Spirituality and Social Work Communicator, 2*(1), 12–14.

Marty, M. E. (1980). Social service: Godly and godless. *Social Service Review, 54,* 4463–4481.

Melton, J. G. (1993). The development of American religion: An interpretive view. In J. G. Melton (Ed.), *Encyclopedia of American religion* (pp. 1–24). Detroit: Gale Research.

Meystedt, D. M. (1984). Religion and the rural population: Implications for social work. *Social Casework, 65,* 219–226.

Millison, M., & Dudley, J. (1990). The importance of spirituality in hospice work. *Hospice Journal, 6*(3), 63.

Morell, C. (1996). Radicalizing recovery: Addiction, spirituality, and politics. *Social Work, 41,* 306–312.

Nabigon, H., & Mawhiney, A. (1996). Aboriginal theory: A Cree medicine wheel guide for healing First Nations. In F. J. Turner (Ed.), *Social work treatment: Interlocking theoretical approaches* (4th ed., pp. 18–38). New York: Free Press.

Nakashima, M. (1995). Spiritual growth through hospice work. *Reflections, 1*(4), 17–27.

Netting, F. E. (1984). Church-related agencies and social welfare. *Social Service Review, 58,* 404–420.

Niebuhr, R. (1932). *The contribution of religion to social work.* New York: Columbia University Press.

O'Brien, P. J. (1992). Social work and spirituality: Clarifying the concept for practice. *Spirituality and Social Work Journal, 3*(1), 2–5.

Pals, D. L. (1996). *Seven theories of religion.* New York: Oxford University Press.

Parr, R. G., & Jones, L. E. (1996). Point/Counterpoint: Should CSWE allow social work programs in religious institutions an exemption from the accreditation nondiscrimination standard related to sexual orientation? *Journal of Social Work Education, 32,* 297-313.

Raines, J. (1996). Toward a definition of spiritually-sensitive social work practice. *Society for Spirituality and Social Work Newsletter, 3*(2), 4–5.

Reid, P. N., & Popple, P. R. (Eds.). (1992). *The moral purposes of social work: The character and intentions of a profession.* Chicago: Nelson-Hall.

Religious Freedom Restoration Act of 1993, P. L. 103-141, 107 Stat. 1488.

Ressler, L. (in press). The relation between church and state: Issues in social work and the law. *Social Thought.*

Robbins, S., Chatterjee, P., & Canda, E. R. (in press). *Contemporary human behavior theory: A critical perspective for social work.* Boston: Allyn & Bacon.

Russel, R. (in press). Spirituality and religion in graduate social work education. *Social Thought.*

Sermabeikian, P. (1994). Our clients, ourselves: The spiritual pespective and social work practice. *Social Work, 39,* 178–183.

Sheridan, M. J., & Bullis, R. K. (1991). Practitioners' views on religion and spirituality: A qualitative study. *Spirituality and Social Work Journal, 2*(2), 2–10.

Sheridan, M. J., Bullis, R. K., Adcock, C. R., Berlin, S. D., & Miller, P. C. (1992). Practitioners' personal and professional attitudes and behaviors toward religion and spirituality: Issues for education and practice. *Journal of Social Work Education, 28,* 190–203.

Sheridan, M. J., Wilmer, C. M., & Atcheson, L. (1994). Inclusion of content on religion and spirituality in the social work curriculum: A study of faculty views. *Journal of Social Work Education, 30,* 363–376.

Siporin, M. (1982). Moral philosophy in social work today. *Social Service Review, 56,* 516–538.

Siporin, M. (1985). Current social work perspectives on clinical practice. *Clinical Social Work Journal, 13,* 198–217.

Siporin, M. (1990). Welcome to the *Spirituality and Social Work Communicator. Spirituality and Social Work Communicator, 1*(1), 3–4.

Smith, E. D. (1995). Addressing the psychospiritual distress of death as reality: A transpersonal approach. *Social Work, 40,* 402–412.

Smith, E. D., & Gray, C. (1995). Integrating and transcending divorce: A transpersonal model. *Social Thought, 18*(1), 57–74.

Spencer, S. (1956). Religion and social work. *Social Work, 1,* 19–26.

Towle, C. (1965). *Common human needs* (rev. ed.). New York: National Association of Social Workers.

Walz, T., Sharma, S., & Birnbaum, C. (1990). *Gandhian thought as theory base for social work* (University of Illinois School of Social Work Occasional Paper Series I). Urbana-Champaign: University of Illinois.

Williamson, W. B. (Ed.). (1992). *An encyclopedia of religions in the United States.* New York: Crossroad.

Yellow Bird, M. J. (1995). Spirituality in First Nations story telling. *Reflections, 1*(4), 65–72.

FURTHER READING

Canda, E. R. (Ed.). (in press). Special issue on spirituality in social work. *Social Thought.*

Canda, E. R. (Ed.). (1996). Special issue on spirituality [entire issue]. *Reflections: Narratives of Professional Helping, 1*(4).

Krill, D. F. (1990). *Practice wisdom: A guide for helping professionals.* Newbury Park, CA: Sage Publications.

Edward R. Canda, PhD, is associate professor, School of Social Welfare, University of Kansas, Lawrence, KS 66045.

For further information see

Christian Social Work; Church Social Work; Clinical Social Work; Ethics and Values; Human Development; **Jewish Communal Services;** Natural Helping Networks; Person-in-Environment; Progressive Social Work; Self-Help Groups; Social Development; Social Work Practice: Theoretical Base.

Key Words	
diversity	religion
morality	spirituality
mysticism	

T

Temporary Assistance to Needy Families
Mimi Abramovitz

In August 1996, Congress enacted the Personal Responsibility and Work Opportunity Reconciliation Act of 1996 (P.L. 104-193), known as the Personal Responsibility Act (PRA). Among other things, the act abolished the cash assistance program known as Aid to Families with Dependent Children (AFDC). AFDC, which had provided income support for poor children and their mothers since its inception as Title IV of the 1935 Social Security Act (IV A U.S.C. §401), was replaced by block grants for Temporary Assistance to Needy Families (TANF). The details of TANF, also known as Title I of the PRA of 1996, were just beginning to emerge at the time of this writing. The law, which becomes fully operative between October 1997 and July 1998, weakens the principle of entitlement, the linchpin of the welfare state in the United States. The transformation threatens to bring much harm to poor and working class people, especially women and children.

THE FALL OF AFDC

The 1935 Social Security Act was passed by Congress during the Great Depression to provide income for food, clothing, shelter, and other basic necessities. The landmark legislation, which launched the modern welfare state in the United States, authorized the federal government to assume responsibility for providing a minimal level of economic support to many, but not all, individuals and families in the nation. The Social Security Act established two very different approaches to economic security: social insurance and public assistance. The two social insurance programs, Old Age Retirement Insurance and Unemployment Compensation, are universal, nonstigmatized, and popular, unlike the original means-tested public assistance programs—that is, Old Age Assistance; Aid to the Blind; Aid to Dependent Children; and Aid to the Permanently and Totally Disabled, which was added in 1954. In 1974, all the public assistance titles, except the highly controversial AFDC program, were consolidated into a federalized income support program known as Supplemental Security Income (SSI). These and other entitlement programs, such as Medicaid (1965) and Medicare (1965), guaranteed a minimum of income and support to people in need.

For nearly 50 years most Americans accepted the idea that the federal government should play a major role in supporting individuals and families when the market economy could not ensure adequate levels of income and employment. The welfare state expanded

accordingly. However, by the mid-1970s, globalization and deindustrialization, along with major social and political changes, eroded the "American dream" that provided many people with economic security and a sense of hope. In the increasingly conservative political climate of the 1980s and 1990s, politicians and policymakers began to challenge the role of government in wider society—some because they opposed government regulations in general, others simply to win votes. The Reagan administration launched an attack on the welfare state as part of its broader plan to promote economic recovery and social stability by cheapening the cost of labor, restoring the traditional family, shrinking the federal government, and curbing the influence of popular movements that might fight back (Abramovitz, 1992).

The assault on AFDC—the least popular of all the social welfare programs—became the "stalking-horse" for a wider attack on all social programs. Begun in the 1980s, the assault was continued by President Clinton, who, in his 1992 campaign for the presidency, promised to "end welfare as we know it" and then, as president in 1996, declared that the "era of big government is over." While welfare reform inched its way through congressional politics, President Clinton allowed the states to "experiment" with AFDC changes to prove that he was committed to changing the program. By May 1996 about 75 percent of all AFDC recipients nationwide were covered by programs designed under these waivers, most—although not all—of which were extremely punitive (Center on Social Welfare Policy and Law, 1996b).

The Republican Contract with America of 1994 upped the ante on welfare reform by trying to end welfare entirely. In 1996, in the midst of a heated presidential election campaign, Congress, with considerable bipartisan support, passed the PRA, which embodied the punitive spirit, if not all the details, of the Republican contract. Signed by President Clinton in August 1996, despite considerable opposition from his cabinet and his constituents, the new federal welfare law abolished the safety net that had protected poor women and children, however meagerly, for 60 years. The legislation also eliminated the federal entitlement to AFDC and paved the way for a continued assault on the more popular social welfare programs.

REQUIREMENTS FOR RECEIVING CASH ASSISTANCE

Entitlement to Assistance

Under the former AFDC program, the federal government entitled individuals to aid. In exchange for the guarantee of federal money, states had to serve all qualified persons who applied for assistance. However, with a single stroke, the PRA ended this federal commitment to the downtrodden. It abolished AFDC; removed the obligation to serve all those in need; and, for the first time, put a cap on federal funds provided to the states. Although the new law grants vast new powers to the states, it does not free them from all federal controls. Instead, it shifts the federal role from one of protection to one of punishment. Indeed, TANF either obligates or permits the states to restrict eligibility for benefits based on the number of years a person has been on welfare (time limits), his or her participation in a work program (work requirements), his or her citizen status and childbearing decisions, and any existing convictions for a drug felony. Instead of cushioning individuals and families from the vagaries of the economy and crisis in family life, the new federal welfare policy will regulate the behavior of the poor even more than before.

Time Limits

An unprecedented change made by TANF is the imposition of a time limit on the receipt of welfare. Under AFDC people received assistance as long as they satisfied the program's eligibility rules, which were set by the individual states under federal guidelines. The new federal law limits federal funding for individuals to a lifetime maximum of five years, or less at the state's option, and imposes a 5 percent cut in federal funds on states that do not comply with the time-limit rule. The states can exempt 20 percent of their TANF caseload from the time limit on the basis of hardship, but they cannot use federal funds to provide noncash benefits (for example, vouchers) to children once they reach the time limit. It is unclear at this point if states will be able to use their own funds to assist adults whose time limit expires. The harsh penalty for noncompliance and the fact that, prior to TANF, nearly 30 states had secured federal approval to try out some kind of time limit suggest that most states will comply with the new rule. The Congressional Budget Office estimated that even with the hardship exemption included, by the year 2004, between 2.5 and 3.5 million children could be adversely affected by the time limit (Super, Parrott, Steinmetz, & Mann, 1996).

Income Limits

TANF also eliminated the federal income test that previously determined eligibility for AFDC. To qualify for assistance under the former rules, a family's gross income had to be less than 185 percent of the state's need standard, and their income after deductions could not exceed 100 percent of this measure (Larin & Porter, 1992). The low need standard and means test ensured that AFDC served only the poorest of the poor and kept the program's enrollment down. By 1990, only 60 percent of all children in poverty received assistance, down from 80 percent in 1973 (U.S. House of Representatives, 1994). In contrast, TANF allows each state to set its own income rules. Given the lack of funding, there is great likelihood that the TANF means test will be even more restrictive than its predecessor.

Work Requirements

TANF dramatically intensified the already stiff work requirements attached to the receipt of cash benefits. AFDC was enacted to help single mothers stay home with their children. However, the program's long history of stigma, low benefits, and strict eligibility rules acted as an unofficial work requirement that routinely deterred many applicants from applying for aid, thereby channeling them into low-paying jobs. The 1967 Work Incentive Program (WIN) formalized AFDC's work rules by rewarding women who participated in welfare job training programs. These rules were intensified by the Job Opportunity and Basic Skills (JOBS) program established by the Family Support Act of 1988, which mandated that women on welfare work to receive aid. However, many states could not meet the JOBS enrollment quotas because of a lack of jobs, funds, and child care. Instead, many opted for the less expensive, and more punitive, job search and workfare programs. The latter required recipients to work off their benefits at or below the minimum wage.

TANF's work rules are even more coercive. In addition to time limits, the new law narrows the definition of work activities the government will fund, ruling out many of the skills-building and training options, including higher education, allowed by the former JOBS program. The state must put adult recipients to work after two years of assistance (or less, at the state's option) and can place them in workfare programs if they have not found a job after two months. Single mothers (even those with very young children) must work a minimum of 20 hours per week in fiscal year (FY) 1997, a requirement that increases to 35 hours in FY 2002. In addition to these tougher rules, TANF also allows states to pay a wage subsidy to employers who hire welfare recipients, thereby lowering their labor costs. Although the history of such subsidies is not promising, profits remain in private hands (Offner, 1996).

TANF penalizes both individuals and states that do not comply with the work rules. Except for parents who cannot find or afford child care, adults can lose some or all of their cash benefits, as well as access to Medicaid (U.S. House of Representatives, 1996). States must enroll a steadily rising number of recipients in work programs: 25 percent of all single-parent families in FY 1997, increasing to 50 percent in FY 2002. For two-parent families, the rate increases from 75 percent in FY 1997 to 90 percent in FY 1999. The Congressional Budget Office estimated that by 2002 the states will have to spend $5.6 billion to fulfill these federal work participation quotas, excluding child care costs. This is $4.1 billion more than what states spent on their JOBS program in 1994, yet TANF has budgeted $12 billion less than what the states will need over the next six years (Center for Law and Social Policy, 1996; Super et al., 1996). States that fail to meet federal quotas face reduced federal funds ranging from 5 percent in the first year to a maximum of 21 percent thereafter.

TANF also contains some adverse incentives. States that reduce their caseload are rewarded with lower work participation quotas. Because the caseload can be shrunk in many ways, the caseload reduction credit creates a strong but perverse incentive for states to find ways to decrease the number of recipients without operating a costly work program. Federal law forbids shrinking the caseload by tightening eligibility, but the burden of proof will lie with a retrenched U.S. Department of Health and Human Services and in any case will be difficult to establish (Center for Law and Social Policy, 1996; Super et al., 1996).

Unemployed Parents

In 1962 a small number of two-parent households became eligible for AFDC in a program known as Aid to Families with Dependent Children with Unemployed Parents (AFDC–UP). To qualify, the breadwinner had to be incapacitated, working fewer than 100 hours a month, and the household had to meet a host of other strict requirements. AFDC–UP was voluntary for the states until 1988, when the JOBS program made it mandatory. TANF abolished AFDC–UP, which was serving about 360,000 families in 1994, along with AFDC (U.S. Department of Health and Human Services, 1995b).

Deprivation of Parental Support

The former AFDC eligibility rules required that a child be deprived of support or care as a result of the death, absence, or incapacity (mental or physical) of a parent. Almost 85 percent of the 9.8 million children receiving welfare in 1994 were eligible because of the absence of a parent. Depending on the state, the supervising relative may be the child's father, mother, grandparent, aunt, uncle, sibling, stepparent, or stepsibling. However, the societal gender division of labor ensured that in 1994, 92.4 percent of the 5 million children receiving AFDC funds were being cared for by a woman, more than 75 percent of whom were the child's mother (U.S. Department of Health and Human Services, 1995b). Subject to significant restrictions noted both previously and later, TANF funds may be used to assist whatever types of families a state chooses. Because states need not cover any specific group, they can pick and choose among them. For example, states might exclude two-parent households or make payments based on completion of certain tasks or compliance with behavioral mandates.

Presence and Age of Children

AFDC served only families with minor children who were eligible for assistance from birth to their 18th birthday, although many states also assisted pregnant mothers. When the youngest child reached age 18 (or, at the state's option, age 19 if a full-time student), the family's benefits ceased. Although TANF continues these rules, the cessation of benefits when a mother's last child reaches age 18 will create even greater financial hardship for poor women. Before TANF, women who became ineligible for AFDC on these grounds had no place to turn for income support if they lacked work skills and good health, were too young to collect social security benefits, or were ineligible for Supplemental Security Income (SSI). There are no federal programs to aid able-bodied adults younger than age 62 with no children in the home. Some cities and states provide small amounts of local assistance to this group, but these forms of assistance are currently under fire. In addition to the elimination or retrenchment of these and other already meager local programs, the PRA of 1996 placed new restrictions on SSI and food stamps, leaving few positive options for childless women in their forties and fifties who cannot find paid work.

Child Support

For years federal law made the receipt of AFDC conditional on a mother's willingness to cooperate with the state in its effort to establish paternity of a nonmarital child, to obtain child support payments, and to assign support rights to the state. Child support payments that were less than the AFDC grant went directly to the government, with $50 of each payment passed through to the family in addition to its regular AFDC check (U.S. House of Representatives, 1992). TANF stiffened these controls. It tightened child support enforcement procedures by, among other things, creating a central registry to provide interstate tracking of those obliged to pay support; reduced by 25 percent the grant to women who do not cooperate with the increasingly detailed paternity and child support enforcement procedures; denied aid to families who do not

assign child support rights to the state; and eliminated the $50 pass-through to women on welfare, unless states pay for it with their own funds (Borkowski, 1996; Center on Social Welfare Policy and Law, 1996a).

Most observers agree that noncustodial parents should be expected to support their children. However, the situation becomes quite complex in the welfare arena, as poor women tend to partner with poor men. Some women will simply find it harder to qualify for aid because of the new, stricter rules. Others may find that TANF jeopardizes an existing relationship between a child and his or her father or opens the door to male violence against women (NOW Legal Defense and Education Fund, 1996). States that fail to comply with these new rules stand to lose from 1 percent to 5 percent of their TANF grant.

Childbearing Behavior

AFDC had a long history of trying to regulate the childbearing behavior of poor women by making receipt of aid conditional on conformity to moralistic behavioral standards. However, in the 1960s the "man-in-the-house" rule (if a caseworker found evidence of a man in the home, it was assumed that he was supporting the children, and the welfare check could be reduced or canceled); the "suitable-home" rule (states used various, often vague and moralistic, behavioral criteria, such as presence of a nonmarital child, to define homes as unsuitable and therefore ineligible for aid); and midnight raids (special investigative units of the welfare department—not caseworkers—would make surprise midnight visits to homes of women on welfare to determine whether there was a man in the house), which penalized women who had relationships with men or bore children outside of marriage, were largely discredited and discontinued. Such provisions reappeared in the early 1990s, when the cost and modest outcomes of work programs, along with the shift in the political climate, led states to stigmatize single mothers and penalize out-of-wedlock births as a way to reduce their welfare rolls. By 1996, beginning with New Jersey, more than 15 states had won federal approval for the child exclusion rule (also known as the family cap), which allows them to deny aid to children conceived or born while their mother was on AFDC. North Carolina, for example, stopped increasing the welfare grant for most children born to an AFDC family; Connecticut limited the increment for such children to one-half the average amount of the regular increase for an additional child. Other states created similar variations on the theme.

TANF strongly endorses the use of government dollars to promote behavioral change. Its preface states that the law was designed "to end dependence of needy parents on government benefits by promoting job preparation, work, and marriage; to prevent and reduce the incidence of out-of-wedlock pregnancies and to encourage the formation and maintenance of two-parent families" (U.S. House of Representatives, 1996, pp. 9–10). TANF permits (but does not require) all states to deny aid to children born on welfare. If current waivers are indicative of what is to come, more and more states will adopt child exclusion rules. According to the U.S. Department of Health and Human Services (1995b), about 26 percent of the 9.2 million children on AFDC in 1993 were born while the mother was on welfare. Under the new law, no funds would be provided for their care.

TANF also tries to regulate women's reproductive choices with an "illegitimacy" bonus. During fiscal years 1999 through 2002, states that show a net decrease in the number of nonmarital births (without an increase in abortions) will receive a financial bonus. The top five states qualify for an extra $20 million. If fewer than five states qualify, the grant rises to $25 million each. If the states actually compete for this extra money, the impact of the effort to reduce nonmarital births will extend far beyond the amount of money actually spent on the bonus. TANF also requires the secretary of the U.S. Department of Health and Human Services to establish and implement a strategy based on abstinence programs to prevent out-of-wedlock teenage births and to ensure that at least 25 percent of communities have this type of teenage pregnancy prevention program.

Immigrant Status

Before the PRA of 1996, undocumented immigrants were ineligible for most major entitlement programs. However, documented immigrants, including noncitizens, qualified for many government benefits, because they paid taxes and served in the military. Immigrants use benefits at the same rate as citizens—5 percent—but 44 percent of the federal savings resulting from the PRA come from cuts to immigrant entitlements. The PRA cut benefits for future and current immigrants enrolled in AFDC and other programs by more than $22 billion. Legal immigrants in the country before the enactment of PRA (August 22, 1996), with limited exceptions for both those currently receiving benefits and those in need of benefits in the future, will be denied TANF, SSI, and food stamps. The states have the option to continue or to deny these benefits to current immigrants. Immigrants who enter the country on or after August 22, 1997, will not be eligible for most means-tested programs (SSI, food stamps, Medicaid) for the first five years after entry; exceptions include refugees, those seeking asylum, and those on active military service or in possession of an honorable military discharge. The state will deem the income of the immigrant's sponsor available for the immigrant's support until the immigrant attains citizenship or has worked 40 qualifying quarters—regardless of whether the sponsor's income is actually used for this purpose. The PRA also prohibits state and local governments from using their own funds to assist undocumented immigrants (Super et al., 1996). Pregnant immigrant women can also lose access to prenatal nutrition benefits provided by the Women, Infants, and Children program (WIC). One of the few federal programs to serve undocumented aliens, access to WIC reduces health care costs of children after birth (Super et al., 1996). When President Clinton signed the PRA of 1996, he promised to "fix" some of the anti-immigrant provisions. Advocates of poor people or local officials who do not want to bear the costs when federal funds are cut will probably take the provisions to court. The outcome of efforts to restore immigrant rights to cash assistance programs will depend on many factors, most of them political.

ADMINISTRATION AND FUNDING

The Social Security Act did not require the states to have an AFDC program, but most states signed on to participate. At the time of TANF's enactment, AFDC existed in all 50 states, the District of Columbia, Guam, Puerto Rico, and the Virgin Islands (U.S. House of Representatives, 1992). Known as a grant-in-aid to the states, AFDC and other public assistance programs were administered and funded jointly by the federal government and the states; 15 states also involved local governments in the daily operations of AFDC.

Administration

To receive federal funds the states had to operate AFDC statewide, develop uniform standards, and serve all applicants who met the prevailing state and federal criteria. However, AFDC left considerable administrative powers to the states. Within broad federal guidelines, states had to establish their own eligibility rules, standards of need, benefit levels, income limits, administrative procedures, and behavioral mandates. By securing federal approval for a waiver, they could also experiment with programs that did not meet federal guidelines. The plan developed by the states had to be approved by the Social Security Administration and was considered a contract or agreement between the two parties.

TANF also requires a written state plan but does not subject it to federal approval. TANF asks each state to

- show that its welfare program is operating in all political subdivisions (but the program can vary from one jurisdiction to the next)
- establish objective criteria for determining eligibility and delivering benefits (although it need not provide families with any specified type of benefit)
- indicate whether it has decided to privatize the program by contracting for program administration to charities, religious organizations, or other private entities. Shortly after the passage of the PRA, Lockheed and other for-profit corporations began to bid for the potentially lucrative contracts (Bernstein, 1996). The fact that corporations such as Lockheed were seeking to replace lost Department of Defense contracts with welfare department contracts angered opponents of "corporate welfare." Advocates of poor people pointed out that the government was willing to support big business while it cut benefits for poor people.

Funding

As stated earlier, AFDC was jointly funded by the federal government and the states. Except for Guam, Puerto Rico, and the Virgin Islands, all participating states and territories received an open-ended federal appropriation drawn from income tax dollars. The reimbursement rate to the states (subject to change every two years) ranged from 50 percent to almost 80 percent of costs for benefits paid out and 50 percent of costs for administration and staff training. Some states required localities to finance some of the nonreimbursed costs.

TANF creates a dramatically new financial structure for cash assistance programs. First and foremost, TANF abolishes the guarantee of federal aid to the states, aid that has previously increased automatically when recessions, population growth, or other social trends caused caseloads to rise. This guarantee became the linchpin of the modern welfare state, because it enabled the states to help all needy applicants who qualified for help. In sharp contrast, the TANF block grant freezes federal funding at $16.4 billion per year from FY 1996 to FY 2003, which is $1.2 billion less than the states would have received collectively under AFDC, a shortfall that will reach about $1 billion a year by 2002 (Super et al., 1996). TANF dollars for income support and work programs will be allocated based on a state's past spending for these programs, without regard to changes in the state's needs. States can choose to calculate their federal funding based on the average of federal payments for these programs in 1992 through 1994, federal payments in FY 1994, or federal payments in FY 1995. These formulas provide states whose caseloads fell after 1994 (because of coercive policies or improved local economies) with a temporary fiscal windfall, until a recession or population growth increases their caseload. State costs will rise as well, because TANF requires the states to expand enrollment in their work programs.

Under pressure from state governors, TANF established several contingency funds. The largest—$2 billion—is earmarked for those states that experience a recession between 1996 and 2001. During this period, states with high unemployment rates or sharp increases in food stamp participation can apply for funds equal to 20 percent of their base grant. Another $800 million fund was created for states that face exceptionally high population growth during this period. There is also a $1.7 billion loan fund. However, these small funds cannot address the need. During the relatively mild recession of 1990 to 1992, federal AFDC spending increased by $6 billion—triple the amount of the TANF five-year contingency fund. Current projections suggest a 4.6 percent increase in the nation's population between 1996 and 2001, which is more than four times greater than the growth of TANF's population fund. Insufficient funding virtually ensures that large numbers of children whose parents cannot find a job will be denied assistance under TANF, unless states commit more of their own funds. However, according to a Cato Institute report, tax cuts, spending limits, and other signs of fiscal conservatism are on the rise in many states (More & Stansel, 1996).

In addition to federal funding shortfalls, TANF allows the states to withdraw substantial amounts of state resources from basic income support and work programs. AFDC required states to contribute 20 percent to 50 percent of the program's costs, with wealthier states paying more than poorer ones. For each federal dollar not matched with state funds, states lost between $1 and $4 in federal funds. TANF's weak maintenance-of-effort provision eliminates AFDC's stronger incentive to spend. States must maintain funding at 75 percent of what they spent on work, income support, and child care programs in 1994 to receive the full federal block grant; this requirement rises to 80 percent of 1994 spending for states that fail to meet the law's work requirement. However, states may transfer up to 30 percent of the TANF block grant to the child care and development block grant; of this, 10 percent can be channeled to the Title XX social services block grant. Given that other federal funds for these politically popular social services targeted to better-off individuals and families have been cut by 15 percent, the temptation by the states to transfer the funds will be strong. Although TANF disallows its funds to be used for families with incomes above 200 percent of the poverty line, the Center on Budget and Policy Priorities has predicted that because of enforcement difficulties, the transfer provision could lead states to withdraw $40 billion from welfare and work programs for the very poor between FY 1996 and FY 2002 (Super et al., 1996).

MYTHS AND FACTS DRIVING WELFARE REFORM

The welfare reform drive that resulted in TANF reflected deep, but often misinformed, concerns about the size and cost of providing cash assistance to the poor. It was widely assumed that AFDC—called "welfare" by the public and "the system" by recipients—was a large, ever-expanding program that supplied many undeserving people with overly generous benefits. The public was encouraged to blame the growth of AFDC on the "irresponsible" work, marital, and childbearing behavior of poor women and the mounting deficit on

spending for AFDC. However, prevailing data suggest that these public perceptions seriously oversimplified and distorted the issues.

AFDC Caseload: Large and Ever Expanding
The widely held belief that AFDC is a large and ever expanding program helped build support for replacing it with TANF. However, the public perception of the size and growth of AFDC was not fact based. The AFDC caseload jumped sharply from 1.9 million families in 1970 to 2.9 million in 1972. However, from 1972 to 1990 the number stabilized, fluctuating from a high of 3.9 million during economic downturns to a low of 3.1 million families in better times. By the end of the 1980s, because of stagnating wages; corporate downsizing; high rates of unemployment; and decreased access to food stamps, unemployment insurance, and other benefits, the number of families in need soared, as did the number of families receiving AFDC. The AFDC caseload grew again in the early 1990s during a recession, reaching 4.3 million families in 1991 and 5 million in 1994. The number of recipients dropped off to 4.8 million in 1995 as a result of both state cuts and the end of the economic downturn (U.S. Department of Health and Human Services, 1996; U.S. House of Representatives, 1994). In summary, the expansion of AFDC between 1970 to 1995 is best understood as an inevitable outcome of normal population increases, fluctuating economic conditions, changes in the rules of other social programs, and other forces over which individuals had little or no control. In earlier periods political pressure and grassroots turbulence also influenced the expansion and contraction of AFDC (Epsing-Anderson, 1990; Orloff, 1993; Piven & Cloward, 1971). However, then, as now, the number of recipients was always limited by the stigma surrounding AFDC and public hostility to the program.

Those who blamed AFDC's growth spurts on the allegedly irresponsible values and behavior of poor people failed to note that more than two-thirds of the 14.2 million AFDC recipients were children, 75 percent of whom were under age 10. The children on AFDC accounted for 14 percent of the U.S. population under age 18 and 63 percent of the children in poverty (U.S. Department of Health and Human Services, 1995b; U.S. House of Representatives, 1994). The welfare critics also ignored that the program grew slowly throughout most of the

1970s and 1980s and that in most of the years between 1970 and 1995, the caseload made up only 4 percent to 5 percent of the total U.S. population. This was about the same percentage as received SSI and far less than the percentage receiving social security, Medicare, unemployment insurance, and food stamps. The critics did not complain that in 1990, 49 percent of the people in the United States received some type of direct government payment. In addition, many middle- and upper-class families claimed indirect government benefits through tax deductions for dependents, housing, health care, and education (Abramovitz, 1983; Wines, 1994). The enormous subsidies and tax breaks given by the government to large corporations drain the U.S. treasury far more than do social benefits, but these are never regarded as a handout.

Program Costs: Fast Growing and Draining the Federal Treasury

The myths surrounding the size of AFDC are matched by misperceptions about its cost. In 1995 total federal and state spending for AFDC amounted to $25 billion, up from $21 billion in 1990 and $16.5 billion in 1985 (U.S. Department of Health and Human Services, 1996; U.S. House of Representatives, 1994). Contrary to popular wisdom, few of these dollars go to administrative expenses. In 1995, for example, 88 percent of the $25 billion went for benefits and 12 percent for administration; these percentages have remained relatively unchanged since the early 1970s (U.S. Department of Health and Human Services, 1996).

The second misperception about AFDC spending is that it absorbs too much of the federal budget, leading some to blame it for the deficit. However, the federal government spent about $14 billion for AFDC in 1995, or less than 1 percent of its more than $1.5 trillion budget (Congressional Budget Office, 1995). This percentage has remained steady since the mid-1980s, and in previous decades spending for AFDC never amounted to more than 1.7 percent of all federal expenditures (Center on Social Welfare Policy and Law, 1996c). Although AFDC has absorbed fewer public dollars than was popularly imagined, its cost has always sparked controversy, and frequently it became a "lightning rod" for those opposed to all social welfare spending.

Cash Benefits: Living "High on the Hog"

A third misperception about AFDC pertains to its benefits. Critics from the right regularly argued that AFDC benefits were overly generous. However, in 1994 the average AFDC payment for a three-person family (not adjusted for inflation) was $377 per month, up from $275 in 1980 and $178 in 1970. Set by the states, these benefits varied widely nationwide. The average payment for a family of three ranged from a low of $121 in Mississippi to a high of $846 in Alaska (U.S. Department of Health and Human Services, 1995a). AFDC recipients were also entitled to food stamps and Medicaid, although a few states deducted the value of food stamps from the AFDC payment.

Between 1970 and 1994, the notoriously low AFDC benefit failed to keep pace with inflation, causing the real purchasing power of the grant to plummet 47 percent. Although food stamps offset some of the loss, only in Alaska and Hawaii did the AFDC and food stamp package lift a family of three above the 1994 poverty line of $11,800 a year. In Mississippi, the lowest benefit state, the package equaled only 43 percent of this amount, which is widely considered to be underestimated (U.S. House of Representatives, 1994).

In all but 10 states, the average AFDC benefit for a family of three fell below the state's own official standard of need, which ranged from a high of $1,648 a month in New Hampshire to a low of $320 per month in Indiana (U.S. House of Representatives, 1994) and was typically set far below the state's actual cost of living (Larin & Porter, 1992). From July 1970 to January 1992, the median benefit rose from $232 a month to $579 a month, or 149 percent. Although this may appear to be a large jump, during the same period the Consumer Price Index jumped 275 percent (U.S. House of Representatives, 1994). The Family Support Act of 1988 asked the states to re-evaluate their need standards and report their findings to the U.S. Department of Health and Human Services at least once every three years, but the reporting requirement was subsequently dropped (Larin & Porter, 1992).

AFDC's low benefits are likely to dwindle further now that TANF gives the states greater control over welfare benefits but less money to spend on them. TANF actually permits a state to provide *no* income support benefits at all and instead to limit itself to services such as homeless shelters, work farms, and poorhouses. Now that the federal prohibition on reducing benefits below 1988 levels is gone, some states have already proposed to slash the welfare grant and provide different amounts to different groups. Even before TANF, some states had cut their grants, and other states, such as New York, applied for a waiver to drop benefits below what existing federal law permitted. The package of cash assistance and food stamps will shrink as well, because Title VIII of the PRA of 1996 reduced the food stamp benefit and tightened its work requirements (Super et al., 1996).

Advocates for the poor have consistently called for a national minimum benefit to eliminate interstate inequities and to make the grant more adequate. An early version of the Family Support Act included higher benefits, but this proposal did not survive the political process. Over the years welfare rights advo-cates have successfully challenged the states in court for failure to match AFDC benefits state need standards, but these court victories have not resulted in higher benefits. In July 1996, the Urban Institute reported that if the proposed welfare bill became law, the income of one in five U.S. families with children (8.2 million families) would fall an average of $1,300 a year. The legislation, it concluded, would push 1.1 million children and 2.6 million people into poverty and deepen the destitution of those already impoverished (Super et al., 1996). This helps explain why active welfare rights organizations are still calling for a guaranteed annual income.

Time Spent on Welfare: Lazy Freeloaders Trapped by Welfare

Myths also abound about the work values of the poor. The introduction of punitive time limits and stiff work requirements derives from stereotypic images of women on welfare as lazy freeloaders who consistently choose welfare over work. TANF imposes strict new rules despite widely cited studies showing that most AFDC families spend only a few years on welfare (Ellwood & Bane, 1983). Indeed, less than half the families of AFDC received benefits for more than a total of 36 months overall, counting all the times on welfare. Most families use AFDC for no more than two years at a time and in many cases, the period of continuous receipt of benefits is even shorter (Center on Social Welfare Policy and Law, 1996c). The picture of welfare use is confusing because there are really

two populations to consider and two time frames. During the course of a year, most welfare families spend only a short time on AFDC. However, on any one day of that year, the majority of recipients on welfare are in the midst of a long stay. In brief, while the majority of women move on and off welfare rather quickly, a smaller group end up using the program for a long time. Of the first group, many package welfare and work simultaneously or sequentially on the basis of changing life circumstances. The women who leave welfare and then return to the rolls do so because of factors that are often beyond their control: a lost job, failed relationship, poor health, unexpected family problems, and changes in the condition of the local economy (Pavetti, 1993; Spalter-Roth, Hartmann, & Andrews, 1992).

Research on intergenerational use of welfare is basically inconclusive. Although daughters of welfare mothers are more likely than daughters of nonrecipients to use welfare as adults, the findings are mixed as to the number of welfare daughters who turn to AFDC later on. In their review of the literature, McLanahan and Garfinkel (1989) found one study (Gottschalk, 1988) that reported that within seven years of leaving home, about 60 percent of the welfare daughters used welfare for at least 12 months. However, another study found that only 36 percent of the daughters did so (Duncan, Hill, & Hoffman, 1988; U.S. House of Representatives, 1994). The percentage of welfare daughters is higher among African American than white women and higher among unmarried than divorced women. Because most studies did not control for confounding variables, even where intergenerational welfare use is high, it is unclear whether the cause is welfare, poverty, or something else.

AFDC and Marriage: Welfare Causes Family Breakup

In addition to a having a faulty work ethic, women on welfare are portrayed by welfare critics as lacking "family values." Based on the belief that AFDC encouraged families to break up, TANF made promotion of marriage and two-parent households one of its stated purposes. However, studies of welfare and family composi-tion have found that AFDC was not a major force in the breakup of U.S. families. Ellwood and Bane (1985) reported that from 1968 to 1980, almost half the AFDC awards started after a separation or widowhood—conditions that plunged women into poverty—or after unmarried childless women gave birth. According to the U.S. Bureau of the Census (1992), a decline into poverty significantly increases the chances that a two parent family will break up. Only after the marriage dissolved was the mother–child unit eligible for AFDC. This report confirmed the results of earlier studies that found that welfare benefits have little or no consistent impact on marital stability (Moffitt, 1991; Wilson & Neckerman, 1986). Time series data have also failed to find a fixed relationship between welfare and family structure.

AFDC and Childbearing Choices: Having Children for Money

TANF also seeks to prevent and reduce nonmarital pregnancies on the belief that poor women have children to receive money and that AFDC encouraged excessive childbearing and large families. As noted earlier, TANF permits states to deny aid to children born to mothers on welfare, institutes more stringent paternity establishment, funds abstinence programs, and rewards states that reduce their nonmarital birth rate. One stereotype driving these changes holds that women on AFDC have inordinately large families. However, the average AFDC family includes only two children, the national average. Moreover, as part of the overall decline in family size, welfare families have also become smaller. In 1994, 73 percent of 5 million AFDC families had two or fewer children, compared with 49 percent in 1969. Likewise only 10 percent had four or more children in 1994, down from 32.5 percent in 1969 (Duvall, 1987; U.S. Department of Health and Human Services, 1995a).

Critics also hold AFDC responsible for the rising rate of nonmarital births among poor women. However, studies have suggested that 40 percent to 50 percent of women turned to AFDC after their marital or financial circumstances deteriorated, and in most cases they had been caring for at least one child for about two years (Center on Social Welfare Policy and Law, 1996a). Government figures indicate that 77 percent of the children receiving AFDC were born before their mother was on the rolls. Likewise, Williams (1992) noted that all the mothers she surveyed said that the ability to receive AFDC had no effect on the decision to have a child. Earlier studies from the mid-1970s found that women on welfare were less likely to refrain from using contraceptives, less likely

to desire an additional pregnancy, and less likely to become pregnant than women not on public assistance (Wilson & Neckerman, 1986).

Trend data also refute the notion that AFDC promoted nonmarital births. Although the number of such births is higher among poor people, their rate has increased among both poor and middle-class women. Second, the value of welfare benefits and the rate of nonmarital births rose together in the 1960s and early 1970s, but the nonmarital birth rate continued to rise after the value of welfare benefits fell. Third, states with higher benefits do not have higher nonmarital or teenage birth rates (Jencks & Edin, 1990; Moore, 1992; Shapiro et al., 1991; Wilson & Neckerman, 1986). In addition, despite their more generous welfare benefits, European countries have far lower teenage pregnancy rates than the United States (Smeeding, 1991).

General demographic data indicate that births to single mothers have increased among women in all walks of life. Between 1960 and 1990, while the share of all births that were nonmarital more than quintupled, rising from 5 percent to 29 percent, the annual nonmarital birth rate rose from two births for every 100 single women to four. Although the increase in the annual nonmarital birth rate was significant, it was much smaller than its increased share of the total birth rate. The explanation for the difference suggests that contrary to popular opinion, rising birth rates among single mothers reflect demographic shifts rather than looser morals. During the same 30 years more and more women of child-bearing age delayed getting married, and the annual birth rate for married women dropped from 16 percent to 9 percent of all births. Delayed marriages and the declining fertility of married women shrank their share of all births statistically. Thus, when demographers took their count, the percentage of all births to unmarried women was much higher than that of births to married women. For example, from 1930 to 1960, among African American women, the share of nonmarital births rose from 23 percent to 65 percent, although the annual birth rate for single African American women declined from 10 percent in 1960 to 9 percent in 1990. Among white women, the share of nonmarital births rose from 36 percent to 60 percent while the annual birth rate rose from 1 percent to 3 percent. Many social and economic changes in the United States help to explain the rise of nonmarital births among white women and the higher but declining rates among African American women. However, the data on the relationship between the value of welfare benefits and nonmarital birth rates noted above suggest that welfare is not one of them (Center on Social Welfare Policy and Law, 1996c).

AFDC: A Proxy for Race
The stereotypic image of the "promiscuous black welfare queen" lies at the heart of the welfare reform debate despite data suggesting more complex realities (Christensen, 1996, p. 14). The racial composition of the program varies widely by state. The proportion of AFDC families who are white ranges from 0.2 percent in Washington, DC, to 97.1 percent in Vermont. In the nine states that serve more than 100,000 AFDC families, the proportion of white families ranged from a low of 18.1 percent in Texas to a high of 58.4 percent in Ohio (Center on Budget and Policy Priorities, Center on Social Welfare Policy and Law, & Children's Defense Fund, 1992).

The racial composition of AFDC has also changed over time. The proportion of AFDC families who were white rose from 38 percent in 1973 to 42 percent in 1983, after which it fell back to 37 percent in 1994. In contrast, during the same period, the African American share of the caseload fell steadily from 46 percent in 1973 to 44 percent in 1983 to 36 percent in 1994. Currently, the percentages of African American and white people on welfare are nearly equal. The major growth in the AFDC rolls during the past 20 years took place among Latinos, whose numbers increased from 13 percent of all families in 1973 to nearly 20 percent in 1994. Native Americans hovered around 1 percent and Asians around 3 percent of the total caseload (Duvall, 1987; U.S. Department of Health and Human Services, 1995a; U.S. House of Representatives, 1994).

The way that the numbers are counted also makes a difference. In 1990, in any one month about half of African American and Latino families received benefits (Congressional Budget Office, 1991). However, over time, that is, throughout the entire year, many more white families than African American and Latino families received benefits (Center on Social Welfare Policy and Law, 1996c). Because AFDC is a means-tested program that serves only poor people, the overrepresentation of families of

color on welfare relative to their numbers in the population and the underrepresentation of whites reflects the degree to which each group is vulnerable to poverty.

The higher poverty rates for families of color and the fact that whites move off welfare faster than African American and Latino families stems from the relationship between racism and poverty. Contrary to popular misconception, people of color still suffer unequal treatment on the basis of race in employment, education, housing, the courts, and the health care system, to mention only some spheres of American life in which individual prejudice, exclusionary policies, and the more subtle impact of institutionalized racism (and xenophobia) are at play (see for example, Applebome, 1996; Hacker, 1992; Schemo, 1994; Unequal Sentencing, 1996). Instead of addressing these and the underlying causes of poverty among all groups in our society, "talking about welfare has been a way for mostly white pundits, policy makers, and ordinary white Americans to acceptably refer to the nearly subconscious racialized stereotype of women of color's sexuality; a way to exploit for political gain some of America's deepest racial fears and resentments; and to pay homage to the old, theocratic undertow in American politics, all the while remaining within polite 'mainstream' or even 'liberal' discourse" (Christensen, 1996, p. 14).

Welfare Magnets
In addition to work and family issues, welfare reform has been driven by the erroneous belief that higher welfare benefits draw women from one state to another like a magnet. However, in reality, very few poor families move from state to state, and those who do are as likely to settle in states with lower AFDC benefits as they are to move to states with higher benefits. For example, from 1982 to 1988, slightly more poor women of childbearing age moved from California to Texas—where AFDC benefits were one-third lower—than moved from Texas to California. Researchers have found that labor market conditions and weather patterns play a larger role in poor people's decision to move than welfare policy (Center on Social Welfare Policy and Law, 1996c). They have also reported that (1) the high cost of moving (for example, transportation expenses, a security deposit for a new apartment, and time spent in transit without income from employment or AFDC), (2) lack of

information about income opportunities in other states, and (3) the presence of family and friends in their current location all make it very unlikely that welfare recipients decide to move based on more attractive benefits elsewhere.

HISTORY OF AFDC

Mother's Pensions

The idea of providing aid to single mothers and their children stems from the 1909 White House Conference on Children, which recommended that children of "worthy" mothers who are deprived of breadwinner support be kept with their parents and given aid "as may be necessary to maintain suitable homes for the rearing of children" (Abramovitz, 1996a, p. 7). Advocates of mother's pensions hoped the new program would empty the increasingly costly orphanages that were filled with children whose parents were alive but were too poor to provide for them; they also hoped that the pension program would be more generous and dignified than the prevailing system of local relief for widows and their children.

From 1911 to 1920, 40 states enacted mother's pension laws in a movement spearheaded largely by women reformers, the forerunners of social workers. By 1935, all but two states had such a law. However, because implementation was optional, fewer than half the counties nationwide actually offered a pension prior to the 1935 Social Security Act. Those that did tended to reserve the grants for the "deserving" poor—that is, those who passed a test of moral conduct as well as a test of financial need. As a reflection of prevailing attitudes toward race and gender, most recipients of mother's pensions turned out to be widowed and white. Only a few states aided deserted, divorced, or unmarried mothers or women of color (Bell, 1965). Despite the plan to help them to stay home, most "pensioned" mothers worked for wages, because they could not subsist on the program's meager benefits. Mother's pensions became the philosophical and operational model for the Aid to Dependent Children program that was added to the 1935 Social Security Act.

AFDC and the 1935 Social Security Act

The deterioration of the economy, mounting social unrest, and massive unemployment during the Great Depression forced President Franklin Roosevelt and Congress to enact the Social Security Act six years after the 1929 stock market crash. The act was part of a larger effort to stimulate purchasing power, stabilize the political economy, quiet social unrest, and maintain the legitimacy of the government. By shifting social welfare responsibilities from the states to the federal government, this landmark legislation launched the modern U.S. welfare state—albeit much later than in most other Western industrialized nations.

The needs of women were not a high priority for the architects of the Social Security Act. The original act covered only retired workers, most of whom at that time were men. The men's nonemployed wives and children were not insured until the Social Security Act was amended in 1939 to include benefits for a worker's dependents. Although many African American women worked for wages in 1935, the major occupations open to them at the time—farm labor and domestic work—were excluded from the Social Security Act, leaving those workers without any coverage at all.

The initial version of the social security legislation was more comprehensive than the final bill. Congress struck a more far-reaching proposal mandating the states to furnish families with subsistence "compatible with health and decency" in deference to Southern legislators who feared resulting higher benefits would force the South to raise the pay of black tenant farmers and otherwise match the higher Northern wage standards (Bell, 1965). Southern legislators also succeeded in defeating the more inclusive eligibility provisions requiring the states to provide relief to any citizen who met the age and need criteria (Abbott, 1938). That the National Industrial Recovery Act (1933), the Agricultural Adjustment Act of 1933, the Fair Labor Standards Act of 1938, and other New Deal programs similarly excluded African Americans, giving support to those who argue that President Roosevelt was unwilling to use political capital to settle race issues or to provide more than limited support for civil rights (Kirby, 1972; Wye, 1972).

The Social Security Act also distinguished among women as "deserving" or "undeserving" of aid. On the basis of an idealized image of womanhood, the act's programs favored married or previously married women and women who lacked a breadwinner through no fault of their own (such as widows and wives of sick, disabled, and temporarily unemployed men) over single mothers, abandoned wives, and women whose breadwinner did not provide adequate support. The "undeserving" women tended to be poor or immigrant women or women of color whose poverty and other life circumstances prevented them from following the mainstream's idealized version of wife and motherhood (Abramovitz, 1996a).

The categorization of women as deserving or undeserving of aid based on standard definitions of women's roles deeply influenced the development of the AFDC program. Were poor women who applied for income support "proper" women who would provide "good" care for their children, or were they "deviants" who should be penalized for violating work and family norms? If not for the women's network in the 1930s (which included Eleanor Roosevelt), AFDC might never have become part of the Social Security Act. Poor mother's were a special concern of this group, which had already fought for and won mother's pensions (1911 through 1920), establishment of the Children's Bureau (1912), passage of the Sheppard–Towner Act, also called the Maternity Act (1921), and positions in the Roosevelt administration (Muncy, 1991; Ware, 1981; Witte, 1963). Unfortunately, the early reformers were products of their time and, like many others, accepted prevailing views of worthy and unworthy womanhood.

AFDC, 1935 through 1977

From the start the AFDC program penalized women for departing from the prescribed roles of wife and mother. Individual states took longer to implement AFDC than other public assistance programs and set benefits well below those for elderly and blind aid recipients. Until 1950, the AFDC grant included funds for children but not their mothers, forcing many women to work outside the home. Beginning in 1939, the survivors' insurance component of the social security program began to provide benefits to a worker's widow and children, as well as to some divorced women. This left AFDC for the abandoned, separated, and unmarried women who were viewed by society as less deserving of aid because they departed from conventional wife and mother roles. Because racial discrimination barred African American men from the social security pension, their widows had no choice but to apply for AFDC. However, by the 1940s, many states, mostly in the South, refused to extend AFDC benefits to African American women, so that employers would be supplied with the low-cost labor force they needed, especially female domestic workers (Bell, 1965).

By the 1950s, a variety of complex social, economic, and demographic changes led never-married mothers and African American women to became overrepresented in the AFDC program (Trattner, 1989). The African American caseload grew because of poverty, dislocations following the mechanization of Southern agriculture (which forced more than 20 million people off the land between 1940 and 1970), and subsequent employment discrimination in the North as well as in the South. In the late 1950s, the changing and expanding caseload combined with McCarthyism to fuel another harsh attack on public welfare, especially AFDC (Axinn & Levin, 1982).

Regulating Women's Sexuality and Childbearing

As a result of prevailing but inaccurate views that most women on welfare were African American and that African American and poor women were by definition "immoral," in the 1940s and 1950s, state welfare departments intensified their use of behavioral standards as a condition of aid (Myrdal, 1944). By 1960, the man-in-the-house and suitable-home rules that equated unmarried motherhood with unfit motherhood were used in about half the states to deny AFDC to thousands of poor mother-only families. Under pressure from civil rights and welfare rights activists, the federal government eventually limited, but did not disallow, the use of these moral fitness rules. Bell (1965) suggested that the mounting hostility to AFDC during the years after World War II, and some of its virulence, were in part a backlash to the growing strength of the civil rights movement. By 1967, in the wake of urban uprisings, Congress made AFDC policy more punitive. The Social Security Amendments of 1967 (P.L. 90-248) reintroduced behavioral standards as a condition of aid by imposing a freeze on the number of "illegitimate" children who could receive AFDC. However, the freeze, which covered children of never-married women but not children of deceased or unemployed fathers, became too politically controversial to implement.

Work Incentives

The poverty and social problems that followed World War II increased the demand for welfare among the poor (Ehrenreich, 1985). Faced with larger welfare rolls and unable to make "immoral" behavior a condition of aid, the states looked for new ways to reduce welfare costs. The Social Security Amendments of 1956 included social services provisions, but no funds were appropriated. However, the 1962 amendments (P.L. 87-534) to the act authorized federal funds for counseling and employment services in the hope that such services would move women from welfare to work. The amendments, which the social work profession played a role in securing, included a new work incentive: AFDC recipients could keep a portion of their earned income. The amendments also established the AFDC–UP program for a limited group of unemployed fathers. However, the shift to services and work incentives did not redress the so-called "welfare crisis." The rolls continued to grow as a result of inadequate funding for the promised services, administrative barriers, the lack of both jobs and child care services, and a serious misdiagnosis of the causes of poverty and welfare use. Critics blamed both poverty and mounting welfare costs on the never fully implemented "soft" social services and "irresponsible" behavior of poor people. In response to the call for new and stiffer work requirements, in the mid-1960s Congress experimented with work incentives and the Community Work Experience Program, a harbinger of today's workfare. Among other things, to the extent that it occurred, moving women from welfare to the labor market helped increase the supply of low-paid workers and to keep wages down.

The more punitive 1967 amendments created the Work Incentive Program, or WIN, which stiffened the work rules of AFDC by making participation in a work program a condition of aid. Nonexempt welfare mothers were required to enter a job-training or work placement program, with the promise of help with child care, employment, and social services. WIN II, enacted in 1971, added more punitive sanctions for nonparticipation. By all accounts, WIN placed too few women in jobs; cost too much; and suffered from inadequate child care services, lack of appropriate jobs, sex and race discrimination, and administrative flaws (Rein, 1982) similar to those faced by the subsequent Family Support Act of 1988. On the other hand, WIN directly or indirectly sent many women into low-paid jobs. In 1977

President Jimmy Carter unsuccessfully attempted another major welfare reform program, the Program for Better Jobs and Income, which included work incentives, strict work rules, a public works program, and differential treatment for "deserving" and "undeserving" poor people (Handler & Hasenfeld, 1991).

Welfare Reform: From Reagan to the Family Support Act of 1988

Despite the limited success of WIN, work-oriented welfare reform became the hallmark of the Reagan administration, which promoted economic recovery by redistributing income from the poor to the rich. Seeking to increase profits by lowering wages, reducing the overall standard of living, and weakening the influence of trade unions, the Reagan administration launched an attack on unions, the minimum wage, and the welfare state. To make sure that people chose low-paid jobs over welfare, the administration concluded that it was necessary to lower social benefits. The Omnibus Budget Reconciliation Act of 1981 (P.L. 97-35) cut domestic programs, strengthened AFDC work requirements, and encouraged states to bear responsibility for social welfare. The Deficit Reduction Act of 1984 (P.L. 98-369) reversed some of the more restrictive AFDC provisions but left the basic package intact (U.S. House of Representatives, 1992).

Family Support Act of 1988

The Family Support Act of 1988 (P.L. 100-485), especially JOBS, transformed AFDC from a program to help single mothers stay home with their children into a mandatory work program. Reminiscent of earlier efforts, JOBS required mothers to go work or school or to enter a job-training program in exchange for benefits and some employment-related services. Welfare mothers who refused to participate faced reduced or terminated benefits. Like its predecessors, the JOBS program foundered on rising unemployment, a proliferation of low-paid jobs, a weak labor market, discrimination, a lack of health benefits, the absence of affordable child care, and too little investment in the program's service component (Riccio & Friedlander, 1992; U.S. General Accounting Office, 1987, 1991). The JOBS programs also suffered from a lack of state funds; a host of implementation problems (Hagen & Lurie, 1992); the poor health and limited education of some women on welfare; and the presence of young children at home, which makes employment difficult for any woman, but especially one with limited means (U.S. General Accounting Office, 1987, 1991).

Paving the Way to TANF Welfare Reform in the 1990s

State waivers. The Family Support Act of 1988 legitimized the use of federal dollars to leverage behavioral change and paved the way for a second round of welfare reforms that targeted the work, marital, childbearing, and parenting behavior of poor women. During the drawn-out debate over President Clinton's proposal to "end welfare as we know it," many states applied for waivers to experiment with their own programs.

Drawing on the myths about welfare and work, nearly 30 states applied for and won approval for federal waivers that allow them to impose a lifetime limit on AFDC recipiency, which opened the door to lifetime limits on TANF benefits. Based on negative perceptions of single motherhood, the states also won approval for programs designed to promote marriage, limit family size, improve parenting, and otherwise promote "family values." They rewarded marriage by exempting a stepparent's income when calculating the AFDC benefit but denying the same advantage to mothers who married the biological father of their children, on the grounds that fathers, unlike stepparents, are by definition responsible for providing support. More than 15 states penalized single mothers by denying aid to children born to women on welfare. A few states also considered making the use of levonorgestrel (Norplant), a long-lasting contraceptive implant, a condition of aid. Some also secured federal waivers for "learnfare" and "healthfare" programs, which were designed to regulate the parenting behavior of poor women by docking their AFDC check if their children had too many absences from school or did not receive their immunization shots in a timely fashion. The states also initiated "reforms" to penalize women on welfare who moved from low to higher benefit states and to prevent immigrants, both those with and those without proper papers, to receive aid; both of these reforms later ran into trouble in the courts.

The Contract with America. The November 1994 elections swept the Republican Party into office and placed the "Contract with America" on the congressional agenda. The welfare reform plank of the contract intensified the prevailing behavior modification ideas proposed by President Clinton. Along the way the Republicans began to place even greater emphasis on "family values," strongly recommended the child exclusion, and argued strenuously that ending welfare would effectively stigmatize "illegitimacy" and single motherhood. Even more dramatic, the contract breathed new life into the idea of ending entitlements. Its "devolution revolution" called for stripping major social welfare programs of their entitlement status, replacing federal social welfare funding with block grants to the states, transferring social welfare responsibility from the federal to the state governments, privatizing social programs, and otherwise weakening the underpinning of the U.S. welfare state.

Harsh and punitive welfare reforms gained ground during the 1990s, despite 20 years of research showing that the configuration of welfare benefits does not shape women's work, marital, parenting, or migration decisions (Moffitt, 1991); two decades of failed efforts to mount effective welfare-to-work programs (Rein, 1982); and more recent evaluations showing that welfare-to-work programs resulted in only modest gains (Riccio & Friedlander, 1992). The dismissal of both the large body of research and the poor history of coercive measures suggests that the current assault on AFDC, like previous ones, may be serving political rather than social welfare ends. These ends include legitimizing the work ethic (Piven & Cloward, 1971), punishing women viewed as departing from prescribed wife and mother roles (Abramovitz, 1996b), keeping welfare benefits lower than prevailing wages (Cloward & Piven, 1993), creating the impression that the government is doing something about poverty (Handler & Hasenfeld, 1991), and deflecting attention from the underlying causes of the nation's mounting economic distress rooted in, among other things, the downsizing of firms, the deindustrialization of work, and the export of production abroad. Bashing the poor also helps obscure the fact that increased economic insecurity among the working and middle classes—evidenced by the feminization of poverty, the rise of the working poor, the decline of the middle class, and the complaints of "angry white men"—has fueled the divisive politics of hate that are tearing the country apart.

ALTERNATIVE APPROACHES

Most of the major welfare reforms since the 1970s have focused on encouraging or forcing AFDC mothers to work or to limit their child-bearing. However, Congress has periodically considered a more positive alternative: some version of a negative income tax (an income subsidy provided to taxpayers in the form of a grant that raises their income to some specified level).

Family Assistance Plan

In 1969, President Nixon introduced one version of the negative income tax known as the Family Assistance Plan (FAP). It promised $1,600 minimum annual income (about 45 percent of the prevailing poverty level) for families of four through tax rebates, allowed recipients to keep other government benefits, and provided fiscal relief for the states. Proposed by a conservative president and designed for poor families with children regardless of the family head's employment status, FAP was ultimately defeated because of liberal opposition to its low minimum grant (the National Welfare Rights Organization called for a $5,500 minimum) and conservative fears that a guaranteed income would undercut the supply of low-wage workers and blur the line between the deserving and the undeserving poor (Handler & Hasenfeld, 1991).

Earned Income Tax Credit

In 1975, Congress enacted the Earned Income Tax Credit (EITC), a wage subsidy for the working, but not the welfare, poor. The initial credit, which refunded 10 percent of earned income up to $8,000, was originally conceived as a "work bonus" to offset social security taxes paid by low-wage workers (Handler & Hasenfeld, 1991). Underused for many years, EITC became permanent in 1979 and was made more generous over time. It gained the attention of advocates in the mid-1980s and was adopted by President Clinton in the early 1990s. The Clinton plan expanded the credit to ensure that a family of four with a full-time minimum-wage worker would be lifted out of poverty by a combination of the EITC and food stamps. The plan also provided a smaller credit to childless workers.

Tax credits represent a step toward a more universal and unstigmatized system of income support. As an employment-based benefit, such plans have the potential to help working poor people, including employed welfare mothers, who can combine wages and welfare (Spalter-Roth et al., 1992). However, EITC does not cover nonworking welfare mothers or other poor people who have no income as a result of lack of employment. Downsizing, deindustrialization, outsourcing jobs, and other features of the current economic restructuring have slowed the creation of new jobs, contributed to high rates of unemployment during much of the last two decades, and otherwise impaired the capacity of the labor market to provide jobs for all those seeking work. It is widely accepted that the official unemployment figures fail to count many long-term jobless workers—called "discouraged workers" by the U.S. Department of Labor—because they have given up looking for a job after months of pounding the pavement.

Programs in Other Countries

Western industrialized capitalist countries have mounted effective social programs. One well-known study during the 1980s (Smeeding, 1991) looked at seven countries (Canada, Australia, Great Britain, Germany, the Netherlands, France, and Sweden) with pretransfer poverty rates (that is, poverty rates before counting the impact of income support programs) similar to that of the United States. The study found that the income maintenance programs in these countries reduced poverty by an average of 16.5 percentage points, compared with only 6.6 percentage points in the United States. As for welfare, U.S. programs for poor women lifted fewer than 5 percent of single mothers with children out of poverty, compared with 89 percent in the Netherlands, 81 percent in Sweden, 75 percent in Great Britain, 50 percent in France, 33 percent in Germany, and 18.3 percent in Canada. Among single-parent families with children in the United States, poverty dropped fewer than 4 percentage points, whereas poverty plummeted nearly 30 percentage points in the other countries (Blank, 1988; Smeeding, 1991). The European programs work better than America's because those countries invest more money, provide higher benefits, pay child allowances that are not tied to mothers' work efforts, recognize the special needs of single-parent families, and rely on comprehensive programs for all people rather than income-tested programs just for the poor. The effort to retrench these programs in the 1980s and

1990s faced stiff opposition. Even when the programs were cut, the safety nets inherent in the programs emerged much less tattered than those in the United States.

POTENTIAL FOR "REAL" REFORM

If one considers only income support, an agenda for real welfare reform in the United States might include immediate, midterm, and long-term goals. With the passage of TANF, the first step must be damage control. This means minimizing harm by seeking reversal of the program's worst features. In January 1997, the national coalition that mounted the campaign to pressure President Clinton to veto welfare reform has begun a second crusade, this time demanding that he fulfill his promise to fix the problems inherent in this reform. On a more proactive front, real welfare reform would involve raising the public assistance grant, establishing voluntary employment and training programs targeted to skilled jobs, and including college attendance in the definition of acceptable work activities. Still longer-term goals include a national minimum public assistance standard equal to the official poverty line for all families, regardless of family structure; creation of jobs in the public and private sectors that pay above the minimum wage; tax benefits for families with college students; and comprehensive health and child care services.

Universal Family Policy

A more far-reaching change would replace existing public assistance programs with a universal family policy for all families, regardless of family structure. This policy would protect individuals and families from the risk of lost income and reduced capacity to provide care to family members. The Social Security Act programs—both insurance and public assistance—historically have covered the risks of loss of income as a result of retirement, unemployment, illness, disability, and the absence of breadwinner support. Those who crafted the Social Security Act assumed that the income would cover the needs of caretaking as well. However, because of massive changes in demographics, family structure, and women's roles, traditional caretakers are less available to perform their roles. A growing number of families can no longer provide adequate care for children, ill family members, and elders. Declining or lost wages; the growth

of women's labor force participation, dual-earner households, and single-parent families; and nonsupporting fathers have placed new and multiple demands on caretakers, most of whom are women. This reduced caretaking capacity is neither a temporary nor an emergency condition—nor, in most cases, is it a matter of choice. Instead, the need for caretaking supports has become a permanent feature of family life.

If reduced caretaking were recognized as a normative risk because of events largely beyond individual control and were treated similarly to the loss of income for reasons of old age, unemployment, illness, and disability, it could become the basis for a universal family benefit. Such a system might include financing for child care; family leave; flextime; elder care; and cash assistance in the form of child support, negative income taxes, and a family or child allowance. Some of these programs have already been instituted in piecemeal ways. By addressing all families, this approach could mainstream poor single mothers into larger nonstigmatized programs and eliminate the need for a separate cash assistance program for them. It would also implicitly acknowledge that unpaid caretaking work in the home, like paid work in the labor market, is both a service and a contribution to wider society.

Political Action

Promoting any of these agendas for change requires political action by welfare clients, the social work profession, and many others. The forerunners of social work participated in the reform movements that forced expansion of the social welfare provision before World War I and again in the 1930s. In the 1960s, poor African American and some white single mothers organized the National Welfare Rights Organization in alliance with middle-class reformers and legal service attorneys and won a major expansion of the AFDC program (Brenner, 1989; Davis, 1993; Kotz & Kotz, 1977; West, 1981). In the 1990s, welfare mothers around the country began to organize as in years past to improve AFDC, resist punitive welfare reforms, and create a comprehensive and universal income support system that recognizes society's responsibility for meeting basic human needs. This organization is critical. The historical record shows that social policy rarely changes in a progressive direction without pressure from below.

REFERENCES

Abbott, G. (1938). *The child and the state, II*. Chicago: University of Chicago Press.

Abramovitz, M. (1983). Everyone's on welfare: "The role of redistribution in social policy" revisited. *Social Work, 28,* 440–447.

Abramovitz, M. (1992). The Reagan legacy: Undoing class, race and gender accords. *Journal of Sociology and Social Welfare, 19*(1), 91–110.

Abramovitz, M. (1996a). *Regulating the lives of women: Social welfare policy from colonial times to the present* (rev. ed.). Boston: South End Press.

Abramovitz, M. (1996b). *Under attack, fighting back: Women and welfare in the United States*. New York: Monthly Review Press.

Agricultural Adjustment Act of 1933, Ch. 25, title 1, 48 Stat. §1.

Applebome, P. (1996, December 29). After years of gains, minority students start falling behind. *New York Times,* p. A12.

Axinn, J., & Levin, H. (1982). *Social welfare: A history of the American response to need*. New York: Harper & Row.

Bell, W. (1965). *Aid to dependent children*. New York: Columbia University Press.

Bernstein, N. (1996, September 15). Giant companies entering race to run state welfare programs. *New York Times,* pp. A1, A26.

Blank, R. M. (1988). Women's paid work, household income and household well-being. In S. E. Rix (Ed.), *The American woman, 1988–1989: A status report* (pp. 123–161). New York: W. W. Norton.

Borkowski, M. (1996, August 1). Points of disagreement and agreement on the welfare bill. *New York Times,* p. A22

Brenner, J. (1989). Towards a feminist perspective on welfare reform. *Yale Journal of Law and Feminism, 2,* 99–129.

Center for Law and Social Policy. (1996). *The welfare bill's work requirement*. Washington, DC: Author.

Center on Budget and Policy Priorities, Center on Social Welfare Policy and Law, & Children's Defense Fund. (1992). *Selected background material on welfare programs*. Washington, DC: Author.

Center on Social Welfare Policy and Law. (1996a, August 20). Temporary Assistance to Needy Families block grant—Highlights. *Welfare News,* pp. 2–6.

Center on Social Welfare Policy and Law. (1996b, June 3). Waivers continue to transform AFDC. *Welfare News,* p. 4.

Center on Social Welfare Policy and Law. (1996c). *Welfare myths: Fact or fiction*. New York: Author.

Christensen, K. (1996). *Sex, lies and welfare reform or what we talk about when we talk about AFDC.*

Unpublished manuscript, State University of New York, Purchase.

Cloward, R., & Piven, F. F. (1993). A class analysis of welfare. *Monthly Review, 44*(9), 25–31.

Congressional Budget Office. (1991, December). *CBO staff memorandum: A preliminary analysis of growing caseloads in AFDC*. Washington, DC: Author.

Congressional Budget Office. (1995). *An analysis of the president's budgetary proposals for fiscal year 1996*. Washington, DC: U.S. Government Printing Office.

Davis, M. (1993). *Brutal need: Lawyers and the welfare rights movement, 1960–1973*. New Haven, CT: Yale University Press.

Deficit Reduction Act of 1984, P.L. 98-369, 98 Stat. 494, 26 U.S.C. §1 et seq.

Duncan, G., Hill, M., & Hoffman, S. (1988). Welfare dependence within and across generations. *Science, 239,* 467–471.

Duvall, H. (1987, August). *Trends in AFDC recipient characteristics, 1967–1986* [Mimeo]. Paper presented at the workshop for the National Association for Welfare Research and Statistics.

Ehrenreich, J. H. (1985). *The altruistic imagination: A history of social work and social policy in the United States*. Ithaca, NY: Cornell University Press.

Ellwood, D. T., & Bane, M. J. (1985). The impact of AFDC on family structure and living arrangements. *Research in Labor Economics, 7,* 137–297.

Epsing-Anderson, G. (1990). *The three worlds of welfare capitalism*. Princeton, NJ: Princeton University Press.

Fair Labor Standards Act of 1938, Ch. 676, 52 Stat. 1060, 29 U.S.C.A. §201 et seq.

Family Support Act of 1988, P.L. 100-485, 102 Stat. 2343.

Gottschalk, P. (1988). *A proposal to study inter-generational correlation of welfare dependence.* [Mimeo]. Madison: University of Wisconsin Institute for Research on Poverty.

Hacker, A. (1992). *Two nations: Black and white: Separate, hostile and unequal*. New York: Charles Scribner's Sons.

Hagen, J. L., & Lurie, I. (1992). *Implementing JOBS: Initial state choices*. (Summary report). New York: Nelson A. Rockefeller Institute of Government, State University of New York.

Handler, J. F., & Hasenfeld, Y. (1991). *The moral construction of poverty: Welfare reform in America*. Newbury Park, CA: Sage Publications.

Jencks, C., & Edin, K. (1990). The real welfare problem. *American Prospect, 1,* 31–50.

Kirby, J. (1972). The Roosevelt administration and Blacks: An ambivalent legacy. In B. Bernstein & A.

Matusow (Eds.), *Twentieth century America: Recent interpretations* (pp. 265–288). San Diego: Harcourt Brace Jovanovich.

Kotz, N., & Kotz, M. (1977). *A passion for equality: George Wiley and the welfare rights movement.* New York: W. W. Norton.

Larin, K. A., & Porter, K. H. (1992). *Enough to live on: Setting an appropriate AFDC need standard.* Washington, DC: Center on Budget and Policy Priorities.

Maternity Act, Ch. 135, 52 Stat. 224 (1921).

McLanahan, S., & Garfinkel, I. (1989). Single mothers, the underclass and social policy. *Annals of the American Academy of Political and Social Science, 301,* 92–104.

Moffitt, R. (1991). *Incentive effects of the U.S. welfare system* (Special Report Series #48). Madison: University of Wisconsin Institute for Research on Poverty.

Moore, K. S. (1992, January). Facts at a glance. *Child Trends,* pp. 5, T2.

More, S., & Stansel, D. (1996, July 26). A fiscal policy report card on America's governors: 1996. *Policy Analysis,* No. 257, 103.

Muncy, R. (1991). *Creating a female dominion in American reform, 1890–1935.* New York: Oxford University Press.

Myrdal, G. (1944). *An American dilemma.* New York: Harper & Brothers.

National Industrial Recovery Act. 40 U.S.C. §401, §403(a), and §408 (1933).

NOW Legal Defense and Education Fund. (1996). *From the front lines: The impact of violence on poor women.* New York: Author.

Offner, P. (1996). Jobfare, familiar and failed. *New York Times,* p. A27.

Omnibus Budget Reconciliation Act of 1981, P.L. 97-35, 95 Stat. 357.

Orloff, A. S. (1993). Gender and the social rights of citizenship: The comparative analyses of gender relations and welfare states. *American Sociological Review, 58,* 303–328.

Pavetti, L. A. (1993). *The dynamics of welfare and work: Exploring the process by which young women work their way off welfare.* Cambridge, MA: Kennedy School of Government, Harvard University.

Personal Responsibility and Work Opportunity Reconciliation Act of 1996, P.L. 104-193, 110 Stat. 2105.

Piven, F. F., & Cloward R. M. (1971). *Regulating the poor: The functions of public assistance.* New York: Pantheon.

Rein, M. (1982). *Dimensions of welfare policy: Why work strategies haven't worked.* New York: Praeger.

Riccio, J., & Friedlander, D. (1992). *GAIN: Program strategies, participation patterns, and first year impacts in six counties.* New York: Manpower Demonstration Research Corporation.

Schemo, D. J. (1994, March 17). Persistent racial segregation mars suburbs' green dream. *New York Times,* p. A1.

Shapiro, I., Gold, S. S., Sheft, M., Strawn, J., Summer, J., & Greenstein, R. (1991). *The states and the poor: How budget decisions in 1991 affected low-income people.* Washington, DC: Center on Budget and Policy Priorities; and Albany, NY: Center for the Study of the States.

Smeeding, T. M. (1991, September 25). *Cross national perspectives on income security programs. The war on poverty: What worked?* Testimony at hearing before the Congress of the United States Joint Economic Committee. (Luxembourg Income Study, Center for the Study of Population, Policy and Public Policy.) Syracuse, New York: Syracuse University.

Social Security Act (1935). IV A U.S.C. §401.

Social Security Act Amendments of 1956. Ch. 836, 70 Stat. 807.

Social Security Act Amendments of 1962. P.L. 87-534, 76 Stat. 155.

Social Security Act Amendments of 1967. P.L. 90-248, 81 Stat. 821.

Spalter-Roth, R. M., Hartmann, H., & Andrews, L. (1992). *Combining work and welfare: An alternative anti-poverty strategy.* Washington, DC: Institute for Women's Policy Research.

Super, D., Parrott, S., Steinmetz, S., & Mann, C. (1996). *The new welfare law.* Washington, DC: Center on Budget and Policy Priorities.

Trattner, W. (1989). *From poor law to welfare state: A history of social welfare in America.* New York: Free Press.

Unequal sentencing [Editorial]. (1996, April 15). *New York Times,* p. A14.

U.S. Bureau of the Census. (1992). Studies in households and family formation: When households continue, discontinue and form. In D. J. Hernandez (Ed.), *Current population reports* (Series P23-129, No. 129). Washington, DC: U.S. Government Printing Office.

U.S. Department of Health and Human Services, Administration for Children and Families. (1995a). *Characteristics and financial circumstances of AFDC recipients, FY 1994.* Washington, DC: Author.

U.S. Department of Health and Human Services, Administration for Children and Families. (1995b). *Overview of the AFDC program, fiscal year 1994.* Washington, DC: Author.

U.S. Department of Health and Human Services, Administration for Children and Families. (1996). *Time trends, fiscal years 1986–1995, AFDC.* Washington, DC: Author.

U.S. General Accounting Office. (1987). *Work and welfare: Current AFDC work programs and implications for federal policy.* Washington, DC: Author.

U.S. General Accounting Office. (1991). *Welfare to work: States begin JOBS, but fiscal and other problems may impede their progress.* Washington, DC: Author.

U.S. House of Representatives, Committee on Ways and Means. (1992). Overview of entitlement programs: Background material and data on programs within the jurisdiction of the Committee on Ways and Means. In *1992 Green book.* Washington, DC: U.S. Government Printing Office.

U.S. House of Representatives, Committee on Ways and Means. (1994). Overview of entitlement programs: Background material and data on programs within the jurisdiction of the Committee on Ways and Means. In *1994 Green book.* Washington, DC: U.S. Government Printing Office.

U.S. House of Representatives. (1996). *Personal Responsibility and Work Opportunity Reconciliation Act of 1996* (Conference Report to HR 3734, 104th Congress, 2d Session, Report 104-725). Washington, DC: U.S. Government Printing Office.

Ware, S. (1981). *Beyond suffrage: Women in the New Deal.* Cambridge, MA: Harvard University Press.

West, G. (1981). *The National Welfare Rights Organization: The social protest of poor women.* New York: Praeger.

Williams, L. A. (1992). The ideology of division: Behavior modification welfare reform proposals. *Yale Law Review, 102,* 719–746.

Wilson, W. J., & Neckerman, K. M. (1986). Poverty and family structure: The widening gap between evidence and public policy issues. In S. Danziger & D. H. Weinberg (Eds.), *Fighting poverty: What works and what doesn't* (pp. 232–259). Cambridge, MA: Harvard University Press.

Wines, M. (1994, November 20). Taxpayers are angry. They're expensive too. *New York Times,* p. E5

Witte, E. E. (1963). *The development of the Social Security Act.* Madison: University of Wisconsin Press.

Wye, C. (1972). The New Deal and the Negro community: Toward a broader conceptualization. *Journal of American History, 59,* 621–639.

Mimi Abramovitz, DSW, is professor, School of Social Work, Hunter College of the City University of New York, 129 East 79th Street, New York, NY 10021.

For further information see

Aid to Families with Dependent Children; Child Support; Families: Demographic Shifts; Federal Social Legislation from 1961 to 1994; **Federal Social Legislation from 1994 to 1997;** Hunger, Nutrition, and Food Programs; Income Security Overview; Jobs and Earnings; JOBS Program; Poverty; **Social Welfare Expenditures: Private;** Social Welfare Expenditures: Public; Social Planning; Social Security; Social Welfare Policy; Welfare Employment Programs: Evaluation; **Working Poor.**

Key Words

Aid to Families with Dependent Children	Temporary Assistance to Needy Families
public assistance	welfare reform
	women

W

Working Poor
Cynthia J. Rocha

In the United States, poor people are generally thought of as being unemployed or on welfare. Yet there are many people who work, are not on welfare, and still remain poor. The U.S. House of Representatives Committee on Ways and Means (1990) reported that almost 4 million people worked full-time but remained in poverty in 1986. In 1994, of the 24 million adults 17 years of age and older living in poverty, almost 10 million worked some part of the year (May & Porter, 1996). The working poor are typically overlooked by government policies that address poverty. The number of working poor will only increase as low-wage industries continue to expand and welfare reform moves more and more welfare recipients into low-paying jobs (Coulton, 1996). This entry addresses the issues surrounding the working poor. Measures by which the working poor are defined and the characteristics of poor workers are discussed. Recent trends that affect poor workers are summarized, and the causes for these trends are examined. Stresses particular to the working poor are described, and current policy responses to the problem are discussed. Finally, future policy directions to alleviate the problems of poor workers are offered.

DEFINITIONS AND CHARACTERISTICS OF THE WORKING POOR

Defining the Working Poor
The *working poor* are generally defined as individuals who work full-time jobs but still fall below the federal poverty threshold. However, this definition is incomplete without including the underemployed, those part-time workers who want to work full-time jobs (Mishel & Bernstein, 1994). The poverty threshold, originally derived by the Social Security Administration in 1964, is based on the estimated annual cost to a family for a minimally adequate diet. This estimate is multiplied by three to include other living costs and is adjusted for the number of children under 18 years of age in the household. The poverty threshold is adjusted annually for inflation according to changes in the Consumer Price Index (CPI) to represent the same real purchasing power each year (Plotnick, 1989). The official poverty definition counts cash income from all public or private sources before taxes but does not take into account public or private noncash benefits such as food stamps.

The current poverty threshold has been criticized as inadequate in that it either overestimates or underestimates poverty in the United States. Critics who claim that the threshold overestimates poverty argue that tying the poverty line to the CPI ignores substitutions

that can be made by households to keep costs down (Popple & Leighninger, 1993). Another argument for overestimation is that the poverty line does not take into account in-kind welfare benefits (for example, food stamps, Medicaid, and public housing subsidies) that are used by the poor (Butler & Kondratas, 1987). Conversely, many social scientists argue that the poverty line is too low and therefore underestimates the extent of poverty. For example, Plotnick (1989) pointed out that the official poverty line does not subtract income taxes or social security taxes in assessing family poverty. Analysts question whether the amount derived from the economy food budget used to calculate the poverty threshold realistically provides a nutritionally adequate diet (Popple & Leighninger, 1993). Geographic differences in cost of living also are not considered in the poverty threshold, which further calls into question the adequacy of the measure. The inadequacies of the poverty threshold have led many researchers to define poor workers by a number of other measures, including a wage that is less than 70 percent of the median income (Marshall & Marx, 1991) or a wage that falls below the bottom 10th percentile range of all workers (Shapiro & Parrott, 1995); *near-poor* workers have been defined as those having wages that fall below 150 percent or 200 percent of the federal poverty guideline (Rocha, 1994). For this entry the official U.S. government definition—a wage of up to 100 percent of the poverty threshold—is used.

Demographics of Poor Workers

The working poor constitute the fastest growing population in poverty in the United States. In 1990 nearly two of three poor families with children had one or more workers in the family, many of whom worked full-time. In fact, more than 40 percent of new families falling into poverty have two parents who work (Williams, 1994). Although most working families have remained housed, sharp reductions in welfare benefits to the working poor since 1981 have increased the number of working families who have joined the ranks of the homeless (Gulati, 1992).

The working poor population is diverse. Of the 10.1 million poor workers in 1993, 55 percent were white, 22 percent were African American, and 20 percent were Hispanic. African American and Hispanic workers are about three times more likely to fall into poverty as non-Hispanic whites. According to Shapiro and Parrott (1995), poverty wages is one reason for the higher poverty rates of minorities. From 1979 to 1987, minority workers were 33 percent more likely to be working below the poverty line than white workers. This trend constitutes a reversal of the pattern in the 1960s and 1970s, when the proportion of jobs paying higher wages increased for African Americans (Harrison & Gorham, 1992).

About 53 percent of poor workers are women (Shapiro & Parrott, 1995). Female-headed households are overrepresented among the working poor. For example, the U.S. median family income for all families was $35,939 in 1991, but female-headed households had a median income of only $16,692 (U.S. Bureau of the Census, 1992). The U.S. Department of Labor (1993) reported that in 1992, women's median weekly earnings were 75.4 percent of men's earnings. Female-headed households have increased from 10 percent of the total households in 1960 to more than 16 percent in 1985 (Pressman, 1990). Although poverty rates for all single mothers are high, working has not lifted female-headed families out of poverty; more than 51 percent of children in homes with a single mother working live in poverty (Allen-Meares & Roberts, 1995). Female-headed families are the fastest growing population in poverty. This trend has led to predictions that by the year 2000, the poverty population will be composed primarily of women and their children (Dolgoff, Feldstein, & Skolnik, 1993).

According to Shapiro and Parrott (1995), educational and skills deficits contribute to the poverty wages of poor workers. Although one-third of working poor people have less than a high school education, a high school education does not guarantee escape from poverty. In 1994, 10.9 percent of high school graduates lived below the poverty level (May & Porter, 1996). A U.S. Bureau of the Census (1995) report on training and economic status found that the gap in education and earnings is widening. In 1993 monthly earnings for people not completing high school averaged $508, whereas high school graduates averaged $1,080, and college graduates averaged $2,339.

Although knowledge and skill deficits contribute to workers' poverty, more education cannot be seen as the sole answer to the dilemma of the rising numbers of people who work but remain poor. Rank (1994) pointed out in his analysis of welfare dependency that lack of education alone does not cause welfare use but does place the individual in an economically vulnerable position. Even if all workers had a higher educational level, there would still be low-wage jobs to fill. Low-wage work results from broader economic, social, and political forces that lie beyond the direct control of the individual.

CAUSES FOR THE INCREASING NUMBER OF POOR WORKERS

Trends in income and wealth distribution demonstrate some of the stark differences among workers in the United States. In 1994 the lowest 20 percent of families commanded only 3.6 percent of all income in the United States, whereas the top 20 percent commanded 49.1 percent of income (May & Porter, 1996). Assets are distributed even less evenly, with the top 10 percent of wealthy families holding 72.1 percent of assets (Oliver & Shapiro, 1990). During the 1980s the living standards of many families improved, but these gains were not distributed evenly. According to Bradbury (1990), average income for all families rose 8.3 percent in the 1980s. In her analysis of average income from 1979 to 1988, Bradbury reported that the richest 20 percent of Americans gained 14.7 percent in income, whereas the poorest 20 percent lost more than 5 percent in income.

Working poor families lost ground in the 1980s, making less money than at any time in history (Bureau of Labor Statistics, 1996).

While the rich got richer and the poor got poorer, the middle class lost ground as well. In an analysis of 27 years of census data, the Center on Budget and Policy Priorities (May & Porter, 1996) found that the middle 20 percent of families fell from 17.3 percent of income held in 1967 to 15.0 percent of income held in 1994. In fact, at every distribution level except the top 20 percent, household income fell from 1967 to 1994 (Table 1). While the middle class inched lower, the richest households were the only category gaining in income, increasing the gap between the rich and the poor (May & Porter, 1996).

Increases in Low-Paying, Temporary, and Part-Time Employment

Harrison and Gorham (1992) estimated that between 1979 and 1987, high-wage employment rose by only about 2 percent, whereas the number of people working below the poverty line grew by almost 40 percent. The working poor are overrepresented in the lowest paid occupations, including service, low-skilled blue collar, and agricultural jobs (U.S. Bureau of the Census, 1991). About 30 percent of poor workers are employed in service positions, and 22 percent work in low-skilled blue collar jobs (Shapiro & Parrott, 1995). There has been some shift in the United States toward low-income industries such as retail and service; this sector of the job market accounted for 70 percent of all new jobs from 1979 to 1989 (Mishel & Bernstein, 1994). Blank (1994) reported, however, that real wages have declined for both manufacturing jobs and service-sector jobs. Less-skilled workers who

find jobs in manufacturing industries face reduced wage opportunities as well. Reasons for this phenomenon include increasing internationalization, which places less-skilled U.S. workers in competition with less-skilled, lower-paid foreign workers; technological changes, which have increased the demand for more-skilled workers in the United States; and a decline in unionization, which has depressed the wages of the least-skilled workers.

The growth of temporary agencies and the practice of "contracting out" have also affected low-wage workers. *Contracting out* is the process whereby corporations, government industries, or other organizations subcontract part of their work to outside firms (Helper, 1990). When a private or public corporation issues a contract for a service, jobs that previously produced adequate wages with benefits are often lost to smaller contracting firms or to temporary services organizations that offer low wages and no benefits and frequently cut full-time hours down to part-time (Howley, 1990). The population of temporary employees, now the fastest growing category of workers, is estimated to be between 27 million and 37 million workers (Heclo, 1994).

Part-time employment (less than 35 hours per week) has increased in recent years from 16.6 percent of the workforce in 1973 to 18.8 percent in 1993 (Mishel & Bernstein, 1994). This increase has been almost entirely involuntary, reflecting the preferred use of part-time workers by employers and not the preference of the workforce for shorter hours. In part-time and temporary employment, wages are lower, fewer benefits are offered, and little opportunity for advancement is available.

Minimum Wage and Inflation

Although more workers are employed in lower-paying occupations, the rise in full-time workers receiving poverty-level wages is predominantly a result of the decline in the value of the minimum wage. The *minimum wage*, first set in 1938, is a price floor imposed by the federal government on the labor market (Grossman, 1996). Workers' real earnings decrease over time when the minimum wage is not adjusted by Congress for inflation. Figure 1 shows the minimum wage from 1960 to 1995 in unadjusted dollars and adjusted 1995 dollars.

To understand how the minimum wage has changed over time, it must be compared in

TABLE 1

Percent Distribution of Aggregate Household Income, 1967–94

Year	Lowest Fifth	Second Fifth	Middle Fifth	Fourth Fifth	Highest Fifth
1967	4.0	10.8	17.3	24.2	43.8
1970	4.1	10.8	17.4	24.5	43.3
1975	4.3	10.4	17.0	24.7	43.6
1980	4.2	10.2	16.8	24.8	44.1
1985	3.9	9.8	16.2	24.4	45.6
1990	3.9	9.6	15.9	24.0	46.6
1994	3.6	8.9	15.0	23.4	49.1

SOURCE: May, R., & Porter, K. H. (1996). *Poverty and income trends: 1994*. Washington, DC: Center on Budget and Policy Priorities.

dollars that have been adjusted for inflation. As shown in Figure 1, although the minimum wage was $1 per hour in 1960, it was worth $5.15 in 1995 dollars. From 1965 to 1980, the minimum wage rate was increased eight times, from $1.25 to $3.10, keeping up fairly well with inflation and maintaining its value in real dollars. The value of the minimum wage, in 1995 dollars, during this 15-year period ranged from $5.15 in 1960, to a high of $6.64 in 1969, and $5.73 in 1980. After 1980, however, the real value of the minimum wage declined rapidly, reaching an all-time low in 1995 of $4.25. From 1981 to 1989 there were no increases in the minimum wage, and from 1990 to 1995, the minimum wage was increased only twice. During the 15-year period from 1980 to 1995, inflation continued to rise, causing workers' wages to decline in real dollars. The proportion of workers whose wages did not lift them above the poverty level rose from 12.1 percent in 1979 to 16.2 percent in 1993.

In 1996 the annual income from full-time work at the minimum wage was $9,890. For a family of three, whose poverty threshold was $12,980 per year, a full-time minimum wage worker earned only 76.1 percent of the poverty level. For a family of four, whose poverty threshold was $15,600, a full-time minimum wage worker earned only 63.3 percent of the poverty level (Bureau of Labor Statistics, 1996).

In the absence of automatic adjustments for inflation, changes in the minimum wage continue to be a political battleground between conservative and liberal forces. The lack of adjustments has caused the wage rate to decline in buying power over time. For nine

years during the Reagan and Bush administrations, the minimum wage was never raised, accounting for the large dip in real income for poor workers during that time (Bureau of Labor Statistics, 1996).

Under the Clinton administration, the minimum wage was increased in October 1996 to $4.75 per hour and will increase again to $5.15 per hour in the fall of 1997. However, because inflation also continues to rise, workers will not gain much in real income. For example, even with the increase in 1996, the minimum wage will provide an income that is only 76.1 percent of the poverty level for a family of three and 63.3 percent of the poverty level for a family of four (May & Porter, 1996).

Declining Benefits
The problem of lower pay and fewer hours of work is compounded by the decreasing benefits offered to employees through their place of employment. Although the trends in benefits such as pensions and retirement accounts have not been well documented in the literature, employer-provided health care benefits show a disturbing trend. In 1992, 38.9 million people were uninsured (Mishel & Bernstein, 1994). The percentage of Americans covered by employment-related health insurance declined from 62 percent in 1988 to 57.2 percent by 1993. Current coverage for the working poor is even more discouraging and also shows a downward trend in recent years. In 1988, 35.5 percent of working poor families were covered by employment-related health insurance; by 1993 this figure had declined to 30.3 percent (Shapiro & Parrott, 1995). In 1992, 9.8 million children lived in families with no health insurance (Mishel & Bernstein, 1994).

Some of the decline in health insurance coverage is caused by companies that increasingly hire part-time workers and provide fewer benefits because these workers are not full-time employees (Ellwood, 1988). Other factors include jobs that either do not include health care benefits or include health insurance at a price that families cannot afford (Mishel & Bernstein, 1994).

CONSEQUENCES FOR WORKING POOR FAMILIES
Although the stress associated with working while in poverty is relatively undocumented, it is clear that the working poor must simultaneously grapple with the negative effects of poverty and the stressors associated with

FIGURE 1

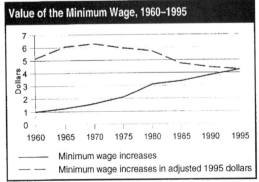

Value of the Minimum Wage, 1960–1995

——— Minimum wage increases

– – – Minimum wage increases in adjusted 1995 dollars

SOURCE: Bureau of Labor Statistics. (1996). *Value of the minimum wage over the last 40 years*. Washington, DC: U.S. Department of Labor. Available online at http://www.dol.gov/dol/esa/public/minwage/chart2.htm.

work. The working poor earn too much to benefit from many of the government subsidies provided to recipients of Aid to Families with Dependent Children (AFDC) but not enough to purchase needed services, such as child care and health care, in the private market.

Child Care

Child care is a major financial strain for working poor parents. The lack of reliable and dependable child care assistance often leads poor workers to lose their jobs (Bowen & Neenan, 1992; Lazere, 1996). Seguino (1995) found that 31 percent of AFDC recipients who had left a previous job did so because of difficulties with child care.

According to Moscovice, Craig, and Pitt (1987), in more than one-fourth of the poor families in their study, children under age 13 were left on their own so that the parents could work. Poor families who pay for child care pay more than one-fourth (27 percent) of their income (Shapiro & Parrott, 1995), compared with all families who, on average, spend about 9 percent of their income on child care (Marshal & Marx, 1991). In Sarri's (1985) study 87 percent of working women surveyed needed child care. Occasionally, older children were kept out of school so they could baby-sit their younger siblings.

Health Care

Although there is little research that assesses the health care of poor workers, there are comparisons of health care use between poor and nonpoor families. Poor workers who lack health care benefits receive less preventive health care. Wolfe (1994), for example, found that poor people were less likely to be vaccinated and that poor children were three times less likely to see a dentist than children in higher income families. Wolfe also found that among the poor, the uninsured poor, rather than the insured poor, use less health care. People living in poverty have poorer health and see physicians less frequently. The inadequate living conditions (for example, housing and nutrition) of poor people cause poorer health (Patrick, Stein, Porta, Porter, & Ricketts, 1988). Evidence also indicates that poverty hinders the life chances and intellectual development of children, who are adversely affected before birth because of the poorer health and nutrition of their mothers (Pressman, 1990). Pressman also found that poor women are

more likely to give birth prematurely and have lower-birthweight babies.

For working poor families, the stress of a potential illness is exacerbated by high costs of health care, even when families have health insurance. Rocha (1996) found that even those workers who have health benefits may not be able to afford insurance deductibles or meet cost-sharing requirements if their wages are too low. More than 45 percent of the patients studied in a public clinic had some form of insurance. Of the 10 percent who were privately insured, almost 75 percent had annual incomes below $20,000. The high rate of public clinic use, instead of a private physician's office, by these insured patients indicates that the out-of-pocket expenses associated with health insurance may keep low-wage workers from using their private insurance benefits.

Economic Distress

For poor workers, economic crises are a constant dilemma. Stress is often a problem for working poor families, who deal with the problems of poverty and work-related issues as well. Voydanoff and Donnelly's (1988) research on the consequences of economic distress on family and marital relationships illustrated the potential effects on working poor families. They found that economic distress decreased both family and marital satisfaction. Coping resources did not significantly buffer the negative effects of economic distress for women or for men.

The economic consequences of inadequate wages carry through into retirement. Social security retirement benefits are calculated by using the worker's average indexed monthly earnings (Ozawa, 1982). Retirees who have earned low wages receive a smaller subsidy, and therefore a smaller monthly retirement check, than higher wage earners when they retire.

Stress on Family Functioning

The rise in child poverty in the United States has occurred simultaneously with reduced spending on social services (Danziger & Danziger, 1995). Moreover, poor workers who make at or slightly above minimum wage may not qualify for subsidized mental health care. Yet there is a strong relationship between family poverty and child development problems. Economic constraints can reduce the quality and quantity of parenting because of financial and psychological stresses (Danziger & Danziger, 1995). Furthermore, Korenman, Miller, and Sjaastad (1995) found that chronic poverty has a negative effect on children's cognitive and socioemotional development, including verbal memory, math, and reading achievement, resulting in behavior problems. The consequence may well be that poor working families in most need of services have the least access.

CURRENT POLICY RESPONSES FOR THE WORKING POOR

Few policies are designed specifically for the working poor. Several programs, including food stamps and housing and child care subsidies, extend their services to working poor families and thereby provide a safety net for them. The Earned Income Tax Credit (EITC) is the only program specifically designed to benefit poor workers.

Food Stamps and Housing Subsidies

Many working poor families are eligible for food stamps, but less than 40 percent take advantage of this option (Shapiro & Parrott, 1995). One reason for the lack of use is the strong welfare stigma attached to receiving food stamps (Weaver, 1988). Other reasons may include the difficulty of leaving work to apply for food stamps and the unwillingness to report earnings each month to the welfare office. In a study of AFDC recipients who became employed through the Job Opportunities and Basic Skills Training (JOBS) program, Hagen and Davis (1995) found that 62 percent still received food stamps because their average income was below the poverty level. Under the Personal Responsibility and Work Opportunity Reconciliation Act of 1996 (P.L. 104-193), food stamp benefits are slated to be cut for working poor families, which will further erode their economic well-being (Greenstein, 1996). Overall, the new law provides for $27.7 billion in food stamp cuts (Center on Budget and Policy Priorities, 1996). Food stamp benefits are to be cut by almost 20 percent by 2002, with average benefits declining from 80 cents per person per meal to 66 cents per person per meal.

Housing assistance is another potential resource for poor workers. However, as Mulroy (1995) noted, most low-income households do not receive rent subsidies. Although working poor families may meet the income guidelines, housing assistance is not guaranteed to those who need it. In the 1990s waiting lists for families who qualify have grown so dramatically that two-thirds of U.S. cities have closed their lists to new applicants. For a family of three on a waiting list, a two- to five-year wait to receive subsidized housing is typical. For example, in North Carolina in 1991, 2,000 households were on the waiting list in Charlotte alone, and the list was closed to all new applicants (Aulette, 1991).

Earned Income Tax Credit

The EITC provides a wage supplement to low-income working families with children and is paid for through the federal government in the form of a tax subsidy. The EITC, enacted in 1975, is a refundable tax credit and has been adjusted yearly for inflation since 1987. Presidents Reagan, Bush, and Clinton all supported increases in the EITC to offset the erosion in wages among low earners and a series of increases in payroll taxes (Shapiro & Parrott, 1995). With the new expansions in 1996, the EITC can bring a family of two or three out of poverty (Ozawa, 1995).

The EITC subsidizes earned income at a decreasing rate up to a maximum amount of income. For example, for $11,000 in earnings in 1995, the maximum credit was $3,370. The credit is reduced by 21.06 cents for each dollar earned until income reaches $27,000, at which point the credit is $0 (Ozawa, 1995). As Ozawa indicated, the EITC benefits not only the working poor but also the working near-poor. In 1996 the number of eligible taxpayers reached 13 million. Of those, 7.6 million had incomes above the federal poverty line. When the EITC began to be adjusted for inflation in 1987, it became an important way for working poor families to keep their income level from falling.

The EITC is not without its problems and critics, however. First, the EITC does not distinguish between workers who work full-time all year for low wages and part-time workers. Moreover, although the credit is successful at alleviating federal income tax burdens, families still must pay social security taxes of 7.65 percent (Ozawa, 1995). Third, unless the minimum wage is adjusted for inflation, the benefits will slowly erode as inflation increases. Nevertheless, the EITC is a positive step, and the recent changes in the EITC have expanded it to include more families since 1990 and to bring smaller families above the poverty line.

The Joint Economic Committee (1996) issued a report stating their strong conviction that the EITC be reduced and reformed. Republican senators William Roth (DE) and Don Nickles (OK), members of the committee, introduced legislation in 1995 to slow the growth of the EITC. They cited an 800 percent increase in the program from 1985 to 1994, negative work incentives, insignificant effects on the labor supply, massive fraud, and marriage disincentives as reasons for reform. Clearly the program is under attack by some just as it has been expanded enough to move some working poor families out of poverty.

THE FUTURE OF POOR WORKERS: SOME POLICY ALTERNATIVES

How the current federal welfare reform legislation, the Personal Responsibility and Work Opportunity Reconciliation Act will affect the working poor is still unknown. After the last federal welfare reform attempts in 1981 (the Omnibus Budget Reconciliation Act, P.L. 97-35) and 1988 (the Family Support Act, P.L. 100-485), the population of poor workers continued to grow. The reforms largely train welfare recipients for low-paying technical and service jobs, relegate them to the ranks of the working poor, and cause competition for the lower-paying occupations (Coulton, 1996). As the working poor population continues to grow, feasible policy alternatives become even more important.

Many policy alternatives have been suggested by social scientists to alleviate the economic hardship on poor working families. Increased housing subsidies are one answer to the critical shortage of affordable low-income housing stock (Gulati, 1992). Further expansions in the EITC are also suggested as a way to help working poor households escape poverty (Caputo, 1991; Plotnick, 1989). Child care tax credits could be revised to assist low-income working families with day care expenses. The current child care tax credit primarily benefits middle-class families because low-income families who do not pay taxes are not eligible for the credit (Berrick, 1991). Family or children allowances have also been discussed extensively in the professional literature. These types of allowances are universal grants provided to all families, regardless of income, based on the number of children in each family

(Meyer, Phillips, & Maritato, 1991). Children or family allowances are already used in most other developed countries, including most European countries and Canada (Hanratty, 1992; Jones, 1995; Pressman, 1992).

Three other policy alternatives may help alleviate some of the burdens on poor workers, enhance their opportunity to live above the poverty threshold, and provide a safety net by increasing their resource base. The first policy alternative combines self-employment opportunities through community-based microenterprise loans with asset-accumulating individual development accounts (IDAs). The second alternative is to set the minimum wage at an acceptable level, at or above the poverty line, and adjust it annually for inflation. The third policy option is to provide a safety net by moving toward a system in which health care is accessible and affordable for all workers.

Community Investment Strategies

Given the economic realities of global competition and low-paying jobs, education will help some of the working poor increase their skills and find higher-paying occupations. Although the demand for skilled labor will increase, "the job structure will not shift markedly toward higher paying jobs" (Mishel & Bernstein, 1994, p. 194), in part because the increase in the supply of college-educated workers will outpace the demand for college graduates. Wage inequality will continue to grow unless there is a sizable improvement in productivity growth.

The challenge is to promote a more community-focused strategy by empowering poor workers with increased skills, but also by expanding social and economic opportunity. Although traditional economic development strategies, such as tax incentives and business subsidies for attracting new industry into inner-city neighborhoods, are essential, new, innovative ideas for building healthy neighborhoods and communities are needed. Two innovative ideas that have been suggested in the literature and partially supported by federal legislation are (1) creating greater opportunity for self-employment through microenterprise loans and (2) acquiring assets through IDAs.

The microenterprise movement. In a time of shrinking wages and dwindling federal funding and responsibility, Weil (1996) listed several important ways to empower people by creating healthy communities: "Building family self-sufficiency . . . means more than just helping people develop skills in interviewing for jobs; it also relates to working with communities to create enterprises, microenterprises, and cooperatives that fill longer term niches in the local and global markets, that create and support community infrastructure, and that strengthen the nonprofit and community-based services sector to continually invest in the development of human capital" (pp. 489–490).

A federal microloan demonstration project was established in 1992 to assist women, low-income, and minority entrepreneurs and business owners to start and operate successful small businesses. The project targets people who lack credit for traditional loans (Micro Loan Demonstration Program, 1992). Microloan programs work through intermediaries to provide small loans to prospective small businesses (Small Business Administration, 1996a). Loan amounts range from $100 to $25,000. Depending on the earnings of the business, the loan maturity may be as long as six years. The intermediaries, a variety of nonprofit organizations, are eligible for grants from the federal government for marketing, management, and technical assistance to borrowers, and loans from the Small Business Administration for making short-term, fixed-interest-rate microloans for small business startup.

Examples of microenterprises in the United States are scarce in the professional literature. Examples found on the Internet include a bead and craft shop, a bridal consulting business (Johnston, 1995), and rural local market development (Rural Local Markets, n.d.). Third World microenterprise loan programs have expanded greatly since the mid-1980s, however, and examples from Africa, Asia, and Latin American are available in the literature (Rhyne & Otero, 1992). Third World examples include agriculture programs (Adams & Pischke, 1992); vendor opportunities; and small-scale industrial workshops, such as shoemaking shops, uniform shops, and recycleries (Sahley, 1995).

Investing in self-employment strategies such as microenterprises provides opportunities for workers to make higher earnings and have a chance to move beyond a poverty wage. As Weil (1996) suggested, these strategies represent the kind of major investment needed in programs that enable families to get out of poverty and gain economic security. Presently, all 50 states have some form of microloan program in place (Small Business Administration, 1996b). To continue government involvement and expand federal resources, evaluation of these enterprises is essential

Individual development accounts. According to the U.S. Bureau of the Census (1993), household economic well-being depends on both income and asset accumulation. Sherraden's (1991) theory of asset-based social welfare illustrates the importance of economic resources for social well-being. Assets are not simply income stored to be used for future consumption; they are important above and beyond income and are likely to be transferred from generation to generation. The accumulation of assets has been found to lead to attitudes and choices that promote employment, increase confidence about the future, and promote the creation of social capital through connectedness with the community (Coulton, 1996).

An example of asset-based social welfare policy is the IDA proposed by Sherraden (1991). IDAs, by design, "promote orientation toward the future, long-range planning, savings and investment, individual initiative, individual choice and achievement of life goals" (p. 220). IDAs target savings for purchasing a home, obtaining postsecondary education, or starting a small business.

The new federal welfare reform legislation, Reconciliation P.L. 104-193, includes the option of creating IDAs for welfare recipients. All amounts contributed by recipients must be derived from earned income, and investments in the IDAs will not reduce benefits. The federal government does not provide matching funds directly, but federal law allows block grant funds to be used by states for matching contributions. In an attempt to provide IDAs to working poor populations, several demonstration projects have begun. In St. Louis, the Charles Stewart Mott Foundation provided startup funds for the St. Louis Reinvestment Corporation to plan an IDA program. Participants' income must be at 80 percent or less of the median family income established by the federal government (Center for Social Development, 1996). This program, still in the planning stages, establishes the basis by which the working poor may begin to accumulate assets and develop a financial "safety net."

Adjusting the Minimum Wage for Inflation

Adjusting the minimum wage for inflation has been a recurrent topic in public debate. The idea almost became law during the Carter administration in 1977 (Weaver, 1988). Indexing the minimum wage to inflation was on the congressional agenda in the 1970s during a period of high inflation and after the minimum wage had not been raised through ad hoc increases for seven years. Originally, legislation sought to index the minimum wage to the CPI so that when prices rose more than 3 percent, the minimum wage increased by that amount plus 1 percent (Weaver, 1988). After outcries of impending disemployment effects from economists and business interests, the legislative initiative was revised to index the minimum wage to 60 percent of the manufacturing wage, and support for indexing the minimum wage to the CPI was withdrawn. The bill was further amended to provide a seven-year increase in the minimum wage, with no indexing component. The revised measure was approved and for seven years the minimum wage remained stable, only to fall miserably in the 1980s, with no increases between 1981 and 1989.

Conventional economists oppose raising the minimum wage at all, let alone indexing the wage to adjust for inflation. Their arguments center around a theoretical assumption that artificially increasing the minimum wage in a market economy will increase unemployment (Mincy, 1990). Empirical studies, however, have found negligible disemployment effects from wage increases (Card & Krueger, 1994; Mincy, 1990). In fact, Card and Krueger (1995) found that increases in the New Jersey minimum wage actually increased employment. Automatic indexing of the minimum wage is one way to guarantee workers a wage above the poverty level (Rocha, 1997). Given the current research findings, adjusting the minimum wage for inflation may actually help rather than harm business. From a business standpoint, instead of making large increases in the wage of 25 cents to 50 cents after long periods of stagnation, it may be better to raise the wage in smaller increments, following cost-of-living adjustments. As the cost of living increases for housing, groceries, and other commodities, the minimum wage would be adjusted to keep up with these expenses.

Providing Health Care Benefits for All Workers

Although these economic strategies will help poor workers rise above the poverty level and gain resources to invest in the future, families may face financial disaster without health insurance. Health care benefits are essential for a healthy, functioning workforce. Health benefits are an important consideration for women who want to leave welfare, as well as for anyone starting a small business. Poor workers and self-employed workers are the least likely workers to have health benefits.

Self-employed workers clearly have fewer benefits than are provided to wage and salary workers. The most visible and important benefit, health coverage, is provided to roughly three-fourths of wage and salary workers but to only 38 percent and 16 percent, respectively, of self-employed men and women (Mishel & Bernstein, 1994).

There are several alternative models for providing health care for all Americans. Gorin and Moniz (1992) outlined two models: the pay-or-play model and the single-payer model. First, under pay-or-play models, employers supply health insurance through private insurers or contribute to a fund that would then be used to subsidize private insurance coverage for uninsured people. Other play-or-pay schemes include expanding Medicaid to cover individuals not covered by employer-provided insurance or private insurance or eliminating Medicaid all together.

In the second model, the single-payer model, the government is the sole insurer. There are also a variety of single-payer models that range from eliminating private insurance and using a single public program to cover everyone to limiting private insurance to cover certain uncovered services, such as cosmetic surgery. The Children's Defense Fund (CDF) (1991) proposed a commitment by both government and business. The CDF suggested that the federal government expand public health insurance (Medicaid) to all poor and near-poor families with income less than 200 percent of the poverty level, while the private sector provide subsidized health insurance with dependent coverage to all employees, regardless of pay level.

Two current attempts to provide health care to all workers were recently rejected in Congress. The Clinton administration's call for a nationalized, comprehensive managed care

plan was strongly linked to workforce participation (White House Domestic Policy Council,
1993). NASW proposed a single-payer model for
health care reform and developed a comprehensive national health care plan that was
introduced in the U.S. Senate in 1992 (Mizrahi,
1995). Both national health care plans, however, were defeated in Congress in favor of
state-controlled managed care plans that do
not guarantee health care for all workers.

CONCLUSION

The working poor in the United States are in a
precarious situation. They are at risk because
of the combined stresses of poverty and low-
wage workforce participation. Few government
programs provide a safety net for this group.
Education is one way for some to escape a life
as a poor worker, although larger economic
forces will always keep some workers in low-
paying occupations. Policy alternatives—for
example, adjusting the minimum wage for
inflation, creating self-employment incentives,
and the expansion of the EITC—are ways of
helping the working poor escape poverty.
IDAs also may increase the ability of the
poorest workers to save for postsecondary
education, ownership of a home, or self-
employment. Other policy initiatives, such as
food stamps and child care and housing
subsidies, can lessen the economic burden on
families. Health care financing for poor
workers is a continuing problem. Without this
necessary benefit, the working poor will
continue to experience health care crises that
undermine their health and economic well-
being. The United States must make a commitment to its poor workers to maintain a healthy
workforce and a strong economy.

REFERENCES

Adams, D. W., & Pischke, J. D. (1992). Microenterprise credit programs: Deja vu. *World Development, 20,* 1463–1470.

Allen-Meares, P., & Roberts, E. M. (1995). Public
assistance as family policy: Closing off options for
poor families. *Social Work, 40,* 559–565.

Aulette, J. (1991). The privatization of housing in a
declining economy: The case of Stepping Stone
Housing. *Journal of Sociology and Social Welfare,
18,* 151–164.

Berrick, J. D. (1991). Welfare and child care: The
intricacies of competing social values. *Social Work,
36,* 345–351.

Blank, R. (1994). The employment strategy: Public
policies to increase work and earnings. In S. H.

Danziger, G. D. Sandefur, & D.H. Weinberg (Eds.),
Confronting poverty: Prescriptions for change. New
York: Harvard University Press.

Bowen, G. L., & Neenan, P. A. (1992). Child care as an
economic incentive for the working poor. *Families
in Society, 73,* 295–303.

Bradbury, K. L. (1990, July/August). The changing
fortunes of American families in the 1980's. *New
England Economic Review,* pp. 25–40.

Bureau of Labor Statistics. (1996). *Value of the minimum
wage over the last 40 years.* Washington, DC: U.S.
Department of Labor. Available online at http://
www.dol.gov/dol/esa/public/minwage/chart2.htm.

Butler, S., & Kondratas, A. (1987). *Out of the poverty
trap.* New York: Free Press.

Caputo, R. K. (1991). Patterns of work and poverty:
Exploratory profiles of working-poor households.
Families in Society, 72, 451–460.

Card, D., & Krueger, A. B. (1994). Minimum wages and
employment: A case study of the fast-food industry
in New Jersey and Pennsylvania. *American
Economic Review, 84,* 772–792.

Card, D., & Krueger, A. B. (1995). *Myth and measurement: The new economics of the minimum wage.*
Princeton, NJ: Princeton University Press.

Center for Social Development. (1996). CSD update.
*A Newsletter for the Center for Social Development, ,
1*(1), 2.

Center on Budget and Policy Priorities. (1996, August
12). *The depth of the food stamp cuts in the final
welfare bill.* Washington, DC: Author. Available
online at http://epn.org/cbpp.food/html.

Children's Defense Fund. (1991). *The state of
America's children, 1991.* Washington, DC: Author.

Coulton, C. J. (1996). Poverty, work and community:
A research agenda for an era of diminishing federal
responsibility. *Social Work, 41,* 509–520.

Danziger, S. K., & Danziger, S. (1995). Child poverty,
public policy and welfare reform. *Children and
Youth Services Review, 17*(1/2), 1–10.

Dolgoff, R., Feldstein, D., & Skolnik, L. (1993).
Understanding social welfare (3rd ed.). New York:
Longman.

Ellwood, D. T. (1988). *Poor support: Poverty in the
American family.* New York: Basic Books.

Family Support Act of 1988. P.L. 100-48 5. 102 Stat.
2343.

Gorin, S., & Moniz, C. (1992). The national health care
crisis: An analysis of proposed solutions. *Social
Work, 37,* 37–44.

Greenstein, R. (1996). *Raising families with a full-time
worker out of poverty: The role of an increase in the
minimum wage.* Washington, DC: Center on Budget
and Policy Priorities.

Grossman, J. (1996). *Fair Labor Standards Act of 1938:
Maximum struggle for a minimum wage.* Washing-

ton, DC: U.S. Department of Labor. Available online at http://www.dol.gov/dol/esa/public/minwage/history.htm.

Gulati, P. (1992). Ideology, public policy and homeless families. *Journal of Sociology and Social Welfare, 19*(4), 113–128.

Hagen, J. L., & Davis, L. V. (1995). The participants' perspective on the Job Opportunities and Basic Skills Training Program. *Social Service Review, 69,* 655–678.

Hanratty, M. J. (1992). Why Canada has less poverty. *Social Policy, 23,* 32–37.

Harrison, B., & Gorham, L. (1992). Growing inequality in African American wages in the 1980's and the emergence of an African-American middle class. *Journal of Policy Analysis and Management, 11,* 235–253.

Heclo, H. (1994). Poverty politics. In S. H. Danziger, G. D. Sandefur, & D. H. Weinberg (Eds.), *Confronting poverty: Prescriptions for change.* New York: Harvard University Press.

Helper, S. (1990). Subcontracting: Innovative labor strategies. *Labor Research Review 15, 9*(1), 89–99.

Howley, J. (1990). Justice for janitors: The challenge of organizing in contract services. *Labor Research Review 15, 9*(1), 61–71.

Johnston, J. (1995, November/December). To boldly loan where no banker has loaned before. *Business Ethics Magazine.* Available online at http://condor.depaul.edu/ethics/bizethics.html.

Joint Economic Committee. (1996). *Earned income tax credit.* Available online at http://www.senate.gov/comm/JEC/general/eitcpap.html.

Jones, R. M. (1995). The prices of welfare dependency: Children pay. *Social Work, 40,* 496–504.

Korenman, S., Miller, J., & Sjaastad, J. (1995). Long-term poverty and child development in the United States: Results from the NLSY. *Children and Youth Services Review, 17*(1–2), 127–155.

Lazere, E. B. (1996). *Maine's families: Poverty despite work.* Washington, DC: Center on Budget and Policy Priorities.

Marshall, N. Y., & Marx, F. (1991). The affordability of child care for the working poor. *Families in Society, 72,* 202–211.

May, R., & Porter, K. H. (1996). *Poverty and income trends: 1994.* Washington, DC: Center on Budget and Policy Priorities.

Meyer, D. R., Phillips, E., & Maritato, N. L. (1991). The effects of replacing income tax deductions for children with children's allowances: A microsimulation. *Journal of Family Issues, 12,* 467–491.

Micro Loan Demonstration Program. (1992). 15 U.S.C. 636, Title 15, chap. 14A, 1A, i & ii.

Mincy, R. B. (1990). Raising the minimum wage: Effects on family poverty. *Monthly Labor Review, 113*(7), 18–25.

Mishel, L., & Bernstein, J. (1994). *The state of working America: 1994–95.* New York: M. E. Sharpe.

Mizrahi, T. (1995). Health care: Reform initiatives. In R. L. Edwards (Ed.-in-Chief), *Encyclopedia of social work* (19th ed., Vol. 2, pp. 1185–1198). Washington, DC: NASW Press.

Moscovice, I., Craig, W., & Pitt, L. (1987, September). Meeting the basic needs of the working poor. *Social Service Review,* 420–430.

Mulroy, E. A. (1995). Housing. In R. L. Edwards (Ed.-in-Chief), *Encyclopedia of social work* (19th ed., pp. 1185–1198). Washington, DC: NASW Press

Oliver, M. L., & Shapiro, T. M. (1990). Wealth of a nation: A reassessment of asset inequality in American shows at least one third of households are asset-poor. *American Journal of Economics and Sociology, 49,* 129–151.

Omnibus Budget Reconciliation Act of 1981, PL. 97-35, 95 Stat. 357.

Orchansky, M. (1969). How poverty is measured. *Monthly Labor Review, 92*(2), 37–41.

Ozawa, M. N. (1982). Who receives subsidies through social security, and how much? *Social Work, 27,* 129–134.

Ozawa, M. N. (1995). The earned income tax credit: Its effect and its significance. *Social Service Review, 69,* 563–582.

Patrick, D. L., Stein, J., Porta, M., Porter, C. Q., & Ricketts, T. C. (1988). Povery, health services and health status in rural America. *Milbank Quarterly, 66*(1), 105–137.

Personal Responsibility and Work Opportunity Reconcilliation Act of 1996. P.L. 104-193, 110 Stat. 2105.

Plotnick, R. D. (1989). Directions for reducing child poverty. *Social Work, 34,* 523–530.

Popple, P. R., & Leighninger, L. (1993). *Social work, social welfare and American society.* Boston: Allyn & Bacon.

Pressman, S. (1990). America's new poverty crisis. *Forum for Applied Research and Public Policy, 5*(2), 47–55.

Pressman, S. (1992). Child exemptions or child allowances: What sort of antipoverty program for the United States? *American Journal of Economics and Sociology, 51,* 257–272.

Rank, M. R. (1994). *Living on the edge: The realities of welfare in America.* New York: Columbia University Press.

Rhyne, E., & Otero, M. (1992). Financial services for microenterprises: Principles and institutions. *World Development, 20,* 1561–1571.

Rocha, C. (1994). *Effects of poverty on working families: Comparing models of stress by race and class.* PhD dissertation, Washington University, George Warren Brown School of Social Work, St. Louis.

Rocha, C. (1006). Use of health insurance in county-funded clinics: Issues for health care reform. *Health & Social Work, 21,* 16–23.

Rocha, C. (1997). Factors that contribute to economic well-being in female headed households. *Journal of Social Service Research, 23*(1), 25–32.

Rural Local Markets—Phase II. (n.d.). *Recommended research and demonstration project.* Washington, DC: Rural Center, Mid-East Commission. Available online at http://www2.ncredc.org/ncredc/grants/newgrants/localmarket2.html.

Sahley, C. M. (1995). NGO support for small business associations: A participatory approach to enterprise development. *Community Development Journal, 30*(1), 56–65.

Sarri, R. C. (1985). Federal policy changes and the feminization of poverty. *Child Welfare, 64,* 235–246.

Seguino, S. (1995). *Living on the edge: Women working and providing for families in the Maine economy, 1979–1993.* Orono: University of Maine, Margaret Chase Smith Center for Public Policy.

Shapiro, I., & Parrott, S. (1995). *An unraveling consensus? An analysis of the effect of the new congressional agenda on the working poor.* Washington, DC: Center on Budget and Policy Priorities.

Sherraden, M. (1991). *Assets and the poor: A new American welfare policy.* New York: M. E. Sharpe.

Small Business Administration. (1996a). *Financing your business.* Available online at http://www.senat.gov/~sbc/103pubs.

Small Business Administration. (1996b). *Microloan lender participants.* Available online at http://www.sbaonline.sba.gov/gopher–local–information/microloan–len.

U.S. Bureau of the Census. (1991). Poverty in the United States: 1988–1989. In *Current population reports* (Series P60-171). Washington, DC: U.S. Government Printing Office.

U.S. Bureau of the Census. (1992). Poverty in the U.S.: 1992. In *Current population reports* (Series P60-185). Washington, DC: U.S. Government Printing Office.

U.S. Bureau of the Census. (1993). Asset ownership of household: 1993. In T. J. Eller & W. Fraser (Eds.), *Current population reports* (Series P70-47). Washington, DC: U.S. Government Printing Office.

U.S. Bureau of the Census. (1995). What's it worth. Field of training and economic status: 1993. In R. R. Bruno (Ed.), *Current population reports* (Series P-70/2/51). Washington, DC: U.S. Government Printing Office.

U.S. Department of Labor, Women's Bureau. (1993). *Facts on working women.* Washington, DC: U.S. Government Printing Office.

U.S. House of Representatives Committee on Ways and Means. (1990). Overview of entitlement programs. *In 1990 Green Book.* Washington, DC: U.S. Government Printing Office.

Voydanoff, P., & Donnelly, B. W. (1988). Economic distress, family coping and quality of family life. In P. Voydanoff & L. C. Majka (Eds.), *Family and economic distress: Coping strategies and social policy.* Newbury Park, CA: Sage Publications.

Weaver, R. K. (1988). *Automatic government: The politics of indexation.* Washington, DC: Brookings Institution.

Weil, M. O. (1996). Community building: Building community practice. *Social Work, 41,* 481–500.

White House Domestic Policy Council. (1993). *Health security: The president's health security plan—The complete draft and final report.* New York: Times Books.

Williams, B. L. (1994). Reflection on family poverty. *Families in Society, 75,* 47–50.

Wolfe, B. L. (1994). Reform of health care for the nonelderly poor. In S. H. Danziger, G. D. Sandefur, and D. H. Weinberg (Eds.), *Confronting poverty: Prescriptions for change.* New York: Howard University Press.

Cynthia J. Rocha, PhD, is assistant professor, College of Social Work, University of Tennessee, 219 Henson Hall, Knoxville, TN 37996.

For further information see

Aid to Families with Dependent Children; Community Needs Assessment; Employment and Unemployment Measurement; Families Overview; Families Demographic Shifts; Federal Social Legislation from 1961 to 1994; **Federal Social Legislation from 1994 to 1997;** Health Care: Financing; Homelessness; Housing; Hunger, Nutrition, and Food Programs; Income Distribution; Jobs and Earnings; JOBS Program; Poverty; Rural Poverty; Social Security; Social Welfare Expenditures: Public; **Temporary Assistance to Needy Families;** Unemployment Compensation; Welfare Employment Programs: Evaluation; Women Overview.

Key Words

individual development accounts	poverty
	underemployment
minimum wage	working poor

World Social Situation

Richard J. Estes

The social work profession has a distinguished history of service in international development, and its commitments to international development are both extensive and varied. Social workers can be found in virtually every corner of the world, applying their knowledge, values, and skills to a broad range of social, political, and economic problems. Consistent with the perspective of those who preceded them, today's international practitioners share a vision of social work as a profession in the service of promoting increased social justice and world peace for people everywhere. This entry explores the varied nature of the social problems on which social workers in international practice focus. Many of these problems, such as poverty, racism, and hunger, are deeply rooted in the structure of the existing international social order, but other problems (for example, social caste, sexism, classism, and ageism) persist simply out of habit or tradition. Still other problems, though, emerge as a response to the impossible social conditions in which the world's most deeply impoverished people live. In all of these situations, social workers in the international community are seeking to redress the most serious injustices.

PROBLEMS AND PARADOXES

The world social situation is characterized by extraordinary paradoxes. *Social progress*, defined as net improvements in the capacity of governments to provide for the basic social and material needs of their populations, has been impressive for some countries since 1970. However, many societies have been marred by recurrent intraregional wars, civil conflicts, chronic human rights violations, corrupt governments, deepening poverty, and growing numbers of political and economic refugees. Population growth continues to be rapid, as is the rate of urban migration. The landscape of the planet has been seriously compromised as well: Large numbers of the world's peoples are struggling against the effects of rapid deforestation, exhausted soil and animal resources, recurrent floods, and other natural and man-made disasters.

The Promise

The response of the world's governments to the current social situation has been direct and forward-looking. Their commitments have been expressed in an unprecedented number of international declarations and agreements that emphasize

- achieving a better balance between social and economic development
- returning people and people's organizations to the center of development
- formulating new development paradigms that better reflect the planet's diverse cultures, traditions, and histories

- promoting increased protection of the planet's fragile biodiversity and dwindling natural resources
- responding to the special needs of historically disadvantaged population groups, especially women, children, and people of color
- undertaking major initiatives to eliminate absolute poverty and other forms of socially debilitating "maldevelopment" by the year 2000 or as soon as will be practical thereafter
- working toward more equitable sharing of the planet's abundant material resources.

The Reality

Progress toward attainment of the planet's social development goals has fallen far short of what was anticipated (United Nations Children's Fund [UNICEF], 1997; United Nations Development Programme [UNDP], 1997; World Bank, 1996). The issue of resource scarcity aside, since 1990 comparatively few governments have demonstrated the political will required to chart new directions for either their own people or the larger world community. As a result, world social progress is disappointingly slow, although some recent dramatic changes have occurred in certain developing countries in Asia, Africa, and Latin America (Estes, 1995, 1996a, 1996b).

SOCIAL DEVELOPMENT TRENDS IN THE WORLD'S MAJOR REGIONS

The development trends shown in Figure 1 reflect average scores achieved by each of the world's seven largest geopolitical regions since

FIGURE 1

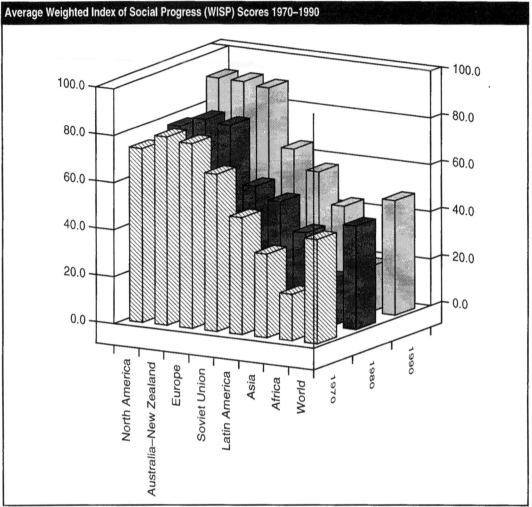

Average Weighted Index of Social Progress (WISP) Scores 1970–1990

SOURCE: Estes, R. J. (1988). *Trends in world social development.* New York: Praeger.

1970 on the Weighted Index of Social Progress (WISP) (Estes, 1988). Among other factors, the WISP measures levels of national and international social progress in a broad range of socioeconomic indicators that are of concern to social workers and other social development practitioners: infant and child mortality, literacy levels, access to primary health care, population trends, economic growth rates, the changing status of women, seriousness of diversity-related social conflict, the incidence of serious natural and man-made disasters, the availability of formally structured social welfare programs and services, and other factors that are known to impinge directly on human development. The WISP contains a total

of 46 highly reliable indicators of national and international social development, which are divided into 10 subindexes of social development practice: education, health status, women's status, defense effort, economic, demographic, geography, political participation, cultural diversity, and welfare effort.

North America

North America's strongest performances on the WISP occurred on the political participation, education, economic, health status, women's status, and demographic subindexes. The region's performance on the welfare effort subindex also is strong but fell well below the accomplishments of other highly developed regions such as Europe and Australia–New Zealand. North American scores on the geography subindex are consistently problematic because of the region's vulnerability to a disproportionate number of natural disasters. (Although extensive property damage results from these disasters, human casualty rates tend to be low because of the region's highly advanced early warning and civil defense measures.)

North America's most substantial 20-year gains occurred on the defense effort, political participation, demographic, and cultural diversity subindexes. Twenty-year losses occurred on the women's status, welfare effort, and geography subindexes. These losses are small, however, and in practical terms reflect a comparative steady-state situation. Thus, North America remains one of the most advanced regions in the world. Social progress advanced steadily between 1970 and 1990 such that, today, no major differences exist between North America and the world's two other most socially advanced regions, Europe and Australia–New Zealand.

The region's continuing major social issues include

- sustaining at least moderate patterns of economic growth in the context of reasonably full employment
- continuing to absorb large numbers of culturally diverse political and economic immigrants
- responding adequately to the unique cultural needs of an increasingly diverse population and workforce
- financing the health and economic security needs of a rapidly aging population
- rebuilding urban infrastructures and economic structures
- realigning the goals, content, and structure of systems of primary and secondary education
- reducing high levels of infectious disease, violent crime, and substance abuse
- reversing a current trend toward growing economic inequality and poverty, especially among historically disadvantaged groups
- promoting fuller popular participation in political decision making
- building more effective—and perhaps more efficient—public-private partnerships for human services delivery

- resisting growing tendencies toward international isolationism.

Social workers are providing substantial, multidimensional leadership for these reforms in all areas of the region, with the result that social work, at least in the United States, has become a fully recognized and licensed profession.

Australia–New Zealand
The region made up of Australia and New Zealand achieved the world's highest composite WISP scores in 1970. In 1990 the region remained one of the three most socially advanced regions. In all, the region performed well above world averages in 1990 on nine of the WISP's 10 subindexes: political participation, welfare effort, education, women's status, demographic, economic, cultural diversity, health status, and defense effort. Because of their equally large combined geographic area, Australia and New Zealand show vulnerability on the geography subindex.

The region's most significant 20-year WISP gains occurred on the political participation, defense effort, cultural diversity, economic, and education subindexes. These gains reflect broad-based social improvements since 1970. However, the region's most significant 20-year social losses were equally substantial, especially on the geography, women's status, and health status subindexes. Erosion also occurred in the region's welfare effort subindex performance. All of the region's social losses must be considered serious: In general, they reflect a retreat by the region's governments from the advanced network of social programs that characterized these countries during earlier decades.

The Australia–New Zealand region is undergoing rapid and dramatic social and economic reorganization, with changes that promote

- a smaller role for government in managing the national economy
- transfer of responsibility for social welfare programs and services from the national government to local communities, individuals, and nongovernment organizations
- increased emphasis on personal investment and savings as a means of financing both public- and private-sector initiatives

- return of land, economic assets, and other natural and man-made resources to the region's aboriginal peoples
- greater recognition of the importance of social, political, and economic partnerships with Asian and other Pacific nations, rather than Europe, as the foundation for the region's future economic progress.

In addition to advancing these reforms, the governments of Australia and New Zealand are experiencing dramatic increases in population diversity as a result of migration into the region of large numbers of people from other parts of Asia and the Pacific. These migrations are having a profound impact on the region's political and economic systems and, in turn, on social services. Social work practice in the region is turning from a perspective based on European heritage to an Asian–Pacific perspective.

Europe

Europe is undergoing profound social, political, and economic change (Estes, in press). The region's transformations are driven by the increasing globalization of the world economy, the collapse of the former Soviet Union in 1991, and Europe's rapidly changing social composition. Since 1991 the region's membership has been expanded by 26 "new" countries, such as the newly autonomous Baltic states, including Latvia and Lithuania; the Commonwealth of Independent States, including the Slovak Republic, Slovenia, Croatia, and others; and the former Warsaw Pact countries of Eastern Europe, including Poland, Hungary, Bulgaria, and others.

Europe performed strongly in 1990 on nine of the WISP's 10 subindexes: welfare effort, demographic, political participation, health status, women's status, education, economic, cultural diversity, and geography. The region's performance on the defense effort subindex was less impressive, but it does show improvement over 1970 and 1980 levels. The most impressive 20-year gains on the WISP were in the political participation and defense effort subindexes. The region experienced small 20-year net losses on the demographic and welfare effort subindexes, but these losses are not significant.

Europe's current reform efforts are far-reaching and unprecedented. They touch on virtually every aspect of European life. To date, the region's most significant reforms include

- reclassification of 26 successor states of the former Soviet Union as "European" countries
- creation of the federated European Union (EU)
- establishment of an empowered European Parliament
- steps toward the implementation of a common currency (the ECU) by 2000
- ratification of a social charter that extends to all citizens of the EU a common set of social protections that transcend national boundaries
- devolution of significant political power from central to local governments
- increased participation of individuals, employers, and local governments in financing locally controlled human services programs (especially in health care, income support, housing, and education)
- emergence of a viable independent sector as a coproducer of services previously provided only by the public sector—especially in the transportation, communications, education, and human services sectors.

The complexity of the reforms initiated by European governments is illustrated by the public expenditures data for industrial countries in Table 1. These data show, for example, that the region's central governments, on average, control nearly half of the total economies of their countries and, on average, employ one person in every five in the workforce. For much of this century these governments also depended on high tax rates and aggressive redistribution methods to finance public services in health, education, housing, and income security. As a result of their welfare accomplishments, however, the majority of the region's governments have amassed large national debts in combination with slow-to-moderate rates of economic growth and persistent high unemployment.

Whether successful over the long term or not, Europe's experimentation with reform of its major social institutions will have a profound impact on other economically advanced countries. The region's reform movements already are reshaping the nature of European social work practice and education in a more socially diverse, transregional, and international Europe.

TABLE 1
Public Sector Economic Activity of Selected OECD Countries, 1990–96

Region Countries	Current General Government Revenue, as % of GDP	Current General Government Expenditure, as % of GDP	Government Final Consumption Expenditure, as % of GDP							Net Government Saving, as % of GDP	Employment, as % of Total Employment
			Total	Defense	Public Order and Safety	Education	Health	Social Security and Welfare	Housing and Community Amenities		
Asia–Pacific	33.2	31.9	14.0	1.6	1.3	3.5	1.8	0.8	0.5	1.3	14.9
Australia	33.5	36.9	18.2	2.2	1.3	3.8	3.1	1.0	0.3	-3.4	16.6
Japan	32.90	26.9	9.7	0.9	—	3.2	0.5	0.6	0.7	6.0	5.9
New Zealand	—	—	—	—	—	—	—	—	—	—	22.1
Europe	46.2	48.6	19.8	2.3	1.4	4.6	4.2	2.3	0.5	-2.4	19.6
Austria	47.3	47.8	19.0	0.9	0.9	4.3	5.1	3.5	0.0	-0.5	22.4
Belgium	50.9	54.6	16.8[a]	2.6[a]	1.6[a]	6.2[a]	0.5[a]	1.0[a]	0.2[a]	-3.7	19.3
Denmark	58.3	61.1	26.3	2.0	1.0	5.8	5.3	6.6	0.2	-2.9	31.8
Finland	52.5	58.9	23.3	1.8	1.3	5.8	5.1	3.7	0.6	-6.3	24.8
France	46.8	51.0	17.9	3.0	0.8	4.6	3.1	1.4	1.1	-4.2	24.8
Germany	45.7	45.6	18.3	2.2	1.5	3.5	5.6	2.2	0.3	0.0	14.9
Greece	40.2	51.2	19.8	4.9	—	3.1	2.3	0.3	—	-11.1	—
Iceland	35.9	34.9	20.6	0.0	1.3	4.0	6.6	1.6	0.8	1.0	19.4
Ireland	40.1	41.7	—	—	—	—	—	—	—	-1.6	14.3
Italy	44.9	50.9	17.8	1.9	1.9	4.7	3.7	0.7	0.5	-6.0	16.2
Luxembourg	52.9	45.0[a]	—	—	—	—	—	—	—	7.9	10.8
Norway	55.3	52.9	21.5	3.2	0.9	5.5	4.9	2.3	-0.1	2.4	28.7
Portugal	36.0[b]	34.7[b]	15.1[b]	1.5[b]	2.0[b]	4.4[b]	2.4[b]	0.7[b]	0.4[b]	1.3[b]	14.7
Spain	40.1	43.7	15.6	1.5	1.2	3.0	3.7	1.7	0.9	-3.6	15.1
Sweden	59.0	67.3	27.9	2.4	1.5	5.3	5.2	6.4	0.6	-8.3	32.6
Switzerland	36.0	36.7	—	—	—	—	—	—	—	-0.7	14.1
The Netherlands	52.0	53.2	15.3[b]	2.7	—	4.6[b]	—	0.7[b,c]	—	-1.2	12.7
United Kingdom	36.8	42.7	22.0	3.8	2.2	4.4	5.7	1.8	0.6	-5.9	16.9
North America	37.0	41.2	17.1	—	—	—	—	—	—	-4.2	17.5
Canada	42.2	46.5	—	—	—	—	—	—	—	-4.3	20.4
United States	31.7	35.8	17.1	—	—	—	—	—	—	-4.1	14.5
All countries	44.1	46.4	19.0	2.2	1.4	4.5	3.9	2.1	0.5	-2.2	18.8

Source: Data from Organisation for Economic Cooperation and Development. (1996). *OECD in figures 1996 edition* (pp. 44–45). Paris: Author.
Notes: OECD = Organisation for Economic Cooperation and Development; GDP = gross domestic product; — = not available.
[a]1986.
[b]1989.
[c]Includes social security.

Latin America

Development in Latin America is progressing at an especially slow pace, although important changes are occurring (Estes, 1996b). Since 1970, for example, the region's most important 20-year social development accomplishments occurred on the demographic, welfare effort, political participation, and women's status subindexes. Although these gains were important, they were eroded by regional losses on the economic, cultural diversity, health etatus, and education subindexes. Latin America' defense effort scores, although more favorable than those of the rest of the world, remained unchanged for the 20-year period.

The region's 20-year pattern of social gains and losses reflects the intermittent nature of Latin America's development. The asynchronous nature of the region's development is closely associated with

- Latin America's recent history of intraregional wars, civil unrest, and political instability
- continuing high levels of external indebtedness and low rates of economic growth
- high inflation and high unemployment
- intractable poverty, especially for residents of the region's unsustainable urban agglomerations
- slow social, political, and economic progress for women
- inattention to the special development needs of children and youths (for example, preventive health, preparatory education, and housing security)
- comparative neglect of the region's most urgent needs by international donors and development assistance organizations.

Latin American social workers are performing heroically in meeting the challenges before them, especially in the absence of critical social infrastructure. Social work practice within the region continues to focus on social reform and seeks mainly to redress chronic problems of injustices between the region's rich minority and poor majority populations. Land reform efforts have been somewhat successful, and, on balance, a broader spectrum of health and education services is becoming available to the region's large population of rural poor people. Fertility control, housing, skills training for employment, informal education, and agricultural

reform are major concerns of social work activity in the region's urban areas.

Asia

Asia's strongest performances on the WISP occurred in the cultural diversity, economic, and health status subindexes. The region's performance in these subindexes closely approximates those of the world as a whole. This is not surprising, because 60 percent of the world's population resides in this region (Estes, 1996a).

Significant 20-year gains occurred in the defense effort, economic, cultural diversity, women's status, demographic, and geography subindexes. Gains also were observed in the education subindex. Regional progress in these subindexes is impressive and reflects the outcome of substantial social investment by many Asian governments. These gains also reflect the growing influence on public policy of the region's rapidly developing private sector. However, Asia's losses on the welfare effort and political participation subindexes are worrisome, given the concentration in the region of 70 percent of the world population living in absolute poverty, the region's stated priority of promoting increased popular participation at every level of political decision making, and the region's far-reaching economic goals, including the export of their products and contract labor to more developed regions.

Despite Asia's enormously varied national realities, social work practice in the region tends to share many goals in common:

- elimination of absolute poverty and its associated social pathologies, including homelessness, begging, hunger and malnutrition, high mortality rates among infants and children, and illiteracy
- creation of more sustainable economic systems, especially at the local level
- increased popular participation in politics
- restoring and strengthening traditional family and community systems
- more mobility and more educational and employment opportunities for women
- increased legal and social protection for the most vulnerable populations (for example, aged people, people with disabilities, children and youths, and religious and ethnic groups)
- emphasis on responsible child spacing and family planning within the context of local cultures and religious mandates

- effective land reform and renewed attention to agricultural development and food self-sufficiency.

Urban social workers in Asia's poorest countries also are leaders in the resolution of the social dislocation problems associated with the migration of large numbers of people to the region's urban centers: congestion, inadequate housing, underemployment and unemployment, violence, sexual promiscuity, substance abuse, divorce, and so forth. These problems often coexist with the emergence of slums and their characteristic absence of basic social and physical infrastructure (roads, streets, access to clean piped water, schools, emergency health services, and the like). In the region's richer countries (such as Japan, Hong Kong, Singapore, Taiwan, and South Korea), the services problems faced by Asian social workers are not unlike those experienced in Western countries—for example, serving an aging population, financing human services, and establishing new partnerships between the public and private sectors.

The social development challenges facing the Asian region are complex and will not readily yield to simple solutions. The intervention models that are being developed by the region's innovative social workers are of great interest to social workers in other parts of the world, even in comparatively rich industrialized countries. Social workers often make possible the transfer of the most promising of these new social technologies, such as poverty alleviation methods, noncollateralized microcredit arrangements, microenterprise development, low-technology approaches to health care, energy conservation, nonformal education, and the like.

Africa
The African region experienced 20-year net losses on six of the WISP's 10 subindexes: political participation, demographic, women's status, economic, geography, and defense effort. These losses are significant and reflect not only the general state of social stagnation in the region but also the major social reversals that Africa has experienced since earlier decades of development. As a result, Africa remains the world's least developed region despite two decades of preferential international development assistance (Estes, 1995).

Despite a generally negative assessment of development trends for the region as a whole, small but important 20-year social gains were recorded for the region on the health status, welfare effort, education, and cultural diversity subindexes. Net improvements in these subindexes reflect understanding by Africa's political leaders of the need for substantial new investments in human development as a precondition for accelerated economic development. However, the region's gains in these sectors will be difficult to sustain without simultaneous advances in the economic, women's status, demographic, and political participation subindexes.

WORLD SOCIAL LEADERS AND SOCIALLY LEAST DEVELOPING COUNTRIES
Table 2 identifies world social leaders (SLs), middle-performing countries (MPCs), and "socially least developing countries" (SLDCs). The criteria used to assign countries to these categories are overall performance on the WISP in 1990, the consistency of WISP performance since 1970, and individual country performance on the WISP relative to all 124 countries included in the study.

Leaders in Social Development
On the basis of their overall WISP performances, 25 countries are classified as world SLs. Most of these countries are in Europe and North America—and, in the case of Japan, in Asia. Australia and New Zealand—countries whose majority populations and social systems originated in Europe—are also included. Four former Warsaw Pact countries are classified as SLs: the former German Democratic Republic, Hungary, the former Czechoslovakia (now the Czech Republic and Slovakia), and Poland. No Central or South American country has been identified as an SL.

In general, SLs are countries with market economies and multiparty political systems (Estes, 1990). Most share similar ideological commitments on a broad range of social, political, and economic issues: With the exception of Japan, they also share long histories of progressive social legislation that have resulted in comprehensive, mostly universally available, social welfare programs and services (U.S. Department of Health and Human Services, 1995). On average, SLs allocate from 60 percent to 90 percent of central government's total revenues to domestic social

TABLE 2
Country Scores and Rankings on the Weighted Index of Social Progress (WISP), 1970–90

Country	WISP90	Rank WISP90	Position Changes in WISP Ranks 1970–80	Position Changes in WISP Ranks 1980–90	Position Changes in WISP Ranks 1970–90
Social leaders					
Denmark	108	1	−1	2	1
Norway	103	2	−3	4	1
Sweden	102	3	−3	1	−2
Austria	101	4	3	1	4
The Netherlands	100	5	−5	4	−1
France	98	6	3	1	4
Federal Republic of Germany	98	7	5	−6	−1
Italy	97	8	10	−6	4
Finland	97	9	−1	6	5
Belgium	97	10	3	−2	1
Switzerland	96	11	7	2	9
United Kingdom	96	12	−7	0	−7
Ireland	95	13	−4	−2	−6
Japan	95	14	12	−4	8
Canada	93	15	1	3	4
New Zealand	93	16	−7	0	−7
Australia	91	17	−1	−3	−4
United States	90	18	4	1	5
Spain	90	19	7	−2	5
German Democratic Republic	88	20	—	1	—
Greece	87	21	9	−1	8
Hungary	87	22	−7	0	−7
Portugal	87	23	5	3	8
Czechoslovakia	83	24	−8	0	−8
Poland	80	25	−8	0	−8
Middle performing countries					
Bulgaria	79	26	−5	−3	−8
Uruguay	78	27	−4	4	0
Taiwan	75	28	—	11	—
Costa Rica	75	29	6	−1	5
South Korea	74	30	3	16	19
Argentina	73	31	−2	4	2
Israel	73	32	5	0	5
Yugoslavia	72	33	−1	−4	−5
Hong Kong	71	34	—	4	—
Singapore	70	35	9	1	10
Chile	69	36	−19	13	−6
Romania	69	37	−6	−10	−16
Jamaica	67	38	4	−4	0
Mauritius	67	39	—	6	—
Trinidad and Tobago	66	40	−2	2	0
Cuba	65	41	−11	−4	−15
Soviet Union	65	42	−19	2	−17
Colombia	64	43	4	−3	1
Venezuela	63	44	6	−11	−5
Brazil	63	45	−6	−4	−10
Panama	63	46	−7	−3	−10
Thailand	62	47	−1	6	5
Mexico	59	48	−8	6	−2
Sri Lanka	57	49	−5	−2	−7
Dominican Republic	57	50	−1	2	1
Tunisia	57	51	−3	5	2
Ecuador	57	52	−4	−1	−5
Turkey	55	53	−1	2	1

TABLE 2 (*continued*)

Country	WISP90	Rank WISP90	Position Changes in WISP Ranks 1970–80	Position Changes in WISP Ranks 1980–90	Position Changes in WISP Ranks 1970–90
Albania	55	54	−16	−6	−22
Paraguay	53	55	−2	−5	−7
El Salvador	53	56	−8	2	−6
Malaysia	52	57	3	0	3
Philippines	51	58	−6	3	−3
Algeria	50	59	−13	15	2
Jordan	50	60	5	5	10
Honduras	50	61	−19	14	−5
China	49	62	—	11	—
Saudi Arabia	48	63	—	19	—
Peru	48	64	−11	5	−6
Egypt	47	65	−6	3	−3
North Korea	47	66	—	−3	—
Morocco	45	67	−1	5	4
Lebanon	45	68	11	−38	−27
Iran	45	69	1	−3	−2
Libya	44	70	22	−8	14
South Africa	44	71	−16	−12	−28
Mongolia	43	72	—	−2	—
Indonesia	42	73	41	−13	28
Syria	39	74	0	−10	−10
Nicaragua	39	75	−21	3	−18
Zimbabwe	37	76	−16	5	−11
Guatemala	36	77	−12	3	−9
Myanmar[a]	36	78	−25	6	−19
Lesotho[a]	36	79	—	−8	—
Iraq	35	80	−10	−4	−14
India	35	81	1	4	5
Vietnam	34	82	−4	−5	−9
Socially least developing countries					
Haiti[a]	28	83	−17	6	−11
Zambia[a]	28	84	−12	4	−8
Papua New Guinea	28	85	—	−2	—
Congo	27	86	—	5	—
Bolivia	27	87	−4	−20	−24
Pakistan	24	88	−18	15	−3
Senegal	24	89	−23	9	−14
Kenya	24	90	−12	−4	−16
Madagascar[a]	23	91	−10	−12	−22
Cameroon	21	92	−10	0	−10
Rwanda[a]	21	93	−13	9	−4
Bangladesh[a]	19	94	—	7	—
Burundi[a]	18	95	−13	22	9
Togo[a]	17	96	−6	10	4
Nepal[a]	17	97	−8	7	−1
Ghana	16	98	−16	1	−15
Côte d'Ivoire	16	99	−11	−9	−20
Republic of Yemen[a]	15	100	—	14	—
Laos[a]	15	101	—	−5	—
Tanzania[a]	15	102	2	−7	−5
Zaire[a]	14	103	−3	−9	−12
Malawi[a]	13	104	−22	16	−6
Sudan[a]	13	105	−12	−5	−17
Mauritania[a]	13	106	−33	7	−26
Uganda[a]	12	107	−14	0	−14
Cambodia[a]	12	108	−27	0	−27

Continued

TABLE 2 (*continued*)

Country	WISP90	Rank WISP90	Position Changes in WISP Ranks 1970–80	Position Changes in WISP Ranks 1980–90	Position Changes in WISP Ranks 1970–90
Liberia[a]	12	109	–19	–12	–31
Nigeria	11	110	15	–23	–8
Central African Republic[a]	9	111	–10	–2	–12
Benin[a]	8	112	–13	–7	–20
Burkina-Faso[a]	8	113	–4	–2	–6
South Yemen[a]	7	114	–3	–21	–24
Mali[a]	4	115	–20	0	–20
Afghanistan[a]	3	116	—	5	—
Niger[a]	3	117	–13	–1	–14
Sierra Leone[a]	2	118	–33	–8	–41
Somalia[a]	1	119	–25	–7	–32
Guinea[a]	–1	120	–24	–2	–26
Chad[a]	–2	121	–17	2	–15
Angola[a]	–3	122	—	–3	—
Mozambique[a]	–4	123	—	–1	—
Ethiopia[a]	–10	124	–19	0	–19
World	48.8	62.5	–5.0	0.0	–5.5

NOTES: — = Not available.
[a]Classified as least developing countries by the United Nations.

spending. SLs are also distinguished by their sustained high levels of social development.

The countries that can be considered the world's five most socially advanced tend to be comparatively small and culturally homogeneous: Denmark, Norway, Sweden, Austria, and The Netherlands. The populations of these countries range between 4.3 million (Norway) and 15.3 million (The Netherlands) and culturally are predominantly white and Protestant.

SLs enjoy consistently low population growth rates, longer average life expectancy, low rates of infant and child mortality, and high levels of child and adult literacy. The majority of SLs have strong and dynamic economies: Unemployment rates are high in some of the European SLs, but, in general, inflation tends to be low. As a result, per capita income levels in SLs are high, and nearly all SLs enjoy favorable international exchange rates for their currencies. In addition, SL per capita debt levels, although high for some countries, are substantially lower than those in the majority of developing countries. The majority of SLs also are characterized by low levels of diversity-related social conflict (although France, the United Kingdom, and the United States are notable exceptions to this pattern), and only a few have engaged in major wars or other international disputes since the end of World War II. SL public expenditures for defense and

military purposes also tend to be low (Table 1), except in the United States and the United Kingdom, which allocated 18.1 percent and 10.4 percent, respectively, of their central government resources to defense purposes in 1994 (World Bank, 1996).

WISP scores for the SLs averaged 94 (standard deviation [*SD*] = 6.6) in 1990; scores range from a low of 80 for Poland to an exceptionally high score of 108 for Denmark, which retained the highest overall WISP scores for all three time periods. On average, SLs improved their WISP rank positions by one rank (*SD* = 5.5) between 1970 and 1990. Significant 20-year WISP rank position losses, however, were observed for the former Czechoslovakia, Poland, the United Kingdom, Hungary, Ireland, and Australia. Sweden and The Netherlands also experienced losses in their WISP rank positions between 1970 and 1990.

Approximately 17 percent of the world's population in 1995—about 890 million people— reside in the SLs. SL share of the world's total population is expected to decline steadily until at least 2025, by which time only about 13 percent of the world's population will reside in current SL countries.

Middle-Performing Countries
Fifty-seven countries are identified in Table 2 as MPCs. Approximately 3.7 billion people,

about 68 percent of the world's total population, live in the MPCs. All the MPCs are in Asia, Africa, and Latin America, with the exception of the former Soviet Union and certain countries in Eastern Europe, such as Bulgaria, the former Yugoslavia, Romania, and Albania. Three of the world's four largest population centers, China, Indonesia, and India, are grouped with the MPCs.

WISP scores in 1990 for the MPCs ranged from a low of 34 for Vietnam to a high of 79 for Bulgaria; the group's average score is 55.3 (SD = 12.9)—just six points higher than the average score of the world as a whole (mean [M] = 49). The majority of MPCs experienced 20-year net losses in WISP ranks averaging -3.8 ranks per country (SD = 10.7). The most significant positional losses occurred for South Africa, Lebanon, Albania, Myanmar (formerly Burma), Nicaragua, the former Soviet Union, Romania, and Cuba.

The MPCs are highly heterogeneous: Enormous differences characterize the countries grouped at the top and at the bottom of the list. In general, the majority of countries at the top of the MPCs list are well on their way toward becoming SLs (for example, Uruguay, Taiwan, Costa Rica, South Korea, Argentina, Israel, and Singapore). The countries at the bottom of the list are in danger of drifting into SLDC status (for example, Vietnam, India, Iraq, Guatemala, and Zimbabwe). Since 1990 at least two of the MPCs near the bottom of the list—Lesotho and Myanmar—have been officially classified by the United Nations as "least developing countries" (LDCs), a term coined in 1971 to describe the "poorest and most economically weak of the developing countries, with formidable economic, institutional and human resource problems, which are often compounded by geographic handicaps and natural and man-made disasters" (United Nations Department of Public Information [UNDPI], 1996, p. 4).

MPCs in the middle of the list have the potential to move toward either SL or SLDC status. Since 1970 the majority of these MPCs have experienced net losses in their WISP rank positions. Some of these losses have been significant (such as those observed for Albania), but the losses of other middle-ranking MPCs have been more modest, as in Mexico, Sri Lanka, and Ecuador. Current development trends are suggestive of a more favorable near-term outcome for Thailand,

Tunisia, Malaysia, the Dominican Republic, and Turkey.

The proportion of the world's population living in the MPCs is expected to remain constant well into the next century. This group's most rapid population increases will occur within the poorest and least developed of the MPCs. As is already the case today, seven of every 10 people on the planet will reside in MPCs in 2025.

Socially Least Developing Countries
Table 2 also identifies the world's 42 SLDCs. The majority of SLDCS are located in Sub-Saharan Africa and the developing subregions of Asia and Latin America. To date, 32 of the SLDCs have been officially classified by the United Nations as LDCs. WISP scores for the SLDCs range from a low of -10 for Ethiopia to a high of 28 for Haiti. WISP scores for the SLDCs averaged only 13 (SD = 9.7) in 1990, well below the average score of 94 achieved by the SLs for the same time period. Twenty-year net gains on the WISP occurred for only nine of the 42 SLDCs: Burundi, Burkina-Faso, Togo, Nepal, Pakistan, Rwanda, Tanzania, Congo, and Malawi. Only Burundi and Togo advanced their WISP rank position between 1970 and 1990. All other SLDCs experienced net losses in their WISP rank positions between 1970 and 1990. These 20-year positional losses on the WISP averaged -15, with 11 countries (Sierra Leone, Somalia, Liberia, Cambodia, Mauritania, Bolivia, South Yemen, Madagascar, Côte d'Ivorie, Benin, and Mali) experiencing losses of 20 or more WISP rank positions.

Despite some limited but important gains by a few SLDCs since 1970, the pace of social progress in most SLDCs remains painfully sluggish. Their situation continues to be much the same as that described by the Brandt Commission in 1980:

> Many hundreds of millions of people in the poorer countries are preoccupied solely with survival and elementary needs. For them work is frequently not available or, when it is, pay is low and conditions often barely tolerable. Homes are constructed of impermanent materials and have neither piped water nor sanitation. Electricity is a luxury. Health services are thinly spread and in rural areas only rarely within walking distance. Primary schools, where they exist, may be free and not too far away, but children are needed for work

and cannot be easily spared for schooling. Permanent insecurity is the condition of the poor. There are no public systems of social security in the event of unemployment, sickness or death of a wage-earner in the family. Flood, drought or disease affecting people or livestock can destroy livelihoods without hope of compensation.

The poorest of the poor . . . will remain . . . outside the reach of normal trade and communication. The combination of malnutrition, illiteracy, disease, high birth rates, underemployment and low income closes off the avenues of escape. (p. 49)

Approximately 15 percent of the world's population—about 820 million people in 1995—currently reside in SLDCs. Their numbers are expected to continue to increase until at least 2025, by which time more than 20 percent of the world's population will reside in these deeply impoverished nations.

DRAMATIC SOCIAL GAINS AND LOSSES

Dramatic social changes have occurred in the WISP profiles of 73 countries. (A change of more than five WISP ranks in either direction is considered a "dramatic" change for purposes of this analysis.)

Gains

Thirty-six countries increased their WISP scores by at least 25 percent between 1970 and 1990. The initial scores of these countries averaged 37 in 1970, 44 in 1980, and 52 in 1990; hence, broad-based social development increased in these countries by an average of 21 percent between 1980 and 1990 and 64 percent over the entire 20-year period studied. The most dramatic advances in social development occurred for Indonesia, Burundi, Burkina-Faso, and Libya. The changes for Burundi and Burkina-Faso are especially noteworthy because both countries currently are classified officially by the United Nations as LDCs. Significant 20-year social gains also were recorded for three other LDCs: Togo, Nepal, and Tanzania. A 10-year gain of 61 percent occurred in the Republic of Yemen, another officially designated LDC.

Rapid advances also occurred in the development profiles of four SLs: Portugal, Japan, Switzerland, and the United States. These countries succeeded not only in consoli-

dating their past social accomplishments, they also used their successes to move to significantly higher levels of social performance. Gains of this magnitude are especially difficult to achieve because these countries already have advanced social positions. The most significant social accomplishments between 1980 and 1990 occurred in Burundi, Saudi Arabia, the Republic of Yemen, Honduras, Algeria, Pakistan, China, South Korea, Taiwan, India, and Jordan. These 11 countries are ready to achieve even higher levels of social development in the near future, and it is encouraging that countries from the Asian, African, and Latin American regions have achieved such social gains. Also encouraging is the inclusion of China and India in the group of countries that have been developing rapidly since 1980. Together these two population giants contain more than 2 billion people—nearly 40 percent of the world's total population.

Losses

Thirty-seven countries experienced significant 10- and 20-year social losses on the WISP. Countries with the most dramatic 20-year social losses are widely scattered, but those with the most significant losses are concentrated in Sub-Saharan Africa and Southeast Asia. African nations are especially overrepresented on the list, making up 62 percent of all countries identified as having experienced dramatic social losses. Albania and Romania are the only European countries in which significant 20-year social losses occurred. Within Latin America, social losses were observed only for Cuba and Haiti. The most dramatic 20-year social losses occurred in Mozambique, Ethiopia, Angola, Chad, Guinea, Somalia, Sierra Leone, Mali, Republic of Yemen, Liberia, Niger, Cambodia, Mauritania, Benin, and Côte d'Ivorie.

WISP scores with net social losses averaged 28 in 1970 and 20 in 1990, a net decline of 29 percent in average score values between 1970 and 1990 and 36 percent between 1980 and 1990. Thus, 80 percent of all the social losses occurred between 1980 and 1990 (Table 2). In another study, the United Nations found that the gap in development between the world's richest and poorest 20 percent of nations doubled between 1960 and 1991, that is, from 30:1 to 61:1 (UNDPI, 1996). The magnitude of this gap is especially disturbing, given the increasing proportion of the world population living in conditions of absolute poverty.

DILEMMAS UNTIL 2000 AND BEYOND

The world's nations have arrived at a critical crossroads. Considerable progress has been realized in achieving at least some of the planet's social goals, but much remains to be done. The following issues must be resolved if significant progress is to be achieved in the future.

Continuing High Rates of Population Growth

Although lower than in the past, the world's overall rate of population increase averaged 1.7 percent in 1990. At the current growth rate, the worldwide population is expected to reach approximately 6.1 billion people by 2000, 7.0 billion by 2010, and 8.2 billion by 2025. The population growth rate is expected to drop to 1.0 percent by 2025. At the same time, population doubling time—the number of years required to double the existing population—is expected to slow to every 60 years rather than every 45 years, which is currently the case.

Eighty percent of the world's population growth since 1960 has been concentrated in the planet's poorest regions, and 95 percent of this increase has occurred in the poorest countries in these regions. At the same time, the proportion of the world's population living in more developed regions has declined from 31 percent in 1960 to 23 percent in 1990. This trend is expected to continue until at least 2025, when 20 percent of the world's population will reside in more developed regions. In even the most optimistic scenarios, the majority of the world's governments are likely to experience severe challenges to their ability to provide for even the basic needs of so many people.

Population Migration

Population migration—both internal and external—continues to be a dominant feature of world social development. Each type of migration may be either voluntary or involuntary, although the choices available to migrants fleeing poverty, political persecution, wars, and the like are severely limited.

Most of today's international migration is occurring in response to recurrent wars, civil unrest, political persecution, and economic failure, as well as the search for new jobs. Today, 100 million people—one person in every 50 on the planet—are living as involuntary migrants outside their country of origin. Some 27 million of these people are officially classified

by the United Nations as political refugees, and an additional 28 million are considered religious and economic refugees and are not given the same social protection granted by the United Nations to political refugees.

The social, economic, and political impact of migration on the world's governments has been enormous. Migration is accelerating the growth and increasing the complexity of urban population centers, which is giving rise to the number of urban agglomerations in which 10 million or more people reside. Migration is also contributing to the appearance of new slums, shantytowns, and other so-called "temporary" communities in which large numbers of poor people reside. This strains the capacity of local governments to make available even the most basic of services required to sustain large numbers of people in such environments, including water, sanitation, food, and basic health and education services.

In recent years, the migration of large numbers of people from developing to developed countries has given rise to backlash movements directed at both legal and illegal immigrants. These movements have been most regressive in France, Japan, Germany, Switzerland, the United States, the United Kingdom, and elsewhere. In all cases, they are intended to deny access to the services that residents who have come from other countries need to ensure their integration into their new homeland, such as language instruction, education, health care, and employment.

Diversity-Related Social Conflicts

Diversity-related social conflicts remain a central challenge at the top of the social agenda. The most enduring of these conflicts are associated with plurality, race, religion, ethnicity, language and accent, caste, and social class. In all cases these conflicts result from asymmetric power relationships between members of more powerful and less powerful groups, which are intensified during periods of economic downturn and political uncertainty.

Today, serious diversity-related social conflicts can be found in almost every country. These conflicts contribute directly to the rapidly increasing levels of crime and personal violence that exist in most of the world's cities. The situation worsens during periods of economic recession and when opportunities for individual and collective advancement are remote. In all cases, diversity-related social conflicts are intense, dehumanizing, and pernicious. They deprive the world's peoples of precisely the resources needed to bring such conflicts to an end.

Economic Threats

The major threats to further worldwide economic development include unemployment and underemployment, the persistence of meaningless work, the relaxation or absence of occupational health and safety standards, continuing high levels of external indebtedness, widening world poverty, and "aid fatigue" as reflected in the reduced flow of official development assistance from more developed to less developed countries. The precise nature of each of these threats to world economic development has been described fully elsewhere and are only noted here (see UNDP, 1996; World Bank, 1996).

The persistence of these patterns confirms that, for at least the remainder of the 20th century, the majority of the world's poorest countries will be expected to achieve more with less. As a result, more stringent controls are likely to be placed on the choices available to national governments in their efforts to respond to local realities. Official Development Assistance (ODA) is likely to be more conditional than in the past, although greater attention will probably be given to the social components of development. Donor demands for structural adjustment and other macrolevel economic reforms are also likely to intensify. Hence, a broader mix of development partners—especially those drawn from the private sector—will be needed by the world's poorest countries as they seek to implement more ambitious social development agendas with few economic resources.

Global Poverty

Along with population migration, total poverty and absolute poverty remain as dominant features of world social development. According to economic criteria identified by the World Bank (1990), total poverty includes all individuals and families with household incomes of less than $350 per year; absolute poverty refers to those households with annual incomes well below $250 and that are unable to meet their daily water, food, shelter, and other basic needs.

In a highly influential study of global poverty, the World Bank (1990) estimated that

at least 1.2 billion people worldwide live in poverty. Of this number, approximately half the world's poor people were living under conditions of absolute poverty, without the basic material resources required to sustain dignified human life. The study confirmed that

- worldwide, approximately one person in five lives in poverty
- poverty exists in all regions of the world
- poverty is unevenly concentrated in Asia and Sub-Saharan Africa
- the incidence of poverty is increasing.

Poverty in Africa is concentrated in Ethiopia and natural resources-rich Nigeria and Ethiopia, as well as in many smaller, landlocked countries. The majority of these countries have only recently obtained their political independence from European colonial powers. In Asia, poverty is concentrated primarily in the southern and eastern areas: Bangladesh, India, Indonesia, Pakistan, the Philippines, central and western China, and Vietnam.

The United Nations Department of Public Information (1996) estimates that more than two-thirds of the world's poor people live in just 10 African and Asian countries: Bangladesh, Brazil, China, Ethiopia, India, Indonesia, Nigeria, Pakistan, the Philippines, and Vietnam. The majority of the world's poor people are women and children, most of whom reside in rural communities. The situation is especially acute among rural households headed by women whose husbands have migrated to urban centers in search of paid employment.

A study undertaken by UNDP concluded that the number of the world's people living in absolute poverty increased to more than 1 billion by 1993—this despite a sevenfold increase in the wealth of nations over the past half century (UNDP, 1997). The transnational nature of contemporary poverty was poignantly summarized by UNDP (1996) when it concluded that "poverty is no longer contained within national boundaries. It has become globalized. It travels across borders, without a passport, in the form of drugs, diseases, pollution, migration, terrorism and political instability" (p. 2).

Weakened Family and Kinship Systems

Traditional family and kinship systems are undergoing profound changes everywhere in the world. These changes are driven mainly by such economic forces as repeated failures in subsistence agriculture, the availability of relatively higher-paying jobs in urban factories, and new economic opportunities in neighboring and distant countries. Social and political forces also figure centrally in the changes that are affecting traditional family forms—for example, continuing high rates of population increase, an aging population, increasing numbers of women who need to work outside the home, and recurrent wars and civil conflict, among other factors.

Nearly all of these changes have occurred in the absence of adequate social welfare and other support programs (for example, unemployment and housing schemes, job training, income support during periods of work-related injury or illness, child care assistance, and services for dependent elderly people). Without such programs, the world's smaller and increasingly urbanized families have become more vulnerable than in the past. Consequently, millions of people have drifted into poverty and find themselves unable to draw on the traditional family systems that offered social and economic assistance in the past.

Comparatively few of the world's poorer countries are able to absorb the economic and social costs associated with the loss of traditional family and kinship systems. They lack the resources to implement the types of social safety nets that residents of more developed countries take for granted—yet the need for such programs exists and grows more urgent each day.

Rise of Neoconservativism

Regressive neoconservative governments have re-emerged in certain developed countries of the northern hemisphere. The origins of these governments are complex but are rooted mainly in the chronic economic difficulties that these countries have confronted since at least the 1980s: slow to moderate economic growth rates, high unemployment in combination with high inflation, underemployment, increased international competition for export markets, deepening central government deficits, growing national debts, and escalating demands for publicly financed human services and other services.

In general, neoconservative governments are engaged in four types of reforms:

1. reducing the size, scope, and influence of their central governments (downsizing)
2. shifting responsibility for problems in the public sector to lower levels of government (devolution)
3. shifting a larger share of the burden for public problem solving to the private sector (privatization)
4. creating new public-private partnerships to resolve recurrent social problems for which public action alone is judged to be inadequate or inappropriate.

Thus, these governments emphasize reducing the number and scope of public entitlement programs, reconceptualizing consumers and other beneficiaries of public programs as customers of the programs, promoting increased effectiveness of those reduced services that remain under public auspices, and improving the cost-effectiveness of all public programs and services, including welfare and other income-support programs for poor people.

Lower wages, reduced fringe benefits, declines in the unionization of workers, and reduced public subsidies for essential human services are associated with neoconservative movements, as are reductions in ODA to developing countries. Often, ODA that is provided is further conditioned upon the purposes for which the aid may be used. In many countries with neoconservative governments, the trend is toward withdrawal from the conflicts and demands of the outside world on what is perceived to be a shrinking national resources base. However, a few of these governments, such as Denmark, Norway, and Belgium, are maintaining their investments in developing countries; other countries, such as France, Germany, and Japan, are actually making historically high financial investments. Nearly all the neoconservative governments, though, have imposed severe immigration quotas for people from poorer countries.

Paradoxically, powerful neoconservative forces are at work in the world community at a time when many previously developing countries—such as Singapore, Taiwan, South Korea, Hungary, Poland, and the Czech Republic—are ready to be considered as more developed countries. The now-advantaged economic status of these countries clearly is the direct result of decades-long investments by richer countries, which has helped to transform these and other countries into modern states.

Prospects for the Future

After decades of only modest social improvement, once again, the majority of the world's countries are strengthening their capacity to meet at least the basic needs of their growing populations. Many countries are developing at a rapid pace: With time, some can be expected to join the group of more developed countries. Others, though, remain outside the range of social progress. For them, the pace of social progress is exceedingly slow—even backward—relative to the development accomplishments of earlier decades. Intractable problems of poverty, ill health, high population growth, inadequate housing, unstable government, civil conflict, economic uncertainty, and substantially weakened traditional family and kinship systems are more common in such countries.

As the new century begins, the need is apparent for new, more dramatic initiatives that will transform all the world's nations into more caring and socially productive societies. At a minimum, these initiatives must promote the elimination of absolute poverty everywhere, enhanced popular participation at all levels of social organization, and a more equitable sharing of the planet's abundant resources. As partners with governments and with people, social workers must remain faithful to the goals that have informed social work practice for more than a century: social provision, not treatment; social caring, not remediation; social change, not accommodation; and fundamental, but sustainable, transformation of the inhumane institutions and social systems in which so many of the world's people live. Only through faithfulness to the profession's historical mission and ideals can international social workers effectively contribute to the creation of the new global society they seek.

References

Brandt Commission. (1980). *North-south: A programme for survival.* London: Pan Books.

Estes, R. J. (1988). *Trends in world social development.* New York: Praeger.

Estes, R. J. (1990). Social development under different political and economic systems. *Social Development Issues, 13*(1), 5–29.

Estes, R. J. (1995). Social development trends in Africa: The need for a new development paradigm. *Social Development Issues, 17*(1), 18–47.

Estes, R. J. (1996a). Social development trends in Asia: Reflections on 25 years of social and economic development. *Social Indicators Research, 37*(2), 119–148.

Estes, R. J. (1996b). Social development trends in Central and South America: In the shadows of the 21st century. *Social Development Issues, 18*(1), 25–52.

Estes, R. J. (in press). Trends in European social development: Development prospects for the new Europe. *Social Indicators Research.*

Organization for Economic Cooperation and Development. (1996). *OECD in figures: 1996 edition.* Paris: Author.

United Nations Children's Fund (UNICEF). (1997). *The state of the world's children, 1997.* New York: Oxford University Press.

United Nations Department of Public Information (UNDPI). (1996). The geography of poverty. [Available online: http://www.un.org/dpcsd/dspd/dpi1782e.htm]

United Nations Development Programme (UNDP). (1994). *Human development report, 1994.* New York: Oxford University Press.

United Nations Development Programme (UNDP). (1996). *Human development report, 1996.* New York: Oxford University Press.

United Nations Development Programme (UNDP). (1997). *Human development report, 1997.* New York: Oxford University Press.

U.S. Department of Health and Human Services. (1995). *Social security programs throughout the world, 1995.* Washington, DC: Social Security Administration.

World Bank. (1990). *World development report, 1990: Poverty.* New York: Oxford University Press.

World Bank. (1993). *World development report, 1993.* New York: Oxford University Press.

World Bank. (1996). *World development report, 1996: From plan to market.* New York: Oxford University Press.

Further Reading

Billups, J. O. (1990). Toward social development as an organizing concept for social work and related social professions and movements. *Social Development Issues, 12*(3), 14–26.

Clarke, S. (1996). *Social work as community development: A management model for social change.* Aldershot, England: Avebury.

Elliott, D., Mayadas, N. S., & Watts, T. D. (Eds.). (1990). *The world of social welfare: social welfare and social services in international context*. Springfield, IL: Charles C Thomas.

Estes, R. J. (1992). *Internationalizing social work education: A guide to resources for a new century*. Philadelphia: University of Pennsylvania, School of Social Work.

Estes, R. J. (1993). Toward sustainable development: From theory to praxis. *Social Development Issues, 15*(3), 1–29.

Healy, L. M. (1992). *Introducing international development content in the social work curriculum*. Washington, DC: NASW Press.

Khinduka, S. K. (1987). Development and peace: The complex nexus. *Social Development Issues, 10*(3), 19–30.

Midgley, J. (1995). *Social development: The developmental perspective in social welfare*. London: Sage Publications.

Sanders, D. S. (Ed.). (1982). *The developmental perspective in social work*. Honolulu: University of Hawaii, School of Social Work.

Schuerman, F. J. (1993). *Beyond impasse: New directions in development theory*. London: Zed Books.

Spergel, I. (1977). Social development and social work. *Administration in Social Work, 1*(3), 221–233.

Van Soest, D. (1992). *Incorporating peace and social justice into the social work curriculum*. Washington, DC: NASW Press.

van Wormer, K. (1997). *Social welfare: A world view*. Chicago: Nelson-Hall.

World Resource Institute. (1996). *World resources, 1996–1997*. New York: Oxford University Press.

Richard J. Estes, PhD, is professor of social work, School of Social Work, University of Pennsylvania, 3701 Locust Walk, Philadelphia, PA 19104; e-mail: restes@caster.ssw.upenn.edu.

For further information see

Community; **Community Building;** Community Organization; International and Comparative Social Welfare; International Social Welfare: Organizations and Activities; International Social Work Education; **Oppression;** Organizations: Context for Social Services Delivery; Social Development; Social Planning; Social Welfare History; Technology Transfer.

Key Words

economic development	social development
least developing countries	social indicators
	social progress

World Wide Web

See **The Internet: Accessing the World of Information; Social Work Education: Electronic Technologies**

Biographies

Cassidy, Helen (1918–1994)

Helen Cassidy—social work educator, administrator, practitioner—received her MSW from Tulane University in 1939 and began an active career spanning 55 years until her death in 1994. The early years of her career were spent as a medical social worker, first in Louisiana and then in Washington, DC, where she was the field director for the American National Red Cross, serving in three naval hospitals providing care to the armed forces. She then assumed overall administrative responsibility for social services programs and developed innovative approaches to offering coordinated casework/group work services.

Cassidy joined Tulane University's social work faculty in 1950 as a field instructor coordinating the maternal and child health grants. In 1959 she became the coordinator of field instruction. She taught a variety of human behavior, methods, and health courses, culminating in the design of and teaching in the gerontology certificate program. Her career at Tulane was a distinguished one, including a Fulbright scholarship to conduct research in the United Kingdom; service in Spain for the United Nations as an expert in social casework, which resulted in national and international prominence; the development of a field instruction model that has been widely copied in the United States; election as the first female president of NASW in 1966; establishment and co-founding of the hospice movement in New Orleans; and appointment as acting dean of the School of Social Work.

Throughout Cassidy's long career she demonstrated a continuing concern for the welfare and well-being of all her students and fellow social work practitioners. In 1987 she chaired the first national NASW symposium in New Orleans, and in 1988 she was named Alumna of the Year by the Tulane University School of Social Work.

Ronald Marks

Davis, Liane V. (1942–1995)

Liane Davis left a legacy as an advocate, scholar, and teacher whose commitment to social justice was lived out in every area of her life. As the child of social activists, she learned early lessons about justice and nonviolence. After receiving her BA degree from Antioch College, she became a child welfare caseworker in New York City. After completing her MSW degree at Adelphi University, she worked in a city health clinic in the Lower East Side of New York City. A second master's degree in psychology became the stepping stone to her PhD in social psychology from the University of North Carolina at Chapel Hill.

In 1978 she became a lecturer and, later, a faculty member of the School of Social Welfare at the University at Albany, State University of New York. In 1989 she joined the faculty of the University of Kansas School of Social Welfare and became associate dean of academic programs in 1992.

As a teacher, she inspired students to go beyond conventional boundaries and to creatively challenge systems that keep women "in their place." As an administrator, she provided leadership within the school and served as the school's representative on major university committees. She chaired NASW's National Committee on Women's Issues, was a member of the board of the Kansas chapter of NASW, and consulted for services to battered women. In 1995 the Council on Social Work Education honored her for distinguished recent contributions.

As a key figure in the renaissance of women's issues in social work, Davis taught and wrote about women's victimization, leaving a legacy of literature on women made vulnerable by abuse and poverty and on the services needed to support their strengths. Among her many publications, her classic article, "Female and Male Voices in Social Work" (*Social Work,* 1985), was among the first to critique the division between clinical social work practice and social work research from a feminist perspective. Her edited book, *Building on Women's Strengths* (1994), moved beyond analysis of the problems to an exploration of the transformational capacity inherent in the strengths of women. In a career cut short by death from cancer, Davis reflected a commitment to social work that is a beacon for the profession.

Ann Weick

Epstein, Laura (1914–1996)

Laura Epstein developed one of the earliest and most fully developed methods of social work intervention, task-centered treatment. This approach to practice was influential in the development of brief treatment approaches to psychotherapy. Her research is commonly used in graduate schools as a model of how a social intervention method is tested and refined during the initial years of implementation. Later in her career, she examined the influence of social structures and institutions on clinical social work practice in the 20th century.

Epstein was born in the Hyde Park neighborhood of Chicago and lived there most of her life. She earned a BA in psychology from the University of Chicago, as well as an MA from the University of Chicago School of Social Service Administration. Early in her career, she was active in union organizing. At a time when the Communist Party formed unions, Epstein's activities came under the scrutiny of the Federal Bureau of Investigation, and she was prevented from finding a job in social work. During World War II she worked at the war labor board in Chicago and completed statistical studies and assisted in mediating conflicts between labor and management. After the war she took a job at Traveler's Aid of Chicago that launched a career in social work, resulting in numerous books, articles, and national and international presentations. Her book *Brief Treatment* (1993) is used as a primary text for students of social work and other helping professions. She also wrote *Helping People: The Task-Centered Approach* (1988) and *Post Modernism and Social Work* (1995). Epstein's search for more humane and effective therapies influenced many students, practitioners, and clients. She received the University of Chicago School of Social Service Administration Charlotte Towle Medal for Lifetime Achievement in Social Work in June 1996.

Jeanne C. Marsh

Germain, Carel Bailey (1916–1995)

Carel Bailey Germain, scholar, teacher, writer, and theoretician, profoundly altered the shape of social work practice. A native of San Francisco, Germain was a devoted naturalist and was active in the Campfire Girls throughout her girlhood. Her love of and interest in nature had major significance for the future development of social work practice theory. She began her career in social work upon completing her BA degree at the University of California at Berkeley. Eventually, she and her family moved to the

East Coast, and she returned to school, receiving her MSW from Columbia University in 1961.

Her outstanding abilities were immediately recognized, and she quickly assumed a leadership role, becoming assistant director of social work in the Department of Psychiatry at the University of Maryland School of Medicine and teaching at the School of Social Work. At age 49, she entered the doctoral program at Columbia University, completing her degree in 1971.

From that time until her death, Germain occupied a major position in the intellectual life of the profession. She was professor of social work at the University of Connecticut and at Columbia University. Her softspoken, elegant, and reflective presentation and her warm and generous relationships enchanted students and colleagues at these institutions and at many others across the country where she was visiting professor, lecturer, consultant, and workshop leader.

A prolific writer, she published her first juried article while still a doctoral student and went on to publish more than 50 subsequent articles and book chapters, as well as to author seven books. Her thinking and writing always reflected her erudition; her extensive knowledge of social work, the social and biological sciences, literature, and the arts; and her originality, creativity, and willingness to challenge cherished notions.

Germain's first publications, the classic "Social Study: Past and Future," which appeared in 1968, and her 1970 "Casework and Science: An Historical Encounter," challenged the 19th century scientism implicit in linear notions of "study–diagnosis–treatment," laying the groundwork for her future contributions. Germain introduced an ecological metaphor for social work theory and practice in her 1973 "An Ecological Perspective in Social Casework." This was followed by a series of articles exploring the person and environment relationship from an ecological perspective, a theme continued in an edited volume, *Social Work Practice: People and Environments* (1979).

In 1989, with Alex Gitterman, she published the widely used text, *The Life Model of Social Work*, a work that focused on the natural human processes of growth, coping, adaptation, and change. A book applying the ecological perspective to practice in health care followed, and her comprehensive text, *Human Behavior and the Social Environment: An*

Ecological View, was published in 1991. *The Life Model of Social Work: Advances in Theory and Practice,* a major revision of Germain and Gitterman's practice text, appeared in 1996, shortly after her death.

Germain received many honors, including an honorary doctorate in humane letters from Smith College, The Lucille Austin Fellowship at Columbia University, and the Richard Lodge Memorial Prize at Adelphi University. Her papers have been deposited in the social work collection of the Sophia Smith Archives at Smith College, Northampton, Massachusetts, where they are available to scholars.

Ann Hartman

Ginsberg, Mitchell I. (1915–1996)

Mitchell Ginsberg's contribution to social work was formidable, particularly his concern for disadvantaged people who looked to the government for assistance and his interest in the education of future social workers.

Ginsberg helped shape the "War on Poverty" in the 1960s. He headed New York City's public welfare program. He combined employment training, child welfare, family counseling, services to the aging, and economic assistance into a single public department. He headed that program from its inception until 1970. Meanwhile he consulted to numerous congressional committees and the U.S. Department of Health, Education, and Welfare.

In 1953 he joined the faculty of the Columbia University School of Social Work, serving as dean of the school from 1971 to 1981. Also, he assisted the university in discharging its social responsibilities through a program of neighborhood services and as co-director of the Center for the Study of Human Rights.

Ginsberg received many awards and four honorary doctoral degrees from leading universities. He served as president of NASW and as both chair and member of numerous national, state, and city commissions and committees.

Bertram M. Beck

Gottlieb, Naomi R. (1925–1995)

Naomi Gottlieb pioneered the development of new approaches to counteract inequities and stereotyped views of both men and women. After earning her DSW from the University of California at Berkeley in 1970, she joined the

faculty of the University of Washington School of Social Work, where she became extensively involved in three major areas: gender issues in the social work curriculum, evaluation of social work practice, and the PhD program in social welfare. She also served as associate dean with responsibilities for curriculum and faculty matters from 1977 to 1985.

In the mid-1970s she co-authored a grant proposal that led to the creation of the first social work program in feminist practice in the country. She once said of this work: "Becoming a feminist and acting on my commitment to educate students to a feminist approach was one of the most important parts of my professional development—it was not just work, but something I did out of real love and conviction."

In addition, Gottlieb helped initiate and develop the University of Washington School of Social Work's doctoral program and coordinated the program for several years. The educational needs of students were at the forefront of all her actions, and she had a profound commitment to students, particularly to those from disadvantaged backgrounds.

She wrote numerous articles on women's issues and feminist practice, including the book *The Welfare Bind* (1974), and served as editor of *Alternative Social Services for Women* (1980) and *The Woman Client* (1987). She also cofounded *Affilia,* a journal on women and social work, and served as its book review editor.

In recognition of her leadership on women's issues, she was the first recipient of the Belle Spafford Endowed Chair in Women's Studies at the University of Utah Graduate School of Social Work in 1987.

At the time of her death, as a tribute to her profound commitment to students' learning, the University of Washington established the Naomi R. Gottlieb Endowed Fund to provide support for those seeking a PhD in social welfare.

Nancy R. Hooyman

Howard, Oliver Otis (1830–1904)

A native of Kennebec County, Maine, Oliver Otis Howard is an unknown entity in social welfare history and atypical of social welfare reformers in the 1800s. Guided by strong Christian beliefs, he was decorated for his heroics in the Civil War and served as the first commissioner for the Bureau of Refugees, Freedmen and Abandoned Lands. He founded Howard University, served as President

Ulysses S. Grant's "Peace Commissioner" with Native Americans, was sent to the Northwest during the Indian Wars, was appointed superintendent of West Point Military Academy to help dispel race problems at the academy during the 1870s, and was an active member of numerous tract societies.

At age 20 Howard graduated from Bowdoin College and four years later from West Point. In 1861 he became a colonel in the Third Regiment of Maine Volunteers and rose to the rank of general. He fought in numerous battles and played a central role in General William T. Sherman's Atlanta campaign. Following the 1862 Battle of Fair Oaks, in which he lost his right arm, Howard always carried a Bible, tucked underneath the jacket of his right arm, into battle, earning him the nickname "the Christian General."

In 1865 President Andrew Johnson appointed Howard the first commissioner of the Freedmen's Bureau, which in effect, became the nation's first large-scale social welfare effort to cross geographic boundaries. Although President Franklin Pierce's veto of mental health legislation in 1854 deemed social welfare to be the province of the states, the bureau's educational, legal, and health services marked the first significant coordinated welfare effort by the national government. Under Howard's leadership and persistence, the bureau's efforts reached their pinnacle in 1867, but these early gains were short lived, as Howard faced tremendous opposition from southerners and northerners. Responding to these pressures, Congress continually narrowed the bureau's mission and limited its overall effectiveness as a change agent.

Supporters of Howard encouraged his candidacy in the 1868 presidential election, although charges of political corruption and mismanagement of the Freedmen's Bureau were levied against him by his political enemies. Two congressional investigations vindicated him of wrongdoing, but any possibility of national elected office was derailed.

From 1869 to 1874 he served as the third president of Howard University, and from 1881 to 1884 as superintendent of West Point. On his death, a *New York Times* editorial chronicled his military contributions, but no reference was made to his work with and on behalf of southern freedmen.

Ira C. Colby

Keith-Lucas, Alan (1910–1995)

Alan Keith-Lucas was a noted writer, historian, storyteller, and social work educator for more than 50 years. Born in Cambridge, England, he received his BA with honors from Trinity College, Cambridge, an MS in social administration from Case Western Reserve University, a PhD in political science from Duke University, and a DLit from Campbell University. His interests included group care of children, the history of social work, and the integration of religious faith and social work practice.

Keith-Lucas wrote more than 30 books, including *Giving and Taking Help* (1972), *The Church Children's Home in a Changing World* (1962), *Decisions about People in Need* (1957), *The Poor You Have with You Always* (1989), and *Essays from More than Fifty Years in Social Work* (1989). He also wrote more than 150 professional articles or book chapters. He served on the faculty at the University of North Carolina at Chapel Hill's School of Social Work from 1950 to 1975, where he founded the Group Child Care Consultant Services and twice served as interim dean. He established the School of Social Work's off-campus programs that assist professionals in the field to obtain their degrees while working.

Keith-Lucas was internationally known for his unique insights into the needs of children and his persuasive style of teaching. He consulted to more than 100 youth-serving agencies, helping to shape a generation of professionals, particularly in religious-based residential homes. He held strong, often controversial opinions about the positive effects of group child care and advocated for their use throughout his life. Keith-Lucas retired from the University of North Carolina at Chapel Hill in 1975 as an Alumni Distinguished Professor Emeritus of Social Work. For 20 years after his retirement he continued to teach, consult, and write.

Daniel Lebold

Meyer, Carol H. (1924–1996)

Carol Meyer, social work educator and prolific writer, occupied a leadership position in the continuing development and adaptation of social work practice to a changing world for more than three decades. In the tradition of Mary Richmond and Gordon Hamilton, her primary theoretical contribution was the expansion and enrichment of the individualizing or assessment process, a theme that is central in her first published article, "Quest for a Broader Base for Family Diagnosis" (1959), as well as in one of her last works, the widely used 1993 volume *Assessment in Social Work Practice.* A major theme in her teaching and writing was that client need as identified through the assessment process, not agency purpose, should determine the direction of practice.

Drawn to social work during her college years at the University of Pittsburgh by contact with social work pioneers Ruth Smalley and Gertrude Wilson, Meyer went on to earn her MSW at the New York School of Social Work (later Columbia University) and was among the first recipients of a doctoral degree from that institution. She worked to bring quality services to underserved and oppressed populations, paying particular attention to the needs of families and children. Throughout her career, she always set practice in the context of social policy, demonstrating and teaching that practitioners should be ready to tackle social and policy issues, as well as individual change.

A charismatic, engaging, and challenging teacher, lecturer, consultant, and workshop leader, she was a central figure on the Columbia University School of Social Work faculty for 34 years, providing a memorable experience to generations of students and traveling throughout the country to teach, train, and exhort, always with the purpose of advancing the practice of social work.

In her later years, she came to embrace feminist ideas and offered invaluable leadership in her term as editor of *Affilia.* Her influence was widely felt through her extensive publications and her editorship of *Social Work.* Her publications include dozens of articles, book chapters, and monographs appearing in major publications and six books, including *Staff Development in Public Welfare Agencies* (1966), *Social Work Practice: A Response to the Urban Crisis* (1970), *Assessment in Social Work Practice* (1993), and *The Foundations of Social Work Practice: A Graduate Text* (1995, co-edited with Mark A. Mattaini).

Ann Hartman

Ripple, Lillian (1911–1993)
Lillian Ripple, recognized throughout the United States as a social work educator, scholar, and research specialist, was an esteemed graduate of the University of Chi-

cago, where she earned her bachelor's, master's, and doctoral degrees at the School of Social Service Administration. Her career began with volunteer work at Hull House and proceeded through direct practice as a caseworker to specialization in research. After distinguished service as the director of research for the Welfare Council of Metropolitan Chicago, Ripple joined the faculty of the School of Social Service Administration at the University of Chicago. As a researcher who knew practice and as a practitioner who valued research, she was especially effective as an educator. When the School of Social Service Administration established a research center, Ripple, now a full professor, was the obvious choice to serve as its first director. It was in this capacity in 1964 that she produced her pioneering study of continuance and discontinuance in social treatment, *Motivation, Capacity and Opportunity: Studies in Casework Theory and Practice.* At the time, this study was regarded as the definitive work in the field of casework research and was widely used by educators and practitioners.

In 1968 Ripple ended her long association with the University of Chicago and its School of Social Service Administration to become associate director of the Council on Social Work Education (CSWE). Although she gave her attention in this position to all aspects of social work education, she again brought her scholarly and research talents to bear on the special problem of the structure and quality of social work preparation for professional practice. A task force under her leadership produced a report that generated a great deal of discussion within CSWE and NASW. At issue was the concept of a BSW–MSW–DSW continuum. Although no consensus was reached within the educational system, experimentation was encouraged.

After her retirement in 1975, Ripple accepted an appointment as a consultant and trainer for the Central Council for Education and Training in London. Her experience with this organization, which serves in the United Kingdom as the accrediting body for social work education, was mutually rewarding. Her British colleagues enthusiastically concurred with the resolution passed earlier by the CSWE board of directors extolling her talents and expressing their profound respect for her contributions to social work education, practice, and research.

Katherine A. Kendall

Rothenberg, Elaine Zipes (1921–1994)

Elaine Zipes Rothenberg, a nationally re-nowned social work educator, was consistent in her commitment to setting educational and professional standards for social work and to ensuring diversity in faculty and student populations. A New York native, she graduated from Queens College in New York in 1941. Two years later, she received a master of social science degree from the Smith College School for Social Work. In 1960 she joined the faculty of the School of Social Work at the Richmond Professional Institute, which became Virginia Commonwealth University (VCU) in 1968.

After 12 years of service at the School of Social Work, Rothenberg was appointed dean in 1972. During the years of her deanship, she built VCU's School of Social Work into one of national renown. Under her direction, the school developed a PhD program, off-campus programs, a part-time social work education program, and a highly regarded continuing education program. She insisted on, and was successful in, recruiting women and people of color to the faculty and student body long before it was an institutional priority. In 1982, Rothenberg resigned as dean and was asked to serve as the director of the university's self-study. Once the self-study had been compiled and VCU had been awarded accreditation, she was appointed acting vice president for academic affairs and occupied that position until she retired in 1988.

Her role as a leader in the accreditation process of schools of social work from 1974 until 1982 resulted in increasing professionalization and accountability in social work education. Rothenberg's advice and assistance were sought by many schools of social work because of the clarity of her thinking, her vision, and her commitment to social work values.

Florence Z. Segal

Samora, Julian (1920–1996)

Julian Samora was born in Pagosa Springs, Colorado, on March 29, 1920. Until age 27, he lived in Colorado, where he attended Adams State College on a Boniles Foundation grant, receiving a BA degree in 1942. He returned there to begin his teaching career, serving from 1944 to 1955. Scholarships enabled him to continue his education toward an advanced degree in sociology, which he earned in 1947. By then he had firmly established himself in his field of study, pioneering the way as the first

Mexican American in sociology–anthropology. He earned his doctorate in sociology and anthropology in 1953 at Washington University. After teaching preventive medicine and public health for two years at the University of Colorado School of Medicine, he accepted a position at Michigan State University teaching sociology and anthropology. His teaching career culminated at the University of Notre Dame, where he was professor of sociology (1959), the head of the department (1963–1966), director of the Mexican-American Graduate Studies Program (1971–1985), and director of the Graduate Studies Program (1981–1984). He retired from Notre Dame in 1985, having distinguished himself as a researcher and scholar in sociology and Mexican American studies and having left a legacy of scholarship, research, and leadership in his discipline.

Samora was a distinguished teacher who was deeply committed to education and to students. As a mentor to hundreds of students in sociology, anthropology, history, law, and Mexican studies, he was revered and given acknowledgment of the place of honor he held in the academic and the Mexican American communities. He co-founded the National Council of La Raza, an organization working on behalf of national issues affecting Mexican Americans.

Samora authored about 30 journal articles and numerous books. His books reflected the critical issues of the era and were the first of their kind, paving the way for the many studies and writers/researchers who followed. Some of his most well-known publications are *La Raza: Forgotten Americans* (1966), *Los Mojados: The Wetback Story* (1971), *A History of the Mexican American People* (with P. V. Simon) (1977), and *National Study of the Spanish-Speaking People* (1979).

Samora was an outstanding scholar who also served as an editor for *International Migrant Review, Muestro,* and other journals. He served on the President's Commission on Rural Poverty, the Commission on Civil Rights, the Ford Foundation, the National Endowment for the Humanities, the Bureau of the Census, the National Institute of Mental Health, the President's Commission on Income Maintenance Programs, and the American Association for the Advancement of Science.

He was honored with many awards during his lifetime. As his final tribute to research, the establishment of the Julian Samora Research Institute at Michigan State University bears his name, providing lasting visibility to his distinguished career.

Juliette Silva

Schottland, Charles Irwin (1906–1994)

Charles Schottland was a leader in social welfare policy making and administration in state, national, and international agencies and the founder of an innovative school of advanced studies in social welfare at Brandeis University. As an educator he brought a wealth of practical and political experience, mostly in government organizations, to academia.

During the Great Depression Schottland headed California's State Relief Administration and later worked in the Children's Bureau in Washington, DC. In World War II he served as General Dwight D. Eisenhower's chief of a section dealing with displaced people in Europe. He was decorated by five nations for his work in repatriating 5.5 million people. President Eisenhower appointed Schottland Commissioner of Social Security; in that position he initiated significant changes in the social security law. He was active in social welfare organizations at the national level, served as an adviser to several United Nations bodies, and was president of the International Council on Social Welfare.

In 1959 Schottland became the founding dean of the Florence Heller Graduate School for Advanced Studies in Social Welfare at Brandeis University. He brought health and welfare administrators and planners together with social scientists to train policymakers and researchers at the doctoral level. At a time of major changes in social work and social welfare, Schottland emphasized the fast-growing public sector. His accessible, calm style of leadership was a vital ingredient in the school's development. He devoted two of his 20 years at Brandeis to serving as the university's third president.

Schottland had a vast network of professional and personal relationships from his work in the federal government and on the international scene. He brought leading figures from every field of social welfare to teach and lecture at the Heller School. Those who knew him as a dean, teacher, or colleague admired the skillful ways in which he combined his many years of first-hand experience as a policymaker and administrator with an incisive grasp of social problems and programs.

Robert Perlman

Shyne, Ann Wentworth (1914–1995)

Ann Shyne, a leader in the development of contemporary social work research, was born in Troy, New York. She graduated from Vassar College in 1935, obtained her MSW from Smith College School for Social Work in 1937, and received a PhD in social work and social research from Bryn Mawr College in 1943. She was first employed as a social worker for the Austin Riggs Psychiatric Center in Massachusetts. She began her research career in 1945 at the Family Service Association of America, and from 1955 to 1968 she directed research projects at the Community Service Society of New York. She then served as Director of Research of the Child Welfare Association of America until her retirement in 1976.

Shyne was a founding member, officer, and the only female member of the highly influential Social Work Research Group in the 1950s and 1960s. The Social Work Research Group was an NASW-sponsored organization of leaders in U.S. social work research. The group was successful in promoting research on social work practice and on social programs and policies and in the development of research activities and curricula in schools of social work.

Shyne designed and directed numerous foundation and federally funded research projects. Her articles, reports, and monographs based on these projects, as well as her writings on research and practice methods, had considerable impact on family and child welfare services and on social work research. She co-authored such influential publications as *Brief and Extended Casework* (1969, with William J. Reid), *Children Adrift in Foster Care* (1973, with Edmund Sherman and Renee Neuman), and *A Second Chance for Families* (1976, with Mary Ann Jones). These works were instrumental in promoting new approaches to foster care and the development of brief treatment in social work and related fields. In 1988 she received NASW's first Lifetime Achievement Award in recognition of her accomplishments in social work research.

Edmund Sherman
William J. Reid

Specht, Harry (1929–1995)

Harry Specht, nationally and internationally renowned for his scholarship, leadership, and advocacy in social welfare, was one of the most prominent and powerful intellectual voices in his generation of social work educators. A child of the Great Depression, his professional life was marked by an abiding compassion for underprivileged people, which stemmed in part from Specht's early life experiences; the first social workers he had contact with placed Specht and his siblings in foster care. On his own at an early age, Specht worked his way through high school and then through City College of New York, earning an AB in 1951. He obtained his MSW in 1953 from Case Western Reserve University.

Specht began his professional career in New York's settlement houses—Bronx House, Lenox Hill, and the Mt. Vernon Young Men's–Women's Hebrew Association—where he worked with street gangs and other groups. Returning to graduate school in the early 1960s, Specht received his PhD from Brandeis University. He then worked for Mobilization for Youth on the Lower East Side of New York City. In 1964 he moved to California to become the associate director of the Contra Costa Council of Community Services, and several years later he joined the social work faculty at San Francisco State University. In 1967 he was recruited to the faculty at the School of Social Welfare, University of California at Berkeley, where he rose through the professorial ranks; in 1977 Specht was appointed dean of the school, a position he held for 17 years.

Specht wrote more than a dozen books and 50 articles, which were translated into Japanese, Chinese, and German. His book *Community Organizing* (1973, with George Brager and, later, James Torczyner) remains one of the basic texts in its field. Specht's last and most controversial book, *Unfaithful Angels: How Social Work Has Abandoned Its Mission* (1995, with Mark Courtney), takes the profession to task for abdicating its historical mission of service to poor people.

Specht was a senior Fulbright Scholar in 1973 and the recipient of numerous honors, including the 1991 Daniel S. Koshland Award; the 1992 NASW Presidential Award for Outstanding Leadership in Social Work Education; and the Berkeley Citation, the highest honor awarded by the University of California at Berkeley.

Neil Gilbert

Contributors to the Biographies

Bertram M. Beck, MSW
Visiting Professor
School of Social Service
Fordham University
New York, NY

Ira C. Colby, DSW
Professor and Director
School of Social Work
University of Central Florida
Orlando, FL

Neil Gilbert, PhD
Chernin Professor of Social Welfare
School of Social Welfare
University of California at Berkeley
Berkeley, CA

Ann Hartman, DSW
Dean and Professor Emerita
Smith College School for Social Work
Northampton, MA
Distinguished Visiting Professor
Graduate School of Social Service
Fordham University
New York, NY

Nancy R. Hooyman, PhD
Dean
School of Social Work
University of Washington
Seattle, WA

Katherine A. Kendall, PhD, ACSW
Honorary President
International Association of Schools of Social Work
Chief Consultant to the Foreign Equivalency
Determination Service
Council on Social Work Education
Alexandria, VA

Daniel Lebold, MSW
Director of Alumni Relations
School of Social Work
University of North Carolina at Chapel Hill
Chapel Hill, NC

Ronald Marks, PhD
Associate Dean
School of Social Work
Tulane University
New Orleans, LA

Jeanne C. Marsh, PhD
Dean
School of Social Service Administration
University of Chicago
Chicago, IL

Robert Perlman, PhD, MSSA
Professor Emeritus
Heller School
Brandeis University
Waltham, MA

William J. Reid, DSW
Professor
School of Social Welfare
University at Albany
State University of New York
Albany, NY

Florence Z. Segal
Assistant Professor Emerita
Special Assistant to the Dean
School of Social Work
Virginia Commonwealth University
Richmond, VA

Edmund Sherman, PhD
Professor Emeritus
School of Social Welfare
University at Albany
State University of New York
Albany, NY

Juliette Silva
San Jose, CA

Ann Weick, PhD
Dean and Professor
School of Social Welfare
University of Kansas
Lawrence, KS

Appendix 1. NASW Code of Ethics

Approved by the 1996 NASW Delegate Assembly.

PREAMBLE

The primary mission of the social work profession is to enhance human well-being and help meet the basic human needs of all people, with particular attention to the needs and empowerment of people who are vulnerable, oppressed, and living in poverty. A historic and defining feature of social work is the profession's focus on individual well-being in a social context and the well-being of society. Fundamental to social work is attention to the environmental forces that create, contribute to, and address problems in living.

Social workers promote social justice and social change with and on behalf of clients. "Clients" is used inclusively to refer to individuals, families, groups, organizations, and communities. Social workers are sensitive to cultural and ethnic diversity and strive to end discrimination, oppression, poverty, and other forms of social injustice. These activities may be in the form of direct practice, community organizing, supervision, consultation, administration, advocacy, social and political action, policy development and implementation, education, and research and evaluation. Social workers seek to enhance the capacity of people to address their own needs. Social workers also seek to promote the responsiveness of organizations, communities, and other social institutions to individuals' needs and social problems.

The mission of the social work profession is rooted in a set of core values. These core values, embraced by social workers throughout the profession's history, are the foundation of social work's unique purpose and perspective:

- service
- social justice
- dignity and worth of the person
- importance of human relationships
- integrity
- competence.

This constellation of core values reflects what is unique to the social work profession. Core values, and the principles that flow from them, must be balanced within the context and complexity of the human experience.

PURPOSE OF THE NASW CODE OF ETHICS

Professional ethics are at the core of social work. The profession has an obligation to articulate its basic values, ethical principles, and ethical standards. The *NASW Code of Ethics* sets forth these values, principles, and standards to guide social workers' conduct. The *Code* is relevant to all social workers and social work students, regardless of their professional functions, the settings in which they work, or the populations they serve.

The *NASW Code of Ethics* serves six purposes:

1. The *Code* identifies core values on which social work's mission is based.
2. The *Code* summarizes broad ethical principles that reflect the profession's core values and establishes a set of specific ethical standards that should be used to guide social work practice.

3. The *Code* is designed to help social workers identify relevant considerations when professional obligations conflict or ethical uncertainties arise.
4. The *Code* provides ethical standards to which the general public can hold the social work profession accountable.
5. The *Code* socializes practitioners new to the field to social work's mission, values, ethical principles, and ethical standards.
6. The *Code* articulates standards that the social work profession itself can use to assess whether social workers have engaged in unethical conduct. NASW has formal procedures to adjudicate ethics complaints filed against its members.[1] In subscribing to this *Code,* social workers are required to cooperate in its implementation, participate in NASW adjudication proceedings, and abide by any NASW disciplinary rulings or sanctions based on it.

The *Code* offers a set of values, principles, and standards to guide decision making and conduct when ethical issues arise. It does not provide a set of rules that prescribe how social workers should act in all situations. Specific applications of the *Code* must take into account the context in which it is being considered and the possibility of conflicts among the *Code*'s values, principles, and standards. Ethical responsibilities flow from all human relationships, from the personal and familial to the social and professional.

Further, the *NASW Code of Ethics* does not specify which values, principles, and standards are most important and ought to outweigh others in instances when they conflict. Reasonable differences of opinion can and do exist among social workers with respect to the ways in which values, ethical principles, and ethical standards should be rank ordered when they conflict. Ethical decision making in a given situation must apply the informed judgment of the individual social worker and should also consider how the issues would be judged in a peer review process where the ethical standards of the profession would be applied.

Ethical decision making is a process. There are many instances in social work where simple answers are not available to resolve complex ethical issues. Social workers should take into consideration all the values, principles, and standards in this *Code* that are relevant to any situation in which ethical judgment is warranted. Social workers' decisions and actions should be consistent with the spirit as well as the letter of this *Code*.

In addition to this *Code,* there are many other sources of information about ethical thinking that may be useful. Social workers should consider ethical theory and principles generally, social work theory and research, laws, regulations, agency policies, and other relevant codes of ethics, recognizing that among codes of ethics social workers should consider the *NASW Code of Ethics* as their primary source. Social workers also should be aware of the impact on ethical decision making of their clients' and their own personal values and cultural and religious beliefs and practices. They should be aware of any conflicts between personal and professional values and deal with them responsibly. For additional guidance social workers should consult the relevant literature on professional ethics and ethical decision making and seek appropriate consultation when faced with ethical dilemmas. This may involve consultation with an agency-based or social work organization's ethics committee, a regulatory body, knowledgeable colleagues, supervisors, or legal counsel.

Instances may arise when social workers' ethical obligations conflict with agency policies or relevant laws or regulations. When such conflicts occur, social workers must make a responsible effort to resolve the conflict in a manner that is consistent with the values, principles, and standards expressed in this *Code*. If a reasonable resolution of the conflict does not appear possible, social workers should seek proper consultation before making a decision.

The *NASW Code of Ethics* is to be used by NASW and by individuals, agencies, organizations, and bodies (such as licensing and regulatory boards, professional liability insurance providers, courts of law, agency boards of directors, government agencies, and other professional groups) that choose to adopt it or use it as a frame of reference. Violation of standards in this *Code* does not automatically imply legal liability or violation of the law. Such determination can only be made in the context of legal and judicial proceedings. Alleged violations of the *Code* would be subject to a peer review process. Such processes are generally separate from legal or administrative proce-

---

[1] For information on NASW adjudication procedures, see *NASW Procedures for the Adjudication of Grievances*.

dures and insulated from legal review or proceedings to allow the profession to counsel and discipline its own members.

A code of ethics cannot guarantee ethical behavior. Moreover, a code of ethics cannot resolve all ethical issues or disputes or capture the richness and complexity involved in striving to make responsible choices within a moral community. Rather, a code of ethics sets forth values, ethical principles, and ethical standards to which professionals aspire and by which their actions can be judged. Social workers' ethical behavior should result from their personal commitment to engage in ethical practice. The *NASW Code of Ethics* reflects the commitment of all social workers to uphold the profession's values and to act ethically. Principles and standards must be applied by individuals of good character who discern moral questions and, in good faith, seek to make reliable ethical judgments.

Ethical Principles

The following broad ethical principles are based on social work's core values of service, social justice, dignity and worth of the person, importance of human relationships, integrity, and competence. These principles set forth ideals to which all social workers should aspire.

Value: *Service*

Ethical Principle: *Social workers' primary goal is to help people in need and to address social problems.*

Social workers elevate service to others above self-interest. Social workers draw on their knowledge, values, and skills to help people in need and to address social problems. Social workers are encouraged to volunteer some portion of their professional skills with no expectation of significant financial return (pro bono service).

Value: *Social Justice*

Ethical Principle: *Social workers challenge social injustice.*

Social workers pursue social change, particularly with and on behalf of vulnerable and oppressed individuals and groups of people. Social workers' social change efforts are focused primarily on issues of poverty, unemployment, discrimination, and other forms of social injustice. These activities seek to promote sensitivity to and knowledge about oppression and cultural and ethnic diversity. Social workers strive to ensure access to needed information, services, and resources; equality of opportunity; and meaningful participation in decision making for all people.

Value: *Dignity and Worth of the Person*

Ethical Principle: *Social workers respect the inherent dignity and worth of the person.*

Social workers treat each person in a caring and respectful fashion, mindful of individual differences and cultural and ethnic diversity. Social workers promote clients' socially responsible self-determination. Social workers seek to enhance clients' capacity and opportunity to change and to address their own needs. Social workers are cognizant of their dual responsibility to clients and to the broader society. They seek to resolve conflicts between clients' interests and the broader society's interests in a socially responsible manner consistent with the values, ethical principles, and ethical standards of the profession.

Value: *Importance of Human Relationships*

Ethical Principle: *Social workers recognize the central importance of human relationships.*

Social workers understand that relationships between and among people are an important vehicle for change. Social workers engage people as partners in the helping process. Social workers seek to strengthen relationships among people in a purposeful effort to promote, restore, maintain, and enhance the well-being of individuals, families, social groups, organizations, and communities.

Value: *Integrity*

Ethical Principle: *Social workers behave in a trustworthy manner.*

Social workers are continually aware of the profession's mission, values, ethical principles, and ethical standards and practice in a manner consistent with them. Social workers act honestly and responsibly and promote ethical practices on the part of the organizations with which they are affiliated.

Value: *Competence*

Ethical Principle: *Social workers practice within their areas of competence and develop and enhance their professional expertise.*

Social workers continually strive to increase their professional knowledge and skills and to apply them in practice. Social workers should aspire to contribute to the knowledge base of the profession.

ETHICAL STANDARDS

The following ethical standards are relevant to the professional activities of all social workers. These standards concern (1) social workers' ethical responsibilities to clients, (2) social workers' ethical responsibilities to colleagues, (3) social workers' ethical responsibilities in practice settings, (4) social workers' ethical responsibilities as professionals, (5) social workers' ethical responsibilities to the social work profession, and (6) social workers' ethical responsibilities to the broader society.

Some of the standards that follow are enforceable guidelines for professional conduct, and some are aspirational. The extent to which each standard is enforceable is a matter of professional judgment to be exercised by those responsible for reviewing alleged violations of ethical standards.

1.   Social Workers' Ethical Responsibilities to Clients

1.01   Commitment to Clients

Social workers' primary responsibility is to promote the well-being of clients. In general, clients' interests are primary. However, social workers' responsibility to the larger society or specific legal obligations may on limited occasions supersede the loyalty owed clients, and clients should be so advised. (Examples include when a social worker is required by law to report that a client has abused a child or has threatened to harm self or others.)

1.02   Self-Determination

Social workers respect and promote the right of clients to self-determination and assist clients in their efforts to identify and clarify their goals. Social workers may limit clients' right to self-determination when, in the social workers' professional judgment, clients' actions or potential actions pose a serious, foreseeable, and imminent risk to themselves or others.

1.03   Informed Consent

(a) Social workers should provide services to clients only in the context of a professional relationship based, when appropriate, on valid informed consent. Social workers should use clear and understandable language to inform clients of the purpose of the services, risks related to the services, limits to services because of the requirements of a third-party payer, relevant costs, reasonable alternatives, clients' right to refuse or withdraw consent, and the time frame covered by the consent. Social workers should provide clients with an opportunity to ask questions.

(b) In instances when clients are not literate or have difficulty understanding the primary language used in the practice setting, social workers should take steps to ensure clients' comprehension. This may include providing clients with a detailed verbal explanation or arranging for a qualified interpreter or translator whenever possible.

(c) In instances when clients lack the capacity to provide informed consent, social workers should protect clients' interests by seeking permission from an appropriate third party, informing clients consistent with the clients' level of understanding. In such instances social workers should seek to ensure that the third party acts in a manner consistent with clients' wishes and interests. Social workers should take reasonable steps to enhance such clients' ability to give informed consent.

(d) In instances when clients are receiving services involuntarily, social workers should provide information about the nature and extent of services and about the extent of clients' right to refuse service.

(e) Social workers who provide services via electronic media (such as computer, telephone, radio, and television) should inform recipients of the limitations and risks associated with such services.

(f) Social workers should obtain clients' informed consent before audiotaping or videotaping clients or permitting observation of services to clients by a third party.

1.04   Competence

(a) Social workers should provide services and represent themselves as competent only within the boundaries of their education, training, license, certification, consultation received, supervised experience, or other relevant professional experience.

(b) Social workers should provide services in substantive areas or use intervention techniques or approaches that are new to them only after engaging in appropriate study, training, consultation, and supervision from people who are competent in those interventions or techniques.

(c) When generally recognized standards do not exist with respect to an emerging area of practice, social workers should exercise careful judgment and take responsible steps (including appropriate education, research, training, consultation, and supervision) to ensure the competence of their work and to protect clients from harm.

1.05   Cultural Competence and Social Diversity

(a) Social workers should understand culture and its function in human behavior and society, recognizing the strengths that exist in all cultures.

(b) Social workers should have a knowledge base of their clients' cultures and be able to demonstrate competence in the provision of services that are sensitive to clients' cultures and to differences among people and cultural groups.

(c) Social workers should obtain education about and seek to understand the nature of social diversity and oppression with respect to race, ethnicity, national origin, color, sex, sexual orientation, age, marital status, political belief, religion, and mental or physical disability.

1.06   Conflicts of Interest

(a) Social workers should be alert to and avoid conflicts of interest that interfere with the exercise of professional discretion and impartial judgment. Social workers should inform clients when a real or potential conflict of interest arises and take reasonable steps to resolve the issue in a manner that makes the clients' interests primary and protects clients' interests to the greatest extent possible. In some cases, protecting clients' interests may require termination of the professional relationship with proper referral of the client.

(b) Social workers should not take unfair advantage of any professional relationship or exploit others to further their personal, religious, political, or business interests.

(c) Social workers should not engage in dual or multiple relationships with clients or former clients in which there is a risk of exploitation or potential harm to the client. In instances when dual or multiple relationships are unavoidable, social workers should take steps to protect clients and are responsible for setting clear, appropriate, and culturally sensitive boundaries. (Dual or multiple relationships occur when social workers relate to clients in more than one relationship, whether professional, social, or business. Dual or multiple relationships can occur simultaneously or consecutively.)

(d) When social workers provide services to two or more people who have a relationship with each other (for example, couples, family members), social workers should clarify with all parties which individuals will be considered clients and the nature of social workers' professional obligations to the various individuals who are receiving services. Social workers who anticipate a conflict of interest among the individuals receiving services or who anticipate having to perform in potentially conflicting roles (for example, when a social worker is asked to testify in a child custody dispute or divorce proceedings involving clients) should clarify their role with the parties involved and take appropriate action to minimize any conflict of interest.

1.07   Privacy and Confidentiality

(a) Social workers should respect clients' right to privacy. Social workers should not solicit private information from clients unless it is essential to providing services or conducting social work evaluation or research. Once private information is shared, standards of confidentiality apply.

(b) Social workers may disclose confidential information when appropriate with valid consent from a client or a person legally authorized to consent on behalf of a client.

(c) Social workers should protect the confidentiality of all information obtained in the course of professional service, except for compelling professional reasons. The general expectation that social workers will keep information confidential does not apply when disclosure is necessary to prevent serious, foreseeable, and imminent harm to a client or other identifiable person or when laws or regulations require disclosure without a client's consent. In all instances, social workers should disclose the least amount of confidential information necessary to achieve the desired purpose; only information that is directly relevant to the purpose for which the disclosure is made should be revealed.

(d) Social workers should inform clients, to the extent possible, about the disclosure of confidential information and the potential consequences, when feasible before the disclosure is made. This applies whether social workers disclose confidential information on the basis of a legal requirement or client consent.

(e) Social workers should discuss with clients and other interested parties the nature of confidentiality and limitations of clients' right to confidentiality. Social workers should review with clients circumstances where confidential information may be requested and where disclosure of confidential information may be legally required. This discussion should occur as soon as possible in the social worker–client relationship and as needed throughout the course of the relationship.

(f)   When social workers provide counseling services to families, couples, or groups, social workers should seek agreement among the parties involved concerning each individual's right to confidentiality and obligation to preserve the confidentiality of information shared by others. Social workers should inform participants in family, couples, or group counseling that social workers cannot guarantee that all participants will honor such agreements.

(g) Social workers should inform clients involved in family, couples, marital, or group counseling of the social worker's, employer's, and agency's policy concerning the social worker's disclosure of confidential information among the parties involved in the counseling.

(h) Social workers should not disclose confidential information to third-party payers unless clients have authorized such disclosure.

(i)   Social workers should not discuss confidential information in any setting unless privacy can be ensured. Social workers should not discuss confidential information in public or semipublic areas such as hallways, waiting rooms, elevators, and restaurants.

(j)   Social workers should protect the confidentiality of clients during legal proceedings to the extent permitted by law. When a court of law or other legally authorized body orders social workers to disclose confidential or privileged information without a client's consent and such disclosure could cause harm to the client, social workers should request that the court withdraw the order or limit the order as narrowly as possible or maintain the records under seal, unavailable for public inspection.

(k) Social workers should protect the confidentiality of clients when responding to requests from members of the media.

(l)   Social workers should protect the confidentiality of clients' written and electronic records and other sensitive information. Social workers should take reasonable steps to ensure that clients' records are stored in a secure location and that clients' records are not available to others who are not authorized to have access.

(m) Social workers should take precautions to ensure and maintain the confidentiality of information transmitted to other parties through the use of computers, electronic mail, facsimile machines, telephones and telephone answering machines, and other electronic or computer technology. Disclosure of identifying information should be avoided whenever possible.

(n) Social workers should transfer or dispose of clients' records in a manner that protects clients' confidentiality and is consistent with state statutes governing records and social work licensure.

(o) Social workers should take reasonable precautions to protect client confidentiality in the event of the social worker's termination of practice, incapacitation, or death.

(p) Social workers should not disclose identifying information when discussing clients for teaching or training purposes unless the client has consented to disclosure of confidential information.

(q) Social workers should not disclose identifying information when discussing clients with consultants unless the client has consented to disclosure of confidential information or there is a compelling need for such disclosure.

(r) Social workers should protect the confidentiality of deceased clients consistent with the preceding standards.

1.08   Access to Records

(a) Social workers should provide clients with reasonable access to records concerning the clients. Social workers who are concerned that clients' access to their records could cause serious misunderstanding or harm to the client should provide assistance in interpreting the records and consultation with the client regarding the records. Social workers should limit clients' access to their records, or portions of their records, only in exceptional circumstances when there is compelling evidence that such access would cause serious harm to the client. Both clients' requests and the rationale for withholding some or all of the record should be documented in clients' files.

(b) When providing clients with access to their records, social workers should take steps to protect the confidentiality of other individuals identified or discussed in such records.

1.09   Sexual Relationships

(a) Social workers should under no circumstances engage in sexual activities or sexual contact with current clients, whether such contact is consensual or forced.

(b) Social workers should not engage in sexual activities or sexual contact with clients' relatives or other individuals with whom clients maintain a close personal relationship when there is a risk of exploitation or potential harm to the client. Sexual activity or sexual contact with clients' relatives or other individuals with whom clients maintain a personal relationship has the potential to be harmful to the client and may make it difficult for the social worker and client to maintain appropriate professional boundaries. Social workers—not their clients, their clients' relatives, or other individuals with whom the client maintains a personal relationship—assume the full burden for setting clear, appropriate, and culturally sensitive boundaries.

(c) Social workers should not engage in sexual activities or sexual contact with former clients because of the potential for harm to the client. If social workers engage in conduct contrary to this prohibition or claim that an exception to this prohibition is warranted because of extraordinary circumstances, it is social workers—not their clients—who assume the full burden of demonstrating that the former client has not been exploited, coerced, or manipulated, intentionally or unintentionally.

(d) Social workers should not provide clinical services to individuals with whom they have had a prior sexual relationship. Providing clinical services to a former sexual partner has the potential to be harmful to the individual and is likely to make it difficult for the social worker and individual to maintain appropriate professional boundaries.

1.10   Physical Contact

Social workers should not engage in physical contact with clients when there is a possibility of psychological harm to the client as a result of the contact (such as cradling or caressing clients). Social workers who engage in appropriate physical contact with clients are responsible for setting clear, appropriate, and culturally sensitive boundaries that govern such physical contact.

1.11   Sexual Harassment

Social workers should not sexually harass clients. Sexual harassment includes sexual advances, sexual solicitation, requests for sexual favors, and other verbal or physical conduct of a sexual nature.

1.12 Derogatory Language

Social workers should not use derogatory language in their written or verbal communications to or about clients. Social workers should use accurate and respectful language in all communications to and about clients.

1.13 Payment for Services

(a) When setting fees, social workers should ensure that the fees are fair, reasonable, and commensurate with the services performed. Consideration should be given to clients' ability to pay.

(b) Social workers should avoid accepting goods or services from clients as payment for professional services. Bartering arrangements, particularly involving services, create the potential for conflicts of interest, exploitation, and inappropriate boundaries in social workers' relationships with clients. Social workers should explore and may participate in bartering only in very limited circumstances when it can be demonstrated that such arrangements are an accepted practice among professionals in the local community, considered to be essential for the provision of services, negotiated without coercion, and entered into at the client's initiative and with the client's informed consent. Social workers who accept goods or services from clients as payment for professional services assume the full burden of demonstrating that this arrangement will not be detrimental to the client or the professional relationship.

(c) Social workers should not solicit a private fee or other remuneration for providing services to clients who are entitled to such available services through the social workers' employer or agency.

1.14 Clients Who Lack Decision-Making Capacity

When social workers act on behalf of clients who lack the capacity to make informed decisions, social workers should take reasonable steps to safeguard the interests and rights of those clients.

1.15 Interruption of Services

Social workers should make reasonable efforts to ensure continuity of services in the event that services are interrupted by factors such as unavailability, relocation, illness, disability, or death.

1.16 Termination of Services

(a) Social workers should terminate services to clients and professional relationships with them when such services and relationships are no longer required or no longer serve the clients' needs or interests.

(b) Social workers should take reasonable steps to avoid abandoning clients who are still in need of services. Social workers should withdraw services precipitously only under unusual circumstances, giving careful consideration to all factors in the situation and taking care to minimize possible adverse effects. Social workers should assist in making appropriate arrangements for continuation of services when necessary.

(c) Social workers in fee-for-service settings may terminate services to clients who are not paying an overdue balance if the financial contractual arrangements have been made clear to the client, if the client does not pose an imminent danger to self or others, and if the clinical and other consequences of the current nonpayment have been addressed and discussed with the client.

(d) Social workers should not terminate services to pursue a social, financial, or sexual relationship with a client.

(e) Social workers who anticipate the termination or interruption of services to clients should notify clients promptly and seek the transfer, referral, or continuation of services in relation to the clients' needs and preferences.

(f) Social workers who are leaving an employment setting should inform clients of appropriate options for the continuation of services and of the benefits and risks of the options.

2. Social Workers' Ethical Responsibilities to Colleagues

2.01 Respect

(a) Social workers should treat colleagues with respect and should represent accurately and fairly the qualifications, views, and obligations of colleagues.

(b) Social workers should avoid unwarranted negative criticism of colleagues in communications with clients or with other professionals. Unwarranted negative criticism may include demeaning comments that refer to colleagues' level of competence or to individuals' attributes such as race, ethnicity, national origin, color, sex, sexual orientation, age, marital status, political belief, religion, and mental or physical disability.

(c) Social workers should cooperate with social work colleagues and with colleagues of other professions when such cooperation serves the well-being of clients.

2.02 Confidentiality

Social workers should respect confidential information shared by colleagues in the course of their professional relationships and transactions. Social workers should ensure that such colleagues understand social workers' obligation to respect confidentiality and any exceptions related to it.

2.03 Interdisciplinary Collaboration

(a) Social workers who are members of an interdisciplinary team should participate in and contribute to decisions that affect the well-being of clients by drawing on the perspectives, values, and experiences of the social work profession. Professional and ethical obligations of the interdisciplinary team as a whole and of its individual members should be clearly established.

(b) Social workers for whom a team decision raises ethical concerns should attempt to resolve the disagreement through appropriate channels. If the disagreement cannot be resolved, social workers should pursue other avenues to address their concerns consistent with client well-being.

2.04 Disputes Involving Colleagues

(a) Social workers should not take advantage of a dispute between a colleague and an employer to obtain a position or otherwise advance the social workers' own interests.

(b) Social workers should not exploit clients in disputes with colleagues or engage clients in any inappropriate discussion of conflicts between social workers and their colleagues.

2.05 Consultation

(a) Social workers should seek the advice and counsel of colleagues whenever such consultation is in the best interests of clients.

(b) Social workers should keep themselves informed about colleagues' areas of expertise and competencies. Social workers should seek consultation only from colleagues who have demonstrated knowledge, expertise, and competence related to the subject of the consultation.

(c) When consulting with colleagues about clients, social workers should disclose the least amount of information necessary to achieve the purposes of the consultation.

2.06 Referral for Services

(a) Social workers should refer clients to other professionals when the other professionals' specialized knowledge or expertise is needed to serve clients fully or when social workers believe that they are not being effective or making reasonable progress with clients and that additional service is required.

(b) Social workers who refer clients to other professionals should take appropriate steps to facilitate an orderly transfer of responsibility. Social workers who refer clients to other professionals should disclose, with clients' consent, all pertinent information to the new service providers.

(c) Social workers are prohibited from giving or receiving payment for a referral when no professional service is provided by the referring social worker.

2.07   Sexual Relationships

(a) Social workers who function as supervisors or educators should not engage in sexual activities or contact with supervisees, students, trainees, or other colleagues over whom they exercise professional authority.

(b) Social workers should avoid engaging in sexual relationships with colleagues when there is potential for a conflict of interest. Social workers who become involved in, or anticipate becoming involved in, a sexual relationship with a colleague have a duty to transfer professional responsibilities, when necessary, to avoid a conflict of interest.

2.08   Sexual Harassment

Social workers should not sexually harass supervisees, students, trainees, or colleagues. Sexual harassment includes sexual advances, sexual solicitation, requests for sexual favors, and other verbal or physical conduct of a sexual nature.

2.09   Impairment of Colleagues

(a) Social workers who have direct knowledge of a social work colleague's impairment that is due to personal problems, psychosocial distress, substance abuse, or mental health difficulties and that interferes with practice effectiveness should consult with that colleague when feasible and assist the colleague in taking remedial action.

(b) Social workers who believe that a social work colleague's impairment interferes with practice effectiveness and that the colleague has not taken adequate steps to address the impairment should take action through appropriate channels established by employers, agencies, NASW, licensing and regulatory bodies, and other professional organizations.

2.10   Incompetence of Colleagues

(a) Social workers who have direct knowledge of a social work colleague's incompetence should consult with that colleague when feasible and assist the colleague in taking remedial action.

(b) Social workers who believe that a social work colleague is incompetent and has not taken adequate steps to address the incompetence should take action through appropriate channels established by employers, agencies, NASW, licensing and regulatory bodies, and other professional organizations.

2.11   Unethical Conduct of Colleagues

(a) Social workers should take adequate measures to discourage, prevent, expose, and correct the unethical conduct of colleagues.

(b) Social workers should be knowledgeable about established policies and procedures for handling concerns about colleagues' unethical behavior. Social workers should be familiar with national, state, and local procedures for handling ethics complaints. These include policies and procedures created by NASW, licensing and regulatory bodies, employers, agencies, and other professional organizations.

(c) Social workers who believe that a colleague has acted unethically should seek resolution by discussing their concerns with the colleague when feasible and when such discussion is likely to be productive.

(d) When necessary, social workers who believe that a colleague has acted unethically should take action through appropriate formal channels (such as contacting a state licensing board or regulatory body, an NASW committee on inquiry, or other professional ethics committees).

(e) Social workers should defend and assist colleagues who are unjustly charged with unethical conduct.

3.   Social Workers' Ethical Responsibilities in Practice Settings

3.01   Supervision and Consultation

(a) Social workers who provide supervision or consultation should have the necessary knowledge and skill to supervise or consult appropriately and should do so only within their areas of knowledge and competence.

(b) Social workers who provide supervision or consultation are responsible for setting clear, appropriate, and culturally sensitive boundaries.

(c) Social workers should not engage in any dual or multiple relationships with supervisees in which there is a risk of exploitation of or potential harm to the supervisee.

(d) Social workers who provide supervision should evaluate supervisees' performance in a manner that is fair and respectful.

3.02   Education and Training

(a) Social workers who function as educators, field instructors for students, or trainers should provide instruction only within their areas of knowledge and competence and should provide instruction based on the most current information and knowledge available in the profession.

(b) Social workers who function as educators or field instructors for students should evaluate students' performance in a manner that is fair and respectful.

(c) Social workers who function as educators or field instructors for students should take reasonable steps to ensure that clients are routinely informed when services are being provided by students.

(d) Social workers who function as educators or field instructors for students should not engage in any dual or multiple relationships with students in which there is a risk of exploitation or potential harm to the student. Social work educators and field instructors are responsible for setting clear, appropriate, and culturally sensitive boundaries.

3.03   Performance Evaluation

Social workers who have responsibility for evaluating the performance of others should fulfill such responsibility in a fair and considerate manner and on the basis of clearly stated criteria.

3.04   Client Records

(a) Social workers should take reasonable steps to ensure that documentation in records is accurate and reflects the services provided.

(b) Social workers should include sufficient and timely documentation in records to facilitate the delivery of services and to ensure continuity of services provided to clients in the future.

(c) Social workers' documentation should protect clients' privacy to the extent that is possible and appropriate and should include only information that is directly relevant to the delivery of services.

(d) Social workers should store records following the termination of services to ensure reasonable future access. Records should be maintained for the number of years required by state statutes or relevant contracts.

3.05   Billing

Social workers should establish and maintain billing practices that accurately reflect the nature and extent of services provided and that identify who provided the service in the practice setting.

3.06   Client Transfer

(a) When an individual who is receiving services from another agency or colleague contacts a social worker for services, the social worker should carefully consider the client's needs before agreeing to provide services. To minimize possible confusion and conflict, social workers should discuss with potential clients the nature of the clients' current relationship with other service providers and the implications, including possible benefits or risks, of entering into a relationship with a new service provider.

(b) If a new client has been served by another agency or colleague, social workers should discuss with the client whether consultation with the previous service provider is in the client's best interest.

3.07   Administration

(a) Social work administrators should advocate within and outside their agencies for adequate resources to meet clients' needs.

(b) Social workers should advocate for resource allocation procedures that are open and fair. When not all clients' needs can be met, an allocation procedure should be developed that is nondiscriminatory and based on appropriate and consistently applied principles.

(c) Social workers who are administrators should take reasonable steps to ensure that adequate agency or organizational resources are available to provide appropriate staff supervision.

(d) Social work administrators should take reasonable steps to ensure that the working environment for which they are responsible is consistent with and encourages compliance with the *NASW Code of Ethics*. Social work administrators should take reasonable steps to eliminate any conditions in their organizations that violate, interfere with, or discourage compliance with the *Code*.

3.08   Continuing Education and Staff Development

Social work administrators and supervisors should take reasonable steps to provide or arrange for continuing education and staff development for all staff for whom they are responsible. Continuing education and staff development should address current knowledge and emerging developments related to social work practice and ethics.

3.09   Commitments to Employers

(a) Social workers generally should adhere to commitments made to employers and employing organizations.

(b) Social workers should work to improve employing agencies' policies and procedures and the efficiency and effectiveness of their services.

(c) Social workers should take reasonable steps to ensure that employers are aware of social workers' ethical obligations as set forth in the *NASW Code of Ethics* and of the implications of those obligations for social work practice.

(d) Social workers should not allow an employing organization's policies, procedures, regulations, or administrative orders to interfere with their ethical practice of social work. Social workers should take reasonable steps to ensure that their employing organizations' practices are consistent with the *NASW Code of Ethics*.

(e) Social workers should act to prevent and eliminate discrimination in the employing organization's work assignments and in its employment policies and practices.

(f) Social workers should accept employment or arrange student field placements only in organizations that exercise fair personnel practices.

(g) Social workers should be diligent stewards of the resources of their employing organizations, wisely conserving funds where appropriate and never misappropriating funds or using them for unintended purposes.

3.10   Labor–Management Disputes

(a) Social workers may engage in organized action, including the formation of and participation in labor unions, to improve services to clients and working conditions.

(b) The actions of social workers who are involved in labor–management disputes, job actions, or labor strikes should be guided by the profession's values, ethical principles, and ethical standards. Reasonable differences of opinion exist among social workers concerning their primary obligation as professionals during an actual or threatened labor strike or job action. Social workers should carefully examine relevant issues and their possible impact on clients before deciding on a course of action.

4.   Social Workers' Ethical Responsibilities as Professionals

4.01   Competence

(a) Social workers should accept responsibility or employment only on the basis of existing competence or the intention to acquire the necessary competence.

(b) Social workers should strive to become and remain proficient in professional practice and the performance of professional functions. Social workers should critically examine and keep current with emerging knowledge relevant to social work. Social workers should routinely review the professional literature and participate in continuing education relevant to social work practice and social work ethics.

(c) Social workers should base practice on recognized knowledge, including empirically based knowledge, relevant to social work and social work ethics.

4.02 Discrimination

Social workers should not practice, condone, facilitate, or collaborate with any form of discrimination on the basis of race, ethnicity, national origin, color, sex, sexual orientation, age, marital status, political belief, religion, or mental or physical disability.

4.03 Private Conduct

Social workers should not permit their private conduct to interfere with their ability to fulfill their professional responsibilities.

4.04 Dishonesty, Fraud, and Deception

Social workers should not participate in, condone, or be associated with dishonesty, fraud, or deception.

4.05 Impairment

(a) Social workers should not allow their own personal problems, psychosocial distress, legal problems, substance abuse, or mental health difficulties to interfere with their professional judgment and performance or to jeopardize the best interests of people for whom they have a professional responsibility.

(b) Social workers whose personal problems, psychosocial distress, legal problems, substance abuse, or mental health difficulties interfere with their professional judgment and performance should immediately seek consultation and take appropriate remedial action by seeking professional help, making adjustments in workload, terminating practice, or taking any other steps necessary to protect clients and others.

4.06 Misrepresentation

(a) Social workers should make clear distinctions between statements made and actions engaged in as a private individual and as a representative of the social work profession, a professional social work organization, or the social worker's employing agency.

(b) Social workers who speak on behalf of professional social work organizations should accurately represent the official and authorized positions of the organizations.

(c) Social workers should ensure that their representations to clients, agencies, and the public of professional qualifications, credentials, education, competence, affiliations, services provided, or results to be achieved are accurate. Social workers should claim only those relevant professional credentials they actually possess and take steps to correct any inaccuracies or misrepresentations of their credentials by others.

4.07 Solicitations

(a) Social workers should not engage in uninvited solicitation of potential clients who, because of their circumstances, are vulnerable to undue influence, manipulation, or coercion.

(b) Social workers should not engage in solicitation of testimonial endorsements (including solicitation of consent to use a client's prior statement as a testimonial endorsement) from current clients or from other people who, because of their particular circumstances, are vulnerable to undue influence.

4.08 Acknowledging Credit

(a) Social workers should take responsibility and credit, including authorship credit, only for work they have actually performed and to which they have contributed.

(b) Social workers should honestly acknowledge the work of and the contributions made by others.

5. Social Workers' Ethical Responsibilities to the Social Work Profession

5.01 Integrity of the Profession

(a) Social workers should work toward the maintenance and promotion of high standards of practice.

(b) Social workers should uphold and advance the values, ethics, knowledge, and mission of the profession. Social workers should protect, enhance, and improve the integrity of the profession through appropriate study and research, active discussion, and responsible criticism of the profession.

(c) Social workers should contribute time and professional expertise to activities that promote respect for the value, integrity, and competence of the social work profession. These activities may include teaching, research, consultation, service, legislative testimony, presentations in the community, and participation in their professional organizations.

(d) Social workers should contribute to the knowledge base of social work and share with colleagues their knowledge related to practice, research, and ethics. Social workers should seek to contribute to the profession's literature and to share their knowledge at professional meetings and conferences.

(e) Social workers should act to prevent the unauthorized and unqualified practice of social work.

5.02 Evaluation and Research

(a) Social workers should monitor and evaluate policies, the implementation of programs, and practice interventions.

(b) Social workers should promote and facilitate evaluation and research to contribute to the development of knowledge.

(c) Social workers should critically examine and keep current with emerging knowledge relevant to social work and fully use evaluation and research evidence in their professional practice.

(d) Social workers engaged in evaluation or research should carefully consider possible consequences and should follow guidelines developed for the protection of evaluation and research participants. Appropriate institutional review boards should be consulted.

(e) Social workers engaged in evaluation or research should obtain voluntary and written informed consent from participants, when appropriate, without any implied or actual deprivation or penalty for refusal to participate; without undue inducement to participate; and with due regard for participants' well-being, privacy, and dignity. Informed consent should include information about the nature, extent, and duration of the participation requested and disclosure of the risks and benefits of participation in the research.

(f) When evaluation or research participants are incapable of giving informed consent, social workers should provide an appropriate explanation to the participants, obtain the participants' assent to the extent they are able, and obtain written consent from an appropriate proxy.

(g) Social workers should never design or conduct evaluation or research that does not use consent procedures, such as certain forms of naturalistic observation and archival research, unless rigorous and responsible review of the research has found it to be justified because of its prospective scientific, educational, or applied value and unless equally effective alternative procedures that do not involve waiver of consent are not feasible.

(h) Social workers should inform participants of their right to withdraw from evaluation and research at any time without penalty.

(i) Social workers should take appropriate steps to ensure that participants in evaluation and research have access to appropriate supportive services.

(j) Social workers engaged in evaluation or research should protect participants from unwarranted physical or mental distress, harm, danger, or deprivation.

(k) Social workers engaged in the evaluation of services should discuss collected information only for professional purposes and only with people professionally concerned with this information.

(l) Social workers engaged in evaluation or research should ensure the anonymity or confidentiality of participants and of the data obtained from them. Social workers should inform participants of any limits of confidentiality, the measures that will be taken to ensure confidentiality, and when any records containing research data will be destroyed.

(m) Social workers who report evaluation and research results should protect participants' confidentiality by omitting identifying information unless proper consent has been obtained authorizing disclosure.

(n) Social workers should report evaluation and research findings accurately. They should not fabricate or falsify results and should take steps to correct any errors later found in published data using standard publication methods.

(o) Social workers engaged in evaluation or research should be alert to and avoid conflicts of interest and dual relationships with participants, should inform participants when a real or potential conflict of interest arises, and should take steps to resolve the issue in a manner that makes participants' interests primary.

(p) Social workers should educate themselves, their students, and their colleagues about responsible research practices.

6. Social Workers' Ethical Responsibilities to the Broader Society

6.01 Social Welfare
Social workers should promote the general welfare of society, from local to global levels, and the development of people, their communities, and their environments. Social workers should advocate for living conditions conducive to the fulfillment of basic human needs and should promote social, economic, political, and cultural values and institutions that are compatible with the realization of social justice.

6.02 Public Participation
Social workers should facilitate informed participation by the public in shaping social policies and institutions.

6.03 Public Emergencies
Social workers should provide appropriate professional services in public emergencies to the greatest extent possible.

6.04 Social and Political Action
(a) Social workers should engage in social and political action that seeks to ensure that all people have equal access to the resources, employment, services, and opportunities they require to meet their basic human needs and to develop fully. Social workers should be aware of the impact of the political arena on practice and should advocate for changes in policy and legislation to improve social conditions in order to meet basic human needs and promote social justice.

(b) Social workers should act to expand choice and opportunity for all people, with special regard for vulnerable, disadvantaged, oppressed, and exploited people and groups.

(c) Social workers should promote conditions that encourage respect for cultural and social diversity within the United States and globally. Social workers should promote policies and practices that demonstrate respect for difference, support the expansion of cultural knowledge and resources, advocate for programs and institutions that demonstrate cultural competence, and promote policies that safeguard the rights of and confirm equity and social justice for all people.

(d) Social workers should act to prevent and eliminate domination of, exploitation of, and discrimination against any person, group, or class on the basis of race, ethnicity, national origin, color, sex, sexual orientation, age, marital status, political belief, religion, or mental or physical disability.

Appendix 2. Reader's Guides

Following are the Reader's Guides from the 19th Edition, updated wherever appropriate to include the new entries featured in this *Supplement*. New entries appear in boldface.

Child Sexual Abuse Overview
Child Sexual Abuse: Direct Practice

Children and Youths
Adolescence Overview
Adolescent Pregnancy
Adolescents: Direct Practice
Adoption
Child Abuse and Neglect Overview
Child Abuse and Neglect: Direct Practice
Child Care Services
Child Foster Care
Child Labor
Child Sexual Abuse Overview
Child Sexual Abuse: Direct Practice
Child Support
Child Welfare Overview
Childhood
Children: Direct Practice
Children: Group Care
Children: Mental Health
Children's Rights
Families (see Reader's Guide)
Gay and Lesbian Adolescents
Juvenile and Family Courts
Juvenile Corrections
Runaways and Homeless Youths
Youth Services

Clinical Social Work
Assessment
Brief Task-Centered Practice
Brief Therapies
Clinical Social Work
Cognition and Social Cognitive Theory
Cognitive Treatment
Crisis Intervention: Research Needs
Diagnostic and Statistical Manual of Mental
    Disorders
Direct Practice Overview
Ecological Perspective
Ethnic-Sensitive Practice
Generalist and Advanced Generalist Practice
Gestalt
Goal Setting and Intervention Planning
Group Practice Overview
Interviewing
Licensing, Regulation, and Certification
Managed Care Overview
Person-in-Environment
Psychosocial Approach
Recording
Termination in Direct Practice
Transactional Analysis

Community
Charitable Foundations and Social Welfare
Children's Rights

Citizen Participation
Community
Community-Based Corrections
Community Building
Community Development
Community Needs Assessment
Community Organization
Community Practice Models
Health Planning
Housing
Human Rights
International and Comparative Social
    Welfare
Peace and Social Justice
Planning and Management Professions
Policy Analysis
Social Justice in Social Agencies
Social Planning
Technology Transfer

Computer Use
Archives of Social Welfare
Computer Utilization
Continuing Education
Expert Systems
Information Systems
**The Internet: Accessing the World of
    Information**
Recording
**Social Work Education: Electronic
    Technologies**

Courts and Corrections
Adult Corrections
Adult Courts
Community-Based Corrections
Criminal Behavior Overview
Criminal Justice: Class, Race, and Gender
    Issues
Criminal Justice: Social Work Roles
Domestic Violence
Domestic Violence: Gay Men and Lesbians
Domestic Violence: Legal Issues
Family Views in Correctional Programs
Female Criminal Offenders
Gang Violence
Health Care: Jails and Prisons
Homicide
Juvenile Corrections
Juvenile Courts
Legal Issues: Confidentiality and Privileged
    Communication
Legal Issues: Low-Income and Dependent
    People
**Legal Issues: Recent Developments in
    Confidentiality and Privilege**
Police Social Work

Appendix 3. Acronyms

AA	Alcoholics Anonymous
AAFP	American Academy of Family Practice
AAFRC	American Association of Fund-Raising Counsel
AAGW	American Association of Group Workers
AALL	American Association for Labor Legislation
AAMD	American Association on Mental Deficiency
AAMFT	American Association of Marriage and Family Therapists
AAMR	American Association on Mental Retardation
AAMSW	American Association of Medical Social Workers
AAP	affirmative action program
AAPSW	American Association of Psychiatric Social Workers
AARP	American Association of Retired Persons
AASSW	American Association of Schools of Social Work
AASSWB	American Association of State Social Work Boards
AASW	American Association of Social Workers
AB	Aid to the Blind
ABE	American Board of Examiners in Clinical Social Work
ABW	average body weight
ACEHSA	Accrediting Commission on Education for Health Services Administration
ACLU	American Civil Liberties Union
ACM	anticult movement
ACOAs	adult children of alcoholics
ACOSA	Association of Community Organization and Social Administration
ACSUS	AIDS Cost and Service Utilization Survey
ACSW	Academy of Certified Social Workers
ACT-UP	AIDS Coalition to Unleash Power
ADA	Americans with Disabilities Act of 1990
ADAMHA	Alcohol, Drug Abuse, and Mental Health Administration
ADC	Aid to Dependent Children
ADC	adult day care
ADL	activities of daily living
ADHD	attention-deficit hyperactivity disorder
AFAR	American Foundation for AIDS Research
AFDC	Aid to Families with Dependent Children
AFDC-UP	Aid to Families with Dependent Children—Unemployed Parent program
AFL-CIO	American Federation of Labor-Congress of Industrial Organizations
AFRAIDS	fear of AIDS
AFSCME	American Federation of State, County, and Municipal Employees
AFSW	Association of Federation Social Workers
AFT	American Federation of Teachers
AGI	adjusted gross income
AHA	American Hospital Association
AID	Agency for International Development
AIDS	acquired immune deficiency syndrome
AIM	Aid to Imprisoned Mothers
AIME	average indexed monthly earnings
AIRS	Alliance of Information and Referral Systems
ALMACA	Association of Labor and Management Consultants on Alcoholism
AMA	American Medical Association
AMFAR	American Foundation for AIDS Research
ANCSA	Alaska Native Claims Settlement Act
AoA	Administration on Aging
APA	American Psychiatric Association
APMs	annual program meetings

APS	adult protective services
APTD	Aid to the Permanently and Totally Disabled
APWA	American Public Welfare Association
ARC	AIDS-related complex
ARROW	Americans for Restitution and Righting of Old Wrongs
ASAP	Automated Screening and Assessment Package
ASCO	Association for the Study of Community Organizations
ASH	Action on Smoking and Health
ASL	American Sign Language
ASO	AIDS services organizations
ASPA	American Society for Personnel Administrators
ASSIST	American Stop Smoking Trial
AUPHA	Association of University Programs in Health Administration
AZT	azidothymidine
BCRS	Bertha Capen Reynolds Society
BLS	Bureau of Labor Statistics
BSW	bachelor of social work
CAB	Citizens Advice Bureau (British)
CAP	Community Action Program
CAPTA	Child Abuse Prevention and Treatment Act
CARE	Community and Resource Exchange
CARE	Comprehensive AIDS Resources Emergency
CARE	Cooperative for American Relief Everywhere, Inc.
CASA	court-appointed special advocate
CASP	Comprehensive Annual Services Plan
CASS	computer-assisted social services
CASSP	Child and Adolescent Services Programs
CCC	Competence Certification Commission
CCDBG	Child Care and Development Block Grant
CCETSW	Council of Education and Training in Social Work
CCIP	Center for Children of Incarcerated Parents
CCMC	Committee on the Costs of Medical Care
CCMS	Child Care Management Service
CCS	Crippled Children's Services
CCSSO	Council of Chief State School Officers
CDC	Centers for Disease Control and Prevention
CDF	Chapter Development Fund
CD-I	compact disk—interactive
CD-ROM	compact disk—read-only memory
CEOs	chief executive officers
CES	Current Employment Statistics
CETA	Comprehensive Employment and Training Act
CEUs/CECs	continuing education units/credits
CFC	Combined Federal Campaign
CHAMPUS	Civilian Health and Medical Program of the Uniformed Services
CHAP	Children Have a Potential
CHAP	Comprehensive Homeless Assistance Plan
CHAS	Comprehensive Housing Affordability Strategy
CHIP	Comprehensive Health Insurance Plan
CHP	Comprehensive Health Planning and Public Health Services Amendments
CIA	Central Intelligence Agency
CIAS	Committee on Inter-Association Structure
CIP	Council of International Programs
CLAIM	Chicago Legal Aid for Imprisoned Mothers

CMHC	community mental health centers
CMHCA	Community Mental Health Centers Act
CMHS	Center for Mental Health Services
CMHSA	Community Mental Health Services Act
CMV	cytomegalovirus
CNHI	Committee of One Hundred for National Health Insurance
COA	Commission on Accreditation
COAs	children of alcoholics
COBRA	Comprehensive Omnibus Budget Reconciliation Act
CODAs	children of deaf adults
COI	Committee on Inquiry
COMPSYCH	computerized software service for psychologists
CON	certificate of need
COPA	community-oriented primary care
CORE	Congress of Racial Equality
CORPA	Council on Regulating Post-Secondary Education
COS	Charity Organization Societies
COSAs	children of substance abusers
COSSMHO	Coalition of Spanish-Speaking Mental Health Organizations
CPAI	Correctional Program Assessment Inventory
CPC	child protective services
CPI	consumer price index
CPS	Child Protective Services
CPS	Current Population Survey
CPS	curriculum policy statement
CRA	Community Reinvestment Act
CREP	Cuban Refugee Emergency Program
CSA	Child Support Assurance
C-SAP	Centers for Substance Abuse Prevention
C-SAT	Centers for Substance Abuse Treatment
CSCE	Commission on Security and Cooperation in Europe
CSFII	Continuing Survey of Food Intakes by Individuals
CSHCN	children with special health care needs
CSOs	Community Service Organizations
CSWE	Council on Social Work Education
CVS	chorionic villus sampling
CWA	Communications Workers of America
CWEP	Community Work Experience Program
CWLA	Child Welfare League of America
CWS	Child Welfare Services
D&D	design and development
DAWN	Drug Abuse Warning Network
dB	decibels
DBMS	database management system
DD	design and development (of interventions)
ddC	dideoxycytidine
ddI	dideoxyinosine
DEA	Drug Enforcement Administration
DHEW	Department of Health, Education, and Welfare
DHHS	U.S. Department of Health and Human Services
DII	Disability Insurance
DipSW	Diploma in Social Work
DMA	Department of Memorial Affairs
DNA	deoxyribonucleic acid
DNR	Do Not Resuscitate

DoD	U.S. Department of Defense
DRG	diagnosis related group
DSM	*Diagnostic and Statistical Manual of Mental Disorders*
DSS	decision support system
DSW	doctor of social work
DUI	driving under the influence
DVB	Department of Veterans Benefits
DVI	digital video interactive
DWI	driving while intoxicated
EAP	employee assistance program
EAPA	Employee Assistance Professionals Association
EBRI	Employee Benefit Research Institute
EBT	electronic benefits transfer
ECA	Epidemiologic Catchment Area
ECOSOC	Economic and Social Council
EEO	equal employment opportunity
EEOC	Equal Employment Opportunity Commission
EIC	earned income credit
EITC	earned income tax credit
ELAN	Education Legislative Action Network
ELISA	enzyme-linked immunosorbent assay
E-Mail	electronic mail
EMSC	emergency medical services for children
ENIAC	Electronic Numerical Integrator and Computer
EOA	Economic Opportunity Act
EPA	Environmental Protection Agency
EPO	exclusive provider organization
EPSS	electronic performance support system
ERISA	Employee Retirement Income Security Act of 1974
ES	effective size
ESL	English as a Second Language
FAO	Food and Agriculture Organization
FAP	Family Assistance Program
FAS	fetal alcohol syndrome
FBI	Federal Bureau of Investigation
FDA	Food and Drug Administration
FEHPA	Federal Employees Health Benefits Act
FEMA	Federal Emergency Management Agency
FERA	Federal Emergency Relief Administration
FHA	Federal Housing Administration
FICA	Federal Insurance Contributions Act
FIDCR	Federal Interagency Day Care Requirements
FLE	Family Life Education
FLSA	Fair Labor Standards Act
FmHA	Farmers Home Administration
FMLA	Family and Medical Leave Act
FNS	Food and Nutrition Service
FOSR	Function, Organization, and Structure Review
FPAs	Family Program Administrators
FSA	Federal Security Administration
FSAA	Family Service Association of America
FTC	Federal Trade Commission
FWAA	Family Welfare Association of America
FY	fiscal year
FYSB	Family and Youth Services Bureau

GA	General Assistance
GAI	guaranteed annual income
GAIN	Greater Avenues to Independence
GAO	U.S. General Accounting Office
GARF	Global Assessment of Relational Functioning
GDP	gross domestic product
GED	general equivalency diploma
GEM	Geriatric Evaluation and Management
GNP	gross national product
GRECC	Geriatric Research Education and Clinical Centers
GRID	gay-related immune disorder
4-H	Head, Heart, Hands, and Health
HCFA	Health Care Financing Administration
HI	Hospital Insurance
HIP	Helping Incarcerated Parents
HIV	human immunodeficiency virus
HIV/AIDS	HIV disease
HMO	health maintenance organization
HRD	(National) Health, Planning, and Resources Development Act
HRR	Human Rights Report
HRSA	Health Resources and Services Administration
HSAs	health system agencies
HTML	hypertext markup language
HUD	U.S. Department of Housing and Urban Development
Human SERVE	Human Service Employees Registration and Voter Education
Hz	hertz
I&R	information and referral
IASSW	International Association of Schools of Social Work
ICD	International Classification of Diseases
ICSSW	International Committee of Schools of Social Work
ICSW	International Congress of Social Welfare
ICWA	Indian Child Welfare Act
IDA	injection drug abusers
IDEA	Individuals with Disabilities Education Act
IDU	injecting drug use
IEP	individualized educational program
IFSW	International Federation of Social Workers
IHHS	In-Home Health Services
IHS	Indian Health Service
ILO	International Labour Organization
INS	Immigration and Naturalization Service
IPEC	International Programme on the Elimination of Child Labour
IPO	independent practice organization
IQ	intelligence quotient
IRCA	Immigration Reform and Control Act of 1986
IRS	Internal Revenue Service
IS	information system
ITV	interactive television
IUCISD	Interuniversity Consortium on International Social Development
IUD	intrauterine devices
iUPAE	Independent Union of Public Aid Employees
IV	intravenous
IVD	interactive video disk
JCAHO	Joint Commission on Accreditation of Healthcare Organizations
JJDPA	Juvenile Justice and Delinquency Prevention Act

JOBS	Job Opportunities and Basic Skills Training
JTPA	Job Training and Partnership Act
LAN	local area network
LEAA	Law Enforcement Assistance Administration
LRU	La Raza Unida
LULAC	League of United Latin American Citizens
LULU	locally unwanted land uses
MADD	Mothers Against Drunk Driving
MAG	Mothers Against Gangs
MAGIC	Merced Automated Global Information Control
MALDEF	Mexican American Legal Defense and Education Fund
MAP	membership assistance program
MAPA	Mexican American Political Association
MASH	Make Something Happen
MCC	Metropolitan Community Church
MCH	maternal and child health
MCHS	Maternal and Child Health Services
MDRC	Manpower Development Research Corporation
MIS	management information system
MORE	Member-Organized Resource Exchange
MPSW	military psychiatric social worker
MRI	magnetic resonance imaging
MSA	metropolitan statistical area
MSSP	Multipurpose Senior Services Project
MSW	master of social work
NA	Narcotics Anonymous
NAACP	Nation Association for the Advancement of Colored People
NABSW	National Association of Black Social Workers
NACW	National Association of Colored Women
NAEYC	National Association for the Education of Young Children
NAMI	National Alliance for the Mentally Ill
NAOSW	National Association of Oncology Social Workers
NAPWA	National Association of People with AIDS
NARCEA	National Aging Resource Center on Elder Abuse
NASHP	National Academy for State Health Policy
NASPAA	National Association of Schools of Public Affairs and Administration
NSSA	National Association of Schools of Social Administration
NASSW	National Association of School Social Workers
NASUA	National Association of State Units on Aging
NASW	National Association of Social Workers
NCATE	National Council for Accreditation of Teacher Education
NCCC	National Conference of Charities and Correction
NCCS	National Center on Charitable Statistics
NCF	National Civic Federation
NCRA	National Council for Children
NCHS	National Center for Health Statistics
NCLC	National Child Labor Committee
NCN	NASW Communications Network
NCOI	National Committee on Inquiry
NCOLGI	National Committee on Lesbian and Gay Issues
NCOMA	National Committee on Minority Affairs
NCORED	National Committee on Racial and Ethnic Diversity
NCOWI	National Committee on Women's Issues

NCPCR	National Center for the Prevention and Control of Rape
NCRP	National Committee for Responsive Philanthropy
NCSPP	National Center for Social Policy and Practice
NCSW	National Conference of Social Work
NCSWE	National Council on Social Work Education
NCVS	National Crime Victimization Survey
NFB	National Federation of the Blind
NFSCSW	National Federation of Societies for Clinical Social Work
NGO	nongovernmental organization
NGT	nominal group technique
NHIP	National Health Insurance Program
NHIS	National Health Interview Survey
NHO	National Hospice Organization
NIAAA	National Institute on Alcoholism and Alcohol Abuse
NIADC	National Institute on Adult Day Care
NIDA	National Institute on Drug Abuse
NIDS	National Inventory of Documentary Sources
NIH	National Institutes of Health
NIMH	National Institute of Mental Health
NIT	negative income tax
NLRA	National Labor Relations Act
NLRB	National Labor Relations Board
NLS	National Library Service
NLS	national longitudinal survey
NMES	National Medical Expenditure Survey
NMHA	National Mental Health Association
NPR	national public radio
NRA	normal retirement age
NRM	new religious movement
NSFG	national surveys of family growth
NTEE	National Taxonomy of Exempt Entities
NVRA	National Voter Registration Act of 1993
O&M	orientation and mobility
OAA	Old-Age Assistance
OAA	Older Americans Act of 1965
OASDI	Old-Age and Survivors and Disability Insurance
OASI	Old-Age and Survivors Insurance
OBRA	Omnibus Budget Reconciliation Act
ODP	Orderly Departure Program
OJJDP	Office of Juvenile Justice and Delinquency Prevention
OJT	on-the-job training
OMB	Office of Management and Budget
OSAP	Office of Substance Abuse Prevention
OSIQ	Offer Self-Image Questionnaire for Adolescents
OXFAM	Oxford Committee on Famine
PACE	Political Action for Candidate Election
PAR	population-attributed risk
PASSO	Political Association of Spanish-Speaking Organizations
PATCH	Planned Approach to Community Health
PCP	*pneumocystis carinii* pneumonia
PET	positron emission tomography
PIA	primary insurance amount
PIE	person-in-environment
PIN	personal identification number
PIRC	Prevention Intervention Research Center

PKU	phenylketonuria
POS	purchase of service
PPO	preferred provider organization
PSID	Panel Study of Income Dynamics
PSIR	presentence investigation report
PSR	psychosocial rehabilitation
PTSD	posttraumatic stress disorder
PVO	private voluntary organization
PVS	persistent vegetative state
PWA	people with AIDS
QMB	qualified medical beneficiary
RDA	recommended dietary allowance
REA	Retirement Equity Act of 1984
RFP	Request for Proposal
RICO	Racketeer Influenced and Corrupt Organization (1970 statute)
RLIN	research libraries information network
RMP	regional medical program
RMP Act	Regional Medical Programs Act
RR	risk ratio
RTR	Reintegration Through Recreation
SAMHSA	Substance Abuse and Mental Health Services Administration
SCLC	Southern Christian Leadership Conference
SCMWA	State, County, and Municipal Workers of America
SDI	strategic defense initiative
SE	supported employment
SEIU	Service Employees International Union
SEM	standard error of measurement
SERVE	Service Employees Registration and Voter Education
SES	socioeconomic status
SGA	substantial gainful activity
SHARE	Source of Help in Airing and Resolving Experiences
SHPDA	state health planning and development agency
SIC	Standard Industrial Classification
SIECUS	Sex Information and Education Council of the United States
SIPP	Survey of Income and Program Participation
SMHAs	State Mental Health Authorities
SMI	Supplementary Medical Insurance
SNCC	Student Non-Violent Coordinating Committee
SOFAS	Social & Occupational Functioning Assessment Scale
SOS	Secular Organization for Sobriety
SOSAD	Save Our Sons and Daughters
SPL	sound pressure level
SPRANS	Special Programs of Regional and National Significance
SRO	single-room occupancy
SSA	Social Security Administration
SSD	single-subject (or -system) design
SSDI	Social Security Disability Insurance
SSEU	Social Service Employees Union
SSI	Supplemental Security Income
STD	sexually transmitted disease
STEPA	Street Terrorism Enforcement Prevention Act
SVREP	Southwest Voter Registration Education Project

SWIM	Saturated Work Initiative Model
SWOT	Strengths, Weaknesses, Opportunities, and Threats
SWRG	Social Work Research Group
TANF	Temporary Assistance to Needy Families
TB	tuberculosis
TDHS	Texas Department of Human Services
TFP	Thrifty Food Plan
TIAC	Temporary Inter-Association Council of Social Work Membership
TVA	Tennessee Valley Authority
UAW	United Automobile Workers
UCR	Uniform Crime Reports
UFWA	United Federal Workers of America
UN	United Nations
UNDP	United Nations Development Program
UNESCO	United Nations Education, Scientific, and Cultural Organization
UNHCR	United Nations High Commission for Refugees
UNICEF	United Nations Children's Fund (formerly United Nations International Children's Emergency Fund)
UNRRA	United Nations Relief and Rehabilitation Agency
UOPWA	United Office and Professional Workers of America
UPWA	United Public Workers of America
USCC	U.S. Catholic Conference
USCRA	U.S. Coordinator for Refugee Affairs
USDA	U.S. Department of Agriculture
USINS	US. Immigration and Naturalization Service
USNCHS	U.S. National Center for Health Statistics
UWASIS	United Way of America Services Identification System
UWI	University of the West Indies
VA	Veterans Administration
VCR	videocassette recorder
VET Centers	Vietnam-era Veterans Outreach and Counseling Centers
VHA	Veterans Health Administration
VISTA	Volunteers in Service to America
VOCA	Victims of Crime Act
VS	vital signs
VSC	voluntary surgical contraception
VSIS	Voluntary Cooperative Information System
WAN	wide area network
WASP	white Anglo-Saxon Protestant
WHO	World Health Organization
WHO/GPA	World Health Organization Global Programme on AIDS
WHO/SPA	World Health Organization/Special Programme on AIDS
WIC	Special Supplemental Nutrition Program for Women, Infants, and Children
WIN	Work Incentive Program
WPA	Works Progress Administration
YMCA	Young Men's Christian Association
YWCA	Young Women's Christian Association

Index

1997 Supplement to the Encyclopedia of Social Work, 19th Edition
Designed by G. Quinn Information Design
Composed by Wolf Publications, Inc., in Cheltenham Book and Helvetica
Printed by Boyd Printing Company, Inc., on 60# Windsor

Order These Fine Reference Works from the NASW Press

The Encyclopedia of Social Work, 19th Edition, 1997 Supplement,
Richard L. Edwards, Editor-in-Chief.
The new supplement brings the *Encyclopedia of Social Work, 19th Edition* up-to-date
with the most current concerns in social work. With 400 pages of new information,
the supplement features new entries on timely topics such as managed care and
social work, electronic technologies and the Internet, spirituality in social work, the
working poor, and more—for a total of 30 all-new entries and 15 new biographies,
plus the 1996 *NASW Code of Ethics.*

ISBN: 0-87101-277-4. Item #2774. 1997. Price $37.95

The Encyclopedia of Social Work, 19th Edition, *Richard L. Edwards, Editor-in-Chief.*
Nearly 300 comprehensive entries—almost 3,000 pages—inform the reader about
virtually every aspect of social work with a depth and breadth that are unmatched in
any other social work volume. Features include 142 biographies; 80 Reader's Guides;
charts, graphs, and tables; freestanding cross-references; and key words for every
entry. Your choice of hardcover, softcover, and CD-ROM* formats.
Hardcover — ISBN: 0-87101-255-3. Item #2533. 1995. Price $159
Softcover — ISBN: 0-87101-256-1. Item #2561. 1995. Price $129
CD-ROM — Item #D34. Updated 1997. Price $279*

*The CD-ROM, revised in 1997, features 65 updated *Encyclopedia* entries, 30 all-new
entries, and 15 new biographies; *The Social Work Dictionary, 3rd Edition; Social Work
Almanac, 2nd Edition, Revised,* featuring nearly 100 updated tables; the 1996 *Code of
Ethics;* and much more.

The Social Work Dictionary, 3rd Edition, *by Robert L. Barker.*
This 1995 edition surpasses its predecessor with 60 percent more content. It presents a concise, alphabetized listing of 5,000 social work definitions, organizations,
concepts, values, and historical events. One of the most valuable tools ever written
for the human services professional—from the beginning student to the seasoned
expert.

ISBN: 0-87101-253-7. Item #2537. 1995. Price $34.95

Social Work Almanac, 2nd Edition, *by Leon Ginsberg.*
The latest facts and figures have been rigorously researched and compiled to update
this practical compendium of statistical data related to social welfare. The second
edition is over 61 percent larger, with 69 percent more tables and 73 percent more
figures.

ISBN: 0-87101-248-0. Item #2480. 1995. Price $34.95

Title	Item#	Price	Total
___ Encyclopedia of Social Work, 1997 Supplement	2774	$ 37.95	_____
Encyclopedia of Social Work, 19th Edition			
___ Casebound version	2553	$159.00	_____
___ Softcover version	2561	$129.00	_____
___ CD-ROM version	D34	$279.00	_____
___ Social Work Dictionary, 3rd Edition	2537	$ 34.95	_____
___ Social Work Almanac, 2nd Edition	2480	$ 34.95	_____

Subtotal _____
add 10% postage and handling _____
Total _____

I've enclosed my check or money order.
Please charge my   NASW Visa*   Other Visa   MasterCard

Credit Card Number _____ Expiration Date _____

Signature _____
      *Use of this card generates funds to support work on behalf of the social work profession.

Name _____

Address _____

City _____ State/Province_____

Zip _____ Country _____

Phone_____ E-mail _____

NASW Member # (if applicable) _____

(Payment must accompany this order. Please make checks payable to NASW Press.)

Return to—

NASW PRESS
P.O. Box 431
Annapolis JCT, MD 20701
USA

Or call toll free—
1-800-227-3590
(In Metro., DC, area call 301-317-8688)

Fax your order to
301-206-7989